Voices of a Nation

A History of Mass Media in the United States

Fourth Edition

Jean Folkerts, School of Media and Public Affairs
The George Washington University

Dwight L. Teeter, Jr., College of Communications
The University of Tennessee

with chapter biographies by

Keith Kincaid
The George Washington University

Allyn and Bacon
Boston   London   Toronto   Sydney   Tokyo   Singapore

Vice President, Editor-in-Chief: Karen Hanson
Series Editor: Molly Taylor
Series Editorial Assistant: Michael Kish
Composition and Prepress Buyer: Linda Cox
Manufacturing Buyer: Julie McNeill
Cover Administrator: Kristina Mose-Libon
Editorial-Production Service: Omegatype Typography, Inc.
Electronic Composition: Omegatype Typography, Inc.

Library of Congress Cataloging-in-Publication Data

Folkerts, Jean.
    Voices of a nation : a history of mass media in the United States / Jean Folkerts,
Dwight L. Teeter, Jr.—4th ed. / with chapter biographies by Keith Kincaid.
        p.   cm.
    Includes bibliographical references and index.
    ISBN 0-205-33546-2 (alk. paper)
    1. Mass media—United States—History.   I. Teeter, Dwight L.   II. Kincaid,
Keith.   III. Title.
P92.U5 F58   2002
302.23'0973—dc21

                                                                      2001046053

Printed in the United States of America

10 9 8 7 6 5 4 3 2 1   06 05 04 03 02 01

Brief Contents

Contents

PART 2   MEDIA IN AN EXPANDING NATION   139

CHAPTER 6   EXPANSION UNIFIES AND DIVIDES   141

CHAPTER 7   COMMUNICATION ISSUES IN THE ANTISLAVERY MOVEMENT AND THE CIVIL WAR   173

PART 3   MEDIA IN A MODERN WORLD   307

CHAPTER 11   PROGRESSIVISM AND WORLD WAR I   309

CHAPTER 12   MEDIA AND CONSUMER CULTURE   355

PART 3   CORPORATE POWER AND GLOBALIZATION   449

CHAPTER 15   ELECTRONIC IMAGES IN A COLD WAR   451

CHAPTER 16   AFFLUENCE AND ACTIVISM   477

Preface

> One has always to reckon with the generation that has gone before. I think where one gets one's real intellectual impetus is reacting against ideas one has felt strongly.
>
> —Richard Hofstadter, "Interview: 1960"

A textbook about history is, at least to some extent, a comment on "reckoning" with the generations that have gone before. The study of history is more than the memorization of dates, facts, and people's names. Studying history is an attempt to understand what has gone before. Such study requires familiarity with methods of historical inquiry and the recognition that the mind of the person inquiring can affect the results of the inquiry itself. That is to say, how we ask the questions can determine the answers.

Only a few decades ago, most historians were male—products of graduate schools dominated by middle- to upper-class men. Those men generally asked questions about how superior men in the past had conceived ideas and how they had structured nations and policies around those ideas. In the 1960s, when more women and minorities attended graduate schools, those individuals began to ask different questions about the past. Therefore, the picture of the past changed.

Communications history as presented in the classroom can take many forms. It can be a study of great men and women journalists, publishers, and broadcasters. It can be a study of publishing and broadcasting as a political enterprise or as an economic enterprise. One can start with the assumption that in colonial America the press was primitive, and that it has progressed over time to a point of unsurpassed professionalism. Or we can look at the press (print, broadcast, and on-line) as an important societal institution that functions in different ways at various times in history. The historical situation, or the values, goals, aspirations, and physical conditions of the society at a given time, will affect the type of journalism practiced in a given time period, and the type of journalism practiced will have an effect on the society.

This book is intended to introduce students to the nature of historical inquiry and to help them understand how the media developed within the context of history. The authors consider how social, cultural, and economic factors influenced the change in the press over time. Special emphasis is given to the role of women and minorities in altering the course of the mainstream press and in developing their own newspapers and magazines to provide alternative political and social viewpoints. The authors hope that this book will contribute to the broadening of intellectual horizons that is an essential part of a liberal arts education.

The great legal historian James Willard Hurst said that history is analogous to a wrestler's training. History can help citizens keep their balance against sudden onslaughts, to understand that although government often seems to be a shield between mass media and efforts to censor or control, it also has, in times of crisis, turned into an opponent of freedom of expression. *Voices of a Nation* analyzes eddying relationships between media and government.

Voices sees technological innovation as contributing to cultural and social change, change accelerated by the eagerness of business institutions to maximize profits. Media are analyzed as business institutions from colonial times, when groups of printers formed networks to share supplies and contracts, into the late twentieth century when media units "went public," issuing shares on stock markets, getting new masters—stockholders and stockbrokers who demanded that profit margins be kept healthy. Predictably, the "bottom-line" management approach led to charges of hyping entertainment at the expense of providing citizens with the information needed to function as informed citizens.

Throughout this analysis, individuals retain distinction. Particular owners are described as examples of specific developments, journalists and public relations practitioners are treated as significant contributors to a process of information, and audiences are seen as changing factors in the interplay of various media. The authors hope to convey the excitement of the role of media in a modernizing society, the conflicts between traditional values and commercial development, the exuberance with which editors confronted the diversity of city life, and the passion with which Native Americans, suffragists, African Americans, immigrants, and agrarian radicals fought for increased recognition.

Finally, we hope our readers will share with us the conviction that history is not dead—that the cliché "past is prologue" is true. As David A. Shannon observed, the present is only the cutting edge of the past.

New to This Edition

This book is reorganized into four parts: Part I: Media in Early America (Chapters 1–5); Part II: Media in an Expanding Nation (Chapters 6–10); Part III: Media in a Modern World (Chapters 11–14); and Part IV: Corporate Power and Globalization (Chapters 15–18). The authors shifted the chapter on Progressivism and World War I from Part II as it appeared in the third edition to Part III, arguing that World War I and the public relations and communications styles and strategies that developed during the war were indeed part of the modern world. Some of these "modern" approaches emanated from the tenets of progressive thought. Part IV was created to reflect increased corporate power and the globalization of media. Two of the chapters that appeared in Part III in the third edition are included in Part IV of the fourth. This reflects the move toward corporate ownership of the 1950s and the disillusionment with distribution of power that emerged in the 1960s. The authors believe this reorganization brings the book up to date and helps professors bring the past twenty years into coherent focus from an historical viewpoint.

Also new in this edition is expanded material on the Civil War, especially regarding the development of the Confederate Press Association, as well as a revision of the material on the Vietnam conflict, which was rewritten to include new scholarship. The section on the language of journalism in the 1960s was tightly edited to put that development more into perspective with other developments of language and style. The last two chapters contain much new material, with a new perspective of the Telecommuncations Act of 1996 and developments throughout the 1980s and 1990s. Other minor changes have occurred throughout the chapters.

Acknowledgments

Numerous research articles and monographs, written by scholars who have mined voluminous files of newspapers, conducted surveys, completed meticulous content analyses, and focused on detailed aspects of media, form the bibliographic base that enabled us to write an analytical synthesis of the history of U.S. media. We express our gratitude to those authors, who often receive little student or public recognition, and hope that *Voices* will stimulate further appreciation of their work. Both authors thank their teachers and their students, whose insights made this book possible. Neither the teachers nor the students, however, should be held accountable for any shortcomings in this book. Errors of commission or omission may be ascribed solely to Jean Folkerts and Dwight Teeter. The authors would also like to thank the following reviewers: Lois Breedlove, Central Washington University; Wallace B. Eberhard, University of Georgia; and Owen V. Johnson, Indiana University.

Many colleagues and friends contributed to the writing of this book, either by reviewing portions of the manuscript or by sharing their knowledge, their time, and their support. Among those are Owen V. Johnson, Indiana University; Christopher H. Sterling, George Washington University, who lent generously from his personal library; Donna M. Bertazzoni, Hood College; James L. Baughman, University of Wisconsin–Madison; Patricia Bradley, Temple University; George Everett, University of Tennessee at Knoxville; Anthony R. Fellow, California State University, Fullerton; Roy Halverson, Arizona State University; Terry Hynes, University of California at Fullerton; Lee Jolliffe, University of Missouri–Columbia; Stephen Lacy, Michigan State University; Judith Yaross Lee, Ohio University; Jerilyn McIntyre, University of Utah; Stephen Ponder, University of Oregon; Nancy L. Roberts, University of Minnesota; Donald Shaw, University of North Carolina at Chapel Hill; Jeffery A. Smith, University of Iowa; John D. Stevens, University of Michigan; Patrick S. Washburn, Ohio University; and Mary Ann Weston, Northwestern University.

Jean Folkerts also would like to acknowledge Del Brinkman, Lee Young, and Norman Yetman at the University of Kansas; the late Jack Backer; and Robert Bontrager and the late Roberta Applegate of Kansas State University. Elaine Prostak Berland, Webster College, also provided insightful critiques on the 1920s, as well as a deep and abiding faith that this project would succeed and continue. Colleagues at The George Washington University, including Jarol B. Manheim, the late Charles Puffenbarger, Janet Steele, Kerric (Lisa St. Clair) Harvey, Steven Livingston, and Steven Keller, have generously supported this project through gifts of time, use of the book, and careful and insightful critiques. Maria George kept a line from forming outside a closed office door. For help on this edition, Folkerts thanks Maxine Cogar and Jesse Demastrie in the Columbian College Office of the Dean at The George Washington University. Keith Kincaid wrote chapter biographies for Chapters 1–17 and Emily Sherinian wrote the Chapter 18 biography of Katherine Graham. Folkerts also thanks her husband, Leroy Towns, for his love and for sharing his ability as an editor; and her parents, Betty and Leonard Folkerts, for their support through good times and bad. She also thanks her children, Sean and Jenny.

Dwight Teeter thanks his wife, Tish, for her loving and judicious advice and acknowledges a special debt to his one-time graduate adviser, co-author, and all-time friend, the late Professor Emeritus Harold L. Nelson of the University of Wisconsin–Madison. Another historian's voice that has remained with Teeter through the years is that of the late professor Merrill Jensen of the University of Wisconsin–Madison. Thanks also go to a splendid historian who insists he is really a law professor, David A. Anderson of the University of Texas at Austin. Other colleagues who have helped Teeter over the years include William E. Ames, Don R. Pember, Roger A. Simpson, and Jerry Baldasty and Professors John D. Stevens, University of Michigan, and the late MaryAnn Yodelis-Smith, University of Wisconsin–Madison. Janine Jennings, administrative secretary at Tennessee, is to be commended for keeping Teeter organized.

The authors also thank the staff of The George Washington University's Gelman Library, as well as Lucy Cocke, Anne Emery, and Ruth Duvall of Eckles Library at Mount Vernon College. Other library staffs also have contributed, including those of the periodical reading room, and the photo and copyright divisions of the Library of Congress; Professor Roy Mersky, law librarian at the University of Texas at Austin; George A. Talbot, Myrna Williamson, and Christine I. Schelshorn of the iconography collections of the State Historical Society of Wisconsin; and Dean Paula Kaufman, now of the University of Illinois, and her colleagues of the Hodges Library of the University of Tennessee.

Generous help also was received from the public relations departments of the *Chicago Tribune* through the good offices of Jeffrey D. Bierig and from Gloria Gilbert of the *Washington Post*. Also helpful in the photography effort were John Klein of the Milwaukee Journal's picture desk and Howard Fibich, deputy managing editor for news of that paper. And finally, the authors would like to thank Mary Beth Finch, production administrator at Allyn and Bacon, and the team at Omega-type Typography, Inc.

Jean Folkerts
Dwight Teeter

Voices of a Nation

WATERLOO INN.

the first Stage from Baltimore to Washington.

Communication was tied to transportation. During colonial days and in the early republic, stagecoaches carried passengers as well as mail. This T. M. Baynes lithograph, published in 1826, depicts the first Baltimore-Washington stage stopped at the Waterloo Inn. (Division of Prints and Photographs, Library of Congress Collection)

PART 1

Media in Early America

▼

From the earliest days in human history, communication was tied inextricably to transportation. Face-to-face communication was accomplished only when two people were in the same place. The continuation of the oral tradition of telling legends as well as the passing on of current information was achieved only through travel. In early America, information could travel only as fast as a person could walk, a canoe or rowboat or sailboat could move through ocean and river waters, or a horse could run. Information had to be collected and then delivered either to a receiver or to an intermediary—such as a publisher.

When John Campbell began his handwritten newspaper in Boston in 1700, he began an enterprise that by the early 1840s developed into an institution. It was characterized by a network of printers scattered throughout the coastal states and across the Appalachians and by a complex relationship between printers, government, and the socioeconomic system.

The technology for such an enterprise was developed in the fifteenth century when Gutenberg invented movable type, paving the way for a transition from an oral and scribal culture to a culture characterized by print, shared information, and facts that could be validated. Newspapers, first developed on the continent of Europe and then in England, became common carriers of information and created bonds of shared knowledge between the Mother Country and British America.

From the beginning, the press was intricately connected to government. Licensing systems developed in England that precluded criticism of government as "seditious libel" were transported to the New World. Some printers, reluctant in the early years to become involved in controversial local politics, focused on foreign news. However, as the colonies grew stronger and more independent, printers spoke out more freely on political issues and began to champion freedom of the press as a philosophical tenet. Nevertheless, public opinion reigned supreme during the Revolutionary War, and Tory opinion was considered treason. During the years when political parties were beginning to form in early America, newspapers helped to forge party lines and often relied on the parties for financing.

Government and the press also were interrelated by the economics of distribution and the importance of postal legislation. The earliest newspapers were started by postmasters, who had free access to the mail. Later, editors often helped start postal systems in order to expand their distribution. The distribution of newspapers outside the major urban centers occurred primarily along major trade routes.

By the 1750s, politicians of opposing sides confronted the issues of civil liberties, including freedom of the press. Libertarians argued the necessity of protecting printers not only from government but from popular majorities as well.

The development of the press was not tied solely to governmental interaction but also was linked to entrepreneurial enterprise. Printers, who often were shopkeepers and booksellers before they were publishers, established ties through family and friendship networks. These networks were important in the distribution of supplies and newspapers and in earning government printing contracts. More importantly, the existence of this network of printers suggests that one should examine how the shared values of these entrepreneurs were reflected in the press of that time.

Editors recruited their audiences, or subscribers, from the colonial elite and from merchants needing information from abroad. The small urban population of early colonial days supported only a few newspapers. As these newspapers expanded and became involved with the ideology of revolution and espoused republican values, the audience broadened to include more shopkeepers and artisans as well as women.

By the time the Constitution was ratified in 1788, the newspaper press had established itself as a profitable enterprise with an expanding audience and as an institution intricately connected with the new government it had participated in forming.

The beginning of the nineteenth century was characterized primarily by a local press, a development in keeping with a society marked by regional differences and filled with debate over the value of national, centralized power versus local control. The issue of governmental control was political and ideological, with politicians of the period fearing the authoritarianism of centralized power. The struggle over this issue's competing theories had a major impact on the press of the nation, particularly during the period of the Alien and Sedition Acts. The partisan press vociferously argued the competing views as political parties developed their own cohesive ideologies.

The debate was cultural as well as political, however. Early debates over postal law indicated that legislators recognized the effects of communication on modernization. Thus, they argued either for a free flow of information that would bind the nation together or for the preservation of local media voices.

Born into the midst of a nation in transition from a local society to an urbanized nation-state was the penny press, which separated financing from party loyalty and relied on advertising in a growing manufacturing economy. First developed in the 1830s in the commercial center of the nation—the city of New York—the penny press soon circulated in weekly form to distant communities. Editors used new technologies to expand circulation, attract broad audiences, and gather news quickly.

While the penny press was able to attract diverse socioeconomic audiences, it was not an accepted model for press activity throughout the nation. Most newspapers remained local and partisan until the end of the Civil War, and many newspapers retained partisan characteristics well into the twentieth century. Native Americans and African Americans utilized older technology to develop newspapers designed to build community among geographically disparate groups. Bible societies, utilizing new technologies as early as 1820, also spanned geographic boundaries.

By the 1840s, the beginnings of the modern press were under way. Newspaper, book, and magazine publishers and the distributors of pamphlets and other reading matter were adapting new technologies in printing, seeking new methods of transportation to speed the collection of news, and providing a diverse range of publications. The lecture circuit as well continued to be a major force in communication at the local as well as the national level. ▼

CHAPTER 1

Crossing the Atlantic

▼

The invention of movable type in Germany in the fifteenth century spurred a printing revolution that was to shatter social structures and encourage the spread of information among varied social classes. English kings and queens tried to restrain this democratization of knowledge because they feared that diversity of thought would lead to dissension. Such fears were carried to British America in the 1600s, where British colonial officials also attempted to maintain control of information.

Until 1750 in the colonies, oral traditions maintained primary importance. Elite networks of clergy and merchants exchanged business and political information chiefly by word of mouth, and they used letters, messengers, and documents only to verify specific aspects of information. After 1730, newspapers gained in importance but still faced hurdles. Communication was tied directly to transportation, and roads were poor at best. The American colonists, who viewed links to the Mother Country as more important than ties to each other, were slow to develop an internal postal system.

Newspapers were published by printers who sometimes acted as editors and booksellers in order to augment their incomes. Other printers received editorial and financial assistance from prominent elites who acted as editors but who preferred to remain in the background. Printing networks composed of business associates or family members spread the printing business from the New England to the Middle

Atlantic colonies and then to the South. The first newspapers provided historical rather than timely accounts of events and practiced a cautious neutrality advocated by Benjamin Franklin that served both political and business interests. ▼

Printing Revolution as a Catalyst for Social Change

The spreading of news—information about public events—throughout empires and the search for printing techniques date to the birth of Christ. However, not until the European printing revolution in the fifteenth century, the result of the invention of movable type, did social interactions alter the nature of societal structures because of the ability to reproduce text in multiple copies. The desire and need for news, of course, is as old as humankind and can be found early in recorded history. Roman scribes carried written news throughout the empire as early as 59 B.C., "helping to ensure that *Romans* stationed in the provinces retained their identity as Romans," and evidence of printing methods is found in the Middle East as early as 1700 B.C.[1] In A.D. 1295, Marco Polo, an Italian adventurer, first brought word to Europe about printing techniques developed by the Chinese. In South America, the Aztecs hung colored paper banners in the main public square of the capital to spread the news. It was, however, the shift from an oral and scribal transmission of culture to a printed culture in Europe that contributed to the democratization of knowledge, or the spreading of knowledge among various social, political and religious groups. The technological revolution brought about by the printing press encouraged the appearance of new relationships among elites, new occupational groups, new trade networks, and new markets for printed matter.[2]

In a print shop in Mainz, Germany, Johannes Gutenberg invented the movable type that was to revolutionize the process for spreading information. Although today Gutenberg is given credit for his innovation, at the time he might have been classified as the first victim of a capitalistic venture in publishing. Gutenberg, who had used woodcuts for printing pictures, planned to carve individual, movable letters from wood. To accomplish his task, Gutenberg borrowed money from a merchant who saw value in the printer's idea. Gutenberg hired a skilled worker who suggested that wood would produce blurry letters and that metal might be a better medium. Once a mold had been made, a letter could be cast from metal as many times as required. Gutenberg and his assistant, Peter Schoeffer, produced a copy of the Bible by 1455, but just as it was ready for sale, Gutenberg's financier demanded repayment of his loan. Because Gutenberg could not settle accounts, the merchant commandeered the printing press and the metalworker. Gutenberg borrowed money from a friend and built another press. However, most of his profit went to pay back his original loan, and Gutenberg never again achieved financial independence.[3] Gutenberg's invention achieved much greater recognition than he did, and his metalworker, Peter Schoeffer, established an important printing business in Mainz.

Before Gutenberg's invention, European cultures represented a combination of oral and scribal traditions that sustained control by the Catholic church and separa-

Figure 1–1   The kind of press used by Gutenberg. (Division of Prints and Photographs, Library of Congress Collection)

tion among social classes.[4] For centuries, monks in monasteries or lay copyists, primarily in university towns, reproduced manuscripts for distribution among a select group of elites. Hand-copying each manuscript required inordinate amounts of time and created possibilities for shifts and changes within the manuscript. Because manuscripts were rare and expensive, even members of the educated classes often relied on teachers reading aloud from a single book, rather than reading from their own copies. This situation changed dramatically after 1450, when early printed editions—ranging from 200 to 1,000 copies—began to appear and printers' workshops sprouted in every important city in Europe.

The printing revolution affected social relationships, as formerly isolated priests and printers began to work with university professors and as these groups began to have contact with metalworkers and mechanics. Careful and competent printer–merchants began to achieve prestigious positions in the cities. Such printers worked hard to remain on good terms with officials, as well as to secure supplies and labor. The printer's shop became a meeting place and educational center within European towns. Soon, printers began searching for new markets for their products, printing handbills, circulars, and sales catalogs advertising their products, which they sent to neighboring countries.

Movable type contributed to a widespread diffusion of information that loosened the grip of the Catholic church on political, moral, and religious discussions. The ability to reproduce a scientific, technical, or religious manuscript in exact form and in many copies enabled the scholarly community to begin to eliminate errors that had persisted through generations as books were copied and recopied. Further, the scholar no longer was required to be a traveler, moving from book collection to book collection, but could remain at home. Rather than intensively studying a single

Figure 1–2   This reproduction of an engraving by Philip Galle from Jan Van Der Straet's *Nova Reperta* depicts a sixteenth-century book printing shop. The introduction of movable type secularized printing and revolutionized business and social relationships. (Division of Prints and Photographs, Library of Congress Collection)

written text, the scholar was able to compare different printed texts. More importantly, the ability to preserve information by circulating copies of a text gradually led to increased democratization of knowledge, or the decentralization of information, and this development ultimately became the basis for the Enlightenment and a growing reliance on rational thought.5 What once might have remained local, such as a slight change in church liturgy or social thought, now was dispersed regionally, nationally, and internationally.6 The best village storytellers were no longer those who manufactured or remembered the tales of yore, but the literate men who passed on orally what they had read. Thus, the "popular culture" of medieval romances became commonly available to villagers long before it was widely available in published form in the nineteenth century.7

Prior Restraint in England: Publishing Precedent

Newspapers, books, and pamphlets flourished in the various countries of Europe during the seventeenth and eighteenth centuries, extending the printing revolution. Nevertheless, English kings and queens, in their efforts to maintain political and religious control, exercised prior restraint over all publishing. William Caxton, the first printer in England, set up a press at Westminster about 1476, on which he published nearly 100 books. Caxton enjoyed royal patronage and worked at a time when the press had not yet become controversial. Printing, however, soon became a dangerous occupation in England, when Henry VIII, who assumed the throne in 1509, struggled with the pope to determine who would control the destiny of England. Although news accounts of single events appeared in parts of Europe during the late 1400s and early 1500s, the king closely controlled their British publication and it was not until the seventeenth century that such accounts were published in England.

As a young man, Henry VIII was content to remain subordinate to the Catholic church and to the pope, who held supremacy not only in religious affairs but in political life as well. When Henry first challenged the church by requesting a divorce from his first wife, Catherine of Aragon, he asserted the power of the state—national government—over the power of the pope. The Reformation Parliament (1529–1536) dismantled the monasteries that remained loyal to the pope and established Henry VIII as the supreme head of the new Church of England. However, Henry rejected few tenets of Catholicism and continued persecuting Protestants. To maintain his control, Henry imposed prior restraint, a system of prepublication censorship that has had many imitators over the years. When publications eluded the network of censors, Henry's government punished those responsible for "seditious libel." Such punishment could be both unutterably cruel and deadly. In 1529, Henry published a list of prohibited books, and on Christmas day of 1534 he ordered printers to secure royal permission to operate. Starting in 1542, the king's advisors, the Privy Council, also arrested individuals for sedition, or criticism of the government, prevented some individuals from publishing, and required, in essence, permission or a license to operate.

Despite these controls, printing gained a foothold in England. One-third of the books published in sixteenth-century England were printed outside the official channels.[8] With the overthrow of papal domination, clerical lands were seized and sold to noblemen. Many of these gentlemen's sons replaced the abbots who had studied at Oxford and Cambridge, thus promoting an educated *commercial* class, as well as the study and questioning of religious dogma. The Bible, printed in English, circulated freely in parish churches. Parishioners were able to read for themselves and no longer relied as intensely on clerical interpretation. Thus, under Henry VIII, England established national independence and freedom of religious inquiry. These two concepts would color the colonists' view of English domination of their colonial world. Unfortunately, Henry's reinforcement of the idea of sedition, already present in English law, and introduction of prior restraint have left remnants that are still controversial concepts in today's legal world.

When Queen Mary, who succeeded Henry VIII, subjugated England to Spain through marriage and attempted to reinstate papal authority, conflict reigned supreme. The queen in 1557 formalized the licensing procedure by establishing the Stationers Company, an organization of printers and dealers in books, in an attempt to stop the growth of Protestantism. Only select printers were allowed to belong to the Stationers and, therefore, to print. Further, the company policed its own members, ordering searches and seizures of unauthorized works.

Throughout the sixteenth century, licensing and prior restraint were common. Under Queen Elizabeth, all new works had to be submitted before publication for clearance by the queen or another authority. During the early years of her reign, Queen Elizabeth allowed both religions to flourish, but when the pope excommunicated her in 1570 and invaded Ireland with his own troops, Catholics were hanged for treason and Puritans persecuted. Illegal printers forfeited books, binders were fined the substantial amount of up to a day's pay per book, and convicted printers served three months in jail and were banned from future printing. The Court of the Star Chamber in 1570 arrested defendants on whim or mere suspicion. Defendants were examined in private; the government had the right to secretly arrest, confine, and try an alleged offender. If a defendant refused to talk before the Star Chamber, guilt was assumed and the person was imprisoned and punished.

Nevertheless, Elizabeth was a popular queen, and she allowed the use of the printing press to expand. Music and literature were printed and disseminated, and the Bible and Anglican Prayer Book circulated freely. Much of the English population, however, resented her attempt to make Anglicanism a state religion and resisted the curbs on their religious freedom.

Licensing Challenge by Books and Newspapers

By the early seventeenth century, literacy had spread sufficiently to create a demand for historical, religious, and romantic tales to be circulated in print, but authorities still restricted the publication of newspapers, regarding them as dangerous. Most European clergymen, lawyers, and aristocrats could read, as could nearly half of the tradesmen and farmers. Although the professional classes were the most likely of all occupational groups to own books, possibly half of *all* males in England did so. Religious books outnumbered all others, but also popular were romances—"fairy stories, chivalric poems, light fiction"—as well as historical narratives that ranged from myth and legend to travelogs. David Hall categorized these texts as the "traditional" world of print, books that appealed across class lines and preserved ancient interpretations of "community origins and community destiny."[9]

James I and Charles I, whose reigns spanned the period from 1603 to 1649, opposed the development of the newspaper in English. The first English language weekly news sheet, *The Corrant out of Italy, Germany, &c,* was published in Amsterdam in 1620 and imported to England. However, James I soon convinced the Dutch to ban exports of English-language newspapers, and he imprisoned English publishers for attempting to print without governmental approval. Despite the threat of the Star Chamber, printed broadsheets carried news of crimes, catastrophes, and scandals. Cautiously printing no local news, Nathaniel Butter and his associates issued news books from 1621 to 1642. *The Continuation of Our Weekly News* appeared at least twenty-three times, with a probable average circulation of 250 to 500 copies.[10]

During the early 1640s, at the beginning of the English Civil War, newspapers flourished in London until Parliament began to exert greater control later in the decade. By 1644, about 6,000 copies of a dozen newspapers in London circulated to the city's residents. John Milton, a Puritan, took advantage of the short-lived, open political climate to write *Areopagitica,* a plea for a free press. "Give me the liberty to know, to utter, and to argue freely according to conscience, above all liberties," he wrote. Milton addressed his plea to Parliament and argued that licensing of the press restricted the dissemination of truth. Milton's argument, far from truly liberal, was made within the context of his Protestant religion. He did not tolerate freedom of expression for Catholic or atheistic ideas. In 1651, serving as secretary to the commonwealth's Council of State, Milton was an official licenser for the Puritans.[11]

After 1660, the British Parliament attempted a variety of licensing measures, but by the end of the century, British lawmakers discarded such attempts as ineffective. Two years after the restoration of the monarchy in 1660, Parliament passed a licensing act that allowed only twenty master printers in the kingdom, concentrated them in London, and put them under the control of the secretaries of state. Based on the

▼

The Power of Truth

And though all the winds of doctrine were let loose to play upon the earth, so truth be in the field, we do injuriously by licensing and prohibiting to misdoubt her strength. Let her and falsehood grapple; who ever knew truth put to the worse, in a free and open encounter?

—Milton's *Areopagitica*

theory that freedom to print was dangerous to the king and a threat to "faith, loyalty, and morality," the act limited both the right and the ability to print.[12] In 1695, due less to a public outcry for freedom of the press than to Parliament's belief that the existing system did not work to sufficiently control the press, the licensing act was not renewed.

Between 1690 and 1713, eight bills were introduced in Parliament to control the press. They failed, not because the English governing class had abandoned the concept of censorship, but because vested interests in the expanding printing and book trades opposed the concentration of publishing that censorship would cause. Ultimately, the increased volume of printing made controls more difficult.[13]

The lapse of the licensing act in 1695 left controls by the king in place but signaled an open door for the proliferation of newspapers in London, the provinces, and the colonies. By 1704, London had nine newspapers, including a daily, that issued twenty-seven editions each week. Between 1695 and 1712, London newspapers established new markets in the countryside, and London printers migrated to provincial and colonial towns to publish their own newspapers.[14]

The social revolution that had begun with the advent of Gutenberg's printing press by the early 1700s had made trade in information a strong enough economic force to overcome the British inclination to wield censorship power.

British America

Information was a scarce but highly prized commodity in British America. The American colonies grew from tiny settlements of political, religious, and economic dissenters in the early 1600s to an extensive network of intricately governed colonies, which by 1700 supplied much of Britain's raw materials and served as an extensive colonial market for the Mother Country. Colonists immigrated to the New World for economic, religious, and political reasons, creating a diverse population in the American colonies. By the end of the colonial period, the colonies were inhabited by 500,000 slaves, 15,000 Huguenots (French Protestants), 100,000 Germans, and the Scotch-Irish. By 1643, eighteen different languages were spoken in New York alone.[15] Information usually circulated by word of mouth, then was verified through written information in the form of letters or public documents. Not until the Stamp Act controversy of the 1760s were newspapers used widely as conveyors of documents or letters in order to provide greater information than word of mouth could deliver. Written information was scarcely ever available to the slave population, both because of illiteracy and language differences and by specific design as a form of elite, white control.

Definitions of News

"Certainly, our society pays enough attention to the news," wrote Mitchell Stephens in *A History of News.* "We watch news, read news, debate news, marvel at, puzzle over, and curse news." In the seventeenth and eighteenth centuries, colonists told news, listened to news in sermons and in tavern-house conversation, and published

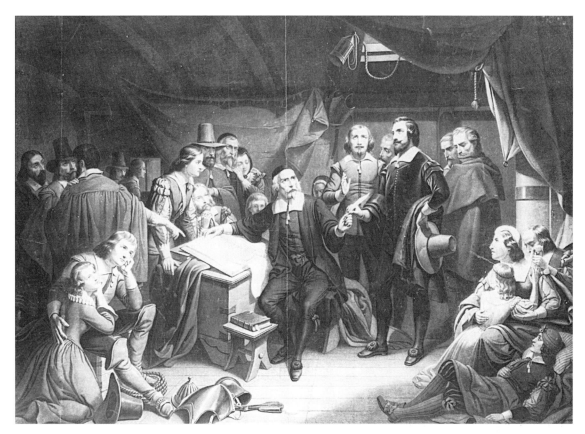

Figure 1–3 Pilgrims signing the compact on board the *Mayflower,* November 11, 1620. From a Gauthier engraving, 1857. (Division of Prints and Photographs, Library of Congress Collection)

news in pamphlet and newspaper form. Scholars have defined news in different ways, some using a broad definition to include casual gossip, while others have defined news as information of a public nature.[16] Stephens, who adopted the broader definition, claimed that individuals are driven to consume news by a "hunger for awareness. . . . The act of telling news brings with it a series of ego gratifications: the opportunity to appear well informed, knowledgeable, current . . . the chance to capture attention, to perform, and win appreciation; and the privilege of branding events with one's own conclusions."[17]

Printed news in British America was rooted in the British tradition and, David Nord claimed, the religious culture of seventeenth-century New England. In that context, news as the reporting of current public occurrences became news that was ordered according to "God's perfect plan." News was meaningful, social, and public. For New Englanders, informed participation in public affairs was deemed essential to a society that required an individual commitment to the public good. Thus, in 1638, when Elizabeth Glover installed the first printing press at Cambridge, she and her printer issued The Freeman's Oath, the formal contract required by citizens of the colony, an almanac, and *Bay Psalm Book* within the first two years of operation.[18] These early publications of the press at Harvard College were not meant simply for individual consumption but rather for fostering the "*public* life of the community."[19]

Publishing news designed to persuade the public of the importance of God's divine plan incorporated several elements, some of which have persisted into twenty-first-century news gathering. Certainly news was not gathered then by professional reporters as we know them today, but Nord pointed out that early works relied heavily on "reportorial empiricism," or the "routine collation and citation of the statements of sources." Similar techniques are a staple of twenty-first-century reporting. "The sources ranged widely," wrote Nord, "from leading scientists to folklore to average people with stories to tell. The role of the writer was not to conduct systematic empirical research but rather to report the empirical statements of others. Such a methodology was empiricism without science. It was, in a word, journalism."[20] Such reporting did not require verification of facts or information. Although the authoritative interpretation of reported news was intended to affirm public authority, the mere existence of published accounts led to a variety of possible interpretations. Thus, Nord claimed that defiance of authority, as well as preservation of

~ Old Bruton Parish Church, Williamsburg, Virginia, and a Sunday gathering in Colonial times. This church was completed in 1715.

Figure 1–4   Sermons delivered at churches such as the Old Bruton Parish Church in Williamsburg were the major legitimate forms of public communication in the early 1700s.

the status quo, emerged from the reporting of public events. That tension of interpretation created a basis for citizenship and participation in community life.

Diffusion of News

The first exchange of news in the American colonies depended on word-of-mouth transactions or letters from ship captains abroad, from official proclamations carried through a colonial postal service reserved primarily for the governmental and religious elite, from formal town meetings and church services, and from less formal tavern or coffeehouse conversations.

Dissemination of information in the colonial period relied heavily on oral messages, which then were verified either through public oratorical events or through letters or documents delivered by messengers. The lack of postal roads and high postal rates determined that most mail officially carried would be related to business or government. In early Boston the clergy were central figures, issuing information and advice from their pulpits and interacting with merchants and public officials to collect information and to make decisions about what information to circulate to the rest of the population. This approach was hierarchical, relying on networks of gentlemen who chose to disseminate only that information that fell into the categories of (1) public instruction and (2) formal public notices. In a society in which face-to-face communication was dominant, the sermon, as the only legitimate form of public address, was generally the vehicle through which such information was disseminated. Elites read the London papers, and it was not until revolutionary times that American newspapers served as major sources of primary information.[21]

In the South, information circulated through elite circles of planters as well as merchant networks. Early southern newspapers, as well as London papers such as the *Tatler* and the *Spectator,* were regarded as essential for developing one's conversational abilities rather than as essential for information. The gentry learned about public affairs through participation, in letters, and from conversation, but they relied on the London papers and early southern news sheets to assure that they were maintaining the English habits of gentility they would have been expected to uphold had they not immigrated to this New World.[22]

The dissemination of written communication depended entirely on transportation. News could be collected only as fast as the ships crossed the ocean or the post rider's horse galloped from New York to Boston. Although a variety of attempts were made during the colonial period to link the colonies and to create communication links with the Mother Country, the colonies remained relatively isolated. In 1736, when William Byrd II wanted to correspond with an old law school friend in Boston, his letter traveled from Virginia to Massachusetts by way of London.[23]

Developing a Postal System

Initiatives to link colonial cities began in 1673, when the New York governor wanted to ensure that he would receive news from England, even in the winter months when ships did not sail as often. His attempts were short-lived, and it was 1692 before the first postal service in the colonies began, privately run under a charter from the king. New York and Massachusetts passed postal acts and initiated service among New York, Massachusetts, and New Hampshire. The post riders also tied together the smaller ports of Massachusetts with the commercial center of Boston.

Other colonies soon joined New York and Massachusetts. In 1693, Pennsylvania passed a postal act. Although Maryland and Virginia passed postal legislation, the legislatures opposed expanding communication routes with the northern colonies. The navigable rivers of Virginia that kept planters in close touch with information from across the Atlantic provided barriers to post riders from the North. Virginians opposed the expensive construction of ferries that would promote land transportation to the north. In 1711, about ten years after John Campbell began the first newspaper, Parliament placed the postal service under government control, but Maryland, Virginia, and the Carolinas remained without service. These colonies finally instituted postal services in the late 1720s and 1730s. A connection between postal services and printers developed in two ways. The earliest newspapers were begun by postmasters, but later, particularly in the southern colonies, printers helped start the postal services that enabled them to mail their newspapers free of charge to other printers and to subscribers.

Information Linked to Trade Routes

Boston, the newspaper center for the first half of the eighteenth century, was home to an important group of printers and booksellers who shared contacts, supplies, and geographic location. These printers, whose businesses were clustered near Boston's busy docks, shipped books and paper along trade routes to various New England states. Jeremy Condy, a Boston bookseller in the 1760s, kept account books indicating that cash was used sparingly in trade and that consignment, bartering of goods and services, and selling on credit were far more common modes of trade. For example, Condy sold paper to Boston publishers Benjamin Edes and John Gill in return for printing and advertising. Condy's ledgers suggested that books and paper traveled farther than did most commercial commodities. Keep in mind, however, that Condy's clients were an elite audience. Although he had customers in more than 134 towns in Connecticut, Rhode Island, Massachusetts, and New Hampshire, each town usually had only two or three customers. These towns were on major trade routes—along the coast, the rivers, or stage routes. Newspapers and booksellers' catalogs traveled along these routes as well. What is strikingly apparent in the account books is that no books traveled to towns *not* located on the trade routes, indicating a line of "cultural demarcation" created by the routes.[24]

Control by Elites

Colonial leaders were little different from the English kings in their fears that diversity of opinion would disrupt the colonies. Therefore, in 1665, a court restricted all Massachusetts printing to Cambridge and required that all print work be reviewed by licensers. Until 1674, no printing was allowed outside of Cambridge.[25]

What happened in Massachusetts was the rule, rather than the exception, in colonial society. Virginia, populated by royalist Anglicans and given to commercial development rather than religious purity, rejected the printing press perhaps even more than New England Puritans. In 1671, the royal governor of Virginia, William Berkeley, thanked God that there were no uncontrolled presses or free schools in his colony, for learning has brought disobedience, and heresy, and sects into the world, and printing has divulged them, and libels against the best government. God keep us from both.[26]

Nevertheless, as early as 1721, authorities ended the licensing of newspapers, and in 1729, the Massachusetts assembly refused to grant the governor permission to institute licensing.

Publishing—A Commercial Enterprise

Printers as Artisans

The social and economic status of printers varied among colonies and from one printer to another, depending on background, training, and whether a printer was able to move into the merchant or landed class. The first newspapers were printed by members of either the artisan or professional class. The status of an artisan fell somewhere below that of the large landowners, wealthy merchants, and professionals, and somewhat above that of the landless laborers and indentured servants. Those printers who also were minor governmental officials probably fell into the lower ranks of the professional class, although it is difficult to know for sure. Class structure was fairly fluid until the middle of the eighteenth century, and although lawyers and clergy, for example, were not considered professionals in the latter part of the sixteenth century, those individuals rose in status over time. Printers who completed their apprenticeships in London probably gained status more quickly than those trained in colonial shops.

Artisans were scarce in colonial America because the development of a trade did not offer the same social mobility as did ownership of land, but such scarcity assured artisans of higher pay than their counterparts in England. Printers often were supported by men of higher standing, who wrote for and helped finance the papers. Printers were hard-pressed to find equipment for their task because England, determined not to let the colonies compete in manufacturing, prohibited many exports of machinery.[27]

Printers learned their trade by the standard method of apprenticeship. An apprentice agreed to work for a set number of years, to serve his masters faithfully, and to remain unmarried while learning his craft. At the end of the set time, the apprentice became a journeyman and perhaps later, a master craftsman. Women were not admitted to the apprenticeship system. However, many women learned printing in the shops of their fathers or husbands, and fourteen women printers were active in the colonies before the start of the Revolution. Most took over established businesses when their husbands died, but at least one woman printer, Mary Crouch, moved her family, type, and presses to another community 1,000 miles away and began a new printing business.[28]

Most printers also were small merchants, and some grew to prominence within their communities. William and Andrew Bradford, Benjamin Franklin, and William Parks, as well as other printers, operated extensive bookselling operations, often dealing directly with London book dealers. They sold other imports as well through their shops, and because currency in the colonies was scarce, they often traded paper and similar items for goods and services. The newspaper and book trades were intricately intertwined. Newspapers advertised books available, and book sales supplemented printers' incomes.

Development of the Book Trade

Colonists read books for pleasure, to maintain a connection to their European past, and to achieve a sense of gentility that was regarded as necessary for upward mobility. Nearly all books in British America during the seventeenth century were imported from England, with the notable exceptions of some religious books and histories published in Cambridge.

In the 1790s, some booksellers shifted their emphasis from making profits from their printing enterprises that accompanied book selling and began to produce American editions of English works. The network of printers struggling to become producers of books acted in what today would be called "restraint of trade" and granted various publishers the right to be the sole producer of an English work. Under these agreements, a single reprint of an English work could circulate up and down the East Coast without competition from other printers. These "men of capital," according to Rosalind Remer, exploited child labor, drove down wages for journeymen printers, and stole intellectual property.[29]

With the expansion of the book trade in the eighteenth century, semipublic libraries were created to serve the population.[30] In Philadelphia, for example, the Library Company was founded in 1731, the Union Library in 1747, and two other libraries in 1757. These libraries operated on a subscription basis. Benjamin Franklin, who opened a printing firm with his partner Meredith in 1728, wrote in his autobiography:

> At the time I establish'd my self in Pennsylvania, there was not a good Bookseller's Shop in any of the Colonies to the Southward of Boston. In New-York and Philadelphia the Printers were indeed Stationers, they sold only Paper, &c., Almanacks, Ballads, and a few common School Books. Those who lov'd Reading were oblig'd to send for their books from England.[31]

In fact, it was Franklin and a group of his friends who each contributed forty pounds to form the Library Company, so that their money could be pooled to import books for joint reading and discussion.

The most common of the imported books were religious works, with school books ranking second in availability. The next largest category of imports was professional books, catering to those in law, medicine, and navigation. Next were those books that could be categorized as *belles lettres*—fiction and poetry.[32] These English works provided a continuity between England and its colonies and between the past and the present.

Many of the early American authors were ministers, publishing their sermons as well as histories. The Reverend Increase Mather's *The Present State of New-English Affairs* was printed in 1689 as a report from Mather to Governor Broadstreet of Massachusetts. Often originally published as pamphlets, such sermons and reports eventually were incorporated into books.

Another dimension of the imported books of that time was revealed in the category known as books for pleasure, often referred to as chapbooks. These books were printed on rough rag paper and, although durable, have not survived because they were "read to death." These cheap booklets competed with almanacs and broadside ballads for acceptance as the most popular of popular literature. Again, tradition was paramount.33 Topics included tales of pirates and highwaymen, cookbooks, household manuals, fortune-telling, and even primitive weather forecasting. Although imports of chapbooks continued until the beginning of the Revolution, during the 1780s increasing numbers of these books were being printed in the colonies.

Newspapers and Pamphlets

By 1739, thirteen newspapers were being published in British America. Relying heavily on news transported from England, these newspapers carried news of the empire to which the colonies belonged and enabled colonists to remain informed about world events that affected their economic, social, and political lives. Publishing English and Continental news, as well as some intercolonial information, the newspapers helped to build a sense of community among members of the heterogeneous and often intolerant colonial population and provided "a vernacular—a common language in both words and pictures"—to allow colonists to express and share political interests.34 Historian Ian Steele described newspapers as "the most powerful and extensive public communications innovation . . . within the English Atlantic empire between 1675 and 1740.35 By the mid-1730s, Boston, a major colonial harbor, was second only to London in the number of newspapers produced. With local and regional markets large enough to support a newspaper enterprise, Boston was fortunate in having a harbor that provided access to news from London, making the city a natural center of newspaper development. Colonial newspapers imitated each other and English newspapers, cautiously avoided political criticism, and cultivated little local identity during the early years. Although the press sometimes profited by government printing contracts, various factions of colonial governments tolerated little criticism, and ventures into local politics brought harassment to colonial editors.

Pamphlets provided another important source for the discussion of public affairs. Philip Davidson claimed that the pamphlet in the prerevolutionary period "was vitally and peculiarly the medium through which was developed the solid framework of constitutional thought."36

By midcentury, Massachusetts, New York, and Pennsylvania—colonies where populations were more concentrated, where the postal service operated under fair circumstances, and where towns, rather than farms, dominated the landscape—boasted the most newspapers. Between 1730 and 1750, newspapers appeared in the southern colonies of Maryland, Virginia, and South Carolina. The growth of newspapers accompanied a rapid expansion in population from 251,000 in 1700 to 1,171,000 in 1750.

Boston News-Letter *as an Historical Account*   As early as 1700, John Campbell—postmaster of the growing town of Boston—was sending handwritten newsletters to governors

New England News
121
4c

Numb. 1.

PUBLICK
OCCURRENCES

Both *FORREIGN* and *DOMESTICK*.

Boston, Thursday Sept. 25th. 1690.

IT is designed, that the Countrey shall be furnished once a moneth (or if any Glut of Occurrences happen, oftener,) with an Account of such considerable things as have arrived unto our Notice.

In order hereunto, the Publisher will take what pains he can to obtain a Faithful Relation of all such things; and will particularly make himself beholden to such Persons in Boston whom he knows to have been for their own use the diligent Observers of such matters.

That which is herein proposed, is, First, That Memorable Occurrents of Divine Providence may not be neglected or forgotten, as they too often are. Secondly, That people every where may better understand the Circumstances of Publique Affairs, both abroad and at home; which may not only direct their Thoughts at all times, but at some times also to assist their Businesses and Negotiations.

Thirdly, That some thing may be done towards the Curing, or at least the Charming of that Spirit of Lying, which prevails amongst us, wherefore nothing shall be entered, but what we have reason to believe is true, repairing to the best fountains for our Information. And when there appears any material mistake in any thing that is collected, it shall be corrected in the next.

Moreover, the Publisher of these Occurrences is willing to engage, that whereas, there are many False-Reports, maliciously made, and spread among us, if any well-minded person will be at the pains to trace any such false Report so far as to find out and Convict the First Raiser of it, he will in this Paper (unless just Advice be given to the contrary) expose the Name of such person, as A malicious Raiser of a false Report. It is Suppos'd that none will dislike this Proposal, but such as intend to be guilty of so villanous a Crime.

THE Christianized *Indians* in some parts of *Plimouth*, have newly appointed a day of Thanksgiving to God for his Mercy in supplying their extream and pinching Necessities under their late want of Corn, & for His giving them now a prospect of a very *Comfortable Harvest*. Their Example may be worth Mentioning.

Tis observed by the Husbandmen, that altho' the With-draw of so great a strength from them, as what is in the Forces lately gone for *Canada*, made them think it almost impossible for them to get well through the Affairs of their Husbandry at this time of the year, yet the season has been so unusually favourable that they scarce find any want of the many hundreds of hands, that are gone from them; which is looked upon as a Merciful Providence.

While the barbarous *Indians* were lurking about *Chelmsford*, there were missing about the beginning of this month a couple of Children belonging to a man of that Town, one of them aged about eleven, the other aged about nine years, both of them supposed to be fallen into the hands of the *Indians*.

A very *Tragical Accident* happened at *Water-Town*, the beginning of this Month, an Old man, that was of somewhat a Silent and Morose Temper, but one that had long Enjoyed the reputation of a Sober and a pious Man, having newly buried his Wife, The Devil took advantage of the Melancholy which he thereupon fell into, his Wives discretion and industry had long been the support of his Family, and he seemed hurried with an impertinent fear that he should now come to want before he dyed, though he had very careful friends to look after him who kept a strict eye upon him, least he should do himself any harm. But one evening escaping from them into the Cow-house, they there quickly followed him found him hanging by a Rope, which they had used to tye their Calves withal, he was dead with his feet near touching the Ground.

Epidemical *Fevers* and *Agues* grow very common, in some parts of the Country, whereof, tho' many dye not, yet they are sorely unfitted for their imployments; but in some parts a more *malignant Fever* seems to prevail in such fort that it usually goes thro' a Family where it comes, and proves *Mortal* unto many.

The *Small-pox* which has been raging in *Boston*, after a manner very Extraordinary, is now very much abated. It is thought that far more have been sick of it then were visited with it, when it raged so much twelve years ago, nevertheless it has not been so Mortal, The number of them that have

337

Figure 1–5   Facsimile of *Publick Occurrences, Both Forreign and Domestick*.

of the New England colonies ringing Massachusetts. His goal was not to meet a fast-breaking deadline but rather to provide an historical account for those far away from European decision making. From this laborious effort to summarize English news grew colonial America's first successful newspaper, the *Boston News-Letter*. Campbell enjoyed special privileges as Boston's postmaster. He gleaned a substantial amount of news from post riders and others who came by the post office, and he could send and receive mail and newspapers at reduced expense. He published with prior permission from government, focusing on foreign news. Although he operated to make a profit, his limited audience of about 300 brought him little subscription money for his effort, despite occasional government subsidies.

After several years of scratching out his newsletters by hand, Campbell must have regarded the creaking wooden-framed press that he used to print the edition on April 24, 1704, as a great luxury. The publication was tiny by twenty-first-century standards—6¼ inches by 10½ inches—smaller than a piece of typing paper but comparable to its English predecessors.

Campbell avoided the local politics that had caused the quick demise of Benjamin Harris' 1690 attempt to publish *Publick Occurrences, Both Forreign and Domestick* and obtained approval of news before publishing. Set in boldface type, just under the newspaper's nameplate, was the prominent statement "Published by Authority." Campbell strived to give his readers a continuing account of news from abroad, but his news often was published from six to thirteen months after its occurrence. Although Campbell often received London accounts more quickly than he published them, he hesitated to leave out information and lacked the finances to print enough pages to include all the news.

The first issue brought the colonists news from England, but it also indicated a growing interest among readers in the relationship between colonies. It contained an extract about James VIII of Scotland from the *London Flying Post;* an account of the queen's speech to Parliament; a few articles from Boston; four paragraphs of marine intelligence from New York, Philadelphia, and New London; and a sole advertisement—for Campbell's newspaper.[37]

Campbell's ad brought no immediate revenue:

> This News Letter is to be continued Weekly; and all Persons who have any Houses, Lands, Farmes, Ships, Vessels, Goods, Wares or Merchandizes, &c., to be Sold or Lett; or Servants Runaway; or Goods Stoll or Lost, may have the same Inserted at a Reasonable Rate; from Twelve Pence to Five Shillings. . . .
>
> All Persons in Town and Country may have said News Letter Weekly upon reasonable terms, agreeing with John Campbell Post Master for the same.[38]

John Campbell edited the *Boston News-Letter* for eighteen of its seventy-two years, but he never managed to make money from the effort. At the end of the first year, he wrote that his paper

> was propounded to be Printed for one year for a tryal . . . to see Income by the Sale thereof at a moderate price would be sufficient to defray the necessary Charge

expended in the procuring and printing of same, which Charge is considerable beyond what most conceive it to be, besides the trouble and fatigue attending it.[39]

Campbell listed some of his expenses, which included gathering information along the continent's edge, with post riders and ships having to cover "almost 500 miles from E. to W. from N. Hampshire to Pensilvania." He also paid correspondents who lived in other seaports "for sending intelligence." Campbell lamented the time, as well as the money, spent. He complained of "Waiting on Masters, Merchants, and others when Ships & Vessels arrive to have from them what Intelligence they can give" and of "Waiting on His Excellency (the Governor) or (his) Secretary for approbation of what is Collected."

Campbell's occasional appeals to the government for subsidies to supplement his paper's meager income was further testimony of his economic insecurity. Despite subsidies, the *News-Letter* suspended publication from March of 1709 until January of 1710.[40]

Although Campbell endeavored to avoid controversy and to please the officials of Massachusetts Bay Colony, he was unsuccessful. Even his abject apologies for one tiny error—putting a comma in the wrong place in a story—did not save his political hide. In 1719, Campbell lost his job as postmaster to William Brooker, who immediately began a new paper, the *Boston Gazette*.

Campbell continued to publish his *News-Letter* after losing his postmastership, keeping the paper going until 1722. He and Brooker overtly competed for subscribers, primarily on the basis of who could provide the latest news. Bartholomew Green, who printed the paper for Campbell during much of the *News-Letter's* existence, took over the paper in 1722.[41] Once Campbell lost his postmastership, the motto under the *News-Letter's* nameplate—"Published by Authority"—also disappeared.

Local Controversy in the New-England Courant   James Franklin, a young printer in charge of producing the *Boston Gazette* during its first year, soon turned to printing controversial materials, and on August 7, 1721, he published the first issue of the *New-England Courant*. The newspaper appeared at the end of a summer distinguished by a raging smallpox epidemic; half the population of Boston was infected, and one person in seven died. The editors noted from the beginning that the paper would be controversial, attacking the Congregational clergy and actively opposing inoculation for smallpox.[42] The *Courant* introduced items of wit and humor, reprinting the popular English essays of Addison and Steele, as well as supplying local humor and news. Further, and significantly, it was the first Boston newspaper to start without benefit of postmaster support. For his efforts, James Franklin served time in jail for seditious libel, a warning to future printers of colonial America.[43]

Franklin and a Newspaper Crusade   Franklin began his *New-England Courant* in 1721 during an economic depression, in a small community, and in competition with five other printers. Controversy was a staple he hoped would help him compete in such an environment. In the long run, repression turned out to be more of a problem for James Franklin than finances. During the early eighteenth century, criticism of government could lead a writer or printer to jail, and government authorities sought, and at times exercised, the stringent power of prior restraint.

▼ **Table 1–1**

New England Courant (2 pages)	*Boston Gazette* (4 pages)	*Boston News-Letter* (4 pages)
History of inoculation (over 1 page)	Letter on the South Sea Company	Foreign news (3¹/₂ pages)
Short letter from a Dr. Herrick on the ineffectiveness of inoculation	Reprint of letter to the *London Journal* regarding peace with the Moors on Gibraltar	Meeting of the Boston Council on smallpox scheduled
Article answering the *Anti-Courant* and defining the purpose of the paper	Gossip and news from London (1 page)	Custom house notices
Report on the South Sea Company	News from the *London Journal* (1 page)	Advertisements:
News from Philadelphia	Meeting of the Boston council on smallpox scheduled	1. Brigantine for sale
Journey of Cadwallader Colden to the New York Council	Advertisements:	2. Notice of pirates
Plague in France	1. Wine for sale	3. Sale of goods including slaves
Report from the custom house	2. Notice of pirates	4. Settling of Harris estate
Advertisements:	3. Sale of various goods including slaves	5. Settling of Heskew estate
1. Announcement refuting the rumor that the physicians were now favoring inoculation	4. Lost items	6. Settling of Kelly estate
2. Advertisement for the *Courant* itself	5. Wine for sale	
	6. Assignment of debts	
	7. Prints and maps from England for sale	
	8. Request for return of books	
	9. Sale of estate	
	10. Rhode Island to exchange counterfeit currency	

In 1719, for example, an Anglican minister, the Reverend John Checkley, challenged the Puritan-controlled government and society of that colony. The governor exercised prior restraint by ordering Checkley not to publish anti-Calvinist writing. The Massachusetts legislature then passed a statute requiring anyone who was suspected of being "disaffected" with the king to swear an oath of loyalty. When Checkley refused to take the oath, he was fined six pounds and ordered by the court to be on "good behavior."[44]

The dissenting minister, Checkley, found an ally in the iconoclastic printer, James Franklin. Both were ready to challenge the Puritan clergy, led by Increase Mather and his son, Cotton Mather. The treatment of smallpox represented a challenge to the existing leadership, rather than an effort to investigate or publish facts to resolve a controversy:

> Defiance was the soul of the *Courant,* the spirited cry of newcomers bumping against an old elite, of artisans mocking the more respectable classes, of provincials picking up the language of London coffee houses, and of eighteenth-century men recovering the nerve to mock and amuse in the face of the grave.[45]

Cotton Mather had learned of experiments in inoculating healthy persons to prevent them from contracting smallpox and urged that this strange-sounding new procedure be used to halt the epidemic. Many Bostonians, however, including all but one physician, countered that inoculation—using blood from persons who had survived the pox—would surely add to the number of deaths from the disease.[46]

Checkley, who wrote most of the material for the first issues, confronted the Puritan advocates of inoculation, saying they were men

> Who like faithful Shepherds take care of their Flocks, By teaching and practicing what's Orthodox,
> Pray hard against Sickness, yet preach up the POX![47]

The Reverend Thomas Walter, grandson of Increase Mather, strongly favored inoculation, and he responded to the *Courant*'s first issue with a single sheet labeled *The Little-Compton Scourge, or The Anti-Courant.* The third issue of the *Courant* accused the Reverend Walter of drunkenness and other improprieties. Franklin, uncomfortable with such attacks, removed Checkley as "editor" of the *Courant* but did not abandon the controversy. The *Courant,* whose supporters soon were dubbed the "Hell-Fire Club," continued to publish anti-inoculation pieces, with supporters of the Mathers using the *Boston Gazette* to return journalistic salvos.

Franklin's Freedom Restrained   After several issues, James Franklin's *Courant* turned away from a virtually exclusive concern with the inoculation controversy and adopted the satirical tone of contemporary British newspapers. James Franklin wrote an essay in letter form, attributing it to "Ichabod Henroost," not at all unlike a "Nathaniel Henroost" piece published earlier in the *Spectator* of London.[48]

James Franklin's journalistic rambunctiousness came at a time when the governor's licensing power was being disputed. During the 1720s a standard section of a governor's set of formal instructions from the king included licensing procedures. When the Massachusetts governor turned to the legislature for approval of his licensing power, the House of Representatives, struggling to secure dominance over the governor, refused to cooperate. As a by-product of the struggle, printers gained some limited freedom.[49]

That freedom was tenuous at best, however, and in 1722, Franklin slyly suggested in the *Courant* that the Massachusetts General Court was not trying hard enough to keep pirates from preying on colonial shipping. Franklin satirically wrote that a ship was being prepared to pursue the pirates "sometime this month, wind and weather permitting."[50]

▼

Benjamin Franklin (1706–1790)

Perhaps no figure from American colonial history is more written about than Benjamin Franklin. But then, Benjamin Franklin published enough during his lifetime to keep scholars busy for centuries. His writings spanned his entire life. His first essay was submitted to a printing shop in Boston owned by his brother, James Franklin. Young Benjamin—only sixteen and an apprentice at the time—slipped it under the door. Franklin's final letter to the press was written just weeks before he died in 1870.

Source: Verner W. Crane, *Benjamin Franklin's Letters to the Press, 1758–1775* (Chapel Hill: University of North Carolina Press, 1950). (Division of Prints and Photographs, Library of Congress Collection)

This reflection on government resulted in a month's imprisonment for James Franklin. While in jail, he continued to run the newspaper with a highly able substitute editor, his younger brother Benjamin. Almost ten years younger than James, Benjamin Franklin had been apprenticed to his brother's printing house for five years, since the age of twelve. With James in jail, the seventeen-year-old Ben got to see first-hand the dangers of confronting an autocratic political structure head-on.

Indeed, a committee of the General Court was named to study the offensive publication called the *New-England Courant.* Early in 1723, the committee reported that the tendency of the paper was to mock religion, profanely abuse scriptures, and affront government. The committee forbade James Franklin to print any unapproved publication and released him on good behavior and sufficient bond. Franklin went into hiding after refusing to obey and was arrested when he reappeared. However, a grand jury refused to indict him. Meanwhile, James publicly released Ben from his indenture, but he had his younger brother sign a secret agreement intended to bind Ben to continued servitude.[51]

So in 1723, if only as a "front man" for his brother, the teenaged Benjamin Franklin began publishing the *Courant.* The younger Franklin's cleverness had never been fully engaged by the routine life of an apprentice printer; since March of 1722, he had been writing essays under the pen name "Silence Dogood."

Through these fourteen essays the young Franklin gently satirized the foibles of human nature.[52] Franklin modeled the essays after those he read in London's *Spectator.* Silence Dogood purported to be a talkative and philosophical widow, who, in high-flown moments, styled herself an "Enemy to Vice, and Friend to Virtue" as well as a "mortal Enemy to arbitrary Government & Unlimited Power."[53] According to Ben Franklin, it took his brother James six months to discover the identity of the essays' author. Ben's far-wiser-than-his-years, amused, and amusing tone colored the introductory prospectus he wrote for his *Courant:*

> The main design of this Weekly Paper will be to entertain the Town with the most comical and diverting Incidents of Human Life, which in so large a Place as Boston, will not fail of a universal Exemplification: Nor shall we be wanting [lacking] to fill up these Papers with a grateful Interspersion of more serious Morals, which may be drawn from the most ludecrous and odd Part of Life.[54]

Silence Dogood Speaks

I DOUBT not but moderate Drinking has been improv'd for the Diffusion of Knowledge among the ingenious part of Man-kind, who want the Talent of a ready Utterance, in order to discover the Conceptions of their Minds in an entertaining and intelligible Manner. 'Tis true, drinking does not improve our Faculties, but it enables us to USE them; and therefore I conclude, that much Study and Experience, and a little Liquor, are of absolute Necessity for some Tempers, in order to make them accomplish'd Orators.

The secret indenture papers had no force, and within months Benjamin Franklin quarreled with his brother and left Boston to seek freedom and his fortune elsewhere.

James Franklin continued his *New-England Courant,* a newspaper that remained sassy but economically unsuccessful. He ended the *Courant* in 1726, moving to Newport, Rhode Island, to become a government printer. In 1732, he established the *Rhode-Island Gazette,* which lasted only a year and evidently was not profitable. His health failed, and James died in 1735 after a long illness. His widow, Anne Smith Franklin—whom he had married in 1724—then ran the printing house successfully, working on such projects, for example, as the printing of the laws of Rhode Island in 1745. Journalism historian Isaiah Thomas wrote that Anne Franklin "was aided in her printing by her two daughters, and afterward by her son when he gained a competant age." The daughters, "sensible and amiable women," were termed "correct and quick compositors at the [type] case."[55] Her son, James Franklin, Jr., became his mother's partner and, after an apprenticeship in Philadelphia with his Uncle Ben, established the *Newport Mercury,* a newspaper that endured into the twentieth century.[56]

Publishing Enterprise in Philadelphia—The Bradford Dynasty

In the 1720s and 1730s, several printers operated in Philadelphia, and at least two newspapers successfully competed. Andrew Bradford, his adopted son William, and Andrew's widow created a dynasty that vied successfully with Benjamin Franklin's printing establishment. These powerful printing networks fostered the development of publishing as a commercial enterprise throughout the Middle Atlantic and southern colonies.

Andrew Bradford, who learned printing in New York in a shop belonging to his father, William Bradford, moved to Philadelphia about 1712. In 1719, the younger Bradford began printing the first newspaper in Pennsylvania, *The American Mercury.* The only printer in Pennsylvania until 1723, he became the postmaster of Philadelphia in 1732.

In 1741, Andrew Bradford published *The American Magazine, or Monthly View of the Political State of the British Colonies.* Its publication date—February 13, 1741—established it as the first magazine in the British North American colonies, but only by three days. Competition came from Benjamin Franklin's *General Magazine, and Historical Chronicle, for all the British Plantations in North America.* These two publications were short-lived, with Bradford's magazine lasting only three months and Franklin's only six.[57] Andrew Bradford's brother, William Bradford, Jr., also was a printer and bookseller in Philadelphia, but he is little remembered today. He was the father of William Bradford III, who was born in New York City in 1719. At the age of fourteen, William III was apprenticed to his childless Uncle Andrew, who adopted him. Andrew and William Bradford III were partners in Philadelphia for a short while, from 1739 to 1740. Young William sailed to London in 1741 to visit a great aunt who had inherited the substantial Sowle printing house in London, where his grandfather had learned printing.[58]

William Bradford III, who earned the title of colonel for his military activity during the French and Indian Wars, began publishing the *Pennsylvania Journal and Weekly Advertiser* in December 1742. The *Journal,* with new type brought from England, quickly became one of the best-appearing papers in the colonies. In direct competition with Bradford was his stepmother, Cornelia. After Andrew Bradford's death, she had gone into partnership with Isaiah Warner. When that partnership had dissolved about two years later, she continued in business for herself for another two years. In 1752, Bradford opened the London Coffee-House at Front and Market streets, which became a major commercial center in Philadelphia. William Bradford III, with his major ties to the London printing houses and booksellers, made bookselling a substantial portion of his business, dealing with London bookdealer John Oswald, who sponsored popular dissenting authors, both in religion and in politics.[59]

In 1762, William Bradford III's son, Thomas, joined his father in the printing house and subsequently became a partner. Thomas assumed total responsibility for the newspaper in 1778, after his father suffered business losses during the War for Independence, especially during the British occupation of Philadelphia from 1777 to 1778. Thomas converted the *Journal* to a daily, and the paper continued until 1814.

Benjamin Franklin in Philadelphia Competition

Often viewed as the Renaissance man who discovered electricity, edited newspapers, and conveyed political messages to France, Benjamin Franklin viewed printing as a business and as a public service. He discussed in print the concept of neutrality, which he considered a matter of both sound business and principle, and he extended a printing network southward by financing several printers as they began news operations. Although he had no direct intention of doing so, he also provided an opportunity for a woman to gain a foothold in the printing business.

Franklin, who had escaped his brother's iron hand by moving to Philadelphia, had gone by way of New York, where he hoped to find work with William Bradford. Bradford sent him to Philadelphia with an introduction to his son, Andrew. Franklin found work with the printer Samuel Keimer and soon became involved in a scheme with Pennsylvania's Governor William Keith to establish a printing house in Philadelphia. Promised letters of credit from Governor Keith, Franklin went to London in 1724 to buy printing equipment. The nineteen-year-old soon discovered the letters of credit had not been written, and he worked for a time at a London printing establishment.[60] He returned to the Philadelphia shop of Samuel Keimer but left in 1728 after a squabble with the older man. After entering the printing business with a friend, Franklin attracted considerable business through a group of friends who formed a debating society called the Junto.

Upon hearing a rumor that Franklin intended to start a newspaper, Samuel Keimer rushed into print with *The Universal Instructor in all Arts and Sciences; and Pennsylvania Gazette.* The grandiose title competed with William Bradford's *American Weekly Mercury,* a publication that Franklin and his friends, attempting to outwit Keimer, had helped make popular by submitting satirical essays called the *Busy-Body Papers.* After nine months of publication, Keimer sold his paper to Franklin and his friend.

In 1729, the twenty-four-year-old Franklin became sole owner of his printing house and the newspaper he titled the *Pennsylvania Gazette.* This paper, with its mission of "Carrying the freshest Advices Foreign and Domestick," was only the most visible part of a growing business. Franklin not only published advertisements, but he also peddled a variety of goods and services from his printing house. He offered stationery, paper, ink, and pens; did bookbinding; and sold books, dried fish, cheese, and chocolate.

Ben Franklin practiced the common colonial printing strategy of cautious neutrality, writing in "An Apology for Printers," published in the *Pennsylvania Gazette* on June 10, 1731, that

> Printers are educated in the Belief, that when Men differ in Opinion, both Sides ought equally to have the Advantage of being heard by the Publick; and that when Truth and Error have fair Play, the former is always an overmatch for the latter: Hence they chearfully serve all contending Writers that pay them well, without regarding on which side they are of the Question in Dispute.[61]

Franklin further argued that printing both sides of an issue was necessary to make a living:

> That hence arises the peculiar Unhappiness of that Business, which other Callings are no way liable to; they who follow Printing being scarce able to do any thing in their way of getting a Living, which shall not probably give Offence to some, and perhaps to many; whereas the Smith, the Shoemaker, the Carpenter, or the Man of any other Trade, may work indifferently for People of all Persuasions, without offending any of them and the Merchant may buy and sell with jews, Turks, Hereticks and Infidels of all sorts, and get Money by every one of them, without giving Offense to the most orthodox, of any sort, or suffering the least Censure or Ill will on the Account from any Man whatever.

Franklin's arguments in his "Apology" contended that a practical approach helped bring in money.[62] His comments were couched in the romantic notion of John Milton's *Areopagitica:* that if all opinions could be heard, given a free and open encounter, truth would "overmatch" error.

Although Andrew Bradford's newspaper and printing house successfully continued, Benjamin Franklin's enterprising spirit and ready wit constituted formidable opposition. His *Pennsylvania Gazette* became the most successful newspaper of the colonial years. In 1732, Franklin first published *Poor Richard's Almanack*, a money-maker—and an advertisement for his printing house—and it lasted for years to come. It combined predictions for the ensuing year, humor, and a seemingly endless fund of self-improvement advice:

> In Things of moment, on thy self depend,
> Nor trust too far thy Servant or thy Friend:
> With private views, thy Friend may promise fair,
> And servants very seldom prove sincere.

> He that would be beforehand in the World, must be beforehand with his Business: It is not only ill Management, but discovers a slothful Disposition, to do that in the Afternoon, which should have been done in the morning.

Extension of Franklin's Network to the Southern Colonies   Franklin's influence stretched into the southern colonies as he sponsored printers in Virginia and South Carolina. William Parks in 1727 began the *Maryland Gazette,* and in 1736 he extended his operation to Virginia, where his office became a central place for the exchange of news as well as the official

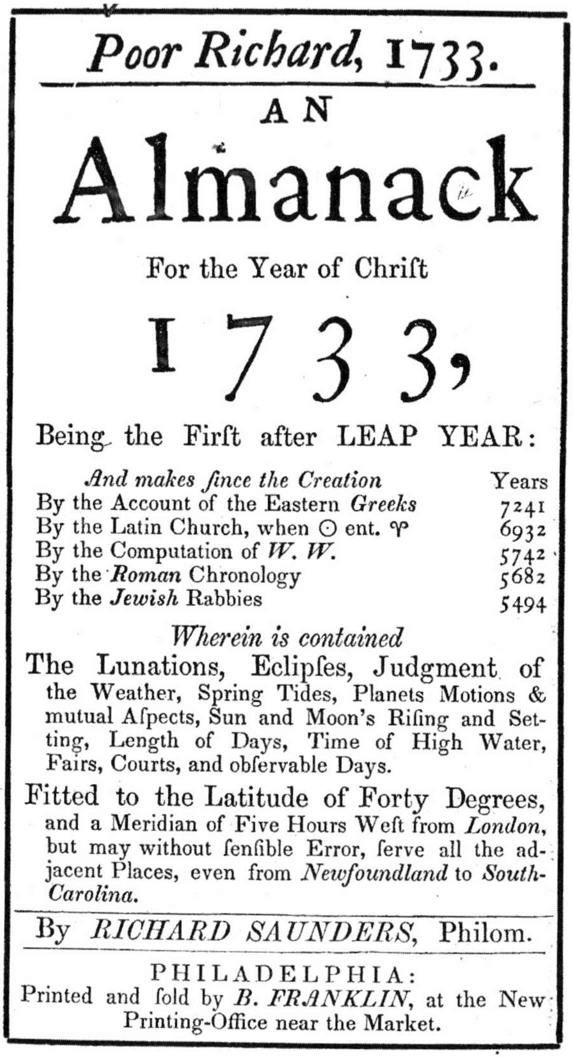

Figure 1–6 *Poor Richard's Almanack,* 1733, was a money-making publication for Benjamin Franklin. (Division of Prints and Photographs, Library of Congress Collection)

Poor Richard, **1733.**

A N

Almanack

For the Year of Chrift

1733,

Being the Firſt after LEAP YEAR:

And makes fince the Creation	Years
By the Account of the Eastern *Greeks*	7241
By the Latin Church, when ☉ ent. ♈	6932
By the Computation of *W. W.*	5742
By the *Roman* Chronology	5682
By the *Jewish* Rabbies	5494

Wherein is contained

The Lunations, Eclipſes, Judgment of the Weather, Spring Tides, Planets Motions & mutual Aſpects, Sun and Moon's Riſing and Set-ting, Length of Days, Time of High Water, Fairs, Courts, and obſervable Days.

Fitted to the Latitude of Forty Degrees, and a Meridian of Five Hours Weſt from *London,* but may without ſenſible Error, ſerve all the ad-jacent Places, even from *Newfoundland* to *South-Carolina.*

By *RICHARD SAUNDERS,* Philom.

PHILADELPHIA:

Printed and ſold by *B. FRANKLIN,* at the New Printing-Office near the Market.

post office. Isaiah Thomas said Parks' salary consisted of 2,000 pounds of produce, which coincides with other reports that goods, rather than cash, often provided the means of exchange between a printer and his clients at the time. As the official printer of the Laws of Maryland, Parks continued to maintain his Maryland printing shop even though he moved to Virginia in 1731. For a time he served as official printer to both colonies. In 1736, he started the first newspaper in Virginia, the *Virginia Gazette.*[63]

The Williamsburg printing office, established nearly a century after printing began in New England, was a major source of information for Virginians during the last four colonial decades. The shop, positioned along Duke of Gloucester Street, the main thoroughfare of the Virginia capital, served as a printing office, bookshop, and post office starting in the 1740s. Religious protest and a well-educated clergy like that which promoted printing in New England did not exist in Virginia, and colonists were content to read the products of English writers, relying primarily on direct imports from London.[64] William Parks imported Bibles, prayer books, and school books from England. By the time Parks died in 1750, his inventory had expanded greatly, and bookselling assumed a greater portion of his business.

In addition to bookselling, Parks contributed to Williamsburg's economy by establishing a paper mill with the assistance of Benjamin Franklin. When the intercolonial postal service reached Williamsburg in 1738, Parks' shop also became the post office, and Parks published a variety of the colony's laws as the official printer for Virginia.[65]

Another southern printer sponsored by Benjamin Franklin was Lewis Timothy, a French Protestant immigrant and French teacher, who served as the official printer to South Carolina and the editor of the *South Carolina Gazette.* The first printers in South Carolina had arrived there in 1731 or 1732, apparently publishing a few issues of the *South Carolina Weekly Journal* and the *South Carolina Gazette,* but two of the papers died during the next year. With the goal of reviving a newspaper that had perished, Franklin established a partnership with Timothy, signing a six-year contract that provided for Timothy's elder son, Peter, to take over in case of his father's death. Under Timothy's management, the *Gazette* resumed publication in February of 1734. Timothy was a commercial success, operating a shop as well as the newspaper and also functioning as official printer. In 1736, he gained a grant for 600 acres of valuable Charleston property. When he died in December 1738, his wife, Elizabeth, successfully took over operation of the newspaper, despite the fact that she bore her sixth child less than a month after her husband died. Benjamin Franklin commented that

> she not only sent me as clear a state as she could find of the transactions past, but continued to account with the greatest regularity and exactitude every quarter afterwards, and managed the business with such success that she not only brought up reputably a family of children but at the expiration of the term was able to purchase of me the printing house and establish her son in it.[66]

In addition to printing international and local news and becoming involved in controversies such as piracy, Elizabeth Timothy also pleaded the plight of women. In November of 1743, after much commentary in the newspaper on the role of women, she printed this verse:

How wretched is a woman's Fate,
No happy change her Fortune knows,
Subject to Man in Every state.
How can she then be free from woes?

In Youth a Father's stern Command,
And jealous Eyes controul her will;
A lordly Brother watchful stands,
To keep her closer Captive still.
The tyrant Husband next appears,
With awful and contracted Brow;
No more a Lover's form he wears,
Her Slave's become her Sov'reign now.[67]

Elizabeth Timothy turned the shop over to her son in 1746. Evidently, she and her husband had been quite successful; in her will she left her son and three daughters a silver watch, two houses, two slaves, and clothing in addition to money that would accrue from selling another house, three slaves, and furniture.[68]

Conclusion

A printing revolution in the fifteenth century paved the way for a transition from a primarily oral or scribal culture to a printed culture. The ability to print simultaneously multiple copies of a work enabled the more accurate transmission of information and encouraged the sharing of identical information. In moving the copying of books from the monasteries and universities to the print shops, literate elites and printers developed new relationships. Printing developed in England despite strict controls on presses and printers, and newspapers flourished particularly during periods when licensing acts were not in effect. In British America, information was a highly prized, scarce commodity that circulated primarily among elites by word of mouth. Letters, messengers, and documents served to verify circulated information.

Despite the heterogeneity of the colonial population, intolerance rather than diversity characterized early use of the printing press, which was used at first to print official proclamations and religious pamphlets. Colonial newspapers appeared at about the same time that English provincial papers began developing. The early newspapers lacked a substantial economic base, focused heavily on foreign news, and cautiously approached the types of local controversy that could bring printers into conflict with licensing acts or governmental authority. James Franklin, in publishing the *New-England Courant,* demonstrated the difficulty of writing about local controversy. Nevertheless, his newspaper represented a departure from the earlier *News-Letter* and *Gazette* by introducing controversy, wit and humor, and coverage of local events. Benjamin Franklin and the Bradfords expanded the printing network to New York, the middle colonies, and the South, and Franklin introduced discussions of the principle and good business practice of neutrality. Cornelia Bradford and Elizabeth Timothy made significant contributions to the printing business, although they were regarded chiefly as continuing their husbands' businesses.

In the period dating from the beginnings of the North American newspaper to the years preceding the War for Independence, active artisans and members of the professional class established print shops in connection with bookselling operations, stationery sales, and newspaper production. Printers were trained through apprenticeships, both in the colonies and in London or the English provinces. Their incomes depended on the success not only of their newspapers but also of their operations as a whole, including the securing of appointments to fill postmaster positions and commissions to print official documents. The printing trade first developed in the cities, such as Boston, Philadelphia, New York, and then Annapolis and Williamsburg. The distribution of newspapers and books followed the major trade routes. Attempts to publish magazines were short-lived.

Endnotes

1. Mitchell Stephens, *A History of News* (New York: Penguin Books, 1988), p. 67.

2. For a detailed discussion of this thesis and the impact of the printing revolution on the Renaissance and the Reformation, see Elizabeth L. Eisenstein, *The Printing Revolution in Early Modern Europe* (Cambridge: Cambridge University Press, 1983). For further exploration of the relationship between elites and nonelites, see David Hall, "The World of Print and Collective Mentality," in John Higham and Paul K. Conkin, eds., *New Directions in American Intellectual History* (Baltimore: Johns Hopkins University Press, 1980), pp. 166–80. See also Eisenstein, *Grub Street Abroad: Aspects of the French Cosmopolitan Press from the Age of Louis XIV to the French Revolution* (Oxford: Clarendon Press, 1992).

3. S. H. Steinberg, *Five Hundred Years of Printing* (New York: Criterion Books, 1959), pp. 21–22.

4. For discussions of the history of literacy, with particular attention to the development of theories of oral traditions and definitions of literacy, see Carolyn Marvin, "Constructed and Reconstructed Discourse: Inscription and Talk in the History of Literacy," *Communication Research* 11:4 (October, 1984), pp. 563–94; and Harvey J. Graff, "The Legacies of Literacy," *Journal of Communication* 32 (Winter, 1982), pp. 12–26.

5. The Enlightenment was an eighteenth-century philosophical movement concerned with criticism of existing institutions and doctrines, usually from a rationalist point of view. Rationalism is based on the theory that reason, rather than spiritual revelation or authority, is the valid basis for action.

6. Eisenstein, *Printing Revolution*, p. 80.

7. Eisenstein, *Printing Revolution*, p. 94.

8. Hall, "Collective Mentality," p. 167.

9. Hall, "Collective Mentality," pp. 171–72.

10. Ian K. Steele, *The English Atlantic, 1675–1740: An Exploration of Communication and Community* (New York: Oxford University Press, 1986), pp. 133–34.

11. Jeffery A. Smith, *Printers and Press Freedom: The Ideology of Early American Journalism* (New York: Oxford, 1988), p. 34.

12. Jeremy Black, *The English Press in the Eighteenth Century* (Philadelphia: University of Pennsylvania Press, 1987), p. 2.

13. Black, *English Press*, p. 9. Smith, *Printers and Press Freedom*, p. 21. Richard D. Brown, *The Strength of a People: The Idea of an Informed Citizenry in America, 1650–1870* (Chapel Hill: University of North Carolina Press, 1996), p. 28.

14. Steele, *English Atlantic*, pp. 136–38.

15. For details of political, economic, and religious emigration, see Jerome E. Reich, *Colonial America* (Englewood Cliffs, New Jersey: Prentice-Hall, 1984), p. 154.

16. Richard D. Brown, *Knowledge Is Power: The Diffusion of Information in Early America, 1700–1865* (New York: Oxford, 1989).

17. Mitchell Stephens, *A History of News*, pp. 3, 18, 20.

18. Marion Marzolf, *Up from the Footnote* (New York: Hastings House, 1977) p. 2.

19. David Paul Nord, "Teleology and News: The Religious Roots of American Journalism, 1630–1730," *The Journal of American History* 77:1 (June, 1990), pp. 9–38.

20. Nord, "Teleology," p. 26.

21. Brown, *Knowledge Is Power*, pp. 27–40.

22. Brown, *Knowledge Is Power*, pp. 44–62.

23. Brown, *Knowledge Is Power*, p. 44. For an analysis of colonial newspaper content, see David Copeland, *Colonial American Newspapers: Character and Content* (Newark: University of Delaware Press, 1997).

24. For a full account of Condy's business, see William L. Joyce et al., eds., *Printing and Society in Early America* (Worcester, Mass.: American Antiquarian Society, 1983), pp. 104–17.

25. For a more positive view of the Puritans, see Samuel Eliot Morrison, *Builders of the Bay Colony* (Boston: Northeastern University Press, 1981).

26. William Waller Hening, *The Statutes at Large Being a Collection of All the Laws of Virginia (1619–1792)* (Richmond: 1809–23), Vol. 2, p. 517, cited in Leonard W. Levy, *Emergence of a Free Press* (New York: Oxford, 1985), p. 18.

27. Reich, *Colonial America*, p. 154.

28. Susan Henry, "Exception to the Female Model: Colonial Printer Mary Crouch," *Journalism Quarterly* 62:4 (Winter, 1985), pp. 725–33, 749.

29. Rosalind Remer, *Printers and Men of Capital: Philadelphia Book Publishers in the New Republic* (Philadelphia: University of Pennsylvania Press, 1996); for a summary of Remer's book and other recent analyses of the book trade, see *The Book, Newsletter of the Program in the History of the Book in American Culture*, no. 39 (July, 1996), Worcester, Mass.: American Antiquarian Society.

30. Edwin Wolf, II, *The Book Culture of a Colonial American City* (Oxford: Clarendon Press, 1988), p. 3.

31. In Leonard W. Labaree et al., eds., *The Autobiography of Benjamin Franklin* (New Haven and London: Yale University Press, 1964), p. 141.

32. Hall, "Collective Mentality," p. 10.

33. See Victor Neuburg, "Chapbooks in America: Reconstructing the Popular Reading of Early America," in Cathy

Davidson, ed., *Reading in America* (Baltimore: Johns Hopkins University Press), p. 82.

34. For comments on "conscious interdependence," see Reich, *Colonial America,* p. 224; Thomas C. Leonard, *The Power of the Press* (Oxford: Oxford University Press, 1986), p. 4; and David Paul Nord, unpublished manuscript, "The American People."

35. Steele, *The English Atlantic,* p. 133. For a comparison of development in various European countries, see Anthony Smith, *The Newspaper: An International History* (London: Thames and Hudson Ltd., 1979).

36. Philip Davidson, *Propaganda and the American Revolution,* pp. 209–10, cited in Bernard Bailyn and John B. Henck, *The Press and the American Revolution,* (Boston: Northeastern University Press, 1981), p. 349.

37. Isaiah Thomas, *The History of Printing in America,* 2nd ed., Marcus A. McCorison, ed. (New York: Weathervane Books, 1970), p. 215.

38. Cited in Thomas, *History of Printing,* pp. 215–16.

39. *Boston News-Letter,* April 2–9, 1705.

40. Jo Anne Smith, "John Campbell," in Perry J. Ashley, ed., *American Newspaper Journalists, 1690–1872, Dictionary of Literary Biography,* vol. 43 (Detroit: Gale Research, 1985), p. 95.

41. Willard G. Bleyer, *Main Currents in the History of American Journalism* (New York: Houghton-Mifflin, 1927), p. 51.

42. *New-England Courant,* August 14–21, 1721, cited in Bleyer, p. 53.

43. The formal charge against Franklin was breach of legislative privilege. Legislators had the ability to charge printers in such a manner, thereby punishing them for offensive, or seditious, writings. For an analysis of the colonial use of legislative privilege against the press, see Jeffery A. Smith, "A Reappraisal of Legislative Privilege and American Colonial Journalism," *Journalism Quarterly* (Spring, 1984) 61:1, pp. 97–103, 141.

44. Clyde A. Duniway, *The Development of Freedom of the Press in Massachusetts* (New York: Longmans, Green, 1906), pp. 84–86, cited in Levy, *Free Press,* p. 29. See also Edmund F. Slafter, *John Checkley; or, the Evolution of Religious Tolerance in Massachusetts Bay,* 2 vols. (Boston: Prince Society, 1891).

45. Leonard, *Power of the Press,* pp. 26–27.

46. Smith, "James Franklin," *Dictionary of Literary Biography,* vol. 43, pp. 214–15.

47. Smith, "James Franklin," *Dictionary of Literary Biography,* vol. 43, p. 213.

48. Bleyer, *Main Currents,* p. 55.

49. Levy, *Free Press,* p. 30.

50. Levy, *Free Press,* p. 30.

51. *New-England Courant,* Feb. 4–11, 1723, quoted in Bleyer, *Main Currents,* p. 59. See also Michael J. Kirkhorn, "Ben-

jamin Franklin," *Dictionary of Literary Biography,* vol. 43, p. 197.

52. Kirkhorn, "Benjamin Franklin," *Dictionary of Literary Biography,* vol. 43, p. 196.

53. Kirkhorn, "Benjamin Franklin," *Dictionary of Literary Biography,* vol. 43, p. 196.

54. *New-England Courant,* February 4–11, 1723.

55. Thomas, *History of Printing,* p. 315.

56. Thomas, *History of Printing,* pp. 315–16; Kirkhorn, *Dictionary of Literary Biography,* vol. 43, p. 217.

57. Frank Luther Mott, *A History of American Magazines, 1741–1850* (Cambridge: Harvard University Press, 1930), p. 24.

58. Isaiah Thomas, *History of Printing,* pp. 374–75; Elsie Hebert, "William Bradford III," *Dictionary of Literary Biography,* vol. 43, pp. 73–74.

59. Stephen Botein, "The Anglo-American Book Trade before 1776: Personnel and Strategies," in Joyce et al., eds., *Printing and Society,* p. 57.

60. *The Autobiography of Benjamin Franklin,* Gordon S. Haight, ed. (New York: Walter J. Black, 1941), p. 62; Michael J. Kirkhorn, "Benjamin Franklin," *Dictionary of Literary Biography,* vol. 43, p. 197.

61. Franklin's argument was directed specifically at religious topics. His comment about writers who paid printers well may have referred to the publishing of pamphlets or to the fact that printers were paid to include polemics in their newspapers.

62. Levy, *Free Press,* pp. 119–20.

63. Thomas, pp. 530, 552–53. See also Lawrence C. Wroth, *William C. Parks: Printer and Journalist of England and Colonial America* (Richmond, Virginia: 1926) and Wroth, *The Colonial Printer,* 2nd ed. (Portland, Me.: 1939).

64. Joyce et al., eds., *Printing and Society,* p. 139.

65. Joyce et al., eds., *Printing and Society,* pp. 135–53.

66. Elizabeth Cook, *Literary Influences in Colonial Newspapers* (New York: Columbia University Press, 1912), p. 6, cited in Ira L. Baker, "Elizabeth Timothy: America's First Woman Editor," *Journalism Quarterly* 54:2 (Summer, 1977), p. 282.

67. *The South Carolina Gazette* (Charleston), 21 November 1743, p. 2, cited in Julie Hedgepeth, "A Quiet Revolution, 1739–1748: How America's First Three Women Newspaper Editors Treated the Topic of Women," paper presented at AEJMC annual meeting, 1990, Minneapolis, Minnesota.

68. Baker, "Elizabeth Timothy," p. 285. See also Jeffery A. Smith, "Impartiality and Revolutionary Ideology: Editorial Policies of the *South Carolina Gazette,* 1732–1775," *Journal of Southern History* 49 (November, 1983), pp. 511–26.

CHAPTER 2

Resistance and Liberty

▼

From the 1730s through 1776, when the Declaration of Independence was signed, printing flourished in the American colonies and expanded the information available to the general populace.[1] Although it was growing in importance, printing did not erode the highly personal information networks of gentlemen elites; however, it did offer a forum of discussion to a wider audience. Printers developed new strategies for making money, for relating to government entities, and for influencing public opinion. Newspapers and pamphlets, in conjunction with tavern-house conversation, were used to raise and discuss political issues, with these materials disseminated along established trade routes. Although loyalist ideas continued to be conveyed through a pro-British press, public opinion imposed harsh penalties on those who dared to speak against the patriot cause. The language of news changed. As political events encouraged colonial resistance to English policy, editorial strategies included exposing the injustices of the old system under English rule and associating English authority with criminal action. The logical arguments of John Dickinson's "Letters from a Farmer in Pennsylvania" appealed to an audience familiar with formal argument and formal documents, and the horrible tales propagated by the *Journal of Occurrences* made use of exaggeration and outright fabrication as political weapons. Thomas Paine's *Common Sense* intensified the level of political argumentation, for the first time directly blaming the king for the injustices visited upon British citizens in America.[2] Impartiality gave way to partisan rhetoric. ▼

Impartiality: Principle or Economics?

Scholars have long debated whether the colonial press was courageous in its criticism of government. Stephen Botein maintained that most printers pursued a strategy of neutrality in politics. Although printers often asserted that their pages were "open to all," they sometimes discouraged the more radical contributions of political factions, or they offered to print pamphlets advancing controversial ideas rather than including the unpopular arguments in their newspapers. Botein reasoned that such a practice decreased rather than intensified the range of discussion. He further claimed that printers who were faced with limited audiences for their products were reluctant to alienate possible customers by restricting themselves to one political group. In addition, some ambiguity in political orientation also enabled official printers to tread carefully among warring colonial legislative factions and through troubled disputes between assemblies and governors. Jeffery Smith maintained that some printers, following the dictates of impartiality, often published ideas with which they disagreed and that nonpartisanship was a form of Radical Whig Republicanism. During the latter half of the eighteenth century, as the colonists became increasingly dissatisfied with English rule, printers fought first against commercial restrictions such as the Stamp Act and then for political control.[3] During the 1740s and 1750s, newspapers became indispensable tools for public political debate. The newspapers were powerful enough to cause local elites, who feared the "unthinking multitude," to attack what they saw as irresponsible attempts by the press to inflame the public mind.[4]

Resistance Personified: The Zenger Trial

In 1735, John Peter Zenger was tried for seditious libel after he criticized activities of the New York governor. This trial became a benchmark for American journalists, although historians have long debated whether it was important because it established legal precedent or because it was symbolic. As you read further through the account presented here of the Zenger trial, you will see that this trial brought before the court issues of fact, law, and truth, and posed the question of whether judge or jury should prevail in seditious libel cases. This often-cited case indicates that despite a generally cautious attitude on the part of some printers, others, such as Zenger, James Franklin, and William Bradford, were indeed courageous—at least at one point in their lives—in their criticism of government. In this case it was the printer, Zenger, who took the risk rather than the silent editor and writer, attorney James Alexander, whose views the printer published in the *New York Journal*. However, the Zenger case technically did not create a legal precedent, and the reasoning expressed by the defense in this case was not enacted into law until about sixty years later. Additionally, the framers of the Constitution initially did not address freedom of speech but added it as the First Amendment to the Constitution. Nevertheless, the principles behind the defense of Zenger ultimately were incorporated into law. The late-eighteenth-century New York politician, Gouverneur Morris, probably overestimated the impact of the trial when he termed its outcome "the germ of American freedom, the morn-

The First Legislative Assembly in America.

James Town, Virginia, August, 1619.

Figure 2–1   The first legislative assembly in America met in Jamestown, Virginia, in August 1619. In the late 1700s, these assemblies exerted power to resist the British and to gain colonial independence. Reproduction of engraving in Goodrich's *History of the United States of America, 1828.* (Division of Prints and Photographs, Library of Congress Collection)

ing star of that liberty which subsequently revolutionized America." Nevertheless, accounts of the Zenger trial were widely reprinted and circulated, emphasizing basic tenets of eighteenth-century liberalism, and marking an important milestone in colonial religious and political freedom.

Bradford as Forerunner

The 1692 trial of William Bradford for printing a seditious pamphlet in Pennsylvania posed the same questions of law, fact, and truth that would arise more than forty years later in Zenger's trial. However, the charges against Bradford were dropped, and the trial never gained the notoriety that the Zenger case would. Isaiah Thomas claimed it was not Bradford's eloquent defense but a juror's inadvertent destruction of evidence that freed the printer. As the jurors viewed a frame of hand-set type, one of the jurors bumped it with his cane, and "the types fell from the frame . . . formed a confused heap, and prevented further investigations."5

Whether the yarn retold by Isaiah Thomas about the scattered type can be believed, it *is* known that Bradford argued fiercely in his own defense. In a sedition trial under English law—which also applied in colonial Pennsylvania—the judge determined the law, and the jury determined the fact. Thus, if a judge decided that a publication or utterance was "Malitious [*sic*] and Seditious," then a crime had been committed. That was the law of the matter. The jury was to determine only the fact of publication; if the material bore a printer's imprint or had been seized in his shop, the printer would be found guilty of a crime and punished.6

For the first time in an American seditious libel prosecution, William Bradford contended that jury members "are to find also, whether this be a seditious paper or not, and whether it does tend to the weakening of the hands of the magistrates." Justice Jennings told the jury that they were "only to try, whether William Bradford printed it or not." Bradford retorted, "This is wrong, for the jury are judges in law as well as the matter of fact."7 Nevertheless, William Bradford soon left for New York. There, as a governmental printer who perhaps did not relish the appearance of a competing newspaper, he happily celebrated Zenger's misfortunes rather than support the printer who faced charges similar to those with which Bradford had contended. Bradford wrote in 1734 that all men should be responsible for their words: "Tis the abuse not the use of the press that is criminal and ought to be punished."8

The *New York Journal*

In 1733, John Peter Zenger agreed to begin publishing a newspaper, the *New York Journal,* to express the views of a political faction headed by James Alexander. The heart of this faction was a group of wealthy New York merchants and landowners whose position and income were jeopardized by the newly appointed governor, William Cosby. William Bradford had denied this group access to his well-established *New York Gazette.*

Zenger was a German immigrant who had been apprenticed to Bradford at the age of fourteen and who then operated his own printing business in New York for nearly seven years.

The political setting was labyrinthine. The Crown-appointed governor had died, which had left Rip Van Dam in control for thirteen months as the acting governor. Van Dam, evidently following what he saw as standard political practice in New York, collected a large amount of money by assessing fees as his salary. In 1732, however, the Crown's appointee, Sir William Cosby, arrived and soon demanded half of the fees Van Dam had collected.

When Van Dam refused to hand over the money, Cosby resolved to take him to court. Using his power as governor, Cosby reconstituted the colony's supreme court into a court of equity, a form of court that had the virtue, in Governor Cosby's eyes, of sitting without a jury. It was clear to Cosby that a local jury would not allow him, the new governor and an outsider, to win his action. When the chief justice ruled that it was illegal for the governor to create such a court, the governor replaced him.

Governor Cosby's high-handed behavior infuriated a number of politicians and led to the formation of the so-called Popular party to oppose him. One member of the party, attorney James Alexander, was particularly threatened by the governor. Cosby owed Alexander money, but he refused to repay his debt and attempted to discredit Alexander in London. Alexander, seeing no alternative method for exposing the governor, subsidized and, in fact, became the chief contributor to Zenger's *New York Journal*, begun November 5, 1733.[9]

Alexander represented a political faction that not only opposed Governor Cosby in a narrow political sense but also advanced the eighteenth-century English and American ideas that government should not exercise arbitrary power. Alexander quoted liberally from the writings of the British political writers John Trenchard and Thomas Gordon, who, beginning in 1720, wrote widely on resistance to arbitrary power and on the need for freedom to oppose government violations of the public trust.[10] *Cato's Letters* by Trenchard and Gordon were an important source of libertarian thought in eighteenth-century England and America. James Alexander recast these arguments—emphasizing the need for freedom of expression—for use in New York.[11] James Alexander's work was unsigned, written anonymously, placing Zenger as its publisher in a vulnerable position. When Governor Cosby decided to silence the offending newspaper, Zenger was arrested and imprisoned under a warrant signed by New York's governor and his council "for printing and publishing several seditious libels."[12] The arrest procedure that was used was regarded as high-handed by many, and the new chief justice could not persuade a grand jury to indict Zenger. The governor then asked his council to convince the assembly to order the burning of certain issues of Zenger's *Journal*. New York City's Court of Quarter Sessions was approached with a similar proposal, and it too refused to act against Zenger.[13] Governor Cosby and the council then ordered the mayor and magistrates of New York City to see to the "burning by the common hangman, or whipper, near the pillory, the libelous papers." Because city officials refused to obey the order, "the papers were therefore burnt by the order of the governor, not by the hangman or whipper, who were officers of the corporation [of New York City]."[14]

In the midst of these irregular procedures, Zenger sat in jail for nine months. He was, however, a mere scapegoat. Although the attorney general arrested him by issuing an "information" on November 17, 1734, Governor Cosby simultaneously offered fifty pounds to anyone who discovered the authors of the "seditious libel."[15] Zenger was not allowed to communicate with anyone except his wife, Anna, who continued Zenger's printing operation until he was released. Although the printer often has been considered a hero, he might also be regarded simply as a German immigrant who was used by rich and powerful individuals in an attempt to bolster their own "flagging social and economic power."[16] Like Franklin, Zenger showed how printers could receive public support.

The Zenger Trial

On August 4, 1735, Attorney General Richard Bradley opened Zenger's case, levying the charges of seditious libel. Zenger's lead attorney and the author of most of the newspaper copy that was being challenged, James Alexander, was disbarred. Meanwhile, however, Alexander drafted a brief for the defense and contacted Andrew Hamilton of Philadelphia, a friend of Benjamin Franklin and believed to be the most able trial lawyer in the colonies. (Some speculate, indeed, that Hamilton's expertise helped give rise to the advice still offered, "Get yourself a Philadelphia lawyer.")[17]

The elderly Hamilton rose among the spectators at the trial and, following the strategy planned by Alexander, began Zenger's defense most remarkably. Attorney General Bradley already had stated the law of libel as it was then understood: Juries would decide only the fact of publication; judges would decide the law, or whether the material was libelous. Nevertheless, Hamilton simply affirmed that Zenger had printed the publications in question, saying that he did not think it proper "to deny the publication of a complaint which I think is the right of every free-born subject to make."[18]

Attorney General Bradley then declared that the jury must find Zenger guilty "for supposing they [the statements] were true, the law says that they are not the less libelous for that; nay indeed the law says their being true is an aggravation of the crime." Hamilton replied that "bare printing and publishing" a paper should not be a libel; rather, the printed words themselves "must be libelous, that is, false, scandalous, and seditious or else we are not guilty."

The prosecution clearly had the law of the times on its side, but Hamilton spoke with great ingenuity and force, arguing that truthful publications should not be punishable. The young Chief Justice DeLancey—perhaps because of his age and inexperience, perhaps because of Hamilton's towering reputation—did not stop the older lawyer's eloquent plea, despite the fact that the law was on the side of the court. Hamilton appealed to the jury as citizens of New York, as honest and lawful men. He maintained that the accusations printed in Zenger's newspaper were known widely to be true, noting that "therefore in your justice lies our safety." He said that although in the Court of the Star Chamber men suffered for speaking the truth, "the practice of informations for libels is a sword in the hands of a wicked king." Quickly chided by Attorney General Bradley, Hamilton altered his statement, claiming that "we are governed by the best of kings" and pleading pardon for his zeal. He also pleaded his own health, telling the court, "And you see I labor under the weight of many years, and am borne down by great infirmities of body." Nonetheless, even though he called himself old and weak, he asserted that he would go "to the utmost part of the land to help quench the flame of prosecutions upon informations." He thus concluded his arguments to the jury:

> the question before the court and you, gentlemen of the jury, is not of small nor private concern, it is not the cause of a poor printer, nor of New York alone, which you are now trying. No! It may in its consequence affect every freeman that lives under a British government on the Main of America. It is the best cause. It is the cause of liberty; and I make no doubt but your upright conduct this day will not only entitle you

to the love and esteem of your fellow citizens; but every man who prefers freedom to a life of slavery will bless and honor you as men who have baffled the attempt of tyranny, and, by an impartial and uncorrupt verdict, have laid a noble foundation for securing to ourselves, our posterity, and our neighbors that to which nature and the laws of our country have given us as a right—the liberty both of exposing and opposing arbitrary power (in these parts of the world, at least) by speaking and writing truth.

At the end of the trial, happy crowds carried Andrew Hamilton, who had won a "not guilty" verdict for Zenger, to the Black Horse Tavern to celebrate a people's victory, but the printer Zenger remained in jail until the next day.[19]

After Zenger

Unwilling to confront popular opinion by striking down the jury verdict, the chief justice and Governor Cosby let the decision stand. Although decisions of juries do not create legal precedent as does a judicial decision, post-Zenger legal proceedings involving seditious libel sometimes admitted truth as a defense. In 1742, when Thomas Fleet of the *Boston Evening Post* suggested that Sir Robert Walpole would be taken into custody, Fleet escaped prosecution by obtaining affidavits that he had received the information from a naval officer.[20] William Parks of the *Williamsburg Gazette* was saved in a similar way. Around 1770, after accusing a member of Virginia's House of Burgesses of stealing sheep, Parks escaped prosecution by producing court records, proving that his accusations were true. Looking back from the vantage point of 1810, Isaiah Thomas wrote that after the incident the member of the House withdrew from public life "and never more ventured to obtrude himself into a conspicuous situation, or to trouble printers with prosecutions for libels." Thomas concluded, "Thus, it is obvious that a free press is, of all things, the best check and restraint on wicked men and arbitrary magistrates."[21]

Colonial Resistance to Economic Policy

Called in England the Seven Years' War, the French and Indian War set the stage for colonial resistance to British control. The war represented the culmination of many years of struggle between England and France over colonial territory in Canada and along the Mississippi River, particularly in the Ohio Valley. The English had long coveted the French fur trade in this region. In 1748, when some Indian tribes agreed to sell furs to the English and not to the French, fighting broke out throughout the area.

In an attempt to unify colonial resources, Benjamin Franklin drew up the Albany Plan of Union in 1754, enabling the colonies to act as a unit under a president-general appointed by the king. However, neither the colonists nor the British were ready for unification. Both the British, fearing a united colonial government, and the colonists, fearing British unified control, rejected Franklin's plan. Although recalcitrant colonial assemblies only reluctantly granted provisions for the British war, after major losses the British defeated the French and signed the Treaty of Paris in 1763.

Figure 2–2   Masthead of the *Constitutional Courant*, September 21, 1765. Benjamin Franklin's Plan of Union was first proposed in 1754, but it was not until 1765 that the "Join or Die" emblem indicated colonial willingness to unite. (Division of Prints and Photographs, Library of Congress Collection)

France surrendered all lands east of the Mississippi to England, and Louisiana to Spain; Spain relinquished control of Florida to the English.

The war left England overextended and burdened by debt, with its colonists weary of English war. England's victories, however, freed colonists from the fear of border wars, which further encouraged their recalcitrance. The war also assisted economic development in the colonies, as colonial manufacturing developed to meet military needs. By the end of the French and Indian War, the ship-building industry of New England was thriving and the number of forges and furnaces surpassed those in England.

The economic well-being of the colonies, combined with ill-considered British tax measures instituted after the war to provide unchallenged trade advantages for England, encouraged cohesive colonial resistance to English policy. The Sugar Act of 1764 taxed refined sugar, wool, wine, and coffee imports and—perhaps an underrated irritant to hard-drinking colonials—prohibited the importation of French wines and foreign rum. The Currency Act of the same year, extending a policy already in existence in the northern colonies, forbade Virginia from issuing paper money as legal tender.

Leading Massachusetts dissidents who organized the Popular party and a wealthy Massachusetts legislator, James Otis, Jr., issued a pamphlet in July 1764 to list grievances against the royal governor and King George III. The pamphlet, "The Rights of the British Colonies Asserted and Proved," had little effect beyond the colonies, but it served as a vehicle to advance what would become a familiar marching slogan: "No taxation without representation." The pamphlet contended that legislatures were bound by God and nature to (1) govern by stated laws; (2) assure that laws be designed with the good of the people as the only ultimate goal; and (3) tax only by consent.[22]

The Stamp Act

The Stamp Act of 1765 infuriated influential persons because it put a ten-pound fee on admittance to the bar (higher than the fee in London) and taxed legal documents, business papers, and newspapers. The colonial press, which had much to lose economically, protested vigorously, and those who sought to comply with the act issued by Parliament were confronted by the harsh coercion of public opinion and mob action.

On October 31, 1765, the day before the Stamp Act went into effect, the *Pennsylvania Journal*'s front page was laid out like a tombstone with the newspaper's nameplate displayed below a large representation of a skull and cross-bones as well as picks and shovels. The motto for the issue was, "EXPIRING: In Hopes of a Resurrection to Life Again." The lower right-hand corner where the stamps were to be placed carried another skull and cross-bones illustration with the legend, "An Emblem of the Effects of the STAMP. O! the fatal STAMP!"[23]

Some papers sailed defiantly along, publishing without stamps. Setting such a pattern were the *New London Gazette* and the *Connecticut Gazette*, with issues for November 1, 1765, appearing without stamps.[24] In New York, John Holt's *New York Gazette, or Weekly Post-Boy* used the motto, "The United Voice of all His Majesty's free and loyal subjects in America—LIBERTY, PROPERTY AND no STAMPS."[25]

Colonial mobs assailed printers who accepted the stamp tax or who tried to avoid it by not publishing. Across a number of colonies, a group known as the Sons of Liberty organized resistance. In August of 1765, horns and whistles sounded in Boston, calling rum-inspired mobs from the taverns to the streets where stamp master Andrew Oliver was hanged in effigy from the Liberty Tree. The mob then destroyed a building erected for the stamp master and cut down and beheaded the effigy.[26] Oliver promised to resign his office, but the rioters were not satisfied. They then proceeded to the home of Oliver's father-in-law, Governor Thomas Hutchinson, and burned it. Governor Hutchinson later referred to one of the leaders, Sam Adams, as "the Grand Incendiary of the Province."[27]

John Holt of the *New York Gazette, or Weekly Post-Boy* was threatened with violence to his person and his property if he stopped publishing his newspaper to avoid the stamp issue. In November 1765, a North Carolina mob compelled Andrew Steuart to print "at Hazard of Life" if he refused. James Johnston of Georgia, however, resisted the popular demand to continue printing and closed his shop from mid-November 1765 to the end of May 1766, when the news reached the colonies that Parliament had yielded to political pressure and had repealed the Stamp Act.

The reaction by and toward colonial printers carried a strong message: the former neutrality that had seemed to be the wisest course no longer was acceptable. Those printers who tried to maintain an impartial stance soon found that their audience labeled them Tories.

Economic Resistance Turns Political

From 1755 until 1774, the years between the passage of the Stamp Act and the convening of the Continental Congress, newspapers and pamphlets played a strong role in politicizing reaction to Britain's economic policies. Messages varied, with the *Boston Gazette* advocating radical action, John Dickinson appealing to reason through his series of letters, and the *Journal of Occurrences* appealing to citizens' emotions and irrational fears.

The *Boston Gazette* as Radical Rag

Benjamin Edes and John Gill, who jointly published the *Boston Gazette* from 1755 until 1775, belonged to a young group of colonial printers who were outspoken in their opposition to economic policies imposed by the British Parliament. In 1765, shortly after the Stamp Act was imposed, the *Gazette* published a four-part series penned anonymously by John Adams. The series was reprinted overseas in the *London Chronicle* and later as a separate pamphlet in England. In this essay, Adams argued the importance of an informed populace. Historian Richard Brown, in *The Strength of a People: The Idea of an Informed Citizenry in America, 1670–1870*, persuasively contends that Adams "presented the issue in stark political terms. It was important that the people possess general knowledge in order to understand natural philosophy and religious truth and maintain a decent level of civility, but more immediately, it was absolutely critical that they acquire knowledge in order to participate in politics."[28]

Adams' essay was only an early indication of the *Gazette's* radical stance. Edes was a member of Boston's "Loyall Nine," the group that clandestinely stirred up the Sons of Liberty to occasional mob work and often met at the Green Dragon Tavern adjoining the *Gazette* office.

Edes and Gill opposed British taxes and began in the fall of 1767 to advocate boycotts of British imports. They worked closely with James Otis, who received an advance copy of John Dickinson's "Letters from a Pennsylvania Farmer." Dickinson hoped that Boston's propaganda factories could rouse the public, making Massachusetts once again the "first to kindle the Sacred Flame."[29] Edes, Gill, and the "Loyall Nine" did not disappoint Dickinson, and they printed the Whig's opposition letters in serial form.

The *Gazette* gained greater notoriety with its coverage of the Boston Massacre, a 1770 incident in which several Bostonians were killed after a scuffle with British soldiers. The *Gazette* printed small Paul Revere woodcuts of four coffins that represented the four people killed by the British soldiers. Recording the incident for the *Gazette* was political agitator Sam Adams, who displayed outrage when the British officer and six of his men escaped heavy punishment after being tried for the murders. John Adams and another Caucus Club intellectual, Josiah Quincy, bravely defended the British soldiers. However, Sam Adams wrote angrily under the pen name Vindex the Avenger when five of the soldiers were released and two others ordered merely to have their hands branded.

Benjamin Edes participated directly in planning the Boston Tea Party.[30] Not only did the *Gazette* print a protest that asked for the return of a tea shipment to Britain but the paper also organized armed guards to prevent the tea from being landed. On the night of the Tea Party in Boston, some men drank punch mixed by Benjamin's son Peter at the Edes home in Brattle Street, and then the men regrouped at the *Gazette* office to disguise themselves by painting their faces and putting on feathered headdresses. It took three hours for the tea to be dumped from 342 chests, destroying 15,000 pounds of East India Company property.[31]

John Gill retired from the newspaper when it suspended business for two months in 1775 during the British occupation of Boston. Edes reinstated the paper in Boston and continued it there until the late 1790s; former partner John Gill began another paper, the *Constitutional Journal*, which he ran until 1787. The *Gazette*'s success caused Massachusetts' Governor Hutchinson to grumble, "The misfortune is that seven-eighths of the people read none but this infamous paper, and so are never undeceived."

Letters from a Farmer: Serial Essays

The twelve "Letters from a Farmer in Pennsylvania," published serially in colonial newspapers in 1767 and 1768, actually were a series of letters written by Philadelphia politician John Dickinson. The specific point of the letters was to persuade an already wary audience that the British taxation of tea, paper, and other goods represented a conspiracy against the colonists—an attempt to impose external measures on the colonies and to deprive them of liberty. Dickinson opposed the kind of rabble-rousing Sam Adams deliberately encouraged, appealing instead to the rational side of the Whig businessman.

Journal of Occurrences: Fact or Fiction?

While the "farmer" from Pennsylvania appealed to reason, the widely circulated diary called the *Journal of Occurrences* disseminated instead news of imaginary and embellished grievances, publicizing a parade of loathsome incidents designed to agitate sentiment against the British. The *Journal*, published during 1768 and 1769, carried highly colored accounts of the actions of British troops, who were in Boston during 1768 and 1769 to maintain control during the aftermath of riots protesting revenue provisions.[32]

▼

Letters from a Farmer

I hope, my dear countrymen, that you will in every colony be upon your guard against those who may at any time endeavor to stir you up, under pretences of patriotism, to any measures disrespectful to our sovereign and our mother-country. Hot, rash, disorderly proceedings injure the reputation of a people as to wisdom, valour, and virtue, without procuring them the least benefit. I pray GOD that he may be pleased to inspire you and your posterity to the latest ages with that spirit, of which I have an idea, but find a difficulty to express: To express in the best manner I can, I mean a spirit that shall so guide you, that it will be impossible to determine whether an *American's* character is most distinguishable for his loyalty to his soverign, his duty to his mother-country, his love of freedom, or his affection for his native soil.

—John Dickinson, from Letter III of *Letters from a Farmer in Pennsylvania*

The *Journal* format was a series of articles, written in diary form and sprinkled with editorial comment. The diary, while focusing extensively on Massachusetts and containing vitriolic attacks on the colony's royal governor, appeared in whole or in part in at least fourteen colonial newspapers and in several periodicals in England.33 It was never printed separately.

The authors of the *Journal* have never been identified. Boston royal officials, however, believed it was the work of Sam Adams and his friends. Historians have suggested possible authors: Henry Knox, who was running a bookstore in Boston; Benjamin Edes, co-publisher with John Gill of the *Boston Evening Post*; William

Figure 2–3   Sam Adams, patriot and rabble-rouser. (State Historical Society of Wisconsin)

Greenleaf, an employee of Edes and Gill's printing house; Isaiah Thomas, then working as a printer in Boston; and Sam Adams' cousin (and later the second President of the United States), John Adams.[34]

The *Journal* celebrated the 1766 repeal of the Stamp Act, but the paper claimed Bostonians had little else to celebrate. In the *Journal*'s opinion, the Townshend Duties (taxes on paper, glass, and other items) were intolerable. Further, the *Journal* objected to customs commissioners' attempts to stop smuggling and to the quartering of British troops in the city of Boston.

The Massachusetts royal governor was incensed by the *Journal*, claiming that "nine-tenths of what you read in the *Journal of Occurrences* in Boston is either absolutely false or grossly misrepresented."[35] He wrote that the diary was calculated "to raise a general clamor against his Majesty's government in England and throughout America" and that the *Journal* was a collection of "impudent, virulent, and seditious lies."[36]

John Holt's *New York Journal* published the first installment of the *Journal of Occurrences* on September 28, 1769. It reported that British ships—men of war and transports—had arrived at Nantasket Harbor from Halifax, Nova Scotia, and that the ships carried about 900 soldiers.[37] The piece also needled British authorities by commenting that inland settlements were left unprotected when troops were moved to Boston.

Once troops landed in Boston in September 1768, the *Journal* described the quartering of troops in the town, repeatedly claiming that British officers often were whipped or executed for desertion and that blacks usually were chosen to administer the whippings.

The most pervasive theme, however, involved tales of soldiers mistreating Boston citizens. Most of these alleged incidents were reported without attribution:

> A Physician of the Town walking the Streets the other evening was jostled by an Officer, when a Scuffle ensued, he was afterwards met by the same Officer in Company with another, both as yet unknown, who repeated his Blows, and as is supposed gave him a Stroke with a Pistol, which so wounded him as to endanger his life.[38]

Other frightening tales included that of a British captain who was said to have attempted "to excite an insurrection."[39] The *Journal* claimed that women were no longer safe and were treated rudely by the soldiers, being "taken hold of" or nearly abducted. An old woman's resistance and screams were all that prevented her from being raped.[40]

News of Congress and of War

When the Continental Congress convened in 1774 to debate proposed reactions to British economic and political constraints, it met in secret, as had most colonial legislatures. This secrecy combined with the constraints of limited postal service caused the various colonies to receive news in bits and pieces, and the information was not always reliable. Once the Congress declared independence in 1776, public opinion dictated less freedom of expression than one might expect. Patriots silenced Tory voices such as that of James Rivington and tolerated little opposing opinion. Often, mob rule triumphed over reason. During the years before and during the Revolution, newspapers and pamphlets were important vehicles in the public debate, with essayists such as Thomas Paine eloquently urging patriots to retain their determination to win their independence.

Congressional Proceedings Secret

In mid-October of 1774, young William Bradford, Jr., of Philadelphia wrote to his Princeton College classmate, James Madison of Virginia. Bradford wanted to tell his friend about the impressive men assembled in Philadelphia in the Continental Congress, but Bradford had difficulty learning what was going on in Carpenters' Hall, where the Congress met. "Their proceedings," Bradford told Madison, "are a profound secret & the doors open to no one; so that were you here as you wish your curiosity would be but poorly gratified."

Young Bradford was in a better position than most Philadelphians to learn what was happening behind the closed doors of the First Continental Congress. His father,

Figure 2–4 Visitors still come to Carpenter's Hall in Philadelphia, meeting place of the First Continental Congress. (Division of Prints and Photographs, Library of Congress Collection)

Colonel William Bradford, and his older brother, Thomas, were the official printers for what young William called "a great concourse of gentlemen from all parts of the continent." His unsatisfied curiosity reflected the effectiveness of the Congress's resolve that "the doors be kept shut during the time of business, and that the members consider themselves under the strongest obligations of honour, to keep the proceedings secret, untill [sic] a majority shall direct them to be made public."[41]

Because most of the colonial legislatures met in secret and released information only after it had been carefully edited, printers were familiar with secret proceedings. Although legislatures and the Congress agreed that the public needed to have information, they were unwilling to allow their own dissension to be covered in the press. The Congress, organized to protest British imperial policies and not a regularly constituted legislature, was eager for publicity. However, this publicity consisted of carefully edited proclamations and petitions to the British Parliament, to the king, and to the inhabitants of Canada and America. As Bradford wrote to Madison, the deliberations of that political body remained secret.

America's printers in 1774 and 1775 did not protest as Congress continued to meet in secret throughout the War for Independence (1775–1783) and during the early national years. Congressional delegates denounced breaches of secrecy, and on one such occasion they fired Thomas Paine as secretary to the Congress's Committee on Foreign Affairs.[42]

News of War Spreads through Colonies

News of the "Shot Heard Round the World"—the outbreak of fighting between British soldiers and American colonists at the Massachusetts villages of Lexington and Concord—circulated through the colonies in contradictory and confusing driblets.[43] The problem of reliability continued throughout the War for Independence, and one acerbic observer, dubious of the accuracy of newspaper accounts, wrote in 1783:

> The four winds (the initials of which make the word NEWS) are not so capricious, or so liable to change, as our public intelligencers; we have on Monday a whisper;—on Tuesday a rumour;—on Wednesday a conjecture;—on Thursday, a probable;—on Friday, a positive;—and on Saturday, a premature.[44]

The fighting began on the morning of April 19, 1775. Philadelphia, the city where the Second Continental Congress met in May to react to the fighting, received no news until five days later. At that time, the *Pennsylvania Packet* had this inconclusive statement:

> We have no papers from Boston by yesterday's post.—The report is, that as the printers were moving their types out of the town the packages were stopped and broken open by the soldiery, and the letters scattered or thrown into disorder, so that no paper could be got ready for the post.[45]

Actual news of the fighting arrived with the post rider from Trenton, New Jersey, at 5 P.M. on April 24.[46]

A week later, the *Pennsylvania Packet* published accounts of the hostilities, presenting bits of information in roughly the order they were received. One piece bore the unwieldy title of "Accounts from Rhode-Island, respecting the late transaction in Massachusetts-Bay, being the substance of several letters arrived at New York, dated April 21, seven o'clock, A.M. 1775."

The "First Account" reported that the British troops had taken boats from Boston to Watertown, Massachusetts, "where they had fired upon the minute men, then proceeded to Concord, examined the magazines there, destroyed about 50 barrels of flour, and spiked up four pieces of cannon." This account added that about three or four hundred men had killed about forty British soldiers and had taken another forty prisoners.

The "Second Account" from Rhode Island said that the colony's governor had called the Assembly to meet because of the attack on "our brethren of the Massachusetts." The third version of the firing near Boston said that "the action was at Lexington, about twelve miles from Boston, to which place about 1200 of the King's Troops had advanced upon 30 minute men . . . then fired and killed 7."

Meanwhile, news came from other colonies. A message dated April 23 from Hartford, Connecticut, said "that we have undoubted intelligence of hostilities being begun at Boston by the regular troops." The letter from Connecticut added that the redcoats went to the house where Mr. [John] Hancock lodged, who with Samuel Adams, luckily got out of their way by secret and speedy intelligence from Paul Revere, who is now missing . . . when they searched the house for Mr. Hancock and Adams, and not finding them there, killed the woman of the house and all the children and set fire to the house; from thence they proceeded on their way to Concord, firing at, and killing hogs, geese, cattle, and every thing that came in their way, and burning houses." This version added that the British soldiers "destroyed one hundred barrels of flour at Concord and took possession of the Court-House."[47]

Declaration of Independence

In May 1776, nearly a year after the outbreaks at Lexington and Concord, the Continental Congress took a bold—and treasonable—step by recognizing the revolutionary assemblies as legal governments. A few weeks later, news reached Philadelphia that the Virginia convention had passed resolutions calling for a declaration that the colonies were free and independent states. On June 7, 1776, Virginia delegate to the Congress Richard Henry Lee submitted the resolution that led toward formal independence:

> RESOLVED, That these United Colonies are, and of right ought to be, free and independent States, that they are absolved from all allegiance to the British Crown, and that all political connection between them and the State of Great Britain is, and ought to be totally dissolved.
>
> That it is expedient forthwith to take the most effectual measures for forming Alliances.
>
> That a plan of confederation be prepared and transmitted to the respective Colonies for their consideration and approbation.[48]

Figure 2–5 The Declaration of Independence was printed in 1776 on the Ephrata Press. (Division of Prints and Photographs, Library of Congress Collection)

On June 11, a committee was appointed to draft a declaration of independence: Thomas Jefferson of Virginia, John Adams of Massachusetts, Roger Sherman of Connecticut, and Robert R. Livingston of New York.[49]

Although the Declaration of Independence was presented to the Continental Congress on July 2, news of the document did not reach some colonies until several weeks later. On July 4, the Declaration of Independence was approved by the Congress, and a copy was sent to the legislatures of the states. It was signed by the delegates on August 2. Both the Bradfords' *Pennsylvania Journal* and David Hall's *Pennsylvania Gazette* announced on July 3, 1776, that "the CONTINENTAL CONGRESS declared the UNITED COLONIES FREE and INDEPENDENT STATES." The first publication of the Declaration of Independence was in the newspaper of Benjamin Towne, a "Sunshine Patriot," who got the news printed first because the *Pennsylvania Evening Post* was triweekly. The declaration was printed by John Dunlap in the *Pennsylvania Packet* July 6. The *Freeman's Journal* in Portsmouth, New Hampshire, printed the declaration on July 20. News reached the southern colonies by August 2.[50]

Public Opinion and Freedom of Expression

During the prerevolutionary period, despite the words of liberty and freedom penned by patriot writers, freedom of expression existed only for those who supported the patriot cause. Those printers who remained loyal to England suffered the wrath of public opinion. Loyalist printers—those who supported Britain, or at least wanted reconciliation rather than conflict—published from the early crises of 1774 through 1783, although during the later years of this period they appeared only in towns held by the British. Between 1776 and 1783, twelve loyalist newspapers appeared in New York, Rhode Island, Pennsylvania, South Carolina, Georgia, and Florida. The newspapers helped provide a sense of normalcy in garrisoned towns, carrying advertisements of local merchants, trumpeting British military achievements, and printing official announcements. Loyalist newspapers rarely countered patriot claims with developed political arguments. They rather accused the colonists of ingratitude and disloyalty, charging them with failure to patiently work out the differences between the Mother Country and the colonies. Loyalist publishers perceived colonial difficulties to be the result of isolated corrupt governors and other unjust authorities, rather than a systematic pattern against which colonists should rebel. The authority of church and state, loyalists maintained, was essential to foster self-discipline and reinforce moral duty among most people, incapable as they were of political leadership. Because the colonists failed to recognize legitimate authority, loyalists argued, the "seeds of sedition are usually sown, and the people are led to sacrifice real liberty to licentiousness which gradually ripens into rebellion and civil war."[51]

The colonists' obvious unwillingness to tolerate opposing opinion damaged their position in loyalist eyes. As patriots talked about liberty, they coerced and intimidated those who spoke against the new order, leading many loyalists to fear that danger came not from Britain but from the radical, new political factions—patriot congresses, committees, and mobs. Further, loyalists worried about the ability of a new nation to survive against powerful European nations without the help of Britain, and they noted the economic benefits of protected trade. Nor did they overlook a nearly 200-year tradition of mutual culture, history, and interests. Manifest disobedience "dissolved the delicate network of social relationships that held human aggression under control and enabled people to live in peace and security," loyalist editors claimed.[52] Loyalists therefore maintained that patriots demonstrated "undisciplined behavior, a childish unwillingness to consider seriously the reasoned arguments of critics, and an aggressive intolerance of dissenting views." That combination, editors argued, demonstrated a fatal weakness of the patriot cause.[53]

James Rivington: Loyalist Publisher

New York loyalist James Rivington, a prosperous bookseller in London, quickly discovered that public opinion would not tolerate oppositional viewpoints. When he arrived in Philadelphia in 1760, he opened bookstore partnerships in Philadelphia, New York, and Boston. In 1773, Rivington began a newspaper in New York, grandly named *Rivington's New-York Gazetteer* or the *Connecticut, Hudson's River, New-Jersey, and Quebec Weekly Advertiser.*

▼

James Rivington (1724–1802)

James Rivington was the best known and most influential Tory editor of the American Revolutionary period. Born in England, he moved to the colonies after squandering his fortune gambling. He began the *New York Gazette* and was so hated that he was forced to sign a statement of loyalty to the Continental Congress and was hanged in effigy in New Brunswick. His offices for the *New York Gazette* were twice ransacked, and Rivington had to flee to England for a time until it was safe for him to return and continue publishing.

Source: R. B. Downs, and J. B. Downs, *Journalists of the United States* (Jefferson, N.C.: McFarland & Company, Inc., 1991) (Division of Prints and Photographs, Library of Congress Collection)

At first, Rivington was noted for publishing a neutral newspaper. Lurking in New York, however, was Rivington's nemesis-to-be, one of the most feared mob leaders of the revolutionary era, Isaac ("King") Sears.

In 1774, Sears, a member of the quasi-secret Sons of Liberty, led a New York City mob in a duplication of the much more famous Boston Tea Party. In response, New York's Lieutenant Governor Cadwallader Colden declared that destroying tea in the New York harbor and other violence by the mob had upset the "principal inhabitants" of New York City. Colden suggested that the mob had gone too far and declared mob leader Sears and his lieutenants to be "in disgrace."[54]

Rivington's *New-York Gazetteer* sided with the "principal inhabitants" of New York City. The August 18, 1774, issue included a letter bearing the printed greeting, "To I—c S—s, Esq.," and was signed, "A Merchant of New York." In the letter, Rivington described Sears as possibly insane and at least a "political cracker, sent abroad to alarm and terrify, sure to do mischief to the cause he means to support."[55]

Sears responded, wanting "to know without delay my abuser, or [I] shall Consider you the Author and do myself Justice." Rivington retorted in the *Gazetteer* that he would not "deliver up any author, without his permission, and I am ready to defend the freedom of the press when attacked in my person."[56]

The outraged Sears accused Rivington of "Sculking behind your press, and pleading its Liberty." He continued, "A press in Such hands as yours, instead of being beneficial to Society, may be Justly considered a nuesance [*sic*], tending to both publick and private Mischief—Free only to do evil, restrained from doing good."[57]

Although the quarrel subsided, an April 1775 dispute with another merchant, Ralph Thurman, provoked Sears to violence. After Sears accused Thurman of selling supplies to British troops, Thurman retorted in a broadside published by Rivington, claiming that perhaps it was Sears who sent ships to supply the redcoats in Boston.

Sears, urging his supporters to arm themselves, was arrested and taken before the mayor of New York. Just as Sears was being taken to jail, however, a mob rescued him and carried him through the streets like a conquering hero.

Rivington threw aside caution, mocking a mob that hanged him in effigy. He denounced the mob as dregs of the city and published a parody of a Sears speech to a mob.

Three days later, on April 23, 1775, when news of the fighting at Lexington and Concord reached New York, the Sears-led mob broke into New York's City Hall and took arms and ammunition. Sears, in glory—the mob at his back—took the keys to the customs house and closed the Port of New York.

On May 10, 1775, Sears led the mob to Rivington's printing house, breaking into his shop and destroying frames of type and copies of a pamphlet. One jump ahead of the mob, Rivington fled to a British ship in New York harbor.

When he returned to New York from the ship, Rivington was taken into custody for a short time, but eventually he was given his freedom and allowed to resume printing. New York's Provincial Congress noted on June 6, 1775, that Rivington had published a handbill begging for pardon and passed a resolution that the printer be allowed to return to his type case without being harmed.

Mob leaders, however, do not always follow the dictates of authority. Sears, who had moved to Connecticut, returned to New York in November 1775. Again leading a mob, Sears smashed Rivington's printing house, ruining his presses. Rivington again escaped, but he fled this time to England. He returned in late 1777, while British troops controlled the city. Reestablishing his newspaper, he called it the *New-York Royal Gazette*. The sheet became synonymous with Toryism throughout the war, and it was known in revolutionist strongholds as "the lying gazette."

At the end of 1783, after the war's conclusion, Rivington begged for forgiveness and asked the Continental army to allow him to remain in New York. The army said yes, but Sears said no. On the last day of 1783, Sears and two companions visited Rivington and ordered him to cease publishing. Rivington's last issue appeared on December 31, 1783, although he continued as a bookseller and stationer in New York for some years. Imprisoned for debt in 1797, the most famous of the loyalist printers died, ironically, on July 4, 1802—Independence Day.[58]

Although mobs sometimes attacked patriots as well as Tories, patriot printers more successfully elicited support through official channels. Samuel Loudon, a patriot who started his *New-York Packet* early in 1776, advertised the publication of a Tory response to Thomas Paine's *Common Sense*. A mob subsequently broke into Loudon's printing house, dragged him out of bed, and carried the pamphlets outside for burning. Loudon protested to New York's Committee of Safety, claiming £75 in damages and contending that he was a patriot and entitled to freedom of the press. The Committee of Safety clearly believed Loudon and soon was paying him £200 per year for carrying its news in his *Loudon's Packet*.[59]

Newspapers and Political Pamphlets: Relative Merits

Newspapers and pamphlets served as important vehicles of public opinion during the revolutionary period. Historian Bernard Bailyn concluded that "much of the most important and characteristic writing of the American Revolution" appeared in pamphlet form. Arthur Schlesinger, on the other hand, emphasized the contribution of newspapers, saying that of the "many ways of kneading men's minds, none . . . equaled the newspapers."[60] Political pamphlets served as a source of revenue for printers deprived of income from the importing of stationery and books from England. In Philadelphia alone, 25 percent of printing income was derived from printing political pamphlets.[61]

Newspapers and pamphlets often contained pieces from other sources in reprint form. Series of newspaper articles frequently were republished as pamphlets, and pamphlets were excerpted or run as a series of articles by newspapers. Occasionally, a newspaper writer would be countered by a pamphleteer with an opposing opinion. Newspaper contributors similarly dissected the arguments presented in pamphlets.

During the War for Independence, debate occasionally focused on the relative merits of pamphlets and newspapers. Dr. Benjamin Rush of Philadelphia took credit for inspiring Thomas Paine to write *Common Sense*, a startling publishing sensation. As Rush put it, he influenced Paine to do something "beyond the ordinary short and cold address of newspaper publication."[62] Paine had originally planned to serialize *Common Sense* in the newspapers, in much the same fashion that John Dickinson had published his influential "Farmer's Letters" in 1767–1768.[63]

Paine, however, feared that his work might not be "generally inserted" in the newspapers, so he turned his manuscript over to Philadelphia printer Robert Bell. From Bell's shop, *Common Sense* was widely circulated. Paine asserted that more than a quarter-million copies of *Common Sense* were sold in the three months after it was first issued.[64]

An enthusiastic reader of *Common Sense* regretted, however, that it had not been published first as a series of newspaper essays. The Reverend John Witherspoon, president of Princeton, wrote that "*Common Sense* has been read by many, yet the news papers are read by many more."[65]

Although pamphleteers and newspaper writers did not earn salaries or wages, they sometimes received gratuities or public offices if they needed money. More often, however, writers were men in public life, who postured rather than hid behind fancy pseudonyms. Much of the time, the authors of pseudonymous writings were quickly identified by their readers, as was John Dickinson, alias the "Pennsylvania Farmer."

Thomas Paine and *Common Sense*

Thomas Paine, a former corset maker, was paid little for his contributions to Robert Aitken's struggling *Pennsylvania Magazine*. Paine, who had worked for Aitken since arriving in Philadelphia, received fifty pounds a year in Pennsylvania currency, twenty pounds less than Aitken's journeyman printer John McCulloch.[66] Paine left

THE END OF PAIN.

Figure 2–6 Thomas Paine was an eloquent writer and champion of the Revolution, but he often was ridiculed, as this drawing published in 1800 indicates. Paine's radical views lost their popularity once the Revolution was over. (Division of Prints and Photographs, Library of Congress Collection)

Aitken's shop in December 1775 on less than cordial terms. Aitken possibly felt that Paine's "seditious writing," which ultimately was published as *Common Sense*, was too hot to handle.

The Continental Congress, fearful that the British would use rivers originating in Canadian territory as routes to cut off the northern colonies from the middle colonies, planned a military expedition in the fall of 1775. If the colonies could control the Canadian lands, they could present a solid front against the British.

The Canadian expedition was disastrous. The few men who survived illness, brutal terrain, and the arduous march into the bitter Canadian winter, were soundly defeated as they attempted to take Quebec. The expedition's leader was killed, and the second in command, Colonel Benedict Arnold, was wounded.[67]

Despite the low spirits of those hoping for independence, Thomas Paine gave the cause of resistance and independence great encouragement by publishing anonymously *Common Sense* on January 9, 1776. In an essay published in the *Pennsylvania Journal* late in 1775, Paine had predicted that "the Almighty will finally separate

▼

Paine Describes the Crisis

These are the times that try men's souls. The summer soldier and the sunshine patriot will in this crisis, shrink from the service of his country; but he that stands it NOW, deserves the love and thanks of man and woman. Tyranny, like hell, is not easily conquered; yet we have this consolation with us, that the harder the conflict, the more glorious the triumph. What we obtain too cheap, we esteem too lightly; 'tis dearness only that gives everything its value. Heaven knows how to put a proper price upon its goods; and it would be strange indeed, if so celestial an article as FREEDOM should not be highly rated.

—Thomas Paine, *The Crisis*, No. 1

America from Britain."[68] However, *Common Sense* went much further, directly attacking King George III. Paine wrote, "Government, like dress, is the badge of lost innocence; the palaces of kings are built upon the ruins of the bowers of paradise."[69] Writing at a time when the king was the strongest remaining link between England and America, Paine dared to call George III a "hardened, sullen tempered Pharaoh" and a "wretch who was able to sleep with the blood of Bunker Hill upon his soul."[70]

Common Sense quickly became the center of a rancorous debate in the newspapers. The success of the pamphlet, wrote historian Harry Stout, was that it was not limited by the constraints of classical style. Paine, repudiating the "language and form of classical discourse," established "a new style that anticipated the wave of nineteenth-century literature" intended for people generally, rather than for an elite audience.[71] Indeed, the revolutionary elite did not regard Paine as particularly influential.

Printer Robert Bell, first publisher of *Common Sense*, was ready to make money from loyalists and patriots alike. He assembled the conservatives' first angry attempts at rebutting *Common Sense* into a pamphlet called *Large Additions to Common Sense*. Writing in the *Pennsylvania Packet*, Anglican minister William Smith, who strongly opposed independence, derided Paine's suggestion that the colonies could expect help from foreign nations. Recalling old English prejudices, Smith asked what assistance American Protestants might expect from "Popish Princes." He labeled Paine guilty of "Common Nonsense."[72] By late spring of 1776, Thomas Paine's *Common Sense* was an unprecedented best-seller in America. The pamphlet was to go through twenty-five separate editions by year's end and reached hundreds of thousands of avid readers at a time when the colonies' total population was little more than 2.5 million.

As Paine biographer Eric Foner wrote, *Common Sense* attacked the British king and constitution at a time when most Americans believed they had or could have the full rights of English citizens and were sprinkling their protests with the language of conciliation. Paine, wrote Foner

articulated the deepest meaning of the struggle with Britain. . . . The success of *Common Sense* reflected the perfect conjunction of a man and his time, a writer and his audience, and it announced the emergence of Paine as the outstanding political pamphleteer of the Age of Revolution.[73]

Newspapers for a Continent

The vigorous political dialogues in the newspapers of colonial America in 1775 and 1776—the words that reflected and fueled the early days of the War for Independence—were important along the entire seaboard of North America. The printers of North America during the late eighteenth century were publishers for a continent. Their newspapers or broadsides or printed sermons or pamphlets traveled by post rider's saddlebag, by stage, and by sailing ship to all of the thirteen colonies and beyond.[74] Writers discussed politics freely, and their opinions on matters affecting the developing revolution, once printed, could be read throughout America. As Merrill Jensen noted, printers "made constant use of scissors so that the same news item or political essay often appears in the newspapers all the way from New Hampshire to Georgia, sometimes with acknowledgment and sometimes not."[75]

Although Philadelphia's able bookbinder and printer, Robert Aitken, never published a newspaper, a record book kept in his shop suggests much about the distances over which printers maintained business contacts and exchanged information. Between 1775 and 1784, Aitken did business with printers located along the Atlantic coast of the new nation, sending them paper and supplies, books, pamphlets, and, occasionally, type. In return, Aitken received either money or merchandise such as books and pamphlets that he, in turn, could sell from his Philadelphia shop.

Because Aitken was based in Philadelphia, of course, the bulk of his business was done with residents of that city. However, in the mid-1770s, Aitken had extensive dealings with Francis Bailey, whose printing operation was located some seventy miles to the west, in Lancaster. Additionally, Aitken had business with printers in South Carolina, Vermont, New Jersey, and the cities of Boston and New York.[76]

In addition to doing business with printers, Aitken also traded with many other stationers, booksellers, and bookbinders, both in Philadelphia and in surrounding areas, including distant Burlington, Vermont.

The Significance of Circulations

In the absence of authoritative information on newspaper circulations—as provided for twentieth-century newspapers by the Audit Bureau of Circulations—historians have made do with publishers' own circulation claims. Annual or semiannual subscriptions were the usual vehicle by which a newspaper was provided with some working capital, and subscription lists usually have been the best source of circulation information. With a yearly subscription, a printer might take half "in advance" at the time a person agreed to take the newspaper. The second half of the subscription price would then be due and payable in six months.[77]

In 1719, the *Boston News-Letter*, then New England's only newspaper, struggled along with fewer than 300 subscribers.[78] By 1754, when four competing weekly newspapers were published in Boston, each apparently had an average circulation of about 600 copies. Isaiah Thomas, publisher of *The Massachusetts Spy* in Boston and Worcester as well as author of the first major history of American journalism, wrote that a subscription list of about 600 was needed for a weekly newspaper to make ends meet.[79]

Beyond these figures, there was a never-never land made up of the claims of biased or self-serving witnesses. James Rivington claimed a weekly circulation of 3,600 for his Tory *New-York Gazetteer* in 1775. The *Boston Gazette* listed its weekly circulation as 2,000 for the same year, whereas Isaiah Thomas's rival *Massachusetts Spy* said that its circulation was 3,500.[80] More than likely, publishers padded their circulation figures to impress their readers.

Historians also have had to contend with the puffs of uncritical biographers. Robert Hurd Kany guessed that the circulation of the *Pennsylvania Gazette* during the partnership of David Hall, Sr., and Benjamin Franklin was between 8,000 and 9,000 copies, far higher than the 1,600 to 1,700 copies estimated for the *Gazette* by Lawrence C. Wroth.[81] Kany's estimate also differed from that of a thorough student of the finances of Benjamin Franklin's printing house, George Moranda, who noted that Kany's estimate was based on Franklin's statement that only one of every five copies of the *Gazette* was paid for. If that five-to-one ratio were to be taken seriously, the *Gazette*'s circulation would have been about 750 during the 1740s. Moranda found a settlement of 137 *Gazette* subscription accounts over the seventeen-year period covered by Franklin's account books.[82]

Such circulation numbers games, however, have done little to measure the importance of the newspapers of the American Revolution. The tiny newspapers, often running only four pages, were read for every single word, even though they often published more advertising than news. These printed sheets were popular diversions in the taverns, coffeehouses, shops, and inns where people read newspapers or heard them read aloud.

The *Pennsylvania Journal*

The circulation pattern of a major late-eighteenth-century newspaper was well described in Colonel William Bradford's "List of Subscribers on the 25th of April et. postea to the *Pennsylvania Journal*."[83] In 1776, William and Thomas Bradford's *Pennsylvania Journal*'s circulation book counted only 2,400 subscribers, of which only 230 lived in Philadelphia. Nevertheless, the *Journal* reached the rich and powerful people of the city, the heads of political factions, and the major merchants. These leaders were closely tied together by business and religious connections and, quite often, by family or marital ties.[84] The 1767 Philadelphia circulation of the *Journal* was almost a "Who's Who" of the city. Subscribers included William Allen, the Tory chief justice of colonial Pennsylvania; Robert Morris, a rising merchant; Benjamin Chew, a wealthy Quaker politician; and Joseph Galloway, political boss of what was called the antiproprietary faction. Also included in the list were a few "new men," people such as Daniel Roberdeau who lacked old-line ties but would become important in the revolutionary struggle. By and large, however, the *Journal*'s Philadelphia circulation in 1767 echoed the names of powerful old families or the men connected to them.[85]

Once out of Philadelphia, the paths traveled by the *Journal* were many and varied. About 400 copies of the paper circulated in the hinterlands of Pennsylvania, whereas other copies left at Captain Long's in Philadelphia were destined for "sundrey places." Other subscribers were important political leaders or newspaper publishers. Eight newspapers listed in Bradford's circulation book as having been sent to "Connecticutt" were addressed to the following: "The Post Master in Hartford, Thomas Green Printer Do. Timothy Green Printer New London, Parker & Company Printers O' New Haven, Silas Deane, Esq'r. [an important merchant and politician] and Alexander and James Robertson Printers, Norwich."[86] One of the two copies of the *Journal* sent to Westmoreland County, Virginia, was addressed to Richard Henry Lee, one of the most powerful politicians of the American Revolution. For the *Pennsylvania Journal* and for the emerging nation's other newspapers, circulation patterns that included newspaper printers, postmasters, and important politicians ensured maximum impact.

Recording Early History: Isaiah Thomas

Much of what is known about early American printers—except for the body of published work that has survived them—is the result of research by the first historian of American publishing, Isaiah Thomas. Author of the often-quoted *History of Printing in America* that was published in 1810, Thomas also founded what is today a great research library, The American Antiquarian Society of Worcester, Massachusetts.

The youngest of five children, he was apprenticed to Boston printer Zechariah Fowle in 1756, some four years after Thomas's father had died. The apprentice printer was just six years old, and he served Fowle until he was twenty-one.[87] Following a quarrel with Fowle in 1765, Thomas left for Nova Scotia, and after working in several colonies as a printer, he returned to Boston and Zechariah Fowle's printing house in 1770.

This time Thomas used Fowle's equipment for the publication of a smaller-than-usual newspaper, a triweekly that would compete with four other newspapers—all weeklies—in Boston. On August 7, 1770, Thomas's *Massachusetts Spy* began regular

▼

Colonial Sensationalism

Americans! Forever bear in mind the BATTLE OF LEXINGTON!—where British troops, unmolested and unprovoked, wantonly and in a most inhuman manner, fired upon and killed a number of our countrymen, then robbed, ransacked, and burnt their houses! nor could the tears of defenseless women, some of whom were in the pains of childbirth, the cries of helpless babes, nor the prayers of old age, confined to beds of sickness, appease their thirst for blood!—or divert them from their DESIGN OF MURDER and ROBBERY!

—Isaiah Thomas, *Massachusetts Spy*, May 3, 1775

Figure 2–7 Isaiah Thomas, early journalism historian, taken from the marble bust by B. H. Kinney. The bust is owned by the American Antiquarian Society. (State Historical Society of Wisconsin)

publication. After three months, Thomas bought out Fowle, changing his paper's format from a quarter-sheet to a half-sheet and its publication frequency from three times to twice weekly.[88]

Like many printers, Thomas headed his paper with the motto "Open to all Parties, but Influenced by None," but he soon moved to the patriot side. When he bought Fowle's equipment, he secured loans from those colonists who were protesting British measures. John Hancock had financial responsibility for the press, and rather wild-eyed, radical individuals such as Joseph Greenleaf and Thomas Young became frequent contributors. Thomas felt sufficiently cornered to consider moving as far away as Bermuda.

Thomas and one of his contributors, who wrote under the pen name Mucius Scaaevola, were ordered to appear before Governor Thomas Hutchinson, but Thomas refused three times to attend. The governor's council then faced a legal dilemma: How could Thomas be found in contempt of the council and jailed when

Figure 2–8 Front page of the December 23, 1773, issue of *The Massachusetts Spy*. (Division of Prints and Photographs, Library of Congress Collection)

he never actually appeared before that body? After several alternative approaches were used to indict Thomas, charges were dropped.[89]

Meanwhile, Thomas wrote, it was apparent that British troops and the colonials would soon attack each other. Tories and British soldiers threatened Thomas for his antiestablishment *Massachusetts Spy.* Seeing trouble coming, Thomas packed up most of his printing equipment and sent it in wagons to Worcester during the night of April 16, 1775. Two nights later, Thomas signaled Paul Revere, who rode through the countryside to warn Americans that British troops were leaving Boston to destroy the military stores collected by protesting colonials at Concord, eighteen miles away.

This dislocation caused by war led to Thomas' becoming one of the foremost publishers in America and making his fortune. Late in 1775, Thomas was named postmaster for Worcester, and, by the end of the war in 1783, he had overcome his debts and was prospering with his newspaper and with a profitable almanac, book bindery, and bookstore.[90] Thomas, whose business was to become something of an early-nineteenth-century publishing conglomerate, by 1801 had net assets estimated at $150,000, one of the largest personal fortunes in the nation.

Conclusion

During the French and Indian War, American colonists gained economic independence through the development of manufacturing. However, they soon faced new forms of taxation by England, which strived to make colonialism pay by assuring increased trade advantages to the Mother Country. The first major reaction by the press was in response to the Stamp Act of 1765, which taxed paper and placed a definite economic hardship on colonial printers and lawyers.

Public opinion dictated that the common stance of impartiality would no longer benefit printers, and in some cases the public demanded that the printers publish without stamps, threatening those who halted publication. Nevertheless, public opinion did not, in those early days of protest, demand a revolution.

During the ten years before the Declaration of Independence in 1776, printers grew more partisan. Some writers, such as John Dickinson, authors of the *Journal of Occurrences*, Edes and Gill of the *Boston Gazette*, and Sam Adams, appealed to various audiences for rational, as well as violent, responses to British control.

Meanwhile, the Continental Congress and colonial legislatures conducted secret proceedings, releasing information to selected public printers. News of the first shots fired in the War for Independence traveled from colony to colony, as printers established a trade network that sold newspapers and stationery products along the Atlantic coast. Printers also published political pamphlets that conveyed political views but also were a major source of income for many printers. Newspapers thrived during the years just prior to the War for Independence, and circulations of about 600 were judged to be satisfactory to sustain a profitable newspaper.

Endnotes

1. Stephen Botein, "'Meer Mechanics' and an Open Press: The Business and Political Strategies of Colonial American Printers," *Perspectives in American History* 9 (1975), pp. 140–50.

2. Thomas C. Leonard, in *The Power of the Press* (Oxford: Oxford University Press, 1986), pp. 35–53, develops fully the argument that colonial printers exposed the injustice of the old system, particularly in regard to associating English rule with criminal behavior. For a discussion of how elite ideology interacted with popular will to form the revolution, see Harry S. Stout, "Religion, Communications and the Ideological Origins of the American Revolution," *William and Mary Quarterly* 34 (1977).

3. For an alternative view to that of Stephen Botein, see Jeffery A. Smith, "Impartiality and Revolutionary Ideology: Editorial Politics of the *South Carolina Gazette*, 1732–1775," *Journal of Southern History* 49 (November,

1983), pp. 511–26. Smith argues that for thirty years before the 1765 passage of the Stamp Act the *Gazette* delivered controversy and "expanded the opportunity for public debate" (p. 23). For expansion of Smith's thesis, see his book, *Printers and Press Freedom: The Ideology of Early American Journalism* (New York: Oxford University Press, 1988). Leonard Levy, in *Legacy of Suppression: Freedom of Speech and Press in Early American History* (Cambridge: Belknap Press of Harvard University Press, 1960) argues that printers had failed to oppose the restrictions of seditious libel until the violent sentiment of patriots created an issue impossible to avoid.

4. Gary Nash, *The Urban Crucible* (Cambridge: Harvard University Press, 1986), pp. 123–27. Charles Clark cites the 1739 outbreak of the War of Jenkin's Ear with Spain and the first American tour of evangelist George Whitefield as the key points when American newspaper

editors began to focus editorial content on locally generated news and opinion. See Charles Clark, *The Public Prints: The Newspaper in Anglo-American Culture 1665–1740* (New York: Oxford University Press, 1994).

5. Isaiah Thomas, *The History of Printing in America*, Marcus McCorison, ed., 2nd ed. (New York: Weathervane Books, 1970), pp. 354–55.

6. Thomas, *History of Printing*, p. 344. See Norman Rosenberg, *Protecting the Best Men: An Interpretive History of the Law of Libel* (Chapel Hill: University of North Carolina Press, 1986), p. 35.

7. Thomas, *History of Printing*, p. 350, evidently citing, as did Rosenberg, at p. 283, *New England's Spirit of Persecution Transmitted to Pennsylvania [sic] . . . in the Trial of Peter Boss, George Keith, Thomas Budd, and William Bradford . . .* (Philadelphia, 1693).

8. *New York Gazette*, no. 432, January 28–February 4, 1734, cited in Stanley Katz's introduction to James Alexander's *A Brief Narrative of the Case and Trial of John Peter Zenger*, 2nd ed. (Cambridge: Harvard University Press, 1971), p. 13.

9. For a thorough description of the background of the Zenger case, see Catherine L. Covert, "'Passion Is Ye Prevailing Motive': The Feud behind the Zenger Case," *Journalism Quarterly* 50:1 (Spring, 1973), pp. 3–10.

10. Levy, *Free Press*, pp. 109–12; Arthur M. Schlesinger, *Prelude to Independence: The Newspaper War on Britain, 1764–1776* (New York: Knopf, 1958), p. 137.

11. Paul Finkelman, "The Zenger Case: Prototype of a Political Trial," in Michael R. Belknap, ed., *American Political Trials* (Westport, Connecticut: Greenwood Press, 1981). For an interpretation suggesting that the operating principle in the Zenger case was truth rather than freedom of expression, see David Paul Nord, "The Authority of Truth: Religion and the John Peter Zenger Case," *Journalism Quarterly* 62:2 (Summer, 1985), pp. 227–35.

12. Thomas, *History of Printing*, p. 487.

13. Katz, *John Peter Zenger*, pp. 41–42, 45; Levy, *Emergence of a Free Press*, p. 40.

14. Thomas, *History of Printing*, p. 488.

15. *New York Weekly Journal*, November 18–25, 1734; Willard G. Bleyer, *Main Currents in the History of American Journalism* (Cambridge, 1927), p. 65f.

16. Catherine L. Covert, "Journalism History and Women's Experience: A Problem in Conceptual Change," *Journalism History* 9:1 (Spring, 1981), p. 4.

17. Vincent Buranelli, *The Trial of Peter Zenger* (New York: NYU Press, 1957), p. 49.

18. All quotations from Andrew Hamilton's defense are cited in Katz, *John Peter Zenger*, pp. 62–101.

19. Covert, "Journalism History and Women's Experience," p. 4.

20. *Boston Evening Post*, March 8, 15, 1742; Levy, pp. 32–33.

21. Thomas, *History of Printing*, p. 553.

22. Merrill Jensen, ed., "Introduction" to *Tracts of the American Revolution, 1763–1776* (Indianapolis: Bobbs-Merrill, 1967), pp. xxii, 26–27. For a good summary of various historical explanations of causes of the American Revolution, see Gordon S. Wood, "Rhetoric and Reality in the American Revolution," *The William and Mary Quarterly* 23:3–32 (January, 1964). Wood argues that the revolution occurred because of internal colonial social strains that caused elites to feel and express a sense of tyranny beyond the reality of the restrictions Britain imposed. See also Wood's *The Radicalism of the American Revolution* (New York: Knopf, 1992).

23. *Pennsylvania Journal and Weekly Advertiser*, no. 1195, October 31, 1765.

24. Arthur M. Schlesinger, *Prelude to Independence: The Newspaper War on Britain, 1764–1776* (New York: Knopf, 1958), p. 77.

25. *New York Gazette or Weekly Post-Boy*, November 7, 1765.

26. Cass Canfield, *Sam Adams' Revolution* (New York: Harper & Row, 1976), p. 11.

27. W. V. Wells, *Life and Public Services of Samuel Adams*, 3 vols. (Boston, 1866), vol. 1, p. 237, cited in Bleyer, *Main Currents*, p. 82. For an analysis of revolutionary radicalism, see Patricia Bradley, *Slavery, Propaganda and the American Revolution* (Baton Rouge: University Press of Mississippi, 1998).

28. Brown, *Strength of a People*, p. 56.

29. Warren-Adams letters, December 5, 1767, W. C. Ford, ed., *Collections of the Massachusetts Historical Society*, XLII–LXXIII (1917–25), vol. 1, p. 3.

30. Rosemarian V. Staudacher, "Samuel Adams," in Perry J. Ashley, ed., *Dictionary of Literary Biography*, (Detroit: Gale Research, 1985) vol. 43, p. 182.

31. Staudacher, p. 182; Schlesinger, *Prelude*, pp. 179–81.

32. See John C. Miller, *Origins of the American Revolution*, rev. ed. (Palo Alto: Stanford University Press, 1959), p. 260; and Edward Channing, *History of the United States, Vol. 3: The American Revolution, 1761–1878* (New York: Macmillan, 1930), pp. 95–96, 99.

33. Arthur M. Schlesinger, *Prelude*, Appendix D, pp. 312–13.

34. See O. M. Dickerson, *Boston under Military Rule, 1768–1769* (Boston: Chapman & Grimes, 1936), p. ix.

Schlesinger, in "Review of Boston under Military Rule," *New England Quarterly*, 10 (1938), p. 387, and in *Prelude to Independence*, p. 312, argues that neither Isaiah Thomas nor John Adams should be listed as possible authors of the *Journal*. Schlesinger says that Thomas was then employed as a printer in Charleston, South Carolina, and that Adams had said in June, 1771, that he himself had not "written a line in a newspaper" for the preceding two years, covering much of the period during which the *Journal of Occurrences* appeared.

35. Philip Davidson, *Propaganda and the American Revolution* (Chapel Hill: University of North Carolina Press, 1941), p. 237.

36. Dickerson, *Boston under Military Rule*, p. ix.

37. *New York Journal*, October 13, 1768.

38. *New York Journal*, October 13, 1768.

39. *New York Journal*, November 10, 17, 1768, and May 4, June 1, 1769.

40. *New York Journal*, Supplement, June 8, 1769.

41. October 17, 1774, in William T. Hutchinson et al., eds., *The Madison Papers* (Chicago, 1962) vol. 1, p. 126. See also *Journals of the Continental Congress*, vol. 1, p. 126.

42. Worthington C. Ford et al., eds., *Journals of the Continental Congress 1774–1789*, 3 vols. (Washington, D.C., 1904–1937), vol. 13, Jan. 6–16, 1779, pp. 30–37.

43. Frank Luther Mott, "Newspaper Coverage of Lexington and Concord," in Edwin H. Ford and Edwin Emery, *Highlights in the History of the American Press* (Minneapolis, 1954), pp. 86–99.

44. *Pennsylvania Packet*, Philadelphia, August 9, 1783, "On the Advantage and Amusement derived from the reading of News-papers," reprinted from the *Edinburgh Evening Post*.

45. *Pennsylvania Packet*, April 24, 1775.

46. J. Thomas Scharf and Thompson Westcott, *History of Philadelphia*, 3 vols. (Philadelphia, 1884), vol. 1, p. 299.

47. *Pennsylvania Packet*, May 1, 1775.

48. *Journals of the Continental Congress*, vol. 5, p. 425.

49. Carl L. Becker, *The Declaration of Independence* (New York: Vintage, 1959), pp. 135–37.

50. Schlesinger, *Prelude to Independence*, p. 283.

51. *Boston Post-Boy Advertiser*, Dec. 26, 1774, cited in Janice Potter and Robert M. Calhoon, "The Character and Coherence of the Loyalist Press," in *The Press and the American Revolution*, Bernard Bailyn and John B. Hench, eds. (Boston: Northeastern University Press, 1981), p. 239.

52. Potter and Calhoon, *Press and Revolution*, p. 262.

53. Potter and Calhoon, *Press and Revolution*, p. 249.

54. Cadwallader Colden to Governor William Tryon, Sept. 7, 1774, *Colden Letter Books*, vol. 2, 1765–1775, New York Historical Society Collections, vol. 10 (New York, 1878), p. 361.

55. *New-York Gazetteer*, August 18, 1774.

56. *New-York Gazetteer*, August 18, 1774.

57. *New-York Gazetteer*, September 2, 1774.

58. Dwight L. Teeter, "'King' Sears, the Mob, and Freedom of the Press in New York, 1765–76," *Journalism Quarterly* 41:4 (Autumn, 1964), pp. 539–44; Michael Sewell, "James Rivington," *Dictionary of Literary Biography*, vol. 43, pp. 398–401.

59. Teeter, "'King' Sears," pp. 543–44.

60. Bernard Bailyn, *Pamphlets of the American Revolution, 1750–1765* (Cambridge: Harvard University Press), p. 1; Schlesinger, *Prelude*, pp. 45–46.

61. Botein, "Meer Mechanics," p. 216.

62. Benjamin Rush to James Cheetham, in Lyman H. Butterfield, ed., *The Letters of Benjamin Rush*, vol. 2 (Princeton, New Jersey: Princeton University Press, 1951), p. 1007.

63. Jensen, *Tracts of the Revolution*, p. 1.

64. "The Forester," Thomas Paine, in *Pennsylvania Gazette*, April 10, 1776; cited in Schlesinger, *Prelude*, p. 253.

65. Schlesinger, *Prelude*, quoting "Aristides" (Dr. John Witherspoon) from *Pennsylvania Packet*, May 13, 1776.

66. Arnold K. King, *Thomas Paine in America*, unpublished Ph.D. dissertation, University of Chicago, 1945; Robert Aitken, *Waste Book*, Library Company of Philadelphia manuscript collection, November 19, 1775, entry, p. 284.

67. Page Smith, *John Adams*, 2 vols. (New York, 1962), vol. 1, p. 239.

68. Philip H. Foner, ed., *The Complete Writings of Thomas Paine*, 2 vols. (New York: 1945), vol. 1, p. 4.

69. Foner, *Complete Writings of Paine*, p. 25.

70. King, *Thomas Paine*, p. 98.

71. Stout, "Religion, Communications and the Ideological Origins of the American Revolution," pp. 536–37.

72. *Packet*, March 25, 1776.

73. Eric Foner, *Tom Paine and Revolutionary America* (New York: Oxford University Press, 1976), p. 87.

74. William Bradford, "List of Subscribers on the 25th of April et. postea to the *Pennsylvania Journal*," Bradford papers, Historical Society of Pennsylvania. See also Carol Sue Humphrey, *"This Popular Engine": New England*

Newspapers during the American Revolution, 1775–1789 (Newark: University of Delaware Press, 1992).

75. Merrill Jensen, *The New Nation*, p. 430; see also Carl Bridenbaugh, "Press and Book in Philadelphia," *Pennsylvania Magazine of History and Biography* 65 (January, 1941), p. 7.

76. Robert Aitken's *Waste Book*, Library Company of Philadelphia manuscript collection.

77. *Pennsylvania Journal*, Philadelphia, January 25, 1775.

78. Schlesinger, *Prelude*, p. 303.

79. Thomas, *History of Printing*, pp. 8, 17.

80. Schlesinger, *Prelude*, pp. 303, 304.

81. Robert Hurd Kany, *David Hall: Printing Partner of Benjamin Franklin*, Ph.D. thesis, Pennsylvania State University, 1963.

82. George Moranda, *The Finances of Benjamin Franklin's Printing House*, M.A. thesis, School of Journalism and Mass Communication, University of Wisconsin–Madison, 1964, pp. 100–101.

83. Bradford papers, Historical Society of Pennsylvania.

84. William S. Hanna, *Benjamin Franklin and Pennsylvania Politics* (Palo Alto, California: 1964), pp. 3–4.

85. Hanna, *Franklin and Politics*, pp. 3–4.

86. Bradford, "List of Subscribers."

87. Isaiah Thomas, *Three Autobiographical Fragments* (Worcester, Massachusetts: American Antiquarian Society, 1962), published on 150th anniversary of the founding of the society, p. 19.

88. Terry Hynes, "Isaiah Thomas," *Dictionary of Literary Biography*, vol. 43, p. 439.

89. Thomas, *History of Printing*, pp. 167–68.

90. Hynes, "Isaiah Thomas," *Dictionary of Literary Biography*, vol. 43, p. 444.

CHAPTER 3

Forming a New Nation

▼

By 1787, the new nation had survived a dozen years of cataclysmic change. The nation had experimented with independence and more than one form of government, and it had begun to construct a party and information system that would shape the course of the nation. The political and information systems were intertwined as colonists debated the concept of people governing themselves versus that of the government ruling people. In this climate, the political role of the press emerged as a watchful eye on government power.

After the battles at Lexington and Concord in April 1775, the thirteen colonies declared themselves to be united in an independent nation, then went on to fight and win that independence. In late 1777, while the fighting flared and died down, the Continental Congress approved the Articles of Confederation, and the new nation signed the Treaties of Amity and Commerce with France early in 1778. By 1779, all states except Maryland accepted the Articles of Confederation; when Maryland finally signed in March 1781, the articles took full effect.

The articles had been in operation only six years when the Constitutional Convention convened in Philadelphia in May 1787, its goal to refine the governing plan dictated by the articles. Discussions were held behind closed doors, and the press had access only to what delegates were willing to release. Congressional delegates, once in Philadelphia, devised a new constitution rather than revising the articles.

In June 1788, after a ten-month ratification struggle, nine states adopted the second Constitution of the United States, a document still in full force today. On June

LITH. & PUB. BY N. CURRIER,   *Entered according to Act of Congress in the year 1848 by N. Currier, in the Clerks office of the District Court of the Southern District of New York.*   152 NASSAU ST. COR OF SPRUCE N.Y.
Steuben.   *Knox.*   *Washington.*   *Gov. Clinton.*   *Hamilton.*

WASHINGTON TAKING LEAVE OF THE OFFICERS OF HIS ARMY,

AT FRANCIS'S TAVERN, BROAD STREET, NEW YORK, DEC. 4th 1783.

"With a heart of love and gratitude, I now take leave of you. I most devoutly wish that your latter days may be as prosperous and happy, as your former ones have been glorious and honorable".

Figure 3–1   When he parted from his officers in 1783 at the end of the Revolution, Washington spoke: "With a heart of love and gratitude, I now take leave of you. I most devoutly wish that your latter days may be as prosperous and happy as your former ones have
been glorious and honorable." Washington's speech at St. Francis's Tavern on Broad Street in New York City is depicted here in a
Currier & Ives replica.(Division of Prints and Photographs, Library of Congress Collection)

25, Virginia became the tenth state to ratify, although the slim margin of 89 to 75 signaled the reservations that Virginians held, particularly about the absence of a Bill
of Rights. James Madison, however, urged Virginians to ratify the Constitution without attaching strings, pledging himself to obtain the necessary amendments once the
document went into effect. Madison's assurances, wrote historian Irving Brant, "did
not win the antis, but swung the doubtful and brought victory."[1]

Historians' analyses of the press during this postrevolutionary period have
focused primarily on the debates over whether a Bill of Rights would be included in
the Constitution. Most of the discussion has attempted to determine whether colonial printers had freedom in practice, whether they were free from laws of seditious
libel, and whether the framers of the Constitution possessed a clearly developed theory of freedom of the press. Although colonial printers labored first under licensing

restrictions and then under the possibility of indictments for seditious libel, toward the end of the period they also experienced considerable freedom to criticize the government. During the Revolution, popular opinion acted as more of a restraint than did legislation. Historian Jeffery Smith noted that public demand was responsible for the First Amendment but that political theorists also saw the need to protect the press from the public.[2]

The new nation faced political struggles from within and threats from abroad as it strived to adjust to social and political change as well as establish itself as an independent force in a world of competing interests. Although the constitutional ratification struggle officially ended in 1788, the political infighting between the Federalists, led by Alexander Hamilton, and the Anti-Federalists, or Republicans, led by Thomas Jefferson, continued until the War of 1812.[3] The Federalists, who controlled the presidency until 1801, tried through persuasion and legislation to acquire public support. When the Federalists failed to convince the public that Jeffersonian politics would undermine the fledgling nation, Jefferson's party gained ascendancy. Some historians have argued that Jefferson's inauguration represented a final phase of the Revolution that assured a democratic resolution to a period of conflict and adjustment.[4]

Political infighting created a political press, although with commercial overtones. Editors sided with parties and often were funded by them, thus causing the editors to focus less on advertising and commercial development than on party creation and nation building. Despite the political focus, however, entrepreneurs such as John Dunlap shaped newspapers that were successful enough to evolve from weeklies into dailies and that responded to the growing public demand for information. ▼

Constitutional Politics and the Press

As political figures and editors turned their attention to nation building, editorial and political voices joined to support various forms of government. Benjamin Franklin, as a printer, an editor and a statesman, drafted one of the first confederation plans in 1754 and presented it to the Albany Congress, called in an effort to create treaties with the Iroquois during the French and Indian War. Although the colonies and Britain rejected that plan, Franklin in 1775 submitted a second plan to the Continental Congress. The movement toward independence clearly included a search for a form of government that would bind together the states as they emerged from colonial status. The brilliant Philadelphia lawyer John Dickinson, author of the "Letters from a Pennsylvania Farmer," had hoped for conciliation with Britain. By mid-1776, however, Dickinson saw that independence was inevitable. The Continental Congress appointed Dickinson—in June of 1776—to head a committee to draft a plan of union. Dickinson took the lead in writing a plan to put the colonies "in a league of Friendship with each other."[5] This proposal—the Articles of Confederation—now known as the nation's first constitution, was presented to Congress on July 12, 1776, just eight days after publication of the Declaration of Independence. Congress adopted the articles on November 15, 1778.

Submission of the articles to the states—with nine states required for adoption—proved to be a lengthy process. Finally, on March 1, 1781, after Maryland's adoption, Congress announced that the Articles of Confederation were in effect.

The articles created a unicameral legislature. The number of delegates from each state varied, but each state had only one vote. Congress possessed sole authority to declare war and conduct foreign relations, supervise Indian affairs, regulate weights and measures, and create post offices. Both Congress and the states could coin money. Most significantly, in reaction to English economic policies, Congress could not tax or regulate commerce. No executive or judicial branches existed. Although the Dickinson-drafted articles asserted the primacy of congressional power over the states, the states still retained a strong measure of ultimate control.[6] Politicians who wanted more centralization of power, and those who believed the articles were insufficient to govern an expanding new nation, continued to agitate for change, but the articles were difficult to amend, requiring unanimous state agreement on each change.

The next six years were difficult ones for the new country. In an attempt to recover from the loss of traditional trade patterns with Britain and the empire, the colonies devised new patterns of trade with France, Holland, Sweden, and China. Farmers in western Massachusetts rebelled because the state raised taxes despite difficult economic times and required further that taxes be paid in hard cash. Daniel Shays led a group of farmers in an attempt to seize control of the county courts to prevent foreclosures. In 1787, as the states voted to send delegates to the Constitutional Convention in Philadelphia, the Massachusetts militia was putting down this rebellion. Other issues causing public unrest included the lack of a consistent money supply and uneven actions by state governments, some of which had issued paper money and others that had not.

No day-to-day account of the proceedings of the Constitutional Convention greeted the public each morning in the newspapers of the day: The convention, convened in Philadelphia from May 25 until September 17 of 1787, met behind closed doors. In fact, General Washington complained to delegates when he found a copy of agenda proposals lying on the floor, "I must entreat gentlemen to be more careful, lest our transactions get into the newspapers and disturb public repose by premature speculations."[7] Despite their inability to sit in on the proceedings, members of the press generally supported the new constitution. Of the approximately 100 newspapers being printed in the states in 1787, only a dozen opposed ratification.[8]

The new constitution was a controversial document. Two major issues were at stake: (1) the level of power granted to the national government versus that reserved for the states and (2) the absence of a Bill of Rights.

The Fight for Ratification: Federalists vs. Anti-Federalists

The supporters of the Constitution—the Federalists—argued for a strong national government and exaggerated the financial and political ills that might occur under the Articles of Confederation. Opponents, or Anti-Federalists, argued that the new Constitution would create a centralized and despotic government and give no guar-

▼

Plea for Strong Federal Government

Nothing is more certain than the indispensable necessity of government; and it is equally undeniable that whenever and however it is instituted, the people must cede to it some of their natural rights, in order to vest it with requisite powers. It is well worthy of consideration, therefore, whether it would conduce more to the interest of the people of America that they should, to all general purposes, be one nation, under one federal government, than that they should divide themselves into separate confederacies and give to the head of each the same kind of powers which they are advised to place in one national government.

—John Jay, *Federalist Papers*, No. 2

antees for freedom of speech, religion, press, assembly, and the right to petition government. Although the Federalists maintained that a Bill of Rights was unnecessary because powers not specifically given to the national government would be preserved by the states, they knew they faced serious opposition when three delegates to the Constitutional Convention—George Mason and Edmund Randolph of Virginia and Elbridge Gerry of Massachusetts—refused to sign the Constitutional document.

To encourage ratification of the Constitution, Alexander Hamilton, John Jay, and James Madison, in a series of articles signed "Publius," eloquently argued the Federalist position. Widely reprinted in newspapers throughout the new states, the articles appeared from late October 1787 into April 1788. Called the Federalist Papers, these articles were aimed primarily at New York and probably did little to gain ratifying votes for the Constitution; but they became important historical documents that outlined the position of the Federalist faction. New York ratified the Constitution only after the necessary number of states—a total of nine—had already voted to ratify.[9] All in all, eighty-five newspapers showed strong support for ratification by persuasively arguing that creation of a new constitution was essential to creating a new republic and to preserving liberty and property.

John Jay, a New Yorker born to wealth and power, was prevented by illness from contributing more than five of the Publius essays. A former president of the Continental Congress, he had served as a minister to Spain during the War for Independence. Frustrated by what he saw as the lack of a strong national voice in foreign affairs, he pushed for the stronger central government that would be established by the Constitution of 1787. Jay in 1789 became the first chief justice of the Supreme Court of the United States.

Hamilton and Madison were unlikely compatriots. A handsome and ambitious New Yorker with less-than-promising beginnings—he was born out of wedlock in the West Indies—Hamilton would have preferred a stronger Constitution than the one proposed, but he fought for its adoption over the weaker Articles of Confederation. Hamilton's approach and personality sparked controversy; some historians disparaged his contempt for common women and men, and John Adams referred to

▼

An Anti-Federalist Warning

Friends, Countrymen and Fellow Citizens: Permit one of yourselves to put you in mind of certain liberties and privileges secured to you by the constitution of this commonwealth, and to beg your serious attention to his uninterested opinion upon the plan of federal government submitted to your consideration, before you surrender these great and valuable privileges up forever.

—"Centinel," *Independent Gazetteer*, October 5, 1787

him as the "bastard brat of a Scotch pedlar." Hamilton was, however, "a natural journalist and pamphleteer. . . . His perspicacity, penetration, powers of condensation and clarity of expression were those of a premier editorial writer."[10] Virginia statesman James Madison, often called the Father of the Constitution and of the Bill of Rights, supported Hamilton's view, but he nevertheless took pains to ease Anti-Federalist fears of a consolidated national government, arguing that the state governments would remain "constituent and essential parts of the federal government."[11] Despite his Federalist position, Madison promised, partly in deference to his good friend Thomas Jefferson, to write and secure the adoption of a Bill of Rights in return for ratification votes.

Anti-Federalists opposed what they perceived to be the national centralization of government primarily by arguing for the inclusion of a Bill of Rights, a concept with distinct popular appeal. Protection of civil liberties rated high among colonists who remembered all too well having to shelter British troops in their homes. Undoubtedly concerned with politically exploiting the issue's popular appeal, however, Anti-Federalists also genuinely lamented the absence of a Bill of Rights. Anti-Federalist leader John Smilie of Pennsylvania expressed the fear that "an aristocratical Govt. cannot bear the Liberty of the Press."[12] There is some indication that memories of Zenger's trial sparked argument that in the absence of a Bill of Rights provision judges might harm the press without being held in check by a jury.[13]

A series of Anti-Federalist essays labeled "Centinel" and Virginian Richard Henry Lee's "Letters from a Federal Farmer" argued that unless specific guarantees of freedom of the press were added, government powers under the national Constitution would supersede rights previously taken for granted and could destroy press freedom.

These appeals helped secure a Federalist promise to accept a Bill of Rights in the form of amendments, a promise that encouraged reluctant states, such as Virginia, to ratify the Constitution.[14]

The Bill of Rights: Congress Shall Make No Law

In June 1788, nine states adopted the Constitution. Many of the legislators who arrived in New York for the first session of Congress came with specific plans to introduce amendments to the Bill of Rights. James Madison responded to Thomas

Jefferson's concerns about the lack of protection against governmental intrusion. Although Madison argued that public opinion, as it had expressed itself during the revolution, determined civil rights more than did legislation, he also recognized the value of Jefferson's argument. "The political truths declared in that solemn manner acquire by degrees the character of fundamental maxims of free Government," he wrote, "and as they become incorporated with the national sentiment, counteract the impulses of interest and passion."[15] Madison drafted the document that the states, in December 1791, ratified with little recorded debate as the Bill of Rights.[16] The First Amendment as passed guarantees that Congress can not infringe on specific freedoms, but it makes no reference to what the states can do.[17] Further, the First Amendment addresses a variety of rights, including, but not exclusively protecting, freedom of the press:

> Congress shall make no law respecting an establishment of religion, or prohibiting the free exercise thereof; or abridging the freedom of speech, or of the press; or the right of the people peaceably to assemble, and to petition the government for a redress of grievances.

The remaining nine amendments include protections for the right to carry arms, to trial by jury, to be secure from unreasonable searches and excessive bail, and to reserve rights to the states that are not specifically granted to the federal government.

Figure 3–2   James Madison, from a painting by Gilbert Stuart. (State Historical Society of Wisconsin)

Enlightenment Philosophy and the Bill of Rights

Public opinion in support of a Bill of Rights evolved within a framework of enlightenment philosophy. Small wonder. The language of individual rights, borrowed in part from eighteenth-century French *philosophes* such as Voltaire and Rousseau and based on John Locke's social contract arguments, helped justify the American Revolution in the first place. Enlightenment notes sounded throughout the Declaration of Independence.

Americans who made the revolution borrowed ideas to support their arguments against authority and for greater freedom of expression. Especially important were the writings of "Cato," the pen name of Britishers John Trenchard and Thomas Gordon. Cato's writings appeared in the *London Journal* from 1720 to 1722 and in the *British Journal* in 1723. The essays ended with Trenchard's death in 1723, but editions of *Cato's Letters* were many and popular, in both Britain and in the American colonies.[18]

As legal historians David Rabban and Jeffery A. Smith have noted, the English "Radical Whigs"—including Trenchard and Gordon as well as Joseph Priestly and Richard Price—provided intellectual ammunition for the dissident colonists. "The [English] Radical Whig tradition and the emerging popular ideology," Rabban wrote, "were part of a common intellectual tradition that stressed the importance of free political expression to popular sovereignty and effective government."[19]

So Cato's letters by Trenchard and Gordon were not just about freedom, they were about freedom for a public purpose. Cato's famous words, "Freedom of Speech is the great Bulwark of Liberty," were published in a letter that also said: "The Administration of Government is nothing else, but the Attendance of the Trustees of the People upon the Interest and Affairs of the People."[20] To Trenchard and Gordon—and to the many American dissidents and revolutionists who borrowed their arguments—freedom of expression was the precondition for an informed public, a public with a say in government. At the time the Bill of Rights was passed, Thomas Jefferson argued that the role of learning was "to illuminate, as far as practicable, the minds of the people at large" so that "they may be enabled to know ambition under all its shapes, and prompt to exert their natural powers to defeat its purposes."[21] Madison joined Jefferson in arguing that "Knowledge will forever govern ignorance: And a people who mean to be their own Governors, must arm themselves with the power which knowledge gives." It was the press that was to give the nation's citizens the knowledge with which to confront and shape their government and to preserve individual liberty.

Evolution of the Commercial Press

Advertising was a staple of the colonial press, which supported itself through a combination of advertising and subscriptions, along with book sales and other commercial operations a printer might use to subsidize newspaper printing. By 1800, as dailies became more common, twenty of the twenty-four published dailies carried the word *Advertiser* in their nameplates. That percentage declined during the next twelve years, as newspapers focused increasingly on partisan politics, relying less on advertising and subscriptions for support. Nevertheless, colonial editors and those operating in the early Republic recognized the value of advertising, although they probably did not envision the commercialization of society that it ultimately would represent. John Peter Zenger's *New York Weekly Journal* in 1743 carried more than a page of advertising, and after 1760 newspapers regularly carried as much as 50 percent advertising.[22] Advertisements were small and private affairs; those who advertised regularly used the same copy over a period of a year, and display advertising consisted only of a heading printed in larger type than the regular text. Advertisers generally were subscribers who viewed the papers as "common carriers," or vehicles through which to exchange commercial information as well as political and social content. Concerns about ethics in advertising rarely arose until after 1800, when mass-produced goods began to separate the publisher from the advertiser. Then publishers began to debate the problems associated with advertising such products as patent medicines. In 1805, when a young girl died after taking a patent medicine, the *New York Evening Post* temporarily banned advertisements for quack nostrums.[23]

Information Demand and Developing Dailies

As commerce grew in the cities and the postal service capable of delivering newspapers expanded, dailies became viable economic enterprises. The first abortive attempt at a daily in the United States in 1783 preceded a seven-year period of experimentation with semiweeklies and triweeklies, which began competing with weekly newspapers. By 1790, thirteen dailies were published in Philadelphia, Charleston, New York City, and Baltimore. Seven still existed at the turn of the decade.[24]

By 1800, urban publishers, because of lower costs of production, were able to produce a six-day-a-week newspaper at only about twice the cost of a country weekly. Both local journals and dailies focused on foreign affairs; thus, subscribers to urban dailies could obtain information more quickly than if they read the country journals, which took most of their news from the same publications as the dailies but were published less frequently. In the ensuing years, the advantage urban publishers enjoyed with their lower production costs would become a subject of debate as Congress determined postal rates for printed matter.

Benjamin Towne, a pudgy man remembered as a turncoat during the War for Independence, published the first daily newspaper in North America, the *Pennsylvania Evening Post*. The scruffy little sheet, converted to a daily from a triweekly, lasted only seventeen months after its first issue on May 30, 1783. The newspaper merely struggled along, and in 1784, many years before newsboys sold papers on the streets, it was said that Towne had to peddle the last issue of his paper on Philadelphia's streets, crying, "All the news for two coppers."

John Dunlap: Business Success

John Dunlap was a successful Philadelphia printer and entrepreneur, similar to Benjamin Franklin and Isaiah Thomas. Franklin, Thomas, and Dunlap all moved successfully into society first as printers, then as booksellers and bookbinders, and all three grew wealthy from their printing and merchant enterprises. As the demand for printed materials grew after the Revolution, Dunlap shrewdly converted a tri-weekly newspaper into a successful daily, relying on his business contacts and political acumen as he packed the newspaper with advertisements as well as political announcements.

Like Franklin and Thomas, Dunlap began life in poverty and was apprenticed to a printer early in life. Born in County Strabane, Ireland, in 1747, he was apprenticed at the age of ten to his Uncle William in Philadelphia. By the age of seventeen, he had taken charge of the printing house, because his printer-uncle had gone to England to study to become an Anglican priest. When John Dunlap was nineteen, his uncle began selling the shop to him in installments; at this time Dunlap was so strapped financially he slept on a blanket under the shop's counter. After five years of doing little more than printing handbills, pamphlets, and sermons, Dunlap started the weekly *Pennsylvania Packet, or the General Advertiser.*

From its beginning late in 1771 until it became a daily on September 21, 1784, the *Packet* represented a remarkable success story. John Dunlap associated with some of Philadelphia's most prominent individuals as a member of the First Troop of the Philadelphia Light-Horse—nicknamed the Silk-Stocking Cavalry—and proved himself to be a good soldier at the battles of Princeton and Trenton in 1776 to 1777.

In 1776, Dunlap secured printing contracts from Congress. Dunlap also printed for Pennsylvania's Council of Safety, the quasi-official body that took over in the months when colonial structures lapsed and a new government was established under the Pennsylvania Constitution of 1776.

Not all of Dunlap's business dealings were above reproach. Dunlap printed loyalty oaths that the Council of Safety required of suspicious individuals. If Tories—for political reasons—or Quakers—for religious reasons—refused to sign the oaths, the council confiscated their property. Dunlap, who also printed paper money for Pennsylvania, then used such rapidly depreciating money to buy the lands of persons who would not take the oath. He purchased much of the estate of Pennsylvania Tory Joseph Galloway, who fled during the Revolution.

Although Dunlap left Philadelphia in September 1777 when the British occupied the city and did not return until the following June, he industriously continued his public printing business. Moving his shop to Lancaster, Dunlap increasingly took over congressional printing from his rival Robert Aitken, who abandoned his printing operation during the British occupation. Dunlap did most of the congressional printing from 1779 until 1783. In addition, Dunlap appears to have received more revenue from printing for Pennsylvania's assembly in 1778 and 1779 than did any other printer.[25] Dunlap, with his young partner David C. Claypoole, continued to run a flourishing printing business in Philadelphia from 1780 to 1784. During most of that period, Claypoole's name appeared alone on the *Pennsylvania Packet,* with Dunlap's name reappearing on September 21, 1784, just as the newspaper became a daily.

Dunlap changed the name of the paper when it became a daily, renaming it the *Pennsylvania Packet and Daily Advertiser.* It was full-sized (for its time) and was packed with advertisements and government announcements as well as essays clipped from English papers, news reports, and letters. The *Packet* devoted the September 19, 1787, issue to the first printing of the U.S. Constitution.

During his printing career, Dunlap amassed a fortune, buying sizeable parcels of real estate. In 1788, Governor Edmund Randolph of Virginia, who rented one of Dunlap's better properties, also signed the documents for Dunlap to purchase 131,000 acres of land in what is now Kentucky. When Dunlap died in 1812, his estate was estimated at more than $300,000.[26]

Political Press and National Politics

The press continued along many of the traditional lines of publishing already established in the colonial and revolutionary period. The newspapers reflected intensified party divisions and antagonisms between the Federalists and Anti-Federalists, just as the revolutionary press had reflected the bitter disputes between Tories, Whigs, and Patriots. Although sometimes the results of a partisan press were vitriolic diatribes, also represented were attempts to understand and interpret varying philosophies of government and to establish a party system that would retain the freedom of the people to govern as well as stabilize a fledgling nation. Although few of the newspapers of the period survive, there are nevertheless some indications that the rural press was less partisan than urban papers. In 1804, for example, the postmaster general admonished his deputies to encourage subscribers to take local papers, claiming that "the establishment of country presses, where the printers do not enter into the rage of party, is of great public use."[27] Also, newspapers in Kentucky and Pennsylvania developed during the period not only to spread political information but also to boost new communities and to publish legal notices.

The primary departure from the old way was reflected in the fact that Federalist newspapers were allied with a party in power—a party having formal, administrative, and governmental control. Although in 1798 the Federalists passed the Alien and Sedition Acts to restrict freedom of information, financial support of the press by various factions probably stimulated a diversity of political views. If one accepts that assumption, one can argue that press partisanship actually helped broaden freedom of the press. Both Federalists and Republicans regarded the press as essential to spreading their doctrines and thus used newspapers as a means of building political cohesion and a sense of nationalism. In such an atmosphere, editors were not always printer-entrepreneurs, and they often produced political newspapers without the familiar accompaniment of bookshop and job-printing businesses. In 1817, John Calhoun recognized the importance of newspapers and the distribution of information when he entreated Congress to "bind the republic together with a perfect system of roads and canals. Let us conquer space. . . . It is thus that a citizen of the West will read the news of Boston still moist from the press. The mail and the press are the nerves of the body politic."[28]

Federalist Newspapers

On April 15, 1789—fifteen days before George Washington took the oath of office on Federal Hall's balcony in the city of New York—John Fenno published the first issue of the *Gazette of the United States*. The newspaper boldly supported the Federalist cause and President Washington, and it walked the administration's line. When the national government moved from New York to Philadelphia in November 1790, Fenno's newspaper moved too. Fenno's paper was the "most official" of the Federalist papers, and one of the most moderate as well.

Fenno, a school teacher from Boston, viewed himself as an "editor," not a printer or publisher.[29] He acknowledged that he had writing help from "literary characters"; paramount among these were Secretary of the Treasury Alexander Hamilton and Vice President John Adams. Despite overt Federalist financial support that helped Fenno establish his newspaper, he proclaimed it to be "a National, Impartial, and Independent Conveyancer to all parts of the Union, of News, Politics, and Miscellanies." At three dollars a year, the paper was expensive and for common laborers would have absorbed about a week's pay.[30]

Fenno's circulation differed little from successful prerevolution circulations. Operating first in New York, with a 1790 population of 33,000, and then in the nation's largest city, Philadelphia, with a population of 42,000, Fenno's circulation was 1,400 in December 1791.[31] One-hundred-twenty copies were sent free to editors and postmasters throughout the nation.[32]

Despite subsidies, Fenno faced financial difficulties and appealed regularly to Secretary of the Treasury Hamilton to keep his newspaper functioning during its first five years. By early 1797, the subscription price—in part because of inflationary pressures—had risen to eight dollars a year. Its front page was given over completely—as was often the style of the day—to brief advertisements. Peter Blight offered "A Quantity of Brandy, FIRST & 2d proofs" plus gin, rum, "Window-glass, in boxes, of different sizes Hazlenuts in sacks."

Fenno's newspaper carried continuing reports from the debates in the House of Representatives on tariffs, taxation, and smuggling, as well as foreign news. When Thomas Jefferson resigned on the last day of 1793 amidst charges of scandal in the Federalist administration, Fenno's paper supported Secretary of the Treasury Alexander Hamilton against the opposition newspaper's charges that under Hamilton, the bankers, the speculators, the privileged, and wealthy merchant interests gained far more than was their due.

Fenno represented a middle although highly partisan ground. On the more vituperative side was William Cobbett with *Porcupine's Gazette*, and on the more moderate was Benjamin Russell with the *Columbian*. Russell's moderation existed only in the highly charged atmosphere of the early Republic, however, and in 1798 when a Federalist Congress passed the Alien and Sedition Acts, Russell wrote, "It is Patri-

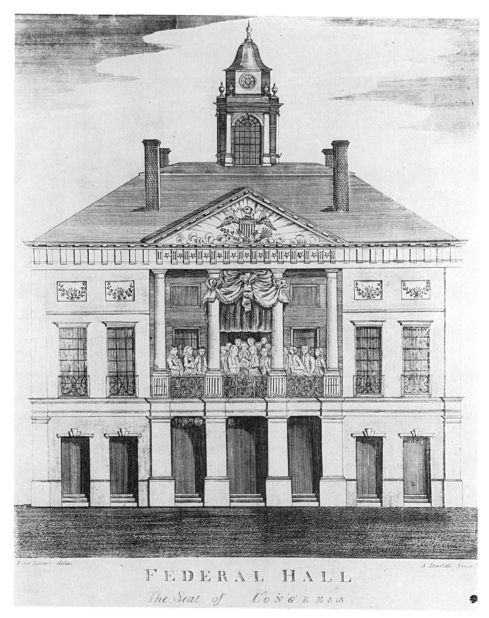

FEDERAL HALL
The Seat of Congress

Figure 3–3   Federal Hall, the seat of Congress in 1790. (Division of Prints and Photographs, Library of Congress Collection)

otism to write in favor of our Government; it is Sedition to write against it."[33] Cobbett, a British journalist, in 1797 produced a prospectus for a *Porcupine's Gazette.* Cobbett proposed to dispute what he believed to be falsehoods against Britain, and he promised to meet editors of newspapers that forwarded such material "on their

Figure 3–4   William Cobbett, the "Porcupine." (Division of Prints and Photographs, Library of Congress Collection)

own ground; to set foot to foot; dispute every inch and every hair's breadth; fight them at their own weapons, and return two blows for one."[34]

Cobbett did not restrict the festering quills of the *Porcupine's* political attacks to the Jeffersonians, however, and by 1799 President John Adams considered deporting Cobbett under the Enemy Alien Act of 1798. Such action turned out to be unnecessary, however, because Cobbett, whose Philadelphia assets were seized in a $5,000 libel judgment, returned to England in 1800.

Jeffersonian (Republican) Newspapers

The *National Gazette*, edited by the "Poet of the American Revolution," Philip Freneau, provided an effective newspaper voice for the Anti-Federalists and, later, for the Jeffersonian Republicans. A 1771 graduate of Princeton, Freneau had roomed there with James Madison. In 1791, Madison and Jefferson persuaded Freneau to move to the nation's capital city, Philadelphia, for the salary of $250 a year.

Madison and Jefferson expected that Freneau would establish a newspaper to fire answering journalistic volleys at John Fenno's *Gazette of the United States*. Indeed, Freneau did attack Federalist men and measures. He lambasted Hamiltonian-Federalist financial measures, including the Bank of the United States, and made fun of the aristocratic airs of the Federalists, airs which seemed to Freneau to reflect a fondness for monarchy.

Freneau's satirical thrusts struck home, and his support of the French won him enemies. Hamilton, writing anonymous letters for publication in the *Gazette of the United States*, accused Secretary of State Jefferson of using public monies to pay an editor who had turned against the government. Hamilton claimed Jefferson had departed "from the rules of official propriety and obligation, and from the duty of a discreet and patriotic citizen."[35]

President Washington indicated to Jefferson that he wanted Freneau fired from his job as a translator clerk in the State Department.[36] Later, in 1793, Washington referred to charges that Jefferson was responsible for the *National Gazette*'s attacks on the president and the government. Jefferson wrote to Washington, pleading that he had no direct influence on Freneau's paper. Jefferson swore that he never wrote for the *National Gazette* unless his name, or that of his office as secretary of state, was used with a written statement.[37] Jefferson's letter to Washington added that

> He (Freneau) & Fenno are rivals for the public favor. The one courts them by flattery, the other by censure, & I believe it will be admitted that one has been as servile, as the other severe. . . .
>
> No government ought to be without censors [critics]: & where the press is free, no one ever will.

The *National Gazette* lasted only two years, suspending publication on October 26, 1793, after Jefferson made known his intent to resign as secretary of state. Its

---

▼

Philip Freneau (1752–1832)

Although he lived an eventful and varied life, Phillip Freneau is best known as the poet of the American Revolution. He wrote volumes of poetry—one collection numbered 1,200 pages—including some written during the time he spent on a British prison ship. Later, his Princeton roommate James Madison along with Thomas Jefferson convinced Freneau to start a newspaper (*National Gazette*) to combat a powerful Hamiltonian newspaper. Jefferson would later comment that Freneau "saved our Constitution which was galloping fast into monarchy." But George Washington, the target of Freneau's criticism in the *National Gazette,* would term him "that rascal Freneau."

Sources: *The Cambridge History of English and American Literature in Eighteen Volumes (1907–21). Volume XV. Colonial and Revolutionary Literature; Early National Literature, Part I;* and A. Leitch, *A Princeton Companion* (N.J.: Princeton University Press, 1978). (Division of Prints and Photographs, Library of Congress Collection)

demise was doubtless ensured not only by the reluctance of subscribers and advertisers to pay their debts but also by the yellow fever epidemic scourging Philadelphia that fall. The *National Gazette*, quite clearly a money-loser, nevertheless had a circulation of more than 1,500 that reached throughout the union.

Six months before the paper suspended publication, Jefferson gave it high marks: "[Freneau's] paper has saved our constitution which was galloping fast into monarchy."[38] Freneau, by no means the most vitriolic of the editors in a vituperative age, nevertheless taunted President Washington into an uncharacteristic outburst during a Cabinet meeting when he denounced "that rascal Freneau."

Freneau, like Fenno, was not alone in occupying one side of the political fence. The outrageous Anti-Federalist paper, the *Aurora*, matched the vitriol of Cobbett's Federalist *Porcupine*. The *Aurora*'s editor, Benjamin Franklin Bache, grandson of the diplomatic and successful Benjamin Franklin, was one of the most ferocious journalists in American history. Bache grew up near his grandfather and accompanied him to France during Franklin's service as ambassador. The younger man became angered at what he perceived to be slights by the Federalists to his grandfather, who had grown suspicious of the aristocratic group of officers under Washington.[39] When Franklin died in 1790 and Bache inherited the publishing house, he began a newspaper to oppose Federalist thought and action. The newspaper, grandiloquently called the *General Advertiser, and Political, Commercial and Literary Journal*, was soon mercifully shortened to *General Advertiser* and later also was known as the *Aurora*.

Bache's residence in France clearly helped shape his sympathies, and his paper favored France and his friend, the soon-to-be discredited French envoy, Citizen Genet. By the end of 1793, Freneau's *National Gazette* had disappeared, and Bache's newspaper emerged nationally as the prime Jeffersonian Republican paper. In late 1796, the *Aurora* cast a savage light on President Washington's farewell address:

> If ever a nation was debauched by a man, the American nation has been debauched by Washington. If ever a nation has suffered from the improper influence of a man, the American nation has suffered from the influence of Washington. If ever a nation was deceived by a man, the American nation has been deceived by Washington. Let his conduct then be an example to future ages. Let it serve to be a warning that no man may be an idol.[40]

The combative Bache—dubbed "Lightning Rod Junior" in reference to his grandfather's experiments with electricity—declared that Washington's retirement was cause for celebration and that "there ought to be a JUBILEE in the United States."[41]

Publication of such sharp criticism of the beloved Washington proved dangerous. A shipbuilder thrashed Bache, and later John Ward Fenno, son of the editor of the Federalist's chief paper, attacked Bache in the streets. Undaunted, Bache published a secret letter from the French foreign minister Duc de Talleyrand, which he accused the administration of hiding in order to avoid negotiating with France. Federalists accused Bache of treason; the poison-penned Federalist editor William Cobbett claimed the "infamous Lightning-rod, jun. was a hireling of, and in correspondence with the despots of France."[42]

Benjamin Bache did not publish the *Aurora* unaided. His wife, Margaret Markoe Bache, proved to be an able manager; and in 1796, William Duane, a thirty-six-year-old wanderer who had published a newspaper in Calcutta, India, joined Bache as assistant editor of the *Aurora*.

In September 1798, while being prosecuted on charges of sedition, Benjamin Franklin Bache remained in Philadelphia to continue publishing his newspaper. Yellow fever struck the city, and Bache died within a week of contracting the disease. After a brief suspension of the *Aurora*, Margaret Bache as publisher and William Duane as editor resumed publication. The two married in 1800 and continued the newspaper until 1822 as a Republican voice.

Lingering Legacy of Seditious Libel

Where the crime of seditious libel is in force, the public and the press cannot be free. Seditious libel—sometimes called "sedition"—has fancy legal definitions, as the one in *Black's Law Dictionary*:

> In English law. A written or printed document containing seditious matter or published with seditious intention . . . an intention to bring hatred or contempt, or to excite disaffection against, the King or the government.

Of course, when emotions run high—as in times of war hysteria—government prosecutors can find the requisite "intent" in words that in calmer times would be ignored. When tensions are high, even innocuous criticisms of government have been held to be "seditious."

As historian Norman L. Rosenberg has suggested, a broader concept—*political libel*—should be considered. As he has correctly pointed out, the law that is used as an excuse to silence a dissident or to jail a journalist is not what matters. What matters is that the protester has been stifled or imprisoned. In the pages that follow, the legal troubles of swashbuckling publisher Eleazer Oswald are discussed. Efforts were made to prosecute him for seditious libel, but when those attempts failed, he finally was jailed for contempt of court.

Professor Rosenberg's point is this: Fashions and techniques for suppressing dissent change over time. As discussed in more detail later in this chapter, early in this nation's history the *federal* Alien and Sedition Acts were used to impose criminal sanctions—fines and imprisonments—on editors. After those statutes were repealed, sedition prosecutions were tried at the *state* level. When those prosecutions fell from favor, some editors found themselves battered—and even sued out of business by barrages of *civil* damage actions—libel lawsuits seeking money. Where political expression is concerned, the *form* of an attempted suppression is not the point. What matters is the *fact* of attempted suppression, whether it comes as a criminal prosecution for seditious libel, a judge's contempt-of-court order, a civil damage suit for defamation, a postpublication prosecution, or a prepublication injunction—the now rare prior restraint order.[43]

The Power of Public Opinion

Eleazer Oswald was a violent man with a hot temper and a tendency to shout "Freedom of the Press" when it best suited his own interest. His story demonstrates not only the importance of a continuing network of printers, often based on family relationships, and the power of public opinion in postrevolutionary America, but it also confirms the continued threat of seditious libel prosecutions in the early Republic. Persecutions for what Oswald printed made him a likely candidate for supporting the side that demanded a Bill of Rights. An additional factor favoring such a political inclination was the fact that Oswald was an entrepreneur, operating a paper mill with William Goddard.

Born in Falmouth, England, in 1755, Oswald sailed to New York in 1770. He apprenticed himself to printer John Holt of the *New York Journal, or General Advertiser,* and later married Holt's daughter, Elizabeth.[44]

After a stint in the army in 1775, Oswald joined William Goddard in Baltimore as a partner. Goddard, a former employee of Oswald's father-in-law, John Holt, and Oswald apparently had become friends while organizing the postal system in New York. Oswald had been contemplating joining Goddard in business for some time.[45]

Goddard and Oswald operated a paper mill at Elk-Ridge Landing near Baltimore, leaving the *Maryland Journal* in the capable hands of Goddard's sister, Mary Katherine Goddard. Goddard's sister operated the *Journal* in her own name; as Isaiah Thomas wrote, she ably conducted a printing house and published the *Journal* for more than eight years and was "an expert and correct compositor of types." She also operated Baltimore's post office during that time. Soon after the Oswald–Goddard alliance was formed, the *Maryland Journal* printed the first installment of Major General Charles Lee's "Some Queries Political and Military." The "Queries" sharply attacked Washington but were suspect because Lee had been court-martialed for his role in the Battle of Monmouth in June 1778. Philadelphia editors had refused to print the letters, evidently fearing that criticism of the popular Washington would bring out the mob.[46]

On July 8, 1779, two days after the paper containing the "Queries" appeared, a mob of thirty men led by several Continental officers broke into William Goddard's home. Goddard and Oswald fled twenty-five miles on horseback to the state capital at Annapolis, where they asked for protection and demanded impeachment of the Baltimore magistrates who had refused to protect them.[47] The matter subsided after a hearing before the Council of Maryland, although the newspaper fired a parting shot on a printer's right to publish:

> Restraints on the Press in any Cases, except Libels and Treason, narrow and debase the liberal Sentiments of the Soul, and curb the rising efforts of Genius: It is a Mockery of the Understanding to call that Country free, where this Restraint is tolerated, approved of, and supported.[48]

After his unpleasant sojourn in Baltimore, Oswald moved to Philadelphia in 1781 to make his fortune. He established a printing house and took over the Bradfords' famous London Coffee House, an excellent center for gathering information from merchants and travelers. Oswald began publishing the *Independent Gazetteer* on April 13, 1782. The first issue of Oswald's paper contained the printer's vow that his newspaper was "independent of Party, upon Principles of Public Utility."[49] However, these aims required more restraint than Oswald had to offer. Oswald's hot-headed publishing led to several threatened libel suits during the first few months of the *Gazetteer's* existence. He soon ended up in court for criticizing Pennsylvania Chief Justice McKean's handling of the trial of a soldier who had thrashed an election inspector for demanding a certificate that proved the soldier had signed a loyalty oath. Oswald's account of the high fine brought him before the chief justice, an appearance that Oswald duly recorded in his newspaper.[50]

Chief Justice McKean submitted charges to a grand jury three times, seeking an indictment of Oswald; and three times, the grand jury refused to indict the printer. On January 7, 1783, the grand jurors presented a written statement to the chief justice, denouncing his actions in bringing repeated charges against Oswald.

Meanwhile, Oswald expanded his printing business, acquiring the *New York Journal and State Gazette* at the death of his father-in-law, John Holt, in 1784. Elizabeth Holt, Oswald's mother-in-law, managed the paper during 1784 and 1785, but Oswald took charge the next year. His name appeared in the nameplate until January 26, 1787, when Thomas Greenleaf bought an interest.[51]

During the struggle over ratification of the Constitution, Oswald's *Independent Gazetteer* printed twenty-four articles signed by "Centinel." Oswald also carried letters for the Anti-Federalists from New York to Virginia during the spring of 1787, at a time when the Constitution's opponents charged that Federalists sabotaged the mails in order to disrupt antiratification efforts.[52]

An attempt to muzzle Oswald and his anti-Federalist *Gazetteer* in 1788 (*Respublica v. Oswald*) is still recognized as an important contempt-of-court case. The attack on Oswald came through the Pennsylvania Supreme Court and his old foe, Chief Justice Thomas McKean. On July 14, 1788, while publishing "Centinel's" articles, Oswald was ordered to appear before the Supreme Court and was jailed for contempt. Chief Justice McKean sentenced Oswald to pay a £10 fine and to spend a month in prison. As Oswald was taken away to jail, his backers gave him three cheers.[53]

From his jail cell Oswald lashed out against McKean, using the *Pennsylvania Packet* to denounce the chief justice's use of the contempt power as "UNPRECE-DENTED, ILLEGAL & UNCONSTITUTIONAL, & WICKED & ARBITRARY . . . tending to pull down FREEDOM OF THE PRESS; to abolish the immortal TRIAL BY JURY. . . ."[54] Once out of jail, Oswald pleaded unsuccessfully for Chief Justice McKean's impeachment. Failing that, Oswald threatened to beat the judge and was again arrested, but he was released after promising to be a good citizen.[55]

In 1792, Oswald traveled to England to settle the affairs connected with the death of one of his wife's relatives, but the revolution in France attracted him to the continent. Oswald wrote in 1793, "the anxiety I felt for the Success of the [French] Revolution, determined me to defer my Return to America and to come to France and offer my Services. . . ."[56] Oswald returned to the United States in 1794 wearing a French uniform and a tricolored ribbon in his hat. He died on September 30, 1795, at the age of forty, after contracting yellow fever. Given the tempestuous outlines of his life, it was no wonder that his old antagonist, McKean, called him "such a seditious turbulent man."[57]

Alien and Sedition Acts

Although the Bill of Rights specifically promised to protect the citizens' rights to speak, crises in the early Republic led not to tolerance of diverse opinion but rather to legislation designed to silence opposition to the central administration's point of view. When John Adams was inaugurated as the second president of the United States on March 4, 1797, the First Amendment had been in effect for more than five years. During those years, the relationship between the United States and France had deteriorated dramatically. French raids on American shipping had outstripped the British raids of earlier years. France had treated American diplomatic emissaries with open contempt, at the same time trying to exact funds from the new country in order to help France with its many-sided war erupting from the French Revolution.

Nationalism and anti-French enthusiasm grew, and the Federalist leadership increasingly equated political opposition with disloyalty to country. The Federalists disliked the French sympathies of the Republican party in general and of Republican journalists in particular. In fact, some Republicans were immigrants and had not yet applied for citizenship, and the Federalists increasingly looked for methods to silence the opposition. In that setting, Congress passed and President Adams signed provisions affecting aliens and also freedom of expression.[58]

The Naturalization Act   This legislation, passed on June 18, 1798, extended the period of residence necessary to become a citizen from five to fourteen years, with the proviso that five of those fourteen years had to be spent in the state or territory where the individual was being naturalized. The single conciliatory feature of the law applied to persons who were living in the United States before 1795, who had a year in which to take advantage of the preexisting five-year naturalization law.

The Enemy Alien Act   This legislation placed despotic powers in the hands of the president, allowing him to deport all males over fourteen who were subjects of any government at war with the United States or who had threatened United States territory. The legislation, in effect, would have allowed Adams to deport all French-speaking unnaturalized citizens in the United States if he had chosen to declare France's actions as acts of war.

The Sedition Act   The Sedition Act made it illegal to conspire to oppose measures of the government. This law specifically included any persons who, with criminal intent, "shall counsel, advise or attempt to procure any insurrection, riot, unlawful assembly, or combination," whether or not the activity had the proposed effect. Punishment for violating the law was a fine of up to $5,000 and imprisonment for up to five years.

The second section of the act hit at the heart of newspapers and published opposition voices:

> That if any person shall write, print, utter or publish, or shall cause or procure to be written, printed, uttered or published, or shall knowingly and willingly assist or aid in

writing, printing, uttering or publishing any false, scandalous and malicious writing or writings against the Government of the United States, or the President of the United States, or either house of the Congress of the United States, with intent to defame the said government, or either house of the said Congress, or the said President, or to bring them, or either of them into contempt or disrepute; or to excite against them, or either of them, the hatred of the good people of the United States, or to stir up sedition within the United States . . . shall (upon conviction) be punished by a fine not exceeding two thousand dollars, and by imprisonment not to exceed two years.

The law provided for truth as a defense and the right of the jury to determine the law and the fact of the case. An expiration date for the Sedition Act, approved on July 14, 1798, was included in the legislation. The law was in force until March 3, 1801.

Supporters defended the Sedition Act by arguing that such restrictions were necessary because of possible war with France and that press freedom as guaranteed by the First Amendment meant absence of prior restraint, not the ability to "make false, scandalous, and malicious publications against the government."[59] Some historians have argued that this act represented an improvement over the common law of sedition, because it allowed a jury to decide both the law and the fact of a case, and it made truth a defense. Further, the intent of speakers or writers, plus the criminal tendencies of their words, would be taken into account.

Such safeguards, however, saved few Anti-Federalists. Federalists appointed the federal court judges (along with marshals and bailiffs) and controlled jury selection processes. The matters of "intent" of the speaker or writer and the "tendency" of words, far from being items of mitigation for the defendant, were indeed easily interpreted as evil in troubled times.[60]

James Morton Smith, leading scholar of the Alien and Sedition Acts, put these laws in chilling perspective, noting that they raised the basic question of whether residents of the United States were to be free to criticize their government:

> The meaning of the First Amendment did not crystallize in 1791, when the Bill of Rights was added to the Constitution. Not until the years from 1798 to 1801, when the Sedition Act was debated and enforced, did the limits of liberty of speech and press become an issue which focused attention squarely on its definition as a part of the American experiment in self-government.[61]

The Virginia and the Kentucky Resolutions, 1798 and 1799   The Republicans protested the Alien and Sedition Acts in 1798 and 1799 by passing the Virginia and Kentucky Resolutions. James Madison secretly wrote the Virginia Resolutions, and Jefferson clandestinely supplied the Kentucky Resolutions. Both sets of resolutions claimed that the Sedition Act violated the Constitution. The Virginia Resolutions of December 14, 1798, declared that the national government's defiance of the Constitution would "transform the present Republican system of the United States into an absolute, or at best, a mixed monarchy." Not only did the Alien and Sedition Acts subvert government by uniting legislative and judicial powers with the powers of the president, those acts exercised a power "not delegated by the Constitution, but on the contrary,

[was] expressly and positively forbidden" by the First Amendment. The resolutions maintained that the power of the Alien and Sedition Acts "is levelled against the right of freely examining public characters and measures, and of free communication among the people, thereon, which has ever been justly deemed the only effectual guardian of every other right."[62] Ostensibly passed over Republican objections as a temporary defense measure, the law in reality "was the work of a party with brazen disregard for the Constitution and was used to prosecute the leading Jeffersonian Republican journalists," wrote Jeffery A. Smith in his study of war and press freedom.[63]

356   AMERICAN NATIONALITY ASSURED.   [1801

JEFFERSON GOING TO HIS INAUGURATION.

Figure 3–5   Thomas Jefferson arrives at the new capital in Washington to attend his inauguration as President in 1801. (Division of Prints and Photographs, Library of Congress Collection)

Prosecutions   Perhaps the most remarkable aspect of the Sedition Act prosecutions was their scope. In 1790, about 100 newspapers existed, and by 1800 that number had grown to 235.[64] Between 1798 and 1800, about twenty-five persons, primarily Republican journalists and printers, were charged under federal or state sedition laws.[65] Newspaper editors and politicians alike were prosecuted. A prime target for prosecutorial eagerness was "Lightning rod, jun.," Benjamin Franklin Bache. On June 26, 1798—the same day that the Sedition Bill was introduced in the U.S. Senate—Bache was indicted under a claim of violating a federal common-law crime.[66] Bache was personally obnoxious to the Federalists because of his name-calling; Abigail Adams had been urging passage of a sedition law to deal with the editor who described her husband as "old, querulous, bald, blind, crippled, toothless Adams."[67] The incident triggering the common-law prosecution of Bache was the *Aurora's* publication of diplomatic correspondence, charging that the Adams administration had forged or tampered with that correspondence before showing it to Congress. Arrested on June 26, 1798, Bache was allowed to remain free until June 29, when his bail was set at $4,000.[68]

Bache's trial was set for October 1798, but a greater power than the Federalist prosecutors interceded: Bache died of yellow fever on September 10, 1798. The *Aurora* continued its fight against the Federalists, with editor William Duane later becoming a sedition target although he was never brought to trial.[69]

By all odds the most ludicrous prosecution was that of Luther Baldwin, a resident of Newark, New Jersey. With Congress adjourned in July of 1798, President and Mrs. Adams left the vaporous heat of Philadelphia, riding in an open carriage. Preparations had been made to celebrate the President's passage through the streets with cheers of "Huzzah!" and as the Adams's carriage pulled off into the distance, the faraway booming of cannon firing a salute could be heard.

One customer of a Newark tavern observed that the cannon were firing at the President's arse. Luther Baldwin, perhaps too long in the tavern, said he did not care if they fired *through* his arse. Federalists overheard the remark, and the unfortunate Baldwin was prosecuted and fined $150 for sedition.[70]

Vermont congressman Matthew Lyon probably garnered the most colorful nicknames in the sordid history of the Sedition Act. This restless immigrant from Ireland was elected to Congress and objected vigorously to the passage of the Sedition Act, predicting he would be the act's first victim. Lyon, one of Vermont's legendary Green Mountain Boys in the Revolutionary War, was briefly removed from the military, evidently on ill-considered charges of his leaving his post while on duty; after he was reinstated, he went on to serve heroically in battle. Nevertheless, Federalists made slighting references in newspapers about his military record. When Federalist congressman Roger Griswold of Connecticut denigrated that record, Matthew Lyon spat in Griswold's face, right in the House of Representatives. Federalist efforts to get the two-thirds vote needed to remove "Spitting Lyon" from Congress failed.[71]

Lyon responded to the attack with a letter to a Federalist newspaper, criticizing the President's "unbounded thirst for ridiculous pomp, foolish adulation, and selfish avarice."[72]

That commentary, along with similar attacks on the presidency, brought Lyon within range of being prosecuted under the Sedition Act. Lyon, meanwhile, tiring of not being able to get his responses to Federalist newspaper attacks accepted for publication, established his own paper in 1798 with the marvelous title *The Scourge of Aristocracy and the Repository of Important Political Truths*. Lyon's protests that the Sedition Act was unconstitutional did him no good, nor did his assertion that his articles were harmless and published without bad intent. Lyon was convicted by a Federalist judge, jailed for four months, and fined $1,000.[73]

After Lyon's conviction, Federalist newspapers crowed that by punishing Lyon for licentiousness, true freedom of the press was being saved.[74] Republican papers such as William Duane's *Aurora* declared that Lyon was a martyr, a hero of press freedom. His jailing in a vile, cramped cell won sympathy for Lyon, as did the letters he wrote from his cell, widely published by Republican newspapers. While still in jail, Lyon was reelected to Congress by a comfortable margin, and he emerged from jail a hero.

The Sedition Act Expires   Prosecutions did not end with the expiration of the Sedition Act in 1801. In 1803, Harry Croswell, editor of the Federalist *Wasp*, was charged under a state charge of seditious libel. Croswell had claimed that Jefferson had paid James Callender (who had been convicted under the Sedition Act) to call Washington a traitor, robber, and perjurer. Alexander Hamilton, a supporter of the Sedition Act, defended Croswell before the New York Supreme Court. Although maintaining that governments could be defamed, Hamilton argued that seditious libel law should not be used to stifle truthful criticism of public men and public measures. Although Croswell was convicted despite Hamilton's efforts, the New York legislature responded by passing a libel act the same year that made truth a defense and gave the jury the power to decide both law and fact.

Conclusion

The early years of the Republic were marked by attempts to stabilize a nation undergoing political and economic turmoil. Emerging from a wartime economy, leaders faced the task of stabilizing an untried political system in the face of a previously colonial economy, with few trade agreements left intact. Disputes over centralized power versus states' rights and civil liberties were grounded in enlightenment theory and Radical Whig republicanism that shaped a concept of a people who governed, rather than a people who were governed. Under this radical governing plan, the press emerged as a dominant force in educating the people to govern.

New economics, new politics, and a growing demand for information provided a commercial backdrop that encouraged the development of daily newspapers within a framework of newspapers and pamphlets financed by advertising, subscription, government printing subsidy, and party funds. As the nation began a new century, a party system and an information system, though young and fluid, were ready to meet the challenges of a developing commercial economy.

Endnotes

1. Irving Brant, *The Bill of Rights* (Indianapolis: Bobbs-Merrill, 1965), p. 41.

2. Jeffery A. Smith, "Public Opinion and the Press Clause," *Journalism History* 14:1 (Spring, 1987), pp. 8–17. For an

excellent review of the debates regarding the degrees of freedom the colonial press experienced, see the Introduction to Smith, *Printers and Press Freedom: The Ideology of Early American Journalism* (New York: Oxford University Press, 1988). Smith argues persuasively that colonial publishers practiced aggressive journalism for decades before the Revolution and suggests that a libertarian press ideology, based on experience and Radical Whig and Enlightenment thought, was forged prior to passage of the First Amendment.

3. Alexander Hamilton died after a duel with Aaron Burr in 1804. Jeffersonian Republicans have no relationship to the Republican party of the twentieth century. The current Republican party was begun in the middle of the nineteenth century.

4. Richard E. Ellis, "The Meaning of Jeffersonian Ascendancy," in Stanley N. Katz and Stanley Kutler, *New Perspectives on the American Past, 1607–1877* (New York: Little, Brown, 1972), pp. 171–72.

5. Worthington C. Ford et al., eds., *Journals of the Continental Congress 1774–1789*, 34 vols. (Washington, D.C.: U.S. Government Printing Office, 1904–1937), vol. 5, pp. 546–47.

6. Merrill Jensen, preface to *The New Nation: A History of the United States during the Confederation, 1781–1789* (New York: Knopf, 1958), pp. xii–xiii.

7. Cited in Francis X. Clines, "Celebrating a Constitution or Violating Its Spirit?" *New York Times*, Sunday, November 3, 1985, p. 4E.

8. Robert E. Rutland, "Newspaper Opposition to the Constitution, 1787–1788," Historical Research Panel, Association for Education in Journalism, Eugene, Ore., August 27, 1959, p. 2.

9. Alexander Hamilton, John Jay, and James Madison, in Edward Meade Earle, ed., *The Federalist* (New York: Modern Library, 1937), p. x.

10. Claude G. Bowers, *Jefferson and Hamilton* (Boston: Houghton-Mifflin, 1925), p. 26.

11. *Federalist*, No. 45.

12. John Bach McMaster and Frederick Stone, *Pennsylvania and the Constitution* (Lancaster, Pennsylvania, 1888), p. 770, cited in Jackson Turner Main, *The Antifederalists: Critics of the Constitution* (Chapel Hill: University of North Carolina Press, 1961), p. 160.

13. *Independent Gazetteer*, Philadelphia, November 16, 1787.

14. Main, *The Antifederalists*, p. 255.

15. James Madison to Thomas Jefferson, October 17, 1788, in *The Papers of Thomas Jefferson* 14:19, 20, cited in Jeffery A. Smith, "Public Opinion and the Press Clause," *Journalism History* 14:1 (Spring, 1987), p. 15.

16. For a discussion of how Madison's document was altered in the debate, see David A. Anderson, "The Origins of

the Press Clause," *UCLA Law Review* (February, 1983), pp. 455–541. See also Jeffery A. Smith, "Prior Restraint: Original Intentions and Modern Interpretations," *William and Mary Law Review* (April, 1987).

17. In 1925, the Supreme Court of the United States in *Gitlow v. New York* applied the press clause of the First Amendment to the states.

18. See Smith, *Printers and Press Freedom*, pp. 24–25, 46.

19. David Rabban, "The Ahistorical Historian: Leonard Levy on Freedom of Expression in Early American History," *Stanford Law Review*, 37 (February, 1985), p. 801.

20. Rabban, "Ahistorical Historian," p. 824; see also Smith, *Printers and Press Freedom*, pp. 24–25, 102.

21. For a complete description of the enlightenment philosophy and for citations for quotes used in this section, see Smith, *Press Freedom*, pp. 42–53.

22. Alfred McClung Lee, *The Daily Newspaper in America* (New York: Macmillan, 1937), pp. 32, 59–60.

23. Lee, *Daily Newspaper*, pp. 314–16.

24. Lee, *Daily Newspaper in America*, p. 43.

25. Dwight Teeter, "A Legacy of Expression: Philadelphia Newspapers and Congress during the War for Independence, 1775–1783," unpublished Ph.D. dissertation, University of Wisconsin (Madison), 1966; "John Dunlap: The Political Economy of a Printer's Success," *Journalism Quarterly* (Spring, 1965) 52, pp. 3–8, 55; "John Dunlap," in Perry J. Ashley, ed., *Dictionary of Literary Biography* 43, pp. 174–79.

26. Benjamin Rush, *The Autobiography of Benjamin Rush*, George W. Corner, ed. (Princeton, N.J.: Princeton University Press, 1948), pp. 319–20.

27. Richard B. Kielbowicz, "The Press, Post Office, and Flow of News in the Early Republic," *Journal of the Early Republic* (Fall, 1983), p. 269. One must be aware, however, that the postmaster was an Anti-Federalist and perhaps assumed that rural papers would tend to support his party rather than the opposition.

28. Cited in Kielbowicz, "The Press, Post Office, and Flow of News in the Early Republic," p. 280.

29. Willard G. Bleyer, *Main Currents in the History of American Journalism* (New York: Houghton-Mifflin, 1927), p. 106.

30. *Gazette of the United States*, April 15, 1789. For a wage/subscription comparison, see Alfred McClung Lee, *The Daily Newspaper in America* (New York: Macmillan, 1937).

31. *Gazette*, December 7, 1791.

32. Bleyer, *Main Currents*, p. 107.

33. *Columbian Centinel*, Boston, October 5, 1798. James Morton Smith, *Freedom's Fetters: The Alien and Sedition Laws and American Civil Liberties* (Ithaca, N.Y.: Cornell

University Press, 1956), p. 179n, also found that statement quoted in the *Albany Centinel* for October 12, 1798.

34. Cobbett's prospectus appeared in the *Gazette of the United States* on February 13, 1797. For a full discussion of Cobbett, see Karen K. List, "The Role of William Cobbett in Philadelphia's Party Press, 1794–1799," *Journalism Monographs* 82 (May, 1983).

35. *Gazette of the United States*, September 15, 1792.

36. Bleyer, *Main Currents*, p. 110.

37. Jefferson to Washington, 1793, in Paul Leicester Ford, ed., *Writings of Thomas Jefferson*, vol. 6, p. 106.

38. Jefferson to Washington, 1793, in Ford, p. 231.

39. Margaret A. Blanchard, "Benjamin Franklin Bache," Perry J. Ashley, ed., *Dictionary of Literary Biography*, vol. 43, pp. 14–15. See also Jeffery A. Smith, *Franklin and Bache: Envisioning the Enlightened Republic* (New York: Oxford University Press, 1988).

40. The *Aurora*, December 23, 1796.

41. The *Aurora*, March 6, 1797.

42. *Porcupine's Gazette*, June 1798, cited in Smith, *Freedom's Fetters*, pp. 194, 195.

43. Norman L. Rosenberg, *Protecting the Best Men: An Interpretive History of Libel* (Chapel Hill: University of North Carolina Press, 1986); Dwight Teeter, "The First Amendment at Its Bicentennial: Necessary but Not Sufficient?" *Journalism Quarterly* 69:1 (Spring, 1992), p. 23.

44. The best account of Oswald's life is in "Eleazer Oswald, Lieutenant-Colonel in the Revolution, Printer in Baltimore and Philadelphia, Soldier of Fortune in the French Revolution," in Joseph Towne Wheeler, *The Maryland Press, 1777–1790* (Baltimore: The Maryland Historical Society, 1938), pp. 19–36.

45. Oswald to John Lamb, Philadelphia, October 15, 1778, Lamb Papers, Box 2, New York Historical Society.

46. For the complete text of the "Queries," see John Richard Alden, *General Charles Lee: Traitor or Patriot?* (Baton Rouge: Louisiana State University Press, 1951), pp. 279–81.

47. Alden, *Traitor or Patriot?* p. 282.

48. *Maryland Journal*, August 3, 1779, cited in Ward L. Miner, *William Goddard, Newspaperman* (Durham, N.C.: Duke University Press, 1962), p. 179.

49. *Independent Gazetteer*, April 13, 1782.

50. *Independent Gazetteer*, October 1, 1782.

51. Wheeler, *The Maryland Press*, p. 34.

52. Wheeler, *The Maryland Press*, p. 31; Main, *The Antifederalists*, pp. 226, 249–250.

53. Rutland, "Newspaper Opposition to the Constitution," p. 9; and Thomas Richard Meehan, "The Pennsylvania

Supreme Court in the Law and Politics of the Commonwealth 1776–1790," unpublished Ph.D. thesis, University of Wisconsin (Madison), 1964, pp. 491–92.

54. *Pennsylvania Packet*, July 26, 1788.

55. *Independent Gazetteer*, November 3, 1788.

56. Eleazer Oswald to the National Convention, Paris, September 1, 1783, *Pennsylvania Magazine of History and Biography*, 4, (1880), p. 252.

57. Thomas McKean to William Augustus Atlee, Philadelphia, September 17, 1788, William Augustus Atlee Papers, Library of Congress.

58. For an account of the tensions of the period, see Smith, *Freedom's Fetters*.

59. Jeffery Alan Smith, *Printers and Press Freedom: The Ideology of Early American Journalism* (New York: Oxford University Press, 1987), p. 59.

60. Smith, *Freedom's Fetters*, pp. 421–22; Levy, *Free Press*, p. 297.

61. Smith, *Freedom's Fetters*, p. 426.

62. Henry Steele Commager, ed., *Documents of American History* (New York: Appleton-Century Crofts, 1949), p. 182. Jefferson's motives may have been two-fold: (1) to protest the Sedition Act and (2) to ensure the supremacy of states' rights.

63. Jeffery A. Smith, *War and Press Freedom: The Problem of Prerogative Power* (New York: Oxford University Press, 1999), p. 37.

64. Alfred McClung Lee, *The Daily Newspaper in America* (New York: Macmillan, 1937), p. 711.

65. Smith, *Printers and Press Freedom*, p. 58.

66. Smith, *Freedom's Fetters*, pp. 188–92.

67. Cited in Page Smith, *John Adams* (Westport, Conn.: Greenwood Press, 1969), vol. 2, p. 361.

68. Smith, *Freedom's Fetters*, p. 202.

69. Smith, *Freedom's Fetters*, p. 204. See also Jeffery A. Smith, *Franklin and Bache: Envisioning the Enlightened Republic* (New York: Oxford University Press, 1990).

70. Smith, *Freedom's Fetters*, p. 271.

71. Smith, *Freedom's Fetters*, pp. 223–24.

72. *U.S. v. Lyon, Wharton's State Trials*, p. 333; case No. 8646, *The Federal Cases* (St. Paul, 1895), vol. 15, pp. 1183–1191.

73. *U.S. v. Lyon, Wharton's State Trials*, p. 335.

74. See *Connecticut Courant*, November 26, 1798; Spooner's *Vermont Journal*, October 15, 1798, cited in Smith, *Freedom's Fetters*, p. 236.

CHAPTER 4

Diversity in the Early Republic

▼

Between 1800 and 1830, reading matter circulated widely throughout the United States. It was, indeed, the Age of Reading. By the 1830s, most white males in all parts of the country and white women in the North could read. Mass literacy for white, southern women was achieved by 1840.[1] Technology, in the form of new printing techniques and better transportation and distribution systems, combined with literacy to propel the new Republic into a society of information abundance.

Citizens of the early Republic, while still attentive to public oratory as a means of acquiring knowledge, turned to printed matter for a more efficient means of communication. The religious publications of an earlier period, daily as well as weekly newspapers, and an expanding form of secular though moralistic fiction assured citizens that they could be entertained as well as informed. Recognizing the popularity of fiction, critics questioned whether widespread reading benefited society. Some ministers argued that reading bred slothful habits, especially among women. Nevertheless, the forms of communication expanded, with books, magazines, and newspapers multiplying.

This nineteenth-century information economy of abundance began to slowly alter the social hierarchy of American culture. Through reading and public lectures, the middle class sought the gentility that during the colonial period had been reserved for the aristocratic class. In addition to coveting the social status that wide reading could help bestow, citizens also expressed a hunger for religious knowledge that was encouraged by the Great Awakening, a period so named because it stimulated individual thought in religious matters. While the elite maintained control of those materials published for the purpose of imparting knowledge—religious and school books—"recreational information was propelled by the demands of the many and tailored to popular fashions, tastes, and capacities."[2] The entertainment industry, even in its very early days, responded to public taste rather than elite determination. Richard Brown, in *Knowledge Is Power*, noted that distinctions had always been made between high and popular culture, but never before had popular materials circulated so widely in print. In an economy of abundance, diversity of language, thought, style, and form characterized the political press and entertainment-oriented books and periodicals. The public debate over national versus local governmental control continued and was especially revealed in debates over postal policy. The forces for modernization recognized the importance of a free flow of information, while others argued to maintain local identification and local circulation of materials. The diversity of the audience increased, with Native Americans, immigrants, and African Americans seeking information and entertainment in print. ▼

Newspapers and an Informed Public

By the early 1800s, statesmen, townspeople, and farmers regarded printed matter as an important source of information. Indeed, intellectuals and politicians alike envisioned newspapers and other periodicals, along with public oratory, as the means for maintaining the informed citizenry essential to a democratic government in the face of geographical, political, and social distance.[3] Public, and especially written forms of communication, were considered an economical way to stay informed. Writing in 1835, Robert B. Thomas, editor of the New England *Farmer's Almanack*, chided his fellow workers to "guard against contracting a fondness for being off; ay, off from the place of his business, the place of his interest, the place of his family, the place of his love." He noted that going from place to place to gather information was no longer necessary. "The way to have this accomodation [*sic*] is to take a newspaper, and then the news will come to you, even to your very door; and your family will also receive a benefit in reading the paper. Look to it."[4] Print in this and other contexts was considered more efficient—getting your information from a newspaper took less time than "free" word-of-mouth knowledge. This transition from reliance on word-of-mouth diffusion of information to printed verification of information meant that "[i]mpersonal scraps of printed paper replaced well-known acquaintances and respectable citizens as reliable sources."[5] Newspapers were considered reliable because readers, although well aware of the heightened partisan rhetoric printed during the political faction battles, knew they could expect the press to publish accurate reproductions of documents and the texts of oral debates.

Modernization and the Postal Dilemma

"For the first quarter of a century under the Constitution," wrote historian Richard Kielbowicz, "the commitment to promote the circulation of news through the mails stood virtually unchallenged." Federalists, who appointed partisans to many postmasterships during the early years of the Republic, supported low postal rates for newspapers because they believed that the circulation of information would promote a strong central government by fostering nationalism and party cohesion. Republicans, or Anti-Federalists, hoped to use the mails to circulate information about Federalist abuses of power. As publishing technology facilitated the production of magazines and fostered national circulation of publications by associations, the postal policy debate took on competitive economic and cultural dimensions.

Congressional debates over postal policy reflected an increasing dependance on printed news and a continuing controversy over the relationship of urban development to traditional country life. From colonial days onward, printers exchanged newspapers free through the mails, a mechanism that dictated the major exchanges of news until the telegraph and the press associations assumed that function in the mid-1800s. Under the provisions of the 1792 postal act, Congress set newspaper postal rates far under the letter rate, but representatives argued about the advantages of a flat rate versus one based on the distance mail would travel. Those arguing for a flat rate envisioned a modern society in which a wide circulation of information would allow "the whole body of the citizens . . . to see and guard against any evil that may threaten them."[6] Other congressmen argued that publishers should bear some of the transportation costs that increased with distance. Further, they contended that flat rates would enable urban publishers to compete unfairly with their rural colleagues. These legislators sought to preserve "the values of country life from an encroaching urban culture."[7] After much discussion, Congress compromised with the Post Office Act of 1792, which established two rates for newspapers. Newspapers sent up to 100 miles paid one-cent postage, and those mailed farther were charged one-and-one-half cents. Similar provisions were incorporated into the 1794 postal law, although one change allowed newspapers to circulate within a state for one cent. Throughout the 1830s, debates over postal policy and newspapers continued, with those who opposed Jackson and his preference for local centers of power arguing for free postage for newspapers in order to allow city sheets to circulate uninhibited. Country editors joined the Jacksonians to resist successfully the move to reduce or eliminate postage, arguing that city newspapers could then employ all the advantages of technology and advertising to put the country papers out of business.

Although magazines were excluded from the 1792 postal act, the 1794 law provided they could be sent "where the mode of conveyance and the size of the mails will admit of it."[8] Magazine postal rates were much higher than those for newspapers, with subscribers paying in postage as much as 20 to 40 percent of the subscription price. Postmasters in later years took advantage of the interpretative clause in the postal act to encourage certain publications at the expense of others. Postmasters generally recognized frequently issued publications with political content to be newspapers. Postmaster General Gideon Granger dictated that a magazine was any other publication issued at regular intervals.[9] By 1815, the postmaster decreed that magazines and pamphlets were too bulky for the mail and should be excluded altogether, allowing only religious publications to circulate in that fashion. Unfriendly postal rates and policies for magazines persisted until midcentury, discouraging the circulation of nationally based magazines.

Continuing Political Tradition

Political newspapers during the early nineteenth century followed the Federalist–Anti-Federalist lines set immediately after the Revolution. They sought to cover Congress and fought against rules of secrecy, yet they often were highly dependent on governmental printing contracts. Newspapers continued to support political factions, a practice well demonstrated in the elections of 1824.

The *National Intelligencer*

Partisan journalism continued as the norm after Jefferson's election, but a newspaper of record, the *National Intelligencer*, begun by Samuel Harrison Smith in 1800, developed methods for extensive coverage of Congress. The *Intelligencer*'s extensive verbatim excerpts of debates in the House and the Senate were exchanged with newspapers around the nation. This practice provided an invaluable fund of in-depth information to other papers until the *Intelligencer* was sold by one of Smith's successors, W. W. Seaton, in 1864.

   Smith began the newspaper when President Jefferson persuaded him to leave his Philadelphia publishing venture to set up shop in the new national capital—the

Figure 4–1   An early national, political newspaper, the *National Intelligencer,* was located at Ninth and E Streets, N.W., in Washington, D.C. (Division of Prints and Photographs, Library of Congress Collection)

"malarial swamp," as John Adams once called Washington, D.C. During his Philadelphia days, Smith learned shorthand from Joseph Gales, Sr., one of the first reporters to cover sessions of Congress and who had acquired the *Independent Gazetteer* after Eleazer Oswald died in 1794.[10] Gales, fearful of Philadelphia's repeated yellow fever outbreaks, sold the paper to Smith in 1797 and moved to North Carolina where he founded another Jeffersonian paper, the *Raleigh Register.*

The House of Representatives had been open to the press and the public since the beginning, but the Senate continued to meet secretly. In 1800, when the nation's capital was moved to Washington, the new galleries in the House were so far from the floor that it was difficult to hear the delegates. Smith tried to secure a desk inside the rail, but he was refused. Until the next congressional election, when Smith finally was granted his request, he reported information given to him by the clerk of the House. His troubles were not over, however, and he was expelled from the House for a session following his report that James Lane had been arrested for disorderly conduct after applauding from the gallery.[11] In addition, the Federalist judiciary attempted to indict him for libel, but a grand jury refused. Smith responded, "Inasmuch as governments may err, every citizen has a right to expose an error in HIS OPINION comitted [*sic*] by them."[12] By 1802, however, Smith's position was secure as he was readmitted to the House and admitted to the Senate.

Smith's triweekly newspaper was a remarkable accomplishment, supporting "liberal policies in a conservative manner." The shorthand reporting from Congress provided a service not otherwise available to editors throughout the young nation.[13] Smith produced the paper single-handedly, except for printing. He wrote the news, reported the debates, clipped excerpts from other newspapers, solicited advertising, and kept accounts. In 1809, however, Smith left the business for banking and sold his newspaper to a trusted associate. In 1808, Joseph Gales, Jr., son of the man who taught Smith shorthand, joined the staff as "stenographer." By January 1809, the younger Gales became a partner, and in August 1810, he assumed full responsibility for the newspaper.

The *National Intelligencer* of Gales and Seaton

The *National Intelligencer*, under Joseph Gales, Jr., continued to be the nation's most important—and politically potent—newspaper for at least a decade. Gales was only twenty-four years old when he took over the *Intelligencer*. However, the rigors of putting out the triweekly put an exhausted Gales in his bed for a lengthy recuperation in 1812, and his brother-in-law William Winston Seaton moved from the *Raleigh Register* to become a partner in the *Intelligencer*. The Gales–Seaton partnership was to last forty-eight years, through truly cataclysmic changes in the nation.

Although the *Intelligencer* offered a gold mine of information on government, with Seaton taking shorthand notes on the debates in the Senate, and Gales covering the House, the paper went through difficult financial times. Smith, as owner of the *Intelligencer*, had done congressional printing (worth perhaps $5,000 a year in 1801) and some printing work for executive departments. When Congress began to award printing and stationery contracts to the lowest bidders, non-newspaper printers gained much of the business until 1819, when a patronage system was reestablished by Congress. Subscribers and advertisers apparently were longer in promises than hard cash, and such government printing as the newspaper received was not enough for the partners to turn a solid profit. Even so, the paper was regarded as both a valuable service and an organ of the presidential administration, starting with that of Jefferson and continuing through the administrations of Madison (1809–1817) and Monroe (1817–1825).

Madison's tenure found a nation in the throes of awkward adolescence and spoiling for a fight. Although President Madison retained a lingering distrust of standing armies and large navies—associated in his mind with British colonial rule—the nation under his leadership took up arms against the Indians and defended itself against other nations' interference with its shipping. In response to congressmen referred to as the War Hawks, Madison urged annexation of Canada and Florida.

At the onset of the War of 1812, Gales and Seaton volunteered for service in a District of Columbia infantry company while continuing to publish their newspaper, alternating roles so that while one served under arms, the other edited. The size and quality of the paper suffered, and friends maintained that the men would be of more service to their country by returning to their former roles as full-time editors.[14]

The *National Intelligencer* worked hard to prepare its readers for war, editorializing to remind the nation of its grievances against the British: the impressment of seamen as well as interference with U.S. trade and U.S. efforts to keep the peace, including embargoes and other trade restrictions. However, other newspapers posed considerable opposition to the *Intelligencer*'s stance. The *Columbian Centinel* of Boston and the *Boston Repertory* both declared the Declaration of War on June 18, 1812, to be dreadful news.

When the British fleet and British soldiers reached Washington, most of the *Intelligencer*'s printers were called away from their work to defend the capital. Troops were badly trained, poorly deployed, and too few in number to be effective. Humiliation mounted upon humiliation, as American gunboats were destroyed so the British could not capture them, and British troops swept into the capital. The government of the United States fled to Virginia, while on August 25, 1814, the British put most of Washington to the torch.

The chief incendiary, Admiral George Cockburn, ordered the *National Intelligencer*'s offices destroyed. Clearly, Admiral Cockburn felt that the newspaper was not merely private property, which generally was spared throughout the city.[15] It was even said that Admiral Cockburn ordered the C's in the type cases smashed so the editors would not be able to print—or denounce—his name.

The *Intelligencer* recovered after the war, although finances remained a troubling issue. By 1818, Joseph Gales, Jr., owed one bank $6,500, a large sum in that day. As he put up the *National Intelligencer* for collateral, Gales told the Bank of the United States that he and Seaton also owed money to private parties because of the difficulty of collecting the $80,000 to $100,000 owed to the *Intelligencer*.[16]

The political ambition of Senator Henry Clay of Kentucky, maneuvering for a presidential bid, helped rescue Gales and Seaton. In 1819, Clay promoted a patronage system that allowed both houses of Congress to select a printer of choice, without regard to low bids. From 1819 until 1846, Clay's patronage legislation directly affected political newspapers in the capital.

▼

Criticism of the Government Springs Eternal

The expenditures for the fiscal year ending June 30, 1857, independent of the public debt, as appears from the report of the Secretary of the Treasury, are $65,032,597.

The first question is, whether those expenditures are greater than what they should be under an economical administration of the Government. We think they are.

—*National Intelligencer*, editorial, August 23, 1858

Not only could each house select its own printer, but other printing projects appeared as the activities of Congress and the executive branch expanded. At times, particularly during the Jackson presidency in the 1830s, the patronage system helped support newspapers that opposed a dominant party. Political horse-trading allowed a number of opposing splinter factions to subsidize newspapers through contracts to print the *Annals of Congress, American Archives,* and the *American State Papers.* Such publishing projects were handled by Whig editors who fought against the Jackson administration at every turn.[17]

Gales and Seaton held House printing contracts from 1819 to 1829 and Senate contracts from 1819 to 1826. In the first five years, they received nearly $160,000, a remarkable amount at a time when a printer's wages amounted to about $500 a year.[18]

The *New York Evening Post*

In an intensely political United States, of course, the *National Intelligencer* was not universally admired. The Federalists of the early nineteenth century loathed anything Jeffersonian. To counteract the influence of the *Intelligencer,* arch-Federalist Alexander Hamilton decided to start a new paper in New York City. By 1800, with 60,000 residents, New York had become the nation's largest urban center,[19] and it already had three Federalist-leaning newspapers and a strong Republican sheet. Nevertheless, Hamilton and some Federalist friends secured the editorial services of William Coleman—a Princeton graduate, an attorney, and a man acclaimed as one of the day's most accomplished public speakers. The Federalist stalwarts signed a founders' list, with each signatory expected to contribute at least $1,000 and a total of $10,000 regarded as necessary for initial capitalization. The first list of subscribers added up to 600, and it included names as prominent as that of John Jacob Astor.

On November 16, 1801, the first issue of the *New York Evening Post* appeared:

The design of this paper is to diffuse among the people correct information on all interesting subjects, to inculcate just principles in religion, morals and politics; and to cultivate a taste for sound literature.[20]

In addition to its weekday efforts—which soon netted it a respectable circulation of 1,100—the *Evening Post* reused its already set type to produce a weekly edition, called the *Herald.* This weekly *Herald* was sent to out-of-town subscribers from

Figure 4–2   Political cartoons appeared in American publications as early as 1798. (Division of Prints and Photographs, Library of Congress Collection)

Boston to Savannah. It featured fewer advertisements but more news and comment than its cousin, the *Evening Post*.

Coleman, perhaps the best-educated journalist of his day, relied heavily on Hamilton's knowledge and also took dictation from Hamilton to write articles. Although the *Evening Post* remained a lively paper, the relationship between Coleman and Hamilton was ended by a duelist's bullet. Aaron Burr, incensed over Hamilton's opposition that may have cost Burr both the presidency and the governorship of New York, fatally wounded Hamilton on July 11, 1804. Coleman continued to edit the newspaper until he was injured in an accident in 1826. The disabled Coleman hired William Cullen Bryant, a recognized poet, embittered lawyer, and literary magazine editor, to assist him. In 1829, Bryant became editor in chief, which he remained until his death in 1878. James Boylan, in a biographical essay on Bryant, captured his contribution:

> William Cullen Bryant brought to American newspaper journalism not only the argumentative and rhetorical skills of the lawyer but the sensibility of the poet. His reputation as one of the few major poets of the early republic has gradually overshadowed, since his death, his career as a newspaper editor, editorialist, and proprietor, to which he gave more than fifty of his eighty-three years. As editor in chief of the *New York*

Evening Post, he left his imprint, that of a classical liberal and humanitarian, on nearly every major national issue from the fight over the Second Bank of the United States through Reconstruction. To nineteenth-century journalism, he lent a civility and literary quality generally lacking in his contemporaries. By the time he concluded his career, he was hailed as New York's first citizen and elder statesman.[21]

Bryant opposed Whig-sponsored tariffs, supported free trade, aligned the newspaper with the Democrats that Hamilton had so opposed, and backed Andrew Jackson for president in 1828. Through the 1840s and 1850s, he shifted from a position of tacit agreement with slavery to eloquently arguing the necessity for its demise. Bryant gave the *Post* an intelligent voice that was respected by business and political leaders.

Competing Papers in the Election of 1824

Jockeying for position during the election of 1824, each candidate representing a different constituency selected a newspaper to espouse his views. John Quincy Adams of Massachusetts, secretary of state under President Monroe, was the son of the second president of the United States. Educated in Europe and graduated from Harvard, he read law and had represented the United States in the Netherlands, Prussia, England, and Russia. He led the American delegation negotiating the 1814 Treaty of Ghent that ended the War of 1812. Adams was supported by the *National Journal*, a solemn, proper newspaper founded in 1823 by Peter Force to support Adams' candidacy for president.

A second candidate, John C. Calhoun of South Carolina, an aristocratic southerner, also claimed extensive government experience. A Yale graduate and attorney, he was elected to the House of Representatives in 1810 and was a leading War Hawk. In 1817, he became President Monroe's secretary of war. When he failed to gain the support of the *National Intelligencer*, Calhoun and his friends founded the *Republican*, edited by Thomas McKenney, to support his candidacy.

Henry Clay of Kentucky, known as the great orator, represented western interests. He advocated a high tariff to protect American manufacturers and supported using proceeds from the tariff to build roads, thus helping farmers and other producers of raw materials to get their goods to market. Clay had helped reach the Missouri Compromise of 1820, setting a pattern by admitting a "slave state" into the Union for every new "free state." Clay was hoping for the support of the *Intelligencer*, because his patronage system of 1819 had been a great financial boon to that newspaper.

William Harris Crawford, also a candidate for President, withdrew his candidacy, but not until he had founded the *Gazette*—a paper edited by an able scholar, Jonathan Elliott, and partially funded by the Treasury Department.

Andrew Jackson of Tennessee, a symbol of the common man, was a hero of the Battle of New Orleans. He stood for the West, but not for the more genteel West of Henry Clay. General Jackson also garnered substantial support among workers in the burgeoning cities of the East. Jackson was fifty-seven in 1824 and had been elected to both the House and Senate from Tennessee. He also served as a judge before retiring. After eight years at his home, the Hermitage in Tennessee, he volunteered to fight in the War of 1812. Nicknamed "Old Hickory," he led troops to a masterful victory in New Orleans; his troops suffered only 16 casualties while inflicting some 2,000 on the British. The District of Columbia had a Jacksonian paper, edited by the mercurial Duff Green—who later turned against Jackson after he became president.

The fortunes of the newspapers of the day to some degree depended on the fortunes of their candidates. The *National Intelligencer*'s coeditor, William Winston Seaton, was a friend of candidate John C. Calhoun, and the *Intelligencer* certainly owed Calhoun a great deal for his 1819 patronage bill. Meanwhile, many suspected the *Intelligencer* of hanging back in hopes of seeing Crawford elected president. After much waffling, the *Intelligencer* announced its support of Crawford, even though he was much weakened from a stroke suffered some ten months earlier.

Soon afterward, John C. Calhoun abandoned the race, and his newspaper, the *Republican*, ceased to exist. In the presidential election, the electoral votes counted on December 1, 1824, showed Jackson leading with 99 votes—surpassing John Quincy Adams with 84, William H. Crawford with 41, and Henry Clay with 37.

Because there was no majority, the election was thrown into the House of Representatives. John Quincy Adams, the prim and high-minded man who said in 1821 that he would never stoop to "cabal and intrigue, or purchasing newspapers, bribing by appointments, or bargaining for foreign missions," was elected when Henry Clay threw support to him. Adams named Clay secretary of state, leading to irate "corrupt bargain" charges by the supporters of Jackson.

The political bargaining and linking of newspapers to candidates was clearly illustrated in the election of 1824. Thereafter, a more independent press began to emerge, although newspapers retained their loyalties to particular candidates and to parties well into the twentieth century. The rise of mass advertising in the 1830s, however, substantially freed leading northern urban newspapers from government and party financial support.

Foreign-Language Press and Diverse Ethnic Backgrounds

From as early as 1739, foreign-language newspapers in the United States provided information from the home countries as well as significant local news for immigrants. Scholars have long debated whether the function of the foreign-language newspapers was to Americanize immigrants or to preserve their home cultures.[22] In his 1884 report, *History and Present Condition of the Newspaper and Periodical Press of the United States*, S. N. D. North commented on the number of foreign-language newspapers in the United States and remarked that the abundance of them "may be regarded as indisputable evidence of the superior intelligence of the class of citizens who seek new homes in the United States." In a less generous spirit, perhaps, he also commented that the success of the newspapers afforded "striking testimony to the tenacity with which the foreign-born citizens of the United States stick to the mother tongue in spite of the difficulties and embarrassments its use involves." North also cited the fact that foreign-language newspapers tended to supply more news from the mother countries than was common for English-language newspapers.[23] Robert Park, in his famous 1922 study, *The Immigrant Press and Its Control*, cited two facets of the foreign-language press: sentiment and need. Park claimed that sentimentality drove immigrants to read papers in their own language largely because they were often forbidden to do so in their home countries. Park also argued that immigrants needed news of the "turbulent cosmopolitan life in modern industrial cities" in which they lived, and the foreign-language press satisfied the need for human expression in the mother tongue.24 Lauren Kessler, in a study of the dissident press, noted that immigrants needed the information necessary to survive—information such as where to find jobs and housing.25 German-language newspapers were the first foreign-language newspapers to appear, although French newspapers were printed as early as 1789, Welsh papers by 1832, Italian papers from 1854, and Norwegian by 1850. Newspapers also appeared in Swedish, Spanish, Danish, Dutch, Bohemian, Polish, Portuguese, and Chinese. Some of these did not appear until later in the nineteenth century. These papers flourished without government interference until the onset of World War I, when government looked anew at the foreign-language newspapers, particularly those published in German, and questioned their loyalty in an atmosphere of world tension.

German-Language Newspapers

Pennsylvania was the home of most of the early German-language newspapers. Carl Wittke, historian of the German-language press in America, traced the first paper to the 1732 publication of the *Philadelphische Zeitung*. In 1739, Christopher Saur published the second paper, *Der Hoch-Deutxcher Pennsylvanischer Geschichtsschreiber oder Sammlung der wichtiger Nachrichten aus dem Natur und Kirchenreich* at Germantown, Pennsylvania. The paper continued for nearly forty years. A German press flourished in Philadelphia in the late eighteenth century, publishing school books and religious tracts as well as a newspaper. These early papers significantly increased German access to American political events. Saur reprinted John Dickinson's *Letters to a Farmer in Pennsylvania* as well as various laws, constitutions, and proclamations.

Before 1830, conditions were not favorable for the printing and distribution of German-language newspapers. Type was scarce, and some German printers still used Roman letters. German farmers had little leisure time for reading, and their children received little education. Further, in 1790 there were only seventy-five post offices in the entire United States, which made distribution difficult.26 The results of Americanization were evident by the 1820s, when most German-language newspapers in Pennsylvania began to use the Pennsylvania German dialect and less often clung to high German.27 The German papers, although they varied politically, more often swung to the Jeffersonians, repudiating the aristocratic leanings of the Federalists. Indeed, as early as 1800, the Jeffersonians circulated pamphlets among the German population, encouraging them to reject the militarism and nativism of the Federalists, who had just succeeded in passing the Alien and Sedition Acts.28

German immigration slowed dramatically between the time of the Revolution and the 1830s; then favorable economic conditions in the United States, promoted by transportation companies in Germany, encouraged further immigration. By 1837, nearly 25,000 Germans were entering the States each year. Not only did the German-language press thrive in Philadelphia during these years, but it grew in New York as well. The *New Yorker Staatszeitung*, which continues to publish today, was begun in 1834 by Gustav Adolph Neumann, a faithful Jacksonian. The *Staatszeitung* befriended the small shopkeeper and laborer, and at first it devoted more space to editorials than to local news. In its early years, it was printed on a hand press and sold for six dollars a year, a price similar to that of other New York papers. Further development of the German press followed German immigration to western Maryland and Ohio. During the 1840s and 1850s, it expanded to Missouri, Illinois, and Wisconsin as well as some of the southern states.

French-Language Newspapers

The first French-language newspaper appeared in 1789 in Boston, its title *Courrier de Boston*. It was printed by Samuel Hall for a Frenchman, J. Naucrede, who taught French at Harvard University. It lasted only six months, but the French-language press continued to flourish, particularly in the province of Orleans immediately after the Louisiana Purchase was completed. By 1810, a triweekly printed in French, a daily in English and French, and three weeklies in English and French were publishing in Orleans. Also in the province were a Spanish weekly and semiweekly. By 1856, four French papers were being published in the United States: two in New Orleans, one in New York, and one in Nauvoo, Illinois. Founded in 1828, the New York paper, *Courrier des Etats-Unis*, was designed to promote attention in French literature, and by 1851 it became a daily. The *Courrier* also was published in weekly editions and sent to Europe and locations in Canada, Louisiana, the Pacific coast, Mexico, the West Indies, and Central and South America—wherever French settlements flourished. The expansion of the *Courrier* took place under Frederic Gaillardet, who took charge of it in 1839. Gaillardet wrote:

> There is a great field to be occupied by a newspaper which can become both the representative and the defender of the French nation in America, which will uphold the traditions of our manners, of our customs, and of our language among the populations of French origin; which can offer itself as a friend and ally to this population in upholding its native idioms and ideas, and in carrying the French diction to all parts of the New World—it will sustain and rally round it all those who speak the language, and of these different scattered members it shall make, if it is possible to do it, one body and one spirit.[29]

Labor Press

During the late 1820s and early 1830s, nearly fifty labor weeklies appeared in the United States. These developed to champion the cause of a nascent labor movement created in response to the emergence of merchant capitalists who sought to exploit labor. One of the earliest and most important of these newspapers was the *Mechanic's Free Press,* a Philadelphia paper with a circulation of about 2,000. Founded in 1828, it survived only two years. The longest running of the newspapers was the *Working Man's Advocate,* published in New York City from 1829 to 1849. The *Mechanic's Free Press* sold for two dollars a year.

The labor press was ridiculed by mainstream editors, who called them editors of the "Dirty Shirt Party," as well as "the slime of this community." Labor editors sought a shorter working day and opposed child labor, arguing that laborers and their children needed time to educate themselves if they were to be citizens in a democracy. William Heighton, editor of the *Mechanic's Free Press,* took his cause to the Philadelphia City Council. The movement for the ten-hour day gained momentum and was championed by labor newspapers in New York, as well as Philadelphia.

Another prominent labor voice, the *Free Enquirer,* published in New York from 1828 to 1835, drew particular attention because one of its editors, Frances "Fanny" Wright, challenged the boundaries of society itself. Wright was a well-educated Scottish woman who publicly opposed slavery, established a commune in Tennessee to prove that African Americans could thrive in decent circumstances, endorsed marriages between African Americans and whites, and announced that women were fully equal to men and should participate in all areas of public life. She also denounced organized religion. Mainstream newspapers labeled her a woman guilty of "incest, robbery and murder."

The labor party and its press faced massive opposition, and in 1832 the Working Men's party ceased to exist. However, the ten-hour day had already been established in Philadelphia and child labor laws followed soon thereafter. In 1834, Pennsylvania also passed a law that created tax-supported public schools for all children. The newspapers died, along with their party, but their legacy was revived in later years when the organized labor movement expanded later in the century.[30]

Native-American Press Responds to European Settlement

During the final stage of the last Ice Age, nearly 27,000 years ago, nomadic hunting bands crossed into Alaska from Siberia, across the now-submerged Bering Land Bridge. These hunting bands formed the beginnings of what ultimately became Native-American nation-states. Between 500 B.C. and A.D. 1500, Native Americans established stable settlements, utilizing both agriculture and hunting as primary modes of subsistence and trade.[31] As European settlers arrived in the early seventeenth century, Native Americans at first greeted them with cautious hospitality, but the European demand for land and control soon imposed new conditions alien to Native American culture. Further, Europeans introduced diseases to which the Native Americans had no immunity, resulting in the depopulation and dislocation of native populations. When Columbus arrived in America, about 14 million Native Americans lived within what is now the United States. Three hundred years later, the Native-American population dwindled to less than 1 million.

The two societies competing for land within the North American continent embraced radically different cultures. Although Native-American nations or tribes varied in religious orientation and cultural patterns, all embraced a mythic oral tradition. "The mythic thinking of northern native people combines the individual intelligence we all have as members of a common species with a cultural intelligence embedded in the wealth of knowledge they carry around in their minds," wrote Robin Ridington. "Their stories tell them how to make sense of themselves in relation to a natural world of sentient beings. Their dreams and visions give direct access to this wealth of information. . . . These hunters act on the basis of knowledge and understanding rather than from orders passed down through a social hierarchy."[32] Within this cultural framework, the oral tradition characterized not only day-to-day communication but the transfer of social heritage as well. Wrote N. Scott Momaday,

> One who has only an oral tradition thinks of language in this way: my words exist at the level of my voice. If I do not speak with care, my words are wasted. If I do not listen with care, words are lost. If I do not remember carefully, the very purpose of words is frustrated. This respect for words suggests an inherent morality in man's understanding and use of language. . . . On the other hand, the written tradition tends to encourage an indifference to language. That is to say, writing produces a false security where our attitudes toward language are concerned. We take liberties with words; we become blind to their sacred aspect.

As Native Americans were removed from their lands, whites scripted orders in official parlance, a written language far removed from the "American Indian oral tradition, far from the rhythms of oratory and storytelling and song."[33]

The move by Native Americans to establish a written language, and subsequently a press, therefore, was a response to white culture rather than a natural evolution of their own cultural traditions. The *Cherokee Phoenix*, the first tribal newspaper to

▼

Sequoyah (ca. 1770–1843)

SE-QUO-YAH

Sequoyah was born part Cherokee in Tennessee around 1770. Initially working as a silversmith and a metal worker, Sequoyah came to believe that the white settlers had a great advantage in having a written system of language, so he decided to begin work on a Cherokee alphabet. He endured early ridicule from tribe members but finished his task in 1821 at the age of sixty. His alphabet contained eighty-six characters and gave the Cherokee the distinction of being the first tribe to have a written language and a newspaper published in its native tongue. Later, the state government of California named the Sequoyah National Forest after him.

Sources: J. L. Stoutenburgh, *Dictionary of the American Indian* (New York: Philosophical Library, 1960); and F. W. Seymour, *The Story of the Red Man* (Freeport, N.Y.: Books for Libraries Press, 1929). (Division of Prints and Photographs, Library of Congress Collection)

appear, was printed in English and in Cherokee, using the eighty-six-character alphabet, or syllabary, developed by Sequoyah, a Native American who, while serving in the army during the War of 1812, recognized certain advantages whites had because of their written language. The Cherokee alphabet was comprised of symbols that represented syllables in the oral language. By 1828, many Cherokee men, women, and children had mastered Sequoyah's syllabary and could read.[34] Thus, prior to the Civil War, several types of Native-American publications were founded, edited, and maintained by Native Americans. Some were owned and operated by tribes; others were Native American–owned, –edited or –operated, sometimes in opposition to tribal leaders; and still others were intertribal newspapers, magazines, and literary periodicals. Tribal governments, therefore, were but one source of financing, and like nineteenth-century white-owned and -edited newspapers, Native-American publications sought financing from outside interests, including real estate and stock companies.

Among the antebellum periodicals published by Native Americans was the *Muzzinyegun*, edited by Henry Rowe Schoolcraft, whose Ojibwa wife wrote much of the poetry and articles on Ojibwa folklore and history. At least four other literary magazines appeared before the Civil War.[35]

Nineteenth-century Native-American newspapers published infrequently, had short lives, and operated with minimal staff and resources. Because few issues were saved, it is difficult to know how many Native-American newspapers existed, but one historian estimated that 250 newspapers were published in Native-American territory before 1900.[36] The papers served an informational and educational function. They carried advertisements, steamboat schedules, and legal notices. Papers were produced from presses in tents, wagons, school houses, and open fields. They averaged fifteen by twenty-four inches in size and were between four and sixteen pages in length. Circulation ranged from 100 to 1,000, and subscriptions varied from one dollar to three dollars per year. Sharon Murphy, historian of Native-American newspapers, noted that editorial policies were explicitly stated in most papers, but varying directories often disagreed in listing the political affiliations of particular sheets. Frequently, the papers were politically outspoken, inviting dispute and bitter controversies.[37]

Native-American journalists also produced about twenty magazines before 1900, and women editors were not uncommon. Despite the efforts of Native-American publications to protest emigration forced on them by the U.S. government, displacement occurred for the five southeastern tribes as well as most other Native Americans:

> Ignoring treaties, property deeds, and the sacredness to Indians of their ancestral homes and burial grounds, the United States government, in the late 1830s, herded more than 17,000 peacefully-living, educated Indians on westward forced marches, to satisfy the greed of land-hungry whites. These forced emigrants were refined, well-established people. Many of their leaders were college educated. Many of them owned large plantations; others were skilled teachers, outstanding craftsmen, successful tradesmen. Over one-fourth of the Indians died en route and many of those who did survive died shortly after resettling. Once wealthy tribes now had nothing. They had been driven at gunpoint by federal troops, from their farms and plantations, to be deposited, with little or no possessions, in new 'homelands.'[38]

The *Cherokee Phoenix*

The *Phoenix* was edited for its first four and one-half years in New Echota, Georgia, by Buck Watie—a man also known as Elias Boudinot, having taken the name of a Philadelphia philanthropist who financed his education at Cornwall, Connecticut. Editor Boudinot's efforts were financed, in part, by the Cherokee National Council with the assistance of the American Board of Foreign Missions.[39] He was paid $300 a year for his services by the Cherokee National Council, but apparently printers were considered more valuable than editors because a pressman was hired at $350 a year. Europeans as well as Cherokees subscribed to the newspaper. The newspaper was published in Cherokee and in English, and it published laws and documents of the Cherokee Nation, accounts of the manners and customs of the Cherokees, interesting news of the day, and miscellaneous articles designed to promote "Literature, Civilization, and Religion among the Cherokees."[40] After a dispute among the political factions organized around the issue of the removal of the Cherokee Nation from Georgia, Boudinot resigned in 1832.[41] The August 11, 1832, issue of the *Phoenix* carried his resignation letter:

> Were I to continue as Editor, I should feel myself in a most peculiar and delicate situation. I do not know whether I could satisfy my own views and the views of the authorities of the nation at the same time. . . . I do conscientiously believe to be the duty of every citizen to reflect upon the dangers with which we are surrounded. . . . to talk over all these matters. . . . I could not consent to be the conductor of the paper without having the right and privilege of discussing these important matters. . . . I love my country and I love my people. . . . and for that very reason I should think it my duty to tell them the whole truth, or what I believe to be the truth.[42]

The *Phoenix* continued until August 1834 when editor Elijah Hicks announced he would suspend the newspaper to raise funds. Hicks had just been released on bond after a libel suit was filed against him for reporting the attack of a Georgia citizen on two Cherokee women. As the Cherokees prepared to move the press to a safer location in Tennessee in early 1835, Georgia authorities seized the press.[43] Theda Perdue suggested that although the *Phoenix* was an important newspaper, it circulated primarily as a propaganda device to whites, designed to convince them that the Cherokee Nation was a progressive force as defined by white America. She argued that because of this goal, the *Phoenix* was not an accurate reflection of Cherokee life.[44]

The *Cherokee Advocate*

Suspension of the *Phoenix* did not destroy the Native-American press, however, and by 1843 the Cherokee National Council authorized a new national newspaper, the *Cherokee Advocate*. John Ross, president of the National Council, purchased a press in Boston, along with type in the Cherokee and English languages. He brought the press to Indian Territory—the present Oklahoma—where the Cherokee had been relocated. By this time, editors had gained stature over printers. William P. Ross, a Princeton University graduate, was named editor at $500 a year. A translator and four printers were paid $300 each. The first issue appeared on September 26, 1844, and carried the slogan, "Our Right, Our Country, Our Race."

The *Advocate*, biased in favor of the political faction in power, covered political issues as well as domestic concerns such as the public school system, the need for jails, elections, and roads. In 1853, the newspaper closed for lack of funds, although the Cherokees removed the press to Fort Gibson for protection during the Civil War and in 1867 authorized repair of a printing office in order to revive the operation.

Images of Native Americans in the Mainstream Press

Minority representation in American life is not a mere function of how many newspapers were published by a particular minority group or how the content of those newspapers strived to shape the views of a particular audience. How minority groups were presented in the mainstream press also served to shape society's ideas about individual groups.

In the case of the Native American, John Coward argues that most coverage was shaped by a powerful ideology that endorsed the concept of Manifest Destiny, "that Indians were destined to give way to Euro-American civilization."[45] Editors commonly portrayed Native Americans at two extremes, either romantic, or savage. Native-American wars were generally underplayed. Humor, literature, and news accounts, all components of nineteenth-century newspaper content, were used in characterizations of Native Americans.

African-American Newspapers as a Response to White Society

During the first sixty-five years of the nineteenth century, 90 percent of African Americans lived in the South. In the North, two-thirds of African Americans were illiterate. African-American people communicated at first through oral means, primarily in the form of sermons, poetry, spirituals, and narratives of escaped or freed slaves. These oral traditions continued as print became yet another vehicle for expression. Under such conditions, the very fact that a black press began and survived is a remarkable feat.

Samuel Cornish and John Russwurm usually have been credited with producing the first black newspaper, *Freedom's Journal*, in 1827, in response to an attack on African-American leaders by Mordecai M. Noah, editor of the *New York Enquirer*. The paper was termed "a thoroughgoing abolitionist sheet" and carried the motto, "Righteousness Exalteth a Nation." The newspaper contained original and reprinted articles, poetry, and news of slavery in the United States as well as in other countries. Russwurm and Cornish were divided over the issue of colonization—whether colonies should be formed in Africa and slaves returned to them—and during the first six months the *Journal* opposed colonization. Once Cornish resigned to return to the ministry, Russwurm reversed the position.

Russwurm graduated from Bowdoin College in 1826, the first African American to graduate from a college in the United States. Before the South enacted additional restrictive measures to control antislavery activity in the 1830s, *Freedom's Journal* circulated through Virginia, Maryland, North Carolina, Louisiana, and Washington, D.C.

Russwurm lost favor because of his position on colonization, and eventually he left the country to become the editor of the *Liberia Herald*. In 1829 when Russwurm left, Samuel Cornish resumed the editorship, changed the name to *Rights of All*, and promised to fight for African-American citizenship. However, lack of finances and support crippled the publication, and it died in October 1829.

Some accounts indicate that several issues of African-American newspapers may have been published in the 1830s, but it was nearly six years after the death of the *Journal* that a continuous publication appeared. The *Spirit of the Times* was founded in New York City and was to be published there for six years. In January 1837, Phillip A. Bell founded the *Weekly Advocate*, which became the *Colored American*. This four-page newspaper, edited by Samuel Cornish of *Freedom's Journal*, lasted until 1842. The *Colored American* focused on a family audience, strove for humanity and justice, attacked colonization, and charged northern newspapers, clergymen, and businessmen with holding slave-holding sympathies. Its circulation reached 2,000, and the paper circulated from Maine to Michigan.

More papers originated during the 1840s, with some lasting for as long as two to twelve years. Among the best were Frederick Douglass' *Ram's Horn*, the *North Star*, and *Frederick Douglass' Paper*. African-American editors continued to initiate publications through the Civil War.[46]

Magazines

The successful establishment of American magazines depended on obtaining content that was significantly different from that of the general press, a paying audience, and a distribution system. The assumption usually has been made that magazines in colonial and revolutionary America did not survive because the magazines consisted primarily of English reprints and that a professional group of writers did not exist in America to produce magazine content. Further, magazine content often seemed elitist, and because prices were high, audiences generally were considered elite as well.

Benjamin Franklin and Andrew Bradford attempted to publish magazines in 1741, but both failed to create economically viable subscription lists. In 1743, Jeremiah Gridley made a more successful attempt and published the *American Magazine and Historical Chronicle* for three years. Five other magazines were started before the Revolution, but none survived long. These included the *Gentleman and Lady's Town and Country Magazine*, which was published in Boston from May through December of 1784 and specifically addressed its appeal to women.[47] In 1800, only 12 magazines existed, but by 1825 their numbers multiplied to more than 100.

The Struggle to Circulate

Perhaps the most severe handicap for magazines was the lack of favorable postal regulation. Magazines such as the *New York Magazine* tended to circulate locally because magazines did not enjoy the favored postal rate status of newspapers. The

Nº X   Engraved for Royal American Magazine.   · Vol. I.

The able Doctor. or America Swallowing the Bitter Draught.

Figure 4–3   Paul Revere's engraving in *Royal American Magazine*, 1774, depicted the British forcing tea down the throats of Americans. (Division of Prints and Photographs, Library of Congress Collection)

1792 postal act required that magazines pay letter rates if sent through the mails. Two Philadelphia magazines—the *Columbian* and the *Museum*—suspended publication. Others survived by creating alternative distribution systems or designs that imitated newspaper formats.

In 1794, the postal act set more favorable mailing rates for magazines but gave postmasters the right to determine whether the mails could handle the added bulk. If subscribers could receive the publications, they paid 20 to 40 percent of the subscription price for postage.

In 1815, the postmaster general decided that magazines and pamphlets interfered with regular mail and excluded all but the publications of "Bible societies." Exempt from the postmaster's ban, religious publications gained the largest national circulations.[48] In 1845 and 1852, Congress took steps to standardize publication postal rates, and decisions about magazines no longer were based on content. An 1863 law created three classes of mail, the second of which covered all periodicals issued at regular intervals from a place of publication to subscribers, although it still discriminated against publications issued less often than once each week.

The *New-York Magazine; or, Literary Repository*

In a recent study, historian David Nord suggested that at least one magazine, the *New-York Magazine; or, Literary Repository*, included content that appealed to working-class groups in the city and that half the magazine's subscribers were artisans and shopkeepers. Only half the subscribers were upper-class merchants and professionals. The editors claimed to design their magazine to appeal to different groups, stating that "[t]he universality of the subjects which it [a well-conducted magazine] treats of will give to every profession, and every occupation, some information, while its variety holds out to every taste some gratification." The editors further claimed that every "class of society" would be able to afford the magazine.[49] Nord concluded that the content did appeal to all but the lowest economic classes because of its Republican themes: virtue portrayed as public virtue, suspicion of luxury, and a belief in the power and democratizing influence of knowledge.

The *Port Folio*

The *Port Folio*, edited by Joseph Dennie, struggled to refine American literary tastes and to establish itself as an educational and political force. It included essays, travel articles, scholarly criticism of all types of writing, and biographies of English and American men of prominence and poetry. Written by Dennie with contributions by John Quincy Adams and other prominent Federalists, The *Port Folio* began publication with a circulation of 2,000 on January 3, 1801, and continued as a brilliant literary weekly until 1809, a year after Dennie lost financial control and the magazine became a monthly. The *Port Folio* continued until 1827. At the beginning, Dennie advertised that the *Port Folio* would be conducted "in the manner of the *TATLER*, politics with essays and disquisitions on topics scientific, moral, humorous and literary." The magazine looked remarkably similar to a newspaper, possibly because of postal restrictions on magazines, or possibly because of its weekly, rather than monthly, publication. Dennie expressed strong British sentiments, believed the separation of the colonies from England had been a mistake, and regularly attacked Jefferson and his doctrines. In July 1803, possibly at Jefferson's direction, Dennie was charged with libel. When the postponed trial finally took place in 1805, Dennie was acquitted, but he emerged less strident politically, and he and others like him recognized the costs of political criticism.[50]

Book Publishing as a Challenge to Cultural Norms

From 1800 to 1850, the number of books available dramatically increased. Advances in technology resulted in books appearing in greater numbers, and these books were printed dually, both in inexpensive and elaborate editions. No longer revered as elite objects, books of all kinds—novels, short fiction, romantic and patriotic verse, travel accounts, etiquette books, advice manuals for young men and women, and gift keepsake books in addition to the standard religious and educational volumes—were advertised, sold on the open market, and circulated widely. The availability of a variety of works challenged the religious control of entertainment and put not only knowledge but entertainment content within a reader's realm of choice.

Despite their popularity, books were rarely distributed through the mails before 1851, when Congress finally admitted books as mailable objects. Prior to that time, packets weighing more than three pounds were excluded from the mails, effectively barring the mailing of some books. In addition, high rates forced most distributors to seek private systems, and in one instance at least, a publisher hired all the passenger seats of the mail stage to ship 500 copies of a book to New York booksellers. Newspapers and magazines circulating through the mails were widely used, however, to advertise books.[51]

In the mid-nineteenth century book publishers emerged at the center of the book trade and coordinated the varied activities involved in securing book manuscripts, publishing, and distributing. William Davis Ticknor, a twenty-two-year-old clerk and bank teller, in 1832 bought a Boston bookstore and created a partnership with James T. Fields, a clerk at the store. Ticknor and Fields sold books from a stand in downtown Boston that later became known—and relatively famous—as the Old Corner Bookstore. Ticknor and Fields continued their bookstore through 1865, but their success was not merely in operating an efficient bookstore. Instead, they began publishing poetry, essays, and fiction and worked with American and English writers such as Longfellow, Whittier, Hawthorne, and Emerson. They were successful because they recognized popular literature, acquired the rights to publish it, packaged it in ways that promoted the concept of literary merit, and sold it nationwide to jobbers and retailers. Thus a pattern was set that remains in place today.[52]

Technology, Production, and Labor

During the early 1800s, printing technology altered forever the relationship of printers to their product and to the public. The wage system began to predominate over the master–apprenticeship system, work became more specialized, and the role of the manager grew increasingly important. As early as 1786, twenty-six Philadelphia journeymen printers went on strike to protest widespread wage reductions, and by 1825 journeymen founded more than a dozen "typographical societies" concerned with wage scales, labor conditions, and benefits. With the invention of the steam press, prior to the financial crisis of 1836, young women could supervise all the press operations that fifty years earlier would have required heavy labor. Stereotyping, invented in 1811, and electrotyping, available in 1841, allowed an impressment to be taken of set type and made into a relatively inexpensive metal plate that could be used repeatedly for different editions of books, thereby diminishing the amount of work required. These innovations also reduced the amount of publisher guesswork. No longer did a publisher have to estimate the number of sales, then reset type and reproduce more copies; rather, inexpensive plates could be retained and additional copies printed as the demand arose. Two paper-making machines (Fourdrinier's in 1799 and Gilpin's in 1816) allowed paper to be produced in continuous rolls rather than sheet by sheet. Other technological developments facilitated the binding process.

These technological innovations cut the cost of hardcover books, which declined by about 50 percent between the late eighteenth century and the Civil War. Nevertheless, a one-dollar book represented one-sixth of an average male worker's weekly wages and more than half of a woman's weekly wages. Even paperbacks, at an average price of fifty cents each, cost more than many workers could afford. In any case, technological innovation, expansion of railroads that promoted distribution, the availability of better illumination for reading at night, and less expensive corrective eyeglasses facilitated an increase in reading.[53]

Relationship to Religion and Values

Not only did the volume of books increase but so did the variety, a feat that disturbed some of the religious personages of the day and that challenged the cultural order. As Mason Locke Weems—better known as Parson Weems—traveled about Virginia and the Carolinas in the early 1800s, taking subscriptions for books at courthouses and churches, he noted that rigidly Puritanical books simply did not sell. Writing to Matthew Carey, the publisher for whom he sold books, Weems asked for a variety of books that, while not religious in subject matter, were religious in tone—conveying moral lessons. Thus, Weems in essence helped to invent "new forms of religious instruction, 'authentic' narratives as opposed to fiction, that compelled readers to experience the disasters that ensued from unlucky or unwise moral straying,"[54] although sometimes these books were, more accurately, violent torture tales. Weems' position directly opposed that of many religious figures who opposed the distribution of fiction and the proliferation of theatre productions. Religious figures feared reading for "mere" pleasure, especially when books were consumed privately at home or in a small company of women. The message was not the issue, they argued; rather, fiction "pandered to active but undirected and uncontrolled imaginations."[55]

Women were voracious readers of novels, but the social message was similar to the religious message: Critics argued that households fell apart when women glued their eyes to a piece of fiction. A popular print of the early nineteenth century depicted a mother, entranced by a novel as the dog made off with the dinner meat, the cat drank the household supply of milk, and the husband and children protested at having no lunch, though it was well past noon.[56]

McGuffey's Textbook Series: Books and Public Education

Schoolbooks had been a mainstay of book publishing in America since colonial days and had been designed for moral education as well as to promote the acquisition of general knowledge. One of the most famous of these was *McGuffey's Reader*, first compiled by William Holmes McGuffey in 1836 to 1837. He advocated public education as a means to moral and spiritual education, to nurture children in Presbyterian Calvinist doctrine and behavior. In McGuffey's reader, God was the central figure as creator, provider, and governor. Children's proper responses were to obey God, fear Him, and be grateful for His goodness. Only by so doing could they enter into immortality within God's grace. The readers also emphasized that people had been given the ability to reason and to choose and that education promoted the acquisition of the knowledge necessary to act "with honor and usefulness." McGuffey's books promoted an optimistic view of human nature and God's natural world, but they also emphasized that people had been born into sin and that children could easily fall from virtue by lying, idleness, or love of money. McGuffey emphasized values and modes of conduct—honesty, obedience, kindness, thrift, industry, patriotism, cleanliness, forgiveness, gratefulness, cooperativeness, curiosity, self-control, meekness, right language, independence, courageousness, frugality, punctuality, temperance, moderation, and truthfulness.

Later editions adapted to serve the needs of an emerging middle class, abandoning the stricter moral constrictions advocated by McGuffey. While in 1837 McGuffey advocated salvation, righteousness, and piety, by 1879 "all that remained were lessons affirming the morality and life-styles of the emerging middle class and those cultural beliefs, attitudes, and values that undergird American civil religion."[57] The values emphasized in the 1879 edition were self-reliance, individualism, and competition. Virtue was no longer seen as its own reward, but material and physical rewards were to be expected for good acts. Hard work and frugality would bring prosperity, and responsibility for that prosperity lay with the individual. Personal choice and commitment—not social, political, or economic systems—determined the course of a person's life.[58]

Conclusion

From the late 1700s through the 1820s, printed matter diversified in type, language, ethnic origin, and content, prompting a shift from a reliance on oral delivery of messages to printed verification of rumors and news. What had been a society of information scarcity became instead a society of information abundance. By 1830, political and economic newspapers were widely available, published both within local communities and city centers. More remarkable perhaps was the wide diversity of form in periodicals and books, despite severe postal restrictions that legislated against all forms except newspapers. Technology fostered rapid development of the printing industry and altered the relationship of labor to management within publishing. Postal policy fostered the development and easy distribution of newspapers, but it restricted the distribution of magazines and books on the basis of form and content.

Endnotes

1. William J. Gilmore, "Literacy, The Rise of an Age of Reading, and the Cultural Grammar of Print Communications in America, 1735–1850," *Communication*, 11 (1988), pp. 23–46.

2. Richard D. Brown, *Knowledge Is Power: The Diffusion of Information in Early America, 1700–1865* (New York: Oxford University Press, 1989), p. 276.

3. Brown, *Knowledge Is Power*, pp. 197–217.

4. *Farmer's Almanack . . . 1839* (Boston, 1838), no. 47, October 1839, as cited in Brown, *Knowledge Is Power*, p. 159.

5. Brown, *Knowledge Is Power*, pp. 266–67.

6. *Annals of Congress*, Second Congress, First Session, pp. 284–86, cited in Richard B. Kielbowicz, "The Press,

Post Office, and Flow of News in the Early Republic," *Journal of the Early Republic* (Fall, 1983), p. 258. See also Richard R. John, *Spreading the News: The American Postal System from Franklin to Morse* (Cambridge, Mass.: Harvard University Press, 1995).

7. Richard B. Kielbowicz, *News in the Mail: The Press, Post Office, and Public Information, 1700–1860s* (Westport, Conn.: Greenwood Press, 1989), p. 3.

8. Richard Peters, ed., *Statutes at Large of the United States of America, 1789–1873*, 17 vols. (Boston, 1850–1873), vol. 1, pp. 70, 178, cited in Kielbowicz, "Press, Post Office, and Flow of News," p. 268.

9. Kielbowicz, *News in the Mail*, p. 122.

10. Harry Stonecipher, "Samuel Harrison Smith," *Dictionary of Literary Biography*, vol. 43, p. 420.

11. William E. Ames, *A History of the* National Intelligencer (Chapel Hill: University of North Carolina Press, 1972), p. 26.

12. *National Intelligencer*, October 26, 1801, cited in Ames, p. 29.

13. Ames, National Intelligencer, pp. 19, 66, 67.

14. Sallie A. Whelan, "William Winston Seaton," *Dictionary of Literary Biography*, vol. 43, pp. 415–16.

15. Ames, National Intelligencer, pp. 98–99; Whelan, "William Winston Seaton," p. 416.

16. Ames, National Intelligencer, pp. 109–11.

17. William E. Ames and Dwight L. Teeter, "Politics, Economics and the Mass Media," in Ronald T. Farrar and John D. Stevens, eds., *Mass Media and the National Experience: Essays in Communications History* (New York: Harper & Row, 1971).

18. United States House Report 298, Twenty-Sixth Congress, First Session, and United States Senate Report 18, Fifty-Second Congress, First Session, cited in Ames, National Intelligencer, p. 111.

19. Allan Nevins, *The Evening Post: A Century of Journalism* (New York: Boni and Liveright, 1922), p. 12.

20. Cited in Nevins, *Evening Post*, p. 19.

21. James Boylan, "William Cullen Bryant," *Dictionary of Literary Biography*, vol. 43, pp. 79–90.

22. Lauren Kessler, *The Dissident Press* (Beverly Hills: Sage, 1984), pp. 91–93.

23. S. N. D. North, *History and Present Condition of the Newspaper and Periodical Press of the United States with a Catalogue of the Publications of the Census Year*, 10th census, vol. 8, 1884, p. 126.

24. Robert Park, *The Immigrant Press and Its Control* (New Jersey: Patterson Smith, 1971), p. 10.

25. Kessler, *Dissident Press*, p. 88.

26. Carl Wittke, *The German Language Press in America* (Lexington: University of Kentucky Press, 1957).

27. Wittke, *German Language Press*, p. 31.

28. Wittke, *German Language Press*, pp. 33–34.

29. North, *History and Present Condition*, p. 128.

30. Rodger Streitmatter, "Origins of the American Labor Press," *Journalism History* 25:3 (Autumn, 1999), pp. 99–105.

31. Neal Salisbury, "American Indians and American History," in *The American Indian and the Problem of History*, Calvin Martin, ed. (New York: Oxford University Press, 1987), pp. 46–54.

32. Robin Ridington, "Fox and Chickadee," in Martin, *The Problem of History*, p. 134.

33. N. Scott Momaday, "Personal Reflections," in Martin, *The Problem of History*, pp. 160, 161.

34. Sharon Murphy and James Murphy, *Let My People Know: American Indian Journalism, 1828–1978* (Norman: University of Oklahoma Press, 1981), pp. 21–22.

35. Daniel F. Littlefield and James W. Parins, *American Indian and Alaska Native Newspapers and Periodicals* (Westport, Conn.: Greenwood, 1984), p. xx.

36. Carolyn Foreman, *Oklahoma Imprints, 1835–1907: Printing before Statehood* (Norman: University of Oklahoma Press, 1936), cited in Sharon Murphy, "Neglected Pioneers: Nineteenth Century Native American Newspapers," *Journalism History* 4:3 (Autumn, 1977), p. 79.

37. Murphy, "Neglected Pioneers," p. 80.

38. Murphy, "Neglected Pioneers," p. 82.

39. Littlefield, *American Indian Newspapers*, p. 84.

40. From "Prospectus for Publishing, at New Echota, in the Cherokee Nation, a Weekly Newspaper, to Be Called the Cherokee Phoenix," broadside (1827), as cited in Littlefield, *American Indian Newspapers*, p. 85.

41. Littlefield, *American Indian Newspapers*, p. 88.

42. Cited in Barbara Luebke, "Elias Boudinott, Indian Editor: Editorial Columns from the *Cherokee Phoenix*," *Journalism History* 6:4 (Winter, 1979), p. 51.

43. Littlefield, *American Indian Newspapers*, p. 90.

44. Theda Perdue, "Rising from the Ashes: The *Cherokee Phoenix* as an Ethnohistorical Source," *Ethnohistory* 24 (Summer, 1977), pp. 207–18.

45. John M. Coward, *The Newspaper Indian: Native American Identity in the Press, 1820–90.* (Urbana: University of Illinois Press, 1999).

46. Cited in Carter R. Bryan, "Negro Journalism in America Before Emancipation," *Journalism Monographs* 12 (September, 1969).

47. Lyon Richardson, *A History of Early American Magazines* (New York: Thomas Nelson and Sons, 1931), p. 228.

48. Kielbowicz, "Press, Post Office and Flow of News," pp. 267–69.

49. *New York Magazine* 1 (April 1790), p. 197, cited in David Paul Nord, "A Republican Literature: A Study of Magazine Reading and Readers in Late-Eighteenth Century New York," *American Quarterly* 40 (March, 1988), p. 7.

50. See James Playstead Wood, *Magazines in the United States* (New York: The Ronald Press Company, 1949), pp. 29–40; and Gary Coll's "Joseph Dennie," *Dictionary of Literary Biography*, vol. 43, pp. 151–59.

51. Kielbowicz, *News in the Mail*, pp. 132–34.

52. Michael Winship, *American Literary Publishing in the Mid-Nineteenth Century: The Business of Ticknor & Fields* (Cambridge: Cambridge University Press, 1995), p. 188. See also William Charvat, *The Profession of Authorship in America, 1800–1870*, ed. Matthew J. Bruccoli (Columbus: Ohio State University Press, 1968).

53. Ronald Zboray, "Antebellum Reading and the Ironies of Technological Innovation," *American Quarterly* 40 (March, 1988), pp. 65–82.

54. R. Laurence Moore, "The Culture Industry in Antebellum America," *American Quarterly* (June, 1989), pp. 219–21.

55. Moore, "Culture Industry," p. 222.

56. Brown, *Knowledge Is Power*, p. 196.

57. John H. Westerhoff, III, *McGuffey and His Readers: Piety, Morality, and Education in Nineteenth Century America* (Nashville, Tenn.: Abingdon, 1978), pp. 18–19.

58. Westerhoff, *McGuffey*, p. 105.

CHAPTER 5

Penny Papers in the Metropolis

▼

In the midst of a society of information abundance and diverse forms of communication, the introduction of newspapers that sold for a penny apiece occurred in the nation's largest commercial city, New York. This commercial venture represented a departure for the press in an industrializing and modernizing nation that was undergoing immense social, cultural, and economic change. The newspapers challenged elite authority within the city by developing a new attitude toward advertising, by aiming at new audiences, and by paying reporters to cover local news. By circulating to diverse audiences within the city and to country audiences through weekly editions, the newspapers sought to break down geographical and local cultural barriers by disseminating news of national interest.

Prior to 1830, the metropolitan press, especially that of New York and other major cities, directed itself toward a commercial and political elite. These early newspapers, dominated by commerce and vehement political editorials, were, as one historian described them, "little more than bulletin boards for the business community."[1] The newspapers cost six cents per issue, and readers paid in advance for a year's subscription. Names such as the *Commercial Advertiser* emphasized these newspapers' particular appeal, and their circulations averaged about 1,500.[2]

With the beginning of Benjamin Day's *New York Sun* in 1833, followed by the *Evening Transcript* in 1834 and by James Gordon Bennett's *New York Herald* in 1835, the "new" New York press represented a rather dramatic change from its elite predecessors and commercial rivals. The penny press, so labeled because each issue sold for a penny, championed the growing city population—immigrants and the middle class—rather than the commercial elite. Its content included day-to-day events such as police-court news within a more traditional format of social and political news. By 1836 and 1837, the penny idea spread to Boston, Philadelphia, and Baltimore. William Swain's *Philadelphia Public Ledger* first appeared on March 25, 1836, and in eight months circulated to 10,000 readers, at a time when the city's previous largest newspaper sold about 2,000 copies.[3]

In order to produce the "new" content for the penny papers, newspaper editors created "new" staffing patterns. Prior to the 1830s, newspaper editors simply took whatever information walked in the door. Ship captains' letters, legal documents, campaign material, and legal documents constituted a good deal of the news. Publishers were primarily printers and collectors of news—not producers or creators. In the 1830s, the pattern began to change, and publishers hired managing editors and reporters, creating a staffing pattern that with modifications and expansion is still in place today. Technology boosted the collection of news as well as the printing and distribution of newspapers. Faster presses and the use of steamships, the railroad, and the telegraph fostered faster, more timely news—printed for greater circulations and delivered more quickly to the readers.

The development of advertising on a larger scale promoted the inexpensive newspaper; and although newspaper editors, relying on advertising instead of political party support, claimed political independence, they often retained strong partisan loyalties. Their assertions of independence related more to the absence of political financing than to the lack or neutrality of political opinion.

Although the independent press claimed to reach the "masses," many groups still perceived themselves to be outside of mainstream society as it was defined and reported by the newspapers. Therefore, specialized newspapers for labor, for various immigrant groups, and for African Americans developed alongside the penny press.

Traditionally, journalism historians have depicted the 1830s as a period of revolution in U.S. journalism. Although this description might be appropriate for the changes in staffing patterns and the speed of newspaper delivery introduced during that period, the revolutionary model does not accurately explain the U.S. press as a whole. Rather, the period from 1820 to 1860 represented both change and continuity: Reporter-originated stories gained prominence over clipped, second-hand news, particularly in urban daily newspapers, and the news was delivered with increased speed, but the content and style of the papers remained rather stable.[4] Major changes did occur in New York, and other cities began to imitate the New York products; reporters and editors trained in the city also carried the idea to smaller cities. Nevertheless, the penny press model rarely was duplicated in the smaller towns of middle America.

Perhaps the most interesting question is why the penny press even came into being. Researchers differ in their interpretations of what caused the penny press, with some attributing the concept to a new focus on the immigrant class and others to more attention to the middle class. Still others relate the evolution of the penny press to broader changes in American society. ▼

Characteristics of the Penny Press

The penny press was distinguished by a variety of characteristics. The most obvious of these traits related to financing, price, and salesmanship. The newspapers sold for a penny a copy, were hawked by street vendors, and were financed primarily through advertising. If debts were incurred, they were based on collateral provided by the value of the newspaper and accompanying property such as presses and buildings. This method of financing differed from the past, when newspaper owners received money either directly from particular political or business interests or through banks supported by particular interests. Another departure from the past was that newsboys sold the penny newspapers on the street, the papers no longer promising discreet delivery.

Advertising: Buyer Beware

The penny press kept the advertising function separate from its subscribers and catered both to the needs of all businesses to advertise and the supposed desires of readers to be apprised of available new products. This orientation toward advertising helped earn the penny press its label of sensationalism. Although sensational advertising existed prior to the penny press, editors of the elite newspapers that preceded the penny press claimed to have screened their advertising. Editors of the new papers adopted a "let the buyer beware" attitude, attracting nearly all comers with a product to sell. The *Philadelphia Public Ledger* announced, for example:

> Our advertising columns are open to the "public, the whole public, and nothing but the public." We admit any advertisements of any thing or any opinion, from any persons who will pay the price, excepting what is forbidden by the laws of the land, or what, in the opinion of all, is offensive to decency and morals. . . . Our advertising is our revenue, and in a paper involving so many expenses as a penny paper, and especially our own, the *only* source of revenue.[5]

Editors who viewed the penny papers as rivals attacked their advertising policies, particularly those regarding patent medicines. In truth, however, many commercial dailies as well as colonial newspapers had carried patent medicine ads before the advent of the penny press. Benjamin Towne's *Pennsylvania Evening Post* in 1784 advertised such genuine patent medicines as Hooper's Female Pills, Turlington's Balsam of Life, and Dr. Anderson's Scots Pills.[6] Fiercely antagonistic toward the New York penny papers, the city's *Journal of Commerce* rejected theatre notices as indecent, and although it accepted ads for patent medicines, at the same time it printed unfavorable comments on the medicines issued by medical societies.[7] Sociologist Alfred McClung Lee suggested that the objections directed at the new advertising represented a shift in the nature of the advertising process itself. In colonial and pre-penny newspapers, those who advertised were also those who subscribed to and financed the journal in which they advertised. An advertisement was seen as a mechanism for spreading information by means of a paid insertion. Under the new system, advertisers simply

Figure 5–1 Early advertisement. (Division of Prints and Photographs, Library of Congress Collection.)

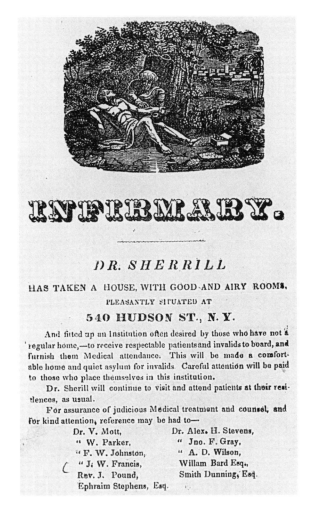

hawked their wares and did not necessarily have a personal relationship to the newspaper or a recognized obligation to the community.

Newspaper ownership was another important factor in the change. Although there were significant exceptions, colonial editors were entrepreneurs—merchants, book dealers, and shop keepers trained in printing either in England or in the colonies. Early Republic editors often were printers hired by political factions to represent a particular point of view. Ownership of the penny press rarely was apolitical, but the first aspiration of the editor was to succeed as a businessman.

Continuity and Change in the Early Nineteenth Century

The issue of whether content in the penny press represented continuity or change has been debated extensively. Some have argued that penny papers changed content, focusing on crime news, on the day-to-day events of the household and the streets, and on local happenings. They have been characterized as "news" papers rather than "views" papers. "One might say," wrote sociologist Michael Schudson,

> that, for the first time, the newspaper reflected not just commerce or politics but social life. To be more precise, in the 1830s the newspapers began to reflect, not the affairs of an elite in a small trading society, but the activities of an increasingly varied, urban, and middle-class society of trade, transportation, and manufacturing.[8]

Some historians have maintained that a change in content was not readily apparent between 1820 and 1860 for the American press as a whole. In analyzing 3,000 sample newspapers, Donald Shaw found that newspapers did not become less political and more social; rather, they focused on politics, social and intellectual aspects of communities, and economic concerns. He argued that social news did not develop in the context of the penny press but that it existed prior to the 1830s. "In terms of press content the story of the 1820–1860 period is one of continuity, not change," Shaw wrote. However, Shaw also noted that the number of stories written by reporters began to replace news gathered from other newspapers. In addition, news began to focus more concretely on local events. The most apparent change was in the employment of reporters to cover news and the developing technology that greatly accelerated the speed with which news was gathered.[9]

The New York Leaders

Benjamin Day and the *New York Sun*

Benjamin Day, an entrepreneur with newspaper and publishing experience, began the *New York Sun* as a business proposition. Throughout its existence, the *Sun* challenged the existing New York papers, expanding advertising, hiring reporters to originate news stories, and experimenting with technology and new business practices. In 1824, when Day was fifteen years old, he began learning the printer's trade in Massachusetts at the *Springfield Republican*. At twenty, he went to New York and worked as a compositor at the *Evening Post* and the *Commercial Advertiser*. With the small savings he accumulated, he began a job-printing business of his own. He subsequently started the *New York Sun*, not out of political or moral principle, but because he thought it would promote his printing business.[10] Other businessmen had tried the same concept—that of a penny paper—and failed, so it was not the first attempt to break away from the more staid metropolitan dailies.

Day issued the first edition of the *Sun* on September 3, 1833, with an old press printing 200 sheets an hour. It was a day of free advertising for those who advertised in the *Sun*. The contents of the paper consisted of rewritten items and ads that Day reprinted from other newspapers. The four-page newspaper was printed on an 11¼-by-8-inch page, slightly larger than a piece of today's standard typing paper. In the first issue, Day announced his ambitions:

> The object of this paper is to lay before the public, at a price within the means of every one, ALL THE NEWS OF THE DAY, and at the same time afford an advantageous medium for advertising. The sheet will be enlarged as soon as the increase of advertisements requires it—the price remaining the same.[11]

The subscription price was $3 per year. Advertisers who signed for a year got ten lines a day for an annual rate of $30.

Two months later Day claimed success, with 2,000 subscribers and a "steadily increasing advertising patronage."[12] On December 17, he acquired a machine press that would print 1,000 impressions an hour, and his circulation surpassed 4,000. With the initial promise of success, Day hired a young reporter, George W. Wisner, and promised him four dollars a week to rise at 4 A.M. to cover daily police-court sessions. Wisner, an ardent abolitionist who sometimes sneaked an editorial into the *Sun*'s pages on the subject of slavery, became half-owner of the *Sun* in 1834. A year later, when Wisner decided to leave New York for the fresh air of Michigan, Day purchased Wisner's share for $5,000.

Day's pattern for success became the historians' formula for describing the penny press. It relied on these essential elements: expanded advertising, a low per-copy price, advanced technology, street sales, and reporters paid to cover local news. As far as Colonel Watson Webb of the old-style *Courier and Enquirer* was concerned, those reporters could have been hired guns. He found the practice of hiring reporters scandalous, the results shoddy, and the success frightening.

When Wisner left Day's *Sun*, the editor hired another reporter, Richard Adams Locke, for twelve dollars a week. Locke was no mere hack, but an educated man interested in recent scientific discoveries and in astronomy.[13] Edgar Allan Poe said Locke's prose style "is noticeable for its concision, luminosity, completeness."[14] His prose style also was adaptable; he wrote poetry, political stories, and stories involving the nature of the universe. It was his interest in philosophy that led him to propose to Ben Day the possibility of a series of stories that would top the

▼

Police Court

Harriet Shultz, charged with committing a violent assault on the person of Henry Shultz, one of her husbands, who appeared against her as complainant; he stated that his wife was generally pretty clever to him, but, by some means or other, she was more ill-natured than usual last night, and took occasion to give him something of a flogging—he stood on the defensive when his wife made the attack, but finding himself unable to cope with her in the matrimonial combat, he bawled "murder," which brought a watchman to his assistance. The injured husband, with the assistance of the watchman, succeeded in capturing his tyrannical rib, and brought her, a prisoner, to the watch-house. On their promising to live together peaceably for the future, they were discharged.

—The *Sun*, September 3, 1833

week's best-seller list—a series that resulted in the now infamous moon hoax. The stories exploited the discoveries of Sir John Frederick William Herschel, the greatest astronomer of his time, who had established an observatory near Cape Town, South Africa. On August 21, 1835, an announcement appeared on page two of the *Sun*:

> *CELESTIAL DISCOVERIES*—The *Edinburgh Courant* says—"We have just learnt from an eminent publisher in this city that Sir John Herschel, at the Cape of Good Hope, has made some astronomical discoveries of the most wonderful description, by means of an immense telescope of an entirely new principle."[15]

Four days later, Locke's first story appeared in the *Sun*. The source cited was a supplement to the *Edinburgh Journal of Science*, which ceased publication before 1835. The first story, leaving readers in great suspense, detailed the new telescope Herschel was using and claimed he had "made the most extraordinary discoveries in

Figure 5–2   Illustrations in the *New York Sun* helped further the moon hoax, perpetuating claims that Sir John Herschel had allegedly seen lunar animals and objects from his observatory at the Cape of Good Hope. (Division of Prints and Photographs, Library of Congress Collection)

every planet of our solar system; has discovered planets in other solar systems; has obtained a distinct view of objects in the moon." The following day, the *Sun* printed four columns of Herschel's great discoveries, which described lunar vegetation, the moon's atmosphere, fine forests, and "continuous herds of brown quadrupeds," similar to the American bison although smaller. Subsequent installments revealed the existence of winged creatures much like men and women on the moon as well as magnificent structures, such as the great Temple of the Moon, built of polished sapphire.

The *Sun* fooled not only the general public but the scientific community as well, including a delegation of scientists from Yale. However, it was Locke himself who exposed the hoax. Gerard Hallock, who was David Hale's partner on the *Journal of Commerce*, sent a young reporter to retrieve extra copies of the *Sun* issue containing the moon story so that the *Journal* could reprint it. Locke warned the young reporter not to reprint the story. "I wrote it myself," Locke said. When the *Journal* revealed the hoax, the *Sun* made light of the whole thing, praising the story's "useful effect in diverting the public mind, for a while, from that bitter apple of discord, the abolition of slavery, which still unhappily threatens to turn the milk of human kindness into rancorous gall." The *Sun* stated that while some called the moon story "an adroit fiction of our own," other readers "construe the whole as an elaborate satire upon the monstrous fabrications of the political press of the country and the various genera and species of its party editors." Locke was known to be annoyed with many of the period's popular books on astronomy, which often mixed fiction with fact. He later claimed he had intended the whole thing to be taken as a satire rather than as truth. "I am the best self-hoaxed man in the whole community," he said.[16]

Dan Schiller suggested in *Objectivity and the News* that the hoax really was a "clever attempt to outwit the papers of New York City."[17] The penny papers were annoyed because the six-penny papers were reprinting the penny papers' stories without credit. Deceived by the detailed scientific description in the stories about the moon, six-penny editors could not ignore the soaring circulation of the moon hoax issues of the *Sun.* When the hoax was revealed, James Gordon Bennett, editor of another famous penny paper, the *New York Herald,* claimed that the *Sun* had gone too far in ignoring the truth in order to make money. Nevertheless, the six-penny dailies, some of which wrote of the moon discoveries as though they had read about them in the *Journal of Science* and not the *New York Sun,* were indeed reduced in stature.

The moon hoax boosted circulation; during publication of the pseudoscientific stories in August 1835, the *Sun* editors claimed a circulation of 19,360. (The largest competitor in New York City was the *Courier and Enquirer,* with a circulation of 4,500.) Advertising consumed so much space that often news appeared in only five of the twenty columns. The publisher sometimes apologized for leaving out advertisements or for having so little space for news. To help the situation, Day expanded the paper in January 1836. It remained a four-page sheet, but the size of the news sheet increased to fourteen by twenty inches. By 1837, the *Sun*'s advertising revenues exceeded $200 a day. These revenues came not from the display advertising we are familiar with today but with "liners," the common form of advertising in the 1830s. Liners looked like this:

A CARD—TO BUTCHERS—Mr. Stamler, having retired to private life, would be glad to see his friends, the Butchers, at his house, No. 5 Rivington Street, this afternoon, between the hours of 2 and 5 P.M., to partake of a collation.

SIX CENTS REWARD!—Run away from the subscriber, on the 30th of May, Charles Eldridge, an indented apprentice to the Segar-Making business, about 16 years of age, 4 feet high, broken back. Had on, when he left, a round jacket and blue pantaloons. The above reward and no charges will be paid for his delivery to
    JOHN DIBBEN, No. 354 Bowery

In June 1837, Benjamin Day sold the *Sun* to Moses Beach, his brother-in-law, for $40,000. For a couple of years during Day's ownership, profits at the *Sun* had been as high as $120,000; the six months net return ending October 1, 1836, as claimed by the *Sun*, was $12,981.88. However, in June 1837, when Day sold the *Sun*, the newspaper was barely breaking even. The editor was only twenty-eight years old and had amassed a sizeable fortune. There was speculation that the drop in advertising was related not to a decreasing popularity for the *Sun*, but instead to the 1835 New York fire, which destroyed more than twenty blocks around Wall Street, and to banking failures during the year.

After the purchase of the *Sun* by Moses Beach, the newspaper continued to be innovative, both in terms of content and new methods of acquiring news. Before becoming involved with the *Sun*, Beach invented a rag-cutting machine for paper mills, but lack of speed in securing a patent prevented him from earning the income he otherwise might have gained from the process. Beach began the use of an express service operated by William F. Harnden to bring news from the harbors, a service that used boats from New York to Providence and rail from Providence to Boston. With the express, New York newspapers could obtain English newspapers from the Boston harbor within a day after the ships landed. In June 1839, as the *Sun*'s own sailing vessels met the incoming steamships moving down the bay, the *Sun* boasted of its speed in collecting the news:

In consequence of our news-boat arrangements we receive our papers more than an hour earlier than any other paper in this city. On the arrival of the Liverpool [July 1, 1839], we proceeded to issue an extra, which will reach Albany with the news twelve hours before it will be published in the regular editions of their evening papers, and twenty-four hours ahead of the morning papers.

While waiting for the telegraph to reach New York, which did not occur until 1846, the *Sun* used horse express, special trains, and carrier pigeons to speed up the collection of news:

Carrier-pigeons have long been remarked for their sagacity and admired for their usefulness. They are, of all birds, the most invaluable, and as auxiliary to a newspaper cannot be too highly prized. Part of the flock in our possession were employed by the *London Morning Chronicle* in bringing intelligence from Dublin to London, and from Paris to London, crossing both channels; therefore they are not novices in the newspaper express.

New technology was necessary to keep up with expanded news gathering and circulation. During the three years that Day owned the *Sun*, he bought two new Napier presses from Robert Hoe for $7,000 so that he could run 3,200 papers an hour on each press. In 1846, Beach bought two new presses at a cost of $12,000, each capable of printing 6,000 copies of the *Sun* an hour.

Within a dozen years, the first penny paper was no longer a small operation. On September 3, 1843, the *Sun* employed 8 editors and reporters, 20 compositors, 100 carriers, 16 pressmen, and 12 folders and counters. Daily circulation was 38,000. The *Weekly Sun* had a circulation of 12,000. The *Sun* still filled four pages, with seven columns per page. Of the twenty-eight columns per issue, about twenty-one were filled with advertising, three with news and editorials, two with court reports, and one with reprints.

The beginning of the Mexican War raised the cost of having news delivered quickly. Battle news from Mexico took about eighteen days to reach New York, traveling by steamer to New Orleans or Mobile, then by railroad to the nearest telegraph. The *Sun* had no correspondent but relied on George Kendall's accounts written for the *New Orleans Picayune*. The expense of each newspaper collecting such news on its own led to a variety of cooperative ventures by New York newspapers designed to reduce costs and speed news gathering. One such venture stemmed from a meeting in the *Sun* offices presided over by Gerard Hallock, editor of the *Journal of Commerce*. Representatives for the *Sun*, the *Herald*, the *Tribune*, the *Courier and Enquirer*, and the *Express* attended the meeting and formed the Harbour News Association to operate a fleet of boats to retrieve news from afar. Other ventures included pooling resources for gathering news in centers such as Washington, Albany, Boston, Philadelphia, and New Orleans.

Beach retired in 1848 at the age of forty-eight and turned the paper over to his sons. The newspaper retained its respectable position through the Civil War and was sold by the Beach family to Charles A. Dana in 1868. Dana spent almost thirty years with the *Sun*. Those thirty years kept the *Sun* in the forefront of developing news gathering and news organization techniques.

Benjamin Day's influence carried farther than New York. Penny papers did not just pop up propitiously in other cities; men trained by Day and familiar with his approach moved to other cities to start those newspapers. William M. Swain, who was Day's foreman on the *Sun*, Azariah H. Simmons, another New York printer, and Arunah Shepherdson Abell, who worked for the *New York Mercantile Advertiser* and who was a close acquaintance of Day's, started the *Philadelphia Public Ledger* in March 1836. The newspaper sold for a penny and claimed to be "neutral in politics." The *Ledger* struggled for nearly a year before its returns were in the black. Once the *Ledger* was on a solid financial footing (where it remained for more than thirty years), Abell, financed in part by his two Philadelphia partners, went to Baltimore in May

1837 to start the *Baltimore Sun*. Writing 100 years later about the *Sun*, the authors of *The Sunpapers of Baltimore* noted that if judged by modern standards, the *Sun* "was almost fabulously bad. But in the realm of the blind, a one-eyed man is king and American journalism, in the early part of the Nineteenth Century, was a realm of the blind. What lay at its own doors it could not by any chance perceive." The authors described the early issues of the *Baltimore Sun*:

> For instance, its early police court stories were frequently characterized by such remarkable statements as 'the defendant, a middle-aged man whose name we did not ascertain,' and again and again cases were reported in every detail *except* the decision of the court. The stories were full of editorial opinion, frequently written in what was intended to be a humorous vein, but which seems pretty heavy-footed to the modern reader, while occasionally the reporter indulged in what any modern newspaper man would identify at a glance as an outrageous fake. Names, dates and addresses, the things in which absolute accuracy is most rigidly exacted by the modern city editor, were treated by the early *SUN* with a casualness which makes a present-day reporter gasp. But on one point *THE SUN* from the very beginning maintained the same policy to which it adheres after a hundred years—it was extremely reluctant to run puffs as reading matter.[18]

James Gordon Bennett and the *New York Herald*

James Gordon Bennett began the *New York Herald* with $500 of capital and a desk made up of wooden planks placed across two barrels. He carved out his place in New York society by being truly irreverent. Impatient with what he considered to be moral hypocrisy, he attacked political and social leaders equally, while at the same time expanding reporting techniques, revolutionizing the coverage of financial affairs, and exploiting technology to speed news gathering.

When he began publishing the *Herald*, Bennett was about forty years old, and some might have termed him, at that point in his life, a failure. A Scotsman, Bennett immigrated to New York in 1822. After a few months of struggling to get work, he moved to Charleston, South Carolina, to work for the *Charleston Courier*, translating Spanish documents as they arrived in port.

In 1823, he went back to New York and wrote for the *Mercantile Advertiser*. He assumed ownership of the *New York Courier*, but within a few months he had returned it to its original owner, unable to turn it into a paying proposition. Bennett then wrote for the *National Advocate* and in 1827 went to Washington as a correspondent for the *New York Enquirer*. In 1829, after the *Enquirer* merged with the *Courier*, Bennett fell out of favor with the new *Courier and Enquirer* publisher and left the paper. In 1832, Bennett tried his hand at publishing once more, but the *New York Globe* failed in a month. From an editorial position in Philadelphia, Bennett then attacked Wall Street bankers as enemies of the people. Returning to New York, he tried to enlist Horace Greeley's backing to start a newspaper, but Greeley turned down the proposition. In the 1840s, Greeley, as editor of the *New York Tribune*, became a competitor of Bennett's.

From the beginning, Bennett had not been popular among the old-line New York editors. He had clashed bitterly with James Watson Webb, publisher of the *Courier and Enquirer*, over the issue of the national bank. Bennett had supported Andrew Jackson's 1832 veto of a congressional resolution to recharter the bank (its charter had been due to expire in 1836) and had accused Webb of accepting political bribes in the form of loans from Nicholas Biddle, the bank's president.

After many attempts at reporting and publishing, Bennett turned to working in his basement office to create a new newspaper, claiming it would support no party. The daily covered Wall Street and attacked its competitors, both old-line newspapers and Benjamin Day's new penny sheet. In August 1835, after an eighteen-day suspension of the paper that was caused by a fire in the printing shop, Bennett invited friends and patrons to stop by with bits of news or advertising, "barring always discoveries in astronomy, which our friends of the *Sun* monopolize."[19] By October, Bennett began to hire help and the twenty columns of the paper included fourteen columns of advertising.

Bennett's florid writing style was put to good use in April 1836, gaining him notoriety and expanded circulation. A young woman by the name of Ellen Jewett was found murdered in a fancy brothel. When Richard P. Robinson, a merchant's clerk, was accused of the hatchet murder, Bennett defended him. The various newspapers in New York disagreed about who was responsible, but the attraction of Bennett's coverage was that he visited the scene of the crime and described the corpse of the beautiful courtesan in detail. Circulation during the stories of the murder varied from 5,000 to 15,000 per day, and Bennett gleefully announced, "We are rapidly taking the wind out of the big-bellied sails of the *Courier and Enquirer* and *Journal of Commerce*." Robinson was acquitted.[20]

Bennett was a truly irreverent man, mocking the social set and attacking other editors. After writing a malicious editorial about James Watson Webb, Bennett was beaten in the street by Webb, an event chronicled by Philip Hone, who was a wealthy merchant and former mayor:

> There is an ill-looking, squinting man called Bennett, formerly connected with Webb in the publication of his paper, who is now the editor of the *Herald*, one of the penny papers which are hawked about the streets by a gang of troublesome, ragged boys, and in which scandal is retailed to all who delight in it, at that moderate price. This man and Webb are now bitter enemies and it was nuts for Bennett to be the organ of Mr. Lynch's late vituperative attack upon Webb, which Bennett introduced in his paper with evident marks of savage exultation. This did not suit Mr. Webb's fiery disposition, so he attacked Bennett in Wall Street yesterday, beat him, and knocked him down.[21]

There were others, in addition to Philip Hone, who considered Bennett a scandalmonger. Bennett's practice of printing news of bankruptcies (one mistake cost him $500 in a libel suit) and his intrusive accounts of exclusive society dinners made him less than popular with the New York social set.

In addition to introducing thorough news coverage of Wall Street and writing florid accounts of murders and social dinners, Bennett made substantial contributions

▼

James Gordon Bennett, Sr. (1795–1872), and James Gordon Bennett, Jr. (1841–1918)

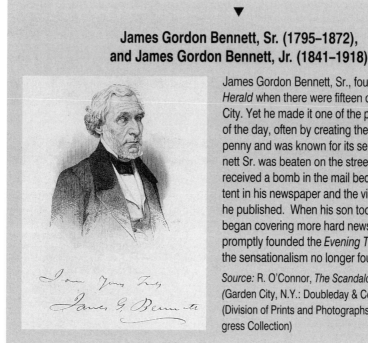

James Gordon Bennett, Sr., founded the *New York Herald* when there were fifteen dailies in New York City. Yet he made it one of the preeminent papers of the day, often by creating the news. It sold for a penny and was known for its sensationalism. Bennett Sr. was beaten on the street and once even received a bomb in the mail because of the content in his newspaper and the violent era in which he published. When his son took over, the *Herald* began covering more hard news items. Bennett Jr. promptly founded the *Evening Telegram* to cover the sensationalism no longer found in the *Herald*.

Source: R. O'Connor, *The Scandalous Mr. Bennett* (Garden City, N.Y.: Doubleday & Company, Inc., 1962). (Division of Prints and Photographs, Library of Congress Collection)

to the field of news gathering. After returning from a European trip in 1837, Bennett hired six correspondents to cover Europe and put correspondents in the field in Mexico, Texas, and Canada. He, like the *Sun* editors, organized a ship news service and contracted with light sailing craft to collect news from foreign ship captains before they landed in U.S. harbors. He also covered court news and experimented with the use of illustrations, primarily in the form of maps and drawings. In 1839, he began printing religious news. His coverage of church conferences was regarded as near sacrilege. Bennett emphasized a personal Christianity and attacked the "new Protestantism that seemed to equate true Christianity with money and empire."[22] Bennett wrote that real Christianity did not consist "in believing the dogmas of any church."[23]

New York society took out its anger on Bennett by organizing a moral war against him in 1840, the same year he was married. The war ostensibly was organized against his attack on prudish language. Words such as *pants, legs, shirts,* and *trousers* were considered forbidden, and Bennett campaigned against what he thought represented insanity of speech. The editor rubbed it in thoroughly: "Petticoats—petticoats—petticoats—petticoats—there—you fastidious fools, vent your mawkishness on that."[24] Philip Hone wrote in his diary, "The evil has reached a pitch of enormity which renders further forbearance criminal, and a simultaneous attack is made upon the libellous paper, its editor, and those who, from fear or a fellow-feeling, support it."[25] A boycott was organized to force hotels and clubs to dispose

▼

Bennett's Marriage Announcement

To the Readers of the Herald—Declaration of Love—Caught at Last—Going to Be Married— New Movement in Civilization.—I am going to be married in a few days. The weather is so beautiful; times are getting so good; the prospects of political and moral reform so auspicious, that I cannot resist the divine instinct of honest nature any longer; so I am going to be married to one of the most splendid women in intellect, in heart, in soul, in property, in person, in manner, that I have yet seen in the course of my interesting pilgrimage through human life.

—James Gordon Bennett, *New York Herald*, June 1, 1840

of Bennett's paper, but circulation continued to hold and in 1840 combined circulation of the daily, a weekly edition, and extras reached 51,000.[26]

In 1841, when President John Tyler assumed office, Bennett decided to open a Washington bureau. In Washington, however, he encountered resistance from Senate leaders and the Washington press. The *Herald*'s correspondents were excluded from the Senate floor on the basis of an old rule that allowed only reporters of local papers to cover the Senate. Bennett responded with a bitter attack:

> It is caused by the selfish and malignant influence of the Washington newspapers, in order to maintain a monopoly of Washington news, and to rob the public treasury, under the color of public printing, in order to gratify their extravagant habits of life.[27]

Bennett noted that the *Washington Globe* was receiving $90,000 and the *Madisonian* $330,000 from the public treasury for printing contracts. A third Washington paper, the *National Intelligencer*, also received government printing contracts. Bennett did not win his challenge immediately, however, and his correspondents were forced to develop inside sources.

In his continuous effort to speed up the collection and delivery of news, Bennett was delighted with the introduction of the telegraph. "What has become of space?" he asked in 1844, after "What Hath God Wrought?" was telegraphed from Washington to Baltimore. "The magnetic telegraph at Washington has totally annihilated what there was left of [space] by steam and locomotives and steamships."[28] In January of 1845, in the midst of the Mexican War, Bennett established a courier system between New Orleans and New York to convey exchanges between the *Herald* and New Orleans. His courier system was faster than the U.S. mails, and he was forced to stop it under a law prohibiting the moving of mail by private means. Bennett was the only New York editor to send correspondents to Mexico. Two New Orleans newspapers, the *Picayune* and the *Delta*, also had correspondents in Mexico.

The personal war on Bennett continued. In 1850, two men who opposed his choice of mayor beat him with whips. A package containing a bomb was delivered to his office.

Libel suits also continued. Promoters sued him for his criticism of an opera company; despite appeals and a reversal, he was found liable and paid $6,000 in damages.

By the 1850s, however, the *Herald* was an established New York institution. Politicians and businessmen alike feared Bennett's power coupled with his apparent southern sympathies and his influence in England. The paper continued to be a fierce competitor to other New York sheets through the years prior to and during the Civil War.

Reasons for Development

Historians have argued a variety of causes for the development of the penny press. Until recently, standard explanations focused on (1) an expanding literate and urban population, (2) the development of technology to support mass circulations, and (3) the brilliance of individual editors. Another explanation, advanced by Walter Lippmann, a prominent journalist during the 1920s and an early media theorist, assumed that the penny press emerged in the context of the natural and inevitable growth and progress of the newspaper industry. Recently, sociologists and historians have begun to search for new explanations. Sociologist Michael Schudson, for example, has written that the penny press developed within the political context of Jacksonian democracy and an expansion of individual rights. Others have regarded it as a commercial development, a product for which the times were right as U.S. manufacturing and commercial development made possible an advertising-based newspaper product. Dan Schiller has argued that rather than appealing to an upwardly mobile middle class, the penny press appealed to a downwardly mobile artisan class. Communications historians Arthur Kaul and Joseph McKerns have linked the development of the penny press to economic and ideological cycles in American life. David Mindich described the evolution of the penny press as a response to Jacksonian violence.

Schudson effectively eliminated expanded technology and literacy as the sole causes for the development of a mass press. Although penny newspapers took advantage of the new technology and, indeed, often supported inventors, the papers existed before the technological developments were in place. The first edition of the *New York Sun* was printed on a flatbed, hand-run press making two hundred impressions an hour. Until 1800, the wooden, hand-powered press had been the standard press in use. It was replaced by an iron press, which was easier to operate and produced better-quality prints. The addition of steam power and the development of the cylinder press were introduced in varying degrees after the turn of the twentieth century.

Frederick Koenig invented a steam press that was first used in England, and by the 1840s steam presses dominated the American big newspaper market. The first rotary press was the "Hoe-Type Revolving Machine," first used by a newspaper when the *Philadelphia Public Ledger* put one of these new presses into service in 1847. Further improvements in the 1850s and 1860s occurred with the adaptation of "stereotyping," or the use of a paper mat made from an impression in order to create cylindrical molds.[29] Another major development came with an improvement by N. L. Robert in the process used to make paper from rags. Robert's Fourdrinier paper-

Figure 5–3 The hand press and hand-set type were in common use in many parts of the country in 1850, despite the introduction of more sophisticated technology. (State Historical Society of Wisconsin)

making machine was first imported to the United States in 1827. Wood pulp as the raw product for paper would not be used in the United States until 1866.[30]

Other technological advances occurred in the transportation system, facilitating the collection and distribution of news. In 1830, the United States had 23 miles of railroad; by 1840, it had 3,000 miles; and by the time of the Civil War, 30,000 miles of track were in place. The telegraph was another important factor in news development. From 16,735 miles of telegraph line in 1852, the wires extended to 110,727 miles in 1880 and to 237,990 in 1902.[31]

Although technology was a critical factor during the nineteenth century in the expansion of the newspaper press, its impact came too late to explain the development of the penny press.

Schudson's argument negating expanded literacy as a primary cause in the development centered on the fact that equally advanced literate societies such as Sweden and Scotland did not produce a penny press. As a singular cause, expanded literacy does not explain the development of the penny press. However, an expanding population—especially such as that in New York at the time—may have contributed to the larger circulations common to the penny press. Certainly, the population of the country was increasing. About 3 million more people lived in the United States than had been there in 1820, representing an increase of about one-third across the decade. The increase, however, represented steady growth, not a departure from the norm. In 1830, 91.2 percent of the population was still rural. By 1840, that figure dropped only 2 percent. The growth in New York did surpass national averages: From 1830 to 1840, New York's population doubled, a rate of growth not equaled by any other city. Daniel Schiller suggested it was the composition of the nation's growing population, rather than the quantity itself, that had the major impact on the development of the penny press.

A third argument posed for the development of penny newspapers is that of inevitability. In 1931, Walter Lippmann suggested that "any nation's press will naturally pass through stages of development."[32] Lippmann described four stages: (1) a monopoly controlled by the government, (2) a press controlled by political parties, (3) a commercially supported press, and (4) a professional press in which newspapers institutionalize "trained intelligence." Lippmann claimed that at the last stage newspapers will divorce themselves from the changing tastes and prejudices of the public itself. What Lippmann did was to study the developments of American newspapers and from these developments, as he viewed them, construct a "natural" or "inevitable" development of all newspapers. Comparative studies have shown that such development is *not* inevitable in all societies.

After debunking the arguments of literacy, technology, and natural tendency, Schudson offered his own explanation of the development of the penny press. He suggested that it developed in the context of Jacksonian Democracy, or the Age of Egalitarianism, which he defined as a period in which the skilled craftsmen, the small and large merchants, and tradesmen were able to wield influence in politics and business. This rise of an urban middle class, Schudson wrote, accounted for the qualities of the penny press—relative independence from political parties; low price; high circulation; and an emphasis on news, timeliness, and sensation.[33]

The commercial aspect of egalitarianism should not be forgotten. James Murphy, commenting on the expansion of the press in the early nineteenth century, said that the "accessible masses of buyers and advertisers and their never-ending sources of story ideas, formed a natural newspaper market." The market, Murphy emphasized, was a greater social equalizer than was politics.[34] However, it was not until several decades after the start of the penny press that expanded advertising made its major impact.

Schiller, in his quest for determining the origins of objectivity in the U.S. press, claimed that the major public for the penny papers were the artisans and mechanics of New York City.[35] Rather than a responding, upwardly mobile, urban middle class purchasing the penny newspaper, Schiller claimed that a downwardly mobile artisan class, shouting its last battle cry, was the buying group. An expanding and changing economy, beginning to move toward national distribution, and a developing transportation system were forcing local artisans to compete with the producers of out-of-town goods. The same steamship that allowed James Gordon Bennett to deliver news more quickly upset the familiar trading patterns within cities and regions. Even the law was changing in regard to workers, with more attention focused on the promotion of business and less on the protection of the laborer. The primary function of law became that of protecting commerce and maintaining law and order. The maintenance of order had its biggest impact on the artisans and mechanics, whose daily lives became suspect. Vagrancy, drunkenness, and other behaviors were not to be tolerated.

In the late 1820s and 1830s, a burgeoning labor press developed in New York, with newspapers such as the *Mechanics' Press* and the *Workingman's Advocate* asking questions about "equality for all," about the politically affiliated press, and about the status of working people in relation to the law. However vigorous it was, the labor press was not able to sustain itself through the depression of 1837, which put nearly 50,000 New Yorkers out of work and left one-third of the labor force unemployed. During that period, the penny press "claimed to speak alike to the politicized and the less-politicized, the journeyman and the merchant," and "appropriated and softened the anger of the labor press into a blustery rhetoric of equal rights, enlightenment, and political independence."[36]

The penny papers flaunted their independence, openly admitted their conversion from politics to business as a source of income, and often supported tradesmen and the right of workers to organize. Schiller argued that focusing on crime news, rather than serving up the sensationalism a mass public desired, was designed to protect the rights of workers and to assure that justice would be meted out equally. The penny press

> focused not only on the integrity of the state but also on the unequal effect of social class on the political nation and, specifically, in the law. The cheap papers had only to station reporters at the police courts to pick through a constant flow of cases that might be used to reveal and dramatize the status of the citizenry's rights.[37]

During the Robinson–Jewett murder case, for example, the penny papers railed against the privileged of the city and asked whether, for the right amount of money, an acquittal could be purchased. Pertinent to this case, Schiller pointed out, was another case at the time, heard by the same judge as the Robinson proceedings, which resulted in the conviction of twenty journeyman tailors for their part in a "conspiracy" to resist wage deductions. The explanation, Schiller argued, for the boisterous crowd at the Robinson hearing was not "in some abstract 'sensationalism,' but in the journeymen's rage against unequal justice, which barred their union as a conspiracy but allowed their masters to combine to lower wages."[38]

The penny papers, however, did not define their major role as taking up the cause of labor. After the depression of 1837 and the decline of the labor press, the penny papers became freer to move into the circles of respectability. Although maintaining a position that championed equality of opportunity and the public good, the penny papers also adhered to the principles of laissez-faire economics and the rights of property. This contradictory philosophy enabled penny papers to rationalize their support of equality for all under the law while at the same time denying the laborer the right to unionize and to strike against employers. Such a position led the newspapers to more conservative stances and provided them with a solid financial base from which to operate.

Kaul and McKerns viewed the emergence of the penny press within the larger context of developing journalistic ethics and ideology in a capitalistic social structure, claiming that "American capitalism has generated cyclical 'long waves' of qualitative structural change in the economy of journalism, prompting economic reconstruction and ideological revitalization in response to life-threatening crises."[39] The authors described a *long wave* as a forty-to-sixty-year period comprised of a time of vigorous growth and expansion followed by a time of sustained stagnation and contraction. For example, a period of expansion occurred from the 1780s to the mid-1820s, followed by a period of contraction from the mid-1820s to the mid-1840s, the period in which the penny press developed. The penny papers, they contended, represented a new medium that radically shifted the "economic infrastructure of newspapers from political patronage to marketplace competition."

During a phase of economic expansion that occurred as the century progressed, however, the size and complexity of newspapers increased and competition intensified, culminating in great newspaper wars like those William Randolph Hearst and Joseph Pulitzer waged in the 1890s. Dependence on the marketplace "produced a formidable turn-of-the-century public backlash that further threatened newspapers' marketplace existence." In an attempt to deal with the economic crisis of the 1830s, newspaper editors resorted to new commercial strategies (dependence on advertising) and to new ideologies (claims to political independence). This American tendency to "translate economic crises into moral terms, commercial strategies into professional ideologies," wrote Kaul and McKerns, "mystifies the linkage of culture to economics." In other words, the American desire to intertwine commercial interest and moral obligation obscures the facts for those of us who look to history to help explain the present.

Most recently, David Mindich described the evolution of the penny press and the events such as Webb's beating of editor James Gordon Bennett within the context of the Jacksonian period as one of the most violent in American history. Mindich argues that President Andrew Jackson personified violence. A hero of the War of 1812, Jackson was known as an unrelenting commander. In 1818, he led an expedition through Florida, which was then owned by the Spanish, and attacked countless Seminole Native Americans without permission from superiors. Forms of violence, such as slavery and Native American "removal," was at its height during the Jacksonian era. Street and mob violence peaked between 1832 and 1837. Philip Hone, who had chronicled Webb's beating of Bennett, called 1834 the "mob year."

Historians differ in their explanations for the violence. Richard Hofstadter called the violence a symptom of a "growing pathology of a nation growing at a speed that defied control, governed by an ineffective leadership." Carl Prince argued that for the first time in the United States, people in urban centers viewed their interests as radically different from that of their neighbors.

In this atmosphere, Mindich argued, the penny press detached itself from "alliances." Party papers had a link to party; penny papers had a link to no persons other than their owners and to a commercial class that advertised in them. Mindich noted that the penny press created a detached forum that appealed to audiences across class and political interests.

> For if we accept Prince's notion that the mid-1830s were violent because for the first time in the nineteenth century neighbors felt that their interests were incompatible, we are struck by the pennies' creation of an opposite paradigm: that neighbors could transcend party and share interests, specifically the interest in buying a detached and nonpartisan paper. The pennies, in replacing divisive ideology and violence with a detached nonpartisanship, had discovered a sound business practice.[40]

Conclusion

The penny press represented a transition from limited-circulation newspapers designed primarily for a commercial and political elite to newspapers with large circulations aimed at expanding audiences, including the middle class and possibly the downwardly mobile artisan class. Publishers of penny newspapers were entrepreneurial businessmen, much like colonial printers, and were not tied by finances to partisan politics as were some editors of the early national period.

During the 1830s, as products became available for distribution, editors relied more heavily on institutional advertising to support their newspapers. Advertising in the press moved away from being a device for subscribers to make simple announcements to a mechanism for developing manufacturers to promote their wares.

Although the content of the press displayed significant continuity with the past, changes were evident, particularly in reporter-originated stories. Editors paid reporters to cover the police court and to develop stories that would boost circulations. Editors focused on expanded news gathering, the development of paid staff, and the organization of cooperative news gathering. The coverage of Washington by New York newspapers challenged the *National Intelligencer*'s monopoly on congressional news.

The penny press emerged during a period of political rhetoric that endorsed egalitarianism. Shifting work and labor patterns created new audiences among the working classes, whereas technology enabled circulations to expand, and the development of manufacturing created a new type of advertising to support newspapers independently of party coffers.

Endnotes

1. Michael Schudson, *Discovering the News* (New York: Basic Books, Inc., 1978), p. 16.

2. Alfred McClung Lee, in *The Daily Newspaper in America* (New York: Macmillan, 1937), p. 730, estimates that in 1830 the eleven newspapers in New York circulated to

16,000 people. For a description of the commercial qualities of newspapers prior to the penny press as well as for a description of early penny newspapers and expansion after 1837, see Alexander Saxton, "Problems of Class and Race in the Origins of the Mass

Circulation Press," *American Quarterly* 36:2 (Summer, 1984), pp. 211–34.

3. Schudson, *Discovering the News*, p. 18.

4. Standard histories such as those already cited in this book tend to describe the 1830s as a major breaking point. Recent research, including Donald Lewis Shaw "At the Crossroads: Change and Continuity in American Press News 1820–1860," *Journalism History* 8:2 (Summer, 1981), pp. 38–50, notes that the New York journalistic world did not represent an accurate picture of the United States press as a whole.

5. Cited in Lee, *The Daily Newspaper in America*, p. 181.

6. Lee, *Daily Newspaper in America*, p. 58.

7. Lee, *Daily Newspaper in America*, pp. 316, 317.

8. Schudson, *Discovering the News*, pp. 22, 23.

9. Shaw, "At the Crossroads," pp. 38–50.

10. Much of the information about the *New York Sun* is taken from Frank M. O'Brien, *The Story of the* Sun (New York: George H. Doran, 1918). The story of the beginning of the *Sun* appears on page 22.

11. The *New York Sun*, September 3, 1833, p. 1.

12. O'Brien, *Story of the* Sun, p. 50.

13. Phil Cohan, "Heavenly Hoax," *Air and Space*, May 1986, pp. 87–95.

14. O'Brien, *Story of the* Sun, p. 66.

15. The story of the moon hoax is detailed in O'Brien, *Story of the* Sun, pp. 68–72.

16. Cohan, "Heavenly Hoax," p. 94.

17. Dan Schiller, *Objectivity and the News: The Public and the Rise of Commercial Journalism* (Philadelphia: University of Pennsylvania Press, 1981).

18. Gerald W. Johnson, Frank R. Kent, H. L. Mencken, and Hamilton Owens, *The Sunpapers of Baltimore* (New York: Alfred A. Knopf, 1937), pp. 34–37.

19. Don Carlos Seitz, *The James Gordon Bennetts—Father & Son, Proprietors of the New York Herald* (New York: Beekman Publishers, 1974; reprinted from Bobbs-Merrill, 1928), p. 44. See also James L. Crouthamel, *Bennett's* New York Herald *and the Rise of the Popular Press* (Syracuse, N.Y.: Syracuse University Press, 1989).

20. Cited in Seitz, *The James Gordon Bennetts*, p. 47.

21. From *The Diary of Philip Hone, 1828–1851*, cited in Seitz, *The James Gordon Bennetts*, p. 49.

22. Judith Buddenbaum, "The Religion Journalism of James Gordon Bennett," unpublished paper presented to the History Division of the Association for Education in Journalism and Mass Communication, Norman, Oklahoma, 1986.

23. James Gordon Bennett, "Religion and Salvation," *New York Herald*, December 14, 1838, p. 2, cited in Buddenbaum, "Religion Journalism."

24. Cited in Seitz, *The James Gordon Bennetts*, p. 74.

25. Hone, cited in Seitz, p. 76.

26. Seitz, *James Gordon Bennetts*, p. 77.

27. Cited in Seitz, *James Gordon Bennetts*, p. 90.

28. Cited in Seitz, *James Gordon Bennetts*, p. 120.

29. Stereotyping was brought to the United States as early as 1811 or 1812 by type founders who learned the process in England. The first book printed from stereotype in the United States was in 1813, and the process was used by the New York Bible Society long before newspapers adapted the technique. See David Paul Nord, "The Evangelical Origins of Mass Media in America, 1815–1835," *Journalism Monographs* 88 (Columbia, S.C.: Association for Education in Journalism and Mass Communication, 1984), pp. 8–9.

30. Schudson, *Discovering the News*, p. 32.

31. Lee, *Daily Newspaper in America*, p. 67.

32. Walter Lippmann, "Two Revolutions in the American Press," *Yale Review* 20 (March, 1931), p. 440, cited in Schudson, *Discovering the News*, p. 39–40.

33. Schudson, *Discovering the News*, pp. 49–50.

34. James Murphy, "Tabloids as an Urban Response," in Catherine L. Covert and John D. Stevens, eds., *Mass Media between the Wars* (Syracuse, N.Y.: Syracuse University Press, 1984), p. 57.

35. Schiller, *Objectivity and the News*, p. 17.

36. Schiller, *Objectivity and the News*, p. 46.

37. Schiller, *Objectivity and the News*, p. 57. See also Alexander Saxton, "Problems of Class and Race in the Origins of the Mass Circulation Press," *American Quarterly* 36 (Summer, 1984), pp. 211–34.

38. Schiller, *Objectivity and the News*, p. 63. For a further analysis of the relationship of the penny press to the cities, see John D. Stevens, S*ensationalism and the New York Press* (New York: Columbia University Press, 1991).

39. Arthur J. Kaul and Joseph P. McKerns, "Long Waves and Journalism Ideology in America, 1835–1985," unpublished paper presented to Association for Education in Journalism and Mass Communication, Memphis, Tenn., August 1985, pp. 5–6. See also David L. Eason, "Review Essay: The New Social History of the Newspaper," *Communication Research* 11 (January, 1984), pp. 141–51; Arthur J. Kaul and Joseph P. McKerns, "The Dialectic Ecology of the Newspaper," *Critical Studies*

in Mass Communication 2 (1985), pp. 217–33; and John C. Nerone, "The Mythology of the Penny Press," *Critical Studies in Mass Communication* 4 (1987), pp. 376–404.

40. See David Mindich, *Just the Facts: How "Objectivity Came to Define American Journalism,"* (New York: New York University Press, 1998). For interpretations of violence during the Jacksonian era, see Richard Hofstadter and Michael Wallace, *American Violence: A Documentary History* (New York: Knopf, 1970); and Carl Prince, "The Great 'Riot Year': Jacksonian Democracy and Patterns of Violence in 1834," *Journal of the Early Republic* 5 (Spring, 1985), pp. 1–19.

FIRST TELEGRAPH LINE
CONSTRUCTED.

The building of the telegraph broke the first link between transportation and communication. Now news could be transported to a home office, thereby speeding the delivery of news to the reader. (Division of Prints and Photographs, Library of Congress Collection)

PART 2 | *Media in an Expanding Nation*

▼

During the early nineteenth century, communication remained tied to transportation, which determined how fast news could be collected and distributed. The telegraph, introduced in the mid-1840s, eliminated geographical barriers and thus produced a new environment for the press.

In 1861, legislative and social structures could no longer ameliorate the conflicts of the nation, and on April 12 the Palmetto Guard of South Carolina fired on Fort Sumter. The press scrambled to cover the various activities of the war and, utilizing technology in new ways, developed new methods of covering the news. The southern press, cut off from its main source of news, the Associated Press, developed its own press organization and altered its traditional approach to reporting. Once more the press debated its relationship to government and the social structure of which it was a part.

During the last half of the nineteenth century and the early years of the twentieth century, newspapers and the periodical press became intertwined with a dramatically changing society experiencing the effects of rapid modernization. First, the role of business grew increasingly important as corporations formed to raise capital for large-scale enterprises—creating national markets, traversing the land with railroad tracks, and converting a largely agrarian society into an urban, national market economy. The political debate of the early half of the nineteenth century had centered on the relationship between local and national government. Although that debate was not resolved, after 1870 the focus shifted to the relationship between government and business. Only the national government could effectively respond to the full development of the telegraph and railroad, technological advancements that eliminated geographical boundaries and spanned many local governmental entities. Secondly, the rapid urbanization that accompanied change during the period spawned the growth of huge cities, which posed new questions for local governments regarding city utilities, sanitation, and transportation.

As mass production quickly replaced artisan craftsmanship, a third major issue confronting society was the growing perception of capital and labor as separate classes. Critics of rapid modernization wondered whether the traditional values of democracy and social mobility could be retained in a society in which commercial values dominated, wealth became more concentrated, and social stratification grew increasingly rigid. Critics also feared that massive immigration from Europe would bring to the United States a class-oriented view of labor. Cultural chaos and corruption typified the negative side of modernization, just as progress and wealth symbolized growth and expansion during the era that Mark Twain labeled "the Gilded Age."

Within this rapidly modernizing society, the newspaper and periodical press developed as large business institutions, although corporate or chain ownership did not expand as quickly as in other industries. Rapid urbanization lent increasing credibility to metropolitan editors, whose outlook was viewed as cosmopolitan rather than local as they advocated progress and used new technologies to advance their own interests. Newspapers became bigger, more costly to start and to produce, and almost totally reliant on commercial advertising. Although political parties had influenced newspapers during the early half of the century, commercial interests transformed the press of the Gilded Age. Favorable postal legislation, new technology, national advertising, and a growing number of writers contributed to a rapidly expanding magazine industry. Magazines appealed to elite interests, to women consumers, and, toward the end of the nineteenth century, to the middle classes interested in reform.

As businessmen, newspaper editors declared their independence from political parties and sought to influence government through the American Newspaper Publishers Association. Publishers cooperated with the U.S. Post Office to achieve favorable postal legislation in Congress. They also sought to control activities involving the organization of labor within the printing shops of newspapers. The Associated Press, through monopolistic agreements with Western Union, dominated the national and international news market. Reporters had little bargaining power over wages and time schedules, and they sought to rationalize their own positions. Although they identified themselves as professionals, their status was more similar to that of laborers.

Newspaper publishers, who identified strongly with local business, frequently formed coalitions with associations or political groups to attack the problems of the metropolis. Although the publishers claimed to be antagonistic to monopolies, at the same time they benefited from the public relations efforts of the railroad companies that issued free travel passes to publishers or from the efforts of others who sought favor with local publishers.

Newspapers celebrated city life and the diversity of urban populations as well as exposed the problems of the city such as corruption and business exploitation. Some publishers created strikingly innovative layouts, complete with photographs and blaring headlines, striving for a dramatic expression of the teeming metropolis. Such sensational treatment offended more traditional newspaper readers, who sought refuge in newspapers with an orientation toward information. Readers found two trends in content. Some newspapers reflected the exuberance of growth and progress, while the others confronted the new order with a mass of rational explanations.

The celebration of progress was not without trauma, and reform groups flourished during the period, fighting partly for what they viewed as the traditional values of early-nineteenth-century democracy and partly for the improved status of groups whose interests had been ignored or denied. Women, African Americans, and agrarian radicals developed their own presses to share information not regarded as "news" by the mass press, to build a sense of community, and to legitimize their organizations. ▼

CHAPTER 6

Expansion Unifies and Divides

▼

Transportation and communication went hand-in-hand with the development of an information system for the new nation. As the nation expanded—across the Alleghenies, onto the plains, into southwest territories, and to the northwest—express mail services, telegraph lines, and railroad tracks assisted the development of towns, the dissemination of market news, the spread of ideologies, and the distribution of information from home states to those pioneers who braved the unknown. With the advent of the telegraph, news and information could surpass the speed of transportation. Transportation and technology affected not only the speed of collection and delivery, but content and language as well.

As the nation expanded, so did the styles and content of its publications. The eastern dailies developed new formats evolving from the penny press. Frontier newspapers, including those published in Spanish, commented editorially on U.S. dominance over formerly Mexican territories, slavery, commercial development, and other issues of interest to those already occupying western lands and to new settlers. Often using old technology imported from the East, frontier newspapers were conceived both as business propositions and as ideological tools.

Despite the technological advances of the telegraph and the railroad, oral culture and the lecture circuit continued as an important part of the information system, not only along the eastern seaboard but in the newly expanding cities and towns of the West. The public lecture replaced the sermon as the primary form of public discourse and was widely extolled as a form of participation in democracy. ▼

Transportation and Communication

Transportation—routes and speed—dictated the gathering and dissemination—and to some extent, the content—of news prior to the development of telegraphy in 1844. During the colonial period, the colonies behaved almost like small city-states in which issues were resolved through public discussion. With the adoption of the Constitution, the states sought to achieve democracy in spite of geography—through communication.[1] For many years, an inadequate postal system hampered communication among colonies and later among states. Feeble attempts at a postal system had been made as early as 1692, and New York and Massachusetts initiated Postal Service between the two states and New Hampshire before 1693. Southern colonies had been slower to develop services; they opposed expanding communication routes with the northern colonies because they regarded Bostonians as troublemakers, agitating against England, and because building such routes was an expensive undertaking. Not until the 1730s did the southern colonies begin to have regular postal delivery. As the country expanded, the postal system became integral to spreading information westward, and it remained the key factor in communication dissemination until the invention and widespread use of the telegraph.

Editors continuously faced transportation problems in collecting news. In the 1830s and 1840s, James Gordon Bennett and other editors experimented with the use of pigeons, sailing craft, and other forms of transportation in order to gather news quickly from Washington and from abroad. Transportation routes determined news content as well. In a study of South Carolina newspapers, Gerald Baldasty wrote that during the first third of the nineteenth century, South Carolina editors depended heavily on the Washington newspapers for news from the capitol. Much of their news came from the *National Intelligencer*, whether or not the South Carolina editors agreed with the views expressed in that Washington paper. However, by the late 1840s, with the development of the telegraph, "the Washington political press provided only a small fraction of national political news to South Carolina papers."[2] While the telegraph broke the transportation link in news collection, publishers still relied

Figure 6–1   This masthead appeared in 1865 on the *Telegrapher,* the newspaper published by The National Telegraphic Union. (Division of Prints and Photographs, Library of Congress Collection)

on transportation for delivering the newspaper. Papers delivered close to home could be carried by horse and rider. Delivery to distant addresses—specifically by editors such as Horace Greeley who sought to expand the circulation of the weekly *Tribune* into the hinterlands—was made possible by postal routes and the railroad.

Postal Express

Newspaper editors both helped initiate postal services and benefited greatly by them. The first postal express, a mail service that traveled faster than ordinary post, was developed in 1825. Several such expresses operated between 1825 and 1861. From the beginning, the U.S. Postal Service, as well as private express services, granted newspapers special privileges. Newspaper postage rates were less expensive than postage rates for other customers, and editors exchanged newspapers at no charge through the mails. This magnanimous gesture was prompted not solely by a philosophical attitude about the importance of newspapers but rather by a commercial

FRANK LESLIE'S ILLUSTRATED NEWSPAPER.   [Oct· 23, 1858.

THE OVERLAND MAIL—THE START FROM THE EASTERN SIDE.

Figure 6–2   The overland mail—the start from the eastern side. Wood engraving. (*Frank Leslie's Illustrated Newspaper*, October 23, 1858)

need. Certain market information acquired by one New England merchant, for example, could provide a definite advantage for that merchant in timing the purchase of southern cotton to be sold to England. That advantage could be eliminated only if all merchants had equal access to market information. The 1825 Express, which operated between Boston, Massachusetts, and Augusta, Georgia, was designed to equalize that kind of information.3

The development of improved mail transportation was accomplished through a blend of public and private enterprise. Between January 14 and February 1 of 1833, David Hale and Gerard Hallock, owners of the *New York Journal of Commerce*, established an express from Philadelphia to New York. Riders would pick up news from Washington and the southern states from the mail in Philadelphia and then forward it to New York by private post rider, beating the *Journal*'s competitors by a day. The post office, embarrassed at being beaten at its own game and wanting to create commercial balance, established its own express on January 31, 1833. In response, the *Journal* moved its express so that it operated from Washington to Philadelphia, passing along its material to the official post office express in Philadelphia and thereby allowing the *Journal* to still beat its competitors by a day. Other New York papers complained and the postmaster general ordered the Philadelphia mail riders not to accept any material from the *Journal*'s Washington express. The *Journal* then attempted an express from Washington to New York, carrying mail between February 12 and March 5 of 1833. When called before a Senate committee, editor Hale testified that although his express was an expensive proposition at $7,500 a month, it was still less expensive to operate than the government's.

The Post Office Act of July 2, 1836, authorized the first nationwide express service. Complaining New York editors spurred passage of the act, as did Postmaster General Amos Kendall, a Kentuckian, who wanted to free readers from their dependence on eastern dailies. As privileged customers, newspaper editors sent digests and proofs free, while one thin sheet of express mail shipped up to thirty miles cost eighteen cents. During the next few years, various routes were operated, including routes from New York to New Orleans, from New York to Washington—with stops in Philadelphia and Baltimore—and from Washington to New Orleans—with stops in Richmond, Columbia, Charleston, Mobile, and Montgomery. Most express routes cut regular mail times in half. For example, in 1835, regular mail traveled from New York to Washington in thirty-two hours; in 1837, by express, the same mail reached its destination in twenty-four hours. In 1839, however, regular mail had speeded up enough that expresses lost their advantage and were discontinued.4

Private express companies competed at times with the Postal Service and at other times operated routes where the post office did not operate. They usually carried newspapers free in return for free advertising.

The Mexican War brought new demands for fast mail service, and from January to March of 1845, James Gordon Bennett operated an express to transport war news from New Orleans to New York. Postmaster General Charles Wickliffe threatened to arrest the New Orleans newspaper cooperating with Bennett for carrying private mail on public postal roads. Probably the most famous private express was the Western Pony Express, which operated during 1860 and 1861. For eighteen months the company carried mail between St. Joseph, Missouri, and San Francisco, California. Before the arrival of the Pony Express, news traveled largely by ship down the Atlantic, to the Isthmus of Panama, then by horse or rail to the Pacific Coast, and by steamers to California towns.

In 1841, the news of President William Henry Harrison's death took three months and twenty days to reach Los Angeles.[5] The first California newspaper, the *Californian*, appeared in 1846, and twelve years later, eighty-nine newspapers and periodicals, including nineteen dailies, published regularly. News still moved slowly, taking twenty-three to twenty-six days to arrive by ship and twenty-two days to arrive overland from St. Louis. In 1860, Pony Express riders cut this time in half by carrying mail 1,900 miles from St. Joseph, Missouri, to Sacramento, California, in about ten days.[6] Newspapers used the expensive Pony Express for bulletin-style information, following it up a few days later with more complete information acquired through the less expensive regular mail routes. For example, Colorado's *Rocky Mountain News* carried a short report on Lincoln's inaugural address, acquired through the express; then the full text was received in a later mailing. Newspapers in Salt Lake City formed a cooperative to jointly use news arriving by Pony Express, thereby cutting their costs.

Telegraph: Technological and Cultural Change

When Samuel Morse opened the nation's first telegraph line on May 24, 1844, with the searing question, "What hath God wrought?" he also opened the modern era of communications, for the first time separating communication from the limits of

▼

Samuel Morse (1791–1872)

Most people know Samuel Morse invented the telegraph, but few are aware of his talents in other areas. Admitted to Yale University at the age of fourteen, he made money by creating portraits. "I employ my leisure time in painting. I have a large number of persons engaged already to be drawn on ivory. . . . My price is five dollars for a miniature on ivory, and I have engaged three or four at that price," Morse once wrote. After graduating, Morse studied under Washington Allston, one of the great artists in America before moving on and creating the machine that made him famous.

Source: S. I. Prime, *The Life of Samuel F. B. Morse* (New York: Arno Press, 1974). (*Photo:* Division of Prints and Photographs, Library of Congress Collection)

geography and transportation.7 The introduction of the technology created fear of the technology itself as well as anticipation of its possibilities. "What might the tele-graph," wondered the nation's populace, "augur for thought, politics, commerce, the press, and the moral life" of the nation?8 Fear was directed at the electrical lines them-selves, and in 1844, when Ezra Cornell was putting in place experimental lines, he was forced to hire an eminent professor to assure the public that there was no dan-ger to their safety.

This fear was outweighed, however, by the expectations of entrepreneurs, who marveled at the possibility of instantaneous communication between the West and the cities of the East. The Reverend Ezra Gannett told his Boston congregation that electricity was both "the swift-winged messenger of destruction" as well as the "vital energy of material creation." Others predicted that the telegraph would link men by a single mind in universal peace and harmony.9 "The telegraph system is invaluable," a business journalist wrote in 1868, "and when the missing links shall have been completed of the great chain that will bring all civilized nations into instantaneous communication with each other, it will also be found to be the most potent of all the means of civilization, and the most effective in breaking down the barriers of evil prejudice and custom that interfere with the universal exchange of commodities."10

After October 1861, with the completion of the transcontinental telegraph, news delivery across the nation was quick and usually reliable. Commemorating the great event on October 24, 1861, the *Sacramento Union* wrote:

> The opening of this line for over 2,000 miles will produce a more marked revolution in the means of transmitting news than has yet occurred in California. The change pro-duced by the establishment of the Pony Express was great; but that produced by the telegraph will prove much greater.11

The telegraph did have a major impact. However, newspapers with limited resources that were off the main telegraph lines still did not have unlimited access to news. When the southern stage route was abandoned at the beginning of the Civil War, the *Los Angeles Star*, for example, found it difficult to obtain news, although a telegraph line linked Los Angeles and San Francisco. The line was often out of order and rates were high.

However, between 1860 and 1862, the Pony Express and the telegraph reduced the time lag between events occurring in the East and news of those events being transmitted to western readers; newspapers used more hard news, made typo-graphical innovations, and became increasingly competitive. Because of high rates, the telegraph resulted in fast but brief accounts of newsworthy events of the Civil War and the politics involved in those events.

Congressional Debate over Control of the Telegraph

Inventor and entrepreneur Samuel Morse tried to interest the government in taking over telegraph lines and preserving them as common carriers of information, but the government refused. Morse had attempted to sell his patent to the U.S. government, because he wanted to avoid uncontrolled speculation. He proposed a plan whereby the U.S. government would buy his patent and license individual companies to build lines. He also proposed that the federal government build a line of its own. Congress subsidized Morse's experimental work but refused to buy him out, despite recommendations in 1845 by the House Ways and Means Committee and the postmaster general. Cave Johnson, postmaster general in 1846, warned that "the evils which the community may suffer or the benefits which individuals may derive from the possession of such an instrument, under the control of private associations or unincorporated companies, not controlled by law, cannot be overestimated."[12] During the early years, many telegraph companies and lines proliferated, but companies with North–South lines suffered greatly during the Civil War, and by 1866 Western Union had a virtual monopoly.

Development of the Associated Press

The origins of the Associated Press (AP) have remained obscure because records are incomplete and historians have been unable to draw a smooth line of development. However, the origins of today's dominant international wire service probably date back to the time when New York editors made various arrangements to share expenses in news gathering. It was the telegraph, however, that accelerated press cooperation. Two press associations developed within a similar time frame in New York State beginning in 1846—one in alliance with the New York, Albany, and Buffalo Telegraph Company that would become the New York State Associated Press, and a second one in New York City. Telegraphic news was available to the newspapers of upper New York state with the building of a successful telegraph line connecting the cities of Buffalo, Syracuse, Oswego, Auburn, Utica, and Rochester. This business corridor was well served by rail and canal, and it linked the metropolitan centers of New York State to the Great Lakes harbors. Telegraph reporters operated independently to sell news to varying papers, but many were unable to afford the high cost of such news. Nevertheless, on February 3, 1846, only a few days after the telegraph line was completed from Utica to Albany, the *Utica Gazette* carried nearly a column of telegraphic news from the state capital, Albany. Editors of several newspapers west of Utica immediately requested subscriptions or exchanges, hoping to gain the advantage of the *Gazette*'s telegraphic news reports. After inquiries by editors, the *Gazette* solicited the support of editors farther to the west to form an association of newspapers for the purpose of hiring a telegraphic reporter in Albany to provide regular news reports. Until the telegraph line was extended farther west, the *Gazette* would express mail proofs of the telegraphic dispatches to other editors. By March 1846, eight newspapers were sharing the cost of a common news dispatch from Albany, and by July 4, the mail link was replaced by completed telegraph wires.[13] The newspapers engaged William Lacy, an employee of the *Albany Argus*, to prepare digests of the New York and Boston papers, to combine them with news from Albany, and to file his reports through the telegraph service. Lacy earned twenty-eight dollars in April 1846 for his efforts, and twelve dollars in June of that year. The New York State AP editors met August 5, 1846, in Utica and proposed a formal arrangement with the telegraph service, offering $72 a week to have it transmit one and one-half hours of news each evening and a brief market report during the day. The final agreement—the result of compromise—indicates that the editors got the news they wanted but at the price of $100 weekly, which they shared equally. They also jointly hired George Snow, a reporter for the *New York Tribune,* as a fifteen-dollar-a-week New York City correspondent. By mid-August, all but three upstate papers belonged to the AP, and the association continued to provide news until 1851, when the papers for a short while purchased news from a New York City agency, Abbot & Winans. By the mid-1850s, however, the New York City AP had recruited the upstate papers away from Abbot & Winans. The upstate papers were separately incorporated in 1867 as the Associated Press of the State of New York and maintained a separate identity in the AP structure until 1897.[14]

The Associated Press of New York City developed through more stages than did the upstate service. The New York City editors fashioned a variety of contracts and agreements on specific routes and for specific types of news, followed by more formal agreements for collecting shared news from the harbors. Of particular interest to the New York editors was news from Halifax, where all foreign ships docked before proceeding to the New York, Boston, or Philadelphia harbors. These agreements evolved into longer-term partnership agreements as the telegraph system expanded. Thus, during 1848 and 1849, stable news gathering operations such as the Harbor News Agreement of 1848 emerged from the intermittent news gathering contracts. The impetus for formalizing agreements came not only from the expansion of telegraph technology but also from the public's overwhelming interest in foreign news, particularly that of the French Revolution. Probably the first major activities of New York City's Associated Press occurred in May 1848, when the *Courier and Enquirer,* the *Sun,* the *Herald,* the *Journal of Commerce,* the *Tribune,* and the *Express* employed a steamer, the *Buena Vista,* to retrieve news from Halifax. The papers also negotiated an arrangement with F. O. Smith's telegraph line to establish a "permanent scheme of rates, line priorities, and rights to the news dispatches as property." The agreement gave the Associated Press exclusive rights to their own dispatches and guaranteed that for $100 for the first 3,000 words, the association could have uninterrupted telegraph transmission of "all the news we may wish to receive" from the telegraph office in Boston, where news from Halifax could be transmitted to New York City. The New York City AP's telegraphic venture was more successful than its employment of the *Buena Vista,* which made three trips to Halifax and was twice beaten by news carried by pigeons. After those three trips, the AP abandoned the express runs but purchased a steamer, which they named the *News-Boy,* to patrol the New York harbor. The *News-Boy* venture lasted only six months. Of the six New York papers involved in the AP, only the *Tribune* did not participate in the *News-Boy* operation. On January 11, 1849, the six newspapers abandoned *News-Boy* in favor of the leased arrangements specified in a formal Harbor News Association agreement.[15]

Similar associations were formed in other cities and regions. In August 1847, a group of southern editors met at Stone Mountain, Georgia, to consider proposals for organizing telegraphic news delivery in the South. This proposal focused on establishing an association of both weeklies and dailies because of the nature of news publishing in the South. Although Georgia's *Macon Telegraph* published a proposal issued at the meeting, no evidence of other activities of such an association has been found. However, it does appear that another association of newspapers, this time in Virginia, developed about this time as well. Nine Boston dailies organized in April 1848 to purchase news from the telegraph company that received messages by steamer in New York. Their agreement was the origin of the Boston Associated Press, later to be enlarged and become the New England Associated Press.

Government's refusal to become involved in telegraphy encouraged the development of competing lines. By May 1850, three competing lines paralleled each other from Boston to Philadelphia, and dual lines competed for business between New York City and Buffalo and between Philadelphia and Washington. While the various regional Associated Press organizations came to dominate news gathering, early telegraphic news gathering was a competitive enterprise engaged in not only by the Associated Press but also by independent enterprises such as that developed by Abbot & Winans. This partnership provided telegraphic news to a variety of newspapers and apparently was created by the telegraph companies themselves.[16] Also providing telegraphic news were independent telegraphic reporters who sold their reports to single newspapers or to groups of papers.

Although the Associated Press at first allowed individual newspapers to make arrangements outside the purview of the AP, increasingly it sought to avoid the costs of competition with agencies such as Abbot & Winans. The search for low costs increasingly led AP to restrict the potential enterprise of its local partners. About 1850, AP hired Alexander Jones as its first general agent. Although he worked as a telegraphic reporter, Jones was also trained as a physician and continued his medical practice during much of his journalistic career. As the AP's general agent, he received and distributed news, paid tolls, employed reporters in major cities, and made copies of information for the press of New York and other cities. The bulk of the news sent was transmitted via telegraph during the late evening hours, so that newspapers would receive their dispatches about 2 A.M. By transmitting in the evening and negotiating for bulk rates, Jones was able to send material at one-third to one-half the regular cost. These early AP reports included legislative summaries from Washington and from New York state's capital, Albany; grain and produce market quotations; marine and harbor shipping news; and short news items. The coverage was gleaned haphazardly, with little systematic effort. AP's one-column news report changed little until the 1850s, when it was expanded by Daniel Craig, AP's second general agent. Craig was a more energetic and ambitious man than Jones had been, and when he replaced Jones in 1851 he sought to eliminate AP's competition and solidify its relationship to the telegraph companies. Craig had been the AP agent in Halifax from 1849 to 1851 and was knowledgeable about AP affairs when he accepted the position of general agent.

Indeed, 1851 was a big year for the AP. That year the *New York Times*, edited by Henry Raymond who had been active in AP affairs as managing editor of the *Courier and Enquirer*, joined the New York AP—becoming the seventh newspaper to join the group. The seven newspapers formed the Telegraphic and General News

Association through a signed agreement. Craig operated on a much more aggressive level than had Jones, and in his first year as general agent he tackled the competitive Abbot & Winans agency while maintaining AP's superiority in getting the news from Halifax. The exclusive agreement that allowed AP to secure such news before anyone else angered competitors, causing Craig to seek protection for the organization by directly leasing telegraph lines, by coercing editors and telegraph operators to cooperate with the AP, and by creating stringent rules to keep editors in line. During 1852 and 1853, a number of small telegraph companies waged war as small capitalistic enterprises fighting for share of market.

Craig also substantially improved the news report as an effort to combat competition. By 1854, the New York AP office had three staff members, correspondents in Liverpool and Halifax, and fifty reporters in various parts of the country. In 1854, Craig circulated a memo to AP agents, noting that the AP wanted all the details that were important—that it wanted only "material facts," not "expressions of opinion." Craig thus began to help define news through important events. Important stories included

> notices of serious Railroad accidents; fires, resulting in large losses of property; ship-wrecks, and other serious maritime accidents; mutinies and piracies; duels; fracases of a serious nature, between individuals distinguished in any way; murders; serious accidents, occurring to individuals well known in the country; movements of the President, or of his cabinet, or of other high Government officers; notices and results of trials of unusual interest; important election news; ship news; notices of proceedings of National, State, political or religious Conventions; extensive robberies; extensive forgeries and swindles; extensive failures; news by foreign arrivals at your place, if of importance; important Legislative proceedings; passages of important laws; riots on a large scale, etc.

Craig noted that the AP was not interested in merely local matters or personalities.[17] Apparently Craig's efforts to compete paid off. The Abbot & Winans organization died about 1855, although little documentation exists to explain why. Through the 1850s, the AP reports remained essentially the same, although the length of those reports varied. The cost to each of the New York papers through the decade was $200 to $230 per week. Toward the end of the decade, charges to all out-of-town clients totaled between $10,000 and $12,000 per week. Craig ruled with an iron hand until his retirement in 1866, cutting off news immediately to publishers who did not pay on time or who complained about the reports. Yet the organization did not achieve structural cohesiveness; rather, it relied in large part on telegraphers for basic business chores, including the recruiting of members, billing, and the transmitting of news. In 1856, a new agreement was adopted, titled the "Regulations of the General News Association of the City of New York," which spelled out the regulations among the seven AP papers, the staff, and out-of-town papers.

From 1847 onward, a southern news report was financed by an association of southern editors, but dispatches to and from the South ended as telegraph lines were cut between the two parts of the nation. The Civil War energized the New York papers, but the AP fared less well, partly because of its reliance on telegraph news. Although the AP negotiated for first release of the information issued by Lincoln, that favored arrangement caused other editors to accuse the agency of being a mouthpiece for the U.S. President. Gerard Hallock, president of the AP, was forced to relinquish control of the *New York Journal of Commerce* and to resign from the AP presidency because of his pro-southern posture. Western editors became increasingly disenchanted with New York control of press reports and began to set the stage for creating a separate organization after the Civil War.

Although the telegraph may well have had as much impact on the flow of commercial information for business use as it did on news dissemination, press reports accounted for a fair portion of the revenues of early telegraph companies. During one week in November 1848, for example, the telegraph office in Milwaukee had receipts of $127, with press reports accounting for $50 of the total.[18] From the beginning, the New York cooperative enjoyed favored rates from the various telegraph companies, and the long and incestuous relationship between Western Union and the Associated Press would become fodder for the Supreme Court in the 1940s.

Communication and the Movement Westward

Movement across the Appalachians into Kentucky initiated western settlement beginning in 1769, settlement that sought news from the East through letters and local news through newly established newspapers. Kentucky became a state in 1792, and during the next forty years settlers moved into Michigan, Minnesota, Indiana, Wisconsin, and other midwestern states. Settlers began moving to Texas and Oregon in the 1820s, a process that culminated in statehood for Texas in 1845 and the settlement of a dispute with the British over Oregon in 1846. California, Utah, and Washington Territory also boasted settlers by this time. By the mid-1850s, settlers poured into Kansas and Nebraska.

The extensive movement westward in the 1840s reflected a period of nationwide interest in expanding settlement and acquiring additional lands. When settlement began in Texas, California, and New Mexico, these territories belonged to Mexico. Britain held major claims to parts of Oregon and Washington. Americans, however, were enamored with the concept of Manifest Destiny, a belief that the United States was destined to expand, conquer, and control. The belief was supported in part by the romantic myth of adventure on the frontier, the desire to develop trade with the Far East (thus the interest in Oregon and California ports), and fears of foreign intervention at isolated borders. Communication from the East was achieved primarily through letters—not newspapers—during the early years of settlement, because newspapers appeared irregularly and depended on available post riders and horses and on expensive equipment that had to be transported across the mountains. Newspapers carried "distant" information, rather than local news, because word of mouth distributed local news faster than did newspapers.[19]

Mexican War: Of Words and Images

Words

The Mexican War earned its place in the history of communication because war news was transmitted for the first time via telegraph. At the start of the war, however, only 130 miles of wire were in place. The only telegraph line, besides an experimental line from Baltimore to Washington, was a single wire connecting New York and Philadelphia. Newspaper publishers, nevertheless, were eager to use the limited facilities. On June 7, 1846, the *New York Herald* recognized the "first flash of the lightning line." The *Herald* reported that it had "received the first flash—the first intelligence, at an early hour last evening—eighteen hours in advance of the mail. The completion is of vast importance. It enables us to give in the morning *Herald* the interesting intelligence from the Rio Grande, one whole day in advance of the old dog-trot way of receiving news from the South."[20] By December 1847, telegraph lines had reached St. Louis, and in July 1848, the *New Orleans Picayune* announced that "telegraph communication between this city and New York, and therefore all the North, is completed by way of Montgomery and Augusta."[21]

Battlefield censorship during the Mexican War established patterns that would be reenergized during the Civil War. Friction with Mexico increased dramatically during the Texas dispute, and after the United States annexed Texas in 1845, Mexico broke off diplomatic relations with the United States. Increased settlement in California and New Mexico irritated the Mexican government, and although the Nueces River had formed the traditional southern boundary of Texas, Texans disputed the boundary line and claimed that the Rio Grande was the southern border. President Polk sent troops to defend the Texas claim at the Rio Grande, further angering the Mexicans. After a failed attempt by President Polk to purchase California and New Mexico, Congress declared war on Mexico on May 13, 1846. Better equipped in terms of men, supplies, and arms, the United States rather easily won the war, occupying New Mexico and California and then moving on to the Mexican capital, Mexico City. On March 10, 1848, the Treaty of Guadalupe Hildalgo gave California, New Mexico, and the Rio Grande boundary to the United States.

During the Mexican War, enterprising printers followed the army, setting up at least twenty-five publications in fourteen occupied cities. These papers provided news for soldiers at the front and civilians at home. Supplementing these war news publications were Mexican newspapers and metropolitan newspapers in the states, which devised elaborate news collections and delivery schemes.[22]

Although the press was relatively free to comment during the Mexican War, at least ten newspapers in the war zone were restricted or closed down. These closings were accomplished under General Winfield Scott's martial law regulations, designed to allow military commanders to enforce behavior within military zones. Scott and other commanders were not partial to either the American or the Mexican press; Professor Sam Riley cited five of each type that were closed. *El Liberal*, a Spanish-language, anti-American newspaper in Matamoros in northern Mexico, denounced the "barbarians from the north." U.S. newspapers commented that the outrageous tone of *El Liberal* was certain proof of freedom of the press in the United

States. The *New Orleans Courier* claimed the continued existence of *El Liberal* was "proof of the respect of our people for the liberty of the press." It did not remain proof for long, however, because the military shut down the press.

Images

Publishers and showmen recognized the power of visuals, and they used primitive photographic techniques, paintings, and dramatizations to depict the Mexican War. Daguerreotype technology having been invented, photographers followed soldiers in the Mexican War and returned with small photographic plates. However, the photographers were severely limited by their equipment, and their photographs earned little recognition in the history of public communication. Tiny, difficult-to-view images on daguerreotype plates competed with the panoramic visual displays that captured the public imagination. A few daguerreotype images from the war still exist, with formal military portraits and views of buildings predominating. However, a few plates suggest genuine war images—troops marching through an occupied town and a young soldier's grave.

These small images, nevertheless, found it difficult to compete with lithographs designed to tell entire stories, painted "transparencies," hung from the sides of buildings and lighted from behind with candles, and panoramic shows that combined Broadway theatrical techniques with a variety of visual artifacts. The lithographs often were used as illustrations by magazines to promote the popular mythology of the war, while the transparencies provided dramatic backdrops for public celebrations of military victories. These backdrops were decorated with painted eagles, troops, battleships, and contemporary heroes that stood life-size on the canvas backdrops. Panoramic dramatic shows included the presentation of long, detailed canvases unrolled from one reel to another and accompanied by special-effects lighting, storytelling, and music. Thus, the small daguerreotypes that attempted to depict the war found little favor in the public audience and never became the basis for woodcut prints in the popular press. By the mid-1850s, depictions of the West were common in lantern slide shows, using techniques that projected images from glass plates onto a wall or screen. Andrew J. Russell, who documented with his camera the Civil War and the building of the Union Pacific Railroad, provided slides for his agent Stephen Sedgwick to show throughout the Northeast. Sedgwick related the slide show to the older panoramic shows, noting that the slides moved "in panoramic form, in their relative and proper order."[23]

Frontier Newspapers

Frontier newspapers were started for a variety of reasons, including: (1) the governmental need for the publication of laws, (2) the desire of a literate population for information and general reading matter, (3) the excess production capacity of job printers, (4) the promotion of political points of view, and (5) boosterism.[24] In some cases, particularly in the Southwest, newspapers belonged to indigenous populations and predated Anglo settlement. Although information is not available for every state, in Wisconsin, newspapers often began six or seven years after the establishment of post offices and tended to develop in towns with more stable populations. Their editors used caustic language, mixed styles of type from whatever was available in the type case, and generally used outdated equipment brought from the East.

Because newspapers were expensive to start, a variety of financing plans were used. In Wisconsin during the 1850s and 1860s, the capital investment for a weekly averaged $1,500. The techniques used for financing included subscription drives, chattel mortgages, joint stock companies, and individual investments. Editors financing newspapers with a subscription drive attempted to get subscribers to promise money in response to a prospectus specifying the newspaper's political position. Editors sometimes solicited financing by mortgaging their equipment to companies who sold presses and type. Often, terms were unrealistic and mortgages were sold or foreclosed on. A third method of financing, the joint stock company, was created by stockholders who owned shares and hired an editor. Usually the stockholders held a common interest in ideas and politics as well as in their financial investment. The fourth method included individual politicians or developers financing an editor's venture.[25]

In Iowa and Utah, handwritten newspapers preceded printed ones. Iowa newspapers included news, features, and editorials written for local residents, and editors may have used them to re-create cultural worlds the editors had known before they migrated westward.[26]

Political and Ideological Newspapers

In Kansas from 1855 to 1857 an ideological press developed, based on sectionalist conflict and the slavery issue. Such newspapers preceded the booster town or promotional press that aligned itself with business and attached itself to the power structure of the community. Kansas editors well knew the value of promotion and did not ignore it, but they viewed resolution of the slavery issue as their first task. In the bloody battle for statehood, editors were as extremist as other groups, and their battles of wit and word contributed to the conflict itself rather than to its resolution. Further, the editors did not represent purely Kansas interests, but rather they represented factions outside the state that saw Kansas as a battleground for the perpetuation of sectional disputes.

When Missouri was admitted as a slave state in 1820, the South agreed that any other states to be carved out of the territory above the 36°30' parallel, which bounds Missouri on the south, would be free. Then, in 1850, a compromise was effected to admit California as a free state and to organize New Mexico and Utah as territories, without reservations about slavery. In 1854, the Kansas–Nebraska Act, which allowed settlers of all new territories to decide whether their lands would be slave or free, killed the Missouri Compromise. Into the law was written the right of squatter sovereignty, and, thus, with Missouri on the east and abolitionist fervor in the North rising, the bloody battle for Kansas began. Newspapers that operated in the 1850s and 1860s in "bleeding Kansas" and on the Kansas–Nebraska border serve as good examples of ideological newspapers. The primary issue was slavery, and editors excelled in flagrant thought and word.

Figure 6–3 A sketch of the Free State Convention in Topeka in December 1855, showing attendees with rifles ready in case of attack. (*Frank Leslie's Illustrated Newspaper*, December 15, 1855)

Legh Richmond Freeman and his brother, Frederick Kemper Freeman, were highly political, pro-Democratic southerners, who edited the *Frontier Index* in various Union Pacific railroad construction towns in Nebraska and Wyoming. Representative of frontier language was a notice to advertisers, in which the *Index* was billed as the emblem of American liberty,

> perched upon the summit of the Rocky Mountains; [it] flaps its wings over the Great West, and screams forth in thunder and lightning tones, the principles of the unterrified anti-Nigger, anti-Chinese, anti-Indian party—Masonic Democracy!!!!!![27]

The newspapers in Kansas sharply divided over the slavery issue from the time the territory was created in 1854. Two types of settlers had soon arrived: "free soilers" from the industrialized North and proslavery southerners, primarily Missourians. Two of the most extreme in their positions were the *Atchison Squatter-Sovereign*, organized and edited by J. H. Stringfellow of Missouri, and the *Lawrence Herald of Freedom*, an organ of the New England Emigrant Aid Society, edited by George Washington Brown.

Although Brown bitterly denied that his newspaper was a society organ and the slogan below the flag read "A Family Newspaper—Independent on All Subjects," the newspaper was financed by the New England Emigrant Aid Society. The newspaper sold for two dollars per year—in advance. Its motto was: "Be just: Let all the ends thou aimest at be thy country's, God's and Truth's."

The emigrant aid company's goal was to establish a newspaper at "the first point selected for settlement, which was to be the organ of the company—not a newspaper representing the sentiments and interests of the community."[28] First issued on October 21, 1854, the initial copy was published in Pennsylvania and labeled the *Herald of Freedom*. It carried a dateline of Wakarusa, Kansas Territory. The second issue was published in Lawrence, called "Yankee Town" by Missourians.

The adamantly proslavery John H. Stringfellow competed for readers with Brown. Publisher of the *Atchison Squatter-Sovereign* that began publication on February 3, 1855, Stringfellow devoted his newspaper to "Politics, Literature, Agriculture, Mercantile Affairs and Useful Reading." The motto of the paper was "The Squatter Claims the Same Sovereignty that He Possessed in the States." The first issue included a series titled "Negro Slavery, No Evil."

The *Squatter-Sovereign* and the *Herald* were similar in format, with small headlines and long columns of type. However, the *Squatter-Sovereign* was a bit more splashy, was divided into seven columns, and ran four pages. The *Herald* was eight columns wide, used a slightly smaller type, and ran an average of eight pages. The *Squatter-Sovereign* usually carried nearly two pages of advertising, whereas the *Herald* often carried only about half a column. The lack of advertising in the *Herald* indicated that the newspaper received outside support, because both newspapers claimed circulations of about 2,000 each and the *Squatter-Sovereign* continually made appeals for more support in order to survive financially.

Brown's newspaper was the more solemn of the two, carrying stories about religion in Japan, making promotional appeals for immigrants who would help settle Kansas as a free state, and describing the virtues of the Kansas Territory. The first issue carried "The Freeman's Song" on page one, which fully described the newspaper's position on slavery:

Men, who bear the Pilgrim's name,
Men, who love your country's fame,
Can ye brook your country's shame,
Chains and slavery?

The first issue also carried a story warning settlers to avoid staking claims on treatied land, an anonymous letter noting that in Kansas an acre would produce sixty-five bushels of corn or twenty bushels of wheat, and correspondence concerning the history of the slavery question.

The *Squatter-Sovereign*'s first issue was somewhat different in tone, although fully as rabid on the question of slavery. It lacked the missionary zeal of the *Herald*, had a column titled "The Funny Corner," and carried poetry titled in a lighter vein than "The Freeman's Song": "Tempt Me Not to Drink Again" and "Every Man Has His Faults."

Slavery was the primary issue, and Stringfellow and Brown engaged in mutual denunciation before Brown ever arrived in Kansas. Brown claimed that with the

The Need for Revenue

It is all important that we should have papers of the "right stripe" in the [Kansas] Territory; and it is evident that, for a year or two, they must be supported by the South. We then appeal to our friends for that material aid, which is so necessary to the success of a newspaper. We shall strive to make the Squatter-Sovereign what the true Southern man would wish it—an uncompromising pro-slavery print—and with this end in view, we appeal to our friends to sustain us.

—J. W. Stringfellow, *Atchison Squatter-Sovereign*, April 3, 1855

repeal of the Missouri Compromise, only sufficient northern immigration would prevent Kansas from becoming a slave state. Stringfellow's first issue warned Missourians of Brown's arrival. He noted that leading abolitionists under the name of "Emigration Aid Societies" were arriving, "the avowed purpose of which is to throw into Kansas a horde who shall not only exclude slaveholders from that territory, but in the end abolish slavery in Missouri." Stringfellow was convinced the abolitionists were determined to convert Missouri, then move south: "Missouri vanquished, Arkansas and Texas are looked upon as easy victims." Regarded almost as the site of a foreign news event, Kansas attracted correspondents from the East to cover the border wars. William A. Phillips came to Kansas for the *New York Tribune*, sent by Horace Greeley. His letters were collected in an 1856 volume, *The Conquest of Kansas by Missouri and Her Allies*. Other correspondents such as Thomas Wentworth Higginson of the *New York Tribune*, Samuel F. Tappen of the *New York Times*, and Richard Hinton of the *Boston Traveller* covered "bleeding Kansas."

The Booster Press

Historian Daniel Boorstin claimed that frontier newspapers began as advertising sheets, then turned into news sheets, their primary purpose to advertise nonexistent towns.[29] Although there was some truth in his statement, the booster press performed a wider function—recruiting additional settlers to already established towns in the West.

Many booster editors became leading men of the community. The first publication across the Alleghenies was the *Pittsburgh Gazette*, which first appeared on July 29, 1786, in the Pennsylvania town with a population of 300. It was edited by John Scull and Joseph Hall from Philadelphia. Hall died shortly after his arrival, but Scull became a community leader—a postmaster, bank president, and one of the incorporators of what is now the Western University of Pittsburgh. When he died in 1828, the population of Pittsburgh was 12,000.[30]

In 1787, the first issue of the *Kentucke Gazette* appeared. John Bradford, not related to the colonial printers and who indeed knew nothing of journalism, was recruited by Kentucky settlers to set up a press. He sent his brother to Pittsburgh to

▼

Fight over a County Seat

Although in the interest of humanity, common decency and honest government we desire that this enterprising, God-fearing and progressive city of Ravanna shall be and remain the permanent county seat of this magnificent county, dowered by nature with a climate that makes the most favored part of Italy seem by comparison like a fever-breeding, miasmatic swamp, yet we refuse, in speaking of the denizens of that nondescript collection of bug-infested huts which its few and scabby inhabitants have the supreme gall to call a town, a few miles distant, to descend to the depths of filth and indecency indulged in by the loathsome creature who sets the type for an alleged newspaper in that God-forsaken collection of places unworthy to be called human habitations.

—*Garfield* (Kansas) *County Call*, October 21, 1887

learn printing from Scull. Bradford also became a community leader and gained a good deal of his income from being printer to the territory.[31] Daniel Richards, who came to Milwaukee at the call of a real estate promoter, issued Milwaukee's first newspaper, the *Advertiser*, in 1836. James M. Goodhue issued the *Minnesota Pioneer* on April 28, 1849. It also played a booster role.

Many western printers did a thriving business publishing legal notices. Such business was aided by the Homestead Act, which required homesteaders to print final notices, stating they had fulfilled all obligations on their claims, six times in the paper nearest their claim before their land claim was final.

Spanish-Language Press in the West

The earliest examples of the Spanish-language press on this continent were found in communities colonized by Spain, both in and outside of what is now the United States. Probably the earliest printed newspaper was in Mexico City, printed more than ten years before the inauguration of the *Boston News-Letter*. Links continued between newspapers printed in southwestern territories of the United States and Latin America long after the 1848 Mexican–American War. New Orleans was a multi-language and multicultural port that provided interchange between Latin America and the United States, and it was in this area that the earliest Spanish-language publications probably developed. The earliest known publication within current U.S. boundaries was New Orleans' *El Misispí*, founded in 1808, a four-page publication with English translations of news in Spanish and a page of advertising. It was started by an Anglo firm, William H. Johnson and Company, and printed on the press of the *Louisiana Gazette*. By 1813, at least three other newspapers existed in Louisiana.

Throughout the 1830s and 1840s, a variety of newspapers were published in the Southwest. One of the oldest was *El Crespusculo de la Libertad* (The Dawn of Liberty), published in 1835 in Taos, New Mexico, by a missionary priest named

Antonio Martinez. This weekly tabloid championed the rights of Indians and Mexicans in the area and called for the sharing of land by all people. At the end of the Mexican War, the United States moved quickly to further populate former Mexican-owned lands and to create a power structure to control economic, social, and political development. The number of Spanish-language newspapers grew, with thirty-five operating nationwide in 1884. The newspapers sought to exert social control, to provide activist leadership, and to reflect Chicano life. Those that sought to exert control often were bilingual papers that had much to gain through government subsidies provided for the printing of laws in Spanish. These newspapers also sometimes exploited class differences among people of Spanish descent, representing the views of those Mexicans with ties to the Anglo business community. Nevertheless, Francisco Ramírez, publishing his newspaper in Los Angeles in 1855, gained an activist reputation for challenging Yankee domination of native Californians. In September 1855, he wrote:

> The North Americans pretend to give us lessons in humanity and to bring our people the doctrine of salvation so we can govern ourselves, to respect the laws and conserve order. Are these the ones who treat us worse than slaves?

Such activism was coupled with encouragement for the maintenance of Spanish-language culture and tradition, acknowledging one school as a place where children could learn English without "losing the language of Cervantes." Short jokes, brief comments on passing events, and poetry appeared regularly. The Spanish-language press occasionally warned against assimilation, fostered the organization of barrio self-help units, and reported migrations across the border of families seeking jobs and settlement.[32]

Oral Culture and the Lecture Circuit

Between 1840 and 1860, the public lecture became a significant form of education and communication, particularly in the growing towns and cities of the Northeast and the West. The increased popularity of the public lecture signified the decline of the sermon as the primary form of public discourse and reflected the rise of secular influence. The public lecture also served to extend a middle-class, democratic culture to newly developing areas of the country and to individuals who were moving across class lines.[33] Between 1840 and 1860, more than 3,000 lectures were advertised, and in 1846, the citizens of Boston could choose from twenty-six different "courses" of lectures. The public lecture series, or lyceum, was popular in the Midwest as well. Davenport, Iowa, organized its first lyceum in 1839, the same year it received its charter. Only 250 people lived in the town. By the mid-1840s, the public lecture relied on national rather than local speakers and appealed in particular to young men in their twenties and thirties who were seeking a profession, a piece of the "intellectual life." The rigid apprenticeship system of the eighteenth century had disappeared, and bureaucratic standards for entering law and medicine were yet to appear. Young urban men often moved from one career to another and sought knowledge that might improve the way along the path to success. The public lecture signaled, for the speaker, possession of wisdom and an act in the public good. "Essentially," wrote historian Donald Scott, "a public lecture was a rather complex form of display. It demonstrated specific intellectual character: a lecture not only diffused knowledge which the speaker was thought to be especially qualified to convey but was also expected to be 'original,' . . . the product of one's own inquiry and intellection."[34]

At first, newspapers hesitated to carry news of public lectures lest they steal the lecturer's product, but before long lectures were considered news items, and newspapers printed summaries of speeches as well as advertised them in advance. Some metropolitan newspapers printed excerpts from lectures of prominent men such as Henry Ward Beecher and Ralph Waldo Emerson. The *New York Tribune* had a special section, "Sketches of Lectures," which summarized various lectures throughout the city. In 1841, the *Boston Daily Advertiser* commented, through a reprinted article from the *New York Post*, that the newspaper had avoided publishing articles about lectures so as not to impinge on the speakers' rights, but that other newspapers had begun the practice of reporting the lectures made to different societies.[35] The lyceum lecturers became famous throughout the country and were well paid for their efforts. Bayard Taylor earned more than $6,000 during the 1854–1855 season, almost three times what was then considered a top clerical salary.[36] In this arena, knowledge was considered a public commodity that assisted individual development and contributed to the practice of democratic theory. Popular lecture topics included science—particularly geology and astronomy—travel, and broad themes relating to American life, including matrimony, money, success, and progress. The lecture was expected to entertain as well as to inform, and newspaper accounts usually measured the quality of entertainment as well as content. "The popular lecture," wrote Scott, "not only provided people with the comprehensive vision they wanted; it did so in a form that embodied what was widely referred to as the 'democratic spirit' of American society. As a public event, it appeared to make knowledge readily accessible to the common man. More important, it presented a quintessentially democratic form of knowledge, which gained its legitimacy from the people's sanction rather than by imposition."[37]

The lecture system brought a variety of lecturers to the platform as well as cutting across class and education in terms of audience. "The rules of the lecture system," wrote Scott, "enforced discourse directed toward the political, moral, and spiritual precepts that transcended sectarian, partisan, and social division. And through its continuing test of popularity, the system was thought to create and embody public opinion—the opinion that the public held in common. In addition, the popular lecture was a ceremony, which in form and content brought the public into self-conscious existence. It was a collective ritual that invoked the values thought to define and sustain the community as a whole."[38] Mary Kupiec Cayton noted that particularly in the Midwest, where religious divisions prevailed, Ralph Waldo Emerson's lectures were "bled of any philosophical, political, or religious implications and used as the basis for a secular faith that focused on a materially defined progress, unlimited wealth, and conspicuous social achievement within the framework of a stable and proscriptive set of moral values. . . . The intentions of the groups were sincere, even if the result was to extend their own hegemony over American culture as a whole."39

Evolution of the Penny Press

Horace Greeley's *New York Tribune* and Henry Raymond's *New York Times* emerged as New York leaders during the decades following the establishment of the penny press. The idea of penny newspapers also moved west—to Chicago in the form of the *Chicago Tribune*—as well as to the South. Such newspapers gained large circulations by using technological innovations of the 1830s and 1840s and popular editorial formats, often with a boost-the-community philosophy. The *Tribune* attracted a diverse audience within and outside of New York with its exchange of ideas so varied that Greeley was often considered erratic. Greeley's weekly edition of the *Tribune* circulated widely in the West. The *New York Times* gained a reputation for thorough coverage of political and economic issues and avoided sensationalism. Both newspapers welcomed the formation of the Republican party in 1854 because it allowed them to adhere to what they considered the best of Whig politics but to oppose slavery, to support the growing economic alliance between western and northern states, and to address themselves to wider audiences.

Horace Greeley and the *New York Tribune*

Horace Greeley was known in a variety of capacities between 1841—the year he began the *New York Tribune*—and 1872—the year he ran for President of the United States, lost the campaign, and died a month after the election. He advertised himself as a contentious individual, and he advocated a variety of not-always-consistent ideas. He believed that the United States was destined to greatness and that agriculture and industry combined would produce a great nation in which all people, black and white, could enjoy a share of prosperity. He could be a great moralist, yet he would print articles about sex and crime if they made a point he believed in; he accepted all forms of patent medicine advertising, but he used his profits to expand the editorial department and to hire and train good reporters and writers.

Greeley was involved in journalistic endeavors for many years before he began his highly successful *New York Tribune* in April 1841. He started his career as a printer, worked on the *New York Evening Post*, printed several Whig publications as part of his own printing business, and edited the *New Yorker*, a literary publication with 9,000 subscribers, for seven and one-half years. In 1841, with $1,000 of borrowed money, $1,000 his own money, and a mortgage of about $1,000, he began the *Tribune.*

Greeley's newspaper was the first cheap Whig publication. It consisted of four pages, with five columns each on a sheet about the size of a modern tabloid. Within

Figure 6–4 Two views of Horace Greeley. (State Historical Society of Wisconsin)

two months, he claimed a circulation of 11,000. In September 1841, Greeley began his weekly edition, which quickly circulated to 200,000 subscribers at a cost of two dollars each per year and gained for him a reputation in the West. He offered one-dollar subscriptions to club members—groups of twenty who subscribed together.

The *Tribune* distinguished itself as an intellectual newspaper for a non-elite audience. Greeley was self-taught and took great delight in playing with new ideas; the *Tribune* often explored topics in depth for a period of weeks or months and then dropped those ideas to go on to something new. His fascination with ideas confused his contemporaries and some historians, and his inconsistencies earned him a reputation for being erratic and undependable. He remained active in Whig politics until he joined the Republican party, and although he continued to write for the newspaper, he also traveled the lecture circuit to increase his income. He advocated abstinence from alcohol, popular education, land for the landless, and the abolition of slavery. He adhered to Whig principles of the high tariff, a stable monetary supply, internal improvements, and national pride. Greeley, who supported the Homestead Act as a solution to social ills, encouraged people to abandon New York City

▼

Margaret Fuller Writes from Rome

The bombardment became constantly more serious. The house where I live was filled as early as the 20th with persons obliged to fly from the Piazza di Gesu, where the fiery rain fell thickest. The night of the 21st–22nd, we were all alarmed about two o'clock, A.M. by a tremendous cannonade. It was the moment when the breach was finally made by which the French entered. They rushed in, and I grieve to say, that, by the only instance of defection known in the course of the siege, those companies of the regiment Union which had in charge a position on that point yielded to panic and abandoned it. The French immediately entered and entrenched themselves. That was the fatal hour for the city. Every day afterward, though obstinately resisted, the enemy gained, till at last, their cannon being well placed, the city was entirely commanded from the Janiculum, and all thought of further resistance was idle.

—Margaret Fuller, Letter 33, July 6, 1849, to the *New York Tribune*, as reproduced in
Maurine Beasley and Sheila Gibbons, *Women in Media*

by promoting the phrase, "Go West Young Man, Go West." In the 1850s, he used the pages of the *Tribune* to investigate socialism, and he hired Karl Marx as a London correspondent.

Greeley's paper became known as a school for journalists, much as Dana's *Sun* became known in later years. Henry J. Raymond, who later became editor of the *New York Times*, worked for Greeley. Other Greeley protégés included Margaret Fuller, a transcendentalist writer; Charles Dana, who later edited the *Sun*; and Whitelaw Reid, who eventually took over editorship of the *Tribune* itself. Greeley willingly committed money to improving the editorial side of the paper and in the 1850s hired a dozen editors for special departments. As the years progressed, circulation leveled

▼

Greeley's Prayer of Twenty Millions

We complain that the Union cause has suffered, and is now suffering immensely, from mistaken deference to Rebel slavery. Had you, sir, in your inaugural address, unmistakably given notice that, in case the Rebellion already commenced were persisted in, and your efforts to preserve the Union and enforce the laws were resisted by armed force, *you would recognize no loyal person as rightfully held in slavery by a Traitor*, we believe the Rebellion would therein have received a staggering if not fatal blow. . . . Had you then proclaimed that Rebellion would strike the shackles from the slaves of every traitor, the wealthy and the cautious would have been supplied with a powerful inducement to remain loyal.

—Horace Greeley, *New York Tribune*, August 20, 1862

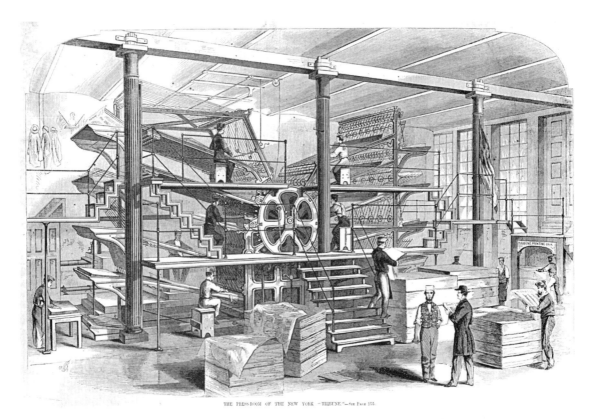

Figure 6–5   *New York Tribune* Press Room, 1861. (*Frank Leslie's Illustrated Weekly*, July 20, 1861)

off and remained steady at about 35,000 to 40,000 for the daily and 100,000 for the weekly. In 1848, Greeley was appointed to Congress to serve out an unexpired term. He ran several times for a House seat, twice for the Senate, and once for New York comptroller, but he always lost his political bids. His last campaign was for the presidency, and although he earned the support of some Liberal Republicans and Democrats, many editors viewed his candidacy with alarm.

Greeley ardently opposed slavery because he felt that the institution was not in the national interest—that it would retard development and destroy the Union. He often received credit for persuading Lincoln to free the slaves through his famous "Prayer of Twenty Millions," but evidence indicates that Lincoln's plans were set long before Greeley published the editorial on August 20, 1862. Lincoln and Greeley were well acquainted, however, and not only met but corresponded about the future of the Union. At the end of the war, Greeley led a campaign to free former Confederate President Jefferson Davis, arguing that a trial would reopen rather than heal the wounds of war. He also supported the move to impeach Andrew Johnson, calling him "America's most degraded son." In 1872, Greeley ran for President on the Liberal Republican and Democratic tickets. The daily and weekly editions of the *Tribune* continued for thirty-one years until Greeley's death in 1872. He was widely known, primarily because of the weekly but also because of his attitude toward westward expansion. Greeley's success could not be measured in business terms, and many claim that if he had not gone into partnership with Thomas McElrath in 1841, the paper would have floundered financially. In 1849, the Tribune Association was organized, with *Tribune* property divided into shares. Some shares were sold to supervisory personnel, and when Greeley died, he owned very little of the Tribune company.[40] Whitelaw Reid became the new editor of the *Tribune*.

Henry Jarvis Raymond and the *New York Times*

Henry Raymond introduced a newspaper to New Yorkers that focused on information and reflected a moderate reporting style. Raymond, born in western New York state in 1820, began his newspaper career while still a student at the University of Vermont by working as a free-lancer for Horace Greeley's *New Yorker*. By 1840, when he received his degree, Raymond had considerable experience in Whig politics and was hired as Greeley's assistant at the *New Yorker*. He added election returns, read foreign newspapers, wrote book reviews, and read proof. Although unhappy with his salary of $600 a year, Raymond was able to earn another $400 from outside work, and he stayed with Greeley as chief assistant of the *New York Tribune*. Raymond objected to Greeley's interest in Fourierism (a form of socialism), and wrote, "Some delectable asses here (among whom I am sorry to say is Greeley) have started a plan for reorganizing society—elevating the social condition of universal dogdom and allowing puppies to hold their proper rank in the scale of being."[41]

Greeley praised Raymond for his hard work and often left him in charge of the newspaper, but Raymond became embittered over his low wages. In 1843, James Watson Webb offered him twenty-five dollars a week and editorship of the *New York Courier and Enquirer*. As assistant to Greeley, Raymond had been earning only twenty dollars a week. Raymond joined the *Courier* and remained until 1851, when he left to begin the *New York Times*. Raymond proposed to his investors a newspaper of wide coverage, including city news, with emphasis on public meetings, sermons, religious gatherings, ship news, and market and stock news. He wanted to avoid what he considered the "crudeness" of Bennett and the radicalism of Greeley. He was aware that the *Tribune* made $60,000 a year and "expressed his decided conviction that a new paper could be started in New York, which would make as much money as the Tribune."[42] Raymond secured the Associated Press franchise, remained a moderate voice, and gained a reputation for good news reporting. After the first year, the newspaper made about $100,000, and on its first anniversary Raymond doubled the paper's size and raised its price to two cents. He returned to political life and in 1854 broke from the Whigs, joined the Republican party, and addressed a conference of party leaders in Pittsburgh, earning himself the title "Godfather of the Republican party." He was credited with outlining principles for the new party, appealing to the party to resist slavery, and giving warning of the approaching Civil War.[43] In 1854, he took a leave from the *Times* when he was elected lieutenant governor of New York. In 1857, when his term was over, he declined offers to run for governor.

By 1857, Raymond moved the *Times* into an improved printing facility. In 1861, he covered the first Battle of Bull Run and spent his time during the war between the battlefields, in Washington and New York. After the war, he supported Andrew Johnson's presidency. Raymond was elected to Congress in 1865. Disappointed with Johnson, Raymond ended his political career in 1867 at the age of forty-seven. When he died in 1869, New York politician Thurlow Weed, Greeley, and Colonel Watson Webb temporarily laid aside their differences to be pallbearers at Raymond's funeral.

The *Times* continued under the editorship of John Bigelow, who was named by the newspaper's three directors: George Jones, Leonard Jerome, and James B. Taylor. Jones, who had been Raymond's partner, saved the paper in 1871 from the hands of William Marcy ("Boss") Tweed, who was trying to shut down the voice that opposed his corrupt New York administration. The *Times*' circulation declined, and the paper suffered bankruptcy before Adolph Ochs bought it in 1896.

Chicago Tribune

The booster press was not confined to the frontier, nor was it the sole province of rural newspapers. As the penny press moved westward, boosterism was one of its primary functions.

The *Chicago Tribune*, which was often credited with exerting a major influence in the election of Abraham Lincoln as President of the United States in 1860 and which gained an archconservative reputation as an anti–New Deal newspaper under Robert P. McCormick, began publication on June 10, 1847. For its first eight years it struggled under the leadership of various owners, at times successful and at times floundering. Before Joseph Medill and Charles Ray assumed part ownership and control in 1854, the paper was in dire straits, partially due to its support of the Know-Nothing party. The nativistic party's attacks on German immigrants and Catholics won little popularity in ethnic Chicago.

Joseph Medill, a Presbyterian Whig, lawyer, and newspaper man, assimilated many ideas of the penny press as editor of the *Cleveland Morning Leader*. Instrumental in establishing the Republican party in the 1850s, Medill and Ray, an Illinois publisher, changed the paper's politics to Republican as soon as they gained financial control over the *Tribune*, which they began editing in September 1855. Medill supervised the news gathering operation, advertising, circulation, and printing, and Ray wrote editorials. They departmentalized the news, ended the antiforeign bias, and argued vehemently to exclude slavery from the territories. Medill viewed Chicago, with its rapidly growing population of 86,000 and an expanding railroad industry, as a booming town that would support a lively newspaper.

Medill and Ray's abolitionist fervor and support of Republicanism led them to cover the Kansas–Nebraska conflict extensively, even holding a free-soil benefit in Chicago and contributing $2,000 to the *Herald of Freedom*.[44]

By rejecting compromise as a solution and promoting continued pressure on the South, the *Tribune* earned a radical reputation in the early days of the Civil War. Before war broke out, Medill traveled to Washington as the newspaper's capital correspondent. During the war, the *Tribune* placed correspondents in the field, with the editors remaining at home to coordinate publication of war news and other information.

Abolitionism and war news, however, were not the only issues for the *Tribune*. The newspaper also exposed local corruption, and in 1865 it condemned corrupt "street railway swindlers."[45]

The *Tribune* was not without competitors in the early years. The *Chicago Democrat*, begun in 1833, and the *Whig Daily Journal* represented other political viewpoints. In 1854, shortly before Medill arrived in Chicago and at a time when other newspapers were moving to a more neutral stance on the slavery and sectional issues, Senator Stephen Douglas of Illinois began another newspaper, the *Chicago Times*, to represent the Democratic viewpoint. By 1855, the city had seven daily newspapers. Throughout the Kansas–Nebraska disputes, the *Times*, which considered politics the mainstay of its editorial content, accused the *Tribune* of supporting a fraudulent government. The *Times* remained loyal to Douglas through the presidential campaign of 1860 and fervently opposed the *Tribune*.

Press Development in the Antebellum South

Press expansion in the South tended to be slower than in the North. However, attitudes about southern "backwardness" have led historians to ignore southern press development and have retarded the acquisition of a good historical base of knowledge for understanding southern publications. During the 1820s, seventeen religious periodicals were founded in Virginia, North Carolina, South Carolina, and Georgia. Southern literary magazines also developed during the period. Antebellum newspapers in the South remained largely partisan and resembled, in large part, the smaller dailies of the North rather than metropolitan models such as the *New York Times* or the *Tribune*. With the exception of a few newspapers, including the *Picayune* in New Orleans, the *Saturday Evening News and General Advertiser* in Washington, D.C., and the *Dispatch* in Richmond, the "penny idea" had not moved South. The number of southern newspapers greatly increased from 1830 to 1860, as they did in

▼

The Language of Boosterism

The growing importance of this metropolis of the West, and the daily extension of its commerce, almost ensure the success of any undertaking which would tend to facilitate our merchants in those dealings which are the foundation of the greatness of our city. With the increase of its commerce, New Orleans itself increases; and in the ratio of this commerce we will see new improvements and ameliorations rise up in every quarter.

—On Establishing a Reading Room, *New Orleans* (La.) *Picayune*, January 25, 1837

the North, and like many northern papers, they needed government and party printing contracts to survive. At the beginning of the war, 800 papers were operating in
the eleven states of the Confederacy. Ten percent, or eighty of those, were dailies.
The typical newspaper was four pages and varied from four to eight columns wide.
The first page carried news and advertisements. Other content included editorials, a
limited amount of telegraphic news, marketing and commercial reports, and serialized fiction. International news was viewed as either equally important as or more
important than local news. Steam presses and other advanced technology had not
moved south to any great extent, and most southern newspapers at the start of the
Civil War were printed on hand presses.[46]

Nevertheless, changes were taking place in the South as well as in the rest of the
country, and urban businessmen banded together in cities such as New Orleans,
Richmond, and Norfolk to promote industrial change that would spur the lagging
agricultural economy in the South. By the 1850s, Thomas Ritchie's venerable *Richmond Enquirer*, a partisan newspaper that represented the urban political elite, competed with James Cowardin's penny paper, the *Richmond Daily Dispatch*. The *Dispatch* claimed to be nonpartisan and focused on city affairs. Cowardin's paper
outdistanced Ritchie's in circulation, selling 18,000 copies in Richmond by 1860.
Cowardin's success was due, in part, to the changing economy in the South. Wrote
David Goldfield, "As cities grew, so did information. Business depended on the effective organization of information from notices of local prices and economic conditions
to descriptions of regional crop failures and national economic trends. Effective
reception and interpretation of such information facilitated commercial relations and
the flow of commerce."[47]

The *Richmond Enquirer* and the Southern Partisan Press

The *Richmond Enquirer* began in 1798 as the *Examiner*, an anti-Federalist organ
established by a prominent Richmond lawyer, but it died in 1804. Thomas Ritchie,
a prominent Virginian, and W. W. Worsley purchased the "good will" of the dying
sheet, along with 500 subscribers, and began issuing their version of the *Examiner*—
renamed the *Enquirer*—on May 9, 1804. Jefferson encouraged editor Ritchie in establishing the paper and hoped that it would aid the development of the Democratic
party. The *Enquirer* was expensive at four dollars a year (the price was soon raised
to five dollars), and payment was required in advance. By 1839, Ritchie was publishing the *Enquirer* three times a week during sessions of the state legislature and
otherwise twice weekly. Six columns of news and advertising appeared on the pages
of the four-page newspaper, including legal notices, the usual patent medicine ads
to restore blood, and local and national news.[48] Ritchie had major competition in
Federalist Richmond from the established *Gazette*. Ritchie's affinity for Jefferson came
in part from his dislike of strong governments and his passion for individual rights.
Unlike many fellow Virginians with a more aristocratic bent, Ritchie supported popular education, legal reform, and the development of Virginia's natural resources as
critical to the rejection of feudalism and the attainment of Republican values. As a

newspaper editor he was successful, partially because in 1814 he was elected the public printer of Virginia and for the next twenty years he printed all acts of the assembly. In addition to his editorial role at the *Enquirer*, from 1820 to 1833 he edited the *Richmond Compiler*, a newspaper devoted to industrial development, and in 1840 he edited the *Crisis*, a paper devoted to educational issues. Although aristocratic in bearing (a wearer of old-fashioned silk stockings), Ritchie supported education for women and women's suffrage. In the early 1830s, he advocated the abolition of slavery, but as the issue became more heated in the 1840s, he defended the institution. In 1845, Ritchie left his son William in charge of the *Enquirer* and moved to Washington to establish the *Union*, remaining there until 1851 when he sold the newspaper. In Richmond, Ritchie had been a prominent community leader and statesman; outside his beloved state—in the nation's capital—he fared less well. Ritchie represented the editor–statesman role well, and a contemporary of his wrote that Ritchie's power "proceeded from a knowledge on the part of the public that he was aiming with his whole soul to promote, as far as he thought right, the public interest and particularly to sustain Virginia in her highly prized principles, and to sustain her in the ascendancy among the states. It strengthened the confidence felt in his disinterested devotion to these things and his freedom from selfish aspirations for himself and his friends."[49] Ritchie's son, William, extended his father's concern for the development of resources, attempting to further a "new era" of industrial development. In 1852, the *Enquirer* maintained that Virginia's railroad network combined with direct trade would make Virginia the "Excelsior State of the Union." Ritchie joined a choir of elite urban businessmen who supported the substitution of business for politics, the development of internal improvements and industrialization to compete successfully with the North, and the use of economic prosperity to preserve political independence.[50]

Conclusion

Communication developments accompanied the movement westward as fast as transportation and technology could carry them. Transportation, improved through the introduction of the express and improved mail systems, shortened the time lag between events occurring in the East and information arriving in the West. The telegraph, which separated communication from transportation, provided news summaries quickly but at considerable expense to western newspapers. The telegraph also sped the development of news brokerage services, including the individual enterprises of telegraphic reporters, private news agencies affiliated with the telegraph companies, and the powerful Associated Press. Through its powerful association of newspapers, the Associated Press helped define news and the language of news, emphasizing fact and resisting opinion. Telegraphic news had to be acceptable to all parties.

The move westward represented hardship for settlers, who struggled against the elements and fought to carve a living from land that proved productive at times, barren at others. As people from the East moved westward, Hispanic populations coped with hostile action and displacement, and their newspapers reflected resistance and compromise. For urban planners, real estate promoters, and others who shaped the urban west, the movement represented both new opportunity and failed dreams. By 1880, all except a few of the eventual urban centers were firmly in place. Each of these urban communities, including many that eventually failed, needed promoters. From the early beginnings of the frontier press came a stable small-town press, significant metropolitan newspapers, and associations of editors active in the political and economic lives of their communities. They were boosters, politicians, reformers, and journalists.

During the late 1830s, the penny press appealed to a diverse audience of varying socioeconomic characteristics. In the early 1840s, Horace Greeley and Henry Raymond established penny newspapers that, although claiming to avoid the sensationalism of Benjamin Day's *New York Sun*, still appealed to a broad audience. Greeley, with the *New York Tribune*, valued the exchange of ideas and endeavored to create an intellectual newspaper for a non-elite audience. Raymond, producing the *New York Times*, disliked what he saw as Greeley's erratic behavior and focused instead on a thorough coverage of events. Joseph Medill carried his profession with him as he moved from Cleveland to Chicago to establish a penny newspaper there. The southern press developed in a less industrialized atmosphere, preserving elements of the partisan press developed in the 1820s and extending the penny press with a focus on urban development to growing urban centers in the South.

Endnotes

1. James Carey, "Introduction," *Communication as Culture: Essays on Media and Society* (Boston: Unwin Hyman, 1989).

2. Gerald Baldasty, "The Charleston, South Carolina Press and National News, 1808–47," *Journalism Quarterly* 55:3 (Autumn, 1978), pp. 519–26.

3. This discussion of the development of postal expresses relies primarily on Richard B. Kielbowicz, "Speeding the News by Postal Express, 1825–1861: The Public Policy of Privileges for the Press," *Social Science Journal* 22:1 (January, 1985), pp. 49–63.

4. For discussions of the tensions evident in federal postal policy of the mid-1800s, see Richard B. Kielbowicz, "Modernization, Communication Policy, and the Geopolitics of News, 1820–1860," *Critical Studies in Mass Communication* 3 (1986), pp. 21–35.

5. Helen L. Moore, "California in Communication with the Rest of the Continent with Reference Chiefly to the Period before the Railroads," in vol. 13 of *Historical Society of Southern California Annual Publications 1924–27* (Los Angeles: McBride Printing, 1924), p. 72, cited in Arthur C. Carey, "Effects of the Pony Express and the Transcontinental Telegraph upon Selected California Newspapers," *Journalism Quarterly* 51:2 (Summer, 1974), p. 320.

Carey's article provides the information included in this chapter on carrying mail to California.

6. See Glenn D. Bradley, *The Story of the Pony Express* (Chicago: A. C. McClurg, 1913).

7. For a discussion of contemporary reaction to the introduction of the telegraph, see Daniel Czitrom, *Media and the American Mind: From Morse to McLuhan* (Chapel Hill: University of North Carolina Press, 1982), pp. 3–29. For an analysis of the cultural implications of the telegraph, see James W. Carey, "Technology and Ideology: The Case of the Telegraph," *Prospects*, Jack Salzman, ed., vol. 8, pp. 303–23. Carey argues that the telegraph created the wire services and introduced standardization of news, which gave the news function of newspapers preeminence over the editorial function. See also Donald L. Shaw, "News Bias and the Telegraph: A Study of Historical Change," *Journalism Quarterly* 44 (Spring, 1967), pp. 3–12, 31; and Robert L. Thompson, *Wiring a Continent: The History of the Telegraph Industry in the United States, 1832–1866* (New York: Arno Press, 1972).

8. As expressed by Czitrom, *Media and the American Mind*, p. 3.

9. Czitrom, *Media and the American Mind*, pp. 7–9.

10. "Influence of the Telegraph on Commerce," *Hunt's Merchant Magazine* 59 (August, 1868), pp. 106–7, cited in Richard B. DuBoff, "The Telegraph in Nineteenth-Century America: Technology and Monopoly," *Comparative Studies in Society and History* 26:4 (October, 1984), pp. 571–86.

11. Cited in Carey, "Effects of the Pony Express," p. 323.

12. Czitrom, *Media and the American Mind*, pp. 21–22.

13. Richard Schwarzlose, *The Nation's Newsbrokers: The Formative Years from Pretelegraph to 1865* (Evanston, Ill.: Northwestern University Press, 1989) vol. 1, pp. 58–61. Schwarzlose's account documents that this New York state association probably predated the formal New York City Associated Press organization, although New York City editors had cooperated in various forms of news gathering enterprises as early as the 1820s.

14. Schwarzlose, *Nation's Newsbrokers*, vol. 1, pp. 63–64.

15. Schwarzlose, *Nation's Newsbrokers*, vol. 1, pp. 100–106.

16. Schwarzlose, *Nation's Newsbrokers*, vol. 1., pp. 118–19. Schwarzlose suggests the arrangement with the telegraph companies because of the absence of any documents indicating disagreements between Abbot & Winans and the companies. This absence is remarkably different from the continual discussions between AP and the telegraphic companies.

17. Schwarzlose, *Nation's Newsbrokers*, p. 180.

18. Bradford W. Scharlott, "Influence of Telegraph on Wisconsin Newspaper Growth," *Journalism Quarterly* 66:3 (Autumn, 1989), pp. 710–15.

19. Hazel Dicken Garcia, "Letters Tell the News (Not 'Fit to Print'?) about the Kentucky Frontier," *Journalism History* 7:2 (Summer, 1980), pp. 49–53, 67.

20. *New York Herald*, May 23, 1846, cited in Robert Luther Thompson, *Wiring a Continent: The History of the Telegraph Industry in the United States, 1832–1866* (Princeton, N.J.: Princeton University Press, 1947), p. 219.

21. *New Orleans Picayune*, July 19, 1848, cited in Thompson, *Wiring a Continent*, p. 220.

22. Tom Reilly, "Newspaper Suppression during the Mexican War," *Journalism Quarterly* 54:2 (Summer, 1977), p. 262. For accounts produced during the Mexican War, see Lawrence Delbert Cress, ed., *Dispatches from the Mexican War* (Norman: University of Oklahoma Press, 1999).

23. Martha Sandweiss, "Undecisive Moments," in Sandweiss and Alan Trachtenberg, eds., *Photography in Nineteenth-Century America* (Fort Worth, Tex.: Amon Carter Museum, 1991), p. 108.

24. See William H. Lyon, *The Pioneer Editor in Missouri, 1808–1860* (Columbia: University of Missouri Press,

1965); and Oliver Knight's review of Lyon's book, *Journalism Quarterly* 42 (Summer, 1965), pp. 478–79.

25. Carolyn Stewart Dyer, "Economic Dependence and Concentration of Ownership among Antebellum Wisconsin Newspapers," *Journalism History* 7:2 (Summer, 1980), pp. 42–46. See also Carol Smith and Dyer, "Taking Stock, Placing Orders: A Historiographic Essay on the Business History of the Newspaper," *Journalism Monographs* 132 (April, 1992).

26. Roy Atwood, "Handwritten Newspapers on the Iowa Frontier, 1844–1854," *Journalism History* 7:2 (Summer, 1980), pp. 56–59, 66–67.

27. *Frontier Index*, May 19, 1868, p. 3. Cited in Thomas H. Heuterman, "Assessing the 'Press on Wheels': Individualism in Frontier Journalism," *Journalism Quarterly* 53:3 (Autumn, 1976), p. 424.

28. William E. Connelley, *Kansas and Kansans* (Chicago: Lewis Publishing Company, 1918).

29. Daniel Boorstin, *The Americans: The National Experience* (New York: Vintage Books, Division of Random House, 1965), p. 127.

30. Boorstin, *The Americans*, p. 126.

31. Boorstin, *The Americans*, p. 127.

32. This discussion relies heavily on the Spanish Language Media Issue of *Journalism History* 4:2 (Summer, 1977). See especially Felix Gutíerrez, "Spanish-Language Media in America: Background, Resources, History," pp. 34–41, 65–66.

33. R. Laurence Moore, "Religion, Secularization, and the Shaping of the Culture Industry in Antebellum America," *American Quarterly* (June, 1989), pp. 216–42.

34. Donald M. Scott, "The Popular Lecture and the Creation of a Public in Mid-Nineteenth Century America," *Journal of American History* 66 (1980), pp. 791–809.

35. Mary Kupiec Cayton, "The Making of an American Prophet: Emerson, His Audiences, and the Rise of the Culture Industry in Nineteenth-Century America," *American Historical Review* 92 (June, 1987), pp. 597–620.

36. Scott, "The Popular Lecture," p. 800.

37. Scott, "The Popular Lecture," p. 806.

38. Scott, "The Popular Lecture," p. 808.

39. Cayton, "The Making of an American Prophet," pp. 619–20.

40. For full-length biographies of Greeley, see Don C. Seitz, *Horace Greeley: Founder of the New York Tribune* (Indianapolis: Bobbs-Merrill, 1926); Henry Luther Stoddard, *Horace Greeley: Printer, Editor, Crusader* (New York: Putnam, 1946); or Glyndon G. Van Deusen, *Horace Greeley: Nineteenth Century Crusader* (Philadelphia: University of Pennsylvania Press, 1953). For an excellent

summary, see "Horace Greeley" by Daniel W. Pfaff in *Dictionary of Literary Biography: American Newspaper Journalists, 1690–1872*, vol. 43.

41. Francis Brown, *Raymond of the Times* (New York: W. W. Norton, 1951), p. 39.

42. Augustus Maverick, *Henry J. Raymond and the New York Press for Thirty Years: Progress of American Journalism from 1840 to 1870* (Hartford, Conn.: A. S. Hale, 1870), p. 90.

43. Meyer Berger, *The Story of the* New York Times *1851–1951* (New York: Simon & Schuster, 1951), p. 21.

44. Lloyd Wendt, Chicago Tribune: *The Rise of a Great American Newspaper* (New York: Rand-McNally, 1979), p. 67.

45. Wendt, Chicago Tribune, p. 200.

46. J. Cutler Andrews, *The South Reports the Civil War* (Pittsburgh: University of Pittsburgh Press, 1985), pp. 24–26.

47. David Goldfield, *Urban Growth in the Age of Sectionalism* (Baton Rouge: Louisiana State University Press, 1977), p. 102.

48. *Richmond Enquirer*, summary of issues in May 1839.

49. Cited in John M. Butler, "Thomas Ritchie," *Dictionary of Literary Biography*, vol. 43, pp. 392–97.

50. See "Epilogue: The Renewed South," in David Goldfield, *Urban Growth*, pp. 271–83.

CHAPTER 7

Communication Issues in the Antislavery Movement and the Civil War

▼

Westward expansion and the emergence of the political and commercial interests of a growing nation, coupled with an active abolitionist movement, symbolized the years before the Civil War. Represented within the antislavery movement were many of the tensions of the communication and political systems of the nation. The role of communication in a social movement, the impact of technology on the printing industry, the use of visuals or iconography in persuasion, the importance of issues of gender, the emergence of a black press, and a growing cultural division on the slavery question characterized the communication issues involved in the abolitionist movement. A growing book trade and a continuing pamphlet trade, along with public lectures and the use of iconography, broadened the range of communication products available for information seekers.

Secession came in South Carolina in December 1860. The election of Abraham Lincoln as President of the United States represented a shift of power to the North and West, to the antislavery factions, and to the Republican party. Electoral college results made it clear that the South, with only a third of the nation's population, would no longer have the power to control decisions regarding slavery, the tariff, or other economic measures. The Democratic party lay temporarily in shreds, as shown earlier by its inability to agree on a strong candidate to confront Lincoln. In April, with the attack on Fort Sumter, the Civil War began.

Covering the war was a challenge for North and South alike. With a few exceptions, correspondents for the expanding U.S. press had not covered a war, and the country itself had little experience in dealing with the press in wartime. Richard McCormick of the *New York Evening Post* had covered the Crimean War; an Associated Press correspondent had covered struggles in Turkey, Palestine, and Egypt; and George Williams had covered the 1858 action against the Mormons. Newspapers responded quickly to the public's desire for war news and devoted a third of the editorial columns to the conflict.

The war increased editors' desire for speed and competitiveness in gathering the news and probably spurred northern urban papers to greater growth, whereas southern papers faced financial hardship and often were destroyed as Union armies advanced through the South. News gathering benefited from expanded use of the telegraph, and correspondents began to move toward the inverted pyramid style of writing, leaving behind their nineteenth-century rhetoric. In the North, newspapers directed war coverage from the home office, and the number of correspondents increased dramatically.[1] ▼

Figure 7–1   The "Lightning Steam Press" along with the electric telegraph, the locomotive, and the steamboat were considered part of the "Progress of the Century" in this nineteenth-century photograph. (Division of Prints and Photographs, Library of Congress Collection)

The Abolitionist Movement: Printed Products in an Age of Change

Abolitionist activity existed in the United States as early as the 1700s, with Quaker groups opposing slavery because it violated their religious principles of brotherly love. While some hoped slavery would be abolished under the newly written Constitution, the three-fifths compromise indicated that compromise rather than principle would rule the day. However, by 1804, Pennsylvania and states north of its boundaries had passed acts of emancipation. Congress ended the foreign slave trade in 1807, the same year that the English Parliament passed a similar law. Abolitionists were a minority, and the movement to free the slaves was not approved by a majority of people until the South actually declared war on the Union. The antislavery movement gathered together freed slaves, white middle-class women disenchanted with boundaries governing women's behavior and rights, ministers, and a variety of volatile reform personalities. Although such diversity might be seen as giving the movement strength, it also fragmented its efforts. Working-class whites often feared the competition a freed African-American labor force would supply, and upper-class whites had difficulty freeing themselves from racial prejudice. Discussions about colonization, or returning blacks to Africa, and varying degrees of emancipation dominated the early years of the movement.

From the beginning, abolitionists valued the impact of printed products. Benjamin Lundy, one of the earliest antislavery editors, edited the *Genius of Universal Emancipation* from 1821 to 1839 in support of colonization, a concept advocated by one of the earliest formal organizations to oppose slavery. The American Colonization Society, organized in 1816, feared that God's wrath over slavery would destroy the Union. Society members compared slavery to the bondage of Israelites in Egypt and argued that as God led the Israelites across the Red Sea, so should blacks be led out of bondage in the United States. Because the colonizationists did not fully accept the concept of equality between the races, they argued that African slaves in the United States, if freed, would sink to the bottom of society, and therefore they strove to create their own promised land for blacks—the land of Liberia along the Atlantic coast of Africa. Exporting blacks to Liberia, colonizationists argued, would preserve the Union by eliminating the racial issue and would provide blacks with an opportunity to create their own society.2

Lundy differed from the colonizationists by believing in equality, and he eventually supported emancipation as the solution to the slavery question. His work attracted many who became principal figures in the abolitionist movement, including William Lloyd Garrison, who quickly moved away from the position of colonization and gradual emancipation to what was considered radicalism—a demand for immediate emancipation and the position that the Constitution was a proslavery document that should be abolished. Garrison and twelve friends formed the New England Anti-Slavery Society in 1831; eventually about a quarter of the members were free blacks. In 1833, the Garrisonians, New York reformers, and Pennsylvania Quakers organized the multiracial American Anti-Slavery Society.

In 1835, utilizing new publishing technology such as the steam press and stereotyping, the American Anti-Slavery Society was able to produce materials at nearly half the cost of the year before. Thus, the group was able, the executive committee reported, to distribute nine times the material at only five times the cost of 1834. The society took advantage of the cheap postal rates reserved for pamphlets and newspapers, and it flooded the country with more than a million pieces of literature. The materials ranged from four monthly journals and a children's newspaper to woodcuts, handkerchiefs, and even chocolate wrappers. To many Americans, North and South alike, wrote David Paul Nord, "the postal campaign was clear evidence that abolitionism was an enormously rich and powerful conspiracy, centered in New York, which was determined to destroy traditional local values and institutions. For them, this nationalization of organization and communication was a threat to the decentralized structure of American republicanism."[3]

Questions about the status of women within the movement precipitated a crisis in 1839, resulting in the establishment of two groups: Garrison's American Anti-Slavery Society, which supported women's leadership, a policy of noncooperation with political institutions, and unorthodox religious views; and the American and Foreign Anti-Slavery Society, headed by Lewis Tappan and James Birney, that excluded women from membership, limiting their participation to female auxiliaries.[4]

William Lloyd Garrison: Radical Mission

Born in Massachusetts in 1805, William Lloyd Garrison was apprenticed at thirteen as a printer in the *Newburyport Herald* office. He quickly became a rapid compositor and wrote his first article anonymously—then set it in type himself. In 1826, at the close of his apprenticeship, he edited several small papers and became involved in the temperance movement. Converted to the work of Benjamin Lundy, he became manager of *The Genius of Universal Emancipation* in 1829. While en route to joining Lundy, he made his first public speech on slavery, remarking that his mission was "to obtain the liberation of two millions of wretched, degraded beings, who are pining in hopeless bondage—over whose sufferings scarcely an eye weeps, or a heart melts, or a tongue pleads either to God or man."[5]

Lundy's position on gradual emancipation was jeopardized in 1828 when Garrison demanded immediate emancipation in an issue of the *Genius*. The newspaper was closed down and Garrison was jailed.[6] In January 1831, when he was twenty-five years old, Garrison began his own weekly journal in Boston, *The Public Liberator and Journal of the Time*. The motto of the *Liberator* was: "Our country is the world—our countrymen are mankind." For thirty-four years, the paper continuously demanded immediate and unconditional emancipation, but it remained loyal to the tactics of nonviolence.

Garrison's position was not a popular one, and Nat Turner's bloody rebellion of 1831 sparked new attacks on Garrison's extremist position. Despite Garrison's continued pleas for nonviolence, many believed that his rhetoric contributed to the insurrection. Nevertheless, Garrison's publications endured. The *National Anti-Slavery Standard* was published weekly in New York for thirty years, and the *Liberator* continued for thirty-five years. Neither paper probably ever exceeded a circulation of 3,000, but they were read, noted, and responded to by supporters and antagonists.

▼

The *Liberator's* Preamble

Whereas, we believe that Slavery is contrary to the precepts of Christianity, dangerous to the liberties of the country, and ought immediately to be abolished; and whereas, we believe that the citizens of New England not only have the right to protest against it, but are under the highest obligation to seek its removal by moral influence; and whereas, we believe that the free people of color are unrighteously oppressed, and stand in need of our sympathy and benevolent co-operation; therefore, recognizing the inspired declaration that God 'hath made of one blood all nations of men for to dwell on all the face of the earth' and in obedience to our Saviour's golden rule, 'all things whatsoever ye would that men should do to you, do ye even to them,' we agree to form ourselves into a Society and to be governed by the following CONSTITUTION.

—The *Liberator*, February 9, 1833

Garrison's paper reported on activities in the African-American community that were not strictly oriented toward antislavery. For example, in 1832, he championed the cause of the Female Literary Association, which met once a week "for the purpose of mutual improvement in moral and literary pursuits." These women were writing and criticizing each others' work. Garrison said one could perceive "intellectual promise" by listening in on the group's conversation, and he commended their efforts to encourage "colored ladies of other places to go and do likewise."[7]

Elijah Lovejoy: The Link between Abolition and Civil Rights

The attempted rebellion of the slave Nat Turner in 1831, coupled with the massive literature campaign of the American Anti-Slavery Society in 1835, created new tensions in the South, and Elijah Lovejoy tested the right to a free press in the border states of Missouri and Illinois. St. Louis, the gateway to the West and a well-established southern city as well, drove Elijah Lovejoy across the river into Alton, Illinois, for expressing anti-Catholic and antislavery views. Lovejoy began publishing the *Observer* in Alton not long before the Illinois legislature, fully aware of the state's dependence on southern commerce, issued a call in January 1837 to resist antislavery activity. After using his newspaper to attempt to establish an antislavery society in the state, Lovejoy was asked to stop printing. When he refused, a mob destroyed his press and the Illinois attorney general ruled the action justified. Lovejoy's printing presses were destroyed twice and his house invaded by proslavery groups. When a third press arrived, Lovejoy was determined to protect it, and so he armed himself; but he was nevertheless gunned down by a mob as his press went up in flames.

Lovejoy's death was the first event to clearly link abolition with civil rights. The American Anti-Slavery Society responded by carrying the motto: "LOVEJOY the first MARTYR to American LIBERTY. MURDERED for asserting the FREEDOM of the PRESS. Alton, November 7, 1837."

Frederick Douglass and the Black Press

Frederick Douglass, former slave and African-American abolitionist, used the press and published books and pamphlets to further the antislavery cause. His best guess was that he was born in February of 1817 in Talbot County on the eastern shore of Maryland. Frederick Douglass knew neither his name at birth, his date and place of birth, nor his white father. Douglass's mother died when he was young, and after his master also died, he was sent away with other slave property. In his new home, he met a kind mistress who attempted to teach him to read, but his master scolded her, saying, "A nigger should know nothing but to obey his master—to do as he is told to do."[8]

Douglass endured slavery under the hands of several masters before he escaped in May 1838 and went to New York City, where he found a benefactor. He supported himself first as a carpenter; then, because of his moving speeches at the Massachusetts Anti-Slavery Society, he became a full-time, paid abolitionist lecturer. In the

Figure 7–2 Frederick Douglass spoke eloquently for the abolitionist cause in the states and abroad. (Division of Prints and Photographs, Library of Congress Collection)

1840s, Douglass was the prize speaker of the Massachusetts Anti-Slavery Society, traveling the lecture circuit with William Lloyd Garrison and Wendell Phillips. Part of Douglass' convincing appeal was his experience as a slave. In his first public address, he captivated his listeners, arguing that emancipation would "blot out the insults we have borne, will heal the wounds we have endured and are even groaning under, will pacify the resentment which would kindle to a blaze were it not for your exertions."9 Douglass told his audience that the worst feature of slavery was not the lash but the separation of friends and families.

In 1845, Douglass traveled to Britain to speak for the society. The British were so impressed by his performance that they raised enough money to buy his freedom. He also continued his own self-education, learning to write well and speak eloquently.

Douglass in 1842 had begun writing for Garrison's *Liberator*. Commenting on a series of letters Douglass wrote to Garrison from abroad, Horace Greeley of the *New York Tribune* said some passages in the letter, "for genuine eloquence, would do honor to any writer of the English language, however eloquent." Thurlow Weed, of the *Albany Evening Journal*, said of the same letter that it gave Douglass "rank among the most gifted and eloquent men of the age."10

In 1845, when he was twenty-seven years old, he published his first autobiography, the *Narrative of the Life of Frederick Douglass*. In August 1847, he became associate editor of *The Ram's Horn* and wrote regularly for the *New York City Standard*. Later that year he began publishing his own newspaper, *North Star*, which continued publication for sixteen years, an unusually long life span for an abolitionist newspaper. Inspiration for the newspaper's name came from the lyrics of a tune sung by runaway slaves, "I kept my eye on the bright north star, and thought of liberty." Douglass printed a prospectus for the paper in the columns of the *Anti-Slavery Bugle*, promising a weekly that would "Attack Slavery in all its forms and aspects: Advocate Universal Emancipation; exalt the standard of Public Morality; promote the Moral and Intellectual improvement of the Colored People; and hasten the day of FREEDOM to the Three Millions of our Enslaved Fellow Countrymen." In 1851, the name was changed to *Frederick Douglass's Paper*.

Douglass's paper was received with mixed reviews. Although his Massachusetts friends were demonstrably happy about the newspaper's publication, James Gordon Bennett of the *New York Herald* suggested that the editor be exiled to Canada and his equipment thrown into a lake. Local hostility, however, was feeble and of short duration. The printers' association welcomed Douglass' paper to Rochester, and the printers and publishers of the city invited Douglass to a celebration of Benjamin Franklin's birthday. Douglass was proud of his printing establishment, which was the first ever owned by an African American in the United States. His press, type, and other printing materials cost between $900 and $1,000 and were, he said, the best that could be obtained in the country. In the modest, single-room office, Douglass' children and a white apprentice set type.

Continuing to lecture on slavery and on women's rights, Douglass published an autobiography in 1855, *My Bondage and My Freedom*. In 1859, he took his message abroad, lecturing in Canada, England, and Scotland. A tireless supporter of the Civil

War, Douglass helped recruit African Americans for a Massachusetts regiment, thereby earning an invitation to the White House from President Lincoln. After the war, he moved to Washington, D.C., and in 1869 began publishing the *New National Era*. In 1872, he served as a presidential elector.

Although Garrison and Douglass began their relationship as friends and political allies, they eventually parted company because of bitter disagreements. Garrison sought dissolution of the Union, rejected the right to vote, and labeled the Constitution a proslavery document. On the other hand, Douglass felt that to abstain from voting was a refusal to exercise a legitimate and powerful means for abolishing slavery. He said the Constitution not only carried no guarantee in favor of slavery but, on the contrary, it was in "its letter and spirit an anti-slavery instrument, demanding the abolition of slavery as a condition of its own existence as the supreme law of the land."[11] When Douglass resisted Garrison's proposition to withhold support to any newspaper that did not accept the Constitution to be a proslavery document, the Garrisonian papers—the *Liberator*, the *Standard*, and the *Freeman*—assailed Douglass, charging him with treachery, inconsistency, and ingratitude.

Douglass turned sixty in 1877, but he didn't hesitate to continue actively working at home and abroad. He was appointed the U.S. marshal for the District of Columbia in 1876 and held the office for five years before becoming the recorder of deeds for the District. He also served as secretary of the Santo Domingo Commission and as the U.S. minister to Haiti.

By January 1882, he had written the last of his three autobiographies. In August of that year, his wife died. In 1884, he remarried and sailed to Europe, Greece, and Egypt to continue his lecture circuit. Highly criticized for his second marriage—to a white woman—Douglass replied that he was quite impartial. His first wife "was the color of my mother, and the second, the color of my father."[12] Douglass died in 1895, attending a women's suffrage convention the day of his death.

In 1963, *Ebony* magazine, on the centennial of the Emancipation Proclamation, used his photograph on the cover of the magazine, editorializing:

> Frederick Douglass, father of the protest movement, is a worthy subject to grace the cover of any publication commemorating the centennial of the Emancipation Proclamation. . . .
>
> After Emancipation was achieved, Douglass went on fighting for a wide variety of reforms in the areas of black voting rights, urban development, pacifism, social justice, and especially women's rights.[13]

Iconography: Persuasive Visuals

The wide use of the printed word—and also pictures—by the abolitionists was unprecedented, although the Bible societies of the 1820s had pioneered such publication efforts. The abolitionists regarded the many prints they used in pamphlets and other publications, as well as the slave emblems produced, as accurate representations of occurrences. The prints ranged from depictions of the separation of slave families to the seizing, branding, selling, and torturing of men, women, and children. Slave emblems had first been used in England, and in 1787 the Committee to Abolish the Slave Trade posed a black male slave as a supplicant, with the motto, "Am I Not a Man and a Brother?" Later that year, Josiah Wedgwood employed his chief modeler to design a cameo, with a black slave on a background of delicate white. Wedgwood distributed the image in England and sent several to Benjamin Franklin, president of the Pennsylvania Abolition Society. Franklin wrote to Wedgwood that he thought the emblem might have as powerful an effect as the political pamphlet.

Figure 7–3   Slave emblem designed by Josiah Wedgwood. (Division of Prints and Photographs, Library of Congress Collection)

The primary abolitionist emblem that evolved and endured pictured a black woman, half nude, chained and kneeling. An 1838 token inscribed with the image carried the slogan, "Am I Not a Woman and a Sister?" The use of graphics was not accidental, and abolitionists recognized their impact. Angelina Grimke wrote, "Until the pictures of the slave's sufferings were drawn and held up to public gaze, no Northerner had any idea of the cruelty of the system . . . and those who had lived at [*sic*] the South . . . wept in secret places over the sins of oppression. . . . Prints . . . are powerful appeals."[14] In 1837, the First Anti-Slavery Convention of American Women passed a formal resolution endorsing the use of prints: "we regard anti-slavery prints as powerful auxiliaries in the cause of emancipation, and recommend that these 'pictorial representations' be multiplied an hundred fold, so that the speechless agony of the fettered slave may unceasingly appeal to the heart of the patriot, the philanthropist, and the Christian."[15]

Women, Voice, and Pen in the Antislavery Movement

In the early 1800s, it was considered inappropriate for women to speak in public, and only a few took up their pen in a public forum. Those who did often worked to support their husbands' printing positions or wrote letters for women in the newly developed "Ladies' Departments" of various periodicals. Women had been active in the American antislavery movement from the beginning, both in exclusively female societies and in societies that included both sexes. In fact, abolitionists were sometimes distinguished for their attitudes about the sexes. Maria Lydia Child explained to her friend and colleague Angelina Grimke that her husband "despised the idea of any distinction in the appropriate spheres of human beings."[16] Defending the master-slave relationship required a structured view of the world that disallowed one's having control over oneself; such a cultural worldview was unacceptable to many abolitionists, who argued that society should have little control over individuals. From such an individualist ideology emerged a feminist strain as well: If slaves were to have control over their own lives, shouldn't women as well? Indeed, it was at the World Anti-Slavery Convention in London in 1840 that Lucretia Mott and Elizabeth Cady Stanton, two women who would signify the women's rights movement in the nineteenth century, concluded that they needed a separate women's rights movement. After crossing the Atlantic to attend the antislavery conference, and after years of devoting their efforts to the movement, the conference voted not to seat the women delegates. Women were not about to bow out of the movement, because they had been mainstays in the antislavery cause and their ability to raise money had earned them positions of power. As early as 1839, the business and finance committees of the Pennsylvania Anti-Slavery Society consisted of four men and three women. By 1850, five of the twelve members of the executive committee were women.[17] Although many women worked within female societies, many did not. Lydia Maria Child, author of the 1833 tract *An Appeal in Favor of That Class of Americans Called Africans* that stated the goal of immediate emancipation, became editor of the American Anti-Slavery Society's *National Anti-Slavery Standard* in 1841.

The antislavery movement therefore awarded women positions of authority and power that were rarely attainable in the mainstream journalistic world. These women also broke the barrier of speaking in public. Lucretia Mott, who spoke freely as one of four female visitors at the founding meeting of the American Anti-Slavery Society in Philadelphia, wrote later, "It was with difficulty, I acknowledge, that I ventured to express what had been near to my heart for many years, for I knew we were there by sufferance; but when I rose, such was the readiness with which the freedom to speak was granted, that it inspired me with a little more boldness to speak on other subjects."[18] The 1837 delegates to the Anti-Slavery Convention of American Women further broke the shackles of pen and voice by passing a resolution offered by Angelina Grimke:

> Resolved, That as certain rights and duties are common to all moral beings, the time has come for woman to move in that sphere which Providence has assigned to her, and no longer remain satisfied in the circumscribed limits with which corrupt custom and a perverted application of Scripture have encircled her; therefore that it is the duty of woman, and the province of woman, to plead the cause of the oppressed in our land, and to do all that she can by her voice, and her pen, and her purse, and the influence of her example, to overthrow the horrible system of American slavery.

Leaders such as Angelina Grimke and Lydia Child came from the educated middle to upper classes of white society, but women abolitionists made some attempts to form bonds with the black women they sought to free. The pampered daughter of Charleston, South Carolina, slaveholders, Angelina Grimke adopted the emblem of the slave woman to symbolize not only the evils of slavery but also the outrage of women's oppression by a patriarchal society. As she matured, she saw herself first as an enchained victim, then as a self-liberated woman. In 1836, she published the pamphlet *An Appeal to the Christian Women of the South*, which caused her to be estranged from her family and banished from her native city of Charleston. Within months she drafted a second document, *An Appeal to the Women of the Nominally Free States*, in which she urged more public action than she had recommended for southern women: "The denial of our duty to act, is a bold denial of our right to act; and if we have no right to act, then may we well be termed 'the white slaves of the North'—for, like our brethren in bonds, we must seal our lips in silence and despair."[19]

Women such as Angelina Grimke, who associated their position with that of the black slave woman, in essence confused the situation. Black women, however, clearly perceived the truth of the difference in position between black and white women; and as the women's rights movement gained in strength, racism drove women apart rather than keeping them together. No black women attended the initial women's rights convention at Seneca Falls, New York, in 1848, and Sojourner Truth was the only black woman to attend the 1851 women's rights convention in Akron, Ohio. Many of the women in attendance pleaded with Frances Dana Gage, president of the convention, to prevent Sojourner Truth from speaking, but Gage ignored them, allowing the old black woman to give her famous "Ain't I a Woman?"

speech. Sojourner Truth distinguished between white and black women by pointing out the hypocrisy of "chivalry": "Nobody ever helps me into carriages, or over mud-puddles, or gives me any best place! And ain't I a woman? Look at me! I have ploughed, planted, and gathered into barns, and no man could head me! And ain't I a woman? I could work as much and eat as much as a man—when I could get it—and bear the lash as well! And ain't I a woman? I have born thirteen children and seen most all sold into slavery, and when I cried out with my mother's grief, none but Jesus heard me! And ain't I a woman?"[20]

Uncle Tom's Cabin: Slavery and the Popular Culture

The 1850s saw a revival of religious fervor and the publication of Harriet Beecher Stowe's *Uncle Tom's Cabin*, which propelled the issue of slavery into the popular culture of the day. The novel was first serialized in the *National Era* beginning in June 1851, and its first appearance in book form was on March 20, 1852, about a week before the last installment appeared in the *Era*. Within three weeks, 20,000 copies of the book had sold, and by January 1853 the number rose to 200,000 copies. Harriet Beecher Stowe received $10,300 as a copyright premium on three months' sales of *Uncle Tom*, a figure thought to be the largest sum ever received by an American or European author from the sale of a work in such a short period of time.

Reaction to the book in the North was quite favorable, and Stowe received laudatory letters from writers such as Ralph Waldo Emerson, James Russell Lowell, and others, although some criticized her for excessive sentimentality. Abolitionists were split on the book; they regarded it as a popular tool to increase people's antipathy to slavery, but they questioned the personality characteristics it ascribed to African Americans and the solutions of colonization it proposed. That racist sentiments were not the peculiar province of southerners alone was apparent in some reviews. The *Cleveland Daily Plain Dealer*, a Democratic newspaper, wrote that *Uncle Tom's Cabin* was misleading and that "[a] pure blooded African when let alone has no aspirations for liberty as we understand it."[21]

Although favorable comment was expressed in the border states and by southerners who had left the South, as the book gained in popularity, southern antagonism also grew. It is difficult to know how widely the book circulated in the South, but there are accounts of book peddlers selling the book in the Carolinas and along the Mississippi River. Students at the University of Virginia, however, publicly burned the book, and other stories abound of booksellers being driven out for offering the book for sale. Southerners claimed that separation of slave families as depicted in the book was overdrawn and that cruelty was not sanctioned by a majority of slave owners. The *Southern Literary Messenger* called it a slanderous work that was spreading across every section of the country as well as crossing the Atlantic. Mrs. Stowe deserved criticism, the author wrote, "as the mouthpiece of a large and dangerous faction which if we do not put down with the pen, we may be compelled one day (God grant that day may never come!) to repel with the bayonet."[22] Outrage was followed by silence, and within two years after the book was published, southern publications declined to mention it in what might have been an attempt at dignified silence.

Uncle Tom's Cabin was widely distributed in theatrical versions without Stowe's permission, who thought such productions violated Christian principles of behavior. Nevertheless, theater versions abounded, seldom following the plot of the book and often exploiting comic elements. One version even sanctioned slavery.

Objections to *Uncle Tom's Cabin* emerged during and after World War II. In 1945, the *Negro Digest* polled African Americans, claiming that a majority considered the play anti-Negro because it showed blacks in a submissive, docile role. In 1963 in the *New Republic*, one writer objected to the book because it reinforced "unfavorable stereotypes of Negroes" and encouraged condescending "pity and neglect." In 1964, Alex Haley, author of *Roots*, made this comment:

> Mrs. Stowe's novel, for all its faults, is redeemed by the fact that it helped to end the institution of slavery. It is a deep irony that a century later, the very name of Mrs. Stowe's hero is the worst insult the slaves' descendants can hurl at one another out of their frustrations in seeking what all other Americans take for granted.[23]

Restrictions on Publishing

In 1832, Virginia legislators reacted to the Nat Turner rebellion and to abolitionist publications by enacting a law that punished those who wrote books or pamphlets "advising persons of colour within this state to make insurrection." The law provided for punishment of thirty-nine lashes for the first offense and death without benefit of clergy for the second offense.[24]

Virginia was not the only state to invoke such a law. In 1829, a former slave, David Walker, published in pamphlet form *Walker's Appeal in Four Articles Together with a Preamble to the Colored Citizens of the World.* He advised slaves to use violence to free themselves and, according to one source, "set off legislation to curb expression in several states beginning with Georgia."[25]

By 1835, in response to increased abolitionist printing activity, laws prohibiting the distribution of antislavery literature were so severe that all antislavery societies below the Mason-Dixon line had disappeared.

Restrictions, although sometimes legal in nature, also came in the form of aggressive public opinion. When the Anti-Slavery Society mailed more than a million pieces of literature in 1835, the reaction neared hysteria.[26] In addition to the hostility they encountered in southern society, abolitionists were not always welcome in the North. In 1835, William Lloyd Garrison was assaulted and dragged through the streets of Boston, and another abolitionist barely escaped death after being beaten by a mob in Concord, Massachusetts.

The attacks on abolitionists and on the publication of antislavery materials attracted more supporters than antislavery societies could garner, although some newspapers defended freedom of speech. During the 1830s, the columns of *Niles'*

Weekly Register vigorously protested the proslavery party's attempts to silence its opposition. The *Boston Courier* expressed its support through rhyme:

> Rail on, then "brethren of the south"—
>   Ye shall not hear the truth the less—
> No seal is on the Yankee's mouth,
>   No fetter on the Yankee's press!
> From our Green Mountains to the sea
>   Our voice shall thunder—WE ARE FREE![27]

Even the *New York Herald*, with its pro-South stance, told the South that if it demanded the North "to pass laws infringing the liberty of the press we must tell them frankly that they are running into a similar degree of fanaticism to that which they object to in the abolitionists."[28] However, the mainstream press did not always support the abolitionists' appeals to freedom of speech and press. The abolitionist minister William E. Channing wrote to James G. Birney that the press had "countenanced, by its gentle censures, the reign of force."[29]

The federal government also tried to restrict the spread of "incendiary" literature. In December 1835, President Jackson proposed that Congress be given the right to determine which newspapers were incendiary. Even the proslavery forces recognized his proposal as being unconstitutional, but later that year Postmaster General Amos Kendall, President Jackson, and John C. Calhoun joined forces seeking a federal law to prohibit abolitionist mail from traveling South. The group was not successful, but a combination of southern postmasters and public groups succeeded where legislation did not. When the citizens of Charleston found that in 1835 a considerable number of abolitionist materials were being sent to South Carolina from the American Anti-Slavery Society, they forcibly seized the literature and burned it on the Charleston parade ground. Acting on the postmaster general's advice, the New York and Charleston postmasters announced that they would forward no more antislavery matter to the southern address. Kendall wrote to the Charleston postmaster that although he had no legal authority to exclude newspapers from the mail, he was not prepared to order the South Carolina official to deliver abolitionist materials:

> The post office department was created to serve the people of *each* and *all* of the *United States* and not be used as an instrument of their destruction. . . . We owe an obligation to the laws, but a higher one to the communities in which we live, and if the *former* be perverted to destroy the *latter*, it is patriotism to disregard them.[30]

Congress also instituted a "gag rule," under which all petitions regarding slavery that were received from citizens were not to be presented, printed, or considered by Congress. Abolitionists protested the rule, and they thereby gained a reputation as champions of the Constitution rather than as radicals.

In response to an 1850 amendment to the Fugitive Slave Act of 1793, abolitionists increasingly rejected their former pacifistic approach, and in some cases they even promoted slave insurrections and violent overthrow of the "peculiar institution."

The law required citizens to help apprehend fugitive slaves and imposed severe penalties on those who helped slaves escape. The law jeopardized the position of free African Americans as well, because a suspected fugitive was not guaranteed the rights of calling witnesses, trial by jury, or writs of habeas corpus.

The Civil War

By February 1861, all the states in the entire lower South had left the Union, but the eight remaining slave-holding states—the upper South and border states—hoped for compromise and prayed for peace. They were in a difficult position. If they remained in the Union, they had little power to retain their slave-holding status; yet they were reluctant to put their faith in fire-eating secessionists, regarding secession as impractical. Attempts at compromise failed, however, and on April 12, 1861, the Palmetto Guard of South Carolina fired on Fort Sumter. The Civil War had begun.

The Confederate States of America was made up of eleven states: South Carolina, Georgia, Alabama, Mississippi, Louisiana, Texas, Florida, Arkansas, Tennessee, North Carolina, and Virginia. Delaware, Maryland, Missouri, and Kentucky—slave-holding states before secession—adhered to the Union. The war was longer and bloodier than anyone could have imagined. Of 2.1 million Union men, 360,000 died. About 225,000 of them died from disease. Of 1.6 million Confederate soldiers, 400,000 died.[31]

Reporters and the War

Civil War coverage was provided by telegraphic reporters, reporters hired by individual newspapers, roving correspondents, and "specials." Estimates of cost and numbers vary. Some historians claim the *New York Herald* spent half a million dollars covering the Civil War and had as many as sixty-three correspondents in the field. Others estimate that together, the *Times,* the *Tribune,* the *Post,* and the *Herald* in New York spent $100,000 a year covering the War. The *New York Times* and the *New York Tribune* may have had as many as twenty reporters covering a major battle. The *Chicago Tribune* claimed to have had twenty-seven reporters in the field, although it is not likely that many wrote simultaneously.[32]

On South Mountain, Maryland, a stone arch memorializes 147 artists and reporters who covered the war. The arch reads:

> To the Army correspondents and artists 1861–1865 whose toils cheered the camps, thrilled the fireside, educated provinces of rustics into a bright nation of readers and gave incentive to narrate distant wars and explore dark lands.[33]

Northern correspondents generally were fairly well educated, with several graduates of Harvard, Yale, and other universities among the corps. Many later distinguished themselves as correspondents in other wars, in other areas of newspapers, or as professionals in other fields. Southern correspondents varied. Some newspaper

Figure 7–4   "News from the Front—the Army Correspondent," a pencil and Chinese white drawing by Edwin Forbes, circa 1876. (Division of Prints and Photographs, Library of Congress Collection)

coverage was provided by soldiers in the fields who wrote letters to editors; reporters were not widely employed in the South before the war.

No correspondents on either side were granted noncombatant status, and often they were in as much danger as the soldiers. Standard equipment for reporters included a revolver, field glasses, notebook, blanket(s), a sack for provisions, and a horse; outfitting a correspondent was an expensive venture.

They were, in some cases, a picturesque lot; the *New York Tribune* took special pride in having its correspondents look more dashing than other newspeople. Probably the most colorful, however, was William Howard Russell of the *Times* of London, who arrived in a khaki "himalyan" suit. He was entertained at the White House and covered the first battle of Bull Run. After his account of the "disgraceful conduct of the troops . . . a miserable causeless panic . . . scandalous behavior," however, he lost favor, and the *New York Illustrated News* pictured him as a "swinish boozer who viewed the battle from a safe remove through bleary eyes and a spyglass."[34] Northern newspapers were not ready to accept a negative English account of their beloved northern army.

Competition to get the news first governed the actions of correspondents and, in some cases, wrote Louis Starr, "drove them to bribery, subterfuge, plagiarism, and outright fakery. It fueled the whole news revolution. It left a residue of anecdote and legend which enriched the lore of American journalism."[35] Among the most well known of the northern correspondents were Murat Halstead of the *Cincinnati Commercial,* Henry Stanley of the *New York Herald,* Whitelaw Reid of the *Cincinnati Gazette,* and Albert D. Richardson and George W. Smalley of the *New York Tribune.*[36] More than 100 army correspondents represented the Confederate press during the war. Reporters commonly used pseudonyms, and if they wrote for more than one newspaper, might use several pseudonyms. Felix de Fontaine thus wrote under the pseudonym "Personne," a still anonymous correspondent under the name of "Shadow," and another preeminent southern correspondent, Peter Alexander, under the initials of PWA. Salaries varied from $6 per day to $25 a week. One reporter, during a two and one-half year period, earned about $12,000.[37]

Press in the North

Newspaper editors developed news coverage through expanded use of the telegraph, a home office organization to assign reporters and handle incoming reports, and the use of "specials" or correspondents.

The war dramatically increased the use of and need for telegraph facilities, and the unreliability of the wires caused major problems for correspondents. Telegraph lines were limited to start with, and they frequently broke or were commandeered by the military or commercial business. The uncertainty of telegraph wires also contributed to reporters' changing from a chronological style of reporting to a style that recorded certain facts first, although the degree to which reporters used a "news lead" varied. Telegraphing was expensive, and reporters began to curtail their flowery nineteenth-century style to fit the needs of telegraphic news. The *New York Herald's* account of the battle of Fort Sumter was presented chronologically, and the reader had to struggle through thirty paragraphs to discover that Major Anderson finally surrendered the fort to the Confederates.[38] Dr. Charles Ray's account of the July 1861 Battle of Bull Run, the first major battle of the war, reported the news first: "The battle is lost. The enemy have a substantial victory." The story did not follow in inverted pyramid style but mixed editorial comment with news and finally reverted to a more chronological order. The account continued:

> The result, so unexpected, dangerous and mortifying, is due to causes that the country will bye and bye discuss. Men who have been inattentive observers of the field of operations and of the tendency of the popular mind, will say that popular clamor has outrun military preparation; but this is not true. The well-appointed and magnificent army that is now coming back broken and disorganized into the entrenchments on the opposite side of the river, ought never to have been beaten.[39]

The battle represented some of the difficulties reporters would have in covering the war, as well as some of the misconceptions newspeople and the public held about the certainty of a "short war." When the battle began on Sunday afternoon,

Washingtonians fully expected a rout of Confederate troops. Henry Raymond, editor of the *New York Times*, wired his newspaper at two o'clock that afternoon that a Union victory was in progress. Unfortunately, Raymond filed his report too soon. The Union troops began to straggle back to Washington, defeated and in disarray. Raymond's newspaper was not the only one in error; the New York press on the Sunday night of the battle and the Monday morning after printed accounts of a Union victory. Press accounts had been prepared in Washington early enough to meet the Monday morning-edition deadlines, but censorship of the telegraph wires held up the news. Henry Villard's accounts in the *New York Herald* ran for three days. On July 21, Villard wrote, "I am en route to Washington with details of a great battle. *We have carried the day.* The rebels accepted battle in their strength, but are totally routed. Losses on both sides considerable." On July 22, the *Herald* account read, "Our troops, after taking three batteries and gaining a great victory at Bull's Run, were eventually repulsed and commenced a retreat on Washington."40

   Emphasis on telegraphic news and the high cost of news gathering during the war spurred editors to further develop cooperative news gathering. The Associated Press, known under various names since its organization in 1848, made agreements with Western Union that gave AP preferred treatment and rates and a virtually monopolistic position. In 1858, with the inauguration of the Atlantic cable, AP made arrangements with European news agencies to acquire news. Reuters in Britain, Havas in France, Wolff in Germany, and Stefani in Italy contributed news to the AP. As the AP expanded, an AP franchise became a valuable asset for a newspaper, and western papers had difficulty securing international news without the franchise. In 1862, angered by the dominance of New York newspapers in the Associated Press, a group of western editors formed the Western AP, charging that New York papers overcharged local papers and dictated what news would be in the daily reports and that local newspapers had little power in decision making. Both APs existed until 1892, when the New York AP folded and the Associated Press of Illinois emerged.41

Criticism of Lincoln

Although focusing heavily on news gathering, northern editors did not relinquish their right to editorialize. Thus, Lincoln's friends as well as his enemies criticized the president for the mistakes of his military commanders, for his reluctance to free the slaves, and for the repeated drafting of additional men to the army.

   The *Chicago Tribune*, often credited with helping to elect Lincoln, first demanded military action in the West, then criticized Major General John C. Fremont, who commanded the Western Army headquartered in St. Louis. Prior to Lincoln's Emancipation Proclamation, Fremont had declared martial law and freed the slaves within his military jurisdiction. The *Tribune*, edited by Charles Ray and Joseph Medill, supported Fremont's emancipation position but took him to task for what the paper considered military misjudgment and precipitous action without consulting President Lincoln. The newspaper's position angered abolitionist newspapers such as Greeley's *Tribune*, the *New York Post*, and Chicago rivals the *Times*, the *Journal*, and the *Post*. In response to the attacks, the *Tribune* published an editorial stating that a news-

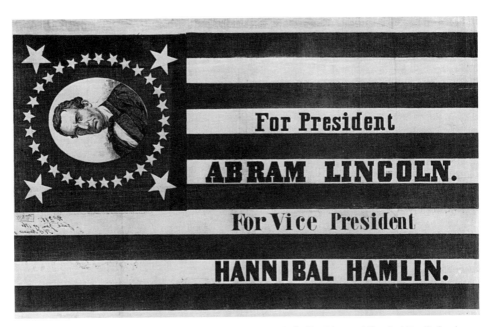

Figure 7–5 Cloth campaign banner supporting Abraham Lincoln for President and Hannibal Hamlin for vice president in 1860. (Division of Prints and Photographs, Library of Congress Collection)

paper during wartime was "regarded as watchmen on the walls" and that military men, as well as civil servants, should not be exempted from editorial criticism.[42]

The Confederate Press

Many changes that occurred in newspapers in the North during the war also characterized changes in southern journalism, but southern newspapers were harder hit with rising news costs and difficulties of obtaining news. In the South, as in the North, newspapers ran more prominent headlines, not often crossing the column rule, but extending for many decks vertically. Southern newspapers were characterized by a marked increase in telegraphic news, "extras," the development of newsboy sales over subscriptions, employment of "specials" or correspondents, and the development of cooperative news gathering. News and editorials gradually replaced the advertisements on page one.

However, the high cost of and sheer lack of newsprint forced editors to print on standard writing paper and, at times, even the reverse side of wallpaper. At the start of the war only 5 percent of the nation's paper mills were located in the South, and once the war was under way, no paper could be imported from the North. Imports from England were unlikely and, as the war progressed, nonexistent. Newspapers that cost $5 to $6 before the war sold for $50 to $60, and, on occasion, reached $125 at the end of the war. Editors reduced the size of their newspapers; by 1865 the

Charleston *Courier* was publishing only a single 10 inch by 15 inch sheet. Editors also used homemade ink substitutes, such as shoeblack.

Manpower was another problem. Of the 800 printers in the South in 1863, by June 1864, 75 percent had been in the army. During the first year of the war forty newspapers in Virginia collapsed; fifty out of sixty in Texas did not survive. Many ceased from lack of economic support, manpower, and supplies, and others were destroyed in the wake of advancing Union armies. By the time Lee surrendered at Appomattox in April 1865, only twenty dailies were still publishing.

The press system in the South had relied on two telegraph lines for its national and international news: the American Telegraph Company's line from New York and Washington that extended to Richmond, Raleigh, Columbia, Macon, Montgomery, and Mobile, and the Southwestern Telegraph Company's line on the western edge of the southern states—from Louisville, Kentucky, through Tennessee, Alabama, and Mississippi to New Orleans. These lines served the primary telegraphic news agency, operated by William H. Pritchard, editor of the Augusta *Constitutionalist* and agent for the Associated Press. However, southern newspapers had retained traditional party allegiances and were considered newspapers of opinion rather than of news. Few southern newspapers employed reporters or fed news to the Associated Press. However, this pattern had begun to shift even before the start of the war. The Richmond newspapers offered a variety of formats for its readers, including a news-oriented penny press product.

In the spring of 1861 telegraph lines were severed between the North and South, and Pritchard set up an office in Montgomery, moving it to Richmond when the location of the Confederate capitol shifted. In 1862, he died and the Southern Associated Press, as it was called, was taken over by his son.

A Rally Cry

The *Richmond Press* had been one of the most developed in the South; like northern papers, once the war began, newspapers quickly rallied to the cause. Throughout the South newspapers expressed a variety of views, but within a limited framework. For example, they criticized specific actions of the Confederate Congress and of President Jefferson Davis, but they rarely approached the issue of slavery.

The war caused a great deal of hardship for many southern newspapers, but some managed to survive and actually flourish. The Richmond *Examiner,* for example, made a net profit of $50,000 during the last two years of the war and maintained a subscription list that far surpassed the boundaries of Virginia. Other Richmond newspapers included the *Enquirer,* which early in the war had a reputation for being an organ of the Davis administration. The *Whig,* as its name implies, was a Whig paper that opposed secession; its editor, however, was forced out in April 1861, and the *Whig* changed its editorial policies overnight. The Richmond *Dispatch,* patterned after the *Baltimore Sun,* represented the penny paper of Richmond. In March 1861, its circulation exceeded that of all Richmond newspapers combined; by the end of the war, it was circulating to 30,000 readers. The *Sentinel,* which first appeared in March 1863, replaced the *Enquirer* as the organ of the administration. Another publication developed during the war was the *Southern Illustrated*

▼

Alcott's Hospital Sketches

My headquarters were beside the bed of a New Jersey boy, crazed by the horrors of that dreadful Saturday. A slight wound in the knee brought him there; but his mind had suffered more than his body; some string of that delicate machine was over strained, and, for days, he had been reliving, in imagination, the scenes he could not forget, till his distress broke out in incoherent ravings, pitiful to hear. As I sat by him, endeavoring to soothe his poor distracted brain by the constant touch of wet hands over his hot forehead, he lay cheering his comrades on, hurrying them back, then counting them as they fell around him, often clutching my arm, to drag me from the vicinity of a bursting shell, or covering up his head to screen himself from a shower of shot; his face brilliant with fever; his eyes restless; his head never still; every muscle strained and rigid; while an incessant stream of defiant shouts, whispered warnings, and broken laments, poured from his lips with that forceful bewilderment which makes such wanderings so hard to overhear.

—Louisa May Alcott, one of many sketches published in the Boston newspaper the *Commonwealth*

News, highly sought after because *Harper's Weekly* was no longer available during the war.[43]

In addition to the Richmond newspapers, strong press centers were located in New Orleans, Charleston, Augusta, Savannah, Atlanta, and Mobile. In Charleston, the *Courier* represented the moderate southern position, whereas the *Mercury* was the mouthpiece for the irascible Robert Barnwell Rhett, Jr., a fire-eating secessionist who was highly critical of Confederate President Davis.

One of the most interesting of the Southern newspapers was the *Memphis Appeal,* sometimes dubbed the "Moving Appeal," which kept ahead of advancing Union armies and published from various cities in Georgia, Mississippi, and Alabama, as well as from a railroad flat car. Valued at $75,000 at the start of the war, the *Appeal* was considered one of the "finest examples of Confederate journalism."[44]

The Confederate Press Association

In 1862, after a year of dissatisfaction with the quality of news being received through Pritchard's southern news gathering agency, a group of editors met in Atlanta to form The Confederate Press Association (the P.A.). Representatives attended from the *Memphis* (Tennessee) *Appeal, Atlanta Southern Confederacy, Savannah Republican, Augusta Constitutionalist, Nashville Republican Banner,* and *Charleston Mercury.*[45] Editors of the *Memphis Appeal* had written that there was "universal complaint" with "the present unorganized and imbecile arrangement." The editor claimed that the news reports were "vague and unsatisfactory, unmeaning, unreliable, and, in many instances, flagitiously false."[46] Editors also believed the existing service was too expensive.

It took a full year, however, before a group of southern editors organized a new agency, the Press Association of the Confederate States of America. Its constitution outlined the purpose of the new organization, "to arrange, put in operation, and keep up an efficient system of reporting news by telegraph . . . under the exclusive control and employed for the exclusive benefit of the members." The initiation fee was $50 and the organization was open to all papers published in the Confederacy. The board hired a general manager, J. S. Thrasher, who traveled to key news centers and hired correspondents who were paid $25 a week. Thrasher advertised for the reporters in newspapers such as the *Atlanta Southern Confederacy:* "Desiring to extend the connections of the Press Association, gentlemen having experience as reporters or correspondents for newspapers, may contribute by sending me by mail information of their previous experience, present residence, customary terms for business and whether short hand writers or not."[47] Thirty-one daily newspapers subscribed to the new organization.

Thrasher exacted promises from the major military commanders to provide news when it was compatible with the public interest. He secured half rates for telegraphing dispatches across military and civilian telegraph lines and employed about twenty news agents to report the news. He instructed reporters to be objective, to discriminate carefully between fact and rumor, and "never to be beaten by a special correspondent."[48]

The association provided weekly reports of 3,500 words for a flat rate of $12. Newspapers were required to pay ten cents a word for additional material. During the first three months the P.A. spent from $17,000 to $18,000 for collecting and transmitting copyrighted news to the dailies and a few tri-weeklies of the Confederacy. The service also acted as a cooperative, with individual newspapers providing information from their own locales.

The P.A. did not wholly succeed in its efforts and failed to give an accurate picture of the seriousness of the northern threat. Reports from Gettysburg in July 1863 at one point gave Lee's army credit for capturing 4,000 Union troops, although ultimately the real story appeared—Lee had suffered serious losses. The association encountered many difficulties with the military and with maintaining the cooperation of the newspapers themselves, but on the whole it succeeded in a way that individual newspapers would not have been able to.

Toward the end of the war, the P.A. had great difficulty securing accurate news accounts. As Sherman marched through Georgia, information was scarce and often wrong. By fall, most accounts were taken from northern newspapers. Four of Richmond's five daily newspapers that had been threatening to abandon the P.A. did so. They formed the Mutual Press Association with James W. Lewellen of the *Richmond Dispatch* as president. The P.A. continued, and in January 1865, reported that the Confederate Congress was discussing peace negotiations. When the Confederacy collapsed on April 9, 1865, the press was barely functioning. The P.A. dissolved and by the fall of 1865, the Associated Press had restored service to most newspapers in the South.

Censorship in the North

Censorship in the North began shortly after the outbreak of the war. It was carried out not only by official decree by the Departments of State and War, but also indi-

▼

Personne Reports from Georgia

Augusta, Ga., March 1, 1862—Notwithstanding all the predictions which the public ear has heard for the last month concerning the fall of Charleston and Savannah, that event appears to be just as far in the distance as the first. In fact, time has so narrowed down the probabilities of a Federal success, that the people of Savannah, at least, are now satisfied of their ability to hold the city against any odds. Yet the preparations for defence still continue. Fortifications against approaches by land are nearly, if not quite complete, and those protecting the water front are deemed equally efficient to resist an attack from that division.

The city is eminently free from excitement—there is marrying and giving in marriages, parties and sociables are mighty woven into the web of social life, while business continues active and undisturbed. Along the river many of the planters have removed their negros, rice and valuables, in accordance with a military order to that effect; but from the town itself there have been comparatively few withdrawals of refugees to the interior. One can hardly say the same for Charleston.

—Felix de Fontaine (Personne), reprinted in the *Collections of the Georgia Historical Society*, June 1959

vidually by commanders of troops. The government successfully prohibited the transmission of news from Washington via the telegraph or the railroad, but it rarely stopped dissemination of news from the fields of battle. Defying the censors had its costs and reporters were arrested, and some court-martialed, for their refusal to cooperate with often rigid restrictions.

After two attempts by Secretary of State Seward and General Scott to quash the telegraphic transmission of news about troop movements, the press and Scott agreed on censorship procedures in 1861, about two weeks before the first major Union defeat at the Battle of Bull Run. Scott agreed that no prior censorship would be required if newsmen would not report by telegraph troop movements, mutinies, riots among soldiers, or predictions of troop movements. On the Sunday afternoon of the battle, Washingtonians drove to Manassas in their carriages, carrying picnics and expecting to watch a rout of rebel troops and an end to the Civil War. What they found instead was a Confederate victory.

As correspondents rushed to correct earlier accounts predicting a Union victory, General Scott imposed strict censorship on the telegraph. Not until reporters found that Monday morning editions of the New York papers carried news of a Union victory did they realize their corrected stories had been stopped. Although Washington newspapers carried the news of the dramatic defeat, out-of-town newspapers were stuck with old and grossly inaccurate information.

Attempts at cooperative agreements broke down on both sides—the military and the press. On August 10, 1861, the war department declared that no information regarding troop movements would be telegraphed from Washington except directly after battles. Newspaper correspondents also were prohibited from writing any

Figure 7–6   "Newspapers in Camp," a pencil and Chinese white drawing by Edwin Forbes. (Division of Prints and Photographs, Library of Congress Collection)

information about troop movements or information "respecting the troops, camps, arsenals, entrenchments, or military affairs within the several military districts."[49] Correspondents printed such information under threat of court-martial and the death penalty in accord with the fifty-seventh Article of War.

In February 1862, telegraphic censorship was transferred from the state department to the war department, and all telegraph lines were transferred to military control. The war department ordered that any newspaper transmitting information not approved specifically by the war department or a commanding general would no longer receive or distribute information or publications by telegraph or rail. Editorial opposition was so strong that the order was modified the next day to allow publication of some "past facts"; a vague post office order issued in March further restricted the press and confused the situation. The war department also harassed several reporters after threatening to seriously enforce its regulations. On April 12, Secretary of War Stanton, in an attempt to standardize censorship, abolished local control and replaced it with a parole system. Correspondents were again prohibited from printing information about the locations of generals, divisions, numbers of troops, kinds of arms, rations, transports used for movements, references to camp locations, or pictorial representations of lines of defense. The restrictions were rigid, but they were not rigidly enforced.

Although criticism or praise of generals often influenced correspondents' access to information, reporters probably faced more difficulties with General William T. Sherman than with any other general. Criticism of Sherman in the 1861 Kentucky campaign started the feud. The *Cincinnati Commercial* called the general "stark mad" and erroneously claimed that he had been relieved of his command. Sherman tried to expel all reporters from his army thereafter, but they were determined to follow him and report his military activities. He is reputed to have said about newsmen:

> They come into camp, poke about among the lazy shirks and pick up their camp rumors and publish them as facts, and the avidity with which these rumors are swallowed by the public makes even some of our officers bow to them. I will not. They are a pest and shall not approach me and I will treat them as spies, which in truth they are.[50]

In December 1862, Sherman's battle with the press culminated in the court-martial of Thomas Knox, a *New York Herald* reporter who violated Sherman's order against reporting an abortive Union attempt to seize Vicksburg, Mississippi. Knox enclosed a map with his story and sent it to a collaborator in Cairo, Illinois, but one of Sherman's aides opened the letter. Knox then went to Cairo by boat and telegraphed a story claiming that Sherman was incompetent. Sherman ordered Knox's arrest and charged him with disobeying orders and giving intelligence to the enemy. Knox was convicted of disobeying orders but escaped the heavier charge, which carried the death penalty, because Sherman could not prove that the reporter gave the enemy information. Knox was told not to return to the war front. Lincoln, however, revoked the sentence and told Knox he had to stay away from the army unless he received permission from General Grant to accompany the troops, permission that Grant would not give without Sherman's approval. Sherman's battle with the press continued, and he once remarked that the only two successful campaigns in the war succeeded because of the absence of newspaper reporters. When Sherman completed his successful march to the sea, he cut the telegraph wires to delay the transmission of information. After the war, it is said that he refused to shake hands with Horace Greeley because the *Tribune* had revealed certain details of his Carolina campaign in 1863, which had resulted in heavy losses.[51]

Lincoln has been lauded for his tolerance of the press because he remanded an order by General A. E. Burnside in June 1863 that would have closed down the Chicago *Times* and prohibited the New York *World* from circulating in the Midwest. However, in 1862 after the war department issued its broad mandate for control of information, Lincoln suspended the writ of *habeas corpus* and allowed military trials for those who discouraged volunteer enlistments, resisted militia drafts, or were generally disloyal.

In May 1864, Lincoln ordered the New York *Journal of Commerce* and the New York *World* closed and their proprietors arrested for publishing a forged presidential proclamation announcing a draft of 400,000 men. Major General John A. Dix investigated the incident and reported to Secretary of War Stanton that the editors were honestly duped. The men were freed after two days when Dix discovered the forgerer, a New York *Times* reporter, Joseph Howard. Howard confessed that the editors had nothing to do with the fraud.[52]

Censorship in the South

The Confederate government kept tight control of information issued from the early Confederate capital of Montgomery, Alabama, from the time of the first declaration of independence from the Union. The meeting of the Confederate Congress in secret session made it even more difficult for correspondents to obtain hard news in the Confederate capital. When the capital was moved to Richmond, Virginia, in late May 1861, reporters followed but the same tight rein on news dissemination continued. During the same month, the Provisional Congress of the Confederate States passed a bill empowering the President to censor telegraphic dispatches, an act that encountered little public opposition. The act authorized agents to censor telegraph messages, required telegraph employees to take an oath of allegiance to the Confederacy, and prohibited coded messages. The act also imposed penalties of fines and imprisonment for persons convicted of "sending news detrimental to the Southern cause by telegraph."[53]

Brigadier General Braxton Bragg, commanding forces in Pensacola, Florida, with the intent of eliminating the federal occupation of Fort Pickens, also was reluctant to give correspondents free rein. The same day that Fort Sumter surrendered, Bragg ordered L. H. Mathews of the *Pensacola Observer* arrested and charged with alerting the enemy to a possible attack on Fort Pickens. Mathews was acquitted and released within a few days, but the incident demonstrated the heavy hand of Bragg in dealings with the press. Throughout the fall of 1861, campaign secrecy was heavily imposed on southern correspondents and they risked being treated as spies whenever they sought information for print. In October, the *Mobile Advertiser and Regis-*

The Press Asserts the Right to Criticize

In response to the *Chicago Times* suppression, the leaders of the New York press community met on June 8, producing a list of four resolutions. The third resolution contained the thrust of the argument:

> While we emphatically disclaim and deny any right as inhering in journalists or others to invite, advocate, abet, uphold or justify treason or rebellion; we respectfully but firmly assert and maintain the right of the press to criticize freely and fearlessly the acts of those charged with the administration of the Government, also those of all their civil and military subordinates, whether with intent directly to ensure greater energy, efficiency and fidelity in the public service, or in order to achieve the same ends remotely through the substitution of other persons for those now in power.

—*New York Times*, June 9, 1863

ter stated, "The Richmond papers announce that all civilians are now rigidly excluded from our lines at Manassas."[54]

By June, the censorship that postmasters had practiced before the war in prohibiting abolitionist and other mails from the North was enacted into law. Sometime between the summer of 1861 and that of 1862 the press and government agreed to voluntary censorship. Newspapers agreed to suppress news of troop movements as well as the locations of forts, munitions, or gunboats. They were permitted to publish any military information regarding the enemy taken from northern newspapers.

Although southern newspaper editors strove to remain cautious and loyal, even they objected when in January 1862 a bill was proposed to subject any newspaper to severe penalties for publishing information vital to Confederate security. The bill did not pass. Military censorship, however, continued to severely restrict reporting.

Photography and Pictorial Illustration

Entrepreneurs, artists, and scientists experimented with various forms of cameras as early as the days of the Renaissance, but not until the 1830s did photographic development proceed sufficiently to allow the recording of permanent images. Louis Daguerre in 1837 designed a process to develop positive photographic plates, which used burnished copper as a base and a thin, silvered negative emulsion with unexposed particles that could be washed away in a solvent. Although the daguerreotype was received with acclaim, the process was limited because copies could not be made and subjects had to stand frozen for twenty to thirty minutes, the time required to expose a plate.

From 1837 to 1840, the development of an improved camera lens provided a more brilliant image, the light sensitivity of photographic plates was increased by recoating the plates with different chemicals, and the harsh tones of the daguerreotype were softened by gilding the plate with gold chloride. These developments made it possible to create portraits that closely resembled the subject, but they did not shorten the exposure time.

Daguerre's progress coincided with the development of a positive–negative process by British scientists William Henry Fox Talbot and Sir John Herschel. Their process allowed for multiple prints. In 1851, however, the emergence of the collodion process, which provided durable glass negatives and a shorter exposure time, revolutionized the portrait business, for which photography was commercially used. Glass plates were coated with collodion, a mixture of guncotton in alcohol and ether, then developed in silver nitrate, exposed while wet, and finally developed. By 1860, the daguerreotype formula had been nearly replaced by a variety of cheaper techniques such as the tintype and paper print. In 1871, the use of dry plates replaced the initial collodion process, cutting exposure time to seconds.

The use of the word *daguerreotype* came to be synonymous not only with the technology and inventor connected with the term, but also with the miniature portraits the technology produced. More descriptive of the emerging technological and cultural process was the word *photography*—with its enclosed word *graph* tying the

Figure 7–7   "Photographer's Wagon" by T. H. O'Sullivan, Carson Desert, Nevada, 1870. (Division of Prints and Photographs, Library of Congress Collection)

process closely to that of printing, writing, and drawing. Photography meant "drawing with light." Popular writers spoke of the process as one of authority, capable of reproducing exact images, verifiable truth. Yet, even as early as 1869, a German scientist pointed to the falsity of photography, noting that lenses distort shapes and perspectives and that colors and shadings may be far from exact. Walt Whitman, editor of the *Brooklyn Daily Eagle*, pointed to yet another result of the emerging technology—that of the creation of studios to display daguerreotypes—new public places for the display of pictures. "What a spectacle!" wrote Whitman. "In whatever direction you turn your peering gaze, you see naught but human faces! There they stretch, from floor to ceiling—hundreds of them. Ah! what tales might those pictures tell if their mute lips had the power of speech! How romance then, would be infinitely outdone by fact . . . a great legion of human faces."[55]

Photographers in the United States usually came from the ranks of graphic artists and sought to record information rather than to produce art. However, the large-format technology that was available precluded the capturing of action shots. During the 1850s, the perfection of shorter-focal-length stereographic cameras enabled photographers to freeze some types of action and ultimately led to the photographing of war. Although Roger Fenton, a British photographer, photographed British army personnel during the Crimean War, the American Civil War was the first conflict to be photographed thoroughly. Mathew Brady, the photographer with the eye of an historian, directed most of the pictorial coverage.

Although technology made it possible to photograph the Civil War—1,500 photographers produced tens of thousands of images in field and urban studios—reproduction technology had not yet arrived to make photographic publication inexpensive. Even during the Civil War, the *New York Herald's* maps had to be hand-engraved in pieces by several engravers in order to meet edition time. Similarly, photographs could only provide models for artists and line engravers; the photographs were used to make the line drawings for reproduction. The absence of adequately reproduced photographs is attested to by the fact that in 1864, after Grant's victories, the Washington press corps did not know the general by sight. Nevertheless, the photographs, for the first time in the history of the Western world, permeated the culture through wood engravings derived from photographs that appeared in *Harper's Weekly* and *Leslie's Illustrated.* These popular journals provided a look at war that might be compared to today's television depictions of modern conflict.

Mathew Brady was a popular portrait photographer during the 1840s in New York, distinguished for his portraits of the country's political and intellectual elite but not well known for business acumen or money management. Known to spend freely, Brady was in financial difficulty at various times during the two decades before the Civil War.

Brady, along with Alexander Gardner, who had directed Brady's Washington studio, and hundreds of other photographers, created a pictorial record of the Civil War. By July 1861, Brady had acquired permission from the federal government to accompany troops at his own expense. He photographed the Union flight at the Battle of Bull Run, following the army with a traveling dark room, supplied with photographic plates, plate holders, negative boxes, tripods, and cameras. Exactly how many of the famous photographs that carried the byline, "by Brady," were actually taken by the man is debatable; Brady hired twenty photographers but always retained the photography credit for himself. One historian suggests that Brady, whose eyesight was failing by the time of the war, may not personally have photographed any of the Civil War.[56] Historians agree, however, that Brady's organization and leadership secured the pictorial history of the Civil War we now have. Because he traveled with Union armies, his photographs of Union soldiers, camps, and battle action are more varied than his coverage of the Confederate Army, which consists primarily of dead and wounded soldiers and destroyed southern towns. Brady's photographs as reproduced by artists gave the public something to digest other than the glory of war, and one *New York Times* writer described it well:

> Mr. Brady has done something to bring home to us the terrible reality and earnestness of war. If he has not brought bodies and laid them on our dooryard and along our streets, he has done something very like it.[57]

The tragedy of Mathew Brady is that at the end of the war, the public no longer wanted to be treated to blood at their doorsteps, and demand for his photos was not what he had expected. Brady continued to try to appeal to an intellectual and political elite as he had done in the past, producing portraits in his well-known formal style.

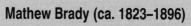

Mathew Brady (ca. 1823–1896)

Mathew Brady, famed Civil War photographer, actually got his interest in photography from Samuel Morse. A friend brought Brady to see Morse, who showed the two young men his daguerreotype. Brady later recalled that after this meeting, his life was "inextricably enmeshed with the infant art of photography." In 1840 Brady enrolled in Morse's photography school, and four years later he had his own studio, winning countless awards in competitive photographic exhibitions. By 1850, well before he began photographing the Civil War, Brady was already one of the most well-known photographers in the world.

Source: J. D. Horan, and G. Horan, *Mathew Brady: Historian with a Camera (*New York: Crown Publishers, Inc., 1955). (*Photo:* Division of Prints and Photographs, Library of Congress Collection)

After the war, Brady also faced growing competition from photographers who sought new audiences, new subjects, and new styles. Napoleon Sarony, a photographer who appealed to a wider audience, specialized not in the elite photographs for which Brady was so well known, but rather for portraits that offered entertainment and recreation. Sarony catered more to the bizarre and eccentric and decorated his studio in the theatrical district with curiosities such as Russian sleighs and Egyptian mummies. Whereas Brady had encouraged celebrities to sit for photographs by giving them free portraits, Sarony's subjects were paid royalties for sitting because he could generate huge profits from the sale of the photographs. Sarah Bernhardt, for example, received $1,500 from Sarony for agreeing to come to New York to sit for a photograph.

By 1896, when both photographers died, Brady was hardly remembered. His finances had been somewhat tenuous before the war, but by refusing to recognize the strength of the popular marketplace, including the tastes of a vast immigrant population, Brady complicated his already fragile financial situation and died in poverty. Sarony, who died during the same year, was eulogized by his friends and fellow photographers in twelve pages of the *Photographic Journal of America.* The *New York Journal* wrote: "No man who has ever lived has done so much to promote photography from the domain of the mechanical arts to that of art proper as Napoleon Sarony."[58] Barbara McCandless, in an essay on early portrait studios, captures the essence of the contributions of these two photographers:

Figure 7–8 "Showman in Camp," at the Culpeper (Virginia) Court House, about September 1863. Pencil drawing by Edwin Forbes. (*Frank Leslie's Illustrated Newspaper,* January 9, 1864)

Brady's portraits of illustrious Americans were intended to provide moral education, giving American citizens examples to emulate as they attempted to better themselves in a new country. But the desire for education went only so far; Sarony extended the celebrity market by satisfying the country's hunger for entertainment. Brady's portraits of illustrious Americans may have been good for the American public's moral improvement, but Sarony's portraits made the public feel comfortable and amused, and entertainment was something the country needed after the strains of the Civil War. Sarony's portraits not only made the fad of collecting celebrity portraits fun; they also conditioned the popular market to an awareness that portraiture in general could be enjoyable, and they set the stage for the greater success of amateur photography.[59]

Conclusion

Although slavery was not the sole cause of the Civil War, it represented a primary cultural division between North and South. The antislavery movement reflected that cultural division in lectures, printed products, and its use of pictures. Using new technologies, the antislavery societies shipped millions of pamphlets and other products through the mails. Many of these publications concentrated on those issues of gender and race that characterized the concerns of the early nineteenth century.

Women achieved positions of power and prominence through public speaking and writing for abolitionist publications—positions that the mainstream press was unwilling to grant them.

In response to antislavery activity, southern state legislatures enacted restrictive legislation, Congress instituted a gag rule, and southern postmasters, encouraged by the postmaster general of the United States, refused to distribute abolitionist materials. Mainstream editors, who responded little to abolitionist appeals to destroy slavery, reacted more intensely when they saw the government impose limitations on publishing and distributing materials.

Newspaper editors entered the Civil War with small staffs in place and with a history of constantly attempting to expand news coverage and the speed with which the news was delivered. They had limited experience in covering wars, however, and the nation had limited experience in dealing with the problems of wartime press coverage.

Northern newspapers continued in the pattern set before the war and increased the size of their staffs, directed war coverage from the home office, and took greater advantage of the telegraph to speed news. Reliance on the expensive and erratic telegraph wires encouraged reporters to put the most critical information at the beginning of stories and to write shorter stories, eliminating the flowery phrases of the past. Nevertheless, despite such encouragement, reporters did not quickly give up their familiar styles. Editors criticized Lincoln, his military commanders, and his strategies for winning the war.

Southern newspapers retained a more partisan flavor, and the high cost of supplies, the unavailability of materials toward the end of the war, and the Union occupation of southern cities took a heavy toll on the Confederate press. Organized under the Confederate Press Association, newspapers did criticize southern military strategy but only within a narrow framework.

Censorship in the North remained in the official channels of the state and war departments, as well as in the hands of commanders in the field. Telegraph lines remained under military control, and reporters were restricted from writing about troop movements and other specific military information. The Confederate government also imposed censorship of the telegraph and of the reporting of military details. Abolitionist and other antislavery materials were excluded from the mails as well.

Pictorial illustration as well as words characterized coverage of the war. Mathew Brady and his crew of twenty photographers followed the army with a traveling darkroom and produced a pictorial record of the war.

Endnotes

1. This chapter synthesizes material from the definitive accounts of Civil War reporting by J. Cutler Andrews, *The North Reports the Civil War* (Pittsburgh: University of Pittsburgh Press, 1955); and *The South Reports the Civil War* (Princeton, N.J.: Princeton University Press, 1970). See also Phillip Knightley, *The First Casualty* (New York: Harcourt Brace Jovanovich, 1975). Knightley portrays Civil War reporters as "ignorant, dishonest and unethical" and

their dispatches as "inaccurate, often invented, partisan and inflammatory" (p. 21).

2. For information on the abolitionist movement, see Louis Filler, *The Crusade against Slavery, 1830–1860* (New York: Harper & Brothers, 1960); Russell Nye, *Civil Liberties and the Slavery Controversy, 1830–1860* (Urbana: University of Illinois Press, 1972); H. L. Perkin, "The Defense of Slavery in the Northern Press on the Eve of

the Civil War," *Journal of Southern History* 9 (February–November, 1943), pp. 501–32; Eugene Genovese, *The Political Economy of Slavery* (New York: Vintage, 1965) and *The World the Slaveholders Made: Two Essays in Interpretation* (New York: Pantheon Books, 1969).

3. David Paul Nord, "The Evangelical Origins of Mass Media in America, 1815–1835," *Journalism Monographs* 88 (May, 1984), p. 23–24.

4. Kathryn Kish Sklar, "'Women Who Speak for an Entire Nation': American and British Women Compared at the World Anti-Slavery Convention," London, 1840, *Pacific Historical Review* 59 (November, 1990), pp. 453–99.

5. V. Tehertkoff and F. Holah, *A Short Biography of William Lloyd Garrison* (London, 1904; rpt. Westport, Conn.: Negro Universities Press, 1970), p. 24.

6. Charles S. Miller and Natalie Joy Ward, *History of America: Challenge and Crisis* (New York: John Wiley & Sons, 1971), p. 297.

7 Elizabeth McHenry, "Forgotten Readers: African-American Literary Societies and the American Scene," in James P. Danky and Wayne A. Weigand, eds., *Print Culture in a Diverse America* (Urbana: University of Illinois Press, 1998), pp. 149–172.

8. Frederick Douglass, *Narrative of the Life of Frederick Douglass, an American Slave* (Boston: Anti-Slavery Office, 1849), p. 58.

9. John W. Blassingame, *The Frederick Douglass Papers* (New Haven and London: Yale University Press, 1979), p. 3.

10. Philip S. Foner, *Frederick Douglass* (New York: The Citadel Press, 1950), p. 77.

11. Rebecca Chalmers Barton, "Witness for Freedom," *Harper's*, June 1948, pp. 172–74.

12. "Frederick Douglass," by Sharon M. Murphy, *Dictionary of American Biography*, vol. 43, pp. 160–68. See also William S. McFeely, *Frederick Douglass* (New York: Touchstone/Simon & Schuster, 1991).

13. Dickson J. Preston, *Young Frederick Douglass, the Maryland Years* (Baltimore and London: The Johns Hopkins University Press). Douglass' multiple autobiographies represented a nineteenth-century practice of famous people writing and updating their life stories.

14. Cited in Jean Fagan Yellin, *Women and Sisters: The Antislavery Feminists in American Culture* (New Haven, Conn.: Yale University Press, 1989), p. 3.

15. Cited in Yellin, *Women and Sisters*, p. 5.

16. Richard Ellis and Aaron Wildavsky, "A Cultural Analysis of the Role of Abolitionists in the Coming of the Civil War," *Comparative Studies in Society and History* 32:1 (January, 1990), pp. 89–116.

17. Sklar, "Women Who Speak," p. 490.

18. Cited in Sklar, "Women Who Speak," p. 489.

19. Cited in Yellin, *Women and Sisters*, p. 35.

20. Cited in Shirley J. Yee, *Black Women Abolitionists: A Study in Activism, 1828–1860* (Knoxville: University of Tennessee Press, 1992), p. 141.

21. Cited in Thomas F. G ssett, *Uncle Tom's Cabin and American Culture* (Dallas: Southern Methodist University Press, 1985), p. !82.

22. Cited in Moira Davison Reynolds, *Uncle Tom's Cabin and Mid-Nineteenth Century United States* (Jefferson, N.C.: McFarland & Company, 1985), p. 12.

23. Citations for the modern period taken from Reynolds, *Uncle Tom's Cabin*, pp. 162–63.

24. *Supplement to the Revised Code of the Laws of Virginia* (Richmond: Samuel Shepherd & Company, 1833), pp. 246–47.

25. Harold L. Nelson, ed., *Freedom of the Press from Hamilton to the Warren Court* (New York: Bobbs-Merrill, 1967), p. 167.

26. Nord, "Evangelical Origins of Mass Media," p. 23.

27. Lucy M. Salmon, "Five Crises in American Press Freedom," *The Press and Society: A Book of Readings* (New York: Prentice-Hall, 1951), p. 69.

28. Salmon, "Five Crises," p. 70.

29. William Ellery Channing, from "The Abolitionists: A Letter to James G. Birney," *Works of William E. Channing* (Boston, 1887), p. 746.

30. Letter of Amos Kendall to the postmaster at Charleston, S.C., August 4, 1835, *Niles Register* 47 (1835), p. 448. Cited in Nelson, *Freedom of the Press*, p. 213. For an interpretation of Kendall's action, see Richard R. John, *Spreading the News: The American Postal System from Franklin to Morse* (Cambridge: Harvard University Press, 1995).

31. For general information on the Civil War, consult David E. Fite, *Social and Industrial Conditions in the North during the Civil War* (New York: Ungar, 1962); Allan Nevins, *The Emergence of Modern America, 1865–1878* (New York: Macmillan, 1927); James M. Woods, *Rebellion and Realignment* (Fayetteville: University of Arkansas Press, 1987); and C. Vann Woodward, *Origins of the New South* (Baton Rouge: Louisiana State University Press, 1951).

32. See Meyer L. Stein, *Under Fire: The Story of American War Correspondents* (New York: Julian Messner, 1968); Wendt, *Chicago Tribune;* and Andrews, *The North Reports the Civil War.*

33. Stein, *Under Fire*, p. 14.

34. Stein, *Under Fire,* pp. 15–16.

35. Louis Starr, *The Bohemian Brigade: Civil War Newsmen in Action* (Madison: University of Wisconsin Press, 1987), p. 232. Copyright first granted to Alfred A. Knopf, who published the book in 1954.

36. For Smalley's reminiscences see *Anglo-American Memories* (New York and London: G. P. Putnam's Sons, 1911). See also Joseph J. Mathews, *George W. Smalley* (Chapel Hill: University of North Carolina Press, 1973). For other correspondents see F. Lauriston Bullard, *Famous War Correspondents* (Boston: Little, Brown, 1914).

37. See Jean Folkerts, "Felix Gregory de Fontaine (1834–1896)," *Dictionary of Literary Biography,* vol. 43, pp. 147–151.

38. Bernard Weisberger, *Reporters for the Union,* (Boston: Little, Brown, 1955).

39. Lloyd Wendt, *Chicago Tribune: The Rise of a Great American Newspaper* (Chicago: Rand McNally & Company, 1979), p. 155.

40. Calder Pickett, ed., *Voices of the Past* (Columbus, Ohio: Grid, 1977), p. 128.

41. For a dramatic but undocumented account of the early years of the Associated Press, see Oliver Gramling, *AP: The Story of News* (New York: Farrar, Straus & Giroux, 1940). For a description of the relationship of AP to European agencies, see Jonathan Fenby, *The International News Services* (New York: Schocken Books, 1986).

42. *Chicago Tribune,* Oct. 3, 1861, cited in Wendt, *Chicago Tribune,* p. 163–64.

43. Andrews, *The South Reports the Civil War,* p. 26.

44. Andrews, *The South Reports the Civil War,* p. 40.

45. *Editor and Publisher,* August 13, 20, and 27, 1949.

46. Floyd Risley, "The Confederate Press Association: A Revolutionary Experience in Southern Journalism?" unpublished paper presented at the Annual Conference of the Association for Education in Journalism and Mass Communication, Phoenix, Arizona, August 2000.

47. Cited in Risley, "Report of the Superintendent," *The Press Association of the Confederate States of America* (Griffin, Ga.: Hill & Swayze's Printing House, 1863); and Atlanta's *Southern Confederacy,* March 26, 1863, p. 2 and May 6, 1863, p. 2. Risley's account of the development of the Press Association is the most recent and most complete analysis of news coverage in the South during the Civil War. See also his work on correspondents, "Bombastic Yet Insightful: Georgia's Civil War Soldier Correspondents," *Journalism History* 24:3 (Autumn, 1998), pp. 104–111.

48. Andrews, *The South Reports the Civil War,* p. 57.

49. Cited in Andrews, *The North Reports the Civil War,* p. 151 (f. 42).

50. Stein, *Under Fire,* p. 18.

51. See Andrews, *The North Reports the Civil War,* pp. 575–84.

52. For an interpretation of Lincoln as restrictive, see Jeffery A. Smith, *War and Press Freedom: The Problem of Prerogative Power* (New York: Oxford University Press, 1999), pp. 99–121.

53. Andrews, *The South Reports the Civil War,* p. 529.

54. *Mobile Advertiser and Register,* October 27, 1861, cited in Andrews, *The South Reports the Civil War,* p. 103.

55. Alan Trachtenberg, "Photography: The Emergence of a Keyword," in *Photography in Nineteenth-Century America,* Martha A. Sandweiss, ed. (Fort Worth, Amon Carter Museum, and New York: Harry N. Abrams, 1991), p. 25.

56. *Civil War Times,* August 1978, p. 20.

57. *New York Times,* 20 October 1862, p. 5.

58. Cited in Barbara McCandless, "The Portrait Studio and the Celebrity," in Sandweiss, *Photography,* p. 70.

59. McCandless in Sandweiss, *Photography,* p. 71.

CHAPTER 8

Modernization and Printed Products

▼

During the decades following the Civil War, the book and periodical industry expanded dramatically as the nation began to forge transportation, telegraph, and manufacturing networks that spanned its geographical territory. Just as the early struggle between the power of the federal government and that of local governments had generated a national debate with the defenders of traditional values poised on one side against the nationalizing forces on the other, so too the struggles to establish national transportation and information networks after the Civil War generated intense disputes. On the one side were those who valued the preservation and advancement of elite culture. On the other were those who favored the benefits of a vast production system—one that promoted not just a limited selection of dignified, quality publications such as those introduced in the 1850s, but a broader spectrum of story papers and dime novels that challenged the elite print culture and spawned the so-called pop culture.

The challenge to the elite culture was reflected not only in the plot lines of the story papers but also in discussions in print concerning how to deal with crime and corruption in the urban metropolis, negotiations involving property rights and labor organizations, and controversy over the appropriate uses of photography. These discussions occurred everywhere—within the editorial content of newspapers and magazines as well as the fictional plots of the exploding book industry—thus shaping the nature of the periodical industry itself.

Expanded technology encouraged high-quality magazine production, fostered high-speed press work, and contributed to the creation of a multiplicity of products—magazines, books, newspapers, and advertising pamphlets. These products benefited from the establishment of national networks that provided brand-name development and the basis for advertising.

In this fast-paced society, all people did not fare equally. The years following the Civil War promised hope for African Americans, and educational reform accompanied the early days of Reconstruction. Soon, however, doors began to close. African-American editors such as Ida B. Wells Barnett protested vociferously, while others muted their voices and sought accommodation. The use of pamphlets continued as an important political strategy, with militant voices such as Barnett's finding an outlet in these popular circulars. ▼

A Magazine Revolution

Although some attempts were made to develop magazines in the colonial and revolutionary periods in the United States, it was not until the mid-1850s that magazines could claim success. Developing technology certainly contributed to the expansion of magazines, but more significantly, Congress enacted postal regulations in 1879 that enabled a less expensive distribution of non-newspaper periodicals. Further, a class of professional writers was emerging to contribute to literary and news publications. The arrival of national advertising agencies and national product advertising significantly broadened the appeal of magazines to national audiences. The number of magazines grew from a total of 700 in 1865 to 3,300 in 1885.

Beginning in the mid-1800s, quality monthlies such as *Scribner's*, the *Century*, the *Atlantic Monthly*, and *Harper's* served up articles on biography, travel, and fiction. The qualities sold for twenty-five to thirty-five cents a copy and sported elegant covers. The cost, a quarter, which seems today to be minimal, was in fact expensive for the times. The magazines, therefore, catered to the wealthy and educated. They often resisted the forces of modernization and tended to be politically conservative, emphasizing a rational, slow approach to changing times and issues.

General-interest magazines and specialized magazines for women developed during the mid- to late-1800s. Weekly magazines such as *Frank Leslie's Illustrated Weekly* and *Harper's Weekly* stressed news and pictures and were, for the most part, more like newspapers than magazines. Women's magazines date to 1792, with the publication of the *Lady's Magazine*. Early women's magazines such as this title provided fashion information, sentimental fiction, and articles on etiquette. The best known of the early women's magazines is *Godey's Lady's Book* noted for its emphasis on fashion and manners. These magazines carried almost no advertising and therefore relied on reader subscription for survival. During the 1870s and 1880s, however, the focus of women's magazines changed, and they began to reflect a modernizing, consumer-oriented society.[1]

Quality Monthlies as Preservers of the Old Order

The quality monthly magazines represented a major development in American periodical literature. Initially associated with publishing houses, such as Harper and Brothers or Scribners', the magazines were viewed as vehicles for serializing books that the publishing companies later published and, therefore, were advertising outlets for the publishing houses. The magazines were supported by subscriptions, newsstand sales, publishing house subsidies, and minimal advertising.

The monthlies played an important role in developing outlets for American writers, creating a forum for American art and art criticism, and finally in establishing markets for national advertising. The offices of quality monthlies "echoed the temper of a gentleman's voluntary association," wrote Christopher Wilson, and editing reflected a cooperative literary venture among editors, authors, and subscribers. Articles generally were not solicited; rather, editors made their selections from voluntarily submitted manuscripts, judging them on their literary qualities and good taste.[2] Because subscription lists for Gilded Age publications were closely guarded as private documents, little can be said about the audiences, although presumably the magazines were aimed at the northeastern elite.

From 1865 to 1870, the number of American periodicals grew from 700 to 1,200 (not including newspapers). By 1870, *Harper's*, which relied heavily on British authors, had a circulation of 150,000. The *Atlantic Monthly*, founded in 1857 with James Russell Lowell as editor, focused on New England contributors and readers. Into this milieu came *Scribner's Monthly Magazine*, which later changed its name to the *Century Illustrated Monthly Magazine*. This *Scribner's* is not to be confused with another quality monthly that was also named *Scribner's*.

Harper's Seeks to Expand the Book Industry

A student once described the *Harper's* of today as a magazine that you would not find at the Kwik-Shop between *True Detective* and *Modern Bride* but rather a magazine you might find at a "quality" newsstand.[3] This description is apt because although *Harper's* has undergone many changes, its reputation for quality has remained throughout its life.

Harper's began in 1850 as a stepchild to the Harper brothers' publishing enterprise in New York. One of its purposes was to be an advertising vehicle for the publishers' selections, both through advertisements and serializations of forthcoming books by popular British authors.[4] From its beginning, *Harper's* attracted the attention of wealthy, upper-middle-class, educated Americans. It offered fiction from the most prominent British authors of the day, including Thomas Hardy, Charles Dickens, and William Thackeray. In addition, the magazine published elegant etchings, travelogs, historical biographies, and scientific essays as well as articles concerned with life's pleasures—yachting, hunting, and vacationing. Navy heroes, newly betrothed maidens, well-mannered children, and pedigreed dogs abounded. The magazine's editors avoided news articles, leaving politics and social reform to the weekly magazines and newspapers.

By 1890, *Harper's* circulation peaked at 200,000. Competition from muckraking magazines slowly forced *Harper's* to change, and editors reluctantly began to include more topical articles among the literary works. From 1885 to 1930, *Harper's* gradually responded to such contemporary issues as American imperialism, national reform, and the "Jazz" era of the 1920s. Nevertheless, it never abandoned its class bias. For example, *Harper's* treatment of subjects such as the country club as a welcome getaway from the bustle of the metropolis ignored issues of membership restriction and focused instead on blue sky and green grass. The country club, wrote the author of a *Harper's* article, "is one of the results of a final ebullition of animal spirits too long ignored in a work-a-day world; it is nature's appeal for recognition of the body in cooperation with the mind."

On the other side of the poverty line, other kinds of clubs existed, but an attempt by one *Harper's* contributor to analyze some of these groups fell flat when its moral tone turned menacing. The author of "Club Life among the Outcasts" depicted as "vagabonds, rowdies and outcasts" those who were either born out of, or were turned out of, respectable society. The author insisted, "Vice must be punished and the vicious sequestered. . . . The best method of handling them is to destroy their clubs and punish them."[5]

Harper's covered the Spanish-American war thoroughly, running a six-part series written by Henry Cabot Lodge. Lodge viewed the Spanish as barbarian and brutal, romanticized the war, and condemned Spain's attempt at imperialism without questioning the motives of the United States in acquiring Puerto Rico, Guam, and the Philippines.[6]

By the turn of the century, *Harper's* became more involved in social issues and printed stories about the education of immigrants, women's feminist activities, and the development of American medicine and evolution. In the midst of the race riots of 1919, the magazine's writers chastised Americans for hiding their heads in the sand and blamed white-controlled newspapers for misrepresenting African-American people as inferior.[7]

Despite varied attempts to be socially relevant, the magazine drifted into financial trouble. In 1953, John Fischer assumed responsibility for *Harper's* as the seventh editor in the magazine's history. He estimated that 85 percent of his readers were college graduates and so kept the tone of the magazine scholarly; nonetheless, circulation and revenues continued to decline. The magazine relied heavily on the publishing company for financial support. A decade later, Willie Morris, controversial ex-editor of the University of Texas' *Daily Texan* and well known as a modern-day muckraker, took over the magazine. Morris promised a public affairs approach, and the magazine began to run long articles, oriented toward social and political change. The magazine's circulation continued to drop and in 1965 the magazine was sold to the Minneapolis Star and Tribune Company. Another editor, Lewis Lapham, took over in 1971, and most of the *Harper's* staff resigned as a stormy controversy raged over the publication of a Norman Mailer essay on women's liberation. During Lapham's tenure, *Harper's* hammered away at the decline and fall of America, but the magazine's readers did not respond, and in June 1980 *Harper's* announced it would fold.[8] High postal rates and production costs put *Harper's* $1.5 million in debt, and advertising revenues dwindled because the ad men found it difficult to define *Harper's* audience, no matter how prosperous it was.[9]

Before the ink dried on *Harper's* obituary, however, a nonprofit organization saved it. The John D. and Catherine T. MacArthur Foundation of Chicago bought *Harper's* for $250,000 and convinced Atlantic Richfield to kick in $3 million for operating expenses. Michael Kinsley, former editor of *The New Republic*, took over and promised to make *Harper's* "scintillating and profitable."[10] Scintillating it may have been, but profitable it was not, and in 1983 *Harper's* brought back Lapham to once again shift the magazine's focus. Under Kinsley's direction, the magazine won the National Magazine Award for "general excellence," but *Harper's* also continued to lose money. Upon returning, Lapham promised a three-part organization for the magazine, including a national op-ed page; annotated texts of speeches, documents, or transcripts of major topics of the day; and a summary of the month's events in science, culture, economics, and politics. Today, *Harper's* continues to struggle along, shored up by foundation funds.

Century Magazine as a Gentleman's Club

Probably the most elegantly printed of the quality monthlies, the *Century*, was an outgrowth of *Scribner's Monthly Illustrated Magazine* developed in 1870 as an independent arm of Scribner's publishing house. The magazine incorporated *House and Home*, which was published directly by the publishing company. The three individuals who were responsible for the magazine were Dr. Josiah Gilbert Holland, a religious man and educator, Roswell C. Smith, an astute businessman, and Charles Scribner, a member of the publishing firm. Smith and Holland insisted on separate editorial control, and the firm was organized with Scribner owning a 40 percent interest and Holland and Smith each owning 30 percent. This organizational policy was significant because the question of independence later became the issue over which *Scribner's Monthly* was dissolved and reestablished as the *Century*. Scribner died only two years after his monthly began. His two sons took over the publishing business and quarreled with Smith and Holland, who wanted to publish books through the magazine company. The sons sold their interest in 1881, and five years later they began *Scribner's Magazine*.

The men who probably deserve most of the credit for the success of the *Century* were Smith, who provided good business management, and Richard Watson Gilder, who edited the magazine from 1881 until his death in 1909. Gilder was a popular poet who had worked for *House and Home* and who had organized the Society of American Artists and Authors as well as the Authors Club of New York. The *Century's* content was similar to that of *Harper's*, with an emphasis on education, religion, history, and biography. The *Century's* entry into the quality monthly market was difficult. *Harper's* had cornered the British market on writers, and American writers were scarce, except for those New Englanders already loyal to the *Atlantic*. The *Century's* unique qualities were its appeal to women and southerners, its focus on visual impact—with its quality paper, elegant covers, and faultless print—and its emphasis on illustration. Evidence exists after 1914 to indicate that the *Century* also attempted to spread its circulation beyond the East. The availability of first-year figures allows us to determine the geographical spread of the magazine's circulation during 1914: the total circulation was 92,000, with 34,000 sales in the Middle Atlantic states, 14,000 in New England, 11,000 in the Far West, and 26,000 in the Midwest from Ohio to Kansas. These figures challenge the claims by some historians that magazines were strictly urban and did not circulate in rural areas.

The magazine emphasized accuracy and became a quality showcase for writers. Gilder, generally a pleasant man to work for, rushed into the office one day with a copy of a new issue in hand, exclaiming, "We ought all to resign!" He had discovered a typographical error. In 1890, the *Century* was at no loss for writers with 10,000 manuscripts reaching the offices every year. Gilder, as editor, could accept fewer than 400.

Gilder was known to be as sympathetic to writers as he was to employees. His staff read every manuscript the magazine received and notified writers immediately of the receipt of their manuscripts. It paid on acceptance—an uncommon practice in the nineteenth century. It sent acceptances on *Century* stationery but mailed rejections in plain envelopes, so as to not damage an author's ego. It also returned all manuscripts—even if an author forgot to enclose postage.[11] Authors were paid as well as at any magazine. Some reports indicate payment was from $10 to $100 per printed page, but rarely did it reach the top of that scale. Mark Twain at his peak was paid only $75 per page by the *Century*.

The magazine, always well managed financially, encouraged employees to buy stock and thus develop a self-interest in the company. The magazine also made great strides in developing national advertising. By the late 1880s, circulation was at 250,000, and it peaked from 1884 to 1887 with a major Civil War series. By 1890, the circulation leveled off at 200,000, and the *Century* outstripped all other monthlies in circulation. Advertisements sold in 1870 at $100 for a regular page and $200 for a page placed next to reading material. By 1880, the standard page rate was $270.

The *Century*'s prestige in arts and letters, as well as its financial success, was mirrored in its offices:

> The *Century* office was the visible symbol of its power and opulence. No other publication in the world was so magnificently housed. The visitor to its fifth-floor home on

---

▼

Celebrating New York

The rich and well-to-do people, of all parts of the country, should be able to find in New York that which will make it a delightful home to them. The opera, the theater, the picture gallery, the museum, the library, the literary and scientific lecture, the choicest eloquence of pulpit and platform, bright and stimulating society in multiplied and multiform organization—all these should combine to make a winter residence in New York so desirable that all who have money and leisure, wherever they may live, will indulge in the luxury.

—Josiah Gilbert Holland, *Scribner's Monthly*, June 1877

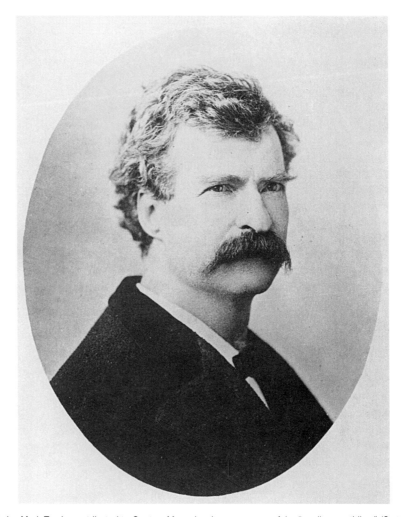

Figure 8–1   Mark Twain contributed to *Century Magazine,* known as one of the "quality monthlies." (State Historical Society of Wisconsin)

Union Square entered a world of polished floors, rich Turkish carpets, broad windows, stained-glass doors, and walls hung with the originals of the monthly's most famous drawings. Only Twain dared keep his hat on and smoke cigars in this atmosphere of elegance and dignity. "You never saw anything like those lovely rooms. And aesthetic furniture," wrote Mrs. S. S. McClure to her sister. "Oh, you Americans are all so rich" was Matthew Arnold's outburst as he gazed about him.[12]

The *Century's* language was as elegant and dignified as its offices, avoiding the harsher situations and aspects of American life. It did not discuss sexual activity, profanity was barred, and other situations that might be "questionable" stayed out of the *Century.* Its political and social stance was conservative, showing concern about corruption and other immoral aspects of American life but focusing on individual responsibility and noblesse oblige.

During the 1890s, circulation dropped to 150,000. It further declined after 1900 to about 125,000, where it leveled off for some years. The competition with mass magazines such as *McClure's* contributed to the demise of the *Century*, with subscribers and advertisers shifting to the less expensive, mass-circulation magazines. Another major factor in the demise of the *Century* was the development of photomechanical engraving and the halftone screen, which allowed mass-circulation magazines to produce pictures at a tenth the cost of their former procedure. For a time, the *Century* refused to lower its standards, although eventually it used the new process as well. In 1899, the same year *Harper's* faced bankruptcy and was bailed out by the banking interests of J. P. Morgan, the *Century* faced financial crisis.

The *Century* managed to last until 1930, when it merged with the *Forum* and ceased its independent existence.

Scribner's: Quality and Beauty

Scribner's Magazine published for fifty-two years—from 1887 to 1939—and adhered to a concept promoted by the quality monthlies—preservation of the social order accompanied by slow, evolutionary change. Priced at twenty-five cents, the magazine sold for a dime less than its competitors—*Harper's*, the *Atlantic Monthly*, and the *Century*. Within two years of its beginnings, its subscriptions totaled 100,000. The magazine covered the arts, travel in the western United States and foreign countries, and natural disasters. Serial stories and other fiction, biographies, and poetry were an integral part of each issue.[13]

The magazine adhered to the concept of social evolution rather than radical social change or revolution. Although it suggested that labor had legitimate grievances, it cautioned against "expecting too much too soon." When dealing with the issue of the women's vote, one article noted that eventually although the laws of all civilized nations would give women a voice in politics, "there seems to be no pressing haste for action. . . . there is a good deal of the old Eve left in the woman of today. And bless her sweet heart, Adam is in no haste to have it otherwise."[14]

▼

Roosevelt and the Rough Riders

One of our men and most of the Spanish dead had been found by the vultures before we got to them; and their bodies were mangled, the eyes and wounds being torn.

The Rough Rider who had been thus treated was in Bucky O'Neill's troop; and as we looked at the body, O'Neill turned to me and asked, 'Colonel, isn't it Whitman who says of the vultures that "they pluck the eyes of princes and tear the flesh of kings?"' I answered that I could not place the quotation. Just a week afterward we were shielding his own body from the birds of prey.

—Theodore Roosevelt, *Scribner's*, July 1898

During the Spanish-American War, *Scribner's* carried stories written by Richard Harding Davis, William Randolph Hearst's firsthand observer who covered the war with artist Frederick Remington. Many of the stories focused on Teddy Roosevelt and his "Rough Riders." As soon as Roosevelt returned from the war and was elected governor of New York, *Scribner's* commissioned him to write his recollections of the war, which appeared in serial form during the first six months of 1899. This series boosted the magazine's declining readership and signaled the beginning of the "heyday" of the magazine (1900–1915).

As the new century opened, *Scribner's* remained fairly oblivious to the muckraking going on around it. The magazine touched briefly on social topics—the problem of the saloon and the immigrant—but made few changes in its format in the early 1900s. Stories focused on the exotic—China and Russia. The magazine also covered the nostalgic—picturesque farming in Iowa and hospitality and pride in the Kentucky hills.

Scribner's described itself in 1908 in an article titled "The Business of a Great Publishing House," claiming it had a "distinct and individual place among periodicals." "No aspect of modern life" was without consideration and "many of the great names representing the transition period from the 19th and 20th centuries have appeared in its pages." Its topics, according to the writer, were history, sociology, the study of the varying conditions of modern life, travel, essays, sports and athletics, music, art, and natural history.[15]

By the 1920s, *Scribner's* circulation declined from 200,000 in the early 1900s to 100,000 by 1911 and 70,000 by 1924. Its use of full-color illustrations and the quality of its paper also declined. Advertising, previously placed at the back of the book, became highly visible from 1920 to 1923, but by 1924 much of it had disappeared. Public issues were given greater emphasis in the 1920s, with arguments that unions were a threat to property rights. Another article lamented the popular "myth" that doctors were overpaid. Shortly before *Scribner's* demise in 1929, Ernest Hemingway's *A Farewell to Arms* appeared, the event many credited for the momentary upturn in circulation occurring that year. New authors, including Langston Hughes, William Faulkner, and F. Scott Fitzgerald appeared in the 1930s, but the magazine continued to lose readers. Circulation dropped below 40,000 by 1936. Although circulation climbed the following year, the magazine continued to lose money, and it stopped circulation after May 1939.

A few months later, *Esquire* bought the subscription list. The name was sold to *Commentator*, and the magazine became *Scribner's Commentator*. In 1942, Joseph Hilton Smyth, the publisher, pleaded guilty to an indictment for accepting money from the Japanese to publish their propaganda in the magazine. Historian Frank Luther Mott described the magazine's unfortunate demise:

> When a respectable magazine dies it should emulate Stevenson's hunter and lay itself down with a will, and not pass its name on for some other periodical to disgrace.
>
> Throughout its long life, however, *Scribner's* was a credit to the name it bore—a magazine notable for its service to American literature and art, and for its urbane criticism of our national life and culture.

Challenge of Modernization

Although a genteel approach characterized the quality monthlies, newspaper editors were more likely to confront the burgeoning new age. A fascination with industrialization crossed geographical and sectional boundaries after the Civil War. Southern editors campaigned for industrialization, and northern urban newspapers increasingly became a part of the industrial world they championed. First, they relied primarily on advertising, in itself a developing industry, for financial support. Second, editors not only commented on the dilemmas of modern industry—labor, technology, consolidation—but they also had to resolve these issues for their own increasingly large businesses. For the most part, newspaper editors responded as reactionary businessmen, using the First Amendment to champion private-property rights as much as freedom of the press. Their traditional attitudes toward individualism, private property, and free enterprise limited their ability to deal with the problems of urbanization, which required an orientation toward a collective public community.[16] Although many editors advocated civil service reform to combat corruption and deplored the impersonalization of the business conglomerate, they were at a loss to provide remedies to the problems of industrialized, modern life in the metropolis. The consolidation of the Associated Press and its relationship to Western Union, which by 1866 held a virtual monopoly of telegraph services, further indicated the broad institutionalization of the press, a business dominated by commercial news values.

Manufacturing/National Distribution Networks

Before the Civil War, manufacturing industries were local or regional in scope and specialized in the processing of raw materials. These industries included flour and grain milling, lumber, and sawmills—businesses that created materials consumers could use to make bread, build houses, or manufacture other products. "It would be hard to conceive of developing a consumer allegiance to the flour of a local grist mill or the lumber of a particular saw mill," wrote advertising historian Daniel Pope. Such local industry advertised only in the form of business notices and did little to encourage the development of advertising as an industry or as a form of consumer culture.

Between 1860 and 1880, the sheer numbers of manufacturing industries grew dramatically, and the type of manufacturing changed as well. Whereas only one pre–Civil War factory—the Merrimack Textile Mill—employed as many as 2,000 individuals in 1854, by 1900 at least seventy plants each employed this many people.[17] As industries became more capital intensive and increased their output, manufacturers needed to sell more products to stay in business.

Other changes accompanied the rapid growth of manufacturing. Transportation networks developed that broadened the market, allowing a volume of goods to be shipped to a single place. Specialized distribution systems created the need for marketing and service in certain geographic areas, and specialized media such as streetcar placards developed to advertise products in particular locales. Urban Americans bought more goods and services, producing fewer of these needs at home.

Large-scale capitalism appeared in response to excess capacity and destabilizing price competition.[18]

Advertising and the Space Buyers

A few entrepreneurs began to see income-earning potential in advertising as early as 1842, but it was not until the latter half of the nineteenth century that advertising became a force in modern periodicals. By the turn of the century, advertising played a major role in defining the United States as a consumer society. During the early years, space buyers dominated the advertising field—not yet an industry—and served as forerunners to the advertising agency. The emphasis was on buying space in volume from a publisher at a discount and, after levying a heavy markup, selling it to advertisers. Volney Palmer, considered to be the first advertising agent, earned as much as a 25 percent commission on his sales, but his business was limited because he demanded exclusive agreements and refused to guarantee payment to publications carrying advertisements he solicited. In 1865, George P. Rowell, operating in

Figure 8–2   The development of brand-name products resulted in advertising, such as this plea to buy Payn's Sure-Raising Flour. The development of nationally marketed products fueled magazine growth. (Division of Prints and Photographs, Library of Congress Collection)

New England, began buying and selling space. He offered businessmen an inch in 100 newspapers per month for an annual fee of $100. He calculated that if he sold half the space he bought, he would net $5,500 on an investment of $7,500.

In 1867, Carlton and Smith, a New York agency, bought space in religious magazines and then resold it to advertisers, soon dominating this specialized market. In 1870, it was estimated that the religious market had a potential of 400 weeklies with a total circulation of five million.[19] A popular employee, J. Walter Thompson, took over the agency in 1878, expanded into the general magazine field, and developed an organization that today is still one of the largest in the field.

In the late nineteenth century, the advertising business had its share of charlatans as well as its share of respectable businesspeople. This fact, coupled with questions about whether an agent's loyalty was to a publisher or to an advertiser, placed the advertising agent in a dubious position. Publishers grumbled about the discounted rates the agent demanded, and advertisers complained that they had no guarantee of circulation rates or placement in the most suitable publications. Although both publisher and advertiser needed the agent to negotiate the buying and selling of space, both also viewed the agent as an exploiter.

During the late 1800s, N. W. Ayer, a major advertising agency founded in 1869, experimented with the "open contract," charging advertisers directly for their work rather than basing their fee on the commission paid by the publisher. However, few agencies followed suit and the commission controversy remained strong through the 1920s.

By 1900, space agents were experiencing many difficulties. Newspaper directories, such as those designed by George P. Rowell, provided advertisers with considerable information about newspapers and other publications, making it possible for them to place their own advertising. Advertisers no longer were quite so blind in regard to their markets. A multiplicity of agents and heavy competition also took their toll, and many of the early agencies collapsed. Newspapers experimented with employing their own people to sell space, a method that worked only for large, metropolitan papers because small, rural newspapers could not afford to send an agent to New York to negotiate for national advertising. Newspaper publishers continued to balk at the heavy commission, and in the 1890s they were often successful in reducing the commission to 10 or 15 percent.

Newspapers as Reflections of Urbanization

Between 1860 and 1878, the growth and modernization of newspapers intensified. Newspapers developed platforms attacking massive corruption in national and local politics, and they responded to widespread industrial and economic change. Editors in the 1870s often reacted to local issues in much the same way magazines would react to national problems in the late 1890s and early 1900s.

By 1870, nearly ten million people lived in the nation's cities, and by 1890 those cities had installed mass transit, a process that spawned urban spread and real estate development. As cities grew and changed, metropolitan newspapers gained increasing credibility as purveyors of news, as mediators in city life, and as social arbiters of the community. The newspaper, from the penny press days until the 1890s, was "intimately connected with the complexity of life in the modern city," Gunther Barth noted in his study of nineteenth-century *City People*. A shift in values saw the minister replaced by the editor as the conscience of the community, with migrants from the countryside and immigrants from abroad looking to the newspaper for information that would help them adapt to city life and to a new language and culture.[20]

Barth wrote that the metropolitan newspaper was the bridge between over-the-fence gossip and telephone chatting. Further, the newspaper was concerned with political aspects of the city: crime and corruption. In the years following the war the focus was on exposing rather than on reforming, but the exposure helped pave the way for serious reform efforts to come later.

Crime, Corruption, and Journalistic Independence

In the 1870s, newspapers intensified their claims of independence from political parties, recognizing that commercial interests now made strong partisan affiliations a liability. Joseph Pulitzer, writing in St. Louis, was one of the first editors to claim that partisan politics in covering local issues no longer paid. As advertisers became more essential to newspapers than did powerful political groups, newspapers covered city life from the bottom up as well as municipal corruption. In St. Louis, Pulitzer criticized the high profits and poor service of gas and streetcar monopolies, published questionable real estate deals, described fraud at the polls, and attacked the traditional institutions of vice—the brothels and the gambling halls.

Thomas Leonard, in his study of political reporting, *The Power of the Press*, suggested that such exposure of local and national corruption evolved from the crime reporting of the early penny papers. For example, when James Gordon Bennett's *Herald* reported the Robinson–Jewett affair in 1836, it connected personal crime to societal stability: "The death of Ellen Jewett is the natural result of a state of society and morals which ought to be reformed. . . . It as naturally springs from our general guilt and corruption as the pestilence does from the waters of death stagnating under an August sun." Leonard noted that "Bennett was just as sure that powerful men were corrupt as he was that fallen women were violent. . . . In turning vice into big news the press of Jacksonian America insisted that an investigation of the sordid facts revealed a general pattern of corruption in society."[21] Leonard further wrote that "The muckrakers of the first years of the new century were the legitimate heirs of the crime story and the first to make the whole nation take notice."[22] Such a contention describes the development of editorial attitudes and news conventions as evolutionary, rather than as representative of isolated characteristics of certain newspapers in a particular period.

Although editors such as Pulitzer may have been responsible for putting a few men in jail and improving some public services, corruption continued largely unabated in the cities.[23] The *New York Times* and *Harper's Weekly*, despite their vivid pictorial and factual criticism of Boss Tweed and Tammany Hall corruption in New York City, were unable to punish most of those who had stolen from the city's treasury or to destroy the city's political machine, although Boss Tweed eventually

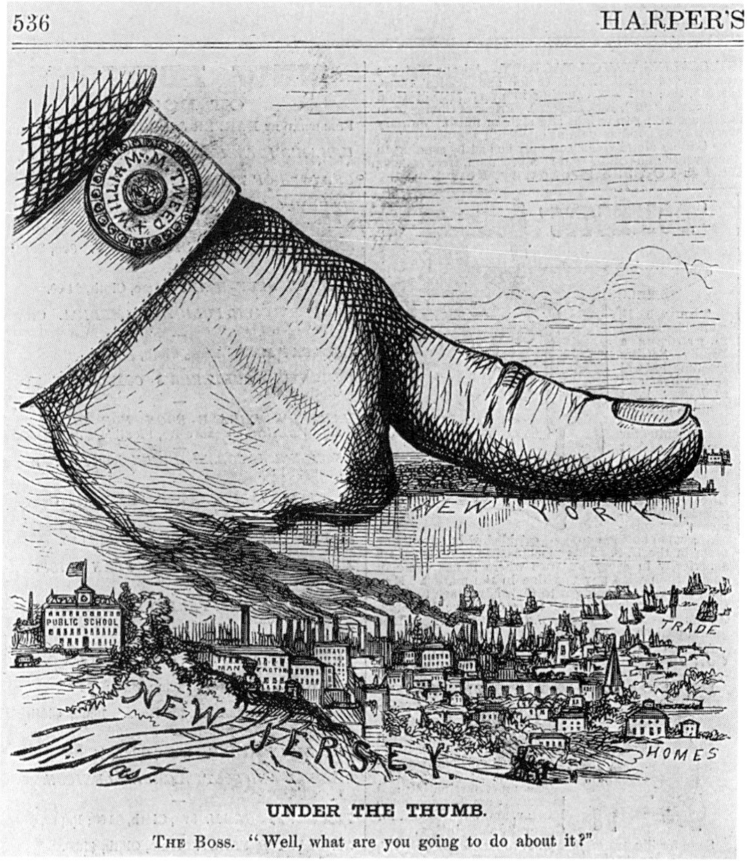

Figure 8-3   This political cartoon, titled "Under the Thumb," was created by Thomas Nast and appeared in *Harper's Weekly* during the summer of 1871. (Division of Prints and Photographs, Library of Congress Collection)

went to jail in disgrace. Once the scandal of a particular situation faded, journalists were seldom able to present remedies or persuade citizens to think about alternative forms of city government.[24] In some cities in the 1890s, this inadequacy was corrected as newspapers limited competition among themselves, decreased their partisanship, and joined forces with broad-based municipal reform groups.[25]

Labor Organization

Newspapers were concerned with labor disputes and unionization from the 1830s on, not only as issues to be discussed in editorial content but also because publishers had to negotiate with labor unions concerning the production and distribution of the newspaper as a manufactured product. The Typographical Association of New York in 1831 began to object to increased mechanization and to child labor, an issue that followed editors into the second decade of the twentieth century. The union also fought against editors' efforts to increase immigrant labor, a practice designed to decrease wages. Although various printers' unions operated with some success until 1837, the financial recession that occurred that year hit labor hard, and by 1840 the New York association folded.

Printers began to reorganize in the 1840s and found support from some editors. Horace Greeley, editor of the *New York Tribune*, was president of the New York Printers' Union that organized in 1850. James Gordon Bennett editorialized in the *Herald* on April 8, 1850, that the "strikes which commenced among the mechanics and workingmen of this city a short time since are still going on, and we must again express our satisfaction at the manner in which these strikes and meetings continue to be conducted."[26] Such support by newspaper editors soon faded, however.

In 1852, the National Typographical Union, predecessor to the International Typographical Union, was officially organized. Membership grew dramatically after the Civil War, and the union worked to assure that as new machinery was developed, union men were trained and ready to operate that equipment. The union focused on specialization, and it effectively adapted in most cases to the introduction of new technology.

As early as 1860, the union promoted the idea of an eight-hour working day for printers, and twenty years later it joined the nationwide, industrywide movement for the eight-hour day. Although some gains were gradually achieved in setting hours for different types of workers, it was not until 1908, after a series of strikes and strong opposition from the American Newspaper Publishers' Association, that the eight-hour day was incorporated into general practice. During the years after World War I, the union movement was labeled un-American and denounced more thoroughly than ever by America's publishers.

Technology, Cost, Speed, and Quality

Rapid developments in newspaper technology after the Civil War paralleled growth in manufacturing as a whole. The introduction of new technology, continued urbanization, and the concept of covering the city's news from the bottom up produced newspapers that were graphically different, that incorporated display advertising, and that continued to expand in new areas such as evening and Sunday editions. Technological advances in wood pulp paper production, stereotyping, the web-perfecting press, and the linotype increased the quality of production and the capital necessary for starting a publication but reduced the cost per subscriber.

Advances made in the processes for converting wood to paper reduced the price of newsprint. Although a variety of attempts to substitute cotton for linen rags, and wood or straw pulp for rags, had been experimented with since 1800, only in the 1860s did successful processes for converting wood pulp take hold.

In 1870, eight wood pulp plants in the United States produced newsprint; by 1880, fifty plants were in operation; and by 1890, eighty-two plants were in production. The price of paper had surged during the Civil War, not only because of shortages caused by the hostilities but also because of collaboration among papermakers and the development of trade associations. The price surged again briefly about 1868, but it then dropped steadily until the beginning of World War II. From the

Figure 8–4   The Linotype Junior was introduced in 1902, sixteen years after its bigger brother was first used at the large dailies. It sold for only $1,500 and took automated typesetting into country shops like this one in Waupaca County, Wisconsin. (State Historical Society of Wisconsin)

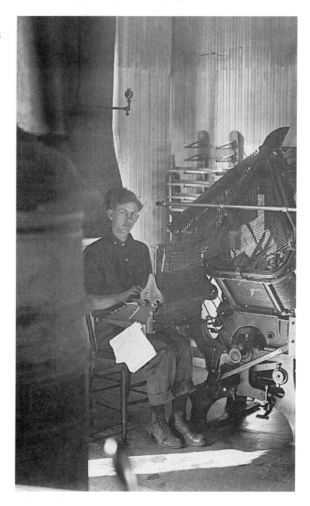

1880s on, there was a sharp increase in newsprint consumption, which reflected increased circulation, additional pages, and a decline in the price of newsprint.

Stereotyping had been a subject of experimentation as early as 1727, and the *New York Herald*, along with *La Presse* of Paris and the *Times* of London, had begun using stereotyped plates. The process employed a papier-mâché mat made from type forms. Because the forms no longer had to be put directly on the press, wear and tear on the type was reduced significantly, resolving what had been a considerable problem for publishers. Just as one example, in 1846 the *New York Sun* needed a complete new set of type every three months in order to make a clean impression.[27] Although some newspapers were using the stereotyping process in the 1850s, the invention of a press developed specifically for the process by R. Hoe and Company provided increased impetus for the use of this technology. The advantages of stereotyping were great, because not only did it cause less wear on type but it also allowed for the removal of column rules and created the possibility of full-page rather than column-bound advertisements.

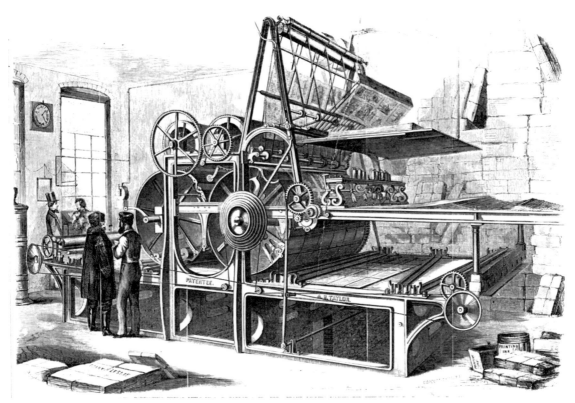

Figure 8–5   This perfecting press was built by A. B. Taylor and Company for *Frank Leslie's Illustrated Newspaper.* (Division of Prints and Photographs, Library of Congress Collection)

By 1870, the web-perfecting press, a press that printed on both sides of a sheet of paper on a continuous roll (a web) of newsprint, came into popular use. Machine cutting and folding also were developed during the 1860s and 1870s, further speeding the process of printing and reducing the labor involved.

The most significant development of the 1880s was the perfection of Ottmar Mergenthaler's Linotype machine in 1886. Operated by a keyboard similar to that of a typewriter, the machine released type matrices, assembled them into a line of type, automatically justified them, and cast them in a "slug" of lead, returning the matrices to the magazine for reuse. Prior to this development, compositors were required to set each piece of type by hand. Each letter had to be handled individually, arranged in a line of type, justified with metal spacers, and returned to the type case. Not only did Mergenthaler's machine increase the speed of setting type, it also solved the problem of type wear and tear.[28]

Dime Novels and Story Papers

In discussing popular forms of literature developed just after the Civil War, Christine Bold noted that popular works "offered to authors and readers models of accommodation, qualified resistance, and negotiation" as ways of responding to the new order.[29] The story papers were the first to benefit from mass transportation and print technology. These papers were cheap, weekly collections of serialized melodramas, international gossip, and news digests. They sold for three to six cents an issue and were designed to obtain the largest possible audience for the smallest possible expenditure. Designed to look like newspapers and therefore able to be mailed under the cheapest postal rate, these sheets continued to appear until the turn of the century. Some, such as the *New York Weekly*, lasted for years (1855–1889) and claimed circulations as high as 350,000 copies each week. Their melodrama included masculine adventures on the sea, in the wilderness, or in war, as well as women's narratives relating trials in the face of sudden poverty, orphanhood, abusive guardians, insanity, or evil suitors. Christine Bold noted that although these fictional women usually endured their trials through Christian action, the stories provided a few illicit thrills before the victory of virtue. The character of the expanding city also colored the tales. E. Z. C. Judson, known best under the pseudonym Ned Buntline, used the rhetoric of mass meetings in New York streets to present political, legal, commercial, and personal cases of the times to audiences of serialized news dramas and fiction.

Dime novels, another commercial product of the postbellum years, had a portable format that ensured their popularity during the years of increased rail travel. They were, indeed, pamphlet novels, sold for five to ten cents each, with illustrated covers. These novels were written almost in assembly-line fashion, with publishers dictating story lines, character, plots, and sometimes specific scenes. They supervised the writers closely, regimenting production in terms of quantity, speed, length, and fixed-payment rates. Dime novelists, laboring in the fiction factories, described their authorship in commercial terms far removed from the aristocratic gentility expressed in the editorial offices of the quality monthlies:

> A writer is neither better nor worse than any other man who happens to be in trade. He is a manufacturer. After gathering his raw product, he puts it through the mill of his imagination, retorts from the mass the personal equation, refines it with a sufficient amount of common sense and runs it into bars—of bullion, let us say. If the product is good it passes at face value and becomes a medium of exchange.[30]

Audiences for the dime novels included soldiers in the battlefields of the Civil War, farmers, mechanics, drummers, boys in shops and factories, and domestic servants. Beadle and Adams, active publishers of the dime novels, advertised their books in the nationally read *New York Tribune*, and some of their publications were favorably reviewed in the *North American Review*. They explicitly said they hoped the books reached "all classes, old and young, male and female." Nevertheless, it appears that the bulk of the audience was constituted by the working class.

Traditional heroic stories of war and the frontier and sentimental plots of the story papers were supplemented by fictionalized tales of outlaws, detectives, male factory operatives, and working "girls." Beadle and Adams also developed the western, depicting the Far West as a site of national, economic, and personal regeneration.[31] Plot lines for women readers clearly depicted the change in women's condition after the Civil War. Typical stories told of a young working woman forced into a loveless and illegal marriage with an upper-class villain, then saved by an upper-class hero who admired her for her personal virtues. Religion ceased to be a central focus, but virtue remained critical. Bold wrote:

> More and more women were joining the work force, often with low-paying factory jobs, and considerable concern was being voiced about the effect of public employment on young women's virtue; in such a climate, the very figuring of the working girl as democratic heroine, her entry into a popular pantheon that included such nationalistically approved types as the hunter, the detective, and the honest mechanic, signaled some level of legitimacy. Fiction that heroized women outside the domestic sphere offered working-class women some kind of accommodation and justification, some means of negotiating the transition from private to public.[32]

Photographs: Question of Technology and Culture

Although pictures had been included in publications during the Civil War years, the necessity of hand-engraving ensured that photographs would not proliferate, or dominate publications in any kind of sensational way. In the early 1870s, photo-engraving made it possible for the *New York Daily Graphic* to carry a full-page picture seventeen by twenty-six inches in size.[33] As papers such as the *Graphic* were able to explode photographs on their cover pages, the photographic revolution became much more than a technological revolution; it became a moral dilemma that caused publishers to shout with joy as well as to weep. Thomas Leonard suggested that the impact of *Harper's Weekly*'s exposé of Boss Tweed was stronger because it was one of the first attempts to encourage an audience to think visually about the political life of a city. Pictures were unfamiliar to American audiences and at the time many public figures were not visually recognizable, even by the press. Furthermore, pictures were regarded as an inappropriate waste of space, and many newspapers through the 1880s fought against including photographs on their pages.[34] Photographs, when used, were carefully posed and conventionally presented, and it took the pen of Thomas Nast to "puncture the pretty pictures" while presenting the Tweed ring as bullies and thugs. Nast played on the city's prejudices and stereotypes, incorporating thug-like Irishmen into his cartoons to signify non-Irish political criminals. As conventions broke down, and Hearst and Pulitzer entered the New York field in the late 1880s, photographs became a valued addition to metropolitan papers.

Associated Press: Wire Service Monopoly

By 1860, the seven New York dailies that had formed the Harbour News Association in 1848 controlled most of the U.S.' foreign and domestic news gathering through their telegraphic news gathering service, the Associated Press (AP). The New York

'A RACE FOR THE WIRES—ENERGY OF THE REPORTERS.

Figure 8-6   A *Harper's Weekly* engraving dated March 21, 1868, depicting "A Race for the Wires—Energy of the Reporters." (Division of Prints and Photographs, Library of Congress Collection)

dailies spent more than $200,000 annually collecting and distributing news, and their customers outside the city paid them back for more than half the expense.[35]

Rebelling at New York's control, in 1865 a group of midwestern publishers organized the Western AP. They complained that the New York group focused too much on the commercial interests of the city and not enough on events concerning the West. They also protested the high cost of cable news from Europe. In 1867, however, AP and the Western AP reached an agreement that respected each service's territorial rights and, in conjunction, reached a monopolistic agreement with Western Union.

Western Union, which in 1866 squeezed out its two remaining competitors, forged agreements with the two AP groups that assured that AP would use the wires of Western Union exclusively and would oppose other telegraph companies. Western Union agreed in return not to engage in news gathering and to grant discount rates to the two associations.[36]

During the latter part of the century, the public, through congressional action, pamphlets, and the press, attacked the monopoly. In 1872, the House Committee on Appropriations pointed out the dangers of the monopoly, and in 1874 a Senate investigation documented instances in which Western Union had cut off transmissions of information critical of Western Union or the AP. The report read:

> The power of the telegraph, continually and rapidly increasing, can scarcely be estimated. It is the means of influencing public opinion through the press, of acting upon the markets of the country, and of seriously affecting the interests of the people.[37]

The Associated Press defended its domination of news access to the wires and the granting of franchises to papers of its choice by declaring that the organization was an association of businesspeople dealing in a commercial commodity—news.[38] Not until the turn of the century would AP face significant competition from a rival news agency.

Pleas for Equality and Progress

The few years after the Civil War represented some gains for African Americans, although the time was short and the gains limited. Black people had immediately given education a high priority, and African American students had flocked to schools and books, both of which had been prohibited under slave codes. Between 1866 and 1869, the American Missionary Association founded seven black colleges. The Freedmen's Bureau helped establish Howard University in Washington, D.C., and by 1877, 600,000 African-American children were attending elementary school. African Americans focused on educational, political, and economic gains during those years. Their reaction to the rapid development of segregation varied from accommodation to militant protest. Land reform, which initially was given some attention by Radical Republicans, never was achieved. Sharecropping originated as a compromise, giving blacks freedom from daily supervision or working under a white overseer but assuring that whites would still control the land and its produce. The system soon became abusive as both blacks and whites suffered from the decline in cotton markets and blacks suffered from the unscrupulousness of white landowners and furnishing merchants.

Republicans won majorities everywhere except in Georgia in the 1868 elections, and sixteen African Americans were elected to Congress. The new governments, however, failed to alter the social structure or distribution of wealth in the South. The number of blacks participating in government raised cries of "Negro Rule" and spearheaded the formation of the Ku Klux Klan in the South. African Americans

Figure 8–7   During and after the Civil War, African Americans left the South to seek a better life. This photograph shows fugitive African Americans crossing the Rappahannock River in Virginia in 1862. (Division of Prints and Photographs, Library of Congress)

continued to participate in government in far lower proportions than they were represented in the population. The claims of "Negro Rule" were grossly distorted. Adopted in 1868, the Fourteenth Amendment conferred citizenship on freedmen and prohibited states from abridging constitutional "privileges and immunities." The amendment also prevented states from taking a person's life, liberty, or property "without due process of law" and from denying "equal protection of the law." The amendment represented major compromises, especially in allowing states to decide whether to give blacks the right to vote.

During the 1870s, many Democrats regained control of state governments. The North, tired of continued conflict with the South, wanted reconciliation with its southern neighbors. The Supreme Court aided the northern retreat from equality for blacks through interpretations of the Fourteenth and Fifteenth Amendments that narrowed their meanings and gave the states power to once again disenfranchise blacks. In 1870 and 1871, federal laws were passed against the Ku Klux Klan, and the Klan went underground, replaced in part by local vigilante groups. In 1872, Congress adopted a sweeping amnesty act that applied to most Confederates.

By 1876, Reconstruction was over, and, despite some political and educational gains, blacks remained dependent on whites for food, work, and land. In 1877, dismayed at the state of affairs in the South, blacks banded together to move to Kansas in what became known as the "Exoduster" movement. After 1880, lynching became a national problem. Even northern newspapers abandoned the blacks. Woodward wrote that the *Nation,* edited by Godkin,

Figure 8–8   This lithograph depicts Reconstruction of the South. (Division of Prints and Photographs, Library of Congress Collection)

thought the government should "have nothing more to do with him," and Godkin could not see how the Negro could ever "be worked into a system of government for which you and I would have much respect." The *New York Tribune*, with a logic all its own, stated that the Negroes, after having been given "ample opportunity to develop their own latent capacities," had only succeeded in proving that "as a race they are idle, ignorant, and vicious."[39]

Lynching in the Late Nineteenth Century

An era of hatred and prejudice from 1889 to 1918 ushered in lynching as a national problem. During this time, 3,224 individuals were lynched, compared to a total of 4,742 between 1882 and 1968. Seventy-eight percent of these individuals were African American.

Lynching was a topic for general newspapers, which focused on the horror and grisly details of specific incidents. For example, the *Springfield* (Massachusetts) *Republican,* on April 28, 1899, reported that "Before the body was cool, it was cut to pieces, the bones were crushed into small bits, and even the tree upon which the wretch met his fate was torn up and disposed of as 'souvenirs.'"[40]

Richard Perloff, in a study of media coverage during the period, argues that although coverage of lynchings may have reflected the prejudice of editors, the majority of editors opposed lynching, believing that it threatened civilization; he argues, however, that media coverage was nearly uniform in its condemnation of "Negroes" as guilty, with special vitriol reserved for those accused of raping white women. Perloff notes that economic factors were at play: Sensational lynchings sold papers. But the most intense of the factors was the racism of the era, "partly steeped in psychoanalytic fears."

Editors faced physical harm if they were critical of the lynchings of Negroes, particularly if the lynching was related to an act against a female member of a good family. Some newspapers and magazines, however, denounced the practice. The *Chicago Tribune* and the *New York Times* pioneered in antilynching efforts, with the *Tribune* beginning its campaign as early as 1882. The *Times* referred to one lynching as "an outrage so terrible and so shameful that it can only be explained as an outbreak of popular delirium."

By the turn of the century, Ray Stannard Baker, in *McClure's,* and other magazine writers argued against lynching. Baker was praised by W. E. B. DuBois for his book, *Following the Color Line,* despite the fact that Baker used common stereotypes of the day and referred to the "animal-like ferocity" of African-American criminals.

In 1918, a number of Georgia's urban dailies supported a state antilynching law. The New South was striving hard to eliminate images of the area as rife with mob violence in its attempt to market itself as a new realm of business elites in a progressive era.

Flourishing African-American Press

Between 1827, when *Freedom's Journal* was first published, and the Civil War, about forty African-American newspapers were published. Although extremely financially burdened and heavily dependent on contributions for survival, these publications fought for the emancipation of slaves and a fuller measure of basic rights for free blacks. After the Civil War ended, the number of black papers expanded, with publications established in eight states that previously had none.

By 1890, 575 African-American papers, including political organs, church papers, and interest group publications, were being published. Several newspapers started in the period—the *Washington Bee, Cleveland Gazette, Philadelphia Tribune,* and *New York Age*—became voices of national influence.[41]

Historians have long recognized that the African-American press helped to celebrate the accomplishments of black people, because the mainstream press rarely printed their basic news such as births or weddings. In addition, the black press discussed issues of racism. Henry Lewis Suggs, however, in his study of the black press in the Midwest, suggested that the existence of an African-American press served a larger goal—that of extending and preserving democracy. He noted that between 1865 and 1900, "an amorphous mass of immigrants, migrants, ex-slaves, exodusters and soldiers symbolized 'citizens without democracy'; nevertheless, the region was transformed by a 'free press' into a marketplace of democratic ideals called Kansas, Nebraska, Oklahoma, Minnesota, and South Dakota." The black press in the Midwest made government more accountable to the people, Suggs found, and "chronicled the evolution of culture and community."

The struggle simply to exist was enormous. The Iowa *Bystander* acknowledged the difficulties of the black press with its motto, "Fear God, Tell the Truth, and Make Money." By 1915 the black press was sufficiently established to comment widely on U.S. foreign policy, including fervent protests against U.S. occupation of Haiti and Marines' behavior there. Other issues ventilated included the rise of black national-ism in Africa and in the Caribbean. Newspaper editors warned of the rise of the Ku Klux Klan in northern states, such as Minnesota, and protested Jim Crow laws and other forms of institutionalized racism.[42]

Chief among these voices, but ignored until recently by historians, were a num-ber of black women writers. Literary figures such as Alice Dunbar-Nelson were active not only in the black women's club movements but also were field organizers for suffrage and became involved in international movements for peace. These women sometimes started their writing careers writing for church publications that educated the community on African-American achievements. Dunbar-Nelson established her career as woman's page editor for the African Methodist Episcopal denomination's *AME Review* and by editing a two-volume compilation of speeches by blacks. Another foremost woman journalist was Ida B. Wells.[43]

Ida B. Wells-Barnett: Voice of Protest

Awards for courage in journalism are given in the name of John Peter Zenger, the printer of colonial New York. At least as appropriately, such awards might be given in memory of Ida B. Wells-Barnett, pioneering crusader for racial justice and women's rights. She was an early example of the power of investigative reporting and a forerunner of the muckraking journalists who energized major magazines and attempted to change society, primarily in the first decade of the twentieth century.

Ida Baker Wells, born to slaves in Mississippi in 1862, was left in charge of a fam-ily of five at the age of sixteen, when her parents died of yellow fever.[44] After caring for her brothers and sisters for two years, she left them with family members and moved to Memphis in 1880. She worked as a schoolteacher for nine years but was drawn to writing. While taking summer classes at Nashville's Fisk University, she wrote for the student newspaper.

Shortly after moving to Memphis, Wells edited a tiny literary publication. This achievement brought her enough notice to enable her to become the editor, when she was twenty-five, of *Living Way*, a weekly black Baptist newspaper. Her goal was to write so clearly and powerfully that she would inspire African Americans—long kept from learning by slaveholders in the South and by prejudice in most of the North—to learn to read and write.[45]

Ida Wells, all of four and one-half feet tall, was a fighter. In 1884, she bought a first-class ticket to make a ten-mile trip on a Chesapeake, Ohio, and Southwestern

▼

Ida B. Wells (1862–1931)

Ida B. Wells was born a slave six months before the Emancipation Proclamation. Her parents died of yellow fever in 1878 and she alone raised six siblings. Wells moved to Memphis where she became a school teacher before moving on to journalism. Originally writing under the pen name Iola, Wells later became editor and part owner of the *Free Speech*. In 1892, three friends of Wells' were lynched. Her spirited editorials led to the burning of her offices and her exile from Memphis. Wells moved to Chicago, where she continued to champion equal rights for African Americans and women.

Source: http://www.chicagohs.org/AOTM/Mar98/ mar98fact2.html. (University of Tennessee, College of Communication Photo Collection)

railroad train. She refused to remain in the front, or "smoking," car and attempted to enter a rear car that the railroad had "set apart for white ladies and gentlemen." The determined Miss Wells refused to hand over her ticket unless seated in the rear car and so was ejected from the train.

This humiliation led her to sue the railroad for forcing her off the train. In its defense, the railroad claimed something Miss Wells clearly did not believe: that both the ladies' car and the smoking car were equal accommodations.[46] She may have been the first African American to sue in a state court after an 1883 U.S. Supreme Court decision invalidated the federal Civil Rights Act of 1875.[47] Wells won her suit before a jury, and a white newspaper, the *Memphis Daily Appeal*, published a story headlined "'A DARKY DAMSEL OBTAINS A VERDICT FOR DAMAGES AGAINST THE CHESAPEAKE & OHIO RAILROAD.'"[48]

Ida Wells' triumph was short-lived. The Supreme Court of Tennessee ruled in 1887 that by offering equal accommodations to this "mulatto woman," "the company had done all that rightfully could be demanded." The state court added: "We think it is evident that the purpose of the defendant . . . was to harass [the railroad] and that her persistence was not in good faith to obtain a comfortable seat for a short ride."[49]

Wells continued to teach until 1891, when she was dismissed. Meanwhile, during the 1880s, she was establishing a presence as a columnist. Wells' career paralleled the rise of black newspapers. By the late 1880s, almost 200 African-American newspapers were published each week, and Wells' column, published under the pen

Figure 8–9 African-American women have been active as journalists and social organizers. Here they are depicted at the Ida B. Wells' Community Housing Project in Chicago. (Office of War Information Photograph, Division of Prints and Photographs, Library of Congress)

name of "Iola," appeared in the most prominent among these papers, including T. Thomas Fortune's *New York Age.*[50]

Once she was fired from her teaching job, Wells bought an interest in a Memphis weekly, *Free Speech.* While traveling in Mississippi, she learned of the lynching of three black businessmen in Memphis. The fighting spirit that led Miss Wells to sue the railroad was aroused even more intensely in that spring of 1892, when she learned that the three black men had been lynched evidently because they had been operating a successful grocery store in competition with a white grocer in Memphis. After white hoodlums sent to wreck the blacks' grocery store were wounded as the storekeepers defended themselves, the three partners—along with 100 other blacks—were arrested and charged with conspiracy.[51]

Lynchings—killings by mob violence—were frequent in the United States at the time. The 1892 Memphis lynching—in a year that saw 255 lynchings around the nation—pushed Wells to action. Ida Wells organized boycotts of white businesses and advised blacks to arm themselves: "A Winchester rifle should have a place of honor in every home."[52]

The lynching of the three storekeepers, of three decent men who had done no wrong, spurred Wells into impressive work in investigative reporting. She studied more than 700 lynchings that had occurred in the United States during the 1880s, concluding that lynching was an excuse to get rid of African Americans who were acquiring property.

Historian Paula Giddings noted that Wells had the courage to write that in sexual liaisons with white women, black men were not solely at fault. Wells declared that black men were lynched for being "weak enough to 'accept' white women's favors."[53] The newspaper co-owned by Wells, still carrying the poignantly hopeful title of *Free Speech*, was put out of business after she reacted to other lynchings with the truth as she saw it:

> Nobody in this section of the country believed the threadbare lie that negro men rape white women. . . . If Southern white men are not careful, they will overreach themselves and public sentiment will have a reaction. A conclusion will then be reached which will be very damaging to the moral reputation of their women.[54]

After that editorial, *Free Speech*'s offices were attacked by a mob; Wells' co-owners escaped but had to leave Memphis. Ida Wells, for the moment, was out of harm's way. She was out of state on business and wound up talking to a leading black publisher, T. Thomas Fortune of the *New York Age*. Realizing that she could not return to Memphis, Fortune allowed her to purchase a 25 percent share in his newspaper in exchange for her *Free Speech* circulation list, presumably a list of about 3,500 names.

Later in the spring of 1892, the *New York Age* carried a huge front-page story, written by Ida B. Wells, about the lynching of blacks. Using research carefully culled from white sources—such as the *Chicago Tribune*—she investigated more than 700 lynchings that had occurred during the decade of the 1880s. The reasons for lynching added up to racism, pure and simple, although the excuses given—mob members accused blacks of various crimes (extrajudicially, of course), including rape and "making threats"—just added up to a rule of terror, a strategy of keeping blacks down.[55]

Wells went on lecture tours in England, publicly charging that many whites in the United States condoned lynchings. In 1894, she became the first black columnist hired by the *Chicago Inter-Ocean*, a major white-owned newspaper.[56]

After two tours of Great Britain lecturing against lynching, Ida Wells purchased the *Chicago Conservator* from Ferdinand L. Barnett, a prominent attorney and political activist. She subsequently bore four children, but she continued to write, although at a slower pace. She investigated and reported on race riots in Illinois for the *Chicago Defender* in 1909, 1910, and 1918, and on similar riots in Little Rock, Arkansas, in 1922.

Ida Wells was also noteworthy in women's club movements, seedbeds of organizing for women's rights. However, her outspokenness and her flinty independence managed to alienate her from her sometime allies, including Frances Willard, the enormously influential head of the Women's Christian Temperance Union, and Booker T. Washington, the African-American leader who favored more conciliatory behavior.[57]

Ida B. Wells deserves closer study for her courageous muckraking against lynching, for her uncompromising adherence to her own standard of justice, for her role in women's rights, and for her role as a publisher as well as a journalist. The outrage she helped stir against lynchings is likely to have had an effect. Paula Giddings contended that the decline in lynchings after 1892 can be attributed directly to her work. "As a direct result of her efforts, the city fathers [of Memphis] were pressed to take an official stand against lynching, and for the next twenty years there was not another incident of vigilante violence there."[58]

Editors and Modernization

Metropolitan editors often were considered voices of modernization, with rural editors taking a back seat, accused of being too traditional and too resistant to change. Modern voices in the South and North championed industrialization and saw the city as the wave of the future. Editors varied, however, in their approaches to change, and although region partially determined an editor's outlook, other factors colored editorial content and newspaper publishing as well. Celebrations of the city varied in execution from Grady's frontierlike town boosting to the championing of industry to the exposing of the ills of modern urban life. Charles Dana, a staunch unionist and a Democrat, cheered the diversity of New York City but still retained a paternalistic slant on his support of the working class, whereas Edwin Godkin published the *Nation* for an elite, sober-minded group.

Henry Grady Boosts Atlanta and the South

In December 1886, Henry Woodfin Grady, prominent southern editor of the *Atlanta Constitution*, told the New England Society in New York City that the "South of slavery and secession" was dead and that rising in its place was a South of "union and freedom."

Grady claimed the New South had "sowed towns and cities in the place of theories and put business above politics." The South Grady described had "fallen in love with work," and had created "close and cordial" relations with black Americans. "The New South," Grady said, "is enamored of her new work. Her soul is stirred with the breath of a new life. . . . She is thrilling with the consciousness of growing power and prosperity."

Although Grady's description of the South was romanticized and exaggerated, he bespoke an attitude common among prominent southern editors, who, in arguing that it was time to put the past behind and to industrialize, represented the modernizing forces of the South. These southern metropolitan editors, "public figures of supreme importance," according to C. Vann Woodward, renowned southern historian, became spokesmen for industrialization and boosted their individual cities

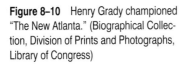

Figure 8–10 Henry Grady championed "The New Atlanta." (Biographical Collection, Division of Prints and Photographs, Library of Congress)

in ways similar to those of the frontier editors of the mid-nineteenth century. In the 1880s, these editors were regarded as metropolitan and progressive, while local editors were considered to be provincial in their concern for strictly local interests.[59] The metropolitan editors of the New South argued that the North should allow the South to rebuild without undue interference, and that rebuilding equaled industrialization.

Labeled the "spokesman for the New South," Henry Grady sang the song of a new land: The only way the South could escape depression and become prosperous was to become industrialized and, therefore, independent of the North and West for the processing of its raw materials. He spoke effectively in the North on the South's behalf and asked that the South be left alone to solve its own problems. In an attempt to minimize the race issue, he tried to persuade northerners that, on the whole, African Americans were treated with kindness and respect. His eulogies to the Old South, his companionship with Joel Chandler Harris, and his promotion of industrial growth represented a balance between modernism and tradition that made him a popular individual indeed. Nevertheless, Henry Grady was foremost a booster of his home city, Atlanta, and many of his political dealings through the *Atlanta Con-*

The New South

The new South is enamored of her new work. Her soul is stirred with the breath of a new life. The light of a grander day is falling fair on her face. She is thrilling with the consciousness of growing power and prosperity. As she stands upright, full-statured and equal among the people of the earth, breathing the keen air and looking out upon the expanding horizon, she understands that her emancipation came because in the inscrutable wisdom of God her honest purpose was crossed and her brave armies were beaten.

—Henry Woodfin Grady, speech as reported by the *New York Tribune*, December 23, 1886

stitution and his wooing of northern sentiment were designed to promote the fortunes of this new and rowdy Georgia city against the conservative claims of older metropolises such as Savannah and Macon.[60]

Henry Grady was born in Athens, Georgia, on May 24, 1850. His father was a successful merchant who became a colonel in the Civil War and was killed in battle. Grady was graduated from the University of Georgia in 1868 and attended the University of Virginia for a year, enrolling in a law course. After several unsuccessful newspaper ventures in rural Georgia, he became a reporter for the *Atlanta Constitution* and a correspondent for the *New York Herald.*

After buying part of the *Constitution* in 1880 with a $20,000 loan from Cyrus Field of Chicago, Grady spent huge sums of money to gather news and continued to report on politics and other major news events. By 1887, the weekly edition of the *Constitution* claimed the largest subscription list in the South, and the following year it boasted the largest circulation for any paper of its type in the United States. Grady avoided personal editorializing and detested the name-calling and other means of stirring up controversy employed by some editors. His emphasis was on news gathering and promotion. He also was one of the first reporters and editors to use the interview technique extensively in reporting and interpreting the news.

Grady also gave immense publicity to southern resources for industrial development, disregarding any subsequent consequences. C. Vann Woodward wrote:

> His oratorical poems picturing "mountains stored with exhaustless treasures, forests, vast and primeval, and rivers that, tumbling or loitering, run wanton to the sea" were one long hum of invocation to preemption and exploitation. "He did not tamely promote enterprise and encourage industry," wrote an admirer; "he vehemently fomented enterprise and provoked industry until they stalked through the land like armed conquerors."[61]

Charles A. Dana: Paternalistic Egalitarian

Charles Dana bought the *New York Sun* from Moses Beach in 1868 for $175,000. His co-owners and backers represented a distinguished group of prominent men, and he earned the reputation of fair play to aspiring journalists. The *Sun* office was known as "the best school of journalism" and the newspaper as "the newspaper man's newspaper."[62]

As a young man, Dana attended Harvard, then became involved in the collective Brook Farm experiment, where he met literary figures such as Nathaniel Hawthorne, Margaret Fuller, Henry Thoreau, and Horace Greeley. At the end of the Brook Farm experiment, he went to work as a typesetter for the *Boston Daily Chronotype* for five dollars a week and in 1847 moved up to city editor of the *New York Tribune* for ten dollars a week. In 1848, he traveled abroad, writing for Horace Greeley and several other editors, earning a combined salary of about forty dollars a week. After about eight months, he returned to become managing editor of the *Tribune.*

During the prewar years, Dana argued for the end of slavery and argued vehemently for the integrity of the Union. During the Civil War, he became assistant secretary of war under Edwin Stanton. He resigned his position in July 1865 and moved to Chicago to edit the *Daily Republican.* After a year he left the paper, which suffered because of inadequate financial backing. When he bought the *Sun* in 1868, he was forty-nine years old.

Dana's *Sun* was the first aggressively independent Democratic newspaper in the city and expressed the ideology of artisan republicanism, a philosophy advocating that all people, including the working class, should share equal rights and full participation in the political system. Dana's willingness to accept the diversity of the city and to champion the working class made him immensely popular in New York City in the 1870s.[63] Dana's paternalistic ideology could not compete, however, when confronted with Joseph Pulitzer's *New York World*, which developed an editorial and news policy that promoted common interests and a "pragmatic, collectivist urban vision."[64]

Dana responded to Pulitzer's challenge with a conservative retreat into the middle class, reestablishing the *Sun* as a newspaper that ultimately defended the rights of capital over those of labor.[65]

E. L. Godkin Appeals to the "Sober-Minded"

Edwin Godkin, born and educated in England, began his journalistic career as a Crimean War correspondent for the *London Daily News.* In 1856, at the end of the war, he traveled to New York and through the southern states, writing letters about slavery and the poor whites of the South to the *London Daily News.* He regarded southern planters as "ignorant provincials clinging with desperation to an institution which was doomed and which was economically unsound," but often thought northern abolitionists were unfair in their "frenzies."[66]

When the Civil War broke out, England sold arms to the Confederates, worried about repayment, and lamented the elimination of cotton shipments from southern ports—cotton that fueled England's textile industries. Godkin, however, had no sympathy for such concerns, and he countered southern sympathy in England with his letters to the *Daily News.*

In 1865, Godkin, together with James Miller McKim of Philadelphia, raised $100,000 to begin *The Nation*, a magazine that proclaimed it would be a journal "of politics, literature, science and art" and that it would report topics "with greater accuracy and moderation than are now to be found in the daily press." *The Nation* called for legislation that would be "likely to promote a more equal distribution of the fruits of progress and civilization," and that would erase artificial distinctions between blacks and whites. Contributors included such literary greats as Henry Longfellow, James Russell Lowell, and John G. Whittier.

Godkin soon encountered difficulty with his backers, each of whom had a singular idea of what *The Nation* should represent.

> The editor learned, as editors nearly always do, that each stockholder had a different conception of the best editorial program. The free traders quarrelled with the protectionists. The abolitionists were chagrined when anything except appeals for the Negro was discussed.

Finally, Godkin himself was subjected to absurd provincial criticism: He was an Englishman and therefore incompetent. *The Nation*, said the Anglophobes, had been financed with British gold and was seeking to undermine the sacred institutions of America. Godkin reorganized the company, relying only on close friends for backers, and continued publishing *The Nation*. The journal, never a great money-maker, provided him with a $5,000 annual salary, a generous stipend but not enough to allow Godkin to live in the style that he preferred. In 1881, *The Nation* became a weekly edition of the *New York Evening Post*, owned by Henry Villard. Godkin became one of three editors of the *Post*, joining Carl Schurz and Horace White. Godkin was fifty years old.

The three agreed, as Godkin wrote, that the *Post* should specialize in "being the paper to which sober-minded people would look . . . instead of hollering and bellering and shouting platitudes like the *Herald* and *Times*." Unfortunately, the three agreed on little else, and when Godkin denounced an 1883 strike of railway telegraphers, Schurz informed Godkin that he could no longer continue working with him.

▼

Note to Workingmen

We believe that sincere respect can only be won by manly honesty, and while we take the workingman's side, we claim also the privilege of being their critics and advisors. This course . . . will render our services doubly useful. It will point out to the workingmen the mistakes they are in danger of committing, and compel the rest of the world, seeing our impartiality, to respect the principles we advocate.

—*New York Sun*, March 17, 1869

Godkin objected to crime news, was offended by public accounts of private matters, and abhorred Dana's *New York Sun*, claiming that it was sensational and scandalous. Dana returned the compliments, shouting that the *Post* was as "heavy as it was dull." Godkin joined the campaign against Tammany Hall, writing articles between 1884 and 1890 without much success. He hated jingoism, admired Grover Cleveland, and condemned the Spanish-American War. By 1899, Godkin was in ill health, and he died in 1902 while visiting England.

Godkin, unlike Dana, was not a friend to his reporters but was known for an aloof austerity. He did not understand the labor movement or problems of the general public. He wholly divorced his journalism from commercialism. "When his freedom was questioned," wrote Edward Mitchell, "he lost his temper completely and refused to give way an inch. It was very seldom questioned, for Godkin's wrath, once aroused, was as noisy as it was sincere. His curses rang through the offices of the *Evening Post*. Even the reporters, who disliked him, smiled as they bent over their tasks. For if Godkin was a free man they were free men, too.

"And [t]he *Evening Post*, under Godkin, was a free newspaper."

Conclusion

The expanded transportation networks and the development of national markets that followed the Civil War created the beginnings of an advertising and subscription base for national periodicals. Developing within this framework of modernization, the quality monthlies sought to preserve the old order, while the dime novels and some newspapers sought to confront the modern world in bold fashion. Newspapers faced corruption and crime in the modern city, but they generally upheld traditional property values in combating the beginnings of organized labor. Newsprint costs rose, then fluctuated, during the Civil War, but the conversion of wood pulp to paper ultimately lowered the costs until after World War I. Stereotyping, the linotype, and web-perfecting presses increased the quality of production and sped the production process. The availability of photographs caused editors to question when they were appropriate and to debate whether they were sensational. The Associated Press thrived in the modern world, forging agreements with Western Union to solidify its hold on national news delivery.

Within the modernizing world, progress was sometimes absent or slow, and African-American editors well knew how slowly the wheels could grind. Ida B. Wells-Barnett spoke loudly on issues of lynching, justice, and freedom for all. Major metropolitan African-American newspapers organized in the years after the Civil War and would ultimately become national voices. Southern editors such as Henry Grady argued that industrialization would ease racial problems, but he offered little concrete evidence or help to black leaders. In the North, many editors abandoned the move to improve the quality of black life.

By the 1880s, editors such as Charles Dana, who championed the working classes of New York City but who remained loyal to the ideology of artisan republicanism, lost circulations in the face of newspapers like those of Joseph Pulitzer, which promoted a collective vision of the urban community.

Endnotes

1. Mary Ellen Waller-Zuckerman, "'Old Homes, in a City of Perpetual Change': Women's Magazines, 1890–1916," *Business History Review* 63 (Winter, 1989), pp. 715–56.

2. Christopher Wilson, "The Rhetoric of Consumption: Mass-Market Magazines and the Demise of the Gentle Reader, 1880–1920," in Richard Wightman Fox and T. J. Jackson Lears, eds., *The Culture of Consumption* (New York: Pantheon, 1983), pp. 39–64. For development of literary journalism as nurtured by magazines and newspapers, see Thomas B. Connery, *A Sourcebook of American Literary Journalism: Representative Writers in an Emerging Genre* (Greenwood, Conn.: Greenwood Press, 1992). For continued development into the twentieth century, see Norman Sims, ed., *Literary Journalism in the Twentieth Century* (Oxford: Oxford University Press, 1990). See also Ronald Weber, "Journalism, Writing, and American Literature," Occasional Paper No. 5, Gannett Center for Media Studies, April 1987 (1–15).

3. Dara Trum, "*Harper's*: Food for Thought 1850–1982," unpublished paper written for "The Magazine in American Society" seminar at Washburn University, 1979, Topeka, Kan., taught by Dr. Jean Folkerts.

4. Theodore Peterson, *Magazines in the 20th Century* (Urbana: University of Illinois Press, 1956), p. 409.

5. Caspar W. Whiting, "Evolution of a Country Club," *Harper's*, December 1894; Josiah Flynt, "Club Life among the Outcasts," *Harper's*, April 1895.

6. Henry Cabot Lodge, "The Spanish-American War," *Harper's*, February–August 1899.

7. See *Harper's*, Elizabeth Breuer, "What Four-Million Women Are Doing," December 1923; Howard Edsall, "Whisky below Decks," July 1929; Ellwood Hendrick, "The Changing View of Evolution," December 1920, and "Sell the Papers: The Malady of American Journalism," June 1925.

8. *Newsweek*, 30 June 1980.

9. *Time*, 28 September 1980.

10. *Time*, 28 September 1980.

11. Arthur John, *The Best Years of the Century* (Urbana: University of Illinois Press: 1981), p. 147.

12. John, *Best Years of Century*, p. 140.

13. The authors are indebted to Cynthia Steele for her unpublished paper, "Chronicle of *Scribner's Magazine*."

14. Robert Grant, "The Art of Living: The Case of Woman," *Scribner's Magazine*, October 1895, p. 476.

15. "The Business of a Great Publishing House," *Scribner's Magazine*, January 1908, p. 134.

16. For a discussion of how the *Chicago Daily News* compared to the *Chicago Times* and *Chicago Tribune* in regard to attitudes toward urban life, see David Paul Nord, "The Public Community: The Urbanization of Journalism in Chicago," *Journal of Urban History* 11:4 (August, 1985), pp. 411–41.

17. Daniel Pope, *The Making of Modern Advertising* (New York: Basic Books, 1983), p. 32.

18. For an analysis of the evolution of a consumer culture, see Michael Schudson, *Advertising, the Uneasy Persuasion: Its Dubious Impact on American Society* (New York: Basic Books, 1986).

19. Pope, *Making of Modern Advertising*, pp. 117, 118.

20. S. N. D. North, "History and Present Condition of the Newspaper and Periodical Press of the United States, with a Catalogue of the Publications of the Census Year," in U.S. Department of the Interior, Bureau of the Census, *Tenth Census* (Washington, 1884), 8, p. 51.

21. *New York Herald*, 13 April 1836, p. 1, cited in Thomas C. Leonard, *The Power of the Press: The Birth of American Political Reporting* (New York: Oxford University Press, 1986). Other quotes from Leonard, p. 149.

22. Leonard, *Power of the Press*, p. 153.

23. Leonard, *Power of the Press*, pp. 177, 178.

24. Leonard, *Power of the Press*, p. 130.

25. David Paul Nord, *Newspapers and New Politics: Midwestern Municipal Reform, 1890–1900* (Ann Arbor, Mich.: University Microfilms, International, 1981).

26. Alfred McClung Lee, *The Daily Newspaper in America* (New York: Macmillan, 1937), p. 138.

27. Lee, *Daily Newspaper in America*, p. 117.

28. See Corban Goble, "Rogers' Typograph versus Mergenthaler's Linotype: The Push and Shove of Patents and Priority in the 1890s," unpublished paper presented to the History Division of the Association for Education in Journalism and Mass Communication, Norman, Okla., August 1986, for controversies involving the development of this technology.

29. Christine Bold, "Popular Forms I," in *The Columbia History of the American Novel*, Emory Elliott, ed., (New York: Columbia University Press, 1991), p. 287.

30. Bold, "Popular Forms I," p. 293.

31. Bold, "Popular Forms I," pp. 294–95.

32. Bold, "Popular Forms I," p. 298.

33. Lee, *Daily Newspaper in America*, p. 128.

34. Leonard, *Power of the Press*, p. 102.

35. Daniel Czitrom, *Media and the American Mind* (Chapel Hill: University of North Carolina Press, 1982), pp. 24–25.

36. Czitrom, *Media and the American Mind*, p. 25.

37. From government reports cited in Czitrom, *Media and the American Mind*, p. 26.

38. Czitrom, *Media and the American Mind*, p. 27.

39. *Nation* 24 (1877), p. 202; and *New York Tribune*, April 7, 1877, cited in Woodward, *Origins of the New South*, p. 216.

40. R. Ginzburg, *100 Years of Lynchings* (New York: Lancer Books, 1962), p. 12, cited in Richard Perloff, "The Press and Lynchings of African Americans," *Journal of Black Studies,* vol. 30 (January, 2000), p. 319.

41. Jannette L. Dates and William Barlow, *Split Image: African Americans in the Mass Media* (Washington, D.C.: Howard University Press, 1990), pp. 344–51.

42. Henry Lewis Suggs, *The Black Press in the Middle West, 1865–1985* (Westport, Conn.: Greenwood Press, 1996), chap. 12.

43. Jinx Marie Coleman Broussard, "Alice Dunbar-Nelson: A Black Woman during the Jim Crow Era," paper presented at the AEJMC 25th Annual Southeast Colloquium, March, 2000; for other recent contributions to the research literature on African-American journalists, see G. T. Hull, *Color, Sex and Poetry: Three Women Writers of the Harlem Renaissance* (Bloomington: Indiana University Press, 1993); and A. Pride and C. C. Wilson, *A History of the Black Press* (Washington, D.C.: Howard University Press, 1997). See also Rodger Streitmatter, *Raising Her Voice: African-American Women Journalists Who Changed History* (Lexington: University of Kentucky Press, 1994).

44. Karen Brown, "The Black Press of Tennessee: 1865–1890," unpublished Ph.D. dissertation, University of Tennessee, 1982, p. 15.

45. Nora Hall, "Ida B. Wells-Barnett," *Dictionary of Literary Biography* (Detroit: Gale Research, 1983) 23: 341–42.

46. *Chesapeake, Ohio & Southern Railroad Co. v. Wells*, 4 S.W. 5, Supreme Court of Tennessee, 1887; Paula Giddings, *When and Where I Enter: The Impact of Black Women on Race and Sex in America* (New York: Bantam, 1984), p. 23.

47. Giddings, *When and Where I Enter*, p. 23.

48. Giddings, *When and Where I Enter*, quoting *Memphis Daily Appeal*, December 25, 1884.

49. *Chesapeake, Ohio & Southern Railroad Co. v. Wells*.

50. Giddings, *When and Where I Enter*, pp. 18, 24.

51. Giddings, *When and Where I Enter*, pp. 18, 24. See also the PBS television production, *Ida B. Wells-Barnett*, narrated by Toni Morrison.

52. Giddings, *When and Where I Enter*, p. 20.

53. Giddings, *When and Where I Enter*, p. 28.

54. Quoted by Hall, "Ida B. Wells-Barnett," p. 343.

55. Hall, "Ida B. Wells-Barnett," p. 343; Giddings, *When and Where I Enter*, p. 29.

56. Hall, "Ida B. Wells-Barnett," p. 343.

57. Giddings, *When and Where I Enter*, p. 180.

58. Giddings, *When and Where I Enter*, p. 92.

59. C. Vann Woodward, *Origins of the New South* (Baton Rouge: Louisiana State University Press: 1951), p. 145.

60. See Harold E. Davis's *Henry Grady's New South: Atlanta, A Brave and Beautiful City* (Tuscaloosa: University of Alabama Press, 1990) for explication of this thesis.

61. Cited in C. Vann Woodward, *Tom Watson: Agrarian Rebel* (New York: Oxford, 1983), p. 90.

62. For biographical information about Dana, see Candace Stone, *Dana and the Sun* (New York: Dodd, Mead & Company, 1938); Edward P. Mitchell, *Memoirs of an Editor* (New York: Scribners, 1924); Frank M. O'Brien, *The Story of the Sun* (New York: D. Appleton and Company, 1928); and Charles J. Rosebault, *When Dana Was the Sun* (New York: R. M. McBride & Company, 1931). For an interpretive account, see Janet E. Steele, *The Sun Shines for All: Journalism and Ideology in the Life of Charles A. Dana* (Syracuse, N.Y.: Syracuse University Press, 1993).

63. Steele, *The Sun Shines for All*, chap. 6.

64. Nord, "Public Community," p. 436. See also George Juergens, *Joseph Pulitzer and the New York World* (Princeton, N.J.: Princeton University Press, 1966).

65. Steele, *The Sun Shines for All*, p. 234.

66. Citations in this section pertaining to Edwin Godkin are taken from Edward Mitchell, "Godkin of 'The Post'," *Scribner's* 96 (December, 1934), p. 329.

CHAPTER 9

Mass Markets and Mass Culture

▼

T he press emerged from the intensely political years of sectionalism, partisan politics, the Civil War, and Reconstruction to confront a new order.[1] The rapid expansion of transportation and communication after the Civil War gave way to an increasingly urbanized society, rapid technological and scientific growth, and corporate consolidation. Resistance to this changed society was evident as critics and labor organizers questioned how the rights of men, women, and children as wage earners within an industrialized society would be preserved.

Emerging from the fray were the captains of industry, leaders of the consolidated corporate giants. Through vertical and horizontal integration of industry, the captains amassed great wealth. They introduced mechanization, which created some new jobs and products but eliminated other jobs in the crafts and subjected laborers to rigid schedules and routine tasks. The captains sympathized little with labor, and in the years of financial panic—1873, 1884, and 1893—they lowered wages while they lengthened hours, and they rarely installed safety equipment or followed safety procedures. Between 1900 and 1917 in the railroad industry alone, 72,000 workers were killed and 2 million were injured.[2]

As corporate capitalism became firmly entrenched, publishers began to conceive of themselves not only as political and cultural voices but as extensions of the nation's marketing system. Advertising became a conduit for promoting an economy of consumption, and magazines such as the *Saturday Evening Post* and the *Ladies' Home Journal* became vital advertising outlets as they took advantage of favorable postal rates and national markets. Magazines and metropolitan newspapers combined to tell stories that reminded readers of their declining control over public affairs—now so often dominated by business interests with advertisements that promoted brand-name products to make teeth whiter, bodies cleaner, and appearances more acceptable. The emphasis on national brands and the development of department stores created a new industry of advertising agents and agencies—an industry that moved beyond the feeble attempts at basic communication made earlier in the century to a more specialized approach toward persuading the consumer. Department stores focused on women as consumers—and as audiences for advertising and publications—and the growth of these stores provided new employment opportunities for women as well.

Editors, consumers, and municipal reformers railed against monopolies even as they supported business in general, promoted growth without always considering the costs, and struggled with how to curtail corruption in city services and government. As the press expanded in numbers and in size, critics questioned the reform positions of editors, asking whether indeed some editors were not captains of industry themselves. Joseph Pulitzer's and William Randolph Hearst's circulation and sensationalism wars of the late 1890s sparked even greater criticism.

Within a growing business environment fraught with labor strikes and other forms of social and intellectual opposition, business sought to win over the public and the press. Incorporating strategies used by early promoters such as P. T. Barnum, who used promotional techniques to attract crowds to his circus, and special interest groups such as the antislavery activists and suffragists, business learned to systematically create an image of public service.

Increased professionalization of journalism, however, excluded some people who had actively participated in disseminating information. New rules purportedly adopted to assure the professional status of the congressional news corps managed to exclude many women and African Americans, who often did not write hard news for daily newspapers. Further, the development of exclusive press clubs left little room for those who did not serve metropolitan dailies. ▼

Advertising and Mass Culture

Those living in the last decade of the nineteenth century witnessed a cultural change perhaps unprecedented in the United States. The nation began a shift from a producer to a consumer economy, and advertising became the single most useful tool to promote consumption. Work patterns changed as people received wages and salaries in factories or corporate bureaucratic structures rather than working for themselves on farms or in small shops where they controlled their hours and patterns of work. Women, although entering the work force in greater numbers, were cast primarily as caretakers of the home. The corporate world of the 1890s envisioned such caretakers primarily as consumers and adapted consumer rhetoric and sales approaches to appeal to women. William R. Leach, in an analysis of the development of the department store from 1890 to 1925, writes, "Forged by merchants in the company of enthusiastic politicians, reformers, educators and artists, this capitalist culture was so powerful as nearly to dwarf all alternative cultures. Advertising gave it shape; a new abundance of commodities established its foundation. The culture of consumption was an urban and secular one of color and spectacle, of sensuous pleasure and dreams. It subverted, but never overturned, the older mentality of repression, practical utilitarianism, scarcity, and self-denial. It slowly encompassed service and comfort as desirable goals, intermingling competition and cooperation, blurring the lines between work and leisure."

The department stores serve well as a focus for describing the development of a culture of consumption because they had integrated concepts of visual display, public service, and advertising. In the 1890s, the department stores not only perfected the visual display of goods but they built their own auditoriums, putting on musicals and plays. In 1904, Leach notes, Richard Strauss conducted the world premier performance of his *Symphonia Domestica* in the dramatic rotunda of Wanamaker's New York store. The department stores contained restaurants, roof gardens, and beauty parlors. Advertising "attempted to endow the goods with transformative messages and associations that the goods did not objectively possess." Thus, writes Leach, "to buy a shawl in a 'Japanese garden'" was to appropriate not only the shawl, but the exoticism of Japan as well.[3]

The concept of public service was promoted to obscure the profit-making aspect of the vast enterprises. In 1897, John Wanamaker proposed that his store was not a "capitalist" or a "Wanamaker" store, but rather a "people's store."[4] The stores promoted institutionalized gender roles but also provided work opportunities for women. From 1890 on, women worked as editors and copywriters for advertising and fashion periodicals, as poster and billboard advertisers in advertising agencies, as dress designers and illustrators, and as directors and owners of cosmetic firms. Men held the highest managerial posts, but women worked in all other levels of the department store bureaucracies. Shopping in the stores also provided diversion and appropriate, secular public activity for middle-class women.

Department stores held a preeminent role in local advertising from 1890 until they experienced a decline in the 1980s. John Wanamaker entered the men's ready-made clothing business in 1861 and by the end of the decade was firmly established as the largest retail dealer in men's clothing in the United States. He was one of the first clients of the Philadelphia advertising agency N. W. Ayer and Son, established in 1869. He guaranteed fixed prices and was noted not only for the policy, but for the use of promotion and advertising in establishing the policy. In 1874, Wanamaker announced his fixed-price policy in a half-page copyrighted ad. Wanamaker's use of advertising was not restricted only to newspapers, although he supported most of the Philadelphia dailies with advertising. His advertising program included such lavish publications as a 200-page guide to the city published in 1887 that provided maps and listed streets, organizations, government offices, ethnic groups, business organizations, and the names and addresses of newspapers. Wanamaker's store was described as the "greatest" of the new general stores in copy that discussed dry-good stores in general. Wanamaker's promotional brochures advanced the public image

▼

John Wanamaker (1838–1922)

John Wanamaker was born the son of a brick-maker. Always driven to succeed, he left school at the age of fourteen to become a errand boy. Later, he began his department store empire with his brother-in-law and created a store that had "thirty-three blocks of counters, numbering 129 in all, and aggregating two-thirds of a mile in length, and in front of which are 1400 stools for the convenience of shoppers. . . ." The main store in Philadelphia counted 70,000 people entering the store in an hour on opening day. At its height, the store had eight acres of floor space.

Source: J. W. Ferry, *A History of the Department Store* (New York: The Macmillan Company, 1960). (*Photo:* Division of Prints and Photographs, Library of Congress Collection)

of the store, but he used newspaper ads to create an intimate relationship with each customer—to sell "one pair of gloves at a time." Wanamaker used display ads, personals, and single-column conversational copy to sell his wares, advancing values of familiarity, honesty, education, economy of size, the importance of price, trust, a sense of partnership, and above all, patriotism. "In Philadelphia," wrote Patricia Bradley, "the advertising, promotion and public spectacle of the John Wanamaker department store had played an important role in spelling out a political metaphor for the coming era in which the interests of large private firms were thought to be interchangeable with those of the public."[5]

Magazines as Vehicles for Advertising

In an atmosphere of woman as consumer and consumerism as patriotism, general interest and women's magazines flourished. They attracted a broader-based audience than did the quality monthlies, aiming at the northeastern elite as well as families of slightly lower income. Editors also sought new regional elite audiences in cities of more than 10,000 people. Unlike the literary editors of the qualities, editors of the mass-circulation magazines often apprenticed in daily journalism and treated their magazines as news commodities, focusing on timely information. They planned their magazines, sought specific contributions from specific writers, and promoted the content as well as the publication. Such editors, wrote Christopher Wilson, "rehabilitated gentle culture by infusing it with managerial skills and work values."[6] These

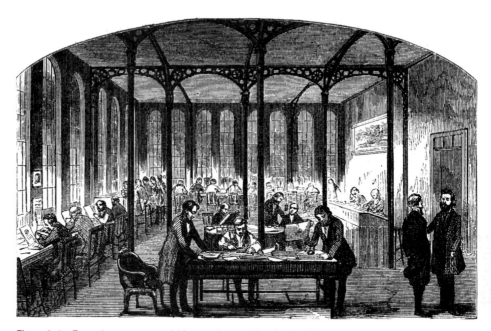

Figure 9–1 Engravings were essential features in magazines in the mid-nineteenth century. Pictured here is the engraving room of *Leslie's Illustrated Newspaper*. (State Historical Society of Wisconsin)

editors covered the realm of business and politics, deliberately aiming at increasing their male readership, and encouraged articles that conveyed tones of authority, authenticity, and expertise. Women's magazines targeted specific audiences, with *Good Housekeeping* aiming primarily at homemakers, whereas *Harper's Bazaar* (1867–present) and *Vogue* (1892–present) sought a more exclusive fashion-oriented audience. The number of magazines published grew from 700 in 1865, to 3,300 in 1885, and to 4,400 by 1890. Between 1890 and 1905, the circulation of monthly periodicals rose from 18 million to 64 million per issue.[7]

The women's publications fell into three categories: mail-order journals, fashion periodicals published by dress-pattern manufacturers, and magazines with contents based on clippings from other journals and newspapers. Six of the magazines started in the last decades of the nineteenth century became circulation leaders. These publications included *Ladies' Home Journal* (1883–present), *McCall's* (1873–present), *Delineator* (1873–1939), *Woman's Home Companion* (1874–1956), *Pictorial Review* (1889–1939), and *Good Housekeeping* (1885–present). *McCall's, Delineator,* and *Pictorial Review* were first published to advance the pattern companies of James McCall, Ebenezer Butterick, and William Ahnelt. These magazines took advantage of urbanization, favorable postal rates, and other factors that promoted the magazine industry as a whole. Advertising was the key factor that allowed for expanded circulation and kept the subscription prices low, and publishers aggressively pursued advertising accounts.

Women's magazines also provided new job opportunities for women. *Woman's Home Companion* was edited by Gertrude Battles Lane, and the *Delineator* had a series of women editors. *McCall's* had five female editors between 1884 and 1918, with one male editor for a brief period in 1911–1912. *Vogue* had only female editors from its beginning.

Initially, magazine editors appealed to advertisers by describing their audiences in romanticized, if not inflated, terms. The Curtis Publishing Company boasted that the *Ladies' Home Journal* was "designed for the home loving," and the *Saturday Evening Post* was designed "for the men and women who desire a wholesome, sane and entertaining treatment of modern life in fiction and fact." Editor George Horace Lorimer said the *Post* appealed to "men with income, and men who are going to have income." During the early twentieth century, however, advertisers began to scrutinize audiences more carefully. If the primary readership of the *Ladies' Home Journal* was women, why should automobile companies such as Peerless, Packard, and Pierce-Arrow buy ad space in the magazine?

To respond to advertiser scrutiny, Curtis formed a Division of Commercial Research in 1911. Its early readership studies appear to be among the first ever done by a publisher. By 1915, Curtis was describing the *Ladies' Home Journal* audience in much more specific terms as families with annual incomes between $1,200 and $1,500. He noted that they were the group most able to use the magazine's assistance. A number of scholars have recognized that assistance as consisting primarily of teaching readers what products to buy and how to buy them. As the Curtis Publishing Company moved deeper into the twentieth century, its publishers, notes Douglas B. Ward, "increasingly viewed readers as consumers, and a publication's readership increasingly became a commodity, a product that was defined, studied and sold."[8]

Ladies' Home Journal

The *Ladies' Home Journal* set a standard for women's magazines for many decades. In addition, it paved the way for magazines to crusade in the public interest. The driving force behind the publication was Cyrus H. K. Curtis, who started the *Ladies' Home Journal* and later the *Saturday Evening Post*. While still a boy, Curtis published his own newspaper. The thirteen-year-old rose at 4 A.M., delivered papers until 7 A.M., attended school, and then spent his evening setting, typing, printing, and selling his four-page paper, *Young America*. When a fire destroyed the Curtis home, and young Curtis' office with it, he quit school to help support his family by working as an advertisement solicitor for the *Boston Times*. He started another newspaper, the *Independent*, in Boston, but that newspaper failed. He then went into partnership with his brother-in-law, Hamilton Mayo, and began publishing the *Tribune and Farmer*. This four-page weekly catered to farmers and sold for fifty cents a year. Curtis attempted to expand the paper by developing a woman's section entitled "Woman and the Home," with reprints of articles from other publications. When Curtis took the new section home to show his wife, she laughed at his choice of content. She became the new editor of the women's section. Curtis' wife, who edited under her maiden name, Louisa May Knapp, assumed the editorship of Curtis' new magazine, initially named the *Ladies' Journal and Practical Housekeeper*, in 1883.

A businessman rather than an editor, Curtis firmly believed that advertising was the key to the production of high-quality magazines offered at a low price. He also used group subscriptions to lure readers. With a group subscription, four readers could subscribe for one dollar. The regular rate was fifty cents a year. This plan doubled his circulation in six months. With this steadily growing subscription base, which was the first to surpass 1 million readers, Curtis was able to turn his attention to selling advertising.[9] Although expanding advertising continuously, Curtis adhered to a policy of not accepting questionable advertising, thus proving that a magazine could be ethical and successful at the same time.

Within six years, monthly circulation of the *Journal* stabilized at 440,000, and Curtis hired a new editor, Edward Bok. Although Bok would be called sexist today for his belief that women arrived at conclusions by instinct rather than by reasoning, he successfully made content decisions that appealed to women.[10] In his magazine he included articles on homemaking, sewing, fashion, cooking, needlework, theater, and celebrities as well as fiction and accounts of a society active in the "Gilded Age." In 1895, he published house plans, and architect Stanford White said that Bok, through his appeals to women, influenced American architecture more than any other individual of his time. From 1898 to 1906, he emphasized social concerns and the possibility of the breakdown of the American family. One article by Theodore Roosevelt, "The American Woman as a Mother," reflected concern for the growing lack of discipline of children, of the man who is not a good husband and father, and the woman who has "lost her sense of duty and is sunk in vapid self-indulgence." He claimed good morals and discipline at home would create a moral, disciplined nation.

In 1893, Bok and Curtis took a bold step and cut patent medicine advertising from the *Journal's* pages. Earlier issues advertised such products as Ayer's Cathartic Pills, which claimed to cure "heartburn, sickness, headaches, and all disorders of the stomach, liver, and bowels."[11] In another issue, a music teacher from North Carolina asserted that a nine-year-old student had become "thin and weak and nervous" due to an awful cough, only to be cured in less than a month's time by Scott's Emulsion.[12]

Despite the *Ladies' Home Journal* 1893 ban on patent medicine advertising, it was not until 1904 that Bok's editorial campaign against the makers of nostrums gained momentum. In the May 1904 issue, Bok wrote an editorial titled "The Patent Medicine Curse," which featured an analysis of the alcohol in various brands of cures. For example, Parker's Tonic contained 41.6 percent alcohol. Bok noted that although most magazines were rejecting patent medicine advertising, it had not yet been legally outlawed. Therefore, Bok continued, it was a woman's duty to refuse to buy any medicine if not fully aware of its ingredients. He also told women who were members of the Women's Christian Temperance Union that they had a special obligation not to allow patent medicine advertisements to be posted on their barns or fences and to end all subscriptions to religious newspapers that continued to run patent medicine advertising. After all, these nostrums were attacking the very soul of a child and "planting the seed of a future drunkard."[13] Alcohol was not the only dangerous ingredient. Among others were morphine, opium, and digitalis—all extremely addictive.

In 1908, Bok began to publish statistics and convincing photographs about venereal disease, a topic hardly mentioned in good homes of the time. He criticized parents for not teaching their children the "evils of some of their actions." He demanded that children be educated about the positive and negative aspects of sex instead of treating it like a closed issue. The *Journal* lost 70,000 readers, but after eighteen months Bok began to receive letters of inquiry instead of protests. He published a series of *Edward Bok Books* that answered the most common questions about sex and paved the way for parents to tell their children the entire story.[14]

Under the leadership of Curtis and Bok, the *Ladies' Home Journal* introduced many "firsts." It was the first popular magazine to sell for one dollar a year or ten cents a month, which was to become the prevailing popular price. It also was the first magazine to originate the idea of changing its cover every month. It was the first to refuse questionable advertising and to contain personal correspondence between the editor and readers. The *Ladies' Home Journal* also introduced, as an award, free education to young men and women who gathered subscriptions. It originated two-, three-, and four-color printing. It was the first magazine to contain a garden department and the first to have a kitchen in which recipes were tested before they were published. Many of the policies forwarded by Curtis and Bok were adopted by other women's and general interest publications of the time.

Although Bok resigned in 1919, the magazine continued to flourish and by 1928 had a circulation of 3 million. It continues today as a major women's magazine, aimed now at women in their fifties, and maintains a circulation of 5.1 million.

Saturday Evening Post

Advertising also played a major role in the development of another Cyrus Curtis magazine, the *Saturday Evening Post*. Under Curtis' watchful eye, with George Horace Lorimer as editor, the magazine appealed squarely to middle America. The magazine lauded businessmen whom Curtis revered and published well-known American writers.[15] In a history of George Lorimer and the *Post*, Jan Cohn wrote that Lorimer set out to "create America in and through the pages of the *Saturday Evening Post*. Week after week he crafted the issues of his magazine as an image, an idea, a construct of America for his readers to share, a model against which they could shape their lives. . . . It can be argued . . . that the *Post* was instrumental in creating and continually reframing a set of attitudes and beliefs that, at least until the time of the New Deal, constituted an American ideology." Lorimer's world was not one of resistance to industrialization, labor strife, or protest; rather it was the "culture of the emerging world of business—business as it hovered between production and consumption and managed to live comfortably with the contradiction between traditional values and present realities." The stories of the *Post* audience—westerns, historical romances, and sports fiction—were "spun out of the collective web of a comprehensible society, a society built on fair play and individual initiative and common sense."[16]

The magazine claimed to have originated as the *Pennsylvania Gazette*, with Benjamin Franklin as its original publisher. However, Samuel Keimer was the original editor of the *Gazette*, and it was a newspaper, not a magazine. Franklin bought the *Gazette* in 1729, and as a newspaper it was defunct by 1815. The *Saturday Evening Post* actually was founded in 1821 by two printers.[17] By 1897, when it caught Curtis' eye, it consisted primarily of reprints from other magazines. Intrigued with the history of the magazine, Curtis bought the *Post* for $1,000, hired George Horace Lorimer as editor, and invested at least $1,250,000 in the *Saturday Evening Post* before it showed a profit. In 1899, the first full-page advertisement appeared. Less than a year later, one issue carried thirty-two columns of paid advertising. Circulation of the five-cent magazine grew quickly from 2,000 at the time Curtis purchased the magazine in 1897 to 315,000 in 1902. Circulation reached 3 million in 1928. Much of the success of the magazine was due to Curtis' promotional techniques, used both in support of the *Ladies' Home Journal* and the *Post*.

George Lorimer edited the *Post* until 1936, when he retired. His long editorship was rivaled by another—that of Ben Hibbs who edited the magazine from 1942 to 1961.

The *Saturday Evening Post* paid on acceptance, and manuscripts were reviewed and decided upon within seventy-two hours of arrival. This practice was favored by writers, and many of the fiction and nonfiction writers of the early 1900s sent manuscripts to the *Post* for review. Among these prominent authors were Joel Chandler Harris, Hamlin Garland, Bret Harte, Richard Harding Davis, and Paul Laurence Dunbar.

1879 Postal Debates and Second-Class Mail

Leading magazine and newspaper publishers in New York and Philadelphia—perhaps a few other large cities as well—met during the 1870s to forge an agreement with Congress to devise a mail system designed to exclude publications issued primarily for advertising purposes and to put magazines on an equal status with newspapers. The move to exclude came partially from postmasters, who operated under chronic deficits, and who found the irregular mailing patterns of the advertising circulars difficult to handle. In addition, magazine and newspaper publishers, by helping to write the legislation, succeeded in carving out a more competitive position for themselves in the new advertising world of the late nineteenth century.[18]

Under existing postal law, magazines were required to pay higher mailing fees than newspapers because the law favored weekly publications. The 1879 Postal Act created the classification system used today, so that printed matter fell into either the second or the third class. In order to fall into the more favorable second-class rate, publications had to appear at regular intervals at least four times a year; be issued from a known office of publication; be formed of printed sheets without substantial binding; and disseminate "information of a public character, or be devoted to literature, the sciences, arts, or some special industry, and have a legitimate list of subscribers." Publications designed especially for advertising or those being circulated without cost were specifically prohibited. The law brought magazines into the fold with newspapers and no longer distinguished between the two by creating more favorable rates for newspapers.

Mass Press for a Mass Audience

The foundations of the modern press were firmly in place, incorporating technologies of rapid printing, mechanized typesetting, cheap papermaking, and photoengraving. Many of these technological improvements that had increased the availability of magazines also affected newspapers. In addition, editors and reporters established news gathering processes such as interviews, beats, and telegraph news. The business function and the editorial process became clearly separate entities, although each influenced the other.[19] Further, the cost of doing business escalated. Newspapers in urban areas frequently sold for $100,000 or more, and some for as much as $250,000.[20]

The newspaper industry, one might say, was on a roll. The number of morning, evening, and Sunday dailies grew steadily between 1880 and 1900, a growth that would continue until the close of World War I. In 1870, only 574 daily newspapers were published, but by 1890 that number grew to 1,536. Weeklies grew as well, with 4,295 weeklies publishing in 1870 and 12,600 in 1890. Simultaneously, circulations grew until in 1900 more than 26 percent of the population subscribed to a newspaper. In 1870, dailies circulated to slightly more than 2.5 million people; in 1890, about 8.5 million daily copies entered the homes of American people. Foreign-language newspapers, in line with the rising immigration levels, grew from 315 in 1870 to 1,159 in 1900. In 1880, 80 percent of the foreign-language journals were German; by 1900, as immigrants arrived from more varied countries, only 64.5 percent were German.[21]

The number of evening newspapers increased rapidly, as editors and advertisers targeted women as the primary purchasers within the home. One trade journal argued:

> The morning paper is the business man's paper, and will never be the home paper so long as women are confronted with household duties. When it is fresh, they are too busy to read it and when they are at leisure, it is old, for the evening paper has been born.[22]

Department stores preferred the evening papers because they were more likely to go to the home and be read by women.

The census of 1880 explained the spectacular growth of the urban press by noting that the "conditions of daily life" required "some general medium of communication between man and man." Also recorded in the census was the fact that the "rate of growth of the news industry seemed unparalleled in any other country of the world and hardly equaled by any other phase of industrial development in the United States."[23]

Newspapers now depended on large circulations and expanded advertising bases, relying little on political party support. However, government job-printing contracts continued to be important sources of income for many editors of small to mid-size papers. Although partisan politics still played an important role in how newspapers addressed the issues, editors were reluctant to emphasize party loyalties if it meant excluding too many strata of the urban societies they served. In some cities, newspapers joined forces with each other as well as with reform groups to achieve nonpartisan municipal control of city services, including utilities and transportation. It was a new kind of politics, in which local issues gained supremacy over party loyalties. In other cities, fragmented political and business groups and party-loyal newspapers failed to bridge their differences, and city services remained in the hands of the politicians.[24]

Newspapers chose a variety of paths along a continuum from sensationalism and entertainment to information and fact-finding. Some newspapers jumped on the successful Hearst-Pulitzer bandwagon. Others shunned either parts or all of it and remained graphically, editorially, and politically conservative. Almost all newspapers, however, became distinct parts of the business communities they served.

Although many of the new techniques grew out of the need to compete with other newspapers in the spectacular cities of the late nineteenth century—and much of the growth in the press took place within the cities—the press was not entirely urban, at least in a "city" sense. Nevertheless, the issues of the city—municipal reform, the status of labor, and the effects of sensational presses—did not escape the smaller towns. Editors such as William Allen White of Emporia, Kansas, rejected the editorial techniques of the Hearsts, professed political independence but remained party-oriented, and championed municipal reform.

Newspapers differed tremendously in treatment of subject matter and in graphic presentation while they catered to audiences as diverse as New York immigrant laborers, Chicago businessmen, and the rural readers of White's *Gazette*. Their purposes varied from entertaining to informing to interpreting as they cajoled readers to vote for their candidates, to support nonpartisan reform, and to admire the dramatic growth of the cities, the western states, and the country at large.

Increased commercialization of the press and the move away from political party dependence fostered an increased interest in news and a decline of the editorial function. Hazel Dicken Garcia saw it as an evolution from content "being idea-centered in the earliest decade [of the nineteenth century] to event-centered by mid-century, and to a diversity dominated by the 'story' in the 1890s."[25]

Accompanying the shift toward news and claims of political independence was a growing discussion of the role of the newspaper and professionalization within the burgeoning trade journals. Although reporters gained new prominence in the news framework, they still received low pay and experienced minimal social status as they began to confront the conflicts inherent with their role. As the shift occurred, some editors worried that newspapers were losing the political power they once held.[26]

The Debate over Information and Sensation

If one describes the 1890s as a period of "New Journalism" evidenced by Joseph Pulitzer's *New York World* and William Randolph Hearst's *New York Journal*, one has to ignore the more generalized claims that in the late 1800s journalists concerned themselves more than before with "facts" and "reality." One also has to ignore the *New York Times*, the *Chicago Tribune*, the Scripps newspapers, and the *Kansas City Star*, which denounced the tactics of Hearst and Pulitzer but nevertheless gained prominence in their communities, succeeded financially, and continued for many years to provide information and to editorialize about a variety of local and national issues. Any student of the journalism of that period has to ask how the two threads—information on the one hand, sensation on the other—are connected.

The *World*, the *Times*, and the *Journal* did not operate in a vacuum but competed within New York with such newspapers as the *New York Herald*—a continuation by James Gordon Bennett, Jr., of his father's publication—and nationally with newspapers started by a number of entrepreneurs, including E. W. Scripps. The

Herald, taken over by the younger Bennett in 1872, was one of the best New York papers at that time. Having pioneered in techniques that increased the speed of both the collection of news and its delivery, the paper had established a secure reputation in the city. Bennett established the Paris edition of the *Herald* in 1887, which grew to be the *International Herald Tribune*. He was probably most well known for sending reporter Henry Stanley to Africa to look for a missing missionary and Stanley's famous greeting, "Dr. Livingston, I presume?" uttered at the successful conclusion of his search.

Scripps, although often called a press lord because of his vast holdings, never sought to establish huge newspapers like those of Hearst and Pulitzer. In 1878, he started the *Cleveland Press* in a rapidly growing Ohio town, and he continued to establish similar small newspapers. He organized one of the first effective newspaper chains and he supported organized labor.

Scripps believed that papers should give working-class readers short, interesting stories in a small format with little advertising. Scripps' formula meant that little in-depth political news would be carried. Further, Scripps minimized costs, including wages, and seldom advocated new equipment. He continuously argued with his editors who wanted to upgrade plant and equipment and expand advertising, emphasizing that "the editorial department embraces 90 percent of the life and vitality of a newspaper."[27]

He established newspapers in towns with little competition, and his corporate officers scrutinized all budgets. To reduce the cost of local news coverage, Scripps required all of his newspapers to belong to his news associations, relying heavily on association news copy and thereby reducing the cost of local coverage. Scripps did not believe in relying on advertisers but rather on business efficiency and subscriber demand.

Scripps detested the sensationalism of Hearst and Pulitzer. He organized the Science Service, a news service that profited from cooperation between journalists and scientists and that was responsible in part for transition from highly sensationalized science news in the latter part of the nineteenth century to professional analysis of scientific developments.[28]

Michael Schudson suggested in *Discovering the News* that a new-found emphasis on facts coincided with a developing American belief that the cure for the ills of the cities and of the society could be found through empirical precision, the advice of the expert, and the application of factual information. Although Americans always had been fascinated by science, as indicated by the *New York Sun's* successful moon hoax, citizens now turned to science as the newest fad, expecting it to solve the ills that government and politics had failed to answer. Reporters, in a search for credibility and respectability, partially justified their role in society as providers of information designed to solve problems.

However, the *World* and the *Journal* did not operate in the problem-solving mentality of the emerging progressive mind. These papers' milieu was the city of New York, a city teeming with immigrants who spoke a variety of languages and little or no English. It was an exciting city that provided literary giants with picturesque paragraphs and social commentators like Jacob Riis with endless material about the abhorrent condition of the slums. It was a city of hope, of color, and of opportunity, as well as a city of graft, corruption, and squalid living conditions. The newspapers of this New York, unlike the respectable *New York Times* that appealed to the business classes, provided entertainment. This is not to say that the business classes did not read the *New York World* or that the working classes did not read the *Times*. Nevertheless, the newspapers had distinctive appeals. Upper-class businessmen and social matrons read the *World* (with perhaps a shade of guilt as they commented on its disgracefulness), and working class people sought the information the *Times* provided. Why was the latter considered respectable and the former not? Schudson wrote:

> Perhaps, then, the *Times* established itself as the "higher journalism" because it adapted to the life experience of persons whose position in the social structure gave them the most control over their own lives. Its readers were relatively independent and participant. The readers of the *World* were relatively dependent and nonparticipant. The experience engendered by affluence and education makes one comfortable with a certain journalistic orientation, one which may indeed be, in some respects, more mature, more encompassing, more differentiated, more integrated. It may also be, in its own ways, more limited; refinement in newspapers, people, and sugar, is bleaching. If the *World*'s readers might have longed for more control of their lives, the readers of the *Times* may have wished for more nutrients in theirs.[29]

Communications theorist John Pauly suggested that public talk about "the news" and the concept of independence allowed Americans to adjust their democratic ideals to the conditions of industrial society and "expressed Americans' belief in the possibility of a morally purified style of commercial journalism that kept faith with earlier political ideals." The ideology of an independent press minimized the severity of political conflicts, proclaimed that metropolitan dailies acted in the public interest, and symbolized a renunciation of the Civil War and a quest for national unity.[30]

Information and Municipal Reform: Concepts of Urban Community

Beginning as early as the 1870s, with the *Harpers' Weekly* and *New York Times* exposés of Boss Tweed, newspapers critically examined local governments. Although the nature of the exposés varied across time, the content often remained similar. Editors generally favored electing better men to office. The "better men" usually came from whichever political party the editor preferred.

As cities multiplied and populations doubled, then doubled again, new problems of sanitation, lighting, and transportation emerged, and editors focused more exclusively on municipal issues as separate from national and state political issues. Historian David Paul Nord, in a study of Chicago and St. Louis newspapers in the 1890s, suggested that reform groups and newspaper editors in Chicago positively affected the development of city services through a broad-based coalition free of party exclusivity. "Reformers learned to use mass communication, largely through newspapers," Nord wrote, "in part because they lacked the elaborate interpersonal communication networks of the political machine." Newspapers, therefore, played "information" and "agenda-setting" roles, rather than persuasive roles. The new politics, Nord wrote,

Figure 9–2   This 1885 lithograph by T. Sinclair and Son depicted representative journals of the United States. (Division of Prints and Photographs, Library of Congress Collection)

was issue-oriented rather than party-oriented; newspapers transcended class and social boundaries to join with consumers, citizens, and taxpayers to achieve specific purposes:

> In this new politics, the newspaper's job was to provide the public with a vision of what the unified, organic city could be. Reform issues, schemes, plans, and proposals were kept always bubbling on the back burners of the public agenda through constant repetition in the newspapers.[31]

Although Chicago's newspapers varied in style and political loyalty, they successfully allied themselves with a broad-based citizens' group, the Chicago Civic Federation, to champion municipal ownership. In St. Louis, also a city of varied newspapers, politics continued to get in the way. Only the *Post-Dispatch*, Pulitzer's paper in St. Louis, supported the fight against privately owned utilities, and even it was not consistent. The other newspapers in St. Louis were mere "house organs" for the street railway companies. Yet, it was not a communication question alone. The failure in St. Louis also was related to the absence of a broad-based coalition that transcended politics and worked with the newspapers to keep municipal issues on the public agenda. Nord's book, *Newspapers and New Politics*, directed historians to look beyond the persuasive influence of prominent newspapers and their editors and to analyze the informational role of newspapers and the cultural-political milieu in which they operated.

Varying degrees of reform were achieved in different cities, and in some areas it was not until the muckraking magazines of the early twentieth century sent reporters to a town that newspapers and officials paid attention to problems. Even then, reform often was slow to arrive and even slower to succeed. In Minneapolis after the turn of the century, Richard Kielbowicz suggested that although the newspapers' and magazines' exposures regarding corrupt but popular officials succeeded eventually in removing certain officials from office, their reports did little to effect changes in laws governing prostitution, gambling, and police operations.[32]

New York Times

Adolph Ochs rescued the *New York Times* from bankruptcy and circulation decline in 1896 when he bought the paper for $75,000. Ochs, who had worked as a typesetter and had successfully edited the *Chattanooga Times*, quickly installed new typographic equipment, bought new typewriters, and added telephones to the office. He reduced the price of the paper, but he never attempted to gain the huge circulation figures of Hearst and Pulitzer. His credo was: "To Give the News Impartially, Without Fear or Favor." Objectivity and accuracy were his bywords, and he sought to turn out a newspaper that was factual and trustworthy. Although Ochs deplored photographs on page one and allowed them only on the occasion of great news events, such as Charles Lindbergh's flight to Paris in 1927 or Franklin Delano Roosevelt's presidential victory in 1932, he introduced an illustrated Sunday supplement featuring the good life in New York. He rejected sensationalism in content and style, and he even refused to allow comic strips within the *Times*.[33]

Ochs hired Carr Van Anda, who became managing editor of the *New York Times* from 1904 until 1925. Van Anda complemented Ochs' style with his interest in scientific achievement and the pursuance of verifiable facts. Van Anda had gained experience on the *Cleveland Herald* and the *Baltimore Sun* and had moved in 1888 to the *New York Sun* as desk man and reporter. After five years as a reporter, Van Anda had become Dana's night editor, and then in 1904 he moved to the *Times*. There he worked twelve hours a day, seven days a week. He retired in 1932 at the age of sixty-seven and died of a heart attack in 1945 when he was eighty years old.

Van Anda set high standards for news reporting and emphasized proper usage, placing a high value on the role of the copy editor. He strove for completeness, accuracy, and objectivity. His motto was that all news is fit to print if handled properly. Van Anda also introduced to America the rotogravure section of the Sunday supplement. He also founded the *New York Times* Index, ensuring that the *Times* would be a newspaper of record.

Kansas City Star

Rather than look for a newspaper to edit, William Rockhill Nelson searched for a city in which to start a newspaper. He was a man willing to take a risk, having earned $200,000 as a road contractor in Indiana by the time he was twenty-five and having lost it all in a business venture with a friend. Nelson and Samuel E. Morss first bought a Fort Wayne, Indiana, newspaper, the *Sentinel*, in 1879 and edited it as an independent Democratic newspaper. Deciding that Fort Wayne lacked the wide scope they needed for their publication, they chose to move to Kansas City, a sprawling and ugly town in 1880. Muddy streets, wooden sidewalks, mule-drawn streetcars, and political corruption characterized the city.

The *Kansas City Star*, an afternoon paper, appeared in September 1880. The four-page paper had narrow columns and sold for two cents—three cents less than its local competitors. Eugene Fields, editor of the competitor *Times*, called the new paper the "Twilight Twinkler."[34] Building a subscription list was no problem for Nelson, but it was difficult to acquire enough advertising to support the increased costs of an expanding subscriber base. Nelson eventually had to borrow money to keep the paper afloat and to install a new perfecting press. During the first year, Morss retired and Nelson became sole owner of the newspaper.

Nelson, like Dana, wrote little for the newspaper, relying on and trusting his reportorial staff. In 1882, he was able to acquire a small evening paper with an Associated Press franchise, which strengthened the *Star*'s news sections. In 1901, he bought the *Times* and published it as a separate morning edition. Nelson's *Star* campaigned against monopoly in the street-railway system, crusaded against city corruption and election fraud, and campaigned for beautification of Kansas City's parks and boulevards. Nelson educated residents about the importance of parks and fought for increased taxes to support such improvements. He fought saloons, offered a reward for the capture of Jesse James, and built model rental homes to demonstrate the possibilities for moderately priced quality construction.[35]

"Anybody can print the news," he declared, "but the *Star* tries to build things up. That is what a newspaper is for."[36] Nelson avoided the sensational devices of the 1890s, and during his lifetime the *Star* never carried colored comics, half-tone illustrations, or large headlines.

Nelson, originally a Democrat, ran an independent newspaper and supported Theodore Roosevelt in 1900, turning to the Progressive party in 1912. In 1914, Nelson began to cope with severe health problems. He died in 1915 from uremic poisoning and stipulated that his fortune be used to establish what is now known as the Nelson Art Gallery.

Information in the Local Press

Municipal reform was not an issue for cities alone, but for smaller incorporated towns as well. William Allen White, editor of the *Emporia Gazette*, advocated governmental control of public utilities as early as 1897 and cautioned Emporia citizens to seek a maximum-rate clause in an ordinance to protect the people from excessive public-utility prices. He also was interested in protecting local business, and he wanted to ensure that the Kansas and Missouri Telephone Company (an out-of-town company)

Figure 9–3 William Allen White edited the *Emporia* (Kansas) *Gazette* from 1895 until he died in the mid-1940s. (State Historical Society of Wisconsin)

would not be granted any favors that a home company would not enjoy. He considered Emporia's municipal ownership of the waterworks to be a successful experiment, which he attributed to the high average intelligence of a community that kept party politics out of this branch of municipal affairs. Nevertheless, White thought that most of the time Republicans were more enlightened than Democrats, and to him the term *businessmen* was usually synonymous with Abe Lincoln's party.

As far as White was concerned, Republicans simply were better businessmen and better social leaders than were Democrats, who to him represented the party that had attempted to destroy the Union and that "bossed" the eastern cities. Surprisingly, many themes that appeared in White's newspaper were similar to those that appeared in the city sheets.[37]

▼

White Praises Republican Businessmen

It was a Republican administration that conceived and executed the idea of brightening the home of the farmer, educating his children, increasing the value of his land, compelling the improvement of the roads and bringing him news of the markets and of the weather, so as to secure him a better price for his crops by delivering his daily mail to him on his farm.

—William Allen White, *Emporia Gazette*, October 24, 1900

Sensation in the Urban Press

Joseph Pulitzer and the *New York World*: Urban Vision

Joseph Pulitzer, born in 1847, earned his way in the world of newspapers by refining sensational techniques, hiring a qualified staff, and achieving one of the all-time largest circulations in New York City. His establishment of the Pulitzer Prize and his endowment of the School of Journalism at Columbia University further secured his reputation. He clamored for fair distribution of wealth and appealed to popular tastes. The keys to his success were his use of technology and his decision to promote the cause of the working class, which needed city services that were likely to be provided only as the result of the public's developing a collective sense of community.[38]

Pulitzer was born in Hungary, the son of a Magyar Jew and a German Catholic. He left home when he was seventeen and after being rejected by the Austrian, French, and British armies, he arrived in the United States in 1864, where he served for seven months in the Union Army. Because he could not find work in New York and spoke very little English, he moved west to St. Louis to seek employment.

From 1865 to 1868, Pulitzer worked at a variety of jobs, finally securing a position on the *Westliche Post*, a German-language St. Louis paper published by Carl Schurz. He started reading law, learned English, and eventually became a U.S. citizen. He was elected to the Missouri legislature, but after shooting a lobbyist who opposed Pulitzer's attempts to reform the awarding of county contracts, his political career ended. Following Schurz's lead into the reform Republican movement, Pulitzer campaigned vigorously for Horace Greeley in 1872, the same year he bought a controlling interest in the *Westliche Post* from Schurz and his partner. He soon relinquished his interest in the *Post* and bought the *Staats-Zeitung*, a bankrupt paper that had an AP franchise. By selling the AP franchise to the *St. Louis Globe* and the machinery from the *Zeitung* to another group, Pulitzer made enough money to retire.

In 1878, Pulitzer purchased the bankrupt *Evening Dispatch* and merged it with the *Post*, published by John Dillon. The newspaper was an immediate financial success, netting $45,000 in 1881. The publisher moved away from the reform Republican camp, dismayed by its inability to create a strong platform, and joined the Democratic party. His aim was to publish the leading Democratic paper in the state, with an emphasis on reform and the middle class. Although Pulitzer left St. Louis in 1883 for New York, he retained ownership of the *Post-Dispatch*.

Figure 9–4 This cartoon, depicting Pulitzer as a leader of Liberal Republicanism, appeared in the *St. Louis Puck* on March 30, 1872. (Division of Prints and Photographs, Library of Congress Collection)

MR. PULITZER AS A LEADER OF LIBERAL REPUBLICANISM.
(Cartoon by Joseph Keppler in the St. Louis *Puck*, March 30, 1872.)

In New York, Pulitzer purchased the foundering *New York World* from Jay Gould for $346,000, a figure considered too high for the 15,000-circulation paper. In 1861, the *World* had absorbed the old *New York Courier and Enquirer*, but despite its longevity it had never made money. In 1883, however, New York's only Democratic voice was that of Charles Dana, and Pulitzer planned to broaden his newspaper's base in order "to talk to a nation, not a select committee."

On May 17, 1883, Pulitzer announced to New York his plan to tax the rich. He printed an editorial platform, which he recommended to politicians "in place of long-winded resolutions."[39] The ten-point platform—very similar, in fact, to the Democratic political platform—attacked corruption and the accumulation of wealth.

Part of Pulitzer's success could be credited to his commitment to hiring good reporters and building a strong staff, although his record for paying reporters well is somewhat in doubt. In 1884, the *World* paid reporters $7.50 a column for space and fifty cents an hour for time, less than that paid by the *Herald*.[40] Pulitzer also apparently would pit two staffers against each other and encourage them to compete for the same position, a practice that fostered distrust and animosity.

▼

Pulitzer's Platform

1. Tax luxuries.
2. Tax inheritances.
3. Tax large incomes.
4. Tax monopolies.
5. Tax the privileged corporations.
6. A tariff for revenue.
7. Reform the civil service.
8. Punish corrupt officers.
9. Punish vote buying.
10. Punish employers who coerce their employees in elections.

Nevertheless, Pulitzer was able to entice an able staff. One popular reporter was Elizabeth Cochrane (Nellie Bly), who as a writer for the *Pittsburgh Dispatch*, wrote so convincingly of Mexican government corruption that Mexican leaders evicted her from the country. After her return, she published *Six Months in Mexico*, then began working for Pulitzer's *World*. Her undercover approach made her famous; in her first venture she masqueraded as an insane woman in order to gain admittance to Blackwell's Island, which resulted in an investigation into the system for caring for New York's mentally ill. She also posed as a woman prisoner to reveal the injustices done to women in prison, she pretended to be a patent medicine manufacturer's wife to expose a bribing lobbyist, and she even danced in a corps de ballet.

Her trip around the world was designed to see if she, while using new forms of commercial transportation, could beat the fictitious Phileas Fogg in Jules Verne's classic *Around the World in 80 Days*; and through it she achieved her highest level of notoriety. She made the trip in seventy-two days, six hours, and eleven minutes. Pulitzer gave her front-page space where she entertained readers with exotic and exciting tales. Her career was cut short by her marriage to a seventy-two-year-old businessman in 1895. After his death, she worked for a time on the *New York Journal* but never regained her popularity. She died of pneumonia at age fifty-six.

▼

In La Belle France

We landed at Bologne. Here, I think, my baggage was examined, but I did not see it done as one of the men in the boat with me took charge of it and also found us places in the train bound for Amiens. In the mean time we went into the restaurant on the edge of the pier and had something to eat. I found the waiters able to speak English and willing enough to take American money. The trip to Amiens was slow and tiresome, but I was fully repaid for the journey by meeting M. Jules Verne and his wife, who were waiting for me at the station in company with *THE WORLD*'s Paris correspondent.

—Nellie Bly, *New York World*, January 26, 1890, reporting her trip around the world

Figure 9–5 Richard Outcault created this "Hogan's Alley" cartoon for Pulitzer's *World* in 1896, before moving to Hearst's newspaper. The cartoon is titled, "Moving Day in Hogan's Alley." (Division of Prints and Photographs, Library of Congress Collection)

Other respected reporters who worked for the *World* included Arthur Brisbane, Frank Irving Cobb, Herbert Bayard Swope, Walter Lippmann, Heywood Broun, and David Graham Phillips. William Randolph Hearst, by promising higher salaries, hired many of these *World* reporters to staff his competing *New York Journal*.

Pulitzer used many of the techniques instituted by Bennett and Day, but he added his own flair. He created "ears" on both sides of the flag, on which he promoted the newspaper and printed tiny news clips; he introduced column-spanning headlines; and he developed a worldwide news service. Pulitzer also introduced the widespread use of photographs, beginning with a four-column cut of the Brooklyn Bridge in May 1883. He used diagrams, drawings, and cartoons. He emphasized the coverage of sports for the working man and stressed women's news, walking a fine line between ignoring and endorsing feminism. The *World*, recognizing the importance of women as buyers, included articles on social etiquette, home decoration, and child care.

Pulitzer also focused more on the working classes than he had in St. Louis and championed crusades for reform aimed at immigrants, the poor, and the working class. By the end of the first year, the *World* had a circulation of 60,000; in 1887, circulation reached 200,000 to become the largest in the United States. Pulitzer was printing twelve to fourteen pages daily and thirty-six to forty-four pages on Sunday. The Sunday edition was a laboratory, used to test new ideas and techniques. In 1887, he added an evening edition, and in 1889, he built the World Building to house his newspaper enterprise.

Pulitzer developed sensationalistic techniques before William Randolph Hearst arrived in New York in 1895. In May 1883, when eleven people were trampled to

Figure 9–6   Front page of the *New York World*, February 17, 1898. (Division of Prints and Photographs, Library of Congress Collection)

death as panic broke out on a pedestrian causeway while a Memorial Day crowd picnicked near the newly constructed Brooklyn Bridge, the *World*'s headline read, "BAPTIZED IN BLOOD."[41] In March 1884, while the *Times*' most sensational frontpage lead headline was, "A PAYMASTER'S OFFICE ROBBED," the *World*'s headlines included dramatic promises of tales such as "AN ENTIRE FAMILY ANNIHILATED BY ITS MURDEROUS HEAD," "DIED A DESPERADO'S DEATH," and "A BRUTAL NEGRO WHIPS HIS NEPHEW TO DEATH IN SOUTH CAROLINA."[42]

However, although Pulitzer was in the business of selling news, he was not without principle. To his secretary he said,

> It is not enough to refrain from publishing fake news, it is not enough to take ordinary care . . . you have got to make everyone connected with the paper . . . believe that accuracy is to a newspaper what virtue is to a woman.[43]

When accused of pandering to public taste to sell newspapers, Pulitzer's reply in the *World* was, "Of course newspapers are made to sell, and in that respect they resemble the highest work of art and intellect as well as the sermons preached in pulpits."[44]

Pulitzer attacked the intellectual elite as well as those who violated the law in order to achieve wealth; he demanded justice and attacked ostentatious displays of wealth, noting that it was "false Americanism" to create an aristocracy.[45] Pulitzer revealed his prejudices about women's education as well as his disdain for intellectual snobbery when he commented on Vassar College's commencement in 1884: "There is something appalling in the amount of transcendental erudition which Vassar College poured out at its Commencement."[46] Pulitzer said the country needed sensible wives and mothers, not philosophers. Pulitzer crusaded against religious bigotry, opposed prohibition as destructive to personal liberty, urged the poor to educate their children rather than sending them to work, and supported labor in its struggles against the corporations. Nevertheless, when unions tried to organize businesses such as his own, he had difficulty understanding the purpose of unionism.

Pulitzer saw his wealth increase, served four months in Congress, and continuously sought the social acceptance denied to him because of his Jewish heritage, his poverty-stricken background, his lack of social graces, and his attacks on the wealthy in the pages of the *World*. In 1890, with his vision failing, he retired from active leadership of the *World*, but he continued to exert absolute control over the paper through constant communication with its editors.

Pulitzer's major challenge came in 1895 with the arrival in New York of William Randolph Hearst, who purchased the *New York Journal*. Hearst raided Pulitzer's office for staff members and imitated many of Pulitzer's inventions. Although Pulitzer had often opposed imperialism in the past, during the Spanish-American War both the *Journal* and the *World* distorted news from Cuba, competing to top each other's circulation figures. In 1898, Pulitzer, disgusted with the sensationalistic treatment being given the war, gave orders to his staff to clean up its act—the time of immoderacy was over. Pulitzer died in October 1911 aboard his yacht, but the *World* continued to publish until 1931, when it was sold to the Scripps-Howard chain. Pulitzer's long-time rival, William Randolph Hearst, wrote an obituary honoring the prominent editor. It began:

> A towering figure in National and international journalism has passed away; a mighty democratic force in the life of the Nation and in the activity of the world has ceased; a great power uniformly exerted in behalf of popular rights and human progress is ended. Joseph Pulitzer is dead.[47]

William Randolph Hearst and the *New York Journal*: A National Platform

William Randolph Hearst, an admirer of Joseph Pulitzer and Pulitzer's main competition during the 1890s and early 1900s, was born into a world vastly different from that of Joseph Pulitzer. He was the son of a wealthy investor and U.S. senator, and had he not flaunted arrogance in the face of his mentors, he would have been a privileged graduate of Harvard University. Hearst was a man of contradiction. Accused of being emotionally childlike and demanding, at times seemingly given to principle while at other times motivated by mere profit or power, he amassed one of the greatest fortunes in the first half of the twentieth century. Although many despised his sensationalism, his promotion of war before and during the Cuban conflict, and his turn to conservative anticommunism in the post-Depression years, he was a man to be reckoned with. When Hearst died, he left a publishing empire with assets of $160 million. His organization published eighteen newspapers in twelve cities, the Sunday newspaper magazine *The American Weekly*, and nine magazines. In addition, his organization owned King Features Service, International News Service, and International News Photos. Hearst owned seven castles and one of the largest private art collections in the United States.

Hearst was born on April 29, 1863. He was the son of an ambitious father and a protective mother, and his painful shyness contrasted with his flamboyance and flair for the dramatic. He entered Harvard in 1882, but he was suspended after a variety of pranks on professors, including one in which he sent to Harvard faculty chamber pots that had the faculty's pictures displayed on the bottoms. While at Harvard, Hearst became business manager of the financially failing *Lampoon* and soon turned it into a profit-making enterprise. Fascinated by newspapers, he secured a letter of introduction to *Boston Globe* publisher Charles H. Taylor and spent many hours in the *Globe* offices. After leaving Harvard, he worked for Pulitzer at the *World* and then returned to the West to edit the *Examiner*, a financially failing newspaper his father used to support his Senate campaign.

Hearst's father, who regarded journalism as less than a wholesome occupation, reluctantly agreed to let his son take over the San Francisco paper. Hearst launched several crusades, hired good and high-priced talent, and began a campaign against the Southern Pacific railroad, whose officials had dominated California politics for many years. Although the *Examiner*'s circulation increased dramatically under Hearst's aggressive news strategy, the paper lost money—$300,000 during the first few years of Hearst's leadership. However, by 1895, the *Examiner* was making money indeed, and Hearst looked for greater challenges.

Figure 9–7 William Randolph Hearst's residence, "Beacon Towers," at Sands Point, Long Island. (Division of Prints and Photographs, Library of Congress Collection)

In 1895, Hearst continued his experiment in New York by purchasing the *Journal*, a newspaper founded in 1882 by Joseph Pulitzer's brother Albert. The paper had struggled through the years as an unprofitable and somewhat scandalous sheet. Within a year, only the *World* remained as a top competitor for Hearst in the New York market, because the circulation of his papers had bypassed those of the other papers. Hearst raided Pulitzer's staff, introduced color printing, and hired Pulitzer's comic-strip producer, Richard Outcault, creator of the Yellow Kid comic strip. Hearst aimed for sensationalism of the highest order and ultimately demanded that the United States engage in a war with Cuba.

In 1900, Hearst began to expand his newspaper chain and to pursue his political ambitions. Although his primary desire was to be President of the United States, he never achieved significant political success in the role of an officeholder. He ran twice for Congress, twice for New York City mayor, and once for the New York governorship. In 1900, he became president of the National Association of Democratic Clubs and was elected to Congress in 1902 and 1904; in 1904, he placed second in balloting for the Democratic nomination for President.

Hearst's unrelenting criticism of President McKinley contributed to his lack of success in politics. The assassination of the President in 1901 followed a series of Hearst attacks and an article by Hearst writer Ambrose Bierce after the assassination of a Kentucky governor: "The bullet that pierced Goebel's breast/Can not be found in all the West;/Good reason, it is speeding here/To stretch McKinley on his bier." After claims that McKinley's assassin Leon F. Czolgosz carried a copy of the *Journal* at the time of the assassination, many subscribers boycotted the Hearst newspapers and Hearst was hanged in effigy.

Hearst still was able to achieve some political success with his election to Congress, but his political career ended in defeat in 1909. Not content to stay out of the fray, however, Hearst plunged into ardent criticism of U.S. support of Britain in 1914 as European powers declared war. Hearst's fear of Japanese domination of the Pacific and of Mexican collaboration with the "yellow peril" resulted in a film made by his International Film Service in 1915 that earned him a pro-German label. The film's bitter attack on the British and the Japanese sparked a Senate Judiciary Committee investigation of Hearst's activities and a Canadian boycott of Hearst's International News Service.

Hearst's empire continued to expand, with more than 38,000 people on the payroll and a $90 million annual operation. Hearst paid top writers well—Arthur Brisbane earned $250,000 a year. However, Hearst publications often were supported by his other enterprises in mining and real estate. The depression strangled the operation, and for several years Hearst feared the possibility of bankruptcy. He turned increasingly conservative and strongly opposed the American Newspaper Guild in the 1930s, became loudly anticommunist, and strongly opposed war with Germany until the bombing of Pearl Harbor in December 1941.

Hearst developed serious heart problems in the postwar years and died August 14, 1951, in Beverly Hills.

Covering the Spanish-American War   The Spanish-American War of 1898 represented the culmination of at least three decades marked by Cuban struggles for independence and U.S. eagerness to acquire additional land and increased power. From 1868 to 1878, the Cubans fought the Spanish and gained some concessions—the abolition of slavery, for example. However, they did not achieve their ultimate goal, independence from Spain. The United States meanwhile maintained a heavy investment in the Cuban economy through the import of sugar. Until 1894, Cuban sugar entered the United States free of duty, but the Wilson-Gorman tariff of 1894, which placed duties on Cuban sugar, disrupted the small country's economy and perhaps contributed to the Cuban agitation for independence.

As a second insurgent uprising began in the 1890s, the Spanish put Commander Valeriano Weyler in charge of the island. Weyler instituted a policy of reconcentration, separating Cubans in camps from the insurgents in the hills. Disease took its toll in the camps, and more than one-fourth of the population died. During the mid-1890s, American investments of $50 million were jeopardized by the conflict, and the $76 million worth of Cuban imports in 1894 declined to $15 million in 1898. While Spain attempted reform in Cuba, Spanish loyalists on the island rioted against the proposed reforms, and the United States sent its battleship *Maine* to the Havana harbor. On February 16, 1898, the battleship exploded. Although recent evidence indicates that the explosion may have resulted from an internal mechanical problem, Americans, including William Randolph Hearst, were quick to blame the Spaniards for the explosion of the ship.

The U.S. government demanded that Spain end its reconcentration policy and declare an armistice. Although Spain agreed to these concessions, Congress declared Cuba independent on April 19, 1898, and authorized the President to use military force to evict the Spanish from the island. Unwilling to relinquish its hold on Cuba, Spain declared war on April 24 against the United States, three days after McKinley blockaded the island. During the short conflict, 5,400 Americans died in Cuba. Only 379 of those deaths resulted from combat; more than 5,000 military personnel died of malaria and yellow fever.

At least a sizeable minority in the United States believed that going to war over Cuba was determined more by extensive sugar investments on the island than a desire to free Cuban citizens. Indeed, despite a good deal of agitation by yellow journalists such as Hearst and Pulitzer, the war resolution passed the Senate by a vote of only forty-two to thirty-five. The sentiment of the Senate was echoed in much of the local press, who eschewed the warmongering of Hearst and Pulitzer.[48] When the Spanish signed the Treaty of Paris in 1898, they granted Cuba its independence; ceded the Philippines, Guam, and Puerto Rico to the United States; and received $20 million for relinquishing the territory. In 1898 and 1899, the United States continued to acquire new land, annexing Wake Island, Hawaii, and Samoa.

Editors were mixed in their approaches to imperialistic motives, and in the early days of the conflict, the *Herald*, the *Post*, the *Tribune*, the *Times*, and even the *World* attempted to analyze the complexities of the Cuban political situation. Pulitzer's first correspondent, William Shaw Bowen, traveled throughout Cuba into insurgent camps and across Spanish lines without restriction because the Spanish respected his fair treatment. Such an approach, however, could not compete with Hearst's jazzy treatment of murderers/victims. One of Pulitzer's biographers, W. A. Swanberg, wrote:

> The majority of the public found it more exciting to read about the murder of Cuban babies and the rape of Cuban women by the Spaniards than to read conscientious accounts of complicated political problems and injustices on both sides.[49]

Some correspondents, such as George Rea of the *New York Herald*, doubted the stories of Cuban oppression. Rea, who had lived in Cuba for five years by the time of the second insurgency, was reluctant to fault the Spanish entirely. Rea accused the insurgent general, Maximo Gomez, of using reporters to perpetrate insurgent lies.[50]

U.S. coverage in favor of insurgency escalated, however, and by 1896 the Spaniards were so incensed by American coverage of the insurgents that they restricted press movement and kept reporters away from the front. In 1896, both Pulitzer and Hearst escalated their calls for war, a tactic followed by immediate increases in circulation. By 1897, Pulitzer's New York circulation was 800,000, and Hearst was close behind with 700,000. Pulitzer's correspondent James Creelman, who later was employed by Hearst, urged President McKinley to act:

> No man's life, no man's property is safe. American citizens are imprisoned or slain without cause. American property is destroyed on all sides. . . . Blood on the roadsides, blood in the fields, blood on the doorsteps, blood, blood, blood! . . . A new Armenia lies within 80 miles of the American coast. Not a word from Washington! Not a sign from the president![51]

The Spanish, irate at Creelman's lack of restraint, evicted him from the island.

In December of that year, Hearst sent a highly celebrated writer, Richard Harding Davis, and the artist Frederic Remington to Cuba. Each was paid about $3,000 a month, a salary that far exceeded the usual $40 a week that Cuban correspondents received.[52] Remington, legend has it, wired Hearst soon after his arrival:

> Everything is quiet. There is no trouble here. There will be no war. I wish to return.
>
> —Remington

Hearst replied:

> Please remain. You furnish the pictures and I'll furnish the war. —W. R. Hearst[53]

Despite Hearst's claims that Davis had penetrated enemy lines, he had in fact seen no action. He wrote to his mother in mid-January that he had not "heard a shot fired or seen an insurgent. . . . I am just 'not in it' and I am torn between coming home and making your dear heart stop worrying and getting one story to justify me being here and that damn silly page of the Journal's. . . . All Hearst wants is my name and I will give him that only if it will be signed to a different sort of story from those they have been printing."[54]

In February 1897, Hearst further angered the Spanish and tried to enlist the American public in his campaign for war with an account of three Cuban women who were searched aboard an American ship off the coast of Cuba. Davis' story that Spanish officers rushed aboard an American vessel, searching for illegal documents, was accompanied by a Remington drawing of Spanish male officers and a naked Cuban woman. Once the ship reached the United States, Pulitzer's *World* reporters interviewed the women, who said they had been searched privately in a cabin by matrons—not by male Spanish officers on the deck of the ship. Davis protested Hearst's treatment of his story, claiming that Remington had not been present and was responsible for the distortion. An irate Congress withdrew resolutions it had introduced to investigate the situation, and the *Journal* was publicly exposed as "fictionalizing" the facts.

Hearst's greatest endeavor to create news as well as report it came with the tale of Evangelina Cisneros, the beautiful Cuban "Joan of Arc," a woman who voluntarily accompanied her imprisoned father in his exile by the Spanish to the Isle of Pines. Although Cisneros claimed that the island governor, Colonel Jose Berrez, had attempted to rape her and that she had been jailed for defending her virtue, some evidence indicates that she had been involved in an insurrection on the island and had framed the Spanish colonel.

The *Journal* wrote a heartrending account of the young woman's brutal treatment by the Spaniards, and she appealed to American women to sign petitions urging the Queen Regent of Spain and the pope to free her from the barbarous hands of the soldiers. When some newspapers, such as the *Commercial Advertiser*, tried to print a more factual account of the case, the public paid little attention. Meanwhile, Hearst sent reporter Karl Decker to free the maiden; he succeeded, dressed the maiden in a sailor's uniform, and escorted her from the island.[55] Once she arrived in New York, Hearst dressed her in the latest fashions and presented her to society and to the President of the United States.

After the explosion of the Maine, Hearst pressed even harder for war, personally funding a junket to Cuba for senators and congressmen, including members of the House foreign affairs and naval affairs committees.[56]

From February to August of 1898, the months of U.S. involvement in the war, Hearst spent seventeen days in Cuba as a foreign correspondent, directing the activities of a staff of twenty. The war had boosted circulation, but by the end of the conflict the *Journal* was still losing money.

Life of a Correspondent   The life of a correspondent, with the exception of a few stars like Richard Harding Davis, was difficult. Few reporters were paid well enough to acquire the needed supplies of a horse, saddlebags, blankets, and adequate food and shelter. The guerrilla-style warfare made it difficult for reporters to talk to insurgents and left them dependent on the guerrillas for food and protection. It was difficult to get information outside official Spanish channels, and many reporters knew they had failed to get accurate information from either side.

After the United States entered the war, reporters relied primarily on cable operators and military officers for information. Cable offices in New York and Key West were manned by censors, and reporters spent some time trying to evade the censors' cuts. Reporters also disliked General William J. Shafter, who led the Fifth Army Corps, the U.S. invading army. Not only did he weigh more than 300 pounds and have a strong body odor that sometimes afflicted people in the sweltering tropics, he also disclosed information reluctantly. Generally, reporters more positively reported the activities of General Wood's Rough Riders, although photographer Jimmy Hare and Davis both said that the Rough Riders' egos occasionally got out of line.[57]

From inland, the only way to obtain information was on horseback or on foot, and in order to get information back to civilization a reporter either had to endure the arduous journey from jungle to shore or hire a courier—whose dependability was suspect at best. Because cable lines between Cuba and the U.S. mainland had been cut at the beginning of U.S. involvement, newspapers chartered dispatch boats to carry correspondents to Key West to dispatch information. The dispatch boats were essential for speedy news delivery, but they cost $5,000 to $9,000 a month. Cable costs also taxed the budgets of newspapers, varying from fifty to eighty cents a word. Melville Stone once claimed that cable costs for one story exceeded $8,000.[58] Newspaper editors urged brevity. In retrospect, news coverage of the Cuban conflict represented dramatic new attempts to obtain information during wartime yet echoed old Civil War dilemmas regarding issues of national security versus the need for information in times of war. Correspondents struggled with the physical aspects of war reporting—coping with the tropical heat, traveling through enemy lines, and living on inadequate rations. In addition, their relationship with editors on the mainland—sometimes involving demands to color the news—often placed reporters at odds with the Spanish as well as with other reporters.

Business Promotes Itself

Although the modern public relations agency is a twentieth-century phenomenon—and indeed Edward Bernays did not coin the phrase "public relations" until the 1920s—public relations, if defined as the "management of communication between an organization and its publics," is a concept that can be dated to ancient times.[59] The rise of the printing press made possible the formation of various publics because this development permitted relatively easy access to shared information, as well as created the possibility for producing information in the name of a public.

Promotional techniques and press agentry common to modern forms of public relations counseling developed in the nineteenth century, although later concerns about ethics reshaped the style with which such techniques were used and certainly far more sophisticated forms of managing public opinion were subsequently developed. Some public relations historians have traced the historical roots of public movements in the United States to Sam Adams, the vociferous patriot who used pamphlets to persuade groups of people to his cause. Adams, they have said, created an activist organization, used a variety of media, employed symbols and slogans, created pseudo-events (the Boston Tea Party), orchestrated conflict, and recognized the need for a sustained saturation campaign.[60] Various volunteer associations, such as the American Bible Society, the abolitionists, and the suffrage organizations used public relations techniques. For example, the use of iconography by antislavery women's groups demonstrated the employment of a public relations technique.

Press agentry, as compared to techniques used by movement groups, has been regarded in a less favorable light, with some critics implying "hoodwinkery" and occasionally other dubious tactics. Press agents have been credited with the creation of characters as diverse as western hero Buffalo Bill Cody and Jenny Lind, the "Swedish nightingale." Foremost among the press agents was Richard F. Hamilton,

Figure 9–8 The typewriter revolutionized newsrooms. This advertisement appealed especially to librarians, who could use the typewriter to create card indices. (Division of Prints and Photographs, Library of Congress Collection)

press agent to Phineas T. Barnum, famous director of the Barnum and Bailey Circus. Even before the formation of the circus in the 1870s, Barnum successfully promoted a variety of scams, such as the story of Joice Heth, whom Barnum claimed had taken care of George Washington nearly 100 years earlier. People flocked to see the ancient black woman, but when she died, an autopsy showed her to be only 80 years old, not 160 as Barnum said she was. Meanwhile, Barnum had been collecting as much as $1,500 a week from those who wanted a look at the pipe-smoking old woman.[61]

The use of similar but more sophisticated techniques for improving corporate images was pioneered by large railroad corporations. In 1850, capitalizing on fears of a coming Civil War, the Illinois Central railroad organized a public relations campaign to construct a North–South railway that the company claimed would bind North and South together "so effactually that even the idea of separation" would vanish from the nation's vocabulary. The company's successful campaign to obtain federal funds for railway construction altered a historic pattern of local business funding for railroad building.[62]

In the late 1870s, in an attempt to alter the public's negative image of powerful business conglomerates, railroad executives paid for "puffery" pieces and issued free railroad passes, which, according to Norfolk and Western Vice President Frederick J. Kimball, was the "cheapest form of advertising we can get." As railroad executives confronted the instability of private rate-fixing agreements in the 1880s, they used their previously established relationship with the press to gain discussion of government regulation of the industry and to create a positive public image of the necessity for governmental regulation. Meanwhile, railroad executives were instrumental in guiding the writing of legislation that resulted in the Interstate Commerce Act of 1886, an act that created a commission sympathetic rather than antagonistic to the industry.[63]

Professionalization and Exclusion

Although being an editor or publisher in the latter half of the nineteenth century signified involvement in a definite profession, being a reporter was more of "a way station on the highway to politics, business, literature or editorial work than a profession itself."[64] Despite the increased amount of news resulting from reporter-generated stories, reporters received low wages, often on space rates, were subject to erratic dismissals, and gained little prestige from their work. Correspondents such as Richard Harding Davis and Jack London, who gained significant reputations as war correspondents, were exceptions rather than the rule. Such treatment propelled journalists to move into editorial capacities or to change professions altogether. In addition, the increased commercialization of the daily press presented a conflict for those reporters who considered themselves to be social critics.

Although some reporters received salaries, more were compensated by the space-rate system, which meant that reporters were paid only for the number of column inches printed. In 1873, the *Nation* editorialized that "there is probably no industry of modern times in which the part played by labor is so large, and the share in the profits received by labor so small."[65] Several studies between 1895 and 1900 placed the wages of journalists between $1,200 and $1,800 a year.[66] In 1884, the trade magazine the *Journalist* claimed that New York reporters received from $15 to $20 per week. Outside New York, reporters received less. By 1900, experienced New York reporters received as much as $60 a week. In smaller cities, $17 to $27 weekly was the norm. Reporters' salaries compared more favorably to those of craftsmen such as plumbers or compositors than they did to professionals such as physicians or teachers. These estimates showed, however, that journalists made more money than the average federal employee in an executive department and about the same amount as a captain in the army. Edwin Shuman, writing in 1903, explained: "Newspaper writing, in the essential qualifications required, is a learned profession; but in its exact comparative insecurity it more nearly resembles a trade."[67]

Reporters engaged in various forms of moonlighting by writing advertisements, working as court stenographers, or producing news and features for independent Sunday papers. It also was possible to supplement one's income by dropping names into stories—including the brand names of products—and by assisting politicians. Because editors checked the opposition newspapers to decide whether their own reporters were being accurate, reporters often cooperated among themselves by agreeing on such details as addresses and the spelling of names, even if these details were incorrect. Reporters employed on a space-rate basis also tended to "overwrite," hoping that by producing more inches they would be paid more.[68]

The career patterns of metropolitan editors also changed toward the latter part of the century; in the earlier years, editors normally started work as young apprentices, worked their way up to own a small paper, then expanded the publication or bought a larger one. Social and economic mobility decreased by the 1890s. From 1875 to 1890, the apprenticeship system faded, and college educations and successful fathers more frequently predicted editorial success. By the latter part of the century, editors usually acquired college degrees, began newspaper work as reporters, and did not always own a controlling interest in the paper for which they worked.[69] In this sense, top editors belonged to a group comparable to that of industrial leaders.

Journalism had always been a male-dominated occupation, although women filled important roles—first in the colonial and early national periods as editors and later, in the nineteenth century, as society reporters and "letter" writers. Colonial women who filled an editorial role usually were caretaker editors—nurturers of a family-owned newspaper from the time of a husband's death until the time a son was ready to assume responsibility for its operation. A few others became editors for different reasons, such as Mary Catherine Goddard who edited and printed a newspaper for her slightly wayward brother.

By the nineteenth century, journalism provided women with greater opportunities than most other professions. Editors hired women reporters to write fiction, poetry, character sketches, and essays. The "sob sisters" who worked for the New York papers were masters of the sensational tearjerker. Nevertheless, discriminatory barriers remained, and the old question of the appropriateness of women appearing in public forums continued even after the Civil War. Mary Clemmer Ames, who began writing a "Woman's Letter from Washington" for the *New York Independent* in 1865 and continued the column for the next twenty years, never applied for membership in the congressional press gallery but remained in the ladies' gallery. "Because a woman is a public correspondent it does not make it at all necessary that she as an individual should be conspicuously public—that she should run about with pencils in her mouth and pens in her ears; that she should invade the Reporters' Galleries, crowded with men; that she should go anywhere as a mere reporter where she would not be received as a lady."[70] Others did not worry about such conventions and embraced the broader world that journalism provided. "The newspaper woman soon learns that the world is bigger than a tea-cup, and in her absorbing work she finds no place for the tittle-tattle of the drawing-room or the gossip of the boudoir," wrote Edith Tupper in 1894.[71]

Attempts to professionalize journalism during the last half of the nineteenth century, however, systematically excluded women and African-American reporters and editors from certain privileges and memberships—such as access to press galleries and press clubs—that were designed to advance individuals within the field. In 1879, 20 women were accredited to the House and Senate press galleries, along with 147 men, but by 1880 all women were excluded. The newly adopted rules of the Standing Committee of Correspondents did not specifically prohibit women, but they tied accreditation to the galleries to activities that at the time were not being performed by women—reporting for daily newspapers and sending dispatches by telegraph. Historian Donald Ritchie wrote, "Women writers failed to qualify under these provisions because they worked for weeklies or posted their columns of Washington society news through the mail. Because editors neither believed women could report political news nor considered their pieces worth the price of the telegraph tolls, their hiring procedures guaranteed that the press galleries would remain exclusively male."[72]

Some women reporters were outraged, and Laura Jones asked why men had the right to restrict the press galleries to masculine use. "Male reporters have a gallery and comfortable seats . . . they have writing-rooms, tables, stationery, pages, and the conveniences, and a door-keeper guards these sacred precincts and perquisites." Women reporters had not even "a ghost of any convenience for writing."[73]

Development of Exclusive Press Clubs

The life of a reporter was fraught with low pay and lack of job security. During the late nineteenth century, reporters formed press clubs to fulfill their need to legitimize their role within society. Reporters leaned toward identifying themselves as professionals and sought with other groups to identify themselves by their skills.

The world of daily journalism was largely a male occupation, although women were hired to write copy aimed at other women. Often the women were physically isolated from the male staff, although on occasion women were allowed into the city pressrooms. Almost all the mainstream clubs excluded women. Jennie June Croly formed her own women's club after being denied entrance in 1868 by the New York Press Club to a dinner honoring Charles Dickens.[74]

Declining social mobility coupled with low job security posed a conflict for those reporters who viewed themselves as professionals. Katherine Lanpher described the metropolitan reporter as "a hard-drinking bohemian who was socially dexterous, traversing the lines of social class with ease, moving in the circles of both the raw and the refined," but who "eked out" his existence amid a "clash of image and reality."[75]

Press clubs performed several services. For example, the Press Club of Chicago, organized in 1880, aimed to elevate the profession and integrate journalists into the professional and social elite of the community. The Whitechapel Club, formed in Chicago in 1889, on the other hand, was a setting for radical political discussions and a theater for satirical pranks.

Prominent editors and publishers such as Melville Stone, Victor Lawson, and Samuel and Joseph Medill belonged to the Press Club, but the "bohemian" reporters of the city also belonged. Despite the diversity of individuals in its membership, this rather formal group tailored its activities to be responsive to society as a whole. The Whitechapel Club, on the other hand, preserved its bohemian status, claimed to be "intolerant of pretense," and served as a radical political forum for ideas that did not

Figure 9–9 Although urban printing plants began to look like modern corporations by the turn of the century, the country newspaper remained a significant force in disseminating news. (State Historical Society of Wisconsin)

appear in Chicago newspapers. Reporters were the mainstay of this organization; publishers and editors were not allowed.

Lanpher suggested that the Chicago clubs served two separate functions. The Press Club of Chicago sought to convey the image of the reporter as a dignified and valued member of society who could easily assimilate into the complex of men's clubs, whereas the Whitechapel Club pressed for recognition of the reporter as a social critic. The clubs thus presented an image of the reporter that was both tangible to those outside the field and acceptable to the reporters themselves. Press clubs did not dissolve the constraints of working on a newspaper-turned-commercial-institution, but they offered journalists a chance to bring about a kind of reconciliation between the constraints with which they struggled and the expectations that they nurtured.[76]

Women's clubs fulfilled similar functions as the men's clubs, giving professional women a chance to interact with each other, but they also gave women power as members of a group that they would not have been able to achieve as individual reporters. The Woman's National Press Association, begun in July 1882, continued until after World War I, when it was replaced by the Women's National Press Club. Three of the founding members of the postwar club were militant suffragettes and three were newspaperwomen. The latter three were Cora Rigby, chief of the Washington bureau of the *Christian Science Monitor;* Carolyn Vance Bell, a syndicated feature writer for the Newspaper Enterprise Association; and Elizabeth King (later Stokes), a reporter for the *New York Evening Post.* Lily Lykes Rowe (later Shepard), the club's first president, said the organization was necessary to combat "the conspiracy of men to keep women off the newspapers—or at least to reduce their number, wages, and importance to a minimum."[77] The club admitted only women actively engaged in magazine, newspaper, and publicity work. After surviving the hard times of the depression in the 1930s, the club flourished during World War II as opportunities opened up for women, who often replaced male reporters who had gone to war. Some members, like Ruth Cowan of the Associated Press, were war correspondents. By 1951, the club was competing actively with the all-male National Press Club, as famous political figures appeared at the banquets and lunches of both groups. Primarily because the women's club exerted political pressure on people like Lyndon Johnson and British Prime Minister Harold Wilson, convincing them not to speak at the National Press Club until it admitted women, the men's club in January 1971 voted to admit women.

Critique of the Press

Hazel Dicken Garcia, in a study of the development of journalistic standards in the nineteenth century, divided criticism of journalistic conduct into three distinct periods: first, an age of political experimentation in which government and party systems were emerging; second, an era of reform activity, technological advances, and increased urbanization; and third, a transition in the economic base from agriculture to industry, nationalization, and a preoccupation with scientific discovery and business. The study examined the early period—1800 to 1830—and concluded that criticism of journalistic conduct focused primarily on a political context in conjunction with the press's primary political role. Much of the discussion centered on whether newspapers should carry the points of view of competing parties. From 1830 to 1850, as an information model emerged, despite increased discussion of an independent press, partisanship continued to dominate. Unlike the British, whose values emphasized deference, fear of the printed word, and the concept of an elite press, Americans by mid-century were "over-awed" by the press, began to discuss values that assumed worth in every reader, and saw the press as serving individuals and a larger society. Nevertheless, conflict over such values remained in the United States. Critics denounced editors for "trivializing" the news. Trivialization, critics argued, gave public notice to ordinary people and was harmful to the community and to the public. Such efforts, the critics said, "misled most people . . . into thinking them[selves] important."

From 1850 to 1889, critics began to analyze the relationship of the press with society and increasingly addressed press abuses. After the Civil War, critics attacked the printing of trivial "gossip" and began to suggest that publishing detailed accounts of weddings and other aspects of people's lives was an invasion of privacy. By 1890, critics agreed that news and opinion must be separated, that care "beyond the profit principle must be exercised in news selection," and that material that violated good taste and judgment should be avoided. Critics and journalists alike, however, differed on their definitions of "good taste." Did crime stories, for example, constitute poor taste? Further, although critics viewed the separation of news and business functions as essential, they were too caught up in the corporate development of the time period to elaborate a great deal on this issue. Nevertheless, they described journalism as difficult, requiring intellectual and moral ability. Their discussions paved the way for journalism education, ethics codes, and other methods of monitoring journalistic conduct.[78]

Conclusion

The last two decades of the nineteenth century represented enormous growth and consolidation in the publishing industries as captains of industry sought to build conglomerates and mass-market their wares. Within this modernizing society, mass magazines appealed to broad audiences of consumers and financed their expanded circulations and technological innovations with advertising that sought to familiarize the public with national brands for consumer goods.

The metropolitan press predated national muckraking magazines that appeared at the end of the nineteenth century and flourished in the early twentieth century, which attacked the corruption that accompanied widespread business expansion and the flirtation between business and politics. The newspapers created new visions of urban communities, dealing with issues of private property, government structures, and municipal services. Although some editors sought to provide information, others introduced a new form of urban sensationalism to capture city readers and create national platforms.

Business began to seek ways to promote itself, first through individual techniques such as those used by P. T. Barnum to create attention for his profitable circus operation, and later by systematic programs to improve the image of business in the eyes of the public.

As journalism began to take on the trappings of professionalism, discrimination against women and African-American editors became institutionalized. Women and African Americans were systematically excluded from House and Senate press galleries and from the rapidly developing press clubs that sought to legitimize journalism in the eyes of the public, as they simultaneously provided social camaraderie for journalists. Journalistic criticism began to focus on issues such as the separation of news and editorial opinion, thus paving the way for journalism education, ethics codes, and other characteristics of professionalization.

Endnotes

1. For an analysis of the cultural transformation of the United States and its relationship to modernization, see Richard D. Brown, *Modernization: The Transformation of American Life, 1600–1865* (New York: Hill & Wang, 1976). Brown argues that modernization is a process that began in the United States at the moment of colonial settlement and continues today. See also Alan Trachtenberg, *The Incorporation of America: Culture and Society in the Gilded Age* (New York: Hill & Wang, 1982).

2. See Naomi Lamoreaux, *The Great Merger Movement in American Business, 1895–1904* (New York: Cambridge University Press, 1985), for a description of the merger movement as a means of business survival. For other interpretations, see Allen F. Davis and Harold D. Woodman, *Conflict or Consensus in Modern American History* (Washington, D.C.: D. C. Heath, 1968) and Samuel P. Hays, *The Response to Industrialism* (Chicago: University of Chicago Press, 1957).

3. See William R. Leach, "Transformations in a Culture of Consumption: Women and Department Stores, 1890–1925," *Journal of American History* 71 (September, 1984), pp. 319–42. See also Leach, *Land of Desire: Merchants,*

Power and the Rise of a New American Culture (New York: Pantheon, 1993), and Willia R. Taylor, *In Pursuit of Gotham: Culture and Commerce in New York* (New York: Oxford University Press, 1992).

4. Leach, "Women and Department Stores," p. 331.

5. See Patricia Bradley, "John Wanamaker and Advertising: Retailing as a Public Trust," unpublished manuscript, for information on Wanamaker's.

6. Christopher Wilson, "The Rhetoric of Consumption: Mass-Market Magazines and the Demise of the Gentle Reader, 1880–1920," in Richard Wightman Fox and T. J. Jackson Lears, eds., *The Culture of Consumption* (New York: Pantheon, 1983), p. 45.

7. Mary Ellen Waller-Zuckerman, "'Old Homes, in a City of Perpetual Change': Women's Magazines, 1890–1916," *Business History Review* 63 (Winter, 1989), pp. 715–56.

8. Douglas B. Ward, "The Reader as Consumer: Curtis Publishing Co. and Its Audience, 1910–1930," *Journalism History* 22:2 (Summer, 1996), pp. 47–53.

9. Walter Deane Fuller, *The Life and Times of Cyrus H. K. Curtis* (New York: The Newcomen Society of America, 1948), pp. 11–13. See also John Tebbel, *The American Magazine* (New York: Hawthorne Books, 1969), p. 181.

10. Tebbel, *American Magazine*, pp. 183–84.

11. *Ladies' Home Journal*, December 1892, p. 32.

12. *Ladies' Home Journal*, December 1892, p. 32.

13. *Ladies' Home Journal*, May 1904, p. 18.

14. James Playstead Wood, *Magazines in the United States* (New York: Ronald Press, 1971), pp. 112–13.

15. Wood, *Magazines in the United States*, pp. 147–65.

16. Jan Cohn, *George Horace Lorimer and the Saturday Evening Post* (Pittsburgh: University of Pittsburgh Press, 1989), introduction.

17. Roland Wolseley, *Understanding Magazines* (Ames: Iowa State University Press, 1969), p. 28.

18. Richard Kielbowicz, "Origins of the Second-Class Mail Category and the Business of Policymaking, 1863–1979," *Journalism Monographs*, no. 96 (April, 1986), p. 22.

19. For a description of the cultural development of the nineteenth-century newspaper, see John Pauly, "The Search for the Ideal Newspaper," unpublished paper presented to the American Journalism Historians Association, St. Louis, Mo., October 1986; "The Professionalization of Newspaper Reading," unpublished paper presented to the American Journalism Historians Association, Tallahassee, Florida, October 1984; "News and the Culture of Democracy," unpublished paper presented to the Popular Culture Association/American Culture Association Convention, Detroit, Mich., April 1980; and "The Ideological Origins of an Independent Press," unpublished paper presented to the American Journalism Historians Association, Las Vegas, Nev., October 1985. Pauly argues that news, as defined by late nineteenth-century and early twentieth-century editors, does not give the public the type of knowledge they need to create a democratic order.

20. Gerald J. Baldasty and Jeffrey B. Rutenbeck, "The Economic Environment of Press Partisanship in the Late Nineteenth Century," unpublished paper presented to the Association for Education in Journalism and Mass Communication Convention, San Antonio, Tex., August 1987, p. 14. See also Baldasty, *The Commercialization of News in the Nineteenth Century* (Madison: University of Wisconsin Press, 1992).

21. All daily figures were compiled from data from the census and Rowell's as cited in Alfred McClung Lee, *The Daily Newspaper in America* (New York: Macmillan, 1937).

22. *Advertising World* (Columbus, Ohio), June 14, 1897, p. 1, cited in Baldasty and Rutenbeck, "The Economic Environment of Press Partisanship in the Late Nineteenth Century," p. 18.

23. S. N. D. North, "History and Present Condition of the Newspaper and Periodical Press of the United States, with a Catalogue of the Publications of the Census Year," in U.S. Department of the Interior, Bureau of the Census, *Tenth Census* (Washington, 1884), 8:51.

24. David Paul Nord, *Newspapers and New Politics: Midwestern Municipal Reform, 1890–1900* (Ann Arbor: University Microfilms, 1981). See also Jeffrey B. Rutenbeck, "Newspaper Trends in the 1870s: Proliferation, Popularization, and Political Independence," *Journalism and Mass Communication Quarterly* 72:2 (Summer, 1995), pp. 361–75.

25. Hazel Dicken Garcia, *Journalistic Standards in Nineteenth-Century America* (Madison: University of Wisconsin Press, 1989), p. 229.

26. Rutenbeck, "The Triumph of News over Ideas in American Journalism: The Trade Debate, 1872–1915," *Journal of Communication Inquiry* 18:1 (Winter, 1994), pp. 63–69.

27. E. W. Scripps to W. B. Colver, April 24, 1910, E. W. Scripps Collection, Series 1.2, Box 12, Folder 12. See also Oliver Knight, *I Protest* (Madison: University of Wisconsin Press, 1966), p. 187; and Gerald Baldasty and Mike Jordan, "Scripps' Competitive Strategy," *Journalism Quarterly* 70:2 (Summer, 1995), pp. 265–75.

28. Gerald Baldasty, *E. W. Scripps and the Business of Newspapers* (Urbana: University of Illinois Press, 1999).

29. For an elaboration of this theme, see Michael Schudson, *Discovering the News: A Social History of American Newspapers* (New York: Basic Books, 1978), pp. 88–120.

30. Pauly, "Ideological Origins of an Independent Press," pp. 4, 8.

31. Nord, *Newspapers and New Politics*, p. 19.

32. Richard B. Kielbowicz, "The Limits of the Press as an Agent of Reform: Minneapolis, 1900–1905," *Journalism Quarterly* 59:1 (Spring, 1982), p. 27.

33. Gay Talese, *The Kingdom and the Power* (New York and Cleveland: World Publishing, 1969), pp. 53, 74.

34. Icie F. Johnson, *William Rockhill Nelson and the Kansas City Star* (Kansas City, Mo.: Burton Publishing Company, 1935), p. 49.

35. Frank Luther Mott, *American Journalism* (New York: Macmillan, 1939), p. 472.

36. Willard Grosvenor Bleyer, *Main Currents in the History of American Journalism* (Boston: Houghton Mifflin Company, 1927), p. 313.

37. Jean Folkerts, "William Allen White as Businessman and Editor during the Reform Years (1890–1900)," *Kansas History* 7:2 (Summer, 1984), pp. 129–38.

38. For a contrast of editors who espoused traditional business values and those who sought a more visionary image of the city as a collective enterprise, see David Paul Nord, "The Public Community: The Urbanization of Journalism in Chicago," *Journal of Urban History* 11:4 (August, 1985), pp. 411–41.

39. *World*, May 17, 1883, cited in W. A. Swanberg, *Pulitzer* (New York: Charles Scribner's Sons, 1967), p. 76.

40. Ted Curtis Smythe, "The Reporter, 1880–1900: Working Conditions and Their Influence on the News," *Journalism History* 7:1 (Spring, 1980), p. 3.

41. *World*, May 31, 1883, cited in George Juergens, *Pulitzer and the* New York World, (Princeton, N.J.: Princeton University Press, 1966), p. 63.

42. Juergens, *Pulitzer*, p. 67–68.

43. Alleyne Ireland, *Joseph Pulitzer, Reminiscences of a Secretary* (New York: Mitchell Kennerley, 1914), p. 110, cited in Juergens, *Pulitzer*, p. 30–31.

44. *World*, May 6, 1884, p. 4, cited in Juergens, *Pulitzer*, p. 69.

45. *World*, December 16, 1883, p. 4, cited in Juergens, *Pulitzer*, p. 187.

46. *World*, June 13, 1884, p. 4, cited in Juergens, *Pulitzer*, p. 227.

47. Swanberg, *Pulitzer*, p. 412.

48. See Robert C. Hilderbrand, *Power and the People* (Chapel Hill: University of North Carolina Press, 1981).

49. Swanberg, *Pulitzer*, p. 117.

50. Mary Mander, "Pen and Sword" (Urbana: Ph.D. dissertation, University of Illinois at Urbana, 1979), pp. 31, 32.

51. *World*, May 17, 1896, cited in W. A. Swanberg, *Citizen Hearst* (New York: Charles Scribner's & Sons, 1961), p. 108.

52. Mander, "Pen and Sword," p. 22.

53. James Creelman, *On the Great Highway*, pp. 177–78, cited in Swanberg, *Citizen Hearst*, pp. 107–8.

54. David Nasaw, *The Chief: The Life of William Randolph Hearst* (Boston: Houghton-Mifflin, 2000), p. 127.

55. *Journal*, October 10, 1897.

56. Swanberg, *Citizen Hearst*, p. 139.

57. Mander, "Pen and Sword," pp. 38–39.

58. Mander, "Pen and Sword," p. 46.

59. For the definition, see James E. Grunig and Todd Hunt, *Managing Public Relations* (New York: Holt, Rinehart, & Winston, 1984), p. 8.

60. Scott Cutlip, "Public Relations and the American Revolution," *Public Relations Review* 2 (Winter, 1976), pp. 11–24.

61. For this story and a short history of public relations organized around four models (press agentry, public-information, two-way asymmetric model, and two-way symmetric model), see James E. Grunig and Todd Hunt, *Managing Public Relations* (New York: CBS College Publishing, 1984). For a captivating account of Barnum's promotional efforts, see Neil Harris, *Humbug! The Art of P. T. Barnum* (Chicago: University of Chicago Press, 1981).

62. See Marvin Olasky, "The Development of Corporate Public Relations, 1850–1930," *Journalism Monographs* 102 (April, 1987), pp. 2–3. For the quotation, see Carter Goodrich, *Government Promotion of American Canals and Railroads, 1800–1890* (New York: Columbia University Press, 1960), p. 171, cited in Olasky, p. 3.

63. Olasky, "Corporate Public Relations," pp. 2–15.

64. Ted Curtis Smythe, "The Reporter, 1880–1900: Working Conditions and Their Influence on the News," *Journalism History* 7:1 (Spring, 1980), p. 8.

65. *The Nation*, 1873, p. 38, cited in William Solomon, "A Study in Contrasts: The Ideology and Reality of Newsroom Work in the Late Nineteenth Century," paper submitted to History Division, AEJMC, 1994.

66. William Solomon, "A Study in Contrasts: The Ideology and Reality of Newsroom Work in the Late Nineteenth Century," paper delivered at annual conference, Association for Education in Journalism and Mass Communication, 1994, pp. 18–19.

67. Edwin Shuman, *Practical Journalism: A Complete Manual of the Best Newspaper Methods* (New York: D. Appleton,

1903), p. 25, cited in Smythe, "The Reporter, 1880–1900," p. 2.

68. Smythe, "The Reporter, 1880–1900," pp. 6–7.

69. Jack Hart, "Horatio Alger in the Newsroom: Social Origins of American Editors," *Journalism Quarterly* 53:1 (Spring, 1976), pp. 14–20.

70. J. Cutler Andrews, "Mary E. Clemmer Ames," in Barbara Sicherman and Carol Hurd Green, eds., *Notable American Women* (Cambridge, Mass.: Belknap Press of Harvard University Press, 1980), pp. 40–42, cited in Donald A. Ritchie, *Press Gallery: Congress and the Washington Correspondents* (Cambridge, Mass.: Harvard University Press, 1991), p. 150.

71. Edith Sessions Tupper, "Women in Journalism," *Journalist* 19 (April 28, 1894), pp. 6–7, in Ritchie, *Press Gallery*, p. 151.

72. Ritchie, *Press Gallery*, pp. 145–46.

73. Ritchie, *Press Gallery*, p. 160.

74. See Maureen Beasley, "The Women's National Press Club: Case Study of Professional Aspirations," *Journalism History* 15 (1988), pp. 112–21.

75. Katherine Lanpher, "The Boys at the Club: An Examination of Press Clubs as an Aspect of the Occupational Culture of the Late 19th Century Journalist," paper presented to the History Division at the Association for Education in Journalism Annual Convention, Athens, Ohio, July 1982.

76. Lanpher, "Boys at the Club," p. 14.

77. Winifred Mallon, "The Whole Truth, as Far as It Goes about Ourselves," typescript dated July 1937, Box 23, WNPCF, National Press Club Archives, p. 1, cited in Beasley, "The Women's National Press Club," p. 115.

78. Taken from Jean Folkerts' review of Hazel Dicken Garcia, *Journalistic Standards in Nineteenth-Century America* (Madison: University of Wisconsin Press, 1989) in *Journalism Quarterly* 67:3 (Autumn, 1990), pp. 606–607, with permission from *Journalism Quarterly*. See also Pauly, "The Search for the Ideal Newspaper," unpublished paper presented to the American Journalism Historians Association, St. Louis, Mo., October 1986. Pauly cites contemporary critiques in the *Arena*, the *Delineator*, the *Literary Digest*, the *Homiletic Review*, and the *Atlantic Monthly*. For an analysis of how journalism developed as an occupation and the theoretical structure that underlies occupation-building, see Patricia L. Dooley, *Taking Their Political Place: Journalists and the Making of an Occupation* (Westport, Conn.: Greenwood Press, 1997).

CHAPTER 10

Reform Is My Religion

▼

Despite the modernization of the metropolitan press, reform newspapers of all kinds continued to flourish in the late 1800s. The suffragists, agrarian radicals, labor, African Americans, and immigrants established their own newspapers in an attempt to disseminate information the mainstream press ignored. Indicative of the intensity of reform movements during the latter part of the nineteenth century was Iowa Greenback-Labor Congressman Leman Weller's cry, "Reform is my religion." The congressman knew the value of a sympathetic press, and supported a variety of reform newspapers in Iowa.

Although the concept of a mass press was firmly in place by the last half of the nineteenth century, the presence of these specialized publications clearly marked the limits of advertising-supported newspapers aimed at a large and diversified audience. A press supported by the marketing of commercial products did not address the needs of the variety of people and groups who lived within the United States. Indeed, these mainstream newspapers depicted a relatively singular view of American life and those who lived outside the mainstream were reflected through its—not their—prism. As John Coward has poignantly illustrated in *The Newspaper Indian,* for example, ethnic and racial groups were often depicted by how well they adapted to an "ideology of progress that animated nineteenth-century America."[1]

Out of this need to portray themselves in their entire complexity, the ethnic, suffrage, black, labor, Native American, and agrarian presses emerged as examples of publications produced by minority voices. To be a majority voice in the 1800s, a citizen had first to be white and male, and second, to own property. Only within this framework were ideas considered seriously and authoritatively by the mainstream press. The publications of minority groups gave more than half the population—white women, African Americans, farmers, and immigrants—a vehicle for expressing their ideas, hopes, aspirations, and solutions, and eventually some of these ideas were incorporated into majority opinion. For example, some Populist legislation of the 1890s, adopted by the Progressive Party in the 1920s, was eventually enacted into law. Further, Margaret Sanger's campaign, in *The Woman Rebel*, to legalize birth control finally resulted in changes in laws that enabled women to make their own decisions about the practice of birth control. These voices and those of others made significant contributions to the diversity and role of the press in America. ▼

Impact of Immigration on Society and Publications

By the late 1920s, at the end of the great migrations to the United States, 35 million new residents had arrived in this country. Although inaccurate records and changing terminology used on those records make it difficult to determine exactly where immigrants came from, ethnic populations became highly visible in a variety of communities, and by 1900 more than half of the industrial labor force in the North was foreign-born. Members of ethnic groups often hoped to return to their home countries, and because some of the immigrants spoke little or no English, the mainstream, English-language press offered them little information or entertainment.

Prior to the massive waves of immigration in the 1890s, the predominant foreign-language press was German. In 1885, 653 of 822 foreign-language newspapers and magazines were German. Although the German press continued to account for more than half the total foreign-language publications in the United States until 1913, newspapers and magazines in a variety of other languages also flourished. Next to the church and the school, the ethnic press served as the single most important social and educational institution in the immigrant communities.

The ethnic press, founded largely by immigrants, peaked in 1917 with a total of 1,325 different foreign-language newspapers in the United States. Throughout the nineteenth century, these newspapers helped immigrants adapt to life in the United States, helped maintain sociocultural heritages, provided unique information not available in mainstream newspapers, enriched American thought, and played an influential political role in their own communities. Many of these newspapers also served as labor voices, importing ideas about labor organization from Europe.

Different newspapers served different purposes. For those who could not read English, the newspapers provided important information that helped immigrants adjust to life in a new country, publishing information about registering to vote, becoming citizens, and conforming to American modes of behavior. Readers could learn from various contributors about the Texas prairies or the wilds of North Dakota, about homesteading laws and regulations. The information function of ethnic newspapers reached a peak during World War I, a time marked by an almost pathological fear of foreigners.

Ethnic newspapers also helped preserve the sociocultural heritage of various groups, fostering the sharing of traditional values and contributing to cultural renewal in different time periods. In addition, ethnic newspapers reported information about immigrants, helping to locate family members and supplying news about countries of origin. Further, these newspapers sometimes served as watchdogs of foreign governments, often learning of and reporting foreign governmental policy before the mainstream newspapers. Ethnic newspapers also played an influential political role in communities, helping to select and support candidates for local office.

Similar to the black, agrarian, and suffrage presses, the ethnic press suffered from financial difficulty. Between World War I and World War II, many newspapers survived not from subscription financing, but from advertising revenues generated by American companies advertising for skilled labor and by department stores hoping to sell to people in certain communities. By the end of World War II, as the old generation died out, subscribers often left ethnic neighborhoods and were assimilated into mainstream suburbia, resulting in a dramatic decline of the ethnic press.[2]

Chicago Press and the "Melting Pot"

Chicago provides an excellent example of the diversity of the publication mix in the late nineteenth century. In 1900, Chicago was the Midwest's most populous city, with slightly over a million in population. Nearly half of Chicago's population was foreign-born, spurring the development of an active foreign-language press. The city was a transportation nexus, a major port, and a link between East and West that made it a leading grain, livestock, lumber, and financial center.[3]

Chicago also boasted a large publishing industry as a central element in its economy. In 1890, Chicago was experiencing the benefits of a newspaper boom during the two previous decades that provided thirteen new or continuing English-language dailies. The City Press Association served fifteen clients, including three German-language dailies and the Western Associated Press. In the *N.W. Ayer & Son's Newspaper Annual* for 1900, about 400 newspapers and magazines were listed for Chicago. Publications in Chicago ranged from the metropolitan dailies—such as the *Daily News*, the *Tribune*, and the *Times*—to papers that reflected other changes of the late nineteenth century. The flourishing business sector was served by an enormous variety of trade magazines, including *American Engineer, American Building Association News, Sewing Machine Advance, Stationer and Printer, Street Railway Gazette, Real Estate and Building Journal*, and *Carriage and Wagonmaker*. Professionalism also characterized the last half of the century, as represented in journals such as *Medical Standard, Journal of the American Medical Association, Journal of Heredity*, and *National Journalist*. Religious publications were another mainstay: *Christian Cynosure, Catholic Companion*, and *Christian Science*, for example. The labor press was active in this city of labor, and newspapers such as the *Daily Labor World* and, after 1908, the *Chicago Daily Socialist*, provided alternative solutions to the problems of industrialization. Women could read the Chicago-published *Ladies Fashion Journal* and *Shopping Magazine;* farmers had the *Farmers' Voice, Farmers' Review,* and *Farm, Field and Stockman;* and even youth had their own publications such as *Young Life.*

The Evolution of the German Press

The German-language press had existed in the United States since the nation's early beginnings, with the 1732 publication of the *Philadelphische Zeitung.* Many of the German-language newspapers acquired a middle-class, status quo reputation by the mid-1850s, marked by cultural, social, and language adaptations to the New World. After the failed socialist revolution in Germany in 1848, an influx of immigrants to the United States, including trained journalists, revitalized the radical press. The new papers began after the influx of '48ers revitalized the German-language press, a development that was largely the result of the transfer of experience, professional skills, and ideology of those editors who had emigrated. After October 1878, antisocialist legislation in Germany made it impossible for the more radical editors to remain, and many emigrated to the United States, thus providing a continuing stream of experienced radical editors. These editors reflected various backgrounds, including members of the working class as well as a small minority of middle-class intellectuals. As the number of immigrating journalists declined, the radical newspapers had a more difficult time surviving because the gap between the newspapers and an audience more assimilated into American culture widened.

After the Civil War, the radical German newspapers had to adapt to the new commercial tone in the United States. They began to open their pages to advertisements and provided general information for their audience, thereby facing competition from both established German-language papers with a more moderate tone and the English-language press.⁴ Many of the radical newspapers, lacking widespread advertising support, were funded by associational or shareholding arrangements. In this climate of uncertain funding, pay scales remained low. Editorial members of the *New Yorker Volkszeitung* earned from eleven to sixteen dollars each week at a time when a typesetter earned about sixteen dollars a week and a foreman, twenty-five dollars. Hartmut Keil wrote that many of the papers faced tough competition and were "threatened by a declining readership, initially because of the lures of upward mobility and the actual growth of the middle class and later because of the increasing numerical preponderance of the second generation, which tended to turn from German-language to English-language publications."⁵

Nevertheless, the German radical press attempted to retain what it considered to be its major goal—the preservation of the German language and German culture. Radical editors viewed the middle-class German papers as having bowed to mass popular tastes and lower standards, especially in regard to German language and literature. Although émigrés from the failed German revolution of 1848 advocated artisan republicanism and free thought, as well as anticlericalism and democracy, by the end of the century the concern over labor exploitation caused the press to attempt a shift to a mass-based, working-class movement.

The Chicago Radical German Press

Between 1870 and 1900, Chicago's socialists and anarchists issued fifty-two newspapers published in eight different languages. Fourteen were German, eleven Czech,

Figure 10–1 The De Pere, Wisconsin, *Volkstem* was produced in this busy shop. (State Historical Society of Wisconsin)

nine English, eight Scandinavian, six Polish, three Lithuanian, and one Italian. The German radical papers competed with two well-established, middle-class German dailies, the Republican *Illinois Staats-Zeitung* and the Democratic *Neue Freie Presse*. Chicago's first socialist newspaper began in 1853 with the issuance of *Der Proletarier*, but by the 1890s Chicago was a major center of radical labor organization, with a section of the International Workingmen's Association. In 1877, after several evolutions in name and form, the association became the Socialist Labor Party, which captured 20 percent of the 1879 mayoral vote and elected one state senator, three state representatives, and five aldermen.

The most enduring of the radical papers were published by the Socialist Publishing Society (SPS), beginning with the weekly *Der Vorbote* in 1874. Others followed, including a Sunday weekly in 1878, titled *Die Fackel*, and in 1879 the daily *Arbeiter-Zeitung*. Between 1874 and 1886, the editors of the publications had working-class, immigrant, union-oriented backgrounds, and half had been journalists before emigration. The SPS papers published national and international telegraphic dispatches, editorials, serialized novels, limited advertising, trade-union news, and reports of local labor and social-revolutionary movements. The *Arbeiter-Zeitung* advertised a handbook on dynamite, nitroglycerin, guncotton, and poisons, and it offered its readers free instruction in the handling of arms. The publications served five different but overlapping audiences, including an immigrant audience, for whom they published reports from Europe, daily market reports for food, railroad timetables, streetcar schedules, and advertisements from railroad companies for cheap, western lands. In this area, the radical papers served much the same purpose as the more established, middle-class German newspapers. Other audiences included workers, trade unionists, party members, and sympathizers with the movement. Content aimed at these groups included advertisements for affordable clothing and home furnishings, labor union news, letters and documents produced by the German Socialist party, and articles on dances, festivals, and picnics that chronicled the "cultivation of a movement culture." Total circulation of the radical press grew from 400 in 1872 to 30,780 in 1886. The 1886 circulation represented more than one-fourth of Chicago's German population, and pass-around circulation may have boosted it to one-third.

Throughout 1885 and 1886, Chicago's union movement mobilized, although representation in the union still reflected only a minority of Chicago's workers. The drive for the eight-hour day was energized by the anarchists, and the Chicago radical press was provocative and inflammatory. On May Day, 1886, the *Arbeiter-Zeitung* called to workers: "Bravely forward! The conflict has begun. An army of wage-laborers is idle. Capitalism conceals its tiger claws behind the ramparts of order. Workmen, let your watchword be: No Compromise! Cowards to the rear! Men to the front! The die is cast." Chicago's businessmen responded to the rhetoric, mobilizing police, the state militia, and private Pinkerton detectives. On May 3, 1886, police forces attacked a group of striking workers, and the next night another group of police marched into Haymarket Square to break up another group. A bomb exploded, and seventy policemen and an unknown number of workers were killed or wounded. The following day, the police arrested everyone they could find in the offices of the Socialist Publishing Society. The movement's most promising leaders, including three editors from the publishing society, were imprisoned or executed. However, the radical press did not perish, and within days the SPS began publishing once more. Other papers soon followed. Nevertheless, circulations declined for the next few years. By 1892, they had begun to climb once more, reaching a total of 33,880 by 1900.[6]

The Suffragist Press

Acquiring the vote for women (suffrage) did not receive major attention from mainstream newspapers until persons outside the movement began to perceive it as a legitimate demand. In Oregon, for example, women gained little coverage of their ideas in the mainstream press from 1870 to 1905. In 1905, when Portland was chosen as the site of the National American Woman Suffrage Association's national convention, the amount and nature of coverage changed.[7] The suffragist press, although divided at times on the scope and tone of women's issues, treated such issues in a serious way and promoted a sense of community among women.[8]

In 1900, many Americans still could not vote. Many immigrants, all African Americans, Native Americans, and women were largely excluded from the political process. Although some local school boards permitted women to vote on school

WASHINGTON, D. C.—THE JUDICIARY COMMITTEE OF THE HOUSE OF REPRESENTATIVES RECEIVING A DEPUTATION OF FEMALE SUFFRAGISTS, JANUARY 11TH—A LADY DELEGATE READING HER ARGUMENT IN FAVOR OF WOMAN'S VOTING, ON THE BASIS OF THE FOURTEENTH AND FIFTEENTH CONSTITUTIONAL AMENDMENTS.—SEE PAGE 347.

Figure 10–2   This 1871 illustration in *Frank Leslie's Illustrated Newspaper* depicts a delegation of female suffragists presenting the case for women's voting rights to the Judiciary Committee of the House of Representatives. (Division of Prints and Photographs, Library of Congress Collection)

issues and in municipal elections, women were basically disenfranchised. It was not until 1920, with the passage of the Nineteenth Amendment, that all women obtained the right to vote in all elections.[9] Throughout the struggle the suffragist press was a vital although limited part of American communication. It existed because the mass press did not, on the whole, cover women's issues from a sympathetic point of view, nor did it adequately chronicle the organization of the women's movement.

The first wave of feminism in the United States began in the 1840s, coinciding with the most intense period of the abolitionist movement. Legally, women were the property of men, isolated in the domestic sphere. Women active in the abolitionist movement appeared more frequently in public life, and African-American publications like the *North Star* and William Lloyd Garrison's *Liberator* called for the enfranchisement of women as well as that of African Americans.

The Beginnings

The women's movement formally began on July 20, 1848, with a meeting in Seneca Falls, New York. After that meeting, a handful of women's publications began to appear. Amelia Bloomer started the *Lily* in 1849 as a temperance (anti-alcohol) publication, later continuing it as a suffrage organ. By 1852, the eight-page monthly was devoted totally to suffrage. Paulina Wright Davis presented women's issues in *Una* from 1853 to 1856, appealing to intellectual women. Two other pre–Civil War suffrage journals were *The Sibyl* in New York and *The Pioneer and Woman's Advocate* in Rhode Island.[10] Although the circulation of the suffrage press was small in comparison to that of its mainstream counterparts, its importance to its audience was expressed by an Ohio reader of *The Mayflower*, the only suffrage paper published during the Civil War:

> How dear your little paper has become to me—how it cheers and strengthens me, even as the voice of a friend . . . it seems endowed with almost human sympathy; perhaps because the writers do not write coldly from the head alone, but warm their glowing thoughts by the pure light of a true and earnest purpose that emanates from the heart.[11]

The Second Wave: Unity, Diversity, and Growth

After the Fourteenth Amendment to the U.S. Constitution was passed in 1868 enfranchising all male voters, a second wave of feminism began. The movement was divided, however, between women who believed they should concentrate on getting the vote and women who longed for more substantial political and social reform. Lucy Stone's moderate *Journal*, which emphasized the importance of the right to vote, attracted only 6,000 subscribers at its peak. By 1893, the official suffrage organization had only 13,000 members. Nevertheless, suffrage journals, small and medium-size, mushroomed across the nation. The suffrage editors lacked support even from the suffrage organizations themselves, which refused to grant funds. Prominent women journalists like Jane Grey Swisshelm, one of the first women journalists to actually work in an office—some called it putting herself on public display—reacted to the suffrage issue with mixed feelings.[12] At least one newspaper emerged as a result of the belief that women's interests would not be served by ordinary papers or typical ladies' magazines, because women's concerns would either be crowded out or mixed up with others of an undesirable nature.

Despite their lack of political and social homogeneity, publications warned women against apathy and encouraged converts to feminism by celebrating women's accomplishments. Women's publications provided women with a sense of community by acknowledging common goals "and shared interests, participation in cooperative activity, self-conscious emphasis on loyalty and commitment." They made available information for those women unable to attend national suffrage conventions.

The newspapers also provided opportunities for women to develop management skills. Women owned, published, and edited the publications. The papers "taught suffragists how to argue, why to sacrifice, when to renounce; they explained

▼

Goals of *The Revolution*

The enfranchisement of women is one of the leading ideas that calls this journal into existence. Seeing its realization, the many necessary changes in our modes of life, we think *The Revolution* a fitting name for a paper that will advocate so radical a reform as this involves in our political, religious and social worlds.

—Elizabeth Cady Stanton, *The Revolution*, January 8, 1868

and exhorted; they glorified both the togetherness of this community and its apartness from the larger society."13

Voices of the Suffragist Press

Suffrage papers ranged from right-to-vote newspapers to publications advocating birth control and free love. The variety of publications showed that although suffrage organizations were developed in eastern states, their publications knew no geographical boundaries. They existed in Oregon, Utah, Illinois, Colorado, Ohio, Arkansas, and Florida. In addition to these individually organized newspapers, about 3,000 publications originally begun as women's professional journals to support various clubs were in existence by the turn of the century. Publications advocating a full range of women's rights issues existed, but suffrage remained the primary focus.14

In 1868, Susan B. Anthony began publishing *The Revolution*, a sixteen-page weekly, which continued for two and one-half years. Anthony, an ardent suffragist, argued that women should not only have the vote but should have expanded rights in social and political arenas. She advocated more radical causes as well, such as free love, abortion rights, and socialism. *The Revolution*'s editor, Elizabeth Cady Stanton, argued for voting rights, liberalized divorce laws, equal pay and equal employment opportunities for women, unionization, and elevation of the place of women in organized religion. The motto, "Men, Their Rights and Nothing More; Women, Their Rights and Nothing Less," was considered too radical and unfeminine by many women, who turned to more moderate publications such as Lucy Stone's *Woman's Journal.*

Begun in 1870, the *Woman's Journal* may have enjoyed a longer life due to its more moderate focus. Its editor, Lucy Stone, was an active abolitionist who lectured for the Garrisonians as well as advocated the cause of women. The *Journal*—coedited by Stone's husband, Henry Blackwell—lasted until 1917, shortly before the passage of the suffrage amendment. Stone died in 1893. After her death, her daughter, Alice Blackwell, continued the publication. The *Woman's Journal* focused on voting rights and used a rational appeal to advocate expanded roles for women. Lucy Stone assured women that a suffragist "could be courageous, dedicated and active," yet still be "a genuine woman, gentle, tender, refined and quiet." The *Journal* emphasized feminism and believed men were necessary as bridge-builders to the rest

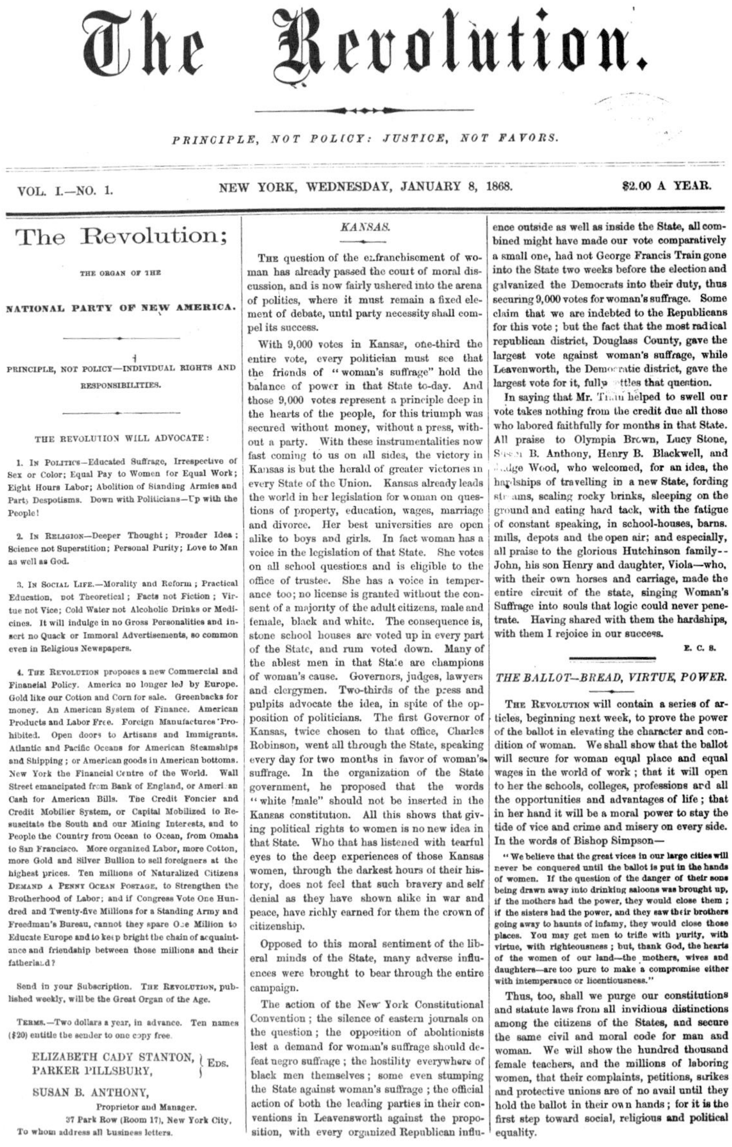

The Revolution.

PRINCIPLE, NOT POLICY: JUSTICE, NOT FAVORS.

VOL. I.—NO. 1. NEW YORK, WEDNESDAY, JANUARY 8, 1868. $2.00 A YEAR.

The Revolution;

THE ORGAN OF THE

NATIONAL PARTY OF NEW AMERICA.

PRINCIPLE, NOT POLICY—INDIVIDUAL RIGHTS AND RESPONSIBILITIES.

THE REVOLUTION WILL ADVOCATE:

1. IN POLITICS—Educated Suffrage, Irrespective of Sex or Color; Equal Pay to Women for Equal Work; Eight Hours Labor; Abolition of Standing Armies and Party Despotisms. Down with Politicians—Up with the People!

2. IN RELIGION—Deeper Thought; Broader Idea; Science not Superstition; Personal Purity; Love to Man as well as God.

3. IN SOCIAL LIFE.—Morality and Reform; Practical Education, not Theoretical; Facts not Fiction; Virtue not Vice; Cold Water not Alcoholic Drinks or Medicines. It will indulge in no Gross Personalities and insert no Quack or Immoral Advertisements, so common even in Religious Newspapers.

4. THE REVOLUTION proposes a new Commercial and Financial Policy. America no longer led by Europe. Gold like our Cotton and Corn for sale. Greenbacks for money. An American System of Finance. American Products and Labor Free. Foreign Manufactures Prohibited. Open doors to Artisans and Immigrants. Atlantic and Pacific Oceans for American Steamships and Shipping; or American goods in American bottoms. New York the Financial Centre of the World. Wall Street emancipated from Bank of England, or American Cash for American Bills. The Credit Foncier and Credit Mobilier System, or Capital Mobilized to Resuscitate the South and our Mining Interests, and to People the Country from Ocean to Ocean, from Omaha to San Francisco. More organized Labor, more Cotton, more Gold and Silver Bullion to sell foreigners at the highest prices. Ten millions of Naturalized Citizens DEMAND A PENNY OCEAN POSTAGE, to Strengthen the Brotherhood of Labor; and if Congress Vote One Hundred and Twenty-five Millions for a Standing Army and Freedman's Bureau, cannot they spare One Million to Educate Europe and to keep bright the chain of acquaintance and friendship between those millions and their fatherland?

Send in your Subscription. THE REVOLUTION, published weekly, will be the Great Organ of the Age.

TERMS.—Two dollars a year, in advance. Ten names ($20) entitle the sender to one copy free.

ELIZABETH CADY STANTON, } EDS.
PARKER PILLSBURY, }

SUSAN B. ANTHONY,
Proprietor and Manager.
37 Park Row (Room 17), New York City,
To whom address all business letters.

KANSAS.

THE question of the enfranchisement of woman has already passed the court of moral discussion, and is now fairly ushered into the arena of politics, where it must remain a fixed element of debate, until party necessity shall compel its success.

With 9,000 votes in Kansas, one-third the entire vote, every politician must see that the friends of "woman's suffrage" hold the balance of power in that State to-day. And those 9,000 votes represent a principle deep in the hearts of the people, for this triumph was secured without money, without a press, without a party. With these instrumentalities now fast coming to us on all sides, the victory in Kansas is but the herald of greater victories in every State of the Union. Kansas already leads the world in her legislation for woman on questions of property, education, wages, marriage and divorce. Her best universities are open alike to boys and girls. In fact woman has a voice in the legislation of that State. She votes on all school questions and is eligible to the office of trustee. She has a voice in temperance too; no license is granted without the consent of a majority of the adult citizens, male and female, black and white. The consequence is, stone school houses are voted up in every part of the State, and rum voted down. Many of the ablest men in that State are champions of woman's cause. Governors, judges, lawyers and clergymen. Two-thirds of the press and pulpits advocate the idea, in spite of the opposition of politicians. The first Governor of Kansas, twice chosen to that office, Charles Robinson, went all through the State, speaking every day for two months in favor of woman's suffrage. In the organization of the State government, he proposed that the words "white male" should not be inserted in the Kansas constitution. All this shows that giving political rights to women is no new idea in that State. Who that has listened with tearful eyes to the deep experiences of those Kansas women, through the darkest hours of their history, does not feel that such bravery and self denial as they have shown alike in war and peace, have richly earned for them the crown of citizenship.

Opposed to this moral sentiment of the liberal minds of the State, many adverse influences were brought to bear through the entire campaign.

The action of the New York Constitutional Convention; the silence of eastern journals on the question; the opposition of abolitionists lest a demand for woman's suffrage should defeat negro suffrage; the hostility everywhere of black men themselves; some even stumping the State against woman's suffrage; the official action of both the leading parties in their conventions in Leavensworth against the proposition, with every organized Republican influence outside as well as inside the State, all combined might have made our vote comparatively a small one, had not George Francis Train gone into the State two weeks before the election and galvanized the Democrats into their duty, thus securing 9,000 votes for woman's suffrage. Some claim that we are indebted to the Republicans for this vote; but the fact that the most radical republican district, Douglass County, gave the largest vote against woman's suffrage, while Leavenworth, the Democratic district, gave the largest vote for it, fully settles that question.

In saying that Mr. Train helped to swell our vote takes nothing from the credit due all those who labored faithfully for months in that State. All praise to Olympia Brown, Lucy Stone, Susan B. Anthony, Henry B. Blackwell, and Judge Wood, who welcomed, for an idea, the hardships of travelling in a new State, fording streams, scaling rocky brinks, sleeping on the ground and eating hard tack, with the fatigue of constant speaking, in school-houses, barns, mills, depots and the open air; and especially, all praise to the glorious Hutchinson family—John, his son Henry and daughter, Viola—who, with their own horses and carriage, made the entire circuit of the state, singing Woman's Suffrage into souls that logic could never penetrate. Having shared with them the hardships, with them I rejoice in our success.

E. C. S.

THE BALLOT—BREAD, VIRTUE, POWER.

THE REVOLUTION will contain a series of articles, beginning next week, to prove the power of the ballot in elevating the character and condition of woman. We shall show that the ballot will secure for woman equal place and equal wages in the world of work; that it will open to her the schools, colleges, professions and all the opportunities and advantages of life; that in her hand it will be a moral power to stay the tide of vice and crime and misery on every side. In the words of Bishop Simpson—

"We believe that the great vices in our large cities will never be conquered until the ballot is put in the hands of women. If the question of the danger of their sons being drawn away into drinking saloons was brought up, if the mothers had the power, they would close them; if the sisters had the power, and they saw their brothers going away to haunts of infamy, they would close those places. You may get men to trifle with purity, with virtue, with righteousness; but, thank God, the hearts of the women of our land—the mothers, wives and daughters—are too pure to make a compromise either with intemperance or licentiousness."

Thus, too, shall we purge our constitutions and statute laws from all invidious distinctions among the citizens of the States, and secure the same civil and moral code for man and woman. We will show the hundred thousand female teachers, and the millions of laboring women, that their complaints, petitions, strikes and protective unions are of no avail until they hold the ballot in their own hands; for it is the first step toward social, religious and political equality.

Figure 10–3 January 8, 1868, issue of *The Revolution*. (Division of Prints and Photographs, Library of Congress Collection)

of society and to the political system. Still, the *Journal* roused women to an indignant sense of self and to the value of the newspaper.

At the other end of the spectrum was a radical publication, *Woodhull and Claflin's Weekly* (1870–1876), considered not only too radical but downright scandalous by

Elizabeth Cady Stanton (1815–1902)

Elizabeth Cady Stanton spent most of her life raising her many children while fighting for women's rights from home. Later in life, Stanton spent two and a half years as the editor of the newspaper *Revolution,* working with her good friend Susan B. Anthony. The first issue was six pages and contained articles and editorials on "anything to do with women." Ten thousand copies of the first edition were distributed. But after two and a half years, money ran out and *Revolution* was sold. Anthony—not Stanton—was saddled with the closing debt of ten thousand dollars.

Source: Elisabeth Griffith, *In Her Own Right: The Life of Elizabeth Cady Stanton* (New York: Oxford University Press, 1984). (*Photo:* Division of Prints and Photographs, Library of Congress Collection)

ADDRESS OF ELIZABETH CADY STANTON BEFORE THE SENATE COMMITTEE ON PRIVILEGES AND ELECTIONS.
THE WOMAN SUFFRAGISTS IN WASHINGTON.
[FROM A SKETCH BY OUR SPECIAL ARTIST.]

Figure 10–4　Elizabeth Cady Stanton testifying before the Senate Committee on Privileges and Elections. First appeared as a wood engraving. (*New York Daily Graphic*, January 16, 1878)

many women. The newspaper was a joint venture of Victoria Woodhull and her sister Tennessee Claflin. Woodhull campaigned for President of the United States through the pages of the weekly, and she and her sister discussed free love, prostitution, abortion, and venereal disease.

Women became more vociferous after the turn of the century, and Margaret Sanger, famous for her campaign to legalize birth control, began publishing *The Woman Rebel* in 1914. Authorities declared an article about contraception "indecent, lewd, lascivious and obscene" under the Comstock (anti-obscenity) Law. Sanger was indicted for sending birth control information through the U.S. mails, forcing her to flee the country. She did not give up, however, and in 1921 she formed the American Birth Control League.

Black Press at the Turn of the Century

Just as suffrage activity found difficulty acquiring space in the mainstream press, the accomplishments of African-American leaders and the day-to-day events of their lives—weddings, births, deaths—seldom appeared in the mainstream daily papers. This void gave rise to the black press, which provided an important social, as well as political function. It became the role of the black press to discuss the issue of whether African Americans eventually would be incorporated into mainstream society. The black press, like the suffrage press, had existed in part to chronicle the activities of people who were ignored or ridiculed by the mainstream press. In addition, reform groups struggled to create discussion over issues such as discrimination and racism. At the turn of the century, African-American leaders began to debate whether accommodating the white power structure or militantly opposing it would be a better strategy in improving the economic and social status of African Americans. This focus on whether and how African Americans would be incorporated into mainstream society characterized the black press of the first half of the twentieth century.

With the end of the Civil War and the passage of the Fourteenth Amendment, African Americans looked forward to an era of freedom, but many of their hopes for political and economic equality were shattered abruptly. By the 1880s, reconstruction and the promise of black equality gave way to segregation and institutionalized racism. In civil rights cases in the 1880s, the Supreme Court declared unconstitutional the 1875 Civil Rights Act, which forbade segregation in public places. Public consensus in both North and South was that African Americans remained at the bottom of society because they deserved to be there.

Booker T. Washington and the Tuskegee Machine

It was in such a climate that Booker T. Washington, president of Tuskegee Institute, rose to prominence as a new leader of African Americans with a speech at the opening of the Atlanta Cotton States and International Exposition. Washington advocated a new position of accommodation between northern whites, southern whites, and

Figure 10–5   Booker T. Washington, speaking to a Louisiana audience. (Division of Prints and Photographs, Library of Congress Collection)

blacks. To the white South, Washington expressed his love and devotion. "I was born in the South," he said, "and I understand thoroughly the prejudices, the customs, the traditions of the South." Washington said "these prejudices are something that it does not pay to disturb," and "that the agitation of questions of social equality is the extremist folly." He renounced northern intervention and advocated that African Americans improve themselves through industrial education and economic opportunity. He reminded the South of the devotion of African Americans during the Civil War and encouraged the South to rely on black labor rather than on those who had produced labor strife in the North. He won the admiration and respect of northern capitalists by denouncing labor unions, revolutionary tactics, and socialism and by professing devotion to the laissez-faire theory of government.[15] His speech, which became known as the "Atlanta Compromise," won the admiration of nearly all whites and espoused a philosophy of equal opportunity, rather than equality, for blacks.

Booker T. Washington became a powerful man. He was the chief distributor of patronage in the South for federal appointments during the administrations of Presidents Theodore Roosevelt and William Howard Taft and a broker for the distribution of northern white patronage. He was invited into southern homes that had barred African Americans since the war's end, and until his death in 1915 he exerted much influence over the black press. Washington developed what became known as the Tuskegee Machine, a national network of editors and other influential African American leaders loyal to Washington. Although many black editors challenged his view, Washington in time exerted a good deal of influence through the distribution of subsidies to a black press, hard pressed to find other financial support.[16]

Opposition to Accommodation

His accommodationist tactics, however, were opposed by many, including William Monroe Trotter's *Boston Guardian*, founded in 1901. Trotter fought with Washington over control of the Afro-American Council, was jailed after a rally, and found himself at the unpleasant end of a libel suit.[17] The *Guardian*, designed to reach intellectuals, was uncompromisingly militant and championed the Niagara Movement, a forerunner to the National Association for the Advancement of Colored People (NAACP).

Later W. E. B. Du Bois became Washington's chief rival. Du Bois, who in 1910 founded the *Crisis*, the magazine supported by the NAACP, described those editors who accepted Washington's subsidies as "bribe-takers" and the "worst type" of blacks.[18] Despite division within the ranks of African-American leaders and editors, the black press thrived. Although about forty black newspapers were started before 1865, more than 1,000 were added from the end of the war to the turn of the century.[19] Many, although vigorous during their lifetimes, did not last long due to economic hardship and social pressure.

Agrarian Press and the Lecture Circuit

Economic hardship of a different sort played a hand in the rise of the agrarian press of the 1890s, which primarily served the Populist party. This party, which grew out of farmers' alliances, first organized in Texas in 1877. The alliances were groups of farmers who banded together after the agricultural depression of the 1870s to protest national policies that they believed hampered their growth. These alliances were not without precedent. Indeed, rural America had a rich history of resistance to economic domination by corporations, railroads, and the "robber barons" of the 1880s. Farmers supported the Union Labor party, in some cases the Socialist party, and joined the Grange, a nonpolitical organization of farmers designed to promote agrarian social life and cooperative business arrangements. The farmers' alliances spread throughout Texas, then through other southern states. Similar organizations developed throughout the Midwest, with Kansas as a key state.[20] Farmers formed cooperatives to combat the crop-lien system that bound southern farmers to the furnishing merchant. (Southern merchants often would lend farmers money for seed in return for their crop. Farmers were never able to repay and save enough money for the next year's crop, so they were continually in debt.) In the Midwest, the emphasis was on eliminating differential railway rates that hampered the shipment of crops.[21]

Members of the farmers' alliances published newspapers to provide information about droughts and crop failures that the mainstream press avoided because they feared such coverage would reduce investments in the West by eastern capitalists. Like the suffrage press, farmers' newspapers also provided a sense of community and presented the alliance movement as a legitimate effort to oppose the dominant political and economic structures. Although the agrarian movement was largely ignored by the eastern metropolitan press, the farmers' activities were noted by midsize dailies in the Midwest. These newspapers tried first to laugh the farmers out of business, but as the agrarian radicals achieved more political success, the press began to take them seriously. Agrarian newspapers, however, were ignored by the editors of mainstream papers and by historians, despite their circulations that in some cases reached 100,000.[22]

Purpose

One of the greatest problems facing the farmers' alliances, and later the Populist Party, was educating farmers about economic issues that directly affected them. By this time, some mainstream newspapers were served by "telegraphic" reports, but most of these newspapers did not carry detailed news about the farmers' plight. In fact, as the farmers' movement gained momentum, the mainstream newspapers actively campaigned against the alliances.

For example, in 1886, the Texas Alliance journal, the *Dallas Southern Mercury*, lamented the drought conditions in west Texas. The *Mercury* requested that each local alliance donate seed and food because "already the depopulation of many sections of the West has begun, and trains of farm wagons with their freight of miserable, half-starved humanity is winding their way over the barren plains eastward in search of food." The Texas State Alliance donated $7,000, its total treasury, to the drive. At the same time, the mainstream daily papers, most conspicuously *The Dallas Morning News*, challenged the reports, claiming that only the cattlemen, not the farmers, would be hurt. The *News,* which represented mostly urban financial interests, was more concerned about declining property values for land speculators and dropping cattle prices than it was about starving farmers.[23]

The reform press struck back at the city dailies with ferocity. The editor of the *Kansas Workman* said the Republican press was "thoroughly unreliable."

> It lacks both honor and intelligence. It is an unsafe teacher. Its ideas of morals are exceedingly low. One day it abuses and the next it praises. One day it exposes fraud and corruption and the next it lionizes the guilty parties. Under its guidance this nation is rapidly approaching the end of nations.[24]

From Lecture to Newspaper

To provide information that the daily newspapers ignored, the farmers' alliances first formed a lecture circuit, sending leaders to small towns and farms to present

▼

How to Start a Reform Newspaper

You will have two sources of income—from subscriptions and advertisements.

A dollar a year is the popular price for a weekly paper. You ought to be able to obtain from 200 to 1,000 subscribers at that price.

Fifty dollars for a column advertisement for one year will be a low rate for you to charge, making it proportionately more for a smaller advertisement or for a shorter time than one year. For local reading notices 5 cents a line is low enough. For business cards of one inch charge $5 per year. You ought to be able to secure four to six columns of advertising all the time in any live town. You can also count on securing from $50 to $100 in railroad advertising which they will pay in transportation—or mileage books. It would be safe to count on at least $300 for advertising. You ought to be able to get $500 out of subscriptions—I am counting about an average county. This will be an income of $800 a year. Now as to expenses.

The paper, say 600 copies, or 25 quires, will cost you laid down at your office about $3 per week. Any boy or young man who has worked in an office a year or so could set the type. Plenty of such can be had at from $1 to $5 per week—say $5. Count incidental expenses at $2 more, making total expenses $10 per week or $520 per year. This leaves a margin of about $300 to pay you for your trouble. At the end of the year you will know enough about the business to dispense with the services of the boy and save that much.

—W. S. Hardy, *National Reformer*, March 1, 1895

speeches about the developing movement. This effort expended too much time and money for a movement that was starving for both. So, instead, the alliances turned to the development of periodicals and newspapers. During the peak years of the movement, the farmers' newspaper, the *National Economist*, attained a nationwide circulation of more than 100,000. Populists had more than 1,000 newspapers in circulation, and in Kansas and Texas—both Populist strongholds—300 newspapers were published. Some, like the *Kansas Advocate*, reached a circulation as high as 80,000, and others, such as Leonidas Polk's *National Farmer*, saw jumps of 1,200 to 12,000 in circulation.[25]

Just as the mainstream press was composed of big circulation leaders as well as smaller, unassuming small-town newspapers, so too was the Populist party press. The papers often were eight pages, with little advertising. The sizes of the newspapers were varied and frequently unusual. Because the papers were published on limited budgets, editors would purchase off-size paper at a discount. The newspapers, like the mainstream small-town and country newspapers, rarely separated editorial content from news content. Stories were not, however, consistently biased toward the editor's viewpoint. Often opposing views were run. The newspapers also contained drawings, songs, poetry, and letters to the editor. It was through the songs and letters that farmers communicated across the miles with each other.

Political Hacks or Journalists?

The Populist newspapers were published in small towns where they usually competed with at least one other weekly, either of mainstream Democratic or Republican persuasion. The editors and the newspapers differed little from their mainstream counterparts, however. Most editors were middle-aged, owned some property—usually a house—and were stable community members. Reform editors tended to migrate west a generation later than did their mainstream counterparts. The main difference

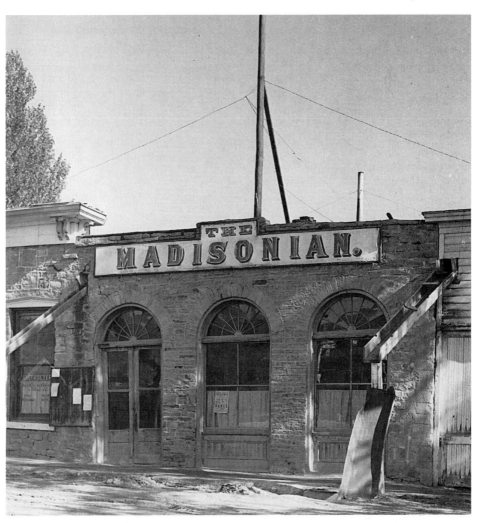

Figure 10–6 Modern technology presented a stark contrast to the country weeklies of 1939. This Virginia City, Montana, newspaper was one of the first in the state. (Division of Prints and Photographs, Library of Congress Collection)

between the reform editors and their mainstream counterparts was their different political philosophies.

The Populist newspapers were criticized heavily by mainstream editors, who claimed that the reform editors simply took up journalism for political purposes. They accused the reform editors of being party hacks—of ignoring the technical quality of their newspapers and of taking money from the Populist party instead of remaining independent or relying on advertising. Reform editors were, indeed, in trouble when it came to advertising. Merchants who supported the dominant Republican and Democratic parties wouldn't buy advertising in the reform newspapers. However, Hardy's instructions indicated that Populist editors expected to support their newspapers primarily from advertising and subscriptions rather than from party coffers.

A technique to improve the quality of the reform newspapers, as well as to spread party-oriented political information, was provided by the National Reform Press Association, founded in 1891. This internal communications network supplied boilerplate, or preprinted material, that could be inserted into any local newspaper. The association lasted until 1897, a year after the popular orator William Jennings Bryan was defeated in his presidential campaign.[26] The press association enabled reform editors to meet with one another and escape the isolation from other editors that they sometimes experienced in their home communities. The publications were many and varied; some gained national circulation, and others circulated to only a few hundred subscribers.

Agrarian Publications

The Progressive Farmer

Leonidas Polk began editing *The Progressive Farmer* in Winston, North Carolina, in 1886. Polk had previously edited North Carolina newspapers, all locally oriented but with an interest in state and national affairs. His experience as North Carolina's first commissioner of agriculture also prepared him for his chosen task of educating North Carolina farmers and their families. The first issues contained news about ensilage and silos, potato culture, beekeeping, egg production, fruit canning, and managing tobacco crops.

Correspondents who were experts about particular subjects wrote to the newspaper, and Polk guided them as an experienced editor. He wrote to one correspondent: "Article too long. Besides you are too fond of theorizing. This is a practical age. Our readers want *facts*. If you have produced an extra yield of Potatoes, Corn, Wheat, Hay, Cotton, Tobacco &c., tell us how you did it and stop. One such *fact* is worth ten columns of *theory* as to how it might be done." Polk also was concerned about the morality of advertising, and promised his readers that advertisements of questionable character would have no place in the *Progressive Farmer*.

In support of farmers' organizations, Polk emphasized their importance in allowing farmers to express their political views, to discuss neighborhood agricultural problems, and to enjoy the advantages of social interchange. By January 1887, just less than a year after Polk began the *Progressive Farmer*, farmers in North Carolina were organized for statewide action.

Polk continued to support agricultural organization through the 1890s, becoming involved in the campaigns in Kansas and other Midwest and Northwest states. The Republican editors of Kansas were not happy to see a radical, out-of-state editor working with local farmers. The *Topeka Capital* attacked him, accusing him of cowardice in the Civil War, of embezzling funds while he was North Carolina's commissioner of agriculture, of letting his partners suffer from his failures in business, and of cheating farmers out of their money. Nevertheless, the efforts of Polk and his Kansas Alliance friends were successful, and they succeeded in replacing John J. Ingalls, a Kansas Republican senator who specialized in patronage and who paid little attention to farmers, with another senator, William Peffer, a member of the alliance and an editor of the *Kansas Farmer.* Polk also supported public education and teacher training for young women.

Polk eventually had to face the same complicated decision as many farmers' alliance editors. As the alliances began to turn political—that is, partisan—the connections among members became frayed along party lines. In North Carolina, there was finally a split between the Democratic and Populist members of the Alliance. Members like Polk had to choose whether to leave the party of their fathers or to abandon the new movement. As Polk became more involved in national Populist politics, he left the editing of the *Progressive Farmer* to others.

Jacksboro Rural Citizen

The *Texas Jacksboro Rural Citizen* represented a far different kind of reform newspaper. J. N. Rogers, the editor, championed the alliance cause in his first issue on September 24, 1880. This rural newspaper, printed during its first few months at the owner's farm, continued as an alliance organ through June 1886, when it changed its name to the *Jacksboro Gazette.*

In the first issue, the editor's statement of journalistic principles indicated that he was more than a mere reformer with no knowledge of journalism. He said he would not accept free advertising disguised as editorial matter. "Omit anything like the 'puff' of one's business, whether it be politics, merchandising or anything that advances the pecuniary or political interests of anyone," Rogers wrote.

In addition to alliance news, this Texas newspaper gave what the editor termed "full and impartial" news and opinions of different parties. Reports discussed crop diversification, planting, and harvesting. "We need articles giving the experience of our farmers and stockmen in this and adjoining counties on stock raising and the cultivation of various crops," the editor wrote.

The newspaper also carried "exchanges" from other newspapers and a good deal of correspondence from its readers. These writers were not people of stature but rather men and women who lived and worked on farms. Thus the newspaper contributed to the community of farmers.

This small paper was more fortunate than some alliance papers its size. Although Rogers became involved in the same political dilemma as Leonidas Polk, he did not approve of the alliance going into politics. As he became more vocal in his disapproval and as the farmers' alliances moved more deeply into politics, he lost alliance support, changed the name of the newspaper, and refused to leave the

Figure 10–7   This 1900 lithograph in *Puck* portrayed William Jennings Bryan, the Populist candidate for President, as swallowing the Democratic party. (Division of Prints and Photographs, Library of Congress Collection)

Democratic party. Consequently, the newspaper did not share the fate of many alliance papers and survived in one form or another until the present day.

The Demise of the Agrarian Reform Press

In 1896, in fear of not being able to accomplish its goals as a separate party, the Populist party joined with the Democratic party to support a joint candidate for President, William Jennings Bryan. In the wake of the subsequent Republican triumph, the Populist press, as an institution, died. Only eight editors attended a meeting of the National Reform Press Association a year after the defeat. In 1891, about six years before, the association had welded more than 1,000 Populist newspapers, providing them with boilerplate material, financial and psychological support, and printed praise of each other. Shortly after the turn of the century and after bitter division within the Populist party over the issue of silver, the party lay in shreds, and its press was buried with it.

Conclusion

Although the captains of industry dominated the commercial landscape during the latter part of the nineteenth century, all in America did not agree with their definition of progress. Various reform ideologies spread, their advocates using old techniques such as the lecture circuit and printed materials made on small hand presses. The mainstream press was thus supplemented by many smaller papers that reached specialized audiences with specialized messages.

Chicago demonstrated many of the forces at work, with a broad array of mainstream, daily newspapers along with numerous specialized magazines and German-language and labor papers that espoused socialist, anarchist, and other labor ideologies.

Women's suffrage papers continued the tradition of female activism that emerged before the Civil War in the antislavery movement, the black press sought to balance accommodation with protest, and the agrarian press fought the conglomerate domination of industries related to agriculture. Within this mix, the mainstream press maintained a dominant voice, often attacking the specialized presses as radical sheets with little impact.

Endnotes

1. John Coward, *The Newspaper Indian: Naïve American Identity in the Press, 1820–90* (Urbana: University of Illinois Press, 1999).

2. This discussion is based on research notes generously provided by Owen Johnson, Czechoslovakian press historian at the University of Indiana, Bloomington. See also Robert Park, *The Immigrant Press and Its Control* (New York: Harper and Bros., 1922; reprinted 1970 by Scholarly Press, St. Clair Shores, Mich.); Edward Hunter, *In Many Voices: Our Fabulous Foreign Language Press* (Norman Park, Ga.: Norman College, 1960); Yaroslav J. Chyz, *225 Years of the U.S. Foreign Language Press* (New York: American Council of Nationalities Service, 1959); and Marion Marzolf, *The Danish-Language Press in America* (New York: Arno Press, 1980). For cultural perspectives on the diversity of print culture in the United States, see James P. Danky and Wayne A. Wiegand, eds., *Print Culture in a Diverse America* (Urbana: University of Illinois Press, 1998).

3 See Norma Green, Stephen Lacy, and Jean Folkerts, "Chicago Journalists at the Turn of the Century: Bohemians All?" in *Journalism Quarterly* 66:4 (Winter, 1989), pp. 813–21. Also see Jon Bekken, "The Working Class Press at the Turn of the Century," in William S. Solomon and Robert W. McChesney, eds., *Ruthless Criticism* (Minneapolis: University of Minnesota Press, 1993), pp. 151–75.

4. For development of this thesis, see *The German-American Radical Press: The Shaping of a Left Political Culture, 1850–1940*, Elliot Shore, Ken Fones-Wolf, and James Danky, eds. (Urbana and Chicago: University of Illinois Press, 1992). See especially Hartmut Keil's "A Profile of Editors of the German-American Radical Press, 1850–1910," pp. 15–28.

5. Keil, in *German-American Radical Press*, p. 25.

6. For a discussion of the Chicago radical German press, see Bruce C. Nelson, "*Arbeiterpresse und Arbeiterbewegung:* Chicago's Socialist and Anarchist Press, 1870–1900," in *German-American Radical Press*, pp. 81–107.

7. Lauren Kessler, "The Ideas of Woman Suffragists and the *Portland Oregonian*" *Journalism Quarterly* 57 (Winter, 1980), p. 4.

8. For a full discussion of the role of the Suffragist press in developing a sense of community among women, see Linda Steiner, "The Importance of Early Suffrage Papers in Creating a Community," unpublished report presented to the Association for Education in Journalism and Mass Communication, Michigan State University, August 1981. See also Steiner's article, "Finding Community in Nineteenth-Century Suffrage Periodicals," *American Journalism* 1:1 (Summer, 1983), p. 15 and Steiner's "Nineteenth-Century Suffrage Periodicals: Conceptions of Womanhood and the Press," in William S. Solomon and Robert W. McChesney, eds., *Ruthless Criticism* (Minneapolis: University of Minnesota Press, 1993), pp. 66–97.

9. Mary Beth Norton, David Katzman, Paul Escott, Howard Chudacoff, Thomas Patterson, and William Tuttle, *A People and a Nation* (Boston: Houghton Mifflin, 1982), p. 550.

10. Lauren Kessler, *The Dissident Press* (Beverly Hills: Sage, 1984), pp. 74–87.

11. Steiner, "The Importance of Early Suffrage Papers in Creating a Community," pp. 12–13.

12. Maureen Beasley and Sheila Gibbons, *Women in Media: A Documentary Source Book* (Washington, D.C.: Women's Institute for Freedom of the Press, 1977), p. 10.

13. This discussion relies heavily on Steiner, "The Importance of Early Suffrage Papers in Creating a Community."

14. For biographical information on other women editors, see Madelon Golden Schlipp and Sharon M. Murphy, *Great Women of the Press* (Carbondale: Southern Illinois University Press, 1983). For classic studies on women's suffrage, see Eleanor Flexner, *Century of Struggle: The Woman's Rights Movement in the United States* (Cambridge: Belknap Press, 1975); Aileen S. Kraditor, *The Ideas of the Woman Suffrage Movement, 1890–1920* (New York: Columbia University Press, 1965); William O'Neill, *Everyone Was Brave: The Rise and Fall of Feminism in America* (Chicago: Quadrangle, 1970); William Chafe, *The American Woman: Her Changing Social, Economic, and Political Roles, 1920–1979* (New York: Oxford University Press, 1972); and Carl Degler, *At Odds: Women and the Family in America from the Revolution to the Present* (New York: Oxford University Press, 1980). These studies focus on the suffrage movement as a white, middle-class, conservative political struggle that abandoned the goals of civil rights at the end of the nineteenth century and focused on obtaining the right to vote. For a more complex view of the women's movement, see Elinor Lerner, *Immigrant and Working Class Involvement in the New York City Woman Suffrage Movement, 1905–1917* (Ann Arbor, Mich.: University Microfilms, 1982); Carole Nichols, *Votes and More for Women: Suffrage and after in Connecticut* (New York: Haworth Press, 1983); Barbara Leslie Epstein, *The Politics of Domesticity: Women, Evangelism, and Temperance in Nineteenth Century America* (Middletown, Conn.: Wesleyan University Press, 1981); and William Leach, *True Love and Perfect Union: The Feminist Reform of Sex and Society* (New York: Basic Books, 1980). For emphasis on the suffrage press, see Karlyn Kohrs Campbell, *Man Cannot Speak for Her: A Critical Study of Early Feminist Rhetoric*, 2 vols. (New York: Praeger, 1989); and Martha M. Solomon, ed., *A Voice of Their Own: The Woman Suffrage Press, 1840–1910* (Tuscaloosa: University of Alabama Press, 1991). Also useful is Lana F. Rakow and Cheris Kramarae, eds., *The Revolution in Words: Righting Women 1868–1871* (New York: Routledge, Chapman, & Hall, 1990).

15. This introductory discussion relies heavily on C. Vann Woodward's *Origins of the New South, 1877–1913* (Louisiana State University Press and the Littlefield Fund for Southern History, The University of Texas, 1951). Quotations are from the 1967 paperback edition. Washington's quotes, cited in Woodward, are taken from his autobiography *Up from Slavery* (New York, 1901) and from his *My Larger Education; Being Chapters from My Experience* (Garden City, 1911). See pp. 357–58 in Woodward.

16. For more information on Washington's dealings with black editors, see August Meier, *Negro Thought in America, 1880–1915* (Ann Arbor: University of Michigan Press, 1964), pp. 226, 230; Emma I. Thornbrough, "American Negro Newspapers," *Business History Review* 11 (Winter, 1966), pp. 483–84; and Louis R. Harlan, *Booker T. Washington: The Making of a Black Leader, 1856–1911* (New York: Oxford University Press, 1972), pp. 254–71.

17. August Meier and Elliott Rudwick, *From Plantation to Ghetto* (New York: Hill & Wang, 1970), p. 206.

18. *Correspondence of W. E. B. Du Bois*, Herbert Aptheker, ed. (Amherst: University of Massachusetts Press, 1973), vol. I, p. 101, cited in Willard B. Gatewood, Jr., "Edward E. Cooper, Black Journalist," *Journalism Quarterly*, pp. 269–75, 324.

19. For information on other black editors, see Stephen R. Fox, *The Guardian of Boston: William Monroe Trotter* (New York: Atheneum, 1971), pp. 31–58; and Armistead Pride, *The Black Press: A Bibliography* (Jefferson City, Mo.: Lincoln University Department of Journalism, 1968). Other prominent editors of the period include Du Bois, of the *Crisis*, Robert S. Abbott of the *Chicago Defender*, W. Calvin Chase of the *Washington Bee*, Edward Cooper of the *Freeman* and the *Colored American*, T. Thomas Fortune of *New York Age*, John H. Murphy, Sr., of the *Afro-American* papers, William Monroe Trotter of the *Boston Guardian*, and Robert L. Vann of the *Pittsburgh Courier*.

20. Lawrence Goodwyn, *The Populist Moment* (New York: Oxford, 1978), p. 33. For background on the Populist movement, see Norman Pollack, who in *The Populist Response to Industrial America: Midwestern Populist Thought* (Cambridge, Mass.: Harvard University Press, 1962) argues effectively for Populism as a class movement, with a broad base including intellectuals and urban labor. For a thorough description of Populist disaffection with the political system, see Pollack's *The Populist Mind* (Indianapolis: Bobbs-Merrill, 1967). For comments on the return of prosperity and the decline of Populism, see John Hicks, *The Populist Revolt* (Minneapolis: University of Minnesota Press, 1931), and Richard Hofstadter, *The Age of Reform: From Bryan to F.D.R.* (New York: Vintage Books, 1955). For efforts on the part of the corporate power structure to thwart Populist efforts, see Goodwyn, *The Populist Moment*. Other sources on Populism include Bruce Palmer's *"Man over Money:" The Southern Populist Critique of American Capitalism* (Chapel Hill: University of North Carolina Press, 1980); and Stanley Parsons' *The Populist Context: Rural versus Urban Power on a Great Plains Frontier* (Westport, Conn.: Greenwood Press, 1973).

21. For example, rates from one major point to another major point were much less expensive per mile than

were rates from rural areas to a major city. It might cost a farmer the same amount to ship his crop from Topeka, Kan., sixty miles west of Kansas City, Mo., as it would cost him to ship it the 496 miles from Kansas City to Chicago. To offset these problems, the farmers wanted government ownership of railroads and other land and monetary reforms. Another major concern was the short money supply. As the movement developed, farmers who joined the Populist party supported the free coinage of silver, a measure they believed would increase the supply of money and help halt the agricultural depression.

22. For development of the thesis that the farmers' alliance newspapers served an important function in building community, providing information the mainstream press ignored, and legitimizing the movement, see Jean Folkerts, "Functions of the Reform Press," *Journalism History* 12:1 (Spring, 1985), pp. 22–25. For other information about the agrarian radical press, see Kessler, *The Dissident Press*, pp. 115–20.

23. *Dallas Southern Mercury*, July 23, 1986, and August 6, 20, 27, 1886; and *Dallas Morning News*, July, August 1886.

24. *Kansas Workman*, October 22, 1886, cited in Seymour Lutzky, "The Reform Editors and Their Press," Ph.D. dissertation, State University of Iowa, June 1951, p. 153.

25. Kessler, *Dissident Press*, pp. 117–18.

26. Bryan was a fusion, or joint, candidate of the Populist and Democratic parties. His nomination reflected a renewed emphasis on the free-silver issue and the relinquishing by the Populists of many other reform measures. The fight over whether to join with the Democrats split the Populists decisively.

With the advent of radio and television, a second link between transportation and communication was broken. Now news could be collected and disseminated over the wires and through the air, regardless of the speed of transportation. By the 1960s, news shows such as this one broadcast by NBC's Chet Huntley and David Brinkley, were capturing the nation's attention. (*U.S. News and World Report* photo, Division of Prints and Photographs, Library of Congress Collection)

PART 3 | *Media in a Modern World*

▼

The nation entered World War I on the verge of a technological revolution that would forever separate communication from transportation. During the war, freedom of expression was severely curtailed even as the mechanisms were being developed to deliver comprehensive messages quickly to wider audiences.

The relationship of government to business that had been debated during the nineteenth century became solidified as the progressive fascination with regulation and the expert held sway. Mass media, now expanded far beyond the periodical press, became integrally interconnected with the business-government relationship. Consolidation accelerated within all forms of media, and as radio and television developed, the federal government and the broadcast industry devised mutually powerful and satisfactory roles. Regulation, nevertheless, represented a critical departure from the First Amendment protection accorded to print media. Although industry recommendations historically dominated governmental regulation, by the 1980s both industry and some individuals in government were advocating the abandonment of broadcasting regulation. The news media continually maintained their right to be free of government censorship, but simultaneously they lobbied the government for preferential treatment regarding labor law and antitrust actions.

The nature of the community also changed as rapid forms of transportation and communication reduced the size of the nation and the world. Although tabloids in the 1920s had still expressed the diversity of urban life and the social agenda characteristic of the progressive years, documentaries of the 1930s were more concerned with the effects of a depression economy. Content and style became interrelated issues, and trends toward increased interpretation in various forms alternated with objectivity as an ideal goal. Journalists explored forms of the documentary through photography and newsreels and introduced political columns and bylines, but they feared the old partisanship of the past and the haunting spectre of nonobjective journalism. The adherence of wire services to the objective form during the anticommunist hysteria of the 1950s, however, convinced many that the old forms promulgated lack of understanding and intolerance.

The introduction of new technology profoundly affected the twentieth century, with portable cameras creating a new journalistic tool. Radio allowed the nation's leaders to bypass editors and exert innovative types of news management. Television brought live pictures of war, poverty, success, and celebration into the nation's living rooms. Audiences rushed to their television sets, sometimes leaving their newspapers behind. Technology altered the face of newspapers as well, but the personal and financial costs of adaptation were severe.

Alternatives to the mainstream media existed throughout the century. Socialist publications and other forms of radical thought flowered in the 1930s, and the black press fought before and during World War II for a double victory at home and abroad. Although consensus politics and culture dominated the late 1940s and early 1950s, individuals such as Dwight Macdonald and I. F. Stone kept alive the voice of dissent. The magazine industry presented another alternative, first in the form of thoughtful opinion magazines, then in the mass-circulation magazines, and finally in specialized information magazines for targeted audiences. ▼

CHAPTER 11

Progressivism and World War I

▼

From the turn of the twentieth century until World War I magazines introduced reform issues into the mainstream of American society. However, with the onset of World War I, reform energies were diverted to winning the war for democracy. Suddenly, the enemy was foreign, rather than domestic. The upheaval of the war reduced citizen tolerance, and rather than generously extend civil rights to others, U.S. citizens responded to immigration, unionization, and a lack of homogeneity with repression of rights rather than extension of civil liberties. The Espionage and Sedition Acts created a legal basis for shutting down newspapers or for restricting their second-class mailing privileges—privileges that reduced the cost of circulation.

Most metropolitan dailies supported the war, often cooperating with George Creel's Committee on Public Information and uttering barely a cry of protest as other newspapers came under the heavy hand of the post office and the courts.

On foreign fronts, the war also had an impact on U.S. media. War correspondents, confronted with heavy censorship, moved from the front to centralized headquarters. Reports were based more heavily on military reports than on first-hand accounts, and issues of censorship dominated editorial decision making.

The technological development of electronic media had begun late in the nineteenth century, and by the time of World War I the technology for radio and motion pictures existed. Motion pictures continued to develop through the war, but governmental holds on the radio waves slowed development of that medium. ▼

Mass-Market Muckraking

Magazine historians generally have explained the development of the muckraking magazines as a form of journalistic exposé aimed at middle-class readers that was interrelated with national reform politics from about 1900 to 1916. Many individuals, including writers, were concerned about the direction the nation's economic growth was taking in 1900. They viewed wealth as being more concentrated than at any previous time in the nation's history, and in fact it was. It is estimated that in 1860, just before the start of the Civil War, there were only three millionaires in the United States, but by 1900, only forty years later, the number of millionaires had increased to about 3,800. About one-tenth of the population owned nine-tenths of the wealth of the nation.[1] In this social context, muckrakers began writing about the social and economic ills of the nation.

The name was bestowed on the magazines by Theodore Roosevelt, who likened the social commentators to the Man with the Muckrake in Bunyan's *Pilgrim's Progress*:

> A man who could look no way but downward with the muck-rake in his hands; who was offered the celestial crown for his muckrake, but would neither look up nor regard the crown he was offered, but continued to rake the filth of the floor.

The term *muckraking* was used by Roosevelt to attack magazine journalists who lacked the optimism he saw as beneficial to the country, but many of the serious muckraking journalists actually were supporters of Roosevelt's third-party Progressive movement. Through cheap, mass-circulation magazines, and occasionally through newspapers, muckraking periodicals reached about 3 million people, primarily urban, middle-class readers. The journalists developed these magazines as responsible tools for public education, informing the people of the close alliance of business and government, giving evidence of corruption, and pointing out the advantages of the privileged. These writers were not trained as historians or as sociologists but as observers, researchers, and writers. They believed exposure would create change and thereby offset revolutionary tactics by underprivileged groups.[2]

Some historians have argued that the muckrakers created or caused much of the public protest that defined the first decade of the twentieth century. However, the muckrakers and the protest movement more likely were intertwined. Some reform groups, like the Anti-Saloon League and the National Municipal Reform League, and attempts to reform civil service practices began before muckraking magazines came into existence. Samuel McClure, one of the most famous muckraking publishers, said he began muckraking with no formulated plan but rather as a response to problems that were beginning to interest people.

The muckrakers were not hoping to create a new society so much as to perfect democracy. Ray Stannard Baker, who wrote many articles about labor organizations for *McClure's* and other magazines, said that he and other muckrakers wrote "not because we hated our world but because we loved it." He emphasized the informational value rather than the reform aspects of his work. Ida Tarbell, who wrote an exposé of the Standard Oil Company, claimed, "the things we were advocating were not advocated with a view to overturning the capitalist system." The muckrakers, although occasionally contemplating the theories of socialism, usually were not interested in revolution. They were full of hope and optimism about American democracy, and they hoped to encourage its development by not letting big business and monopoly control the economics or politics of the country.

The muckrakers saw democracy as a moral force as well as an economic system and believed political institutions should be more responsive to the popular will. They tended to believe that corruption of individual politicians and businessmen was the major problem in American society. In addition to viewing individuals as a source of evil, the muckrakers also held individuals responsible for positive change. The muckrakers therefore expected change would come from the middle class, which would act as a buffer between owners of the major resources and the workers. The muckrakers advocated class harmony and were as upset by violence on the part of miners as they were by the violence of owners.

By 1912, magazine emphasis on reform had declined, and the lack of public interest, deliberate attempts by business to curtail muckraking, and the coming of World War I combined to silence the reform voices.[3] Some writers became disillusioned with reform, but the decline was not merely a result of writers' changing perspectives. The American News Company, the major magazine distributor, discriminated against some of the more radical publications. Big business interests absorbed other publications. When the J. P. Morgan and Thomas Lamont interests (banking) in the form of Crowell Publishing Company purchased *The American Magazine* in 1916, the owners claimed there would be no change in policy. Even Ray Stannard Baker, a writer for *McClure's* and then for *The American Magazine,* saw no reason for the new business connection to disrupt established policies or restrict freedom of expression. The staff of the *American* either was kidding itself, or it did not understand the power of big business.[4] *The American Magazine* did not survive its new ownership.

Other factors also contributed to the decline in reform emphasis by the press. The public grew tired of exposure, and *McClure's* circulation actually increased immediately after its muckraking period, as the muckrakers became heavily involved in promoting World War I. During the 1920s, the newer generation, rather than continuing in the muckraking tradition, became expatriates who directed their scorn against the American middle class. The older muckrakers turned their attention to their own careers and families. Many became biographers and, disillusioned, turned to America's past as well as to travel and religion, losing faith in the masses who failed to respond to middle-class altruism.

McClure's

By the time the muckraking period began in about 1902, *McClure's Magazine* had a history. It had not begun as a muckraking magazine, but instead it initially was published as a general interest magazine, similar to the quality monthlies.

Samuel McClure, a graduate of Knox College in Galesburg, Illinois, began *McClure's* in 1893. His earlier involvement in journalism had been in college publishing, editing a bicycling magazine and creating a news syndicate business. During the summer of 1881, McClure and his friends captured control of the *Knox Student*, and McClure had the magazine chartered by the state. He expanded the magazine, printed book reviews, and organized an intercollegiate news service. Many of his fellow students later joined him in more extensive after-college publishing adventures.

After graduation, McClure worked in Boston and New York, editing the *Wheelman* and writing for the *Century*. In 1893, relying on capital from friends, McClure began his magazine with $7,300 contributed primarily by John Phillips, who later became *McClure's* managing editor. Colonel Pope, a bicycle manufacturer, who owned the *Wheelman*, gave McClure $6,000; Arthur Conan Doyle, the mystery writer, gave $5,000. Of the 20,000 copies that McClure published of the first issue, 12,000 were returned by the distributor, but by 1894 he had 60,000 subscribers and sixty pages of advertising per issue. By 1900, *McClure's* circulation of 370,000 outstripped all his competitors except *Munsey's Magazine*, and by 1907 *McClure's* circulation reached a half million.

From 1895 to 1900, *McClure's* emphasized individual success in American life.[5] Character sketches often revealed the traits of famous political figures and sometimes focused on businessmen responsible for certain monopolistic practices that *McClure's* later denounced during the muckraking period. For example, one article referred to meat-packing magnate Philip Armour as representative of "American life, ideas, ability—representative in success, and . . . personal character."[6] The magazine also referred to Andrew Carnegie, the steel king, as skillful rather than greedy, a man who gave away as much as he earned. The magazine differentiated between good and bad entrepreneurs, good and bad millionaires.[7]

Despite the fact that *McClure's* did not move into the muckraking stage as early as 1894, it was pointing out some problems with industrialization at that time. In July 1894, one writer noted that he could not understand how any human being could tolerate working in the Carnegie Steel plant. "They all die young," the writer said. "Very few men well along in years are found anywhere about the mills. Yet these men go on for a number of years, and anyone of them could do twice the work in the heat that any man could who had worked as the men work in the East."[8]

Why did *McClure's* change? One historian suggested that Samuel McClure, founder and publisher of the magazine, realized in early 1897 that his success-oriented articles did not correspond to the reality of American life. He watched the bitter 1896 presidential campaign and wondered what was missing from his magazine. At first he retreated into the past, emphasizing the individual successes of historical figures. Then he began to assign stories that dealt with complex issues to experienced writers such as Ida Tarbell. In 1897, he wrote an editorial, saying "We, like other men, wish to gain material success, but we want to gain it by those means which appeal to our intellectual as well as to our moral self-respect."[9]

McClure's might have become a muckraking magazine at that point except for the intervention of the Spanish-American War, which absorbed much of the editor's energies. Coverage of the Spanish-American War focused not only on the horrors of war but also on the commercial implications for the United States. Major General Fitzhugh Lee, a former consul general of the United States to Havana, wrote in *McClure's* in June 1898 that human life was being "taken by both contestants under the most aggravating circumstances; and that commerce was being extinguished, entailing great loss to the United States and to the American citizens resident on the island."[10]

In the same issue, McClure explained that many of the publication's June pages had been set aside for war material. He promised that representatives, contributors, photographers, and artists would observe and write "with every branch of the army and navy and at every scene of probable action."[11] *McClure's* would offer personal observation, interpretation, comment, and illustrations, hoping to attain a record "of permanent historical value."

The magazine often speculated about the commercial advantages of controlling Cuba. Speaking about the tobacco industry, one writer said, "Under the fostering care of American enterprise and capital, this industry should develop into many fold its present value, and the time easily come when the laboring man, as well as the millionaire, enjoys his after-dinner 'Havana' or 'Philippine.'"[12] Imperialism, or expansion, was seen by some as a way of providing the luxury to the common American.

It was not until 1901 that the magazine began to evolve as a muckraking magazine.[13] By this time, *McClure's* reflected in many ways the changing of the times. Cities were growing; the West and the South were expanding; immigration was of growing concern; transportation was rapidly developing; emancipation of women was at issue; religion, literature, and art were changing; and labor organizations and vast corporations were developing.

The exaltation of American accomplishment and an emphasis on manifest destiny were pitted against a concern over the increasing chasm between wealth and poverty. It was not until after the Spanish-American war, however, that magazines began attacking expansion as a problem rather than as an achievement.

In 1902, McClure hired Lincoln Steffens, city editor of the *New York Commercial Advertiser*. Steffens joined a capable staff, including Tarbell and Ray Stannard Baker, whom McClure had hired in 1899. Baker was a reporter and editor for the *Chicago Record* and had written free-lance articles for McClure. The three writers—Tarbell, Steffens, and Baker—together with McClure as editor deserve the credit for initiating magazine muckraking, and it was perhaps their influence that made the years 1902 to 1907 a significant period for the magazine. Some historians credit the writers, rather than McClure, for developing the muckraking tradition.

Ida Tarbell was born in 1858, the daughter of Pennsylvania Republicans. One brother, an acquaintance of Lincoln, lost an arm at Gettysburg and another served as a major of "colored troops," appointed by Lincoln.[14] Raised on stories told by abolitionists, Tarbell vividly remembered the tragedy of Lincoln's assassination as well as the adversities of her own family. Rockefeller's Southern Improvement Company forced her father, an oil producer in Titusville, Pennsylvania (where oil production began), out of business, leaving him to labor in the oil fields. It was this background that spurred Ida Tarbell to spend four years researching the life of Lincoln and later to delve into the history of the Standard Oil Company.

Figure 11–1   Lincoln Steffens wrote muckraking articles for *McClure's*, then joined Ida Tarbell and John Phillips to create the *American Magazine*. (State Historical Society of Wisconsin)

Ray Stannard Baker was the oldest son of a Wisconsin family. His father was the president of a land company and sent his son to Michigan State College. Baker's first contact with *McClure's* stemmed from his fascination with Tarbell's Lincoln study. Baker wrote the editor that an uncle of his had been in command of the party that had captured John Wilkes Booth. Baker was commissioned to write an article. During the Spanish-American War, Baker traveled with Stephen Crane and others to the front to write for *McClure's* about scandals in the military administration, about the Rough Riders, and about Theodore Roosevelt. Later, Baker went to Germany to write scientific articles of his own choosing.

The third writer in this muckraking trio was Lincoln Steffens. Born in San Francisco, California, in 1866, the son of naturalized citizens, Steffens grew to adulthood relatively conscious of the political turmoil about him. After graduating from the University of California and studying in Germany, he returned to the United States broke, jobless, and married. After a stint on the *Evening Post*, he was hired by McClure as managing editor, and although his job was not carefully defined, his salary was the same as Baker's—$5,000 per year.[15]

In October 1902, Steffens printed an article, "Tweed Days in St. Louis," and in November, Tarbell began her series on "The History of the Standard Oil Company." In January 1903, the three writers each contributed an article. Steffens wrote "The Shame of Minneapolis," Tarbell continued her history of Standard Oil, and Baker wrote "The Right to Work." These three highly documented articles reflected the writers' talents as well as McClure's commitment to spend time and money on quality editorial copy. In the same issue, an editorial noted that it was "a coincidence that the January *McClure's* is such an arraignment of American character,"16 and that the three articles combined to demonstrate a glaring American contempt for law. Steffens commented on the disgrace of city governments dominated by boss rule; Tarbell discussed capitalists conspiring to break the law; and Baker wrote about how unions deliberately kept nonunion men from working.

By 1906, however, *McClure's* underwent a variety of organizational changes. Sam McClure devised a grandiose plan for a great industrial combination to include a printing plant, an expanded magazine, a publishing company, a life insurance company, a bank, and even ideal housing projects. The result of his plan was that many of the writers and John Phillips, the managing editor, parted company with McClure. At that time McClure bought Phillips' interest and proceeded with his plan. In 1907, the magazine suffered a major loss of circulation and advertising, and McClure abandoned his scheme and worked to secure the magazine's financial health.

By 1911, McClure's health as well as the magazine's business had declined. The magazine changed hands several times and McClure resigned the editorship. In 1915, *McClure's* adopted the quarto size (about 11 by 14 inches) and combined text and advertising. By 1918, *McClure's* increased circulation, reaching its highest point of 563,000. In 1919, with a decline of 20,000 in circulation, the magazine was again sold. Circulation continued to drop, and McClure Publications petitioned for bankruptcy. However, the magazine was not to die so easily. It was purchased once more, and Sam McClure was reinstated as editor. It returned to the old standard (small

▼

Concerning Three Articles . . .

How many of those who have read through this number of the magazine noticed that it contains three articles on one subject? We did not plan it so; it is a coincidence that the January *McCLURE'S* is such an arraignment of American character as should make every one of us stop and think. How many noticed that?

The leading article, "The Shame of Minneapolis," might have been called "The American Contempt of Law." That title could well have served for the current chapter of Miss Tarbell's History of Standard Oil. And it would have fitted perfectly Mr. Baker's "The Right to Work." All together, these articles come pretty near showing how universal is this dangerous trait of ours.

—Editorial in *McClure's*, January 1903

quarto, about 8+ by 11 inches), but it rapidly lost money. In 1926, Hearst money once again revived the magazine, but in 1929 it was combined with another publication. The last two years of the magazine's life bore no resemblance to the early years of *McClure's*.

Munsey's Magazine

Although *Munsey's Magazine* was a muckraking magazine, Frank Munsey's claim to fame was as a consolidator of newspapers rather than as a muckraking publisher. During his lifetime, American newsmen hated him because of his reputation for combining newspapers to make a profit. When Munsey died, William Allen White, a famous Kansas publisher, wrote,

> Frank Munsey, the great publisher, is dead.
> Frank Munsey contributed to the journalism of his day the talent of a meatpacker, the morals of a money changer and the manners of an undertaker. He and his kind have about succeeded in transforming a once-noble profession into an eight per cent security. May he rest in trust.[17]

Although treated unkindly by the newsmen of his day, in some ways Munsey was more visionary than they. His goal was to consolidate, combine, and decrease the competition, a trend that represents business practices even today.

Born in Mercer, Maine, in 1854, Munsey had little schooling and was ill during much of his childhood. At fifteen, he hired himself out to a postmaster for $100 a year. He worked in a country store, where he learned telegraphy. He soon began working for the Western Union Telegraph Company in Portland, Maine, as a night and Sunday operator. Before long, he became manager of the Augusta, Maine, office. In 1882, he launched his first magazine, the *Golden Argosy*, a children's periodical that showed little if any profit. He changed the magazine to *Argosy*, an adult pulp magazine. In 1897, he established the *Puritan*, and in 1900, the *Junior Munsey*. These magazines were merged with *Argosy* in later years.

Munsey founded *Munsey's Weekly* in 1889 and changed it to *Munsey's Magazine* in 1891. The magazine limped along, gathering a debt of $100,000, until, in 1893, Munsey cut the price from twenty-five cents to ten cents an issue in a desperate attempt to boost circulation. The price cut propelled the magazine into a position that enabled it to lead the world in circulation by 1907.[18]

Munsey's business tactics earned him a negative reputation among journalists. He claimed that the same law of economics applied to newspapers as to other businesses, and that small units were no longer competitive. His history of buying and selling was extensive. In 1892, he purchased the *Boston Journal* that published until 1913. In 1901, he bought the *Washington Times* and the *New York Daily News* as the foundation for a proposed chain of daily newspapers to cover several large cities. In 1908, he founded the *Philadelphia Times*, only to abandon it in 1914. He bought the *Baltimore News* in 1908, sold it in 1915, and bought it again in 1917. He acquired the *New York Sun* in 1915. In 1920, he bought the *New York Herald* and its afternoon

Figure 11–2 *Munsey's Magazine.*

counterpart, the *Telegraph*, as well as the *Baltimore Star* and the *Baltimore American*. In that same year, 1920, the *Sun* was absorbed by the *Herald*. Three years later, he bought the *New York Globe* and merged it with the *Sun*. He also sold his Baltimore papers to William Randolph Hearst.

This "dealer in dailies," known for "killing" newspapers, became a millionaire.[19] His dealings paid him more than $20 million. Although other editors criticized him for combining newspapers, he also strengthened these papers. Munsey, for example, poured enough funds into the dying *New York Herald* to give it once again the success it enjoyed under James Gordon Bennett. Then, in 1924, he sold the paper to Ogden Reid of the *New York Tribune* for an unprecedented $5 million.

Munsey's newspapers were conservative, and journalists claimed they lacked distinction because of that position. However, his dailies were clean, respectable, free from bitterness, and fair to advertisers. He supported the Republican party without deviation except for one foray into the Progressive party. When Theodore Roosevelt, Munsey's friend, led the Bull Moose Progressives out of the Republican party in 1912, Munsey followed. Frank Munsey died in 1925. After taxes and payment of debts, his estate was valued at almost $20 million. He had no heirs or family, and most of his money was donated to the New York Metropolitan Museum of Art. During his life he owned eighteen newspapers and twelve magazines.

American Magazine

Although it was a magazine independent of *McClure's*, *American Magazine* certainly had ties to the earlier magazine. Tiring of McClure's schemes for expansion, John Phillips, McClure's able editor, along with Ida Tarbell, Lincoln Steffens, and Ray Stannard Baker, the trio of muckraking writers, broke away from Samuel McClure and began their own magazine. In 1916, they bought *American Magazine*, formerly *Frank Leslie's Illustrated Monthly*, for $360,000. Although their hopes were high, their finances were unstable. Lincoln Steffens wrote to his father, "We are buying an old magazine, which we propose to make the greatest thing of the kind that was ever made in this world."[20] The writers vigorously departed from the old standard of muckraking and approached American life with what Phillips described as "a song of optimism based on facts."[21] Such an approach failed to acquire the needed circulation, and the constant shortage of working capital persuaded the investors to sell the magazine to the Crowell Company in 1911. The Crowell Company was backed by the banking interests of J. P. Morgan and Thomas Lamont. For a year the new arrangement seemed to work fairly well, but in 1915, after numerous disputes over content and with advertisers, most of the staff resigned. From 1915 to 1923, the magazine made a sentimental appeal to a family audience, and circulation passed 1,700,000.

Newspapers in the Early Twentieth Century

Newspapers in the early twentieth century experienced increased costs and publishers raised their prices accordingly. Gone were most of the penny papers from the Hearst and Pulitzer days and in their place were two- and three-cent papers. The cost increase was because of the higher cost of newsprint, higher labor costs, increased volume of news and features, and higher postage rates.

Advertising and Circulation

By the end of World War I the percentage of advertising increased, and advertising paid for a greater percentage of newspaper costs, increasing from 64 percent in 1909 to 75 percent in 1929. More than 4,000 companies were now advertising outside their immediate localities. Mass marketing supplied newspapers and magazines with growing revenues. Linda Lawson, in her study of federal regulation of press business practice, notes that in 1879 publications' revenues totaled $89 million, with 56 percent coming from sales and subscriptions and 44 percent from advertising. By 1914, revenues more than quadrupled, totaling $419 million. Advertising now accounted for more than half of the revenues (66 percent) and subscription and sales for only 39 percent.

Newspapers began to compete ferociously for advertising, and advertisers worked to gain the best possible display for their products. The Royal Baking Powder Company, for example, refused to advertise in publications that carried the advertisements of their competitors. Newspapers were a lucrative business. For example, the *New York World* was worth $10 million by the mid-1890s and netted a $1 million annual profit.

The number of newspapers increased until 1909, then declined. The combined total of morning and evening newspapers peaked in 1909, with 2,600 newspapers. By 1919 there were only 2,441. The major transportation and communication developments that prompted increased numbers of newspapers slowed down. Growth of railroad mileage stabilized, the telegraph was firmly in place and rural free delivery routes grew only slightly in the war and postwar years.

Although the growth in the number of newspapers slowed down, circulation was a different story. The number of readers grew at a rate similar to the rate of growth of the urban population. In 1870 only 11.5 percent of the literate population subscribed to a daily newspaper. By 1930, 45 percent of the literate population subscribed. Newsprint consumption also continued to increase, indicating the growth in the number of pages of dailies. Average circulation of a daily newspaper in 1919 was 13,531. Sunday circulations hovered around 30,000.

The Associated Press provided news for an increasing number of newspapers during the war, but membership slumped slightly after the war. In 1914, nearly 900 news organizations belonged to AP. The number peaked in 1920 at 1,250, then dropped in 1924.

The geographical location of daily newspapers also was changing. In 1880, dailies printed in six cities (New York, Chicago, Philadelphia, Cleveland, Boston, and San Francisco) constituted 51.1 percent of the country's dailies. By 1919 that figure had dropped to 34.7 percent and by 1929 it dropped further to 33.7 percent.

The weekly newspaper picture also showed a decline in number during the war years. In 1909 about 16,135 newspapers were in existence. The numbers fluctuated only slightly until 1917, when the total number dropped to 15,587. The weeklies experienced a steady decline through 1935, when 10,505 weeklies were printed.

Chain ownership was growing, although its greatest period of growth came in the early 1920s. In 1900, 10 chains owned 32 dailies; by 1923, 31 chains owned 153 dailies, or 32.4 percent of all daily newspapers. Newspapers begun in the previous decades continued to be major forces in the South and Midwest. The *Chicago Tribune,* the *Kansas City Star,* the *St. Louis Post-Dispatch* and the *Denver Post* continued as financially strong and independent voices. The *Louisville Courier-Journal* and the *Atlanta Constitution* provided similar strength in the South.[22]

Big Business and Big Power

Amidst this cycle of growth, the questions of who owned the American press and who influenced content became major concerns. Press critics and political reformers intensified claims made since the middle of the nineteenth century that these profitable businesses were owned and controlled by powerful business and political interests. Charges were leveled, not merely of political partisanship, but of business control of content, advertising "masquerading" as news, and exaggeration of circulation figures.

Critics regularly claimed that the richest families in America, along with the most influential corporate leaders and politicians, secretly owned major newspapers and magazines. Critics charged that the business leaders thought the easiest way to buy legislators was to buy the newspapers that could influence people in political power.

Truth underlay the charges. Jay Gould, a railroad magnate, bought the *New York World* in 1879, then sold it to Pulitzer in 1883. Some evidence suggests that Gould might have retained a financial interest in the New York newspaper leader. Henry Villard, a prominent *New York Evening Post* publisher in the 1880s, was also a promoter for the Northern Pacific Railroad. The Rockefeller dynasty, owners of the Standard Oil enterprises, purchased interests in a variety of Ohio newspapers, as well as many in other states. Rockefeller and his associates also financed a number of magazines, including *Outlook*. Allegedly, J. P. Morgan bought interests in many of the muckraking magazines.

Within this atmosphere of big business, critics became increasingly concerned about the blurring of lines between editorial and advertising content. Advertisements sometimes masqueraded as news content. Even William Allen White's *Emporia Gazette* fell prey to the persuasive powers of the Royal Baking Powder Company, who encouraged editors to run front page stories on the dangers of alum in baking-powder products. These stories were actually promotional pieces of alum-free Royal Baking Powder.[23]

In 1907, when the practice of printing "disguised" advertisements was addressed by the Interstate Commerce Commission, the group ruled that "Standard Oil Company buys advertising space in many newspapers, which it fills, not with advertisements, but with reading matter prepared by agents kept for that purpose, and paid for at advertising rates as ordinary news."[24]

The practice had been widely "discussed" in state newspaper associations and at meetings of national trade organizations such as the American Newspaper Publishers Association and the National Editorial Association. By the turn of the century many prominent publishers had condemned and ceased the practice, but the trade associations failed to act.

Publications regularly inflated circulation claims until advertisers and some publishers joined together toward the end of the twentieth century's first decade to seek change. Reform issues emerged not only regarding content but also involving business practices, including regulation of reporting of circulation figures and new attention to the issue of child labor, which included the "newsies" who delivered the then-increasing number of evening newspapers.[25]

Reform Legislation

In 1912, elements of both political parties joined within Congress to pass the Newspaper Publicity Act, the only Progressive-era regulation of the press. In typical Progressive fashion, reformers examined state regulations that might be applicable and they consulted the experts. The law required most publications using the favorable second-class mailing rate to identify their owners and to label advertisements resembling news or editorials. Some publishers lobbied for the bill, wanting to protect their own business interests as well as those of honest advertisers. However, when Woodrow Wilson's postmaster general, Albert S. Burleson, took over in early 1913 and began to enforce the law vigorously, attorneys for the American Newspaper Publishers Association, acting on behalf of two New York newspapers, asked the Supreme Court for a restraining order. When the Court granted the order, publishers predicted it would also declare the law unconstitutional. The Court quickly ruled, however, that publishers who took advantage of favorable postal subsidies could be required to reveal ownership and circulation. Ultimately, honest publishers used the law to reenforce their own legitimacy in the business and opinion/news marketplace, but lack of enforcement and schemes to avoid the provisions of the law also prevailed. Nevertheless, the law provides at least limited accurate information about ownership and circulation and a mechanism for pursuing those who insist on disguising advertising copy as news.[26]

Newspapers and Social Reform

The reform years of the early twentieth century provided content for magazines and newspapers, but they also resulted in pressure on newspapers to treat their employees differently. Child-labor reform groups were concerned about low pay and poor working conditions for newsboys, a concern that culminated in the 1920s in educational programs for news carriers. David Nasaw suggested that newsies were the product of the boom of afternoon dailies that began in the 1880s and continued through the war. Newsboys bought newspapers from the circulation manager at a discounted rate, then sold them to their customers for a specified price. Newspapers depended on the young distributors and fought for their loyalty with Thanksgiving dinners, theater tickets, and baseball leagues. Occasionally, newspapers employed thugs to harass the newsboys of other newspapers, hoping to defeat the competition. Although such violence generally was short-lived and never prevalent, there were incidents reported of Chicago newsboys enduring assaults by adult hoodlums hired specifically to challenge the competition.[27]

Newsboys came from every ethnic group and almost exclusively from the working class. Selling newspapers on the street was a common childhood occupation in all major cities, and newsboys, for the most part, enjoyed the autonomy of being independent dealers away from the watchful and disciplining eyes of teachers and parents. It was a demanding occupation as well, which required boys to exercise judgment about how many papers to buy, where to sell them, and how to get the best tips. If a boy bought too many papers, he made no profit and was stuck with the extras, but if he bought too few, he would alienate his regular customers. Boys chose particular streetcar stops, theatre exits, and other heavily populated districts in order to sell the most papers. They wept, pleaded poverty, or begged for a customer to buy a "last paper" so they could go home to bed—all to gain the tips that gave them their real profit. Reformers urged customers not to tip, nor to encourage the practice of children "begging," but others looked at it differently:

> The more prosperous Americans, on their way home from business or pleasure, saw what they wanted to see in the city left behind. The children of the street were not, to

their eyes, the exploited, deprived children the reformers had described, but a band of little merchants selling their wares. Some were dirty, some ragged; some scowled, some whimpered; but they were all on the streets for a noble cause: to make money for their families—and themselves. Here were scores of children who had adopted the American credo, who believed in hard work, hustle, and long hours, who were on their way up the ladder to success. With the help of kindly benefactors who bought their goods and left tips, these children would raise themselves from poverty to prosperity.[28]

It was not only newsies and reformers who were concerned about the working people on newspapers. Journalists' organizations, comprised of reporters who were concerned about wages and working conditions, began to take shape. These early struggles culminated in the 1930s with the formation of a newspaper guild. Newspapers were not immune from labor strikes as production personnel struck for higher wages and shorter hours.

Figure 11–3   Newsboys formed the distribution network for newspapers during the early twentieth century. These idealized 1916 portrayals of the young workers gained criticism from those who protested that newsboys were exploited children without the protection of child-labor legislation. The newsboy delivering *Grit* reflects news distribution in the small town. (Division of Prints and Photographs, Library of Congress Collection)

"Post-Bellum"

In this poem Dean Collins, a Portland (Oregon) newsie, described the dry news days after World War I that made it difficult for newsboys to sell papers. The poem was printed in a newspaper published by newsboys to raise money for their clubs and activities:

A newsboy with his papers sat sighing on the street
For the cruel war was over and the foe had met defeat.
And the scare-heads in the dailies, they had vanished like a spell,
And the liveliest thing the newsie had was market heads to yell.
"O, maybe Sherman had it right," said he, "but wars must cease—
And Sherman never tried to peddle papers when 'twas peace."

"They used to saw an extra off each half hour by the clock.
And we used to wake the echoes when we whooped 'em down the block.
War may be just what Sherman said it was, but just the same,
If Sherman were a newsie, O, I wonder what he'd think
Of peddling papers after peace had put things on the blink?"

"How can I jar the people loose to buy the sheet and read,
If I start yelling 'bout the rise in price of clover seed?
When they are used to war and smoke and sulphur burning blue,
Will they warm up to read about the W.C.T.U.?
O, Maybe Sherman had it right on war—but wars must cease—
And Sherman never tried to peddle papers after peace."

—*The Hustler*, February 1918, p. 4, cited in David Nasaw, *Children of the City*
(Garden City, N.Y.: Anchor Press/Doubleday, 1985), p. 80.

Postal acts in the early part of the century required newspapers and magazines to make honest statements about circulation and provide specific ownership information. The American Newspaper Publishers Association, organized in 1887 to lobby for legislation favorable to newspapers and against restrictive legislation, gained momentum during the war years and became a significant force in later decades.

Control of Information during the War

In 1914, when the nations of Europe became embroiled in World War I, the United States shunned involvement. War had been brewing for more than a decade, with Germany, Austria-Hungary, and Turkey organized as the Central Powers fighting against those nations that eventually became America's allies: France, England, Russia, and Italy. Members of Theodore Roosevelt's Progressive party, which included the group of journalists who had been involved in muckraking, believed the European nations were fighting over merely commercial disputes. They also believed the role of the United States should be that of a model of peace and democracy, uninvolved in imperialistic wars.

However, in 1917, when the German government threatened American ships and suggested that Germany would involve Mexico in the war, and the Bolshevik revolution in Russia freed the United States from the embarrassment of being allied with a tyrannical power, President Woodrow Wilson went before Congress to argue that the world must be made safe for democracy.

Despite Wilson's plea for democracy, citizens during World War I feared what might result from the period of massive change they had just undergone, and so they sought to create a more restrictive, homogeneous society. In early 1917, in a small rural community in north central Kansas, a group of farmers arrived at the parochial school of a German Lutheran church and painted the schoolhouse yellow, signifying German cowardice. Only months before, the members of the church had seemingly been friends with their neighbors. The Germans were admired for their hard work and thrift. Yet, just a short time later, incidents such as this against German Americans began occurring with increasing regularity. The intensity of the reaction against German people during World War I defied reason. It was, as social historian John Higham wrote, "the most spectacular reversal of judgment in the history of American nativism."[29]

The prejudice against Germans displayed at the Kansas church was manifested in other parts of the country. In his book on the First Amendment, legal historian John Stevens recalled many similar examples from Wisconsin, home for many individuals of German descent.

> Libraries burned German-language books, symphonies removed all German compositions from their repertoires, schools stopped teaching German, and universities fired professors of German. The federal government clamped down on German-language newspapers. By the thousands, citizens, banks, businesses, and even towns lined up to anglicize their names.[30]

What caused this sudden reversal of attitude toward the Germans? Stevens suggested that Americans, partially because they had been able to avoid foreign entanglements, believed the country was unique and that its homogeneity contributed to that uniqueness. The possibility that a sizeable minority of American citizens would disagree on foreign policy, as war threatened, shocked the rest of the populace.[31]

Antagonism toward immigrants also had been on the increase since the economic hard times of the 1880s. Laborers viewed immigrants as threatening to their jobs, and capitalists were afraid immigrant labor would stimulate strikes and other forms of what they termed "anarchism," or disrespect for government and authority. In addition, the German government threatened to sink American ships.

During the early stages of the European phase of the war, German-language newspapers in the United States often supported Germany's victories. Once the United States entered the war, however, most German-language newspapers avoided discussing the war, became pacifist, or supported U.S. policies.[32]

Restrictive Legislation and "Discovering" the First Amendment

World War I is a great irony of history. It was one of the low-water marks for civil liberties in American history. Paradoxically, however, efforts to punish persons suspected of "disloyalty" during the war led the Supreme Court of the United States to consider the First Amendment for the first time in the nation's history. At the beginning of World War I, the only legislation regarding freedom of expression still on the books was the Treason Act and the Conspiracies Act from the Civil War. Neither of these acts punished individuals for uttering disloyal remarks, and both of them required proof of conspiracy to convict. In fact, during the Civil War, President Abraham Lincoln was disturbed because it sometimes seemed that civilians—particularly those associated with the press—had more rights than military personnel, those people who had actually defended the Union. He wrote to a friend, "Must I shoot a simple-minded soldier boy who deserts, while I must not touch a hair of a wily agitator who induces him to desert?"

The situation was different during World War I. In 1917, Congress introduced a draft to increase restrictions on aliens and enacted restrictive legislation: the Espionage Act of 1917, its Sedition Amendment of 1918, and the Trading-with-the-Enemy Act. During the war, at least 2,000 persons were indicted under the Espionage Act alone.

These statutes were passed in a time of overzealous war preparations that could well be termed war hysteria. Feverish emotions led to superpatriotism, excessive prosecutions, and mob violence against persons suspected of "disloyalty. Because Germany was the major and most hated opponent, persons with German accents or German names became targets for discrimination, vandalism, and violence.

The Espionage Act, initially designed to prevent interference with military operations, was aimed at those who attempted to cause "insubordination or "disloyalty or to obstruct enlistment or recruiting.[33] The act also allowed the postmaster to refuse to mail materials thought to violate the act. In 1918, the Sedition Amendment

▼

Wilson Calls for War

The world must be made safe for democracy. Its peace must be planted upon the tested foundations of political liberty. . . .

It is a fearful thing to lead this great peaceful people into war. . . . But the right is more precious than peace, and we shall fight for the things which we have always carried nearest our hearts—for democracy, for the right of those who submit to authority to have a voice in their own governments, for the rights and liberties of small nations, for a universal dominion of right by such a concert of free peoples as shall bring peace and safety to all nations and make the world itself at last free.

—President Woodrow Wilson, war message to Congress, April 2, 1917

expanded the scope of the Espionage Act, making it a crime to write or to publish any "disloyal, profane, scurrilous or abusive language about the form of government of the United States, the Constitution, military or naval forces, the flag or the uniform, or to use language to bring those ideas or institutions into contempt or disrepute. The Sedition Amendment made punishable speech that in World War II would be deemed mere political comment. The Trading-with-the-Enemy Act, passed in 1917, authorized censorship of communications moving into or outside of the United States and required that foreign-language newspapers file translations with the government. Pressures put on foreign-language newspapers during World War I under the Espionage and Trading-with-the-Enemy Act, including massive denials of second-class mailing privileges, resulted in the decline and death of many foreign-language journals.

One elderly Wisconsin editor criticized the army's requirement that all recruits be vaccinated for smallpox, and because he did not file a translation, he was indicted under the Trading-with-the-Enemy Act and the Espionage Act. His son testified that the old man was senile and did not understand the requirement. The son claimed that the newspaper was unimportant and read by only a few of the editor's friends, begged the judge to be lenient, but the judge sentenced the editor to a year a Leavenworth Penitentiary, where he died while imprisoned.[34]

Through such legislation and its harsh application through court decisions came some of the most important decisions made by the Supreme Court regarding freedom of the press. Not since the Alien and Sedition Acts of 1798 had the United States suppressed, to such a great extent, unpopular ideas. The World War I decisions were continued and expanded through the 1920s. The first major legal case to arise out of the Espionage Act was *Schenck v. United States*.[35] Schenck, the general secretary of the Socialist party, sent out about 15,000 leaflets to men who had been called to military service, urging them to oppose the Conscription Act or draft. Those leaflets— just one sheet of paper printed on both sides—don't look dangerous in the twenty-first century. They even included the name and address of the Socialist Party Book Store and Headquarters, which suggests that these shabby radicals believed they had freedom to protest. One side of the leaflet was captioned:[36]

LONG LIVE THE CONSTITUTION
OF THE UNITED STATES

Wake Up, America! Your Liberties are in Danger!

The 13th Amendment, Section 1, of the Constitution of the Untied States says: "Neither slavery nor involuntary servitude, except as a punishment for crime whereof the party shall have been duly convicted, shall exist within the United States, or any place subject to their jurisdiction."

The leaflet consisted of quotations from the Constitution, adding the assertion that the Socialist Party believed that the Thirteenth Amendment forbidding slavery was violated by the "involuntary servitude" of being conscripted into the armed forces.

Mail Privileges Revoked

Publications whose second-class mail privileges were revoked in 1917 after a hearing on account of violation of the Espionage Law, together with the date of revocation.

Arbeiter Zeitung	Buffalo, NY	Oct. 9, 1917
Bull	New York, NY	Aug. 16, 1917
Cultura Obrera	New York, NY	Aug. 28, 1917
Elore	New York, NY	Sept. 24, 1917
Hlas Svobody	New York, NY	Sept. 12, 1917
L'Avvenire	New York, NY	Aug. 15, 1917
Mother Earth	New York, NY	Sept. 25, 1917
The Masses	New York, NY	Aug. 15, 1917
New York Call	New York, NY	Nov. 10, 1917
New Yorker Volkszeitung	New York, NY	Oct. 6, 1917
Novy Mir	New York, NY	Oct. 3, 1917
Obrana	New York, NY	Aug. 28, 1917
Solidarity	Chicago, IL	Oct. 26, 1917
American Socialist	Chicago, IL	Aug. 8, 1917
Das Wochenblatt	Chicago, IL	Mar. 18, 1918
La Parola Proletaria	Chicago, IL	Sept. 25, 1917
The Decatur Labor World	Decatur, IL	Mar. 21, 1918
Il Proletario	Boston, MA	Aug. 28, 1917
Cronaca Sovversiva	Lynn, MA	Aug. 9, 1917
Kova	Philadelphia, PA	Jan. 12, 1918
The Peoples Press	Philadelphia, PA	Aug. 28, 1917
Philadelphia Tageblatt	Philadelphia, PA	Sept. 21, 1917
Die Freie Presse	Glencoe, MN	Jan. 4, 1918
Allarm	Minneapolis, MN	Sept. 26, 1917
Referendum—Four Page Home Print	Faribault, MN	Aug. 11, 1917
Missouri Staats-Zeitung	Kansas City, MO	Feb. 16, 1918
Saint Louis Labor	Saint Louis, MO	Aug. 17, 1917
Social Revolution	Saint Louis, MO	Oct. 3, 1917
El Rebelde	Los Angeles, CA	Aug. 31, 1917
Vorwarts der Pacific Kuste	San Francisco, CA	Oct. 12, 1917
The New Critic	Grand Junction, CO	Oct. 11, 1917
Jeffersonian	Thomson, GA	Aug. 8, 1917
The Thomson Guard	Thomson, GA	Oct. 1, 1917
Watson's Magazine	Thomson, GA	Oct. 12, 1917
Die Washtenaw Post	Ann Arbor, MI	Oct. 10, 1917
New Jersey Freie Zeitung	Newark, NJ	Oct. 6, 1917
Volksfreund und Arbeiter Zeitung	Cleveland, OH	Feb. 23, 1918
The Josephinum Weekly	Columbus, OH	Apr. 6, 1918
Scimitar	Abbeville, SC	Sept. 26, 1917
Charleston American	Charleston, SC	Dec. 20, 1917
The Rebel	Hallettsville, TX	Aug. 7, 1917
The Battle Axe	Danville, VA	Aug. 8, 1917
Spokane Socialist	Spokane, WA	Sept. 12, 1917
The Milwaukee Leader	Milwaukee, WI	Oct. 1, 1917

— National Archives

A conscript is little better than a convict. He is deprived of his liberty and of his right to think and act as a free man. A conscripted citizen is forced to surrender his right as a citizen and become a subject. He is forced into involuntary servitude. He is deprived of the protection given him by the Constitution of the United States. He is deprived of all freedom of conscience in being forced to kill against his will.

Are you one who is opposed to war, and were you misled by the venal capitalist newspapers, or intimidated or deceived by gang politicians and registrars into believing you would not be allowed to register your objections to conscription?[37]

Even though there appears to have been little if any evidence that these leaflets prevented even one man from submitting to conscription, Schenck and his socialist codefendants were convicted of violating the Espionage Act. The Supreme Court unanimously upheld the convictions, with Justice Oliver Wendell Holmes writing for the Court:

We admit that in many places and in ordinary times the defendants . . . would have been within their constitutional rights. But the character of every act depends on the circumstances in which it is done. The most stringent protection of free speech would not protect a man in falsely shouting fire and causing a panic.* * * The question in every case is whether the words used are used in such circumstances as to create a clear and present danger that they will bring about substantive evils that Congress has a right to prevent. It is a question of proximity and degree. When a nation is at war many things that might be said in time of peace are such a hindrance to the effort that their utterance will not be endured.[38]

That remarkable passage did nothing less than *rewrite* the First Amendment. Instead of the unqualified statement, "Congress shall make no law . . . abridging the freedom of speech, or of the press," the Supreme Court sweepingly substituted safety of a government at war for the citizens' right to speak out in protest. In times of war hysteria, an utterance could justify punishing protesters seen to "create a clear and present danger." But that "clear and present danger" language soon wasn't tough enough on protesters to suit a majority of the Supreme Court, and that phrase was not used again—except in opinions dissenting against upholding war protesters' convictions. In its place, the Supreme Court embraced a "bad tendency theory," which allowed prosecutors to make up a presumed intent: If a dissenter spoke in protest, courts could presume a "bad intent that could bring about a harmful result, whether or not any real likelihood of harm could be shown. Consider the case of Jacob Abrams. Abrams ran afoul of the 1918 Sedition Amendment to the Espionage Act. That amendment, repealed during the 1920s, prohibited

any disloyal, profane, scurrilous or abusive language about the form of government of the United States, or the Constitution . . . or the military and naval forces of the United States, or the flag . . . or the uniform of the United States.[39]

Abrams and codefendants were convicted of "distributing" leaflets (they threw them out of a factory building in New York City). A leaflet titled "The Hypocrisy of the United States and Her Allies" did not oppose the U.S. war effort against Germany. Instead, it denounced the United States' joining with other nations to send an expeditionary force into Russia. The leaflet called for munitions workers in the United States to strike so that the bullets they made would not kill innocent Russians. Again, there was no evidence that such leafleteering had any adverse affect on the war effort. The defendants, however, were spitting into the wind with their angry language attacking President Woodrow Wilson and "the plutocratic gang in Washington." That was enough for a federal court jury to convict Abrams and three friends.

In upholding the conviction, the Supreme Court embraced that prosecutor's friend, the "bad tendency" theory. Justice Clarke wrote for the Court in upholding the convictions:

> It will not do to say, as is now argued, that the only intent of these defendants was to prevent injury to the Russian cause. Men must be held to have intended, and to be accountable for, the effects their acts were likely to produce.[40]

Justice Holmes, joined by Justice Brandeis, dissented fervently. They did not believe that Jacob Abrams and his codefendants had created any "clear and present danger" to the war effort. In this dissent, Holmes articulated the "marketplace of ideas" philosophy, a philosophy commonly invoked throughout the remainder of the twentieth century in defense of the First Amendment and freedom of expression. Justice Holmes wrote

> In this case sentences of twenty years imprisonment have been imposed for the publishing of two leaflets that I believe the defendants had as much right to publish as the Government has to publish the Constitution now vainly invoked by them. . . .
>
> But when men have realized that time has upset many fighting faiths, they may come to believe even more than the very foundations of their own beliefs that the ultimate good desired is better reached by free trade in ideas—that the best test of truth is the power of the thought to get itself accepted in the competition of the market, and that truth is the only ground upon which their wishes can be safely carried out.[41]

That dissenting opinion, written with Holmesian power and grace, had greater longer-term impact than it had for Abrams and others who didn't blindly support the waging of World War I by the United. States. Abrams and about 2,000 other dissenters went to prison. This meant that the First Amendment guaranteeing freedom of speech and press meant much less when Holmes wrote those stirring words than it came to mean later in the twentieth century.

Part of the problem was the wording of the First Amendment itself. It said, "Congress shall make no law . . . abridging the freedom of speech, or of the press. . . ." It did *not* say, for example, "New York shall make no law. . . ." In a time of World War I–related superpatriotism and eagerness to stamp out radicals and dissenters, New York passed a statute forbidding "criminal anarchy," defined as the doctrine "that organized government should be overthrown by force or violence, or by assassination of any of the officials of government, or by any other means." Benjamin Gitlow and some other radicals had circulated a pamphlet, *The Left Wing Manifesto,* which urged "revolutionary mass action" to create a government of Communist Socialism.[42]

A jury convicted Gitlow of attempting to overthrow a government under the New York statute, and the Supreme Court upheld his conviction. Gitlow was still in prison during the early 1930s. Although Ben Gitlow paid a heavy price, his name is on the Supreme Court decision known as *Gitlow v. New York* (1925),[43] a decision in which the Court for the first time declared that the First Amendment applied to the states, not merely to the federal government. The Court read the words of the Fourteenth Amendment, adopted in 1868 after the Civil War to protect the rights of newly freed slaves, to include the provisions of the First Amendment. The Fourteenth Amendment to the Constitution says, in part, "No *State* shall make or enforce any law which shall abridge the privileges or immunities of citizens of the United States; nor shall any *State* deprive any person of life, liberty or property, without due process of law; nor deny to any person within its jurisdiction the equal protection of the laws."[44]

Supreme Court Justice Sanford wrote the decision in *Gitlow v. New York,* holding that "freedoms of speech and press—which are protected by the First Amendment from abridgment by Congress—are among the fundamental rights and 'liberties' protected by the due process clause of the Fourteenth Amendment from impairment by the states."[45] This reasoning helped *nationalize* the First Amendment, enabling judges to make it apply across the nation. In 1931, the U.S. Supreme Court's famous decision in *Near v. Minnesota* prevented the city of Minneapolis from halting publication of *The Saturday Press,* a notorious "smear sheet." *The Saturday Press* published charges that racketeering, gambling, and bootlegging were allowed by corrupt law enforcement agencies. The paper, published by J. M. Near and Howard Guilford, expressed contempt and loathing for both Catholics and Jews.[46]

In arguably the Supreme Court's most important First Amendment decision, Chief Justice Charles Evans Hughes denounced prepublication censorship, defining prior restraint as "the essence of censorship."[47] Hughes did not say there could *never* be prior restraint where discussions of government or literature were concerned. He wrote that prior restraint could be used in exceptional cases, such as preventing obstruction of recruiting, halting publications about troop movements in wartime, or stopping incitements to violence and forcible overthrow of government. And further, "the primary requirements of decency may be enforced against obscene publications."[48] Despite these exceptions to the general rule of "no prior restraint," *Near v. Minnesota* provided a substantial underpinning as precedent for a famous Supreme Court decision in 1971 known as the Pentagon Papers case.[49] In that decision, the Supreme Court again ruled against prior restraint.

Efforts to use the First Amendment as a rationale for protecting expression may not have worked to protect dissenters during World War I. Even so, the decisions previously mentioned—*Schenck v. United States* (1919) and *Abrams v. United States* (1919)—set the stage for *Gitlow v. New York* (1925) and *Near v. Minnesota* (1931), cases that expanded the First Amendment to make it applicable to the states. In American law, history matters when it is ennobled as legal precedent protecting and increasing freedom of expression.

Postal Control and the *Milwaukee Leader*

Shortly before the beginning of World War I, broad powers for press control fell into the hands of postmaster Albert S. Burleson. Burleson had the authority to determine what could and what could not be sent through the second-class mails, and he used that authority not wisely but well. The post office activities used to control the press were sanctioned by the Espionage Act of 1917.

The extent of the post office's activities to control "disloyal" publications was substantial. An estimated seventy-five newspapers had been interfered with by the post office by mid-1918, a professor wrote in the magazine *Contemporary Review*, and forty-five of those were socialist papers. Four were suspended, and many others continued only because they agreed not to comment on the war.[50]

The postmaster general's wartime activities ultimately were upheld as legal by a 1921 decision of the Supreme Court of the United States.[51] Even though publications that had their second-class privileges withdrawn had the right to judicial review, the court battles were often so drawn out as to be ruinous to the publishers. The socialist *New York Call* lost its privileges in November 1917, but its court fight did not end until March 1921, when the Supreme Court upheld the withdrawal of mailing privileges from the *Milwaukee Leader*.

The denial of second-class rates did not mean that publications were barred completely from the mails. For a publication that depended on circulation by mail, however, the higher cost of third-class or first-class rates was prohibitive. Second-class rates were eight to fifteen times lower than third-class for printed matter.[52]

As John Lofton noted in his book, *The Press as Guardian of the First Amendment*, "Not only did the *Leader* lose its second-class rate, but the paper was deprived of the right to receive or send first class mail. The withholding of first class mail caused the *Leader* to lose $70,000 in subscription money and $50,000 in local and national advertising. The paper lost approximately fifteen thousand subscribers."[53]

Victor Berger was an important man for a variety of reasons. Born in Austria in 1860, he came to the United States at the age of eighteen. Over the years, he helped found the Socialist party in the United States; was editor of the German-language newspaper, the *Milwaukee Leader*; and was a member of Congress from 1911 to 1913, the first Socialist to serve in Congress. Berger opposed U.S. involvement in World War I like many other Americans. However, as Zechariah Chafee, Jr., noted, "Unlike the great majority of Americans, Berger and other Socialists did not consider the German submarine campaign of February, 1917, a sufficient reason for changing their minds, but maintained that war was justified only in case of invasion."[54]

In October 1917, the third assistant postmaster general withdrew second-class mail privileges from Berger's *Milwaukee Leader*. The *Leader* fought the withdrawal in court, but the U.S. government countered with articles and editorials published in the *Leader* that the post office claimed clearly violated the Espionage Act.

One government exhibit against the *Leader* included a Berger editorial captioned "War and Insanity," which began with this claim: "For the first time, an army has

Figure 11–4   Victor Berger, editor of the *Milwaukee Leader*, opposed U.S. involvement in World War I. (State Historical Society of Wisconsin)

been forced to provide a field insane asylum." Quoting a neurologist, Berger's editorial continued:

> In the present war the number [of cases of battle-induced insanity] frequently reaches 40 to the 1,000 men. Think of it! An army of 1,000,000 men might have 40,000 insane—more than are housed today in all the state hospitals of Illinois, Ohio and Indiana.
>
> It is said that in France there are certain closed cars which are used for the purpose of transporting the insane away from the front, and that there are sometimes long trains made up exclusively of these.[55]

Other newspapers rarely came to the defense of Victor Berger and his *Milwaukee Leader*, and often they seemed to be cheering efforts to keep his newspaper out of the mails. In January 1918, during some of the early actions against publications suspected of being opposed to the war or otherwise "disloyal," the *New York Times* editorially criticized Berger and seemed to ask for harsh enforcement of the Espionage Act. The *Times* approved of a court of appeals decision that upheld the power of the postmaster general to withhold second-class mailing privileges from newspapers he saw as "seditious." The editorial said

> Now . . . Victor Berger will probably be more convinced than ever that our government is not a democracy. The Socialist ex-Representative reached that conclusion when the United States Supreme Court declared the draft law constitutional, and in his paper, [t]he *Milwaukee Leader*, expressed his opinion with what some editors would regard as rather dangerous frankness.[56]

After having wreaked havoc on the *Milwaukee Leader* by manipulating its powers over the mails, the federal government then moved against the *Leader*'s editor. In February 1918, Berger and four other Socialists were indicted for conspiracy to violate the Espionage Act of 1917. In that time of war hysteria, Berger was convicted. Berger's conviction was reversed early in 1921—more than two years after the end of the war—because Judge Kennesaw Mountain Landis (later the commissioner of baseball)—had been obviously prejudiced against Berger and his codefendants. Landis had made derogatory remarks about German Americans during the trial. After the trial, Landis was said to have expressed regrets that the law did not permit him "to have Berger lined up against a wall and shot."[57]

Further, even though Berger was reelected to Congress in 1918 while under indictment for a supposed violation of the Espionage Act, Congress refused to seat him. As Lofton showed, major newspapers had no compunctions about denouncing Berger; evidently, freedom of the press extended only far enough to permit editors such as Berger to agree with those worthy publications about the rightness of World War I. The *New York Times* said that Berger's contentions that he should be seated in Congress had no merit. The *Boston Transcript*, Lofton reported, even endorsed an American Legion resolution calling for Berger to be deported.[58]

Propaganda and the Committee on Public Information

World War I brought with it not only legislation silencing the press but an active propaganda effort promoting American war policy. In April 1917, President Wilson established the Committee on Public Information. Serving on the committee were the civilian director, former newspaperman George Creel—who was paid $8,000 annually for his efforts—and the secretaries of the departments of war, navy, and state. The total cost of the committee's effort came to about $4.5 million, financed from a fund granted to the President for the general defense of the country and by admission fees for committee exhibits and films shown to the public.

The Creel committee's tasks were to change antiwar attitudes to enthusiasm for an organized military operation and to intensify a general feeling of national solidarity.

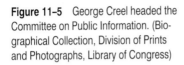

Figure 11–5   George Creel headed the Committee on Public Information. (Biographical Collection, Division of Prints and Photographs, Library of Congress)

In the two years of its existence, the committee mailed 6,000 news releases that generated about 20,000 columns of newsprint each week. It also published an official daily bulletin with a circulation of about 118,000 and sponsored 75,000 speakers who in the small towns of America "roused the righteous wrath" of U.S. citizens toward the Germans.[59]

The Creel committee also established a foreign-language division, which monitored foreign-language newspapers and translated pamphlets into other languages; published a newsletter for schools, *The National School Service*; supported the creation of propaganda films; developed cartoons; created posters supporting the war effort; solicited more than $1.5 million in free advertising in magazines, trade journals, and newspapers; and developed an extensive propaganda effort abroad. John

Mock and Cedrick Larson, who wrote a comprehensive history of the committee's efforts, described the pervasiveness of their approach:

> And every item of war news they [a rural family] saw—in the county weekly, in magazines, or in the city daily picked up occasionally in the general store—was not merely officially approved information but precisely the same kind that millions of their fellow citizens were getting at the same moment. Every war story had been censored somewhere along the line—at the source, in transit, or in the newspaper office with "voluntary" rules issued by the CPI. . . . Patriotic advertising in all of these papers had been prepared by the CPI. . . . Cartoons were those inspired by the Committee staff. At the state fair the family viewed war exhibits under Committee sponsorship, and the movies at the county seat began with one of the Committee's patriotic films and paused briefly for oratory by one of the Committee's Four Minute Men, who had gained his ideas for the talk from the Committee's "suggestions."
>
> At the township school the children saw war photographs issued by the Committee. . . . The postoffice bulletin board was adorned with copies of the Committee's *Official Bulletin,* and posters in the general store and on telephone poles up and down the countryside were those designed by the Committee's artists. . . . On Sunday the pastor thanked Providence for blessings that had been listed by one of the Committee's copywriters.[60]

Creel's appointment was viewed with skepticism by editors, both those on the right and those on the left. Before the war, as a writer for the *Denver Post* and an editor of the *Rocky Mountain News,* Creel vehemently criticized mining companies and the working conditions of miners. Staunch Republican editors accused him of being a socialist and others accused him of being a censor. The *New York Times* described Creel's career prior to the war as "turbulent" and expressed doubt that "he is qualified for any position of authority over the press."[61]

Despite such criticisms, Creel successfully orchestrated press coverage of the war and the effort to positively influence public opinion. In addition to publishing news releases, school bulletins, and other printed materials, he organized exhibits of war and trophies captured from the Germans and charged the public admission to view them. Creel was assisted in his efforts by a variety of liberal, reform-minded journalists and intellectuals, who feared that German militarists posed a new threat to democracy.[62] Charles Dana Gibson designed posters in support of the war that were based on his popular Gibson Girls. Professors from prestigious universities such as the University of Chicago, the University of Illinois, and Columbia University wrote pamphlets and made speeches for the committee. Film stars such as Mary Pickford and Douglas Fairbanks sold liberty bonds.

Within two months after he was appointed, Creel issued regulations to the press requesting voluntary cooperation. He organized news into three categories: "dangerous," or not to be published, news that included information about military maneuvers and threats against the President; "questionable" news that involved technical inventions and rumors, to be published with caution and preferably with the approval of the committee; and "routine" news that required no authorization.

Press reaction varied. The Pittsburgh Press Club organized an intelligence bureau to disseminate war news and to monitor the patriotism of newspapers in twenty-seven Pennsylvania counties. The Hearst papers and the *Washington Post*

Figure 11–6   This 1918 Joseph Pennell poster exhorted citizens to buy bonds to support the war. (Division of Prints and Photographs, Library of Congress Collection)

violated the regulations quite consistently. Cooperation was the rule, however, rather than the exception.

Media Reaction to the War

The United States remained neutral from 1914 until 1917, although it aided the allies, particularly Britain, during the first three years. In 1917, when the German government threatened to sink American ships and to engage Mexico on its side, President Woodrow Wilson asked Congress to declare war. Journalists reacted in various ways.

Just a few of their reactions are described in the following: a biographical sketch of the liberal journalist Walter Lippmann, a discussion of the reaction of major metropolitan newspapers, and a sketch of the socialist publication, *The Masses.*

Walter Lippmann and the Noble Cause

The reaction of the typical liberal journalist to the war was exactly the reaction of Walter Lippmann, a brilliant Harvard graduate who as a college student claimed to be a socialist and who, at the time war was declared, was an editor of the *New Republic*, a liberal journal of opinion financed by benefactors, rather than by advertising. In

·LIFE·   679

His Mother. HERE HE IS, SIR

Figure 11–7   This Charles Dana Gibson drawing appeared in an April 1917 issue of *Life*. In this drawing the mother gives her son to Uncle Sam. (Division of Prints and Photographs, Library of Congress Collection)

1914, Lippmann claimed that wars stemmed from colonialism and imperialism and that the United States should not become involved in Europe's quarrels. He claimed that ignorant rulers led people to war. However, in 1917, on the eve of Wilson's declaration, Lippmann persuaded himself that the war was a noble cause.

> "We are living and shall live all our lives now in a revolutionary world," he wrote the week after America went to war. There would be a "transvaluation of values as radical as anything in the history of intellect." Concepts like liberty, equality and democracy would have to be reexamined "as fearlessly as religious dogmas were in the nineteenth century."[63]

Lippmann's newly found zeal was reflected in his desire to help in the war. He applied for an exemption from selective service and went to work for Secretary of War Newton D. Baker, temporarily severing his ties to the *New Republic*. Although Lippmann promoted the war under Baker's supervision, he was disturbed by the government's censorship of socialist publications. He advocated benign neglect of socialist journalists, fearing censorship would create bitter enemies and leave ugly scars. He suggested censorship should not be left to those who might be intolerant, a comment aimed at George Creel, whom Lippmann did not trust. However, Lippmann also noted that "in the interest of the war it is necessary to sacrifice some" free speech.[64]

Although he had little impact on preventive censorship or the persecution of socialist journals, Lippmann was highly regarded by Wilson and his cabinet and helped draft the President's Fourteen Points, an initial peace proposal. He then joined a group of intellectuals on a special inquiry board and finally traveled to Europe with the Military Intelligence Branch, where he wrote propaganda leaflets to be dropped behind enemy lines. At the peace talks in Paris, he became discouraged by what he regarded as impossible demands by the Allies in carving up European nations, as well as by Wilson's capitulation, and he returned to the United States to argue against Wilson's proposal for the League of Nations. He returned to the *New Republic* and in 1922 joined Pulitzer's *New York World*, which he later edited. At the *World*, Lippmann became widely known as an editorialist and columnist. Lippmann's ardor in supporting the war and his idealism about extending democracy to all nations of the world ended in disillusionment. His later antipathy toward war was apparent in an extensive attack on President Lyndon Johnson's military commitments in Vietnam in the 1960s.

If Lippmann, whose mentor was the old muckraker and socialist radical Lincoln Steffens, could move from a position of antiwar activist to prowar advocate, serving the cause with vigor and enthusiasm, one might wonder about the position of editors who had not objected so greatly in 1914.

Metropolitan Newspapers and the Status Quo

Initial reaction to war in Europe generally was one of dismay coupled with a hands-off policy. The *Detroit Free Press* treated the war as a European phenomenon until German submarines began to attack American shipping. When Wilson declared war, the *Free Press* editorialized that this was a war not against the German peoples, but a war against the "barbarous governmental regime of Berlin."[65] Others were not so generous. The *New York Times* and the *Literary Digest* urged readers to report "any utterances or writings that appeared seditious."[66]

Newspaper attitudes toward censorship varied. When the Espionage Act was first introduced in Congress, many newspapers fought the inclusion of a specific censorship amendment. Once that amendment was eliminated, however, few seemed to recognize the significance of the act itself and the possible impact of the Sedition Amendment. Although cooperation with George Creel's Committee on Public Information was, on the surface, voluntary, Creel certainly had the legislation he needed to back up any requests he made to newspapers that violated his regulations.

E. W. Scripps' chain of newspapers, before the beginning of the war, advocated no U.S. involvement but supported the allies. The Hearst papers heartily opposed the war. Although most newspapers were not overjoyed at the prospect of Creel's regulations, they generally submitted to them.

The technical aspects of coverage were greatly enlarged, and although newspapers probably could not be commended for impartiality and calm reason on the home front (they tended to whip up fear against "hordes of invading Huns"), they could be praised for the zeal with which they pursued coverage of foreign fronts against great censorship odds.

A Challenge to the Existing Order

Some regarded *The Masses* as a socialist rag, others as the intellectual guardian of its time, and still others as simply a vehicle for radical thought and writing. Many of the writers for *The Masses,* including John Reed and Louise Bryant, subjects of the film *Reds;* the poet Carl Sandburg; Upton Sinclair, author of *The Jungle;* and even, for a time, Walter Lippmann, spent the early teen years of the century discussing radical politics in Mabel Dodge's fashionable Greenwich Village flat. Mabel Dodge, not an artist or writer herself, collected radicals as someone else might collect statues or paintings. Those in her coterie included anarchist Emma Goldman, muckraker Lincoln Steffens, people like Lippmann, other intellectuals like Reed—who never abandoned his faith in the Communist party—and Max Eastman, who edited *The Masses* and whose disillusionment came with Stalin's purges in Russia in the 1930s.

Eastman, a graduate of Williams College in Massachusetts and a professor of logic at Columbia, began editing *The Masses* in 1912. He first faced the task of clearing up the magazine's debt. A man of great personal force, Eastman successfully used his charm to recruit money from writers as well as little old ladies who knew next to nothing about socialism but regarded him as a romantic poet.

Under Eastman's leadership, *The Masses* became a successful publication from 1913 to 1916. The magazine published poetry, art, and literature as well as socialist-oriented political articles. Eastman attempted to publish anything he considered interesting that did not compromise *The Masses'* revolutionary character. He wrote in his first editorial notice:

> We plan a radical change of policy for *The Masses,* and we appeal to our subscribers and contributors to help us put it through. . . .

We are going to make *The Masses* a *popular* Socialist magazine—a magazine of pictures and lively writing.

Humorous, serious, illustrative and decorative pictures of a stimulating kind. There are no magazines in America which measure up in radical art and freedom of expression to the foreign satirical journals. We think we can produce one, and we have on our staff eight of the best known artists and illustrators in the country ready to contribute to it their most individual work.[67]

The Masses dealt with the separation of capital and labor by covering labor strikes in a different vein than did metropolitan dailies. In June 1914, Eastman described the Colorado state militia attack on a tent colony of striking miner families:

I put the ravages of that black orgy of April 20th, when a frail, fluttering tent city in the meadow, the dwelling place of 120 women and 273 children, was riddled to shreds without a second's warning, and then fired by coal-oil torches with the bullets still raining and the victims screaming in their shallow holes of refuge, or crawling away on their bellies through the fields—I put that crime, not upon its perpetrators, who are savage, but upon the gentlemen of noble leisure who hired them to this service.[68]

The Masses could not continue in this vein without legal difficulty. The first lawsuit against the magazine occurred after *The Masses* accused the Associated Press of having suppressed a West Virginia strike at the request of the strikers' employers.

Figure 11–8 This antiwar drawing appeared in *The Masses* in 1914. (Division of Prints and Photographs, Library of Congress Collection)

John Reed Writes about Revolution

No matter what one thinks of Bolshevism, it is undeniable that the Russian Revolution is one of the great events of human history, and the rise of the Bolsheviki a phenomenon of world-wide importance. Just as historians search the records for the minutest details of the story of the Paris Commune, so they will want to know what happened in Petrograd in November, 1917, the spirit which animated the people, and how the leaders looked, talked and acted. It is with this in view that I have written this book.

In the struggle my sympathies were not neutral. But in telling the story of those great days I have tried to see events with the eye of a conscientious reporter, interested in setting down the truth.

—John Reed, in the introduction to *Ten Days That Shook the World*, January 1, 1919

Eastman and a second editor were sued for criminal libel, pleaded not guilty, and were released on $1,000 bail. Eventually, the Associated Press dropped the action.

Nevertheless, *The Masses'* difficulties with the legal system continued. Its support of contraception, free love, and feminism drew unkind attention from the post office, and it had difficulty retaining its postal permit. The difficulty increased as Eastman argued against intervention in World War I. *The Masses* argued that revolution was necessary to rout the capitalists, but that World War I was merely a struggle between imperial powers, not a revolution aimed at freeing the proletariat, or the worker. After subsequent attacks on the conscription act (the draft), Eastman and four other editors were indicted under the Espionage Act. Twice, *The Masses'* editors went to trial. Both trials ended in hung juries, but in August 1917 *The Masses* lost its mailing privileges, which forced the editors to suspend publication.

Although *The Masses* could no longer publish, Eastman was not silenced and joined with his sister to publish the *Liberator*. In 1922, Eastman traveled to the Soviet Union, where he was disillusioned by what he termed "the misuse of the sacred scriptures of Marxism. . . . Instead of liberating the mind of man, the Bolshevik Revolution locked it into a state's prison tighter than ever before."[69] When Eastman returned to the United States, he was boycotted not only by those who opposed socialism but also by his friends who could not accept his disillusionment. They branded him a traitor to the cause. In the 1930s, Eastman accused the *New York Times'* correspondent, Walter Duranty, of obscuring the truth about famines, liquidations, and purges within Stalinist Russia. In the late 1930s, when Stalin formed a pact with Adolf Hitler of Germany, others joined in Eastman's disillusionment, and he regained some prestige within the community of writers. Ironically, he worked as a roving editor for the conservative *Reader's Digest*. He continued writing until his death in 1969 and despite his extensive political involvement, he considered his best writing to be two nonpolitical books: *The Enjoyment of Poetry* and *The Enjoyment of Laughter*.[70]

Figure 11-9   This John Sloan drawing appeared in the January 1914 issue of *The Masses* to illustrate "Class War in Colorado." (Division of Prints and Photographs, Library of Congress Collection)

Correspondents at the Front

By World War I, physical conditions had improved for war correspondents, but they faced new challenges of censorship not only from their home governments but from foreign governments as well. During the Spanish-American War, correspondents faced great physical hardships—lack of food, lack of proper quarters, difficulty in obtaining physical access to the places the war was being fought. By World War I, some of these problems were alleviated. Correspondents were well fed and were housed in some of Europe's best hotels.[71]

Although transportation was available, the extensive rerouting of trains and long-distance journeys, sometimes by steamer, proved exhausting to war correspondents. Nonetheless, their biggest problem was the distance of press headquarters from the front and the problems of censorship encountered with the various governments involved. At the very beginning of the war, correspondents moved freely in covering the advance of German armies, but by the fall of 1914 correspondents were kept entirely away from military zones. This ban lasted until April 1915, when the British began to allow a few American reporters behind the lines. Eventually French, Austrian, and German governments also provided glimpses of the front, but the movements of correspondents were strictly regulated. In addition to restricting the correspondents' movements, governments also strictly regulated their copy. In Britain, the willingness of publishers to accept severe controls brought them social prestige and political power, but it also undermined the faith of the public in the press.[72] In 1915, Theodore Roosevelt wrote a letter to the British foreign secretary, claiming that British and French controls of the press were so tight that the only way American reporters could get information was from Germany. Roosevelt told the foreign minister that censorship was hurting Britain's cause in the United States.[73]

One of the most well known American correspondents was Richard Harding Davis, who sailed on the *Lusitania* to Europe in 1914 at the outset of the war. Davis, a famous reporter during the Spanish-American War, went straight to Brussels to report the entrance of the German army into the city.

Davis encountered severe German restrictions in reporting the war and was subjected to arrest and overnight imprisonment after being accused of being a British officer. After the British and French also refused to let him near the front, Davis returned home. "I'm not about to write sidelights," he said. Other correspondents, acting in violation of censorship, had no choice. They were returned home. Some, however, including reporters for the *New York Times*, managed to elude the censors by writing in code. American ingenuity allowed a few uncensored stories to slip through the lines.

After America's entrance into the war, U.S. regulation of correspondents abroad represented a bureaucratic nightmare. Stringent regulations were imposed and reporters who did not cooperate made no progress. Some, like Heywood Broun, returned to New York in 1918, disgusted with the lack of access to information.

Marguerite Harrison: Correspondent, Spy

On the domestic front, many reporters worked in cooperation with the Committee on Public Information. For Marguerite Harrison, a society woman hired at the *Baltimore Sun* to use her connections to improve the society page, the war expanded opportunities to cover hard news. After the war, she went abroad as a journalist and a spy. She was hired part-time at the *Sun* for $16 a week. Within two years her pay increased to $20 a week, and through sheer initiative she quickly became the paper's music and drama critic. Once the United States declared war, Harrison was assigned to cover war-preparedness activities in Baltimore. Harrison described the *Sun*'s efforts to cooperate with the Creel Committee:

> One of the first steps in our mobilization was the organization of a bureau under George Creel for the purpose of directing and co-ordinating our propaganda and publicity services. Every newspaper in the country was virtually mobilized to help win the war.

> News still came first, of course, but the creation of war sentiment and patriotic
> enthusiasm was a close second in importance. Mr. Kent [the managing editor] suggested
> that I write a series of articles calculated to stimulate enlistment and patriotic activities.[74]

Harrison wrote many war-related features, gaining herself a byline. Her articles on camouflage, ship building, and labor disputes, and a series on immigration earned her recognition. Throughout her stories, she conveyed an underlying theme of women's competence in heavy industrial jobs. During the summer of 1918, Harrison decided that she wanted to cover the war in Europe, but at the last minute was denied official permission. In September, she entered the intelligence service in order to gain access to "a war-torn Europe that was off-limits to most civilians."

Harrison took a pay cut when she was commissioned as a captain by the Military Intelligence Division. Although the war ended in November 1918, she was sent to Europe to collect cultural, social, and economic data from postwar Germany. Because of her social position, she was able to move among the upper classes of society in Berlin and Frankfurt. She interviewed many leaders in Germany and Poland, and she made contacts as well among the leaders of the extreme left, including the Russian Bolsheviks.

After returning to Baltimore in 1919, Harrison soon left the United States once again—this time for Russia. While in Russia, she traveled with journalist's credentials from the *Baltimore Sun*, the *New York Evening Post*, and the Associated Press. The AP transmitted Military Intelligence Division funds and messages to Harrison during her stay in Russia.[75]

Harrison interviewed Trotsky and Lenin and traveled throughout much of Russia before she was arrested in April 1920. She was imprisoned in Lubjanka No. 2, the main prison for espionage cases or political prisoners. After ten months in Soviet prisons, she was released in July 1921. She continued her work as a journalist, traveling and producing filmed documentaries. Her work as a journalist in the post–World War I period illustrates the close cooperation during the early twentieth century

▼

The March into Brussels

BRUSSELS, FRIDAY, AUGUST 21, 2 P.M.—The entrance of the German army into Brussels has lost the human quality. It was lost as soon as the three soldiers who led the army bicycled into the Boulevard du Regent and asked the way to the Gare du Nord. When they passed the human note passed with them. . . .

For seven hours the army passed in such solid columns that not once might a taxicab or trolley car pass through the city. Like a river of steel it flowed, gray and ghostlike. Then, as dusk came and thousands of horses' hoofs and thousands of iron boots continued to tramp forward, they struck tiny sparks from the stones, but the horses and the men who beat out the sparks were invisible.

—Richard Harding Davis, *London News Chronicle*

between government and journalists—cooperation which would be considered unacceptable after World War II. The ties between government and journalists just after World War I even involved an organization as massive as the Associated Press in U.S. espionage activities.

Electronic Media's Debut

Technological inroads toward developing radio telephony, as it was called, began as early as 1870, and by the close of World War I, the instruments were ready. In the 1870s, a British scientist named James Clerk-Maxwell discovered that the transmission of radio waves was theoretically possible, and shortly after that a German scientist, Heinrich Hertz, showed that energy actually could be transmitted without connecting wires between two points. Thrilled with the possibility of implementing Hertz's discovery was an Italian youth, Guglielmo Marconi, who saw radio as a means of supplementing or replacing telegraphy. Because the Italians were not interested in his experiments, he went to London, where the British government, because of its colonial empire, was very much interested in the development of improved means of communication.[76]

In 1897, he secured the necessary patents and, backed by English investors, formed the Marconi Wireless and Signal Company. His achievements in areas of the world where it was impossible to lay telegraph wires attracted international attention and resulted in an international radio conference in Germany in 1903.

By the early twentieth century, some pioneering individuals envisioned using wireless telephony to transmit the human voice and music. On Christmas Eve, 1906, Reginald A. Fessenden sent music and voice over the air to previously alerted amateurs and shipboard operators. At about the same time, Lee De Forest invented the audion tube, allowing the modulation and amplification of electrical currents and making small, reliable receivers possible. Prior to World War I and the subsequent corporate ventures into commercial broadcasting, a variety of amateurs broadcast music and other programming across the air waves, and at least four universities made use of the airwaves for educational broadcasting.[77]

Government and Industry Partnership

In 1912, Americans attended an international conference in London, in which the nations represented agreed that each would regulate the use of radio within its own territory. That same year, the U.S. Congress passed the Radio Act of 1912, requiring radio operators to obtain a license from the U.S. secretary of commerce and labor. The secretary issued licenses and frequencies nonselectively and to all comers.

World War I provided a boom in radio research. Wartime military needs provided more systematic, heavily financed research as well as the pooling of patents. Cooperative research between American Telephone and Telegraph, General Electric, and Westinghouse ultimately resulted in the technological sophistication of wireless telephony and the creation of the powerful RCA. Between 1914 and 1918, radio was strictly regulated by the U.S. Navy for use in ship-to-shore communications. During those same years, the navy became increasingly uncomfortable about the fact that a foreign company, British-owned American Marconi, was the sole supplier of most U.S. radio equipment. At the close of the war, the U.S. government applied pressure to General Electric chairman Owen D. Young to propose a new corporation to hold all American patents. General Electric created a $2.5 million fund to buy out American Marconi and, with American Telephone and Telegraph, United Fruit, and Westinghouse Electric, formed the Radio Corporation of America (RCA). David Sarnoff, who had risen from the position of radio operator to commercial manager of American Marconi, became the president of RCA. The companies operated under joint ownership until 1926, when AT&T withdrew from broadcasting.[78]

The creation of RCA and its pooling arrangement strongly affected the development of radio. In essence, the new alliance allowed its members to continue their wartime control over major radio patents. Radio historian Elaine Prostak wrote that the arrangement also "provided member corporations with strong financial bases, a public image of promoting national interest, and friendly relations with the federal government and the military." These factors put alliance members in an advantageous position to influence the field of domestic broadcasting in the 1920s.[79]

Going to the Movies

The modern film industry came of age during World War I, and the economics of war enabled the United States to move rapidly ahead of other countries in the development of film for a commercial audience. In France, Germany, Great Britain, and Italy, countries where film production had flourished, photographic supplies such as cotton, nitric acid, and sulphuric acid were diverted into the manufacture of explosives. Because U.S. involvement in the war was short and marginal compared to that of the European powers, American film producers were at a distinct advantage. The U.S. economy, stimulated by the war, provided a large domestic audience for films, and the industry was guided by a business expertise not available in other countries.[80]

The development of photography was essential to modern film, but people were fascinated with the concept of moving images long before the technology to support photography was developed. The Greeks passed on the concept of the projected illuminated image to the Arabs, and later Leonardo da Vinci in Italy experimented with the camera obscura, or a room with a pin hole that permitted viewing an outside image on the opposite wall. A seventeenth-century Jesuit priest built a portable camera obscura: He added a candle, a lens, and glass slides with images, thereby creating a slide-show entertainment popular throughout Europe. Through the nineteenth century, various individuals developed increasingly sophisticated narrative slide shows.

The next step involved putting pictures on both sides of a wheel and spinning it, creating an optical toy called a Thaumatrope. Various advanced forms of the toy combined a shutter principle, light, and angled mirrors. In the late 1880s in Paris, the

▼
Thomas Edison (1847–1931)

"[T]here is not now and never has been subsequent to the year 1888 any motion picture film machine whatsoever of any relation to the screen art of today that is not descended by traceable steps from the Kinetoscope" (1926).

Although most people remember him for the light bulb, Thomas Edison also began the motion picture industry with the invention of the Kinetoscope. He patented his machine in 1891 and by 1899 had sold 973 of them, as well as films he himself created. *The Black Maria* was probably the earliest film studio, where Edison made films and did early film experiments.

Source: T. Ramsaye, *A Million and One Nights: A History of the Motion Picture,* Volume I (New York: Simon & Schuster, 1926); and R. Phillips, *Edison's Kinetoscope and Its Films: A History to 1896* (Westport, Conn.: Greenwood Press, 1997). (*Photo:* Division of Prints and Photographs, Library of Congress Collection)

Theatre Optique at the Musée Grevin presented stories projected on screen by shining a bright light through long strips of translucent material.

In 1837, Louis Daguerre invented the daguerreotype, which used burnished copper as a base and a thin, silvered negative emulsion with unexposed particles that could be washed away in solvent to create a positive plate. Although he earned a great deal of publicity, the process was limited because there was no way to make copies or prints, and subjects had to stand frozen for twenty to thirty minutes,

Figure 11–10 This 1896 lithograph depicts Edison's Vitascope. The *New York Herald* noted that the vitascope produced life-size pictures full of color that made "a thrilling show." (Division of Prints and Photographs, Library of Congress Collection)

the time required to expose a plate. In 1851, the process was replaced by wet plates, which took only two minutes to expose; by 1871, dry plates cut the time to seconds.

In 1878, Eadweard Muybridge achieved a semblance of motion by setting up a battery of cameras alongside a race track and pulling the shutters several intervals apart. It was only slightly later that the French physician and scientist Etienne Jules Marey devised a camera that produced twelve pictures a second on a single plate. In 1888, gelatin emulsions allowed the photographing of real movement. The production of celluloid began in 1888, another important development during the infancy of the moving picture industry.

From 1891 to 1894, Thomas Edison's labs developed and publicized a new entertainment machine, the Kinetoscope, which moved fifty-foot loops of film in less than a half minute over a series of spools. The machine was about the size and weight of an upright piano. In 1895, Louis and Auguste Lumière made portable equipment and carried their Cinematographe into Eastern Europe, the Far East, and the United States. The Cinematographe and competing machines soon earned a place in vaudeville programs across the United States.

At first, the novelty of captured motion rather than content was the primary focus of film productions, which were about a half minute long. Two American films, produced in 1903 by Edwin S. Porter, *Life of an American Fireman* and *The Great Train Robbery*, were about twelve minutes long and introduced editing techniques, which allowed the film to emerge as its own artistic form.

Films were instantly popular, and by 1907, 3,000 nickelodeons in America were attracting audiences. "There was no better place for this classically democratic phenomenon," wrote film historians Louis Giannetti and Scott Eyman:

> Here, immigrants who couldn't speak English and illiterate laborers attended a new invention, learning about their new land and its customs, transported by the magic of storytelling drama for the first time in their lives, many of them learning English bit by bit, word by word in the bargain. For millions, the movies were art, science, and schooling all in one.[81]

Edison retained significant control over the industry, using lawsuits to preserve and extend his control of patents. By 1908, he had persuaded the major competing companies to join with him in organizing the Motion Picture Patents Company. The members pooled sixteen patents for film, cameras, and projectors. The company secured an agreement with Eastman Kodak to monopolize raw film stock, and they firmly controlled distributors and exhibitors, blackballing those who broke the rules. At first, the pooling arrangement eliminated competition, but by 1912 independent firms, many begun by European immigrants, produced almost half the feature films and were experimenting with longer features and new techniques. During the politically charged late summer of 1912, the government charged the Motion Picture Patents Company with violating the 1890 Sherman Anti-Trust Act and in 1915 declared the group to be illegally restraining trade. By 1915, however, the independents had already gained considerable ground, attracting middle-class audiences by building larger theatres and producing longer, more expensive films.[82]

> All what I see wit' me own eyes I knows an' unnerstan's
> When I see movin pitchers of de far off, furrin' lan's
> Where de Hunks an' Ginnes come from—yer betcher life I knows
> Dat of all de lan's an' countries, 'taint no matter where yer goes
> Dis here country's got 'em beaten—take my oat dat ain't no kid—
> 'Cause we learned it from de movin' pitchers, me an' Maggie did.—

This anonymous poem by a newsboy in 1910 evoked an image of immigrant boys being uplifted by the movies, an impression popular among some civic leaders.[83]

The transition of ten-minute entertainments to "films" was accomplished by 1915, with David Wark Griffith's three-hour production, *The Birth of a Nation*. The film yielded $5 million on an investment of less than $100,000. The editing techniques, the full-story length, and the sensitive construction of visual images made the film an artistic milestone. However, the film also created great controversy because of its "outrageously racist" message. Nevertheless, "[l]ooking beyond the ever-widening social gulf between modern attitudes and those that were the norm in 1915, *The Birth of a Nation* remains a remarkable achievement," wrote Giannetti and Eyman. Griffith made later films, although none achieved the recognition of *Birth of a Nation*. Never a businessman, he suffered financial difficulty, and his inability to change with the changing times left him an embittered alcoholic.

From 1914 to 1916, a few independent distributors, such as the Paramount Group, gained power by contracting with producers such as Adolph Zukor for exclu-

▼

Review of *The Birth of a Nation*

"The Birth of a Nation," an elaborate new motion picture taken on an ambitious scale, was presented for the first time last evening at the Liberty Theatre. With the addition of much preliminary historical matter, it is a film version of some of the melodramatic and inflammatory material contained in "The Clansman," by Thomas Dixon.

A great deal might be said concerning the spirit revealed in Mr. Dixon's review of the unhappy chapter of Reconstruction and concerning the sorry service rendered by its plucking at old wounds. But of the film as a film, it may be reported simply that it is an impressive new illustration of the scope of the motion picture camera.

An extraordinarily large number of people enter into this historical pageant and some of the scenes are most effective. The civil war battle pictures, taken in panorama, represent enormous effort and achieve a striking degree of success. One interesting scene stages a reproduction of the auditorium of Ford's Theatre in Washington, and shows on the screen the murder of Lincoln. In terms of purely pictorial value the best work is done in those stretches of the film that follow the night riding of the men of the Ku-Klux Klan, who look like a company of avenging spectral crusaders sweeping along the moonlit roads.

The "Birth of a Nation," which was prepared for the screen under the direction of D. W. Griffith, takes a full evening for its unfolding and marks the advent of the two dollar movie. That is the price set for the more advantageous seats in the rear of the Liberty's auditorium.

It was at this same theatre that the stage version of "The Clansman" had a brief run a little more than nine years ago, as Mr. Dixon himself recalled in his curtain speech last evening in the interval between the two acts. Mr. Dixon also observed that he would have allowed none but the son of a Confederate soldier to direct the film version of "The Clansman."

—*New York Times,* Thursday, March 4, 1915

sive distribution of the producers' films. In the Paramount case, Zukor, unhappy about working for a distributor, bought out several Paramount partners, took control, and consolidated his power through block-booking. Block-booking required studios to "book" a number of "B"-grade films in order to obtain the popular "A" movies. The next step was to buy theatres and begin to establish vertical integration within the industry. Such was the beginning of the powerful studio system.[84]

Conclusion

The mass markets established at the end of the nineteenth century paved the way for additional types of mass publications in the beginning years of the twentieth century. Muckraking magazines—cheap, mass-circulation publications—targeted the growing wealth of the captains of industry and championed the rights of the laboring classes. Such championship, however, came with a call to the working class to adopt middle-class values and culture and to eschew violence whether it was initiated by corporate captains or labor organizers. The goal of the muckrakers was to restore what they viewed as essential order, similar to that which was prevalent in the early nineteenth century.

Newspapers grew in size and circulation during the same period, but their numbers peaked in 1909 when consolidation and cost factors decreased the number of competing newspapers within metropolitan areas. Newspapers were not immune from reform issues either. They attacked corruption, but when faced with labor issues in their own composing rooms, they tended to react as businessmen with a need to protect property and profit rather than as champions of reform. Truly mass-market publications, metropolitan newspapers relied increasingly on financial support through advertising.

World War I introduced new constraints on the publishing industry, as the post office attacked what it defined as "wayward publications" and as legislators banded together to assure unity by passing the Alien and Sedition Acts. Not since 1798 and the hated Federalist acts had the U.S. Congress passed such restrictive legislation. The effect of the regulations was compounded by propaganda efforts organized by George Creel's Committee on Public Information, a campaign by journalists as well as public officials to control information. Many of the techniques used by the committee became the basis for business and government efforts to manage public opinion.

Technological developments created a basis for radio and motion pictures. The U.S. economy fared better than the economies of European countries during World War I, and filmmakers took advantage of their position to further the motion picture industry, as feature films began to replace the short reels of the past. Although radio technology was advanced far enough to be adapted to commercial use, the vision of broadcasting to the general public—rather than simply ship-to-shore and amateur communications—had not emerged. Further, the government controlled radio technology during the war, fearful of how it might be used.

Endnotes

1. Arthur and Lila Weinberg, eds., *The Muckrakers* (New York: Simon & Schuster, 1961), p. xiii.

2. For an elaboration of this thesis, see David M. Chalmers, "The Muckrakers and the Growth of Corporate Power: A Study in Constructive Journalism," *American Journal of Economics and Sociology* 18 (April, 1959), pp. 295–311.

3. For a discussion of the demise of muckraking magazines, see Robert D. Reynolds, Jr., "The 1906 Campaign to Sway Muckraking Periodicals," *Journalism Quarterly* 56:3 (Autumn, 1979), pp. 513–20, 589.

4. John E. Semonche, "The *American Magazine* of 1906–15: Principle vs. Profit, *Journalism Quarterly* 40:1 (Spring, 1963), pp. 37–44, 86.

5. Fred F. Endres, "The Pre-Muckraking Days of *McClure's Magazine*, 1893–1901," *Journalism Quarterly* 55:1 (Spring, 1978), pp. 154–157. See also Jeanne G. Goldfarb, "*McClure's* in Fact and Legend: Muckraking the Muckraker Historians," master's thesis, University of Kansas, December 1970.

6. Arthur Warren, "Philip D. Armour," *McClure's* (February, 1894), p. 260, cited in Endres, "Pre-Muckraking Days of *McClure's*, p. 154.

7. Endres, "Pre-Muckraking Days of *McClure's*," p. 156.

8. *McClure's*, July 1894, p. 169.

9. *McClure's*, October 1897, p. 1101, cited in Endres, "Pre-Muckraking Days of *McClure's*."

10. *McClure's*, June 1898, p. 100.

11. *McClure's*, June 1898, p. 206.

12. *McClure's*, September 1898, p. 481.

13. Endres, "Pre-Muckraking Days of *McClure's*," pp. 156–57.

14. Harold S. Wilson, McClure's Magazine *and the Muckrakers* (Princeton, N.J.: Princeton University Press, 1970), p. 74.

15. Wilson, McClure's Magazine, p. 89.

16. Wilson, McClure's Magazine, p. 146.

17. George Britt, *Forty Years—Forty Millions, the Career of Frank A. Munsey.* (New York: Farrar & Rinehart, 1935), p. 17.

18. Britt, *Forty Years—Forty Millions*, p. 81.

19. Oswald Garrison Villard, *Some Newspapers and Newspaper-Men* (New York: Alfred A. Knopf, 1923), p. 81.

20. Lincoln Steffens to his father, June 3, 1906, in *The Letters of Lincoln Steffens*, 1:176, 173–74, cited in Semonche, "The 'American Magazine' of 1906–15," *Journalism Quarterly*, pp. 36–44, 86.

21. From John S. Phillips to William Kent, Kent papers collection, cited in Semonche, "The 'American Magazine' of 1906–15," p. 38.

22. Ernest C. Hynds, *American Newspapers in the 1980s* (New York: Hastings House, 1980), p. 75.

23. Sally Foreman Griffith, *Home Town News: William Allen White and the Emporia Gazette* (New York: Oxford University Press, 1989), pp. 82–85.

24. Quoted in "The Advertiser," *Newspaper Maker* (March 5, 1986), p. 3, as cited in Lawson, *Truth in Publishing: Federal Regulation of the Press's Business Practices, 1880–1920* (Carbondale: Southern Illinois University Press, 1993), p. 36.

25. Linda Lawson, *Truth in Publishing.*

26. See Lawson, *Truth in Publishing*, "Publicity as an Antidote for Press Abuses," pp. 141–51.

27. David Nasaw, "The Newsies," *Children of the City: At Work and at Play*, (Garden City, N.Y.: Anchor Press/Doubleday, 1985), chap. 5, p. 65.

28. Nasaw, "The Newsies," p. 86.

29. John Higham, *Strangers in the Land* (New York: Atheneum, 1972) p. 196.

30. John D. Stevens, *Shaping the First Amendment: Development of Free Expression* (Beverly Hills: Sage, 1982), p. 46.

31. Stevens, *Shaping the First Amendment*, p. 45.

32. Lauren Kessler, *The Dissident Press* (Beverly Hills: Sage, 1984), pp. 139, 140.

33. Harold L. Nelson and Dwight Teeter, Jr., *Law of Mass Communications*, 5th ed. (New York: The Foundation Press, 1982), p. 38.

34. Stevens, *Shaping the First Amendment*, p. 49.

35. 249 U.S. 47, 39 S.Ct. 247 (1919). For an alternative view on the Schenck case, see Jeremy Cohen, *Congress Shall Make No Law* (Ames: Iowa State University Press, 1989). Cohen argued that the Schenck case was not decided on First Amendment considerations, but by a Court steeped in tradition expressed as a national intolerance for socialists.

36. Leaflet on file in the National Archives.

37. National Archives.

38. *Schenck v. United States*, 249 U.S. 47, 52, 39 S. Ct. 247, 249 (1919).

39. U.S. Statutes at Large, Vol. XL, 553ff.

40. *Abrams v. United States*, 250 U.S. 616, 621, 40 S. Ct. 17, 19 (1919).

41. 250 U.S. 616, 629, 40 S. Ct. 17, 22 (1919).

42. Zechariah Chafee, Jr., *Free Speech in the United States* (Cambridge, Mass.: Harvard, 1964) [6th printing of 1941 ed.], pp. 318–325.

43. *Gitlow v. New York,* 268 U.S. 652, 666, 45 S. Ct. 625, 630 (1925).

44. U.S. Constitution, Fourteenth Amendment, Section 1. Emphasis added.

45. *Gitlow v. New York,* 268 U.S. 652, 672, 45 S. Ct. 625, 632 (1925).

46. *Near v. Minnesota ex rel. Olson,* 283 U.S. 697, 51 S. Ct. 625 (1931); Fred W. Friendly, *Minnesota Rag* (New York, 1981), and Paul L. Murphy, "*Near v. Minnesota* in the Context of Historical Developments, 66 *Minnesota Law Review* 95 (November, 1981).

47. *Near v. Minnesota ex rel. Olson,* 283 U.S. 697, 713, 51 S. Ct. 625, 630 (1931).

48. *Near v. Minnesota ex rel. Olson,* 283 U.S. at 716, 51 S. Ct. at 631 (1931).

49. *New York Times v. United States,* 403 U.S. 713, 91 S. Ct. 2140 (1971). See also Don R. Pember, "The Pentagon Papers: More Questions Than Answers, *Journalism Quarterly* 48:3 (Autumn, 1971), especially pp. 401–405 for a detailing of the extraordinary circumstances in which this case reached the Supreme Court.

50. Lindsay Rogers, *Contemporary Review,* vol. 114 (August, 1918).

51. *U.S. ex rel Milwaukee Social Democrat Publishing Co. v. Burleson,* 255 U.S. 407 (1921).

52. Zechariah Chafee, Jr., *Free Speech in the United States* (Cambridge, Mass.: Harvard University Press, 1946), p. 300.

53. John Lofton, *The Press as Guardian of the First Amendment* (Columbia: University of South Carolina Press, 1980), p. 176, citing U.S. Congress, Special (House) Committee on Right of Victor Berger to be Sworn In, Hearings, 1: 535, 681, and 719; and Chafee, *Free Speech,* p. 248.

54. Chafee, *Free Speech,* p. 247.

55. Quoted in Seymour, Stedman et al., *The Case of the Chicago Socialists* (brief in the United States Court of Appeals for the Seventh Circuit, October term, 1918), p. 32. *The Case of the Chicago Socialists: In the United States Circuit Court of Appeals for the Seventh Circuit, October Term, A.D. 1918; Victor L. Berger, Adolph Germer, J. Louis Engdahl, William F. Kruse, and Irwin St. John Tucker, Plaintiffs in Error, vs. United States of America, Defendant in Error; Brief for Plaintiffs in Error* (Chicago: n.p., [1919?]), SHSW Cutter collection F83614.B49, p. 3.

56. *New York Times,* January 17, 1918, p. 12. This editorial apparently referred to the decision in *Masses Publishing Co. v. Patten,* 216 F. 24 (1918), overruling Judge Learned Hand's decision in the same case, at 244 Fed. Supp. 535 (1917).

57. Quoted in Lofton, *Press as Guardian,* p. 203.

58. Lofton, *Press as Guardian,* p. 199, citing the *New York Times,* November 12, 1919, p. 12, and the *Boston Evening Transcript,* November 12, 1919, p. 2 of the editorial section. See also Chafee, *Free Speech,* pp. 250–69.

59. Phillip Knightley, *The First Casualty* (New York: Harcourt, Brace, Jovanovich, 1975), p. 123.

60. James R. Mock and Cedric Larson, *Words That Won the War: The Story of the Committee on Public Information, 1917–1919* (Princeton, N.J.: Princeton University Press, 1939), pp. 6, 7.

61. Cited in Mock and Larson, *Words That Won the War,* p. 59.

62. Stephen Vaughn, *Holding Fast the Inner Lines* (Chapel Hill: The University of North Carolina Press, 1980), p. 37.

63. Ronald Steel, *Walter Lippmann and the American Century* (New York: Vintage Books, 1981), pp. 114–15.

64. Steel, *Lippmann,* p. 125.

65. Frank Angelo, *On Guard: A History of the* Detroit Free Press (Detroit: Detroit Free Press, 1981), p. 141–43.

66. Kessler, *Dissident Press,* p. 141.

67. William L. O'Neill, *Echo of Revolt:* The Masses *1911–1917.* (Chicago: Quadrangle Books, 1966), p. 28.

68. O'Neill, *Echoes of Revolt,* p. 150.

69. Daniel Aaron, *Writers on the Left* (New York: Avon Books, 1965), p. 124.

70. The authors would like to thank Bill Frisbie, a student at the University of Texas, for contributing to the research on *The Masses.*

71. Mary Sue Mander, *Pen and Sword: A Cultural History of the American War Correspondent: 1895–1945,* Ph.D. dissertation, University of Illinois at Urbana-Champaign, 1979, p. 62.

72. Knightley, *The First Casualty,* pp. 80, 81.

73. Knightley, *The First Casualty,* pp. 94, 95.

74. Marguerite Harrison, *There's Always Tomorrow,* 1935, p. 85.

75. Catherine Griggs, *Marguerite Harrison,* Ph.D. dissertation, the George Washington University, Spring, 1996. See June 7, 1920, telegram from Milstaff to Solvett; also MID requisition for $500 to reimburse the AP, on the authorization of Mr. L. C. Probart, Manager, Associated Press. File

PF-39205, RG 165 (War Department General Staff, MID, Box 607, National Archives, cited in Griggs, chap. 3, p. 3).

76. For a discussion of the development of radio technology, see Hugh G. J. Aitken, *Syntony and Spark: The Origins of Radio* (Princeton, N.J.: Princeton University Press, 1985), and *The Continuous Wave: Technology and American Radio, 1900–1932* (Princeton, N.J.: Princeton University Press, 1985).

77. Werner J. Severin, "Commercial and Non-Commercial Radio during Broadcasting's Early Years," *Journal of Broadcasting* 22 (Fall, 1978), p. 491.

78. Barnouw, *Tower in Babel*, (Oxford University Press, 1966), pp. 185–86.

79. Elaine Prostak (Berland), "Up in the Air: The Public Debates over Radio Use during the 1920's," Ph.D. dis-sertation, University of Kansas, 1983, p. 31. See also Aitken, *Syntony and Spark*, pp. 472–74.

80. Jack C. Ellis, *A History of Film*, 2nd ed. (Englewood Cliffs, N.J.: Prentice-Hall, 1985).

81. Louis Giannetti and Scott Eyman, *Flashback: A Brief History of Film* (Englewood Cliffs, N.J.: Prentice Hall, 1986), p. 15.

82. Robert Sklar, *Movie-Made America: A Cultural History of American Movies* (New York: Vintage Books, 1975), pp. 35, 36, 40, 87.

83. This stanza of the newsboy's poem is cited in Czitrom, *Media and the American Mind* (Chapel Hill: University of North Carolina Press, 1982), p. 51.

84. Sklar, *Movie-Made America*, pp. 144–45.

CHAPTER 12

Media and Consumer Culture

▼

The 1920s celebrated the introduction of consumer culture. A period character-ized as the flapper age, with prosperity running high, sexual mores changing dramatically, and the world adopting a "devil may care" attitude, the 1920s also featured a dark side: increasing racism and activity by the Ku Klux Klan, rising unem-ployment, fears of immigration, intolerance, and violent struggles between capital and labor.

Although the telegraph broke the link between transportation and gathering news, until the advent of radio, the distribution or dissemination of messages to a mass audience was tied to the transportation system. The introduction of radio into the American household during the 1920s evoked the hopes, fears, and anxieties of a nation already in the midst of cultural disruption. Some hoped radio would pro-vide the technological means to realize utopian dreams of unifying the nation, democratizing society, and ending persistent social problems. Fears surfaced about the lack of face-to-face communication and traditional authority, the growing specter of technology, and increasing alienation. These fears were expressed in ongoing debates in the 1920s about how radio would take shape—how it would affect poli-tics, religion, music, and the arts and whether it would be educational or commer-cially entertainment-oriented.[1]

The motion pictures of Hollywood and the New York tabloids promoted daz-zling modern images, and the consumer orientation of manufacturing was trans-ferred into cultural norms by the rapidly growing, all-pervasive advertising industry.

Using the techniques of persuasion popular in advertising—and successful in converting the populace to support World War I—the public relations industry came of age. Business found a need to explain itself to the public, and the labor strife that had received publicity by the muckrakers reflected badly on the captains of industry. Newspapers increasingly joined the ranks of big business, as chain journalism dominated an increasing percentage of the nation's dailies. African-American newspapers sought equality at home as the war ground to a close. Amidst rapid social change and conflict, Americans faced often contradictory images of themselves and their society as they attempted to adapt to a modern, urban, technological consumer society. ▼

Radio: What Have They Done with My Child?

Radio was a technological innovation that was to change the pattern of communication in the nation. Within less than a decade, radio moved from a technological "miracle" to a household necessity provided by and controlled by corporate interests. Its history is a story of technical development, corporate leadership versus entrepreneurship, industry battles, congressional regulation, and social impact.[2] The debates of the 1920s centered on who would pay for radio development, who would control it, and how it would be used. Legislators and industrial giants viewed radio as a new tool of influence; educators debated its usefulness as a teaching tool; cultural elites worried about the effect it would have on concerts and other cultural events. In many ways, radio became the sounding box for the contradictions of the twenties and, as a new communications medium, played a major role in disseminating debate about those contradictions to Americans who were trying to retain traditional values and behavior and at the same time adapt to modern conveniences and freedoms.[3]

By the end of the 1920s, the fundamental contours of an American system of broadcasting were in place. With little public debate about the significance of the new technology in relationship to freedom of expression, commercial broadcasters quickly took control of the medium and strongly influenced the congressional reg-

▼

What Happened to Radio?

What have you done with my child? You have made him the laughing stock to intelligence, surely a stench in the nostrils of the gods of the iconosphere. Murder mysteries rule the waves by night and children are rendered psychopathic by your bedtime stories. This child of mine is moronic, as though you and your sponsors believe the majority of listeners have only moron minds.

—Lee De Forest, inventor of the audion tube

ulation that was to enhance radio's commercial growth.⁴ The development of radio as a commercial medium, primarily for entertainment, that was loosely regulated by the federal government was neither inevitable nor the result of "happenstance." It resulted from a complex interplay of technology, military and government needs, corporate enterprise, and congressional action within a volatile social and cultural milieu.⁵

Technology Breaks Regional Barriers

Amid the postwar experimentation with receivers and transmitters and the negotiations over patents, Dr. Frank Conrad, like many other amateur operators, received permission to put his amateur station on the air and began playing Victrola music from a small transmitter above his garage in Pittsburgh, Pennsylvania. People responded in droves to his suggestion that they request specific tunes. His success spurred Westinghouse to ask Conrad to build a station, KDKA, which went on the air with advertised programs to help listeners form the "listening habit." Programming was not the primary interest. Westinghouse established the station to sell receivers and goodwill for the company name. On November 2, 1920, KDKA went on the air with a broadcast of the results of the race between presidential candidates Warren G. Harding and James M. Cox, setting into motion what conventionally has been regarded as the birth of broadcasting in the United States. What created radio as a communications medium was not the perfection of technology but rather the realization that a popular market existed and could be reached for a relatively small investment. In the fall of 1921, Westinghouse opened three more stations; General Electric (GE) and RCA established stations in 1922 and 1923.

Radio became so popular that RCA sold $11 million worth of receivers in 1922. By 1925, sales jumped to $50 million. The 5 stations that had existed in 1921 grew to 576 stations by 1923 and to 700 by 1927. By the end of the decade, 618 stations and two networks were firmly in place. Set sales paralleled the growth of stations. In 1924, $45 million worth of sets had been sold, a figure that jumped to $135 million in 1929. In 1923, only 1.5 percent of the households in the United States owned a radio set; by 1930, almost 50 percent owned sets.⁶

It soon became apparent that establishing a broadcast station was an expensive venture, one that could not be supported indefinitely by the sale of radio receivers. Who should pay for the programming became a critical question for the infant industry. As early as 1922, AT&T announced it would sell time to individuals who wanted to send a message over the air. Initially, the public and press reacted negatively. Many observers such as Secretary of Commerce Herbert Hoover envisioned radio as a public service and feared that "if a speech by the President is to be used as the meat in a sandwich of two patent medicine advertisements there will be no radio left."⁷ Despite such reservations, AT&T's station WEAF ventured into what it termed "toll broadcasting," making a pitch for a cooperative apartment complex in New York City. The commercial lasted less than fifteen minutes, was repeated for five days, and cost $100. By the end of 1924, other stations attempted to imitate AT&T's

Figure 12-1   No longer a luxury, by 1929, the radio had become a necessary furnishing in middle-class households. (Division of Prints and Photographs, Library of Congress Collection)

approach, but the company claimed it was a new phase of the telephone business and, as such, was its sole domain.[8]

Disputes over who would control patents, who would manufacture sets, and who had the right to sell advertising and thereby turn radio into a profitable medium created controversy and competition within the industry. The industry also faced technological problems of interference that had not been solved by the allocation of frequencies made under legislation passed in 1912. Foreseeing problems, Secretary Hoover urged Congress to pass new legislation. Between 1921 and 1927, twelve bills that would have repealed the 1912 act and forty others that would have amended it were introduced into Congress. However, Congress failed to act because its members could not agree. Meanwhile, Hoover organized conferences that were attended by industry representatives, educators, engineers, and others to discuss the problems of jammed air waves and proliferating stations that threatened set sales and the industry itself.

As Congress and those attending Hoover's conferences debated the various issues, RCA members sought to renegotiate their earlier cross-licensing agreements. The giants were divided into two groups—AT&T and its subsidiary, Western Electric, or the Telephone Group; and Westinghouse, RCA, and GE, the Radio Group. AT&T claimed it had exclusive rights to manufacture and sell radio transmitters for broadcasting, to sell time for advertising, and to connect stations by wire for network or chain broadcasting. The Radio Group claimed the right to manufacture and sell radio sets to the public, to recoup program expenses from sponsors, and to interconnect stations by any available means. The industry resolved its disputed claims in 1926, with AT&T withdrawing from the broadcast industry. RCA bought AT&T's station, WEAF, for $1 million and guaranteed AT&T $1 million a year by agreeing to use its telephone lines to interconnect stations. RCA, GE, and Westinghouse formed the National Broadcasting Company (NBC), the nation's first network. By adopting commercial sponsorship as well, NBC represented a solid organizational and financial base for the development of radio broadcasting. By January 1927, NBC had two networks in operation—a red network fed by WEAF and a blue network fed by WJZ, formerly a Westinghouse station.

Government and Industry Partnership

At last having settled their own differences, the industry magnates were ready to urge Congress to pass legislation. The networks wanted to solidify their control and assure that the numerous nonprofit broadcasters who had begun operations early in the decade did not control frequencies. These nonprofit broadcasters, who began in the industry "on the ground floor," competed with commercial broadcasters for the air waves. Commercial stations were owned by newspapers, department stores, power companies, and other private concerns. These commercial broadcasters' main goal was to generate favorable publicity for their owner's enterprise. It was not until after the Radio Act of 1927, engineered in large part by the networks and major components of the industry, that the networks were able to establish dominance. Radio historian Robert McChesney points out that although commercial broadcasting officials strongly influenced the Radio Act of 1927, there was no reason to suspect that the law was a mandate for the almost strictly profit-oriented enterprise that developed.[9]

In January, Congress passed the Federal Radio Act of 1927, creating a five-member commission to regulate radio. Congress adopted most of the suggestions made by the commercial radio industry, including the recommendation that broadcasting be left under private control with limited federal supervision of the technical aspects of the medium. Industry officials recommended that the federal government assign licenses, limit the number of stations, abolish low-powered stations (many of these were educational), support trade-name advertising, and issue licenses on the basis of "public interest." Believing that radio was too valuable a resource to be operated as a monopoly, the regulation stated that the airwaves belong to the American people and that stations must operate in "the public interest, convenience, or necessity." Nevertheless, most of the responsibility for programming and the ability to profit was left in private, corporate hands.[10]

The regulation of broadcasting represented a strict departure from the relationship between print communication and government. Licensing was justified on the "scarcity principle": there simply were not enough broadcast frequencies to go around to all comers, so the Federal Radio Commission (FRC) would choose among applicants "in the public interest." Thus it was that a kind of "shotgun wedding" took place between government ownership of the airwaves—a resource in theory belonging to all people (and crossing state and national boundaries, too)—and a media system based on private enterprise.

In August 1928, the FRC reallocated stations to reduce interference. The commission set aside 40 of the available 90 channels as 50,000-watt clear channels that would be occupied by only one station nationally. The other 50 channels were assigned to more than 600 broadcasters who could operate at the same time on lower-power levels. Some broadcasters in the same region would be required to divide up the hours of the day. The requirements to "share" ultimately drove those who had the least favorable times off the air, and by 1929 fewer than 100 stations were on the air. Under these allocations, the networks were the big winners, and by 1931 they accounted for nearly 70 percent of U.S. broadcasting. As the FRC reduced both the power and the hours of nonprofit broadcasting, the commission also reduced the ability of the nonprofits to raise funds. The director of a University of Arkansas station about to shut off its microphones wrote, "The Commission may boast that it has never cut an educational station off the air. It merely cuts off our head, our arms, and our legs, and then allows us to die a natural death."[11] By 1934, the total number of nonprofit broadcasters was reduced to a third of the 1927 figure. The FRC justified its cuts by claiming that only commercial broadcasters truly operated in the public interest, and that nonprofits only produced material for special interests—that is, propaganda messages.

Although the battle was not over, the lines were drawn and the victors were entrenched in powerful positions. Between 1928 and the passage of the Federal Communications Act in 1934, nonprofit broadcasters organized to preserve and increase their number of frequencies. During this period, the National Committee on Education by Radio, elements of the labor movement, religious groups such as the Paulist Fathers—who operated their own station—and the American Civil Liberties Union opposed the increasing commercialization of radio. They argued that the public had not been given a chance to determine the future of the broadcasting industry *in public* but that regulation had been created behind closed doors. Further, they argued that commercial broadcasting would further the interests of the status quo and would not give adequate time to radical or unpopular opinions. McChesney wrote, "The entire opposition movement was propelled by a profound desire to

▼

Lee DeForest (1873–1961)

Lee DeForest was an independent inventor in the age of corporate scientific discovery. DeForest created the audion tube, the basis for a generation of wireless technology, including radio and television. Admiring earlier inventors, such as Edison and Bell, DeForest hoped to achieve fame much the same way, but corporations were doing most of the experiments. DeForest went to work for the American Wireless Telegraph Company of Milwaukee. When the company wanted to use the technology he had pursued with company time and money, DeForest said "I will not let it go into the hands of any company until that company is mine." He was fired.

Source: J. A. Hijiya, *Lee DeForest and the Fatherhood of Radio* (Bethlehem: Lehigh University Press, 1992). (*Photo:* Division of Prints and Photographs, Library of Congress Collection)

create a broadcasting system that would better promote its vision of a democratic political culture."[12] The opposition offered several solutions to the dilemma that was outlined: (1) to set aside a fixed percentage of channels, either 15 or 25 percent, for the exclusive use of nonprofit broadcasters; (2) to have Congress authorize an independent study of broadcasting with the goal of recreating an entirely new broadcasting system; and (3) to establish a series of stations to be subsidized through taxes.

However, the opposition movement faced severe challenges. Commercial broadcasters, backed by substantial funding and influence, established a public relations campaign to define the commercial route as the only true American approach to broadcasting. Further, the American Bar Association organized fully behind commercial interests, opposing any congressional involvement with broadcast policy beyond the bounds suggested by the Radio Act of 1927. Congressional committee leadership also opposed alternative policy, and with the onset of the depression, congressional interest in radio policy waned as interest turned toward economic legislation. Franklin Delano Roosevelt, with more important battles to fight, chose not to oppose entrenched commercial communications interests and, indeed, lobbied against an amendment to the proposed 1934 Communications Act that would have set aside channels for nonprofit broadcasting. In June 1934, President Roosevelt signed the Communications Act of 1934 into law, solidifying commercial, and particularly network, control of broadcasting. The number of nonprofit stations continued to decline, and not until the 1960s did Congress act to establish public radio and television stations.[13]

Newsreels: Facts and Fakery

Newsreels made their debut in 1910 as a worldwide phenomenon. Issued weekly or semiweekly, they presented facts generally selected for their currency and dramatic appeal, and they were shown in more than 15,000 theatres each week throughout the United States. These nine- or ten-minute news capsules featured energetic musical scores and high-speed, invisible narrators.[14] From the beginning, newsreel producers used fakery, re-creation, and staging, devices highly suspect in the journalistic world. While the dramatic quality of the newsreel was high, their journalistic credibility and the level of controversy with which they dealt were low.

The five major newsreel titles were owned by the major movie companies, and they included Pathe's Weekly (later Warner-Pathe News); Fox Movietone News; Universal News; Hearst International Newsreel (later, Hearst Metrotone News, then News of the Day); and Paramount News. American newsreels, at their height, had an estimated U.S. audience of 40 million people and a worldwide audience of at least 200 million. For many people, especially those who could not read, the newsreel provided a major source of news during the three decades before television. Newsreels never made money for any of their owners, and they began a decline in the 1940s when the Justice Department broke up the advantageous block-booking tactics of the movie industry—tactics that made the newsreel an attractive part of a larger package.

Occasionally, independently produced or government-backed newsreels were used in the United States and abroad to expose social ills and to promote various ideologies. Indicative of their worldwide appeal was the Soviet use of newsreels during World War I to depict the war as an agonizing struggle with periods of ups and downs, and after the war to promote Soviet ideology.[15] In the United States, independent companies produced newsreels to comment on various social conditions. One example was the National Film and Photo League's "Workers Newsreel," which documented the national hunger march of December 1932. These, and other efforts, followed in the documentary tradition popular in the 1930s.

Despite some continued use of the newsreel by social and political movements worldwide, by the mid-1920s American commercial producers dominated the worldwide market. By 1927, with the advent of talking pictures, the newsreel became a talkie as well. As historian Raymond Fielding wrote, "For more than half a century, theater patrons got the newsreel with every feature film they paid for, together with a Mickey Mouse cartoon, a Pete Smith Specialty, a Grantland Rice sports reel, or a Fitzpatrick Traveltalk."[16]

After a move by the Justice Department to end block-booking, newsreels began to die. Economic hardships in the industry during the 1940s and 1950s propelled movie companies to sell their least profitable branches, and television news coverage began to successfully compete with the highly staged news provided by the newsreels.

"March of Time"

As a spin-off from a radio program, "March of Time" newsreels began in 1934. "March of Time" was suspect as were other newsreels because it included faked situations and footage, but contrary to standard newsreel style, the "Time" series dealt with controversial subjects. A. William Bluem, student of the documentary, wrote that the series "stretched the limits of journalism by implicitly arguing that the picture as well as the word was, after all, only symbolic of reality. What mattered was not whether pictorial journalism displayed facts, but whether, within the conscience of the reporter, it faithfully reflected the facts."[17]

"March of Time" satirized Louisiana politician Huey ("Share the Wealth") Long, commented on the development of the Soviet state, and depicted an impersonation of Adolf Hitler. Never a profit-maker, "March of Time" was abandoned in 1951. Shortly before the demise of the program, *New York Times* critic Bosley Crowther wrote on July 15

> more than a sentimental sadness over the passing of a cinematic friend will be felt by those toilers in the vineyards who have sweat blood over documentary films. For to them, no matter how they may have snickered at the series' recognized conventional form, the March of Time has stood up as a symbol of real accomplishment in the "pictorial journalism" field.[18]

Going to the Movies

By the 1920s, the film industry was centered in Hollywood, where twenty studios produced features and shorts for a weekly audience of 40 million people. The small-scale capitalism of the first two decades of the twentieth century gave way to monopolistic control by several large movie houses, chain-store marketing, and a self-censorship system designed to keep public criticism at a minimum. The American movie industry dominated the world market by the end of the decade.

Before World War I, the movie industry was self-financed, but profits and stability experienced after the war convinced investment bankers that the movie business was, indeed, business. Banks began to lend funds to the industry to the extent that by 1926 the industry showed invested capital of $1.5 billion. By 1927, seven of the largest corporations were publicly held, with stock traded on the Chicago and New York exchanges.[19] Throughout the decade, the formation of large studios such as Metro-Goldwyn-Mayer and Warner Brothers produced large fortunes. One 1923 film, for example, cost $120,963 and grossed $1,588,545. In the mid-1920s, the 20,000 theatres in the United States grossed about $350 million, and the country produced 82 percent of the world's movies. The silent comedies of Charles Chaplin and Buster Keaton and leading actresses such as Gloria Swanson and Mary Pickford, teamed with Rudolph Valentino and Douglas Fairbanks, reigned supreme.

The decade witnessed the solidification of the industry into large movie companies, with ultimately few films made by independent producers. By 1929, five companies monopolized the industry. Paramount, Warner Brothers, Fox, MGM, and Radio-Keith-Orpheum (RKO) controlled production houses and theatre outlets, and the heads of studios dominated decision making about film topics and production. The studio system, combined with the focus on top stars, reached its peak in the 1930s and 1940s, when moviegoing audiences were at their peak as well.

Figure 12–2 *Life*, a humor magazine of the 1920s, illustrated the use of sound effects for motion pictures in "The Talkie," November 30, 1926. (Division of Prints and Photographs, Library of Congress Collection)

Mass marketing propelled the movie industry in the 1920s. Vertical integration allowed for control from the top down—the design and production of films, the selection of stars, the distribution, and, finally, exhibition in the elaborate movie palaces constructed during the decade. The large studios coordinated advertising with identifiable trademarks, benefited from large-scale economies, and adopted expert business practices such as those practiced by other industries. Film historian Douglas Gomery wrote that "[t]he expansion proceeded in orderly fashion: costs fell, demand increased, profits rose, more theaters were acquired, and so on."[20]

The innovation of feature-length films generated a good deal of public criticism, and in 1915, in *Mutual Film Corp. v. Industrial Commission of Ohio*, the U.S. Supreme

Court declared that exhibiting films was a business, not "press," and thereby not protected by the First Amendment. Film producers, therefore, faced censorship challenges apart from those confronted by print media and radio. Not until 1952 did the Supreme Court reverse its position, ruling that motion pictures were "a significant medium for the communication of ideas."[21] Therefore, special interests, such as the Catholic church, pressured the industry to conform to specified standards of morality. Various cities and states set up censorship boards as early as 1907 to combat what some citizens considered immoral influences. By the early 1920s, with Hollywood scandals erupting—as examples, the drug-induced death of Wallace Reid and the murder of director William Desmond Taylor—the industry organized the Motion Picture Producers and Distributors of America (MPPDA), naming Will H. Hays as its president. In 1934, a group of Catholic bishops formed the National Legion of Decency to warn Catholics against objectionable films. Hollywood responded by enforcing its production code, requiring a seal of approval on each film. Violators paid a $25,000 fine. The code forbade sex, excessive violence, and vulgar language. The system remained in effect until 1968, when the industry adopted the present ratings that designate intended audiences. In 1984, and again in 1992, the industry added ratings, but the primary system remains intact.

By 1928, mediocre films with sound sequences were rapidly outdistancing highly artistic silent films. In 1929, Warners' profits topped $17 million, in comparison to $2 million the year before. Paramount cleared $15 million and Fox $9 million. The stage was set for a rapid expansion in the 1930s into the talking-movie business.

Movies were favorite entertainment fare among the working and middle classes; in Chicago, for example, workers spent more than half their entertainment budgets on movies. Nevertheless, working Chicagoans watched their movies close to home, in neighborhood houses, rather than in the more expensive and palatial movie theatres of the city. Lizabeth Cohen argued that the owners of the neighborhood theatres often lived in the community and that they reinforced neighborhood values in such a way as to mitigate against the influence of mass culture. In the ethnic neighborhoods, theatres combined the showing of popular movies with stage shows and local talent tryouts, and owners often excluded certain races or ethnic groups if they didn't believe they would fit in. By the late 1920s, however, as movies were standardized through the Hollywood studio system and neighborhood theatres were bought by chains, local groups lost their ability to control the dissemination of mass culture. Live shows and local talent groups disappeared, and Hollywood block-booking practices determined what people would see when they went to the theatre.[22]

Advertising and Consumer Culture

Corporate consolidation, increased productivity, and the change from a debtor to a creditor nation accompanied the close of World War I. The growth of the advertising industry promoted the adoption of consumer products and a differentiation of brand names. Coupled with increasingly available credit opportunities through automobile finance companies, banks, and other financial institutions, advertising promoted the purchasing of more consumer goods, particularly major durable goods, than ever before in American society.[23]

By the 1920s, advertising was an established industry, developed in response to changes in business and marketing strategies. Advertisers were becoming aware of their markets, and newspapers were experimenting with hiring employees to sell advertisements. Space agents were experiencing difficulties in attempting to place advertisements, finding themselves in competition with companies' in-house efforts to buy their own advertising space. It became clear that if agencies were to survive, changes were imperative. These changes came by way of added services.[24]

From Space to Agency Service

By the late 1880s, large department stores began to make a commitment to employing advertising copywriters. When Wanamaker's opened in Philadelphia, the store management hired John E. Powers to write advertisements. By 1899, Wanamaker's of New York spent $300,000 in ads. Because they hired their own copywriters and dealt in large volume, such stores could bypass the agency and negotiate directly with the media. Manufacturers dealing with branded goods also began to recognize the value of good advertising copywriting. The developing technology in stereotyping and photography enabled more creative layout and design to take place as well.

Agencies that succeeded in this new market adapted quickly to the change in demand. By 1900, N. W. Ayer regarded preparation of copy as a standard service of the agency. Albert D. Lasker, who in 1898 began to work for the major Chicago agency Lord and Thomas, rapidly expanded the copywriting staff. Lasker bought out the agency in 1912 and gained a reputation for training younger people in the business. Lasker claimed he made his employees so good he could not keep them. Those in the business joked that getting fired from Lord and Thomas was a credential for getting hired elsewhere.[25]

Stanley Resor, trained in economics at Yale, and Helen Lansdowne, a talented copywriter, pioneered new techniques first at Procter and Collier, an agency largely created to service Procter and Gamble products. Resor developed a reputation for coining brand names and educating each social class to imitate the habits of richer people. Lansdowne's superb copywriting complemented Resor's administrative skills. In 1908, Stanley and his brother Walter, along with Lansdowne, opened a branch for the J. Walter Thompson Company in Cincinnati. In 1910, Lansdowne's ads for Woodbury's Facial Soap increased sales by 1,000 percent in eight years. Lansdowne was the first woman to appear before the board of directors of a major company to explain advertising. She wrote the original ads for Yuban coffee, Lux soap, and Cutex nail polish. She claimed to be the first woman to plan advertisements and write copy for national, as opposed to retail, advertising. After Resor and Lansdowne's move to New York, Resor and a group of colleagues bought the J. Walter Thompson Company for half a million dollars; Resor cut the client list by more than two-thirds, focused on large, prestigious accounts, closed some local branches, and reorganized the company. Lansdowne and Resor, friends and colleagues since their early days

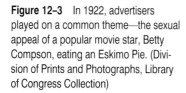

Figure 12-3 In 1922, advertisers played on a common theme—the sexual appeal of a popular movie star, Betty Compson, eating an Eskimo Pie. (Division of Prints and Photographs, Library of Congress Collection)

in Cincinnati, were married in 1917. They continued to divide tasks at the agency, with Resor focusing on administration and client services and Lansdowne on the preparation of advertisements.[26]

Rudimentary marketing surveys had been experimented with at Ayer's as early as 1879, and providing such surveys had become a standard service about 1900. By 1910, other companies had followed suit. Resor pioneered in the field, publishing *Population and Its Distribution,* a collection of demographic and economic data compiled from the federal census. After he bought the Thompson agency, Resor developed departments of planning and statistical investigation. Resor managed "by consensus, distrusting what he called Individual Opinion, and thought that brilliance was dangerous."[27] He abandoned hierarchical authority, preferring instead "cross fertilization" among assorted minds.[28]

The industry was trying to professionalize and made claims to being as valuable to American society as were engineers and physicians. In 1917, the American Association of Advertising Agencies formed; by that year agencies had become powerful institutions, handling 95 percent of all national advertising. Why the agencies were so successful is difficult to analyze. Clearly there were some alternatives. Some of the bigger companies were capable of efficiently creating in-house agencies; boilerplate advertising from the American Press Association provided smaller newspapers with preset advertising copy from a variety of advertisers; and free-lancers were available for work on specific projects. The agencies, however, argued that they had a pre-ferred position with the media in buying space, they offered specialized services, and they provided the advertiser with an independent, unbiased view. As the agencies made these arguments and strove to maintain their position in the advertising exchange, the commission system continued to provoke controversy. The Periodical Publishers Association and the American Newspaper Press Association helped pre-serve the agency/commission system, arguing that the commission kept the agencies loyal to the press, not to the advertiser, and that agencies made it possible for the press to get and keep national advertising. Meanwhile, the American Association of Advertising Agencies developed standard procedures requiring the media to pay commissions only to established service organizations, stabilizing commissions at 15 percent, and discouraging the paying of rebates to clients. By 1918, they had pre-served and stabilized the system, and by the end of World War I, further guidelines were in place. Agencies, as a rule, did not handle competing accounts, they reduced their high-pressure soliciting tactics (taking clients away from other agencies), and they continued to avoid price competition with their rivals.[29]

Another problem, in addition to the dispute over commissions, resulted from unaudited circulations. Advertisers continually complained that publishers inflated circulation statistics and that they had no means of verifying the accuracy of how many individuals their ads actually were reaching. After several attempts by various agencies and a push from Congress, which in 1912 required publications using the mails to print sworn annual circulation statements, the Association of National Adver-tising Managers and the American Advertising Association joined forces in 1914 to create the Audit Bureau of Circulations. Although the bureau had financial difficul-ties in the early years, it was successful in establishing standards for circulation claims and for auditing those claims.

Other changes in the early years of the century were apparent as New York advertising agencies changed their places of business. They moved from an area dominated by publishers to one dominated by business—Madison Avenue. They opened branch offices in various cities and expanded their work force. In 1900, Ayer's had employed 163 people; by 1910, 298 individuals were employed in the agency; in 1920, that number expanded to 426. Billings for Ayer had been $1.5 mil-lion in 1900; by 1921, they surpassed $11 million. The ad agencies, in tune with the progressive period, moved toward systematic, scientific management.

The agency work force was 95 percent male. In 1916, half the men associated with agencies had attended college, and one-fourth held bachelor's degrees. Only one in ten was over fifty, and about half were from the Midwest. They were predominantly Protestant, middle-class, middle-American males. Although women were active in the formation of the industry, as the move toward professionalization took place, women were systematically excluded from professional clubs, and jobs were organized by gender. One of the few women in the advertising business, Helen Rosen Woodward, lamented the industry's change to a more formal business style. She wrote

> Advertising has the solid mentality usual in a large established business with heavy investment. It no longer attracts the lovers of chance, but rather those who look for

safety. It has a pontifical dignity which robs it of much of its earlier fire. If [*sic*] never occurred to any of the pioneers to think about the dignity of advertising. It was much too interesting for that.[30]

Only at J. Walter Thompson did women succeed on a regular basis. The contingent known as the Women's Copy Group controlled much of the advertising copy that emerged from the agency during the 1920s and the 1930s. Yet, management training programs did not include women, women were excluded from executive dining rooms, and all women, unlike the men, shared a common washroom. No special facilities for executive women existed.[31]

By the 1920s, Daniel Pope wrote, agencies were selling "access to American consumers. To use a chilling but revealing phrase of modern marketing, advertising agencies dared to offer their corporate clients a share of the American mind."[32]

Ethics and Regulation

Another hotly debated issue of the early 1900s was that of ethics. Although some publishers and a few agencies had rejected fraudulent advertising, agents took responsibility only for the ads, not for the product. More publishers became involved at the turn of the century; for example, in 1892, Cyrus Curtis rejected all medical ads for the *Ladies' Home Journal*. Some agencies turned away lucrative accounts on ethical grounds. As the truth-in-advertising movement gained credence, agents began to argue that false advertising injured the product's credibility and created financial losses—that the truth paid. Agencies were concerned about their own status as professionals and could little afford claims of false advertising. Although agencies opposed government interference in the 1890s, by the time the Pure Food and Drug Act was passed in 1906, there was hardly any opposition. The act was aimed at penalizing fraud and misstatement, primarily in labeling, and was not aimed at the harmfulness of a product; furthermore, the bill carried few enforcement procedures. However, by 1910, most patent medicine advertisements were placed directly by manufacturers or distributors rather than by agencies.

The first real enthusiasm for a truth-in-advertising movement came with the 1911 convention of the Associated Advertising Clubs of America (AACA), the emotion motivated by the agencies' desire to avoid government regulation. Although postal restrictions and some state laws contained provisions against fraudulent advertising, all required proof of intent to deceive and required that a transaction be complete before the law could be applied. In 1911, *Printer's Ink* ran a series on unfair competition and within that series of articles proposed a model statute banning dishonest advertising—a statute to be enforced by the states that would not require proof of intent to deceive. The article that proposed this statute also suggested that local advertising-club surveillance would be essential to the success of any legislation. By 1921, twenty-three states enacted the statute recommended by *Printer's Ink*, although some exempted publishers from liability, and some required proof of deception. In 1914, Congress passed the Federal Trade Commission (FTC) Act, which made the FTC the most powerful regulator of advertising in the country. Nevertheless, until

1938, with the passage of the Wheeler-Lea Amendment, enforcement required the FTC to prove that a false ad had harmed a competing business.

In 1912, an eighteen-member National Vigilance Committee (NVC) was created from the Associated Advertising Clubs, and many cities established local clubs. Energy was primarily devoted to local cases, the movement was clearly in advertising's self-interest, and there was a heavy dependence on enlightenment rather than on prosecution. Vigilance groups were careful when dealing with large corporations, although the NVC and other groups denied such charges. Under the guise of truthfulness in advertising, the movement also managed to eliminate much comparative price competition.

The movement remained directed at the truthfulness of the words used within ads and never evaluated the social impact of advertising or the ethics of using a variety of persuasive techniques. In fact, Daniel Pope suggested that the decline of the lie led to the introduction of new and more powerful persuasive techniques.

Persuasive Strategies

Advertising copy and persuasive strategies were intertwined with the continuing success of old products and the introduction of new consumer products in the 1920s. Roland Marchand wrote in *Advertising the American Dream* that in a single year "major advertising campaigns rescued two fading products so successfully that the entire advertising industry had to ponder the lessons they offered in modern advertising technique."[33] Fleischmann's Yeast, which had been used primarily to bake bread, was fast becoming a victim of urbanization and the fact that people were buying bread, not making it. The J. Walter Thompson company within a year transformed Fleischmann's into a "potent source of vitamins, a food to be eaten directly from the package."[34] Two years later, the agency assisted in once again transforming the product, this time into a natural laxative. Human interest advertising copy, arranged much like an editorial feature, was a major component in the campaign. In three years, sales increased 130 percent, and the agency called in physicians who recommended eating yeast to counteract "intestinal fatigue." Although the American Medical Association prohibited its doctors from participating in the advertising campaign, European doctors readily testified, and their prestigious names contributed to the campaign's success.

The transformation of Listerine from a general antiseptic to a breath freshener represented another advertising success story of the 1920s. After advertising copywriters had hit upon the term *halitosis*, they explained in ads how a man with wealth, good looks, and charm could lose everything if he labored under the dread "bad breath." Listerine's parent company increased its profits from $100,000 per year in 1920 to $4 million in 1927. In 1926, *Printer's Ink*, a major trade journal, credited the copywriter of the Listerine campaign with having "amplified the morning habits of our nicer citizenry—by making the morning mouthwash as important as the morning shower or the morning shave."[35] Listerine later was promoted as a cure for dandruff, a cure for colds, and a deodorant.

Advertising copywriters did not exist in a vacuum; one of the great dilemmas of the decade was deciding on the true nature of the audience. Did an advertiser aim at the great general mass of people or at the more cultured elite? Many agencies aimed at those who read the tabloids and patterned their copy on techniques used by tabloid and confession magazine writers. Others maintained a more elite position. Advertisers often aimed at women, because although women constituted only about 50 percent of the audience, they were regarded as the family purchasing agents. Men were depicted almost universally as businessmen dressed in business suits. Working-class men never appeared as consumers; in the advertising industry, such people as policemen, factory workers, and government officials did not exist.[36]

Other techniques attracted women consumers. The emphasis on color increased, with kitchen appliances, Hoosier cabinets, and bathroom fixtures produced and advertised in color. The importance of the first impression also was emphasized. Many women in 1920s advertisements lamented the fact they had made a poor first impression in a social or business circle and, therefore, had doomed their husbands' careers forever. Urbanization, mobility, and feared cultural disintegration of the 1920s was incorporated into advertising strategy. According to advertising copy,

> first impressions brought instantaneous success or failure. In a relatively mobile society, where business organizations loomed ever larger and people dealt far more often with strangers, the reasons one man gained a promotion or one woman suffered a social snub had become less explicable on grounds of long-standing favoritism or old family feuds. One might suspect that almost anything—especially a first impression—had made the crucial difference.[37]

By the end of the decade, the full-service agency was firmly in place. The advertising agency had moved from a position in the late nineteenth century in which its primary function was to sell media space to a new position as a sophisticated enterprise that employed businesspeople as well as creative individuals to write copy, design marketing research, and appeal to a variety of consumers by incorporating the social tensions of the day into advertising copy and strategy. The industry had developed its own professional standards, had abolished the more blatant competitive strategies, and had gained legitimacy through a "truth-in-advertising movement."

Public Relations: A Corporate Necessity

Although public relations activities had been visible in ancient and modern societies in a variety of forms, the term, *public relations*, used to describe promotion, press agentry, and publicity, was coined by Edward Bernays in the 1920s. Bernays believed that an understanding of social and behavioral science would lead public relations practitioners to better communicate the public's ideas to management and the ideas of management, or business, to the public.

Bernays' statements came after more than two decades of public criticism of business. The muckrakers during the early days of the twentieth century castigated business, and businesspeople were aware of hostile public opinion. The growth of small individual enterprises had changed business management as well, and corporate leaders recognized that the lack of local control over factories presented new operating obstacles. In the context of hostile public opinion and business management problems, business executives came to respect the impact of public opinion on the conduct of strikes, regulation, sales, and morale. Richard Tedlow wrote that corporate public relations emerged from this context as business leaders realized the importance of controlling news they could not help generating.[38]

By the turn of the century, public relations personnel were regarded as invaluable by the utility industry and other business enterprises, and practitioners became skilled at providing "news" that journalists readily used. Ivy Ledbetter Lee, a newspaper man turned publicist, earned a reputation for "objective" public relations in his work for the Pennsylvania Railroad, the Rockefeller family, and the anthracite coal operators. Lee argued that informing the press and the public, rather than operating in secret, would earn greater public favor, even if the news was not positive, and he earned considerable praise for his efforts to help reporters travel to view a Pennsylvania railroad accident, gather information, and photograph the site.

In 1906, Lee issued a "Declaration of Principles," claiming that all his work was done in the open. He asserted that his material was accurate and that he would assist any editor in clarifying detail. "In brief," Lee wrote, "our plan is, frankly and openly, on behalf of the business concerns and public institutions, to supply to the press and public of the United States prompt and accurate information concerning subjects which it is of value and interest to the public to know about."[39]

Despite his claim to accuracy and objectivity, Lee was despised by many journalists and castigated as "Poison Ivy" by Upton Sinclair in *The Brass Check*. "Journalists were bewildered," wrote Genevieve McBride in an analysis of public relations ethics, "by Lee's ability to deny that persuasion was his purpose but still get publicity, and even accurately predict its news placement."[40]

Ivy Lee's work and the creation of pioneering public relations agencies preceded the massive propaganda efforts of George Creel's Committee on Public Information during World War I. The Publicity Bureau, formed in Boston in 1900, a second agency formed by journalist William Wolff Smith in Washington in 1902, and Parker & Lee, an agency formed by Lee in partnership with George Parker, began to set standards for public relations work. The Creel committee, which employed former journalists and intellectuals, provided a training ground for many who practiced public relations after the war.

Public relations expanded after World War I in a variety of areas, including associational activities as well as corporate business. The war had stimulated the causes for public relations as well as the activities themselves. The Red Cross, the Salvation Army, and the Y.M.C.A. Community Chest developed publicity campaigns based on wartime models. Will Irwin claimed that by 1920 there were nearly a thousand "bureaus of propaganda" in Washington based on such models. Samuel Insull, Chicago Edison's electric power baron, adapted propaganda techniques learned during his tenure in the American branch of the British propaganda office to the Illinois Public Utility Information Committee. By 1923, other utilities followed suit and "were turning out a stream of utility publicity that almost matched the volume of patriotic publicity during the war."[41]

By the 1920s, several corporations were making efforts to adopt a public information model of public relations techniques. Foremost among these was American Telephone and Telegraph Company, which employed Arthur Page in 1927 to emphasize "candid disclosure rather than parochial propaganda."[42]

One of those trained on the Creel committee was Edward Bernays who, with his partner and wife Doris Fleischman, opened his own office in 1919. Bernays envisioned the role of the public relations practitioner as an agent of change—not as an agent of the press. He advocated principle over profit and "personal accountability for professional conduct."[43] Bernays' three books, *Crystallizing Public Opinion* (1923), *Propaganda* (1928), and *Public Relations* (1952), written over a thirty-year period, emphasized the importance of understanding the public and communicating that understanding to business management. Bernays argued that publicity is not the point at which a practitioner starts an activity, but rather the point at which it is ended.[44] Nevertheless, Bernays' early work remained within the realm of publicity and usually was directed toward publicity that generated sales.[45]

The 1920s Newspaper and Nationalization

During the 1920s, newspapers increased their prices and developed a more modern look. This change in newspaper appearance was due to an increased use of syndicated material as well as national advertising, a development made possible by the distribution of papier-mâché mats. Metropolitan dailies ("metros") carried about 60 percent advertising and averaged between twenty and thirty pages. Most dailies were approximately the same size as the newspapers of today and cost three cents each. Metros built branch plants and created neighborhood editions to serve the thriving suburbs. Price jumps after World War I reflected higher newsprint costs, expansion of news and features, and higher postage rates. Further, the cost of labor increased as newspaper editors began to upgrade notoriously low wages.

Chains and Conglomerates

The rapid growth of chain newspaper organizations after 1900 boomed during the 1920s, and the number of chain newspapers doubled between 1923 and 1933. This growth—and apparent monopolization—caused concern among intellectual critics, who worried about information becoming consolidated in the hands of only a few companies.

Commercial agreements among newspapers existed as early as the 1700s, but generally these agreements were designed to handle short-term problems or create short-term gains. In the 1700s, collective agreements were made to hold down the price of labor or to stabilize the price of subscriptions. During the next ten years, a variety of attempts was made to facilitate cooperative news gathering, and after the Civil War several companies developed boilerplate news services, providing ready-made sheets to be included in the weeklies of the country.

By the end of the 1920s, however, chain newspapers had made significant gains against the independents. In 1933, the six largest chains were Hearst, Patterson-McCormick, Scripps-Howard, Paul Block, Ridder, and Gannett. These six giants controlled almost 70 percent of the nation's daily chain circulation and 26 percent of total circulation—independent and chain.[46]

Chief among the chain owners were J. E., G. H., and E. W. Scripps and J. S. Sweeney, who together formed the Scripps Publishing Company, a firm that by 1880 controlled five dailies. E. W. Scripps, the brother who achieved the most fame in the newspaper business, joined with M. A. McRae to launch other group newspaper organizations. By 1920, E. W. Scripps owned twenty-two newspapers. Scripps' method was to lend money to an enterprising young publisher and let the publisher run the paper; if he succeeded, Scripps took 51 percent of the profits; if he failed, Scripps took the loss. Scripps continued to develop his chain organizations, and in 1922 he formed the Scripps-Howard chain with the twenty-five-year-old Roy Howard. This chain grew to twenty-five dailies, most of which were evening papers, by 1930. Howard, who headed the United Press (UP) wire service, had come to Scripps newspapers in Indianapolis and Cincinnati after an earlier stint with the *St. Louis Post-Dispatch* and earned his reputation with Scripps' lively evening-oriented wire service.

Although some newspaper publishers and press critics argued that chain ownership would decrease the diversity of the news media, there was even more concern expressed about conglomerates, or companies with extensive business interests that also owned media properties. The fear was that a company with an interest in a business outside the media would try to influence or dictate how the media treated that business.

One major example from the 1920s is the case of the International Paper Company (IPC), which almost monopolized the American newsprint industry and owned interests in fourteen American newspapers, including the *Boston Herald and Traveler*, the *Chicago Daily News* and the *Chicago Journal*, as well as four Gannett papers. The International Paper Company was owned by International Paper and Power Company (IP&PC), a holding company that also owned large electricity-producing subsidiaries and was considered to be among a small group of large corporations informally labeled the "Power Trust."

In 1928, the Federal Trade Commission, on directions from the U.S. Senate, began an investigation of the IP&PC and seventeen other holding companies. The IPC's newspaper investments were a secret until the FTC hearings, and although no direct evidence was presented, the fear was that the parent company had invested in newspapers in order to assure less press criticism of the power and utility industry. As soon as the hearings made the newspaper investments known, Gannett repaid its loans to IPC and withdrew completely from any dealings with the company. By the end of 1929, IPC had sold all its holdings.

The IPC president argued that there had been no intention to influence public opinion in regard to the utilities industry but that the company had purchased the newspaper companies to assure long-term contracts for its paper business. Gannett testified that his newspapers had opposed the Power Trust and that IPC had put no editorial pressure on him. His dealings with IPC had only to do with tonnage of paper, he testified.

Whether the trust intended to eventually use the newspapers editorially or not is a matter of conjecture, but the investigations and the fear of the possibility of control by business interests set the stage for increased complaints about the corruption of the press in the 1930s.[47]

Content

The information-versus-sensation dilemma of the late nineteenth century continued to appear in the newspapers of the 1920s. Newspapers either maintained an elite attitude, with serious but dull coverage of important national and international news, or they increased their coverage of events associated with the jazz age of the 1920s, and provided little serious news. Newspapers following the latter pattern included more coverage of human interest stories, murders, crimes, natural disasters, train accidents, and sports. Silas Bent, a harsh critic of the metropolitan press in the 1920s, wrote in 1927 that it was not uncommon "to see in New York newspapers as much as twenty columns devoted to a single day's proceedings in two second-rate murder trials."[48]

National Advertising

Newspapers benefited—as did magazines and radio—from the emergence of national advertising in the twentieth century. After the turn of the century, national advertising played an ever-increasing role in the small-town daily, just as it did in the metropolitan newspaper. At first, local retailers designed their own ads for national brand products. Later attempts to gain national advertising through contracts placed directly with the newspaper spearheaded modernization efforts that would enlarge circulations. The messages created by talented individuals such as Helen Lansdowne Resor made their way to the small-town papers, providing visually striking ads for Ivory soap, the National Biscuit Company products, Calumet baking powder, and

What Readers Want

On the editorial page we have only two columns of editorials. But they are crisp and to the point. We have several Harvard professors writing editorials for us. But I do not believe in too much quantity of that sort; for it is the *average* man and woman to whom I want to appeal.

—Edwin A. Grozier, editor, *Boston Post*, speaking to a reporter in 1923 for an *American Magazine* article

Armour oleomargarine. Motion picture advertising accelerated as well. National advertisers requested cooperation from the newspapers, urging them to supply national manufacturers with the names of possible local dealers and to encourage local merchants to advertise certain products such as Sunkist oranges on "Orange Day." Lord and Thomas warned the *Emporia* (Kansas) *Gazette* that "by co-operating on the special Christmas and Orange day large advertisements," the *Gazette* would receive special attention when the agency placed advertising orders. Newspapers, therefore, surrendered a certain amount of independence to national manufacturing organizations that suggested directions for the newspaper to take in advertising and promotion efforts.[49] The widespread use of papier-mâché mats altered the look of the local newspapers, making the newspaper more stylish and cosmopolitan but definitely less local.

Tabloids

The standard view of the tabloids is that they reflected what some termed the declining moral values of the decade, publishing screaming headlines about divorce, murder, and crime. Improvements in photographic technology provided the newspapers with the opportunity to display large pictures. The *New York Daily News* led the way, splashing on page one the execution of Ruth Snyder, first woman to die in the electric chair. The photograph was sensational in content but even more sensational in context, because the photographer talked his way into the execution chamber and took the photo with a camera strapped within a trouser leg.

A newer view of the tabloids suggests that they helped city dwellers to create order in their chaotic lives and to "understand and to cope with their own experience in relationship to a new and increasingly complex society."[50] The tabloid pictures of city life helped citizens to view the city with amazement, even though their day-to-day lives were routine and consisted of factory or assembly-line jobs.

The tabloid was not a creation of the 1920s, nor was it a creation of big-city U.S. editors. A British publisher's experiment with the tabloid format on the *New York World* in 1901 probably was preceded by similar experiments with other British publications. The *New York Illustrated Daily News*, the first regularly published tabloid in the United States, began on June 23, 1919. Published by Chicagoans Joseph Patterson and Robert McCormick, the *Daily News* circulated to 400,000 people within two years. Although the circulation of other New York dailies remained fairly constant from 1919 to 1926, under Patterson's leadership the *Illustrated Daily News* soared to the incredible figure of 1 million by 1926. By 1924, two competing tabloids entered the market: Hearst's *Daily Mirror* and Bernarr MacFadden's *Evening Graphic*. The *Graphic*, never a close contender in circulation, failed after six years. The major innovation of the *Graphic* was the extensive use of photographs and composographs, or faked photos.

The tabloids raised the ire of newspaper publishers and of elite society. The literary world referred to the half-size sheets as "Tabloid Poison," "that new black plague," and "jungle weeds in the journalistic garden." Some claimed, however, that the tabloids were no worse than their full-size metropolitan competitors. "The *News* is cheap and frothy but not, as a rule, antisocial," wrote one critic. "It is, from the social point of view, on a par with a considerable portion of the American press which, like this first of the tabloids, is given its character by triviality and slight constructive content."[51]

The Black Press

Some historians regard the period beginning with World War I and continuing through the 1930s as the time when the black press had its prime influence. From 1900 to 1920, the number of black newspapers grew from 200 to 500. The dramatic story of World War I and its contradictions—African Americans carrying arms in defense of their country, carrying arms with white approval for the first time since the Civil War, coupled with discrimination at home and in the armed forces—gave the black press news content and crusade material. Another major story—that of the migration of African Americans to northern urban communities—attracted comment by editorial leaders of the black press. Coinciding with these news events was a reawakening and rediscovery of black culture that resulted in the renaissance of the 1920s and its promotion of jazz and other cultural developments. War-industry employment improved the overall economy and, with it, the black economy. African-American newspapers, always on the brink of financial disaster, benefited greatly from good economic conditions.

The black press found it difficult to support a war to "make the world safe for democracy," while African Americans in the United States felt that democracy hardly extended to them. Although, on the whole, the black press did support U.S. involvement in the war, black editors vociferously attacked discrimination in the armed forces and in domestic life. Editors such as Robert Abbott of the *Chicago Defender*

▼

INS Reports a Famous Murder

A chilly-looking blonde with frosty eyes and one of those marble, you-bet-you-will chins, and an inert, scare-drunk fellow that you couldn't miss among any hundred men as a dead setup for a blonde, or the shell game, or maybe a gold brick.

Mrs. Ruth Snyder and Henry Judd Gray are on trial in the huge weatherbeaten old courthouse of Queens County in Long Island City, just across the river from the roar of New York, for what might be called for want of a better name, The Dumbbell Murder. It was so dumb.

They are charged with the slaughter four weeks ago of Albert Snyder, art editor of the magazine, *Motor Boating*, the blonde's husband and father of her nine-year-old daughter, under circumstances that for sheer stupidity and brutality have seldom been equaled in the history of crime.

—Damon Runyon, April 19–May 9, 1927

crusaded for integration and equality of opportunity, while others, such as W. E. B. Du Bois, argued for segregated training camps. Du Bois believed segregation was a necessity, and blacks would never be given an equal chance within an integrated training situation. Separate but equal was his battle cry.

George Creel viewed the situation as alarming and tried to persuade black editors that foreign propagandists were stirring up the equal rights crusade. In 1919, the Justice Department claimed that racial propaganda was caused by Russian sympathizers. Black editors, pressured to support the war effort while maintaining their own integrity, met in June 1918 to voice their support of the struggle against Germany.[52] The postwar years were difficult for African Americans. Returning white veterans looking for jobs resented inroads blacks had made during the war, and the resulting tension produced massive race riots in the late teens of the twentieth century.

During the first twenty years of the century, the most significant publications included Marcus Garvey's *Negro World*, sponsored by the Universal Negro Improvement Association. In the 1920s, this newspaper was the first African-American paper to top a circulation of 200,000. Three rivals bypassed that circulation in the 1920s. They were Robert L. Vann's *Pittsburgh Courier*, Carl Murphy's *Baltimore Afro-American*, and Robert Abbott's *Chicago Defender*. The vast majority of African-American papers were small-town southern papers, and editors faced not only discrimination but restrictions concerning freedom of expression. These papers dared not endorse the National Association for the Advancement of Colored People, trade unions, socialism, or black nationalism. Thus, it was left to the big city papers to champion the cause for equality and to promote the northward migration. The city papers initially addressed the African-American elite, but with increased migration to the North and the successful development of a black professional class, the newspapers entered a professional, commercial phase that addressed a mass audience.[53]

Discussed in detail here is the *Chicago Defender*, one of those city newspapers and possibly the paper most responsible for massive northward migrations.

The *Chicago Defender*

The *Chicago Defender* was one of the best known of the African-American papers, particularly in the 1920s. Robert Abbott, who founded the paper in 1905, was born in 1868 to former slaves on St. Simons island off the coast of Georgia.

When he began publishing the *Defender*, it was a one-man operation, although many of his friends donated time and energy to writing, printing, and distributing the paper. The *Defender* covered not only Chicago, but it served as a national chronicler of events in the African-American community. In his autobiography, Malcolm X wrote, "And every time Joe Louis won a fight against a white opponent, big front-page pictures in the Negro newspapers such as the *Chicago Defender*, the *Pittsburgh Courier*, and the *Afro-American* showed a sea of Harlem Negroes cheering and waving and the Brown Bomber waving back at them from the balcony of Harlem's Theresa Hotel."

Albert Kreiling notes that Abbott's *Defender* "stood at the forefront of the commercial black press. Its success signaled the triumph of commercial papers over those for which profit was a minor or nonexistent consideration. The paper carried news

Figure 12–4 Copyreader at work on a 1942 issue of the *Chicago Defender.* (OWI, Farm Security Administration, Division of Prints and Photographs, Library of Congress Collection)

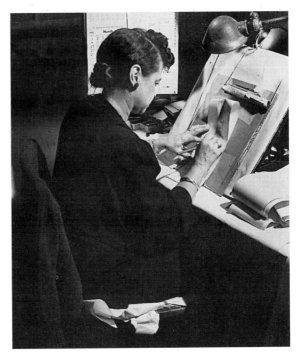

gathering to heights previously undreamed of, as it brought the new commodity of race news to large local and national followings."[54] Abbott used sensational techniques of the day, foreshadowing modern American journalism by compartmentalizing news. Departments in the paper included sports, editorials, women's news, and state news. Abbott advocated the abolishment of racial prejudice—encouraging the representation of African Americans in trade unions, the President's cabinet, police forces, and railway and bus companies; the admission of all Americans, white and black, to public schools; the federally mandated abolishment of lynching; and full enfranchisement of all Americans.

The *Defender* was at its peak during the century's teen years, when race riots broke out in Chicago and other major cities of the nation. At first, it joined in the sensational coverage of other Chicago newspapers. The *Chicago Daily News* falsely claimed that black men had attacked and killed white women, and the *Defender*, just as falsely, informed its readers:

> The homes of blacks isolated in white neighborhoods were burned to the ground and the owners and occupants beaten and thrown unconscious into the smoldering embers.

As the riots continued, the editor sought to calm his readers:

> do your part to restore quiet and order. . . . Every day of rioting and disorder means loss of life, destruction of property, loss of money for you and your families, and for some of us these losses will be large and irredeemable.

When the rioting stopped, Governor Frank O. Lowden appointed a commission of race relations, and Robert Abbott was one of six African Americans appointed to the twelve-member commission. The causes of the riots were many, but one major factor was the heavy migration of southern blacks to the North. Stifled by prejudice and the lack of employment opportunity in the South, blacks responded to the calls of northern newspapers like the *Defender*. Historian William Tuttle reported that Chicago's African-American population nearly doubled from 1916 to 1920 and that perhaps "the most effective institution in stimulating the migration was the *Defender*, which prompted thousands to venture North."55 In October 1916, the *Defender* said, ". . . to the North we have said, as the song goes, 'I hear you calling me,' and have boarded the train singing, 'Good-bye Dixie Land.'"

Abbott finally achieved financial security during the 1920s, and although he changed his mind on a variety of issues, he never wavered on integration. Abbott was proud of his financial success and contributed to the Chicago Urban League, became a life member of the Art Institute of Chicago, and joined a variety of social clubs. During the depression, the *Defender* and its finances declined, but the newspaper survived. When Abbott died, the *Defender* devoted most of its space to his death. However, the racial line was still drawn in Chicago, and although prominent individuals, black and white, attended Abbott's funeral, the *Chicago Tribune* carried his obituary of several paragraphs in the standard obituary columns at the back of the newspaper.

Novels and Pulps

By the twentieth century, the book publishing industry was centered in New York, although companies established during the nineteenth century in Boston, Philadelphia, and Indianapolis continued to thrive. Publishing houses forged relationships with Hollywood, a partnership that created profits both for the publishers and for the film companies. Book clubs helped solve the dilemma of distribution, and the founding of the Book-of-the-Month Club in 1926 and the Literary Guild in 1927 allowed publishers to reach a targeted group of readers through direct mail promotion techniques. Furthermore, from 1852 until 1913, postage rates for books as well as for other types of mail declined, despite the fact that books never enjoyed the special privileges granted to newspapers and magazines.

The novel—and the pulp fiction magazine—made enormous gains during the first decades of the twentieth century. Detective fiction, science fiction, and the western gained attention from readers and editors; each genre, in its own way, defined heroism and individualism in contrast to the faceless, urbanized world of the 1920s. Popular since the end of the nineteenth century, Horatio Alger's rags-to-riches novels of individualistic achievement gave way to the achievement of the athlete, who could build strength and skill to win regardless of family or money. The emphasis on adventure in these books encouraged reading by men and boys, unlike the feminine emphasis found in the popular fiction of the nineteenth century.

Science fiction epitomized modernization—mythologizing technological progress—but it spoke as well to traditional cultures, suggesting that social relations would remain stable despite technological advances. Science fiction covered broad areas, from the technological elimination of human labor to intergalactic travel—the latter an area it tended to emphasize. Juxtaposed against the technological wonders of the universe was the western, featuring the loner, or outside hero, who rectifies the ills within a community in peril, then flees in the dawn of justice. The western resisted urbanization and the dominance of eastern industrial society. The role of the individual in a corrupt, urbanized society was vividly portrayed in the detective novels popular in the 1920s in which individualistic detectives resisted the call of crime and sex in order to apprehend the murderer and preserve their own autonomy.[56]

During much of the nineteenth century, books had been classified under third-class rates rather than the more advantageous second-class. However, during the latter part of the century, many book publishers issued paperbacked books periodically in order to qualify under the more favored rate for magazines. In 1901, after much congressional debate, Postmaster General Charles E. Smith declared that books could not use the second-class rates under any conditions. Several publishers took their case to court. Houghton, Mifflin, and Company argued it should be allowed to mail its Riverside Literature Series under second-class rates. The publisher won its case in the federal district court, but it lost in the higher courts. In 1913, book publishers successfully pleaded with Congress to establish a parcel post, a separate class of postage that addressed packages of heavier weight. Although Congress passed a parcel post rate, it made no provision to include books. However, a year later, a new postmaster general moved books to the fourth-class parcel post rate, providing for books to be delivered via rural free delivery, inaugurated in 1896. This move laid the groundwork for the development of the book clubs in the 1920s, making it possible for publishers to mail packages of books to country residents. In 1928, Congress established a special rate for library books but refused to extend it to what lawmakers called a subsidy for the commercial book business. During World War II, President Franklin Delano Roosevelt administratively lowered the book rate, and lower rates for all books were passed by Congress in 1942.[57]

Conclusion

By the end of the 1920s, most of the modern forms of communication were in place, but a lively debate ensued about how those forms—radio, motion pictures, and newspapers, particularly the tabloids—would affect American life. Critics wondered whether these new forms, which separated the dissemination of information from transportation, would help preserve traditional values or whether they would modernize the world so that it would be unrecognizable to an older generation.

Radio, a social as well as a technological innovation, caused cultural and political leaders to explore the possibilities of the new medium. Within less than a decade, an American system of broadcasting was in place. Initial profits from the sale of sets gave way to a commercialized industry, which relied on advertising for its profits. A proliferation of individual local stations linked by the National Broadcasting Corporation, owned by RCA, dominated the radio industry. The Federal Radio Act of 1927 incorporated most of the demands of the industry, at the same time creating the Federal Radio Commission to administer technical aspects, which stabilized the industry for commercial growth. Although licensing of the broadcast industry introduced stabilization, it also represented a critical departure from the First Amendment protection that had been granted to the print media.

By the end of the 1920s, motion pictures had become full-length entertainments. Once just a few small businesses disseminating twelve-minute novelties, the full-fledged industry now was dominated by five major movie houses in Hollywood. The industry was controlled by monopolistic corporations that dominated production not only in the United States but in the world as well.

Advertising practitioners responded to the development of differentiated products, and by the 1920s they moved from selling newspaper space to creating agencies that provided varied services, from marketing research to copywriting. Agencies soon dominated the business, championed professionalism, moved slowly toward truth-in-advertising policies, targeted women as primary consumers, and incorporated the social tensions of the day in their persuasive strategies.

The development of public relations techniques continued from the latter half of the nineteenth century to enable businesses to boost public awareness of their role as makers and disseminators of news. Skilled practitioners urged business leaders to abandon secrecy and to convince the public of their honorable intentions by explaining situations and policies.

The debate over whether newspapers would provide information or sensation continued throughout the decade. Newspaper chains mushroomed, and fear of conglomerates and dismay over the 60 percent of newspaper content given to advertising evoked criticism. The tabloids, with screaming headlines, reflected the diversity of city life and used advances in photographic technology to attract their readers. African-American newspapers increased circulations and reached what was perhaps their peak of influence in the 1920s. Black metro dailies championed the cause of equality and provided to African Americans day-to-day news of black accomplishments and sorrows.

The book industry flourished as postal regulation became more favorable to sending books in the mail, and the founding of two major book clubs allowed publishers to directly target potential buyers.

Technology triumphed—in many phases of business, in the development of electronic media, in the promotion and distribution of books and periodicals, and in the flooding of even local dailies with nationally syndicated news and advertisements. By the end of the decade, Americans had experienced the onslaught of a commercial consumer culture.

Endnotes

1. Elaine Prostak (Berland), "Up in the Air: The Public Debates over Radio Use during the 1920's," Ph.D. dissertation, University of Kansas, 1983.

2. For an analysis of industry battles and congressional legislation, see Erik Barnouw's classic three-volume work, *A History of Broadcasting in the United States,* vol. 1, *A Tower in Babel* (New York: Oxford University Press, 1966); Philip T. Rosen, *The Modern Stentors: Radio Broadcasters and the Federal Government, 1920–1934* (Westport, Conn.: Greenwood Press, 1980); Daniel E. Garvey, "Secretary Hoover and the Quest for Broadcast Regulation," *Journalism History* 3 (Autumn, 1976), pp. 66–70, 85; and Donald G. Godfrey, "The 1927 Radio Act: People and Politics," *Journalism History* 4 (Autumn, 1977), p. 78.

3. For a discussion of contemporary public debates about educational, political, cultural, and religious use of the airwaves, see Prostak, "Up in the Air."

4. For an extensive account of the debate over the meaning of free speech on the radio, with emphasis on the debate in the legal community, see Louise M. Benjamin, "Radio Regulation in the 1920s: Free Speech Issues in the Development of Radio and the Radio Act of 1927," Ph.D. dissertation, University of Iowa, 1985. See also Robert W. McChesney, "Free Speech and Democracy: The Debate in the American Legal Community over the Meaning of Free Expression on Radio, 1926–1939," unpublished paper presented to the Law and History Divisions, Association for Education in Journalism and Mass Communication, San Antonio, Tex., August 1987.

5. Prostak, "Up in the Air," p. 22. For an important discussion of the complex interplay between opposing forces and the implications of technology, see Daniel Czitrom, *Media and the American Mind* (Chapel Hill: University of North Carolina Press, 1982).

6. Prostak, "Up in the Air," p. 23–24. For figures on station ownership, see Christopher Sterling and John M. Kittross, *Stay Tuned: A Concise History of American Broadcasting* (Belmont, Calif.: Wadsworth, 1978), pp. 510–33.

7. Herbert Hoover at the Third National Radio Conference, October 1924, cited in Sterling and Kittross, *Stay Tuned*, p. 49.

8. Prostak, "Up in the Air," p. 38. See also Catherine L. Covert, "We May Hear Too Much: American Sensibility and the Response to Radio, 1919–1924," in Catherine Covert and John D. Stevens, *Mass Media between the Wars: Perceptions of Cultural Tension, 1918–1941* (Syracuse, NY: Syracuse University Press, 1984); and Mary S. Mander, "The Public Debate about Broadcasting in the Twenties: An Interpretive History," *Journal of Broadcasting* 28:2 (Spring, 1984), pp. 167–85.

9. Robert McChesney, "The Battle for the U.S. Airwaves, 1928–1935," *Journal of Communication* 40:4 (Autumn, 1990), p. 30.

10. For information on the congressional debates, see Daniel E. Garvey, "Secretary Hoover and the Quest for Broadcast Regulation," *Journalism History* 3 (Autumn, 1976), pp. 66–70, 85; Joseph P. McKerns, "Industry Skeptics and the Radio Act of 1927," *Journalism History* 3 (Winter, 1976), pp. 128–31, 136; and Donald G. Godfrey, "The 1927 Radio Act: People and Politics," *Journalism History* 4 (Autumn, 1977) pp. 74–78.

11. Cited in McChesney, "The Battle for the U.S. Airwaves," p. 33.

12. McChesney, "The Battle for the U.S. Airwaves," p. 39.

13. See McChesney, "The Battle for the U.S. Airwaves," and his other works, including "Labor and the Marketplace of Ideas: WCFL and the Battle for Labor Radio Broadcasting, 1927–1934," *Journalism Monographs* 134 (August, 1992); "Constant Retreat: The American Civil Liberties Union and the Debate over the Meaning of Free Speech for Radio Broadcasting in the 1930s," in Stephen A. Smith, ed., *Free Speech Yearbook, 1987*, vol. 26 (Carbondale: Southern Illinois University Press, 1988); and "Free Speech and Democracy! Louis G. Caldwell, the American Bar Association and the Debate over the Free Speech Implications of Broadcast Regulation, 1928–1938," *The American Journal of Legal History* 35 (October, 1991), pp. 351–92.

14. Jacobs, *The Documentary Tradition*, p. 29. See also Erik Barnouw, *Documentary: A History of the Non-Fiction Film* (New York: Oxford, 1983), p. 26; and Raymond Fielding, *The American Newsreel, 1911–1967*, and *The March of Time, 1935–1951* (New York: Oxford University Press, 1978).

15. Barnouw, *Documentary*, p. 52.

16. Fielding, *The March of Time*, p. 4.

17. A. William Bluem, *The Documentary in American Television* (New York: Hastings House, 1965), cited in Jacobs, *The Documentary Tradition*, pp. 104, 105.

18. Cited in Fielding, *The March of Time*, p. 302.

19. For a thorough analysis of the movie industry, see Tino Balio, *The American Film Industry* (Madison: University of Wisconsin Press, rev. ed. 1985).

20. Douglas Gomery, "U.S. Film Exhibition: The Formation of a Big Business," in Balio, *Film Industry*, pp. 218–28.

21. *Mutual Film Corp. v. Industrial Commission of Ohio*, 236 U.S. 230, 244, 35 S.Ct. 387, 391 (1915); *Joseph Burstyn, Inc. v. Wilson*, 343 U.S. 495, 72 S.Ct. 777 (1952).

22. Lizabeth Cohen, "Encountering Mass Culture at the Grassroots: The Experience of Chicago Workers in the 1920s," *American Quarterly* 41 (March, 1989), pp. 6–33.

23. For an analysis of the roles of consumer credit and advertising in the consumer durables revolution of the 1920s, see Martha Olney, "Advertising, Consumer Credit, and the Consumer Durables Revolution of the 1920s," Ph.D. dissertation, Berkeley, 1982.

24. For a critical view of advertising and consumer culture, see Stuart Ewen, *Captains of Consciousness: Advertising and the Roots of Consumer Culture* (New York: McGraw Hill, 1976); and T. J. Jackson Lears and Richard Wightman Fox, eds., *The Culture of Consumption* (New York: Pantheon, 1983).

25. David Ogilvy, *Ogilvy on Advertising* (New York: Crown Publishers, Inc., 1983), p. 191.

26. Stephen Fox, *The Mirror Makers: A History of American Advertising and Its Creators* (New York: William Morrow, 1984), pp. 80–84.

27. Ogilvy, *Ogilvy on Advertising*, p. 192.

28. Fox, *The Mirror Makers*, p. 83.

29. See Pope, *Making of Modern Advertising* (New York: Basic Books, 1983), for a full discussion of why advertising agencies dominated the advertising industry.

30. Helen Woodward, *Through Many Windows* (New York: Harper & Bros., 1926), pp. 348–49, cited in Pope, *Making of Modern Advertising*, p. 180.

31. Fox, *The Mirror Makers*, p. 288–289.

32. Pope, *Making of Modern Advertising*, p. 183.

33. Roland Marchand, "Two Legendary Campaigns," *American Heritage* 36:3 (April/May, 1985), p. 76. See also Marchand, *Advertising the American Dream: Making Way for Modernity, 1920–1940* (Berkeley: University of California Press, 1985).

34. Marchand, "Legendary Campaigns," p. 76.

35. Marchand, "Legendary Campaigns," pp. 76–77.

36. Marchand, "Legendary Campaigns," p. 80.

37. Marchand, "Legendary Campaigns," p. 85.

38. Richard Tedlow, *Keeping the Corporate Image: Public Relations and Business, 1900–1950* (Greenwich, Conn.: JAI Press, 1979).

39. Ray Eldon Hiebert, *Courtier to the Crowd: The Story of Ivy Lee and the Development of Public Relations* (Ames: Iowa State University Press, 1966), p. 48.

40. Genevieve G. McBride, "Ethical Thought in Public Relations History: Seeking a Relevant Perspective," presented to the Public Relations Division, Association for Education in Journalism and Mass Communication, Memphis, Tenn., August 1985.

41. Michael Schudson, *Discovering the News: A Social History of American Newspapers* (New York: Basic Books, 1978), p. 143.

42. Cited in James E. Grunig and Todd Hunt, *Managing Public Relations* (Holt, Rinehart, & Winston, 1984), p. 36.

43. McBride, "Ethical Thought," pp. 5, 8.

44. McBride, "Ethical Thought," p. 7.

45. Tedlow, *Corporate Image*, p. 45.

46. For statistics, see Alfred McClung Lee, *The Daily Newspaper in America* (New York: Macmillan, 1937), pp. 214–15.

47. For a complete description of the International Paper Company investigation, see Cathy Packer, "Conglomerate Newspaper Ownership: International Paper Company, 1928–29," *Journalism Quarterly* 60:3 (Autumn, 1983), pp. 480–83, 567.

48. Silas Bent, "The Art of Ballyhoo," *Harper's* 155 (September, 1927), p. 493, cited in James L. Baughman, *Henry R. Luce and the Rise of the American News Media* (Boston:

G.K. Hall/Twayne), p. 54. This book is cited from the manuscript.

49. See Sally Foreman Griffith, *Home Town News* (New York: Oxford University Press, 1989) for an analysis of the impact of national advertising on the *Emporia Gazette*.

50. James E. Murphy, "Tabloids as an Urban Response," in Covert and Stevens, *Mass Media between the Wars*, p. 55.

51. Douglass W. Miller, "The New York Tabloids," *Journalism Quarterly* 5 (1928), pp. 39–40, cited in Covert and Stevens, *Mass Media between the Wars*, p. 60.

52. Kessler, *Dissident Press*, pp. 41–42.

53. Theodore G. Vincent, ed., *Voices of a Black Nation: Political Journalism in the Harlem Renaissance* (San Francisco: Ramparts Press, 1973), pp. 19–38. See also John D. Stevens, "The Black Press Looks at 1920's Journalism," *Journalism History* 7:3–4 (Autumn–Winter, 1980), pp. 109–113; and Albert Kreiling, "The Commercialization of the Black Press and the Rise of Race News in Chicago," in *Ruthless Criticism,* William S. Solomon and Robert W. McChesney, eds. (Minneapolis: University of Minnesota Press, 1993), pp. 176–203.

54. This discussion relies heavily on the entry of Robert Abbott in the *Dictionary of Literary Biography,* previously cited and written by one author of this text, Jean Folkerts. See also the primary research materials used for the article: Roi Ottley, *The Lonely Warrior* (Chicago: Regnery, 1955); Henry G. La Brie, III, *Perspectives of the Black Press: 1974* (Kennebunkport, Me.: Mercer House Press, 1974); Metz Lochard, "Robert S. Abbott—Race Leader," *Phylon* 8 (Second Quarter, 1947), pp. 124–32; and William M. Tuttle, Jr., *Race Riot: Chicago in the Red Summer of 1919* (New York: Atheneum, 1970). Also see Kreiling, "The Commercialization of the Black Press and the Rise of Race News in Chicago," in *Ruthless Criticism,* pp. 98–121; Theodore Kornweikel, Jr., *"Seeing Red": Federal Campaigns Against Black Militancy, 1919–1925.* (Bloomington: Indiana University Press, 1998).

55. William M. Tuttle, Jr., *Race Riot: Chicago in the Red Summer of 1919* (New York: Atheneum, 1970).

56. Emory Elliott and Cathy N. Davidson, eds., *Columbia History of the American Novel* (New York: Columbia University Press, 1991).

57. For a thorough analysis of the postal controversy over the mailing of books, see Richard B. Kielbowicz, "Mere Merchandise or Vessels of Culture? Books in the Mail, 1792–1942," *Papers of the Bibliographical Society of America* 82:2 (1988), pp. 169–200.

CHAPTER 13

Depression and Disillusion

▼

First of all, let me assert my firm belief that the only thing
we have to fear is fear itself—nameless unreasoning,
unjustified terror.

　　　　—Franklin Delano Roosevelt, inaugural address

I am serving notice that I am firing 25 percent of the staff
now, and when I return from my vacation in Hot Springs I
am going to fire 25 percent more.

　　—Publisher Lucius Tarquinius Russell, *Newark Ledger*

In his inaugural address in March 1933, President Franklin Delano Roosevelt attacked the widespread fear that had gripped the people of the United States, caught in the despair of the depression. The fear, however, was based on reality, as the *Newark Ledger* publisher's remark indicated. The prosperity of the twenties faded as a dream, as 13 million unemployed workers and farmers struggled to feed their families in the face of plummeting prices and the loss of their savings. Among those workers were compositors, reporters, and editors.

The press, as well as stock market analysts, ignored the economic warnings of the late twenties. From 1925 on, the number of commercial failures increased relatively unnoticed, while the automobile and construction industries steadily declined. On Black Thursday, October 24, 1929, Wall Street crashed. A record number of shares sold, but those that sold were priced low, and others remained on the market for lack of buyers. Wild speculation preceded Black Thursday, with considerable buying on margin—investors borrowing 50 to 90 percent of the purchase prices from brokers, who increasingly borrowed from the banks at rising interest rates.

By 1933, corporate profits fell from a 1929 high of $10 billion to $1 billion, and the gross national product dropped by half. During those four years, stockholders and depositors lost $2.5 billion in savings account failures, and farm income was cut in half. In 1930, 4 million Americans were jobless, and by 1933, one-fourth of the labor force—a figure representing 13 million people—was unemployed. From 1928 to 1932, labor income dropped 40 percent.[1]

Despite its vast resources, the press failed to adequately inform the public prior to the stock market crash of 1929. Although the periodical industry would suffer some of the same business losses as other industries, the press proved surprisingly resilient. Newspapers suffered little, radio's profits accelerated, and the technology for television developed throughout the decade. Nevertheless, reporters made few economic gains, and some news staffs responded to the low pay and poor working conditions by organizing the American Newspaper Guild.

The industry remained not only strong but also innovative. The muckrakers and other progressive journalists had relied on a presentation of facts to convince American readers. Artists, filmmakers, and photographers of the 1930s, influenced by international experimentation with the documentary film and newsreel, led a developing documentary movement to chronicle the emotional as well as factual reality of the decade. The camera earned middle-class respectability, and at the beginning of the 1930s nearly 50 million people viewed newsreels and full-length features every week.[2]

The journalism of synthesis and the photojournalistic essay as mastered by Henry Luce in *Time* and *Life* opened new dimensions of interpretation.[3] Some newspapers, codes of ethics, and textbooks suggested that in order to adequately inform the American public, newspapers would have to go beyond presenting facts. Interpretation spawned a new generation of newsmen—the columnists and editorial writers. Newspapers also took advantage of gains in social science, using polls to predict the outcome of elections. Some journalists abandoned the mainstream press and established alternative publications.

President Franklin Delano Roosevelt, the key figure responsible for government intervention during the depression, reinstituted and expanded the government supply of news to the media. His open style and continuous flow of information to members of the press endeared reporters to him, even though his challenges to publishers alienated the industry and encouraged negative editorial-page coverage.[4] ▼

Media Content as Interpretation

As the hard times of the 1930s replaced the roaring excesses of the 1920s, those who held faith in American democracy were losing some of their naïveté. George Creel's propaganda efforts of World War I shook the journalist's faith in facts, and the growing public relations industry persuaded many that even facts were a matter of interpretation. Further, the reporting of facts had not prepared society for the depression.[5]

The Documentary Tradition

One method of interpretation, the documentation of emotion rather than information, was an effort to show "man at grips with conditions neither permanent nor necessary." It appeared worldwide, beginning almost as soon as the moving picture industry sufficiently developed its technical ability to provide entertainment for viewers.[6] In the 1920s, the documentary focused on man's interaction with his environment and on an effort to capture the essence of city life. By 1930, the presentation of political ideology had become a third phase of the documentary film.

At the beginning of the 1930s in Germany and the Soviet Union, where documentary philosophy was determined by the government, technically brilliant films glorified national fervor. In England and the United States, independents, often on the political left, produced most of the documentaries. The Film and Photo League of New York City, for example, documented the inhumanity of evicting people from their homes in a 1934 film, *Sheriff.* As the New Deal progressed, the administration funded documentaries that promoted concepts of conservation and government intervention like Pare Lorentz's production of *The Plow That Broke the Plains* (1936), a report on attempts to alleviate dust bowl conditions for Oklahoma farmers, and *The River* (1937), a documentary of the effects of soil erosion in the Mississippi Basin and the positive effects of the Tennessee Valley Authority, a New Deal reclamation project.[7]

During the 1930s, the documentary became a preferred mode of expression because it appealed to the emotions as well as provided facts, and it informed a generation skeptical of abstract promises who believed "what they saw, touched, handled, and—the crucial word—felt."[8] Practitioners of the new mode included photographers such as Margaret Bourke-White and Dorothea Lange, who photographed American life and working conditions for the Farm Security Administration, as well as other artists employed by the Federal Writers Project and other New Deal agencies and programs. The documentary, wrote cultural historian William Stott, "treats the actual unimagined experience of individuals belonging to a group generally of low economic and social standing in the society (lower than the audience for whom the report is made) and treats this experience in such a way as to try to render it vivid, 'human,' and—most often—poignant to the audience."[9]

Henry Luce, with the development of *Life* magazine in 1936, combined the documentary tradition, the new available technology of the portable camera, the tradition of German picture magazines, and some aspects of 1920s jazz journalism to produce a magazine that soon became the leader in the realm of the photojournalistic essay.

▼

Facts Do Not Spontaneously Take Shape

The development of the publicity man is a clear sign that the facts of modern life do not spontaneously take a shape in which they can be known. They must be given a shape by somebody, and since in the daily routine reporters cannot give a shape to facts, and since there is little disinterested organization of intelligence, the need for some formulation is being met by the interested parties.

—Walter Lippmann, *Public Opinion*

Interpretation in the Daily Press

Interpretation in the daily press, unlike the documentary tradition, was not antithetical to the development of objectivity as a reporting ideal. Newspaper interpretation was more cautious than that of the documentary and expressed emotion less overtly. Recognizing that the citizenry had not been properly forewarned about World War I or about the advent of the depression, journalists began to discuss the need to put facts into context. Such discussion permeated the academic and the professional communities.

Curtis MacDougall's textbook, *Reporting for Beginners*, first published in 1932, reflected the trend toward interpretation. When MacDougall revised the book in 1938, its title changed to *Interpretative Reporting*. MacDougall explained that he changed the title and content because "changing social conditions . . . are causing news gathering and disseminating agencies to change their methods of reporting and interpreting the news." MacDougall wrote that the trend "is unmistakably in the direction of combining the function of interpreter with that of reporter after about a half century during which journalistic ethics called for a strict differentiation between narrator and commenter."[10]

In 1933, the American Society of Newspaper Editors accepted interpretive reporting in a resolution specifying that because world affairs were increasingly complex and because citizens were becoming increasingly interested in public affairs, editors should devote more attention to "explanatory and interpretative news and to presenting a background of information which will enable the average reader more adequately to understand the movement and significance of events."[11]

Michael Schudson, in *Discovering the News*, suggested that journalists responded to the new developments by admitting their subjectivity through signed articles and by developing specialties that would enable them to better interpret facts. Bylines appeared sparingly in the *New York Times* in the 1920s, but they were used liberally by the 1930s. The Associated Press, bylining its first story in 1925, soon followed suit. Although *Journalism Bulletin* in 1924 reported that "[t]ruly the age of specialization is at hand," specialization did not grow significantly until the 1930s.

The acceptance of subjectivity as inevitable did not, however, encourage journalists to abandon objectivity but rather to view it as an ideal. Schudson explained:

> Journalists came to believe in objectivity, to the extent that they did, because they wanted to, needed to, were forced by ordinary human aspiration to seek escape from their own deep convictions of doubt and drift. . . . Surely, objectivity as an ideal has been used and is still used, even disingenuously, as a camouflage for power. But its source lies deeper, in a need to cover over neither authority nor privilege, but the disappointment in the modern gaze.[12]

The Signed Political Column

Developing along with the new interest in interpretation was the signed political column. In the 1920s, David Lawrence, Mark Sullivan, and Frank Kent began to evaluate worldwide political and economic affairs. Heywood Hale Broun's *New York World* column began appearing in 1921, and Walter Lippmann's "Today and Tomorrow" first appeared in the *Herald Tribune* in 1931. By 1937, Lippmann's column was

▼

The Spanish Civil War

BARCELONA, MARCH 17—Barcelona has lived through twelve air raids in less than twenty-four hours, and the city is shaken and terror-struck. Human beings have seldom had to suffer as these people are suffering under General Francisco Franco's determined effort to break their spirit and induce their government to yield.

—Herbert Matthews, writing in the *New York Times*, March 18, 1938

syndicated in 155 newspapers. *The New Republic* noted in 1937 that "much of the influence once attached to the editorial page has passed over to the columnists."[13]

Use of Media Polls

Although by the late nineteenth century major political parties used canvassing widely to determine party allegiances, advances in the 1930s brought improved methods for gathering statistics and refining mathematical techniques. The first efforts to sample opinions of the general population were made by newspapers in the 1840s to predict the outcome of elections, but not until 1896 did polls become serious business. During that year the Chicago press, greatly concerned with the McKinley–Bryan race, sent reporters to sample various segments of the population. The *Chicago Tribune* determined that McKinley was the choice of 82 percent of the factory hands and 86 percent of the railroaders. The *Chicago Record* mailed postcard ballots to all 328,000 registered voters in Chicago and one voter in eight in twelve midwestern states. The *Record* employed mathematicians to analyze the 250,000 return cards, predicting that McKinley would win 57.94 percent of the Chicago vote. Although the prediction was close to the actual Chicago results, the team failed to determine voting percentages in other states.

Newspapers continued their flirtation with polling, and by 1912 a syndicate led by the *Chicago Record-Herald* and the *New York Herald* conducted presidential polls in every state. The Hearst chain polled forty-six states in 1928 and predicted Hoover's win with reasonable accuracy. The *Literary Digest* conducted presidential election polls from 1916 to 1936. Their samples—based on mailings to potential subscribers, then to the public at large—provided reasonably accurate predictions until the Landon–Roosevelt contest of 1936. As a cost-saving measure during the depression, the *Digest* relied on its 1932 mailing list and failed to correct its interpretation of results after Landon supporters responded at a much higher rate than Roosevelt supporters. Afterward, the disastrous prediction that Landon would win led many to discount the validity of mail questionnaires.

Despite the *Literary Digest* disaster, however, refinements in the understanding of random-sampling techniques and the need for advertisers to determine consumer preferences led researchers to continue to develop polling strategies. A reawakening of interest in shifting party membership during the New Deal furthered the cause of polling. George Gallup, Archibald Crossley, and Elmo Roper instituted the modern attitudinal polls in 1935. Roosevelt, intrigued with the concept and pleased that the polls had accurately predicted his 1936 landslide, employed Hadley Cantril, a pollster, to help him time his foreign and domestic policy announcements to appeal to public opinion. The industry flourished until every major pollster and political commentator predicted Thomas Dewey would defeat Harry Truman in 1948. From then until the 1960s, pollsters relied on answering commercial questions to sustain their incomes. In the 1960s, as politicians began to solicit their own secret polls to assist in developing political campaigns, pollsters again moved into the public arena.[14]

News Magazines as Journalism of Synthesis

Another form of interpretation involved the journalism of synthesis, or the interpretive news summary, evidenced by the development of newsmagazines and by the inclusion of weekly summaries in the daily press. Foremost among the developers of the interpretative journalistic summary was Henry Luce, who cofounded *Time* with Briton Hadden in 1923 to summarize information found in the daily press. Luce

JUNE, 1933   5

BUSINESS IS PICKING UP.   *William Gropper*

Figure 13-1   The *New Masses,* a socialist publication, published this lithograph by William Gropper in the June 1933 issue. The cartoon was titled, "Business Is Picking Up." (Division of Prints and Photographs, Library of Congress Collection)

struggled through financial gains and losses during the 1920s, but by the 1930s *Time* was an established financial success.

Luce edged out some competitors such as the *Literary Digest*, but he encouraged others such as *Newsweek*, founded in 1933, and *U.S. News and World Report*, which grew out of the *United States Daily* (1926 to 1933) and other David Lawrence publications. *Business Week*, also a depression baby, was founded in 1929 by McGraw-Hill Publishing Company. *Reader's Digest*, founded in 1922 as a synthesis of articles from other magazines, also flourished in the 1930s.

Dailies followed the lead of Luce and of *Time*, introducing weekend news summaries. In 1931, the *New York Sun* began a Saturday review of the news, the *Richmond News Leader* replaced its Saturday editorial page with an interpretive summary, and in 1935 the *New York Times* began an interpretive Sunday news summary. The Associated Press responded to the development with a weekend review of its own.[15]

Time and Henry Luce

By 1930, *Time* had gained a loyal readership and was so successful that Luce expanded his publishing business by introducing in February a new business magazine, *Fortune*, which lauded the business manager-tycoon. By the middle 1930s, Luce was on his way to becoming a tycoon himself, and in 1936, Luce launched another experiment, the photojournalism magazine, *Life*. Although it initially lost $6 million, it eventually produced enormous profits.

Luce's career was highly influenced by his childhood. Born in China in 1898, he spent his childhood attending a British boarding school at Chefoo on the Shantung north coast, where he was editor in chief of the school paper. In 1912, he went to England to attend St. Albans and then to the Hotchkiss School in Connecticut. He and Hotchkiss classmate Hadden attended Yale together and competed for positions on the *Yale Daily News*. Luce's experience in China as the son of Presbyterian missionaries and his schooling among the upper classes of England and the United States influenced his attitude regarding the necessity of an elite and what he believed to be the proper role of the elite in government. He detested communists even while at Yale, believing in the concept of a morally superior America.

After a year of study at Oxford and a stint on the *Chicago Daily News*, Luce rejoined his friend Hadden in February of 1922 to develop a newsmagazine that would compete with the *Literary Digest*. By October, primarily through their Yale contacts, the two raised $86,000 to start *Time*, and the first issue appeared on March 3, 1923. Giving the news a "jaunty personal point of view," Hadden and Luce sold only 9,000 copies of the first twenty-eight-page issue, which was far below their expectations of 25,000.[16] The magazine remained in the red until 1927.

Luce and Hadden made no pretense at objectivity. They noted in their prospectus that no editorial page would appear in *Time* and that no article would be written to prove a special case but that the editors recognized

> that complete neutrality on public questions and important news is probably as undesirable as it is impossible, and are therefore ready to acknowledge certain prejudices which may in varying measure predetermine their opinions on the news.

The prejudices they listed included a distrust of increasing government authority and expenditures, a respect for old manners, and an admiration for the "statesman's 'view of the world.'"[17] Luce and Hadden continued their competitive friendship until Hadden's death at thirty-one in 1928. After his death, Luce and his associates bought enough shares from Hadden's estate to firmly control Time, Inc.

Time introduced a condensed, telegraphic style that challenged the stodgy papers being written for the upper middle class. Luce instructed editors to write stories with a beginning, a middle, and an ending and to avoid the common inverted pyramid style newspapers had adopted.[18]

Time became famous—or infamous—for its language, dubbed Timestyle. Trick words and inverted sentence structure produced a sarcastic, gossipy tone that, although popular with its audience, also produced its share of critics. T. S. Matthews, a rising editor at *Time* who had worked for the *New Republic*, compared the two magazines:

> The contrast felt between the *New Republic* and *Time* was a contrast between scholarly, distinguished men and smart, ignorant boys. The *New Republic* didn't exist primarily to call attention to itself; it had the nobler motive (or so it seemed to me) of trying to recall Americans to their better senses.

Matthews later called *Time* a "strutting little venture" with a style that was a "ludicrous, exhibitionistic but arresting dialect of journalese."[19] The magazine was criticized for conveying a sense of omniscience; it seldom relied on quotes from authority figures and instead spoke its own mind, despite the fact that it was often wrong. *Time*, for example, predicted before the start of World War II that Hitler would not come to power in Germany.

Time was directed toward an upper-middle-class, male audience. A 1931 survey of readers in Appleton, Wisconsin, showed that 60 percent of *Time* readers had an average annual income of $5,000 or more. The average *Time* family income was $21,000. In 1929 nationwide, only 1 percent of all families earned $10,000 or more, and the average income was $2,335. Advertising in *Time* promoted the expensive hotels and private schools available only to upper middle classes. More bankers read *Time* than any other magazine. Although three out of eight college students were women in 1922, the *Time* prospectus, content, and advertising specifically targeted men. Further, Luce hired women only as researchers, who checked facts, not as writers.[20]

Luce extended his concept of interpretation in the inauguration of *Fortune*, a monthly business magazine. Luce announced the newsmagazine's birth in the last issue of *Time* published before Black Thursday. The monthly would sell at one dollar a copy or ten dollars a year, and it would be produced not by businessmen but by a staff of amateurs, many drawn from Luce's colleagues at Yale. The first 184-page issue sold in February 1930 to 30,000 subscribers. The magazine was a success, and in 1932, in the midst of the depression, Time, Inc., showed profits of $650,000 after taxes. The magazine lauded the business manager, but with writers such as Dwight Macdonald, the poet Archibald MacLeish, and the now legendary film critic and novelist James Agee, *Fortune* expressed skepticism about business, explored the documentary expression popular in the 1930s, and avoided the reactionary tone of other

Henry Luce (1898–1967)

On his passport, in case of death, Henry Luce listed his next of kin as Time, Inc. Luce started *Time* with Briton Hadden, whom he competed with at the Hotchkiss School in Connecticut and later in college at Yale. At both schools, Hadden was editor-in-chief and Luce assistant editor of the school newspapers. However, the two were friends. As Luce once wrote "Briton Hadden is chairman of the News . . . I am managing editor, and am to write a share of the editorials. . . . Happily, I have the greatest admiration and affection for Brit, which, in some measure at least, is reciprocated."

Source: R. G. Martin, *Henry and Clare: An Intimate Portrait of the Luces* (New York: G. P. Putnam's Sons, 1991). (*Photo:* Division of Prints and Photographs, Library of Congress Collection)

business magazines. In 1932, Luce bought *Architectural Forum*, which he kept for more than thirty years although it never made a profit, and in 1936 he inaugurated *Life* magazine.

Luce Politics Pervade Publications

Although Luce was widely regarded as the nation's most powerful publisher during the late 1930s, throughout World War II and during the cold war his influence declined. His magazines appealed largely to the upper middle class and never achieved working-class circulation such as did the *Saturday Evening Post*. Although Luce believed in a morally superior America, he publicized American foreign policy more than he created it.[21]

Luce had actively opposed communism from the beginning of the Bolshevik revolution in 1917. He abhorred the doctrine because it was antireligious, opposed businessmen like himself, destroyed the aristocracy in Russia, and spread throughout his beloved China. In the late 1920s and early 1930s, Luce, like many business leaders and intellectuals, found himself admiring the fascist regime of Italy's Benito Mussolini. In 1928, Luce termed Mussolini the "outstanding national moral leader in the world today."[22]

Laird S. Goldsborough, *Time*'s foreign news editor, drew fire from other *Time* staffers for his support of Franco's ultimately successful attempt to take over Spain. Goldsborough referred to Franco's armies as the "Whites," and to the Loyalists, or the soldiers of the constitutional government of Spain, as the "Reds." Such a position was contrary to that of many of the expatriate writers such as Ernest Hemingway, who traveled to Spain to defend the Loyalists against inroads of fascism. Although Luce, after much opposition to Goldsborough was shown by the staff, removed him as foreign news editor, in 1944 he appointed Whittaker Chambers to the same position. Chambers was known as a former Communist party member who was so anticommunist that *Time* editors were careful not to let him review books on the subject. Chambers is best known for his testimony in the 1950s against Alger Hiss before the House Un-American Activities Committee.

Luce's foreign news may have been most biased in relationship to China. A strong supporter of Chiang Kai-shek, Luce introduced Madame Chiang to the American public, arranging a major press tour for her in 1942, and her face graced the cover of *Time*. Luce assisted relief organizations in forming United China Relief and pressured Roosevelt and other influential leaders to continue military aid to China. His magazines failed to recognize the lack of support for Chiang in his own country. In regard to America's foreign policy in China, Luce was out of step with most prestigious U.S. publishers. Although the Hearst and Scripps chains and Robert McCormick's *Chicago Tribune* agreed with him, most columnists, radio commentators, and the *New York Herald Tribune* agreed that Chiang's position was hopeless.[23]

By 1944, Luce's empire included *Time*, with a weekly circulation of 1,160,000; *Life*, with a domestic circulation of 4 million and foreign circulation of 317,000; *Fortune*, with a weekly circulation of 170,000; *Architectural Forum*, with a circulation of 40,000; radio's "March of Time" broadcast to as many as 18 million U.S. citizens over the NBC Blue Network, of which Luce owned 12.5 percent interest; a daily radio program, "Time Views the News"; and the "March of Time" newsreels that appeared every four weeks in American and foreign theatres.[24]

During the years that followed World War II, Luce's ideological biases filtered through his publications to a greater extent than they had prior to the war. He viewed the twentieth century as the "American century" and attempted to export America's liberties, institutions, and expertise. Although in the early 1940s Luce praised the Soviet Union for carrying the burden of war and for achieving economic progress, by 1946 *Life* adamantly warned its readers of Soviet aggression, and Luce's prominent cold war stance during the 1950s earned him the reputation of an ideologue.

Radio News

During the 1930s, radio began to offer its own forms of interpretation, both through direct broadcasting by important political figures and through news programming designed by the networks. Franklin Delano Roosevelt bypassed the comments of hostile newspaper editors, explaining his policies on radio in "fireside chats" addressed directly to a population besieged by the depression. Structurally, the networks consolidated their control of the industry, and the alliance between industry and government was solidified with the creation of the Federal Communications Commission and the passing of the 1934 Federal Communications Act.

The Battle for the Wires

By the 1930s, radio was a worldwide force. The capacity for international transmission of radio programs was evident in 1929 when Admiral Richard Byrd transmitted news of his Antarctic expedition to Schenectady, New York, and when a symphony concert performed in Queen's Hall in London was heard clearly in the United States. The development of shortwave broadcasting by governments, commercial interests, and the networks contributed quickly to the establishment of transmitters in world capitals and to the evolution of radio news.[25] Radio news, at first mere news bulletins built on a pattern of print news, began to feature talks by politicians or cultural figures. Panel discussions and news commentary successfully won audiences by mid-decade.

The development of news broadcasts put fear in the hearts of newspaper owners and editors, resulting in a press-radio war during the early 1930s. From 1931 to 1934, newspapers successfully prohibited networks from obtaining wire service copy. However, such reactionary activity by newspapers merely spearheaded the development of news departments at both NBC and CBS. Associated Press (AP), an organization dominated and led by newspaper publishers, led the battle against radio news. In 1931, the American Newspaper Publishers Association passed a resolution calling for control of radio news, and at the 1932 national conventions, radio and newspapers confronted each other directly. When United Press (UP) decided to provide CBS with election returns, AP agreed to do so as well, not knowing that UP, fearing the consequences of its action, would back out at the last minute. A third wire service, INS, also installed teletype, resulting in service to CBS from three wire services. After the election, UP and INS continued to sell to broadcasters, but AP refused to serve the networks. In 1933, AP made its reluctance official and passed a specific resolution not to sell news to radio. The organization also pressured influential clients of UP and INS to refrain from servicing the networks.

CBS reacted by creating its own news bureau with 800 stringers. In 1933, David Sarnoff of NBC's parent company RCA, NBC president M. H. Aylesworth, and CBS's William S. Paley sought a peace treaty with the newspapers and wire services. A December 1933 agreement required that networks and stations stop gathering news on their own and limit the times and amount of news they aired.

The decision of the networks not to gather news was short-lived. In 1934, competition from a new service, Transradio Press, offered news from the wire agency Havas in France and England's Reuters as well as domestic news. By the end of 1934,

Transradio had 150 clients. Fear of competition from Transradio and other independent companies drove the wire services to agree to provide news to the new medium, despite publishers' opposition.[26] Radio broadcasts now brought news from Japan, speeches of Adolf Hitler, and reports of the 1938 Nazi occupation of Austria into American homes.

Radio was viewed as a flexible and innovative medium. Initiated as a device for advertising *Time* magazine, a pseudodocumentary radio program—the "March of Time"—popularized news events by using actors to recreate events in various formats. The show appeared on both CBS and NBC and varied from a fifteen- to thirty-minute format. The work of seventy-five staff members and 1,000 hours of labor was required to get each program on the air. One of America's most popular radio shows, "March of Time" was on the air from 1931 to 1945, immortalizing the expression, "Time—Marches On!" Initially Time, Inc., funded the program, but after 1932 it gained sponsors and network support.

The Federal Communications Commission

In 1934, Congress re-created the Federal Radio Commission as the Federal Communications Commission (FCC) and added telegraph and telephone matters to the agency's responsibility. This act repeated the 1927 Radio Act's charge to allocate licensing "in the public interest, convenience or necessity." Nevertheless, despite arguments during the ensuing years by educational broadcasters who claimed that radio had become too commercial, in 1934 Congress granted commercial users continued dominance of the medium through the Federal Communications Act.[27] The commission had no power to censor content, but it did consider a station's past performance when renewing a license. Although the FCC revoked few licenses over the years, critics argued that the threat of license denial could limit the diversity of program content. Broadcasters clearly did not have the same far-reaching range of freedom of expression that was granted to print media.

Congress feared the possible political bias of broadcasters and therefore provided for equal-time provisions for political candidates. Section 315 of the 1934 act granted equal time to candidates, requiring each station that allowed any candidate for public office to broadcast a message to "afford equal opportunities to all other such candidates for that office in the use of such broadcasting station. . . ." Section 315 also denied broadcasters the opportunity to censor material presented by a candidate.

Criticism and Alternatives

The growth of newspaper chains and the formation of powerful and political companies such as Time, Inc., invited criticism from within the industry and from intellectuals and government officials. President Roosevelt claimed that 85 percent of the press opposed him, and he blamed the owners of the papers, not the reporters. Socialist and communist publications flourished, and social movement newspapers such as the *Catholic Worker* challenged the daily press' interpretation of the depression and Roosevelt policies. Although an increasing percentage of newspapers claimed political independence, publishers such as Robert McCormick of the *Chicago Tribune*,

Figure 13-2   FDR addresses a nation. (Trans Lux Theatre, Library of Congress Collection)

William Randolph Hearst, and Henry Luce of Time, Inc., held definite political beliefs and did not hesitate to imbue their newspapers and magazines with their ideologies.

Seldes Attacks the Lords of the Press

George Seldes, a well-known, successful reporter during World War I for the *Chicago Tribune*, launched bitter attacks on metropolitan dailies—the newspapers he called the "monopolistic press." His books *Freedom of the Press* (1935) and *Lords of the Press* (1938), although ignored by many newspaper publishers, became best-sellers. From 1940 to 1950, he published *In Fact*, a newspaper funded through subscriptions only. Seldes refused advertising on the basis that it threatened press freedom as much as government did. Seldes later was accused of association with the Communist party. An acquaintance, Bruce Minton, a contributor to *New Republic*, helped finance Seldes at one point with funds that evidently had been provided by the Communist party. Seldes claimed he did not know the source of the money. Minton severed his relationship with Seldes after a year because he could not control the editorial content of *In Fact*, nor could he persuade Seldes to run communist political commentary. Seldes later was cleared of charges of conspiring with the Communist party.[28]

Seldes urged the development of codes of ethics and pleaded with journalism schools and the newly formed Newspaper Guild to pave the way. He denounced publishers' criticism of Roosevelt's New Deal and labeled the American Newspaper Publishers Association the "House of Lords." Seldes further chided publishers for cultivating tobacco industry advertisers and ignoring research that indicated smoking was harmful to health. Seldes also claimed the great press lords such as Hearst, Chandler, and Gannett were "in bed with business in almost all respects and are using their papers mainly to advance the commercial and political interests of themselves and their cronies."[29] George Seldes lived to be 104 years old. In his later years, the Association for Education in Journalism recognized his contributions to reforming the American press with an award for professional excellence.

The American Newspaper Guild

In 1933, the average reporter earned $29.47 each week, according to government figures. Responding to that figure and to generally deplorable conditions for writers and editors in the newspaper industry, popular syndicated columnist Heywood Broun on August 7, 1933, wrote in the *New York World-Telegram*:

> After some four or five years of holding down the easiest job in the world I hate to see other newspapermen working too hard. It embarrasses me even more to think of newspapermen who are not working at all.

Four months later, Heywood Broun became the first president of the American Newspaper Guild as it organized reporters in response to publishers' opposition to Roosevelt's proposal for a U.S. wage and hour code. Thirty-seven delegates from seventeen cities attended the first convention. Initially, the guild represented only the editorial staffs of newspapers, but it soon expanded to include the commercial staff as well. In 1936, the guild joined the American Federation of Labor, which later merged with the Congress of Industrial Organizations to become the AFL-CIO. Initially, the guild fought for a forty-hour, five-day week; a graded scale of dismissal notices; a minimum wage scale of thirty to thirty-five dollars for newspaper workers with one year's experience; a minimum number of beginners who could be employed; collective bargaining through outside parties; and an annual vacation of two weeks.

Publishers opposed the movement, and after eight students at Washington and Lee University attempted to form a junior guild chapter in March 1934, publishers and university administrators halted further student action. The guild's committee on education reported to the 1935 convention:

> There is a tendency among schools of journalism, to a degree, to be publisher-dominated, either because of endowments from publishers or boards of trustees consisting entirely of publishers. . . .
>
> As a result, journalism students represent a potential reservoir of strikebreakers, existing as a constant menace to the Guilds in the localities of such schools. . . .
>
> Those of us who have attended the schools of journalism are aware of the Horatio Alger philosophy that sometimes pervades them. . . .
>
> The result is that many an immature reporter spends the first years on a newspaper wrestling with his delusions and trying to orient himself to a situation for which he has not been . . . prepared.[30]

In the summer of 1934, the Guild adopted a code of ethics stressing the need for accurate and unbiased news, urging the nonprejudicial reporting of crime news, and opposing the power of privileged groups to withhold news. The code further opposed the printing of publicity items as news, publishing stories that newsmen knew to be false or misleading, accepting money from publicists, and using publisher privilege to influence officials in non-news-gathering situations. Most publishers agreed with the claim of the trade journal *Editor and Publisher* that editorial departments had grown cynical because of their unsuccessful competition with the business department and that labor unionism "smacks of class-conscious propaganda."[31] There were significant exceptions among publishers, however, some of whom agreed that publishers had contributed to conditions that allowed the development of a reportorial union or guild.

PM and Ralph Ingersoll

Many of the conflicts of the depression years were reflected in the high expectations and the quick demise that characterized a New York tabloid newspaper with a magazine format called *PM.* The newspaper, begun in 1939, was to exclude advertising and rely on subscriptions as a financial base, thus eliminating any possibility of being influenced by advertisers. Such an idea, which today might seem radical to media business magnates, was supported by seventeen of America's major business leaders. People such as Chicago department store owner Marshall Field and Sears and Roebuck heirs William and Lessing Rosenwald invested substantial amounts in the experiment. The staffing of the newspaper included hiring professionals from other publications and a variety of nonprofessionals, who argued extensively about the relative merits of capitalism and communism. The first issue benefited from extensive publicity, but *PM* failed because of poor business management, ideological conflict, and opposition from other newspeople.

PM, begun in 1939 by veteran magazine man Ralph Ingersoll, experimented not only with form and content but also with the underlying assumptions of how a newspaper or magazine would be financed. The tabloid newspaper was designed to avoid the sensationalism common to tabloids of the thirties, and was financed through subscription and compartmentalized news. It set up a permanent research staff and covered new beats such as labor, food, radio, and modern living.

Ingersoll began his career as a cub reporter for Hearst's *New York American* in 1923 and soon became managing editor of the *New Yorker.* He moved to *Fortune* as its managing editor and then became general manager of Luce's company, Time, Inc. In the summer of 1942, while publishing *PM,* he enlisted in the army. He was forty-two years old.

Ingersoll's biographer, Roy Hoopes, argued that Ingersoll was the driving force behind the development of *Life* magazine, and when Luce did not reward him with the editorship of that magazine, Ingersoll swore he "would never again lose myself in the creation of a magazine that belonged to someone else—even Harry Luce." After working for the conservative Luce, Ingersoll claimed to have been liberalized by his affair with playwright Lillian Hellman. In *PM*'s prospectus, he wrote, "We do not believe all mankind's problems are soluble in any existing social order, certainly not our own, and we propose to applaud those who seek constructively to improve the way men live together. . . ."[32] By January 1940, Ingersoll acquired $1.5 million and

▼ **Table 13-1**

PM's Original Stockholders

Name	Amount
Marian Rosenwald Stern (Sears Roebuck heir)	$200,000
Howard Bonbright (investment banker)	$100,000
John Loeb (partner in investment firm Loeb, Rhoades, & Co.)	$100,000
Deering Howe (Deere Tractor Co. heir)	$100,000
Garrard B. Winston (lawyer, former undersecretary of the treasury)	$100,000
Elinor Gimbel (department store heir)	$50,000
Marshall Field (Chicago department store heir)	$200,000
Huntington Hartford III (A&P heir)	$100,000
Harry Scherman (chairman of the board of Book-of-the-Month)	$100,000
Dwight Deere Wiman (Deere Tractor Co. heir)	$50,000
William and Lessing Rosenwald (Sears Roebuck heirs)	$100,000
Philip K. Wrigley (chewing gum manufacturer)	$50,000
Chester Bowles (advertising executive)	$50,000
Lincoln Schuster (book publisher)	$50,000
Ira J. Williams (investor)	$50,000
John Hay Whitney (investor)	$100,000

—*Washington Journalism Review*, December 1984. By permission of *Washington Journalism Review*.

more than 10,000 applicants for positions on the new paper. Joseph Medill Patterson, publisher of the *New York Daily News*, declared a circulation war and threatened newsstand dealers if they distributed *PM*. To further complicate the paper's rocky financial situation, staffers could not find the list of 150,000 charter subscribers, only 50,000 fewer than were needed to break even. Although 450,000 copies sold the first day, within eight weeks circulation dropped to 31,000. Marshall Field bought out the other investors and became sole owner of *PM*, with Ingersoll continuing as editor until he joined the army in 1942. When he returned in 1946, he again assumed the editorship for a few months, but he resigned when Field argued to include advertising in the newspaper. In January 1949, the paper folded. Marshall Field commissioned a study to try to determine the reason for the failure. Questionnaires were sent to 200 employees, and most of those replying said bad business management and biased news were the paper's major faults.[33]

The *Catholic Worker* and Dorothy Day

Dorothy Day's journalistic career began while she was a student at the University of Illinois. At first a political activist associated with the Socialist Worker party, and later a converted Catholic, she advocated social action in everything she wrote. While in college, she became a member of the Socialist Worker party and expressed rebellion against her middle-class, proper background by smoking and swearing. She left school at the end of her sophomore year and began working in New York for the socialist *Call*. At the beginning of World War I, she joined the staff of *The Masses*. When it shut down she worked for its successor, *The Liberator*, and entered the social life of Greenwich Village. During the next few years, she joined the expatriates in Europe, then worked in Chicago, New Orleans, and New York. With profits from the movie rights to her first novel, *The Eleventh Virgin*, she bought a cottage on Staten Island, where she welcomed her Greenwich Village friends.

In 1927, shortly after the birth of her daughter, Dorothy Day's life underwent a major transition when she was converted to Catholicism. In 1933, in the midst of the depression, she started the *Catholic Worker*, which published Catholic social activist Peter Maurin's essays and advocated solutions based on radical Christian activism. As editor until the late 1970s, Dorothy Day avoided partisan politics and advocated personal action rather than politics as a means of social change.[34] Because the newspaper contained the word "worker" in the title and because of its strong pacifist views during the Spanish Civil War and World War II, the paper was regarded widely as a communist organ. Circulation reflected opposition to the paper's pacifistic views, dropping from 190,000 in 1938 to 50,500 during World War II.[35] The newspaper fought anti-Semitism, including those views expressed in Father Coughlin's *Social Justice*, and the 1938 Nazi attacks on Jews. It also denounced the U.S. internment of Japanese people during the war.

As early as 1940, the Federal Bureau of Investigation began to investigate Dorothy Day, convinced she was a front for a communist organization; ultimately, however, the FBI became convinced that although radical she was honest and no longer associated with communism. In June 1944, her file apparently was closed. In the fifties, Dorothy Day's newspaper was again investigated by the FBI, and she was jailed several times from 1955 to 1961 for protesting air raid drills. Her imprisonment in 1957 for refusing to participate in an air raid drill finally gained support for the struggling *Catholic Worker* from mainstream newspapers such as the *New York Times* and the *New York Post*, as well as other papers like the *Daily Worker* and the *Village Voice*. The *Catholic Worker* continued to oppose military conflict and led the opposition to the Vietnam War. Dorothy Day died on November 29, 1980, but her newspaper continues today.

Media Content as Entertainment

Radio and Popular Culture

News was only a small part of radio's impact on society. Entertainment programming and commercials dominated radio listeners' conversations. Radio programs were produced primarily by advertising agencies, and by 1932 more time was spent on commercials than on news, education, lectures, and religion combined.

Most of early radio was live programming. For three decades—until the end of the 1950s—radio relied on live music to fill many hours. Because the local stations primarily used local talent, they also showcased the region's culture as expressed through its music. J. Steven Smethers and Lee Jollife, in their study of midwestern radio stations, point out that although stations in the Northeast may have featured civic orchestras, opera singers, or concert violinists who lived in Boston, New York, and Washington, midwestern stations "thrived on homespun melodies from the KMA Cornpickers, the Ozark Ramblers, the Harmony Twins, and Johnny White and his Sons of the West. . . ."

The emphasis on live broadcasting was generated in part by an attitude of the Federal Radio Commission (later the FCC) that declared in a 1928 report, "A station which devotes the main portion of its hours of operations to . . . phonograph records is not giving the public anything it cannot readily have without such a station."[36]

In the 1930s, the various genres already recognized in literature ascended to the radio microphone. Comedy, detective stories, westerns, and melodramas crossed the air waves during the evening programming hours. Radio heroes demonstrated the American values of truth, justice, and goodness. "Major Bowes' Original Amateur Hour" started the amateur craze in 1934, and contests proliferated throughout the decade. "Lux Radio Theatre" showcased Broadway stars.

"War of the Worlds"

On October 30, 1938, 6 million Americans tuned in to CBS's "Mercury Theatre on the Air" to hear what became a famous piece of radio drama, but what seemed at the time to be a genuine news report that Martians had landed in New Jersey. Orson Welles' dramatization "War of the Worlds" concretely demonstrated that American people listened to, and believed in, radio. Welles had planned as a Halloween trick the radio presentation of H. G. Wells' novel about Martians arriving on the shores of the United States, but Welles' use of journalistic techniques convinced many listeners that the invasion was real. Some listeners tuned in late, and therefore did not recognize the program for what it was—fiction. Although popular accounts described listeners who panicked as they waited for the arriving aliens, Hadley Cantril's Princeton University study indicated that only about one-sixth of the listeners—still a million in all—actually were frightened by what they thought was a news program.[37] Realistic news bulletins interspersed with music played live from a hotel ballroom captivated the listening audience. Hundreds of people fled their homes in New York, callers swamped the *Providence Journal* switchboard seeking more information, people gathered in churches in Birmingham, Alabama, to pray, and a power outage that coincided with the broadcast panicked the citizens of Concrete, Washington.

"War of the Worlds" provided a unique opportunity for research, and the Office of Radio Research of Princeton University quickly organized a study immediately after the panic. Hadley Cantril and his associates discovered that those who did not believe the broadcast conducted successful *internal checks*. Although real names and places were used, the facts just did not add up. Some people checked the broadcast against other information, investigating to see if other stations had reports on the invasion or looking up details on the broadcast in the newspaper. However, some people were so frightened that they failed to make successful internal or external checks; in some cases, they simply quit listening. Others adopted an attitude of complete resignation. The researchers found that those who were frightened by the broadcast fell into a category they labeled as *highly suggestive*; those who successfully determined that the program was fictional were said to have high *critical ability*. Hadley Cantril defined it this way:

> By this we mean that they had a capacity to evaluate the stimulus in such a way that they were able to understand its inherent characteristics so they could judge and act appropriately.[38]

Researchers concluded that the impact of the program was due to the sheer brilliance of the performance itself as well as to the confidence Americans had developed in radio and to the drama's historical timing—after Hitler's invasion into parts of Europe. Those with strong religious beliefs or those who were emotionally insecure or lacking in self-confidence were more likely to believe the invasion was real.[39]

Motion Pictures

The movie industry was not immune from the depression. Company profits plummeted, with Warner Brothers losing $14 million in 1932 and Paramount losing nearly $16 million, the latter filing for bankruptcy the following year.[40]

Gangster films, complete with the crime-doesn't-pay moral, gained popularity in the 1930s and avoided the censor's pencil. Producers emphasized the American success story and environmental causes that explained the rise of gangsters. The "suffering proletariat" appeared often in the gangster films:

> The gangster is the man of the city, with the city's language and knowledge, with its queer and dishonest skills and its terrible daring, carrying his life in his hands like a placard, like a club. . . . It is not the real city, but that dangerous and sad city of the imagination which is so much more important, which is the modern world.[41]

Fred Astaire and Ginger Rogers set a standard for dance musicals, making nine films for RKO during the 1930s. "Screwball" comedies and American success stories were other popular genres.

Shirley Temple, a child star, performed in a variety of box-office-hit comedies. In 1932 and 1933, she appeared in *Baby Burlesk*, a series of one-reel comedies. The song-and-dance number "Baby Take a Bow" included in 1934 in her first full-length

Figure 13–3 These movie advertisements encouraged the citizens of Herrin, Illinois, to attend the movies in 1939. (Farm Security Administration photo, Division of Prints and Photographs, Library of Congress Collection)

musical, *Stand Up and Cheer*, made her a star. That same year she received a special Oscar, and from 1935 to 1938 she remained the nation's top box-office star. In 1938, she made $307,014, reportedly more than the president of General Motors. She earned $5 million before she reached her teens.

"I class myself with Rin Tin Tin," she told a Parade reporter in 1986. "People in the Depression wanted something to cheer them up, and they fell in love with a dog and a little girl."[42]

Filmmaker Frank Capra mastered the American-success movie style in "It Happened One Night" (1934) and "Mr. Smith Goes to Washington" (1939). "The movies are energetic, irreverent poems to a civics-lesson America," wrote Louis Gianetti. "Evil is usually represented by one nasty banker or politician; once he is vanquished, the way is clear for the triumph of decency. Capra's world is a middle-class one of marriage, family, the neighborhood—all very much springing from nineteenth century *archetypes*." Capra's message to depression-era moviegoers was "stand up, stick your chest out, fight for what you know is right." [43]

In 1940, John Steinbeck's *The Grapes of Wrath* portrayed the depression-poor Joad family making the trek to California after losing their Oklahoma land. The characters reflected the despair of much of the farming community: "It's not ownin' it. It's bein' born on it, and livin' on it, and dyin' on it. That's what makes it your'n."[44]

The movie industry battled the Justice Department at the end of the 1930s, when in 1938 the government filed suit against all eight movie companies for restraint of trade. Two years later, the department obtained a consent decree against five of the companies. They agreed to limit block booking, blind booking, and other coercive tactics directed at theatre owners. Disputes among workers and actors over wages led to a revived Screen Writers Guild and Screen Actors Guild by the end of the decade.

Media and Government

During the 1930s, the government invaded—or attempted to invade—many aspects of the print and broadcast industries. Motion pictures, although not subject to government control, did not enjoy First Amendment privileges. The passage of the Federal Communications Act in 1934 assured governmental regulation of licensing and the allocation of time for promoting federal political candidates. Franklin Roosevelt's New Deal policies affected the newspaper industry as well as other businesses and instituted labor policies that newspaper publishers abhorred. Further, presidents of the twentieth century viewed the new medium of broadcasting as a venue for reaching the public directly, and they flooded newspaper reporters with information designed to keep them so busy they could not pursue their own stories with investigative fervor.

The Newspaper Industry

The number of dailies continued the decline that began about 1910, dropping from 2,580 in 1914 to 2,441 in 1919, to 2,080 in 1933. Weeklies also declined from about 1916 on, dropping from 13,964 in 1919 to 11,931 in 1935. Circulations showed a slight decline from a 1929 peak. Concentrated in the nation's big cities, 47.4 percent of the nation's dailies in 1929 and 41.8 percent of the nation's Sunday papers originated in six cities.[45] The loss of advertising resulted in a newspaper and periodical revenue decline from $1,580,565 in 1929 to $937,114 in 1933.

However, the total income of the news and periodical industry compared to the income of all other American industries was proportionately higher during the depression years than it had been previously. By cutting wages and paying less for raw materials, newspapers remained relatively stable despite adverse financial conditions. One newspaper reported that operating expenses in 1929 comprised 67 percent of its gross income and in 1932 only accounted for 73 percent of the gross. Evaluating the large, relatively stable, and monopolistic newspaper enterprises, Albert McClung Lee noted in 1937:

> Their publishers believe in such old-fashioned catchwords of democracy as "freedom of the press" largely because the price of the chips defines the character and the number of those who can now play the journalistic game.[46]

Robert McCormick and the National Recovery Act

Robert McCormick, editor of the *Chicago Tribune*, represented the conservative wing of newspaper publishers and led the fight against President Roosevelt's New Deal legislation intended to govern the business aspects of newspapers. McCormick was

Figure 13–4   A Chicago landmark since its completion in 1925, the Tribune Tower is "home" to the *Chicago Tribune*'s staff and to the Tribune Company. (Chicago Tribune photo)

an old Groton school chum of Franklin Delano Roosevelt, and they remained on friendly terms until Roosevelt's initiation of the National Recovery Act (NRA), an attempt by Roosevelt to impose wage, price, and other controls on businesses, including newspapers.

McCormick, who became chairman of the American Newspaper Publishers Association's Committee on Freedom of the Press when it was established in 1928, urged the association to take a stand that the NRA was detrimental to freedom of the press.

Robert R. McCormick grew up in Joseph Medill's newspaper family but not as the chosen son to take over the *Chicago Tribune*. Born in 1880, he was the son of Joseph Medill's daughter, Katherine. When Joseph Medill died in 1899, control of the

Tribune went to Robert Patterson, Medill's son-in-law and the husband of another daughter, Elinor. Patterson's son, Joseph Patterson, who later owned and edited the New York tabloid the *Daily News*, and Robert McCormick took over the *Tribune* after Patterson's death. The two cousins were friends, despite Joe's tendencies toward socialism and Robert McCormick's unswerving conservatism.

McCormick survived major circulation wars in the teen years of the century with Hearst's *American* (which was renamed the *Examiner*), and by 1910 the *Tribune* led Chicago morning circulation with a count of 241,000. It slightly trailed the more popular evening *Daily News*. After a trip to the Russian front and military service in World War I, McCormick became a full colonel and returned to assume even more control on the *Tribune* when Joe Patterson began the *Daily News* in 1919. During the 1920s, McCormick established foreign news correspondents for the *Tribune* and continued his successful management of the newspaper.

Although the depression caused ad lineage at the *Tribune* to decline by half, McCormick was not seriously bothered by hard times. The loss of advertising resulted in a newspaper and periodical revenue decline from 1929 to 1933 of roughly 40 percent. Net profits for *Tribune* shareholders in 1933 were reported by Luce's *Fortune* magazine to be $2,900,000. Joseph Gies, the colonel's biographer, wrote that *Tribune* copy in the early 1930s was hardly controversial: "impassioned demands for reduction in government spending and taxes, and bland appeals for national unity."[47] The *Tribune* dismissed the 1932 veterans' bonus march as Communist-inspired, denounced the veterans for demanding early payment of their bonus, viewed both Roosevelt and Hoover as "firm, middle-of-the-road progressives," and assumed Roosevelt would not undertake any dangerous economic experiments.

By 1934, the *Tribune*'s coverage of Roosevelt was avidly accusatory. Gies noted that

> Stories compared him to Kerenski as an ineffective leader paving the way to bolshevism. Agriculture Secretary Henry Wallace, son of a distinguished family of Iowa Republicans, was compared to Lenin, Mussolini, and Hitler. McCormick saw a coincidence in the birthplace of Felix Frankfurter, which was the same as that of Hitler, Hapsburg-ruled Austria-Hungary, a nativity that left him "impregnated with the historic doctrines of Austrian absolutism."[48]

Unlike Luce, McCormick viewed Hitler as a dangerous leader and informed his readers about the dangers of the Nazi leader. In 1933, stories from the *Tribune*'s Berlin correspondent, Sigrid Schultz, reported "German Decree Annuls Liberty and Civil Rights," "Nazi Terrorism Grows," and "Jewish Stores Closed."[49]

McCormick earned his reputation as a reactionary with his obviously biased coverage of Roosevelt's reelection campaigns, through his activities with the American Newspaper Publishers Association (ANPA) designed to limit government regulation of the newspaper business, and by his involvement with the America First Committee, a group of prominent isolationists, on the eve of World War II.

In 1933, the ANPA confronted Congress directly over passage of the NRA, which provided for establishment of codes of fair competition for all industries. The codes guaranteed the right of collective bargaining and freedom of labor union organization, and they empowered the President to license and to revoke those licenses for individual companies in any industry not cooperating under the NRA. The ANPA submitted a voluntary code, providing for "open shops" in which union and nonunion members could work side by side and exempting newsboys from child-labor restrictions. The voluntary code also exempted reporters and other editorial workers from the maximum-hour provisions of the law. Publishers also included a phrase in the voluntary agreement noting that

> Nothing in the adoption and acceptance of this code shall be construed as waiving, abrogating, or modifying any rights secured under the Constitution of the United States or of any state, or limiting the freedom of the press.

In accepting the publishers' voluntary code with modifications to the child-labor provisions and open-shop clauses, President Roosevelt replied:

> The freedom guaranteed by the Constitution is freedom of expression and that will be scrupulously respected—but it is not freedom to work children, or to do business in a fire trap or violate the laws against obscenity, libel and lewdness."[50]

Such exchanges further alienated publishers from the New Deal. The final version of the Newspaper Code provided a forty-hour week for employees of newspapers in towns with populations of more than 50,000 and set minimum wages. Children of twelve could work as newsboys as long as they worked during daylight hours and were not required to perform duties that would impair their health or interfere with their schooling. News-editorial employees, as well as others, were granted the right of collective bargaining, paving the way for the formation of the American Newspaper Guild in 1933.

McCormick was not the only publisher who was glad to see the Supreme Court declare the NRA unconstitutional in 1935, but his joy was short-lived, for the next year the Wagner Labor Relations Act contained many of the provisions of the NRA, such as collective bargaining. McCormick had little faith in New Deal legislation. When Social Security was instituted in 1935 and many publishers, including his cousin Joseph Patterson, canceled company pension plans, McCormick retained the *Tribune's* plan. McCormick believed that the New Deal would spend the money procured for Social Security on other programs and was convinced he could take better care of his employees than could the federal government. As soon as the guild began to organize the Hearst newspapers, McCormick set his employees' salaries at levels higher than those the guild required.[51]

Presidents and the Press

Although the art of criticizing government or persons within government was the province of journalists from colonial days, the news media faced new challenges when dealing with bureaucracy in the mid-twentieth century. Further, broadcasting was subjected to new governmental regulation that strictly departed from print requirements.

William McKinley, during his presidential years of 1897 to 1901, was the first President to regularly attempt to control the flow of information from the White House to Washington correspondents. Under Roosevelt, from 1901 to 1909, Gifford Pinchot, chief of the U.S. Forest Service from 1898 to 1910 and Roosevelt's conservation adviser, was particularly adept at encouraging newspapers to cover conservation activities. Pinchot, who like many progressives, believed informed readers would make informed decisions, established one of the first press bureaus in an executive branch agency. He directed production of hundreds of publicity pamphlets, newspaper and magazine articles, interviews, lecture tours, and traveling exhibits—all designed to increase public awareness of conservation policy and to further Roosevelt's conservation programs. Pinchot's policies were considered progressive in that they attempted to spread information about conservation and they valued the importance of public opinion.[52]

Although McKinley was interested primarily in gaining favorable recognition of his foreign policy, Theodore Roosevelt used similar methods and his magnetic personality to curry favor for his domestic policies. William Howard Taft, on the other hand, spent four years ignoring and therefore alienating the press. However, Woodrow Wilson, elected in 1912, renewed Roosevelt's practices and instituted regularly scheduled press conferences.[53]

George Creel's activities during World War I furthered government's role in news management, and at the 1919 Paris Peace Conference, President Woodrow Wilson's aide, former muckraker Ray Stannard Baker, was dismayed to discover that the Paris negotiations would be conducted in secret. Although Baker did not object to governments keeping some details from the public, he saw no reason to keep them secret from the press:

> It had been proved over and over again, that no group of men can be more fully trusted to keep a confidence or use it wisely than a group of experienced newspaper correspondents—if they are honestly informed and trusted in the first place.[54]

Michael Schudson suggested that Baker's protest and the continued concern over publicity during the Paris peace talks signified a new relationship between government and the press. "For the first time in the history of American foreign policy," wrote Schudson, "political debate at home concerned not only the substance of decisions the government made but also the ways in which the government made decisions."[55] The press also considered itself, as articulated in Baker's comments, separate from the rest of the public and deserving of additional information.

By the 1920s, regular correspondents often gathered news in Washington from official handouts or briefings. However, perfection of government's use of the media remained in the hands of Franklin Delano Roosevelt, who believed that information was the key to unlock support of his New Deal policies. Roosevelt wisely hired advisors who were familiar with the press, including Louis Howe, former reporter for the *New York Herald*, Marcus McIntyre, former city editor of the *Washington Times*, and

Figure 13–5   Photographers documented the December 1943 Teheran Conference with photographs of Soviet premier Joseph Stalin, the President of the United States Franklin Delano Roosevelt, and England's prime minister Winston Churchill. (Farm Security Administration—Office of War Information photo, Division of Prints and Photographs, Library of Congress Collection)

Stephen T. Early, a former Associated Press reporter and Paramount Newsreel executive. These former newsmen maintained a high level of credibility with the press and close relationships with the President that allowed them during the early years of the depression to circumvent what might have been a more adversarial relationship. Roosevelt's style of keeping open a constant channel of news flow differed so dramatically from Hoover's self-isolation during the last days of his presidency that the press found news gathering an easy and enjoyable task. Further, both Early, as the press secretary, and Roosevelt provided information on the record, rather than forcing reporters to rely on unnamed sources.[56]

For the most part, reporters participated in news management. Their treatment of Roosevelt, for example, showed their continuing willingness to withhold information from the public if only they were allowed to share in the power. The nation's press photographers continuously presented Roosevelt as a strong and vigorous President, despite the fact he was crippled as a result of polio. Through his press secretary and with the help of the Secret Service, Roosevelt managed to control photographers, who agreed not to photograph his wheelchair and other equipment relating to the disease.[57]

However, Roosevelt demanded a high degree of loyalty, tolerating little criticism, and reporters soon became suspicious of government news management, recognizing that information not delivered through the President's well-managed office was information suppressed. Further, reporters were ill-equipped to understand the economic news of the 1930s and relied heavily on the President's often condescending explanations. Roosevelt also violated his early policy of not offering exclusive information to specific reporters, and he often tried to acquire favorable publicity by granting favors to individual newsmen.

By 1936, Roosevelt, who claimed that 85 percent of the press opposed him, focused his criticism on publishers, whom he claimed were motivated solely by selfish concerns. After his overwhelming victory in 1936, he turned to the radio as a preferred medium for conveying his individual message to the nation.

Broadcasters, constantly aware of their vulnerability to government regulation, cooperated fully with Roosevelt's desired use of radio. The networks extended public service time to the administration, broadcasting not only Roosevelt's fireside chats but political education programs as well. By March 1936, at least three government agencies had dramatic radio programs on the air. Broadcasters elected not to comment on administration policy and therefore avoided incurring the same wrath Roosevelt directed at the newspaper press.

The First Lady and Women in the Press

Also adept at relationships with the press, Eleanor Roosevelt instituted press conferences for women only. Although women had made professional strides in the 1920s, during the 1930s when jobs were scarce, employers hired men before women. Women were viewed as second-income earners in a nation without enough jobs to go around. In 1920, 11.9 percent of all professionals had been women, and in 1930 the number had grown to 14.2 percent, but by 1940 the percentage dropped to 13.[58] Women had doubled their numbers in reporting and editing jobs during the 1920s, representing 24 percent of the profession or 12,000 women at the end of the decade. During the 1930s, the number of women in journalism grew by only 1 percent. Women journalists of the 1920s and 1930s often represented "firsts": the first woman to achieve a certain position, or to gain an interview or a privilege. Women still most frequently covered women's issues or worked for society pages.

Mrs. Roosevelt's conferences assured coverage of her and the First Family on the women's pages of newspapers and, because men were excluded, motivated editors to hire women. These efforts contributed to the expansion of women reporters in the capital during World War II. In 1933, only nineteen women had been allowed in the congressional press galleries, but by the end of 1942, sixty-one women were admitted.[59]

Photojournalism

Editors experimented with the use of photographs as early as 1855 in newspapers such as *Frank Leslie's Illustrated Newspaper* and its competitor *Harper's Weekly* (1857). However, the technology of the time necessitated the redrawing of photographs, which then were made into woodcuts. In 1880, as technology emerged to permit the reproduction of half-tones from a printing press, the *New York Daily Graphic* quickly included photographs in its makeup. Nevertheless, it was not until

Figure 13–6 Women became country editors as well as city reporters. In 1939, the editor of the *Valley News* in Brown's Valley, Minnesota, collected news items by telephone. (Farm Security Administration photo, Division of Prints and Photographs, Library of Congress Collection)

the development of the rotogravure press in Germany and the Leica camera after the turn of the century that the photographic capturing of images and reproduction reached the kind of quality that allowed a true "picture" magazine. One of the first of these produced on the American side of the Atlantic was the *New York Times'* weekly rotogravure magazine, the *Mid-Week Pictorial,* which presented photographs of World War I and lasted until 1937. It adopted a photojournalistic format that integrated pictures and text, hired staff photographers, and imitated German picture magazines.[60] The German Leica camera introduced portability, allowed photographers to shoot thirty-six frames before reloading, offered a greater depth of field, and permitted indoor shots without a flash. Although dailies resisted the new technology and issued their photographers Speed Graphics or Graphlexes, which required changing film after each shot, Henry Luce capitalized on the new possibilities in creating a magazine based on the candid photograph and the photojournalistic essay.[61]

Life

Recognizing the possibilities created by portable cameras and building on a tradition of German picture magazines, particularly the picture magazine *BIZ*, Luce created an American photojournalistic magazine that he called *Life*. At first, the magazine relied heavily on agency rather than staff photographers, and its relationship with the Black Star Picture Agency, as well as others, shaped its development as a photojournalistic magazine.

The Black Star Picture Agency was started by German emigrant Ernest Mayer, who in 1929 had become director of the Berlin Mauritius Publishing Company. Mayer's agency published books and sold photographs to German magazines such as *BIZ* and *Munchner Illustrierte Presse*. Mayer's special talent was generating photographic essay ideas by clipping stories from regional newspapers. When Hitler came to power in 1933, Mayer and his Jewish associates were "excluded from all professions exerting an influence over German cultural life . . . (including) theatre, films, radio, literature, and the arts . . . and—most important of all—the press."[62] Mayer, who already had a number of U.S. contacts, emigrated in November 1935, when he was forty-two. In early 1936, he inaugurated Black Star.

The agency became an important component in the development of *Life*, which in its second year of operation had only ten staff photographers while printing about 200 pictures per weekly issue. Eight months before *Life* was published, Black Star signed a contract to supply photographs and photo essays for Time, Inc. Some of these appeared in *Time* magazine before *Life* began in November 1936. Time, Inc., also received first refusal on all pictures imported by Black Star.

Many agency photographers ultimately became *Life* staff photographers, and by 1952 more than a quarter of *Life's* photographers were Europeans who had immigrated to the United States between 1930 and 1940. Half of those had been associated with Black Star.[63] *Life* was important to Black Star as well, comprising about a quarter of the agency's sales during the late 1930s. Other magazines in the United States used photographs, but few showed interest in the photojournalism essay.

Life was instantly successful, selling 435,000 copies of the first issue and achieving a circulation of 760,000 by January 1937. Luce had pegged the advertising rates too low, however, and maintaining the high quality and massive circulation was an expensive endeavor. At first the magazine lost $3 million per year, but by 1939 the magazine broke into the black.

The Cowles family of Des Moines, Iowa, challenged *Life* with the introduction of *Look* in January 1937, but *Life's* head start, its higher quality of paper and production, and its more serious tone carried it past the competition. *Life*, however, was not entirely a serious magazine. Although Margaret Bourke-White's photojournalistic essay on Muncie, Indiana, turned the subject of Lynd's classic sociological study

"Middletown" into a "real" town, *Life* also captured more frivolous sides of life with articles such as "How to Undress for Your Husband."[64]

Margaret Bourke-White

Margaret Bourke-White (1904–1971) earned recognition by providing one of the photographs for the first issue of *Life,* and by becoming the first accredited woman war photographer, the first woman to fly a combat mission, and the first outsider to thoroughly photograph Soviet industry and life.[65] These "firsts" earned her photographic fame, as well as FBI surveillance.

She was first recognized in the 1920s for her documentation of architecture and industry. Bourke-White photographed steel mills, shipyards, banks, and skyscrapers, portraying the capitalistic structure of American industry. One critic observed that her work "transformed the American factory into a Gothic cathedral."[66] Henry Luce hired her as the first photographer for *Fortune* and as one of four original staff photographers for *Life.* Her agreement with Luce allowed her six months of the year to pursue her own work for advertising agencies and other clients.

Bourke-White was always a source of controversy despite her talent and achievements, partly because she espoused liberal causes. In 1944, the House Un-American Activities Committee cited her thirteen times for espousing foreign ideologies and producing un-American propaganda. In the early 1940s, J. Edgar Hoover recommended that Bourke-White be placed on a list of individuals to be considered for custodial detention in time of emergency. The post office monitored her mail, and the customs bureau reported to the FBI whenever she left the country and returned. Despite repeated searches of her luggage, the customs bureau never found incriminating evidence.

When Bourke-White was sent to Korea for *Life* to develop and photograph a human interest story on the impact of the Korean conflict, she voluntarily submitted a statement to the secretary of defense refuting allegations of communist sympathy. She stated:

> I am not a member of the Communist Party, and never have been. I am not affiliated with the Communist Party, and never have been. I have never knowingly been a member of, sponsored, lectured before, or contributed to a Communist-front organization. I have never been sympathetic to the Communist Party or the Communist ideology. I

▼

Margaret Bourke-White

No editorialist writing about the human condition in our time had more to say about deprivation or suffering than she did through pictures. And few philosophers or dramatists penetrated more deeply into the wondrous possibilities of human hopefulness and dignity. . . . Margaret Bourke-White was able to make her camera see past the surface into meaning.

—Norman Cousins, on Bourke-White's death, *Saturday Review,* September 11, 1971

have never voted or campaigned for or provided funds for a candidate of the Communist Party. I have never advocated force or violence to alter the constitutional form of government in the United States.[67]

Bourke-White never learned of the FBI surveillance of her activity nor of the extensive file the bureau maintained about her friendships and affiliations, and the surveillance did not harm her career.

Conclusion

During the depression, the periodical and electronic media industries remained strong, despite declines for newspapers in advertising and circulation. The motion picture industry probably faced the most critical economic problems, with profits plummeting dramatically. Newspapers cut costs and wages to maintain a profit margin, and reporters responded by organizing a newspaper guild to fight for better working conditions and better salaries. Jobs went first to the men, and the gains women had made within the industry during the 1920s held even but did not increase.

The social events and issues of the decade were described and interpreted in a variety of ways. The documentary movement, which chronicled emotion as well as fact, spurred the development of other interpretive techniques. Newswriters added bylines to their stories, editors experimented with news summaries, columnists expounded on political programs, photographers explained with their cameras, and new research methods contributed to measuring public opinion. The variety of innovation sparked a continuing debate in subsequent decades about the validity of objectivity as a professional norm versus the need for interpretation.

Radio expanded its news operations against dramatic protests by newspaper editors and by the end of the decade became a favorite medium for President Roosevelt, whose voice crossed the airwaves with fireside chats and news conferences. Eleanor Roosevelt enhanced the position of women journalists by creating press conferences for women only.

Roosevelt cultivated relationships with print journalists during the early years of his presidency, endeavoring to garner favor for New Deal legislation. Angry with publishers who commented, and often fought against, his programs, he then turned to radio as a means of disseminating government information. Broadcasters, always wary of possible government regulation and uneasy about controversy, opened the air waves to Roosevelt as well as to a variety of government agencies.

Endnotes

1. For a general discussion of the depression and of New Deal legislation, see Mary Beth Norton, et al., *A People and a Nation*, vol. 2 (Boston: Houghton Mifflin, 1982), pp. 700–750. For a more scholarly evaluation, see William E. Leuchtenburg, *Franklin Roosevelt and the New Deal* (New York: Harper Torchbooks, 1963).

2. Edgar Dale, *The Content of Motion Pictures* (New York: Macmillan, 1935), p. 1.

3. James L. Baughman, in a presentation, "Informing the Mass and the Middle: The Journalism of Synthesis in Twentieth Century America," at the annual meeting of the Association for Education in Journalism and Mass

Communication in Norman, Okla., August 1986, suggested "synthesis" as a journalistic theme for the twentieth century.

4. See the introduction to Richard W. Steele, *Propaganda in an Open Society: The Roosevelt Administration and the Media, 1933–1941* (Westport, Conn.: Greenwood Press, 1985).

5. For an elaboration of this theme, see Michael Schudson, *Discovering the News: A Social History of American Newspapers* (New York: Basic Books, 1978), p. 144.

6. The definition of documentary was provided by William Stott, *Documentary Expression and Thirties America* (New York: Oxford, 1973), pp. 8–12, 20.

7. Lewis Jacobs, *The Documentary Tradition* (New York: Hopkinson & Blake, 1971), pp. 12–13, 73, 75.

8. Stott, *Documentary Expression*, p. 73.

9. Stott, *Documentary Expression*, p. 62.

10. Curtis MacDougall, *Interpretative Reporting* (New York: Macmillan, 1938), p. v, cited in Schudson, *Discovering the News*, p. 146.

11. Cited in Schudson, *Discovering the News*, p. 148.

12. Schudson, *Discovering the News*, p. 159.

13. Schudson, *Discovering the News*, pp. 150–51.

14. This discussion relies heavily on Richard Jensen, "Democracy by the Numbers," *Public Opinion* (February/March, 1980), pp. 53–59.

15. Schudson, *Discovering the News*, pp. 145–46.

16. W. A. Swanberg, *Luce and His Empire* (New York: Charles Scribners' Sons, 1972) pp. 42, 53–57.

17. Swanberg, *Luce and His Empire*, p. 53.

18. James L. Baughman, *Henry R. Luce and the Rise of the American News Media*, (Boston: G. K. Hall/Twayne, 1987), p. 27.

19. Cited in Swanberg, *Luce and His Empire*, pp. 122–23.

20. Baughman, *Luce and the Rise of the American News Media*, pp. 34, 49–53, 62–74.

21. See the introduction to Baughman's *Luce and the Rise of the American News Media*.

22. Swanberg, *Luce and His Empire*, p. 70.

23. Baughman, *Luce and the Rise of the American News Media*, p. 156.

24. Swanberg, *Luce and His Empire*, p. 214.

25. David H. Hosley, *As Good as Any: Foreign Correspondence on American Radio, 1930–1940* (Westport, Conn.: Greenwood Press) 1984, pp. 8–9.

26. Hosley, *Foreign Correspondence on American Radio*, pp. 18–22.

27. Erik Barnouw, *The Golden Web* (New York: Oxford University Press, 1968), pp. 28–29.

28. Everette E. Dennis and Claude-Jean Bertrand, "Seldes at 90: They Don't Give Pulitzers for That Kind of Criticism," *Journalism History* 7:3–4 (Autumn–Winter, 1980), pp. 85–86.

29. Dennis and Bertrand, "Seldes at 90," pp. 83–84.

30. Cited in Alfred McClung Lee, *The Daily Newspaper in America* (New York: Macmillan, 1937), p. 683.

31. Cited in Lee, *Daily Newspaper in America*, p. 686.

32. Roy Hoopes, "When Ralph Ingersoll Papered Manhattan," *Washington Journalism Review* (December 1984), pp. 26, 27.

33. Hoopes, *WJR*, p. 32.

34. Nancy Roberts, *Dorothy Day and the* Catholic Worker (Albany: State University of New York Press: 1984), p. 90.

35. Roberts, *Dorothy Day*, p. 119.

36. J. Steven Smethers and Lee B. Jolliffe, "Singing and Selling Seeds: The Live Music Era on Rural Midwestern Radio Stations," *Journalism History* 26:2 (Summer, 2000).

37. Shearon Lowery and Melvin L. DeFleur, *Milestones in Mass Communication Research: Media Effects* (New York: Longman, 1983), p. 70.

38. Cited in Lowery and DeFleur, *Mass Communication Research*, p. 78.

39. See Lowery and DeFleur, *Mass Communication Research*, pp. 58–84, for a thorough analysis of *War of the Worlds*.

40. Louis Giannetti and Scott Eyman, *Flashback: A Brief History of Film* (Englewood Cliffs, N. J.: Prentice-Hall, 1986).

41. Cited in Gianetti, *Flashback*, p. 164.

42. *Parade Magazine*, December 7, 1986, p. 5.

43. Giannetti and Eyman, *Flashback*, pp. 176–77. See also Robert Sklar, *Movie Made America* (New York: Random House, 1975).

44. Giannetti and Eyman, *Flashback*, p. 190.

45. The cities were New York, Chicago, Philadelphia, Cleveland, Boston, and San Francisco.

46. Lee, *Daily Newspaper in America*, p. 173. For supplementary data about the economics of newspapers in the depression years, see pp. 171–73, 203–4.

47. Joseph Gies, *The Colonel of Chicago* (New York: E. P. Dutton, 1979), pp. 117, 123.

48. Gies, *Colonel of Chicago*, p. 129.

49. Gies, *Colonel of Chicago*, p. 130.

50. Edwin Emery, *History of the American Newspaper Publishers Association* (Westport, Conn.: Greenwood Press), 1950.

51. Gies, *Colonel of Chicago*, p. 141.

52. For a full discussion of Pinchot's cultivation of newspaper editors, see Stephen Ponder, "Federal News Management in the Progressive Era: Gifford Pinchot and the Conservation Crusade," *Journalism History* 13:2 (Summer, 1986).

53. This discussion relies heavily on the introduction to Steele, *Propaganda in an Open Society.* See also Robert Hilderbrand, *Power and the People: Executive Management of Public Opinion in Foreign Affairs, 1897–1921* (Chapel Hill: University of North Carolina Press, 1981).

54. Ray Stannard Baker, *Woodrow Wilson and World Settlement*, 2 vols. (London: William Heineman, 1923) vol. 1, p. 137, cited in Michael Schudson, *Discovering the News: A Social History of American Newspapers* (New York: Basic Books, 1978), p. 165.

55. Schudson, *Discovering the News*, p. 165.

56. Steele, *Propaganda in an Open Society*, pp. 9–12.

57. Betty Houchin Winfield, "F.D.R.'s Pictorial Image, Rules and Boundaries," *Journalism History* 5:4 (Winter, 1978–1979), p. 110.

58. Lois Banner, *Women in Modern America—A Brief History* (New York: Harcourt Brace Jovanovich, 1974), p. 143, cited in "The Woman Journalist of the 1920s and 1930s in Fiction and in Autobiography," by Donna Born, presentation to the Association for Education in Journalism and Mass Communication Qualitative Studies Division, Athens, Ohio, July 1982.

59. Betty Winfield, "Mrs. Roosevelt's Press Conference Association: The First Lady Shines a Light," *Journalism History* 8:2 (Summer, 1981), p. 67. See also Ishbel Ross, *Ladies of the Press, the Story of Women in Journalism by an Insider* (New York: Harper & Bros., 1936) and Maurine Beasley, ed., *One Third of a Nation: Lorena Hickok Reports the Great Depression* (Urbana: University of Illinois Press, 1981.)

60. Keith Kenney, "*Mid-Week Pictorial*: Pioneer American Photojournalism Magazine," paper presented to the Visual Communication Division of the Association for Education in Journalism and Mass Communication, Norman, Okla., August 1986.

61. Baughman, *Luce and the Rise of the American News Media*, chapter 6, p. 4.

62. Herman Ullstein, *The Rise and Fall of the House of Ullstein* (New York: Simon & Schuster, 1943), p. 27, cited in C. Zoe Smith, "The History of Black Star Picture Agency: *Life's* European Connection," paper presented to the Visual Communication Division, Association for Education in Journalism and Mass Communication, Gainesville, Fla., August 7, 1984.

63. Smith, "Black Star Picture Agency," p. 2.

64. Baughman, *Luce and the Rise of the American News Media*, pp. 91–102.

65. Robert E. Snyder, "Margaret Bourke-White and the Communist Witch Hunt," *Journal of American Studies* 19:1 (1985), p. 6.

66. Cited in Snyder, "Communist Witch Hunt," p. 5.

67. Margaret Bourke-White, statement to the Office of Public Information, Office of the Secretary of Defense, 15 January 1951, Bufile 100–3518, cited in Snyder, "Communist Witch Hunt," p. 20.

CHAPTER 14

Images of War

▼

During the years of World War II, wire services, newspapers, and broadcast organizations sent correspondents to Asia and Europe to cover international developments. Unlike previous wars, however, this war was broadcast; it was, in many ways, a radio war. The costs of multiple media coverage escalated throughout the war and increased the dominance of the prestige newspapers, the wire services, and the networks. Columnists, cartoonists, and photographers depicted the war, presenting a variety of themes and images. However, nearly all forms of media complied with the government restrictions instituted through the Office of Censorship and the Office of War Information. The Justice Department, the Post Office Department, and the FBI continued their surveillance of "suspicious" journalists and of the black press. Government news management and increased concentration of ownership alarmed publishers such as Henry Luce, who helped fund the Commission on Freedom of the Press, which reaffirmed the importance of a free press in a democratic society and urged publishers to accept the responsibility such a philosophy entailed. Editors, concerned about the lack of information available in other countries, worked to establish a worldwide agreement ensuring freedom of news dissemination. At the end of the war, soldiers returned to a prosperous country and looked for peace and consensus as they moved to an increasingly suburban America.

Although the United States did not declare war and thus become an integral participant in World War II until after Japan bombed Pearl Harbor on December 7, 1941, the beginnings of the conflict dated to the close of World War I. Japan, after experiencing an economic expansion from 1925 to 1929, turned to aggressive action on the Soviet border and in Manchuria during the late 1920s. Internal disputes in China between the Nationalists, led by Chiang Kai-shek, and the communists, led by Mao Tse-tung, crippled the country's resistance to Japanese attempts to control profitable economic relationships with Manchuria. In 1931, Japan attacked Chinese troops and brought Manchuria under its control. The situation grew even more tense in July 1936 when Japan signed an anti-Comintern pact with Nazi Germany, creating a Germany–Italy–Japan axis. Japan threatened to invade central China, and war broke out in 1937.

In Spain, the Republican government struggled to resist Franco's Fascist inroads from 1936 to 1939. England, also facing an economic crisis, fought to keep its empire intact, resisting Indian pleas for independence, appeasing Hitler, and ignoring the Italian invasion of Ethiopia. In 1938 to 1939, Germany seized Austria and areas of Czechoslovakia. During that same period, Germany and the Soviet Union signed the Soviet-Nazi Pact and a few days later separately invaded Poland. In November 1939, the Soviets attacked Finland.   ▼

A Radio War

The need to cover a variety of disturbing world events and the advent of available technology combined with other factors to bring radio news broadcasting to maturity during the 1930s and 1940s. CBS built a remarkable news staff with Edward R. Murrow and his "boys" in Europe and with a behind-the-scenes but powerful group in New York. Murrow, who joined CBS in 1935 as director of Talks and Special Events, went to London for CBS in 1937 as an administrator and coordinator as well as a broadcaster of news. Radio news was so new that when Murrow applied to join the American Foreign Correspondents' Association in London, he was rejected.

Radio coverage was live. Throughout the war Murrow pled to be able to record, but the New York staff argued that live coverage was the "extra dimension" that radio offered.[1] An additional and powerful reason that Bill Paley, the head of CBS, wanted radio to remain live was that he wanted to deter others from recording music and selling it directly to local stations. Demanding that radio be live also meant that Bill Paley could more powerfully control its development.

Murrow remained in London throughout the war. One of Murrow's early recruits was William Shirer, who remained in Berlin in 1940 and who later chronicled *The Rise and Fall of the Third Reich*. Others included Eric Sevareid, Charles Collingwood, Richard C. Hottelet, Larry LeSueur, and Howard K. Smith. Many of these reporters became familiar radio and television voices and were popular throughout the 1950s. By 1939, about 800 radio and newspaper correspondents from the United States covered breaking world events.[2]

Radio news increased during World War II from about 6 percent of network evening programming in 1938 to 1939 to nearly 18 percent in 1943 to 1944. *Fortune* magazine reported that in 1939, 70 percent of Americans relied on the radio as their prime source of news and 58 percent thought radio news was more accurate than that supplied by newspapers. Radio also became an important vehicle in boosting the war effort. In 1945, Kate Smith's singing stint gained pledges for $39 million in war bonds. Radio's pseudo-intimacy gave people a sense of being at, of feeling, an event. Arthur Godfrey wept on the air broadcasting the President's funeral in 1945 as Roosevelt's body was carried down Pennsylvania Avenue, and Americans felt they were present in the nation's capital. Americans turned to their radios for news and commentary on war and related events.

CBS adhered closely to a policy of objectivity until December 7, 1941. Shortly after the Japanese attack on Pearl Harbor, CBS's Paul White in New York announced there would be no further insistence on objectivity. "This is a war for the preservation of democracy," White wrote. "The American people must not only always be kept vividly aware of this objective, but of the value to every man, woman, and child in the nation of preserving democracy."[3] This did not free correspondents, however, to deliver their own opinions, and in 1943, when correspondent Paul Brown criticized President Roosevelt and Prime Minister Churchill for a failure of leadership, his sponsor withdrew support, and Brown resigned in protest. Columnists and commentators, including Dorothy Thompson and Walter Winchell, along with *Variety* and *Editor & Publisher,* criticized the network for not standing behind Brown.

Hans von Kaltenborn

Hans von Kaltenborn, born in 1878 in Wisconsin, became one of radio's first news commentators. Kaltenborn's extensive experience as a newsman on the *Brooklyn Eagle* and as a Washington and Paris correspondent led to the assignment of providing radio-broadcast news analyses on Westinghouse's experimental station WJZ in Newark, New Jersey. In 1923, the *Eagle* began sponsoring Kaltenborn on a regular weekly half-hour commentary over WEAF. His controversial radio broadcasts, which forced him to move from station to station, earned him the nickname, "the wandering voice of radio."[4] In 1930, Kaltenborn left the *Eagle* for CBS. As Kaltenborn broadcast from Spain during the Civil War, listeners heard "machine gun bullets whizzing overhead and the thud of bombs in the distance."[5]

Kaltenborn's name became a household word in 1938 during the twenty days of the Munich Crisis, while discussions continued between British Prime Minister Neville Chamberlain and Germany's Adolf Hitler. Kaltenborn's task was to coordinate reports from CBS's London correspondent Edward R. Murrow and other reporters in Europe. The sixty-year-old Kaltenborn described the twenty days, which he spent either behind a microphone or on a cot in the CBS studio, as a "pressure I had never before experienced in seventeen years of broadcasting."[6] Kaltenborn became a celebrity, receiving honorary doctorates and awards and appearing in cartoons. A *New Yorker* cartoon pictured a captain saying to men leaving a sinking ship: "Hold on men. I've got H. V. Kaltenborn on the radio. He's analyzing our predicament."[7]

In 1940, Kaltenborn began broadcasting daily for NBC and in 1952 was named "Radio Father of the Year." He stopped broadcasting but continued to write. Kaltenborn believed in radio as a force for democracy and as a source for presenting controversy. "If [a news analyst] is worth listening to, he will excite some controversy even if the subject he discusses is not usually considered controversial," he wrote.[8]

Figure 14-1   Hans Von Kaltenborn, who covered the Spanish Civil War, became famous as the coordinator of broadcasts by the "Murrow boys" from Europe during World War II. (State Historical Society of Wisconsin)

Edward R. Murrow

Edward R. Murrow, a Phi Beta Kappa graduate of Washington State College (now Washington State University) in 1930, was a student leader, and after college he became assistant director of the Institute of International Education. Unlike many broadcasters of his time, he had no newspaper experience before becoming CBS's director of talks and education.

Murrow led the way in organizing a network of broadcast correspondents for CBS, setting up the coverage of the European theater of World War II. NBC staffed the major European capitals in a similar fashion, but CBS gained recognition with its staff of fourteen skillful newscasters. Best remembered of all were the Edward R. Murrow "This . . . Is London" broadcasts, accounts which, sometimes during air raids, gave Americans a chilling feel for the war.[9]

In September of 1938, Murrow established his reputation with his reporting and analysis of the German takeover of Czechoslovakia. His live broadcasts were enhanced by the running commentary of H. V. Kaltenborn in New York. In *The Murrow Boys,* Stanley Cloud and Lynne Olson note, "This new kind of journalist was no mere commentator or announcer. He was a full-fledged correspondent who did it all—reported, wrote and spoke on the air." The importance of the radio journalist was being recognized, and Robert Landry in an article for *Scribner's* wrote that Murrow had more influence on America's reaction to foreign news "than a shipful of newspapermen."[10]

Murrow, admired for his courage in refusing to go into air raid shelters while the bombs fell dangerously close to him, dismissed accounts of his valor. Eric Sevareid wrote a few years later that he thought it was Murrow who told him he was afraid to go into the bomb shelters, for fear that once he started, he would not be able to stop.[11] "The only thing that counts," wrote Murrow, "is what comes out of the loudspeaker—and what we're trying to make come out is an honest, coherent account of events. It is not part of our job to please or entertain."

Former CBS television correspondent Marlene Sanders recalled that Murrow was the first to hire television women abroad, advising the first woman he hired, Mary Marvin Breckinridge, "to keep her voice low." The comment was probably in response to a common industry claim that women's voices failed to convey authority. Breckinridge broadcast from Paris until June 1940 when the French government abandoned the city. Other women benefited from Murrow's need for knowledgeable correspondents, and by 1946 the Women's Bureau of the U.S. Department of Labor noted that women constituted 28 percent of the total employees in broadcasting. However, when the war was over, many women lost their positions and the industry continued its claim that audiences did not respond well to female voices.[12]

For two years after the war Murrow was a vice president of CBS and director of public affairs, but he returned to the air in 1951 with his "See It Now" television programs. The most famous probably was his 1954 exposure of Senator Joseph McCarthy during McCarthy's communist-hunting escapades.

Murrow had resisted television, as did the rest of his radio "boys." In 1952, Sig Mickelson, head of the television news division at CBS, asked Murrow to anchor the political conventions that year. Murrow, coupled with Fred Friendly, operated "See It Now" outside the regular confines of the television division and Murrow had the power to say no, which he did. Mickelson, affronted by Murrow's snub, turned to Walter Cronkite as an anchor. Cronkite was an instant hit at both the Democratic and Republican political conventions. In 1954, CBS merged the radio and television news divisions into one. Heading it was Sig Mickelson, who had started with a staff of thirteen, but who was now in charge of 376. Murrow was uncomfortable with television; he battled for content that he thought would "illuminate," "teach," and "inspire." "But it can do so only to the extent that humans are determined to use it to these ends," he wrote. "Otherwise it is merely lights and wires in a box."

In 1961 Murrow joined the Kennedy administration as director of the U.S. Information Agency. He retired for health reasons and died of lung cancer at the age of fifty-seven.

The Wire Services and the War

Until the beginning of World War II, the two major wire services in the United States, United Press (UP) and Associated Press (AP), had maintained various agreements with European agencies such as Havas in France, Reuters in Britain, and Wolff in Germany to trade domestic news for foreign news. However, as Hitler gained control in Europe, devastating the resources of the German and French agencies, the

American wire services dominated the market. AP put 179 reporters in the field, relied on its strong news-picture service built up in the 1930s, and developed a fast-breaking style of news-event coverage. Meanwhile, UP carved out its own expertise in developing the human interest story.[13]

AP's monopoly, which excluded competitors, was finally broken in 1945 when a Supreme Court decision made UP and AP services available to any newspaper or radio station that paid the fee. AP's monopolistic position had been the target of suits in the past, but in 1915, when the *New York Sun* sued the Associated Press because the news gathering cooperative refused to sell its news to nonmembers and would not allow AP members to purchase the *Sun*'s news, the Supreme Court ruled that AP was not a monopoly and therefore not subject to antitrust laws. AP continued its exclusive rules and its exclusive agreements with European news services. World War II made editors more desperate for news, however, and when the powerful Robert McCormick barred Marshall Field and his new pro-Roosevelt newspaper from AP membership, Field went to the attorney general, asking whether the Associated Press constituted a monopoly. For the first time, the issues were framed in First Amendment terms. Judge Learned Hand ruled that any two news reports would never be the same because of the different perspectives of the news gatherers and that "to deprive a paper of the benefit of any service of the first rating is to deprive the reading public of means of information which it should have; it is only by crosslights from varying directions that full illumination can be secured."[14] The Supreme Court upheld the decision upon appeal, and AP members could no longer deny service to competitors nor prevent its members from subscribing to a second service, such as UP. UP no longer had a captive market of those newspapers denied access to AP, but because news was in such demand in the world war period, UP gained subscribers from the group that had previously subscribed exclusively to AP.

After the war, AP continued to expand overseas, competing not only with UP but with Reuters of Britain and the newly developed French service, Agence France-Presse.

Media Play Multiple Roles

In the mid-1930s, about 300 U.S. press and radio correspondents worked outside the boundaries of the country. During the war, the number grew to exceed 2,600, although all correspondents were not in the field at the same time. The depictions of war went beyond the conventional radio and news reports. Cartoonists and columnists chronicled the everyday lives of soldiers and the discrepancies of images at the front with those at home. Photographers recorded the internment of Japanese on American soil, and reports eventually emerged about Nazi concentration camps. Even the movies went to war, as Paramount newsreels depicted the brutality of the Japanese invasion of Chinese soil.

Correspondents and Costs

Coverage of the war in Asia assured that correspondents would be in place as the confrontation escalated into a world war and further assured that the wire services and the prestige press, which could afford the high costs of coverage, would dominate the dissemination of world news. The Associated Press, International News Service, and United Press wired stories home via London at a rate of about thirty-five cents a word.[15] In 1937, United Press coverage of the continuing conflict between China and Japan cost about $2,000 per day. In July of that year, the Associated Press spent $12,000 for all its foreign press coverage, $12,000 more than it had spent in July 1936. For news from China and Japan alone, AP was spending $4,000 per day, plus the costs for transmitting photographs. The first transmission of a photograph from Tokyo to New York took place in August 1937, the process taking ten hours and costing $225.

Costs of coverage continued to escalate throughout the war. By the mid-1940s, CBS and NBC were spending $10,000 a week to bring news round-ups from European capitals. Foreign news costs for the *New York Times* in 1941 exceeded

Figure 14–2   Telegraph desk in the *New York Times* newsroom, September 1942. (Office of War Information photo, Division of Prints and Photographs, Library of Congress Collection)

$1 million, and in 1942 the Associated Press spent slightly more than $1 million for overseas coverage.[16]

Correspondents faced great personal risks. Because of the bombing, they could rarely escape danger even when they were not technically at the front. Joe James Custer, a UP correspondent, suggested that correspondents should train on something other than beer and cigarettes to prepare for physical hardships. Nearly every correspondent in the southwest Pacific, he said, "has had malaria, dysentery and feet and leg sores. . . . It's a hard physical grind, working 24 hours a day, with a nap only now and then. . . . A correspondent is a non-combatant, but if he's surrounded by the enemy . . . he'll be a dead duck." He suggested that correspondents train like the marines train. In March 1943, the *World's Press of London* reported that twenty-three British, British Commonwealth, and U.S. correspondents had been killed, with seven more reported missing and others wounded, captured, and interned. Nine were held as prisoners of war. Of the twenty-three killed, *Editor & Publisher* reported that twelve were U.S. correspondents. After the war, thirty-six correspondents received decorations, including the Silver Star, Bronze Star, Air Medal, and special commendations. By 1948, forty-nine U.S. correspondents were reported to have lost their lives in war-related activities between 1939 and 1945.[17]

Marguerite Higgins

Marguerite Higgins, prominent World War II correspondent, earned an M.A. degree from Columbia University's Graduate School of Journalism in 1942. Upon taking a job as a reporter, she went directly to her employer, *New York Herald Tribune* publisher Helen Ogden Reid, to plead for a job as a war correspondent. Higgins, who went abroad in 1944, was one of the first American correspondents to cover the U.S. capture of the Dachau concentration camp. She also covered the Nuremberg war trials and became the *Herald Tribune's* Berlin bureau chief in 1945. Higgins continued to work hard and challenge herself, maintaining an attitude that paid off as she headed the *Herald Tribune's* Tokyo bureau and won a Pulitzer Prize during the Korean War. When an army colonel in Korea warned her that there might be trouble and she'd have to leave, Higgins replied, "Trouble is news, and the gathering of news is my job."[18] In 1963, Higgins, taking a hard anticommunist line, covered the early days of the Vietnam conflict for *Newsday.* She contracted a tropical disease in Vietnam and died in 1966 at the age of forty-five.

Columnists and Cartoonists

Chroniclers told not only of the events of the war, columnists and cartoonists also told of the lives of soldiers at the front. Bill Mauldin's cartoon characters Willie and Joe talked about the difference between life at the front and life at the rear—wallowing in mud versus staying warm and well fed—and depicted the unpleasant discrepancies between officers and enlisted men. Willie and Joe were critical of bureaucrats at home as well, claiming they sent the boots and jackets to the rear echelon, leaving those at the front in need.[19] Mauldin attacked the pompousness of the military and bureaucracy, but his pictures of the infantry were realistic, noting that soldiers

▼

Marguerite Higgins (1920–1966)

Marguerite Higgins was a female journalist when men dominated the journalism industry. She forged her way through the University of California-Berkeley and Columbia School of Journalism to become a war correspondent for the *New York Tribune*. A professor at Columbia described her as "charming but absolutely ruthless, a flawless combination of sex and brains." After covering several wars, she was buried in Arlington cemetery, with famous figures such as Robert and Ethel Kennedy and Vice President Hubert Humphrey in attendance. When she was buried in Arlington—a national military cemetery—a Washington paper wrote on the front page "And now she is with her boys again."

Source: A. May, *Witness to War: A Biography of Marguerite Higgins* (New York: Beaufort Books, 1983). (*Photo:* Division of Prints and Photographs, Library of Congress Collection)

at the front "shot the enemy in the back, blew him up with mines, and killed him in the quickest and most effective way."

Ernie Pyle

Ernie Pyle, Pulitzer Prize–winning columnist, chronicled the lives of the ordinary soldiers at war, ignoring the already-heralded generals. He died in 1945 in action on Ie Shima in the Pacific. His column was carried by more than 300 daily and 400 weekly newspapers.[20] Pyle began his journalism career at Indiana University working for the school newspaper and then, without finishing college, at Indiana's *La Porte Herald*. Three months after starting work at the *Herald*, Pyle moved to Washington to work for the *News*, where he met Geraldine Siebolds, whom he married. The two

▼

Pyle and the Infantry

I love the infantry because they are the underdogs. They are the mud-rain-frost-and-wind boys. They have no comforts, and they even learn to live without the necessities. And in the end they are the guys that wars can't be won without.

—Ernie Pyle, *New York World-Telegram*, May 3 and 5, 1943

toured the United States in 1926, then moved to New York, where Pyle worked for the *New York Evening World* and the *New York Post*. In 1927, Pyle returned to the *Washington News*, where he served as telegraph editor and wrote an aviation column. In 1932, he wrote his last column before becoming managing editor. "This column," he wrote, "has tried to feel with those who fly. It has recorded the surprised elation of those who have risen rocketlike into renown, has felt despair with those who have been beaten down by the game, has shared the awful desolation of those who have seen their close ones fly away and come back only in the stark blackness of the newspaper headlines." Pyle wearied of editor's work and began once more to write a column, leaving the managing editor's post and traveling across the country. In 1939, Scripps-Howard syndicated the column, and in 1940, Pyle left for London to cover the war. He became famous for his descriptions of the effects of war on London. Then he returned to the United States. After the bombing of Pearl Harbor, he went back to Europe, and during the summer of 1942 he traveled to North Africa to cover the American invasion. Pyle's columns from North Africa described the lives of ordinary soldiers and were collected in a book, *Here Is Your War*, in 1943. Through Italy, to the Anzio beachhead, to England, and with the troops on D-Day, Pyle continued to chronicle the events of the war, often becoming overburdened by the "enormity of all those newly dead." In 1945, after a short visit to the United States, Pyle accompanied troops to the Pacific. When he landed on Okinawa, he wrote what was to be his last column: "The war and weariness of war is cumulative. To many a man in the line today, fear is not so much of death itself, but fear of the terror and anguish and utter horror that precede death in battle." Two days later, Pyle was killed by gunfire. Pyle was known not only for his sympathy with the ordinary soldiers but for his descriptions of the discrepancies of war. He often commented on the difference between attitudes at home and attitudes at the front. Mary Mander's study of war correspondents summed up the differences:

> When the invasion forces were landed on Omaha beach, GIs in Italy were still under enemy artillery and attack, and over and above that, were enduring some of the most miserable weather ever undergone by a man in uniform. Under wretched conditions such as these, the GIs got letters from home in which a relative said, "I'm so glad you're in Italy while the fighting is in France." People such as Bing Crosby, who entertained the troops, told the folks back home that salutes really snap at the front. Meanwhile, back in the foxholes, the soldiers were saying that the folks at home seemed to think the GIs and Germans were dancing the beer barrel polka together.[21]

In response to Pyle's death, President Harry Truman said, "The nation is quickly saddened again by the death of Ernie Pyle. No man in this war has so well told the story of the American fighting man as American fighting men wanted it told. He deserves the gratitude of all his countrymen."[22]

Photography Depicts Two Views of Japanese Internment

By World War II, photojournalism had come of age; and in the spring of 1942, when 110,000 Japanese Americans on the West Coast—70,000 of whom were born in the United States—were "relocated" in ten camps where they spent the duration of the war, the War Relocation Authority hired photographers to document the internment. Among those photographers were Dorothea Lange, famous for her pictures of the depression, and Ansel Adams, known as a landscape photographer.

Both photographed the Manzanar Relocation Center. The record the two produced recorded distinctly different points of view. Adams' pictures, which focused on the small businesses that grew up in the camp, smiling people, and serene landscapes, emphasized the success of the Japanese Americans in adapting to their environment. Lange, on the other hand, showed the oppressive conditions in the camp and attempted to reveal the internment as an injustice.

Few of Lange's photographs were used during the period. Adams' documentation of camp life, *Born Free and Equal*, was published in 1944, and during the same year his photographs were exhibited at the Museum of Modern Art in New York. The exhibit received little attention, and Japanese Americans showed widespread resentment at the work. During the 1960s, Lange's work found more acceptance in a society that recognized a pattern of discrimination against minorities in American life, and in 1972 her work was collected under the title *Executive Order 9066* and widely exhibited.[23]

Coverage of Nazi Concentration Camps

Although the press covered stories of German atrocities toward Jews as early as 1933, many Americans later claimed they had no idea of what was going on in Germany. Most likely it was not the lack of information but a variety of other factors that colored U.S. citizens' perceptions of German behavior. In the early 1930s, American businesspeople envied the growth and expansion of the German economy. Tourists who visited there saw a clean country, devoid of the problems visible in American society. Norman Chandler, attending the 1936 Olympic games, berated Ralph Barnes of the *New York Herald Tribune* and William Shirer of CBS for their critical stories. Reporters feared expulsion from Germany and revenge on their Jewish sources. Readers were wary of false atrocity stories similar to those generated in World War I, greeting them with horror, skepticism, and a belief that the situation within Germany just could not be as bad as it appeared to be. Also blocking perception was a strong strain of anti-Semitism in the United States. These factors combined to color readers' perceptions and although they encouraged editors to cover the news, they also caused the press to moderate the tone of the stories and to avoid treating the Nazi restrictions on Jews as the central theme of German coverage. Repeatedly, the press failed to grasp the extent of the institutionalization of anti-Semitism in the German state, although opposition increased considerably after the Nuremberg laws of 1935 officially disenfranchised Jews and classified them as noncitizens.[24]

In a study of the magazine coverage of the Nazi exterminations of European Jewry from November 1941 to November 1944, when 6 million Jews were systematically annihilated, Arlene Rossen Cardozo found that opinion magazines provided much more coverage and analysis of the Jewish situation than did news or feature magazines. *The Nation*, in particular, repeated the theme that Jews must be removed from Europe in order to survive. The magazine also encouraged the British to lift restrictions on admitting Jews to Palestine and advocated a Jewish homeland as a solution to the problem. Another magazine active in analysis was *The New Republic*.[25]

Nevertheless, American citizens were caught in their own worries with the depression and, with a strain of anti-Semitism running through the country along with a certain amount of skepticism resulting from the untrue atrocity stories told during World War I, they at best were dubious about the tales of horror being reported.[26] In 1945, however, no doubt remained, as *Life* magazine reported on May 7:

> Last week, Americans could no longer doubt stories of Nazi cruelty. For the first time there was irrefutable evidence as the advancing Allied armies captured camps filled with political prisoners and slave laborers, living and dead.[27]

Media and Government

The government was actively involved in monitoring media and encouraging patriotic news messages. Not only did correspondents face censorship at home, but they also dealt with censorship by foreign governments. In addition, the Office of War Information sought cooperation in the broadcast and film industry as well as in the newspaper press. The government also cast cautious eyes toward African-American newspapers, fearing that lack of equality at home might spur antagonism on the part of African-American publishers. At the end of the war, editors cooperated with the government to try to achieve worldwide accords that would guarantee free access to information.

Censorship

Correspondents were, of course, subject to the censorship restrictions of the countries from which they reported. These restrictions were severe at times, especially in Japan and Germany. Once England declared war, the British government also set up fairly strict censorship procedures.

The Federal Communications Act of 1934 gave President Roosevelt the power to take control of radio in a national emergency. Further, in 1941, the Federal Communications Commission (FCC) ruled in the *Mayflower Broadcast Corp.* case that broadcast license holders could not use the airwaves to air their own views on public issues. This doctrine, declared by the FCC at the same time the industry was cautioning its own commentators to avoid expressing personal judgments, did not change until 1949, when the FCC instituted the Fairness Doctrine and held that broadcasters could air a point of view if they made time available for other persons holding different views. Soon after the war began in Europe, Roosevelt declared a limited national emergency. In its own move to cooperate, the National Association of Broadcasters established a regulatory code, requesting the avoidance of "horror, suspense and undue excitement," and ruled out editorializing. The code called for fairness to all "belligerents" and noted that analysis should explain and evaluate facts, rumors, and propaganda, not establish a particular point of view.

Figure 14–3   A California workman reads a war extra. (Office of War Information photo by Russell Lee, Division of Prints and Photographs, Library of Congress Collection)

Within hours after the attack on Pearl Harbor, the U.S. government moved to secure Japanese, Italian, and German correspondents. They were interned at the luxurious Hotel Greenbrier in White Sulphur Springs, West Virginia, until the time they would be exchanged for U.S. correspondents and returned to their countries. The German government reacted to the U.S. internment by arresting twenty U.S. correspondents, and the Japanese held about eleven correspondents for almost two years (1941–1943).

Censorship on the Home Front

Agencies for evaluation of press coverage and dissemination of government news proliferated after Franklin Delano Roosevelt became President. In 1933, the President created the Division of Press Intelligence, which evaluated press coverage of New

Deal policies and synthesized information into bulletins for the President, Congress, and other members of the administration. After 1942, the Office of War Information, together with the Agriculture Department, assisted Roosevelt in gathering information until conservative congressmen, fearful of government manipulation of public opinion, halted much of the work done by the federal agencies. Other government agencies, including Army Military Intelligence and the Bureau of Investigation (renamed the Federal Bureau of Investigation, or FBI, in the 1930s), active in World War I in monitoring newspaper content, continued to investigate journalists and question their levels of loyalty to the country.

By early 1941, correspondents were required to carry a press pass, bearing a photograph, name, institutional affiliation, signature, and fingerprints in order to attend White House conferences and to gain access to many of the other governmental information sources.

The first move toward wartime censorship occurred in January 1941, when Secretary of the Navy Frank Knox asked correspondents to voluntarily censor news about the navy and shipping in general. The request stemmed in part from the U.S. Lend-Lease program, which provided material and munitions to favored nations. Although in April Secretary Knox asked that correspondents not report or photograph the comings and goings of British ships, the request had limited effect.

After the attack on Pearl Harbor, the Espionage Act of 1917, which had not been repealed, was invoked. News of casualties were to be cleared through military channels and communications companies were ordered to halt cable, radio, and telephone traffic to or from Japan, Germany, Italy, and Finland. From the Southeast Pacific, news passed through General MacArthur's headquarters, correspondents in the Central Pacific had to have naval approval, and those in Hawaii had to pass both fleet officers and Honolulu censors.[28] The Defense Communications Board was authorized to take over or close any radio or other communications facility, and navy censorship was imposed on all news entering or leaving the United States. News of weather and of ship and troop movements could not be reported.

Office of Censorship

Censorship procedures gained formality in late December 1941, when the Office of Censorship was organized under the direction of Byron Price, former executive editor of the Associated Press. The staff eventually included 11,500 persons, and its budget for 1943 alone was $26,500,000.[29]

The Office of Censorship had three primary tasks. It administered the Code of Wartime Practices, issued in January 1942, which requested news institutions to adhere to a voluntary censorship code; it monitored news entering and leaving the country; and it handled foreign correspondents reporting the war from the United States. Nine newspapermen, on loan to the government, assisted with the domestic censorship operation, and it is to their credit that complaints by newspaper editors were so few. The Office of Censorship operated quickly, observing the needs of newspapers and broadcast stations to function on deadline; material cabled to the Washington office experienced a turn-around time of as little as seven minutes. The office backed the press in most instances, although it did issue thousands of letters of complaint regarding violations of the code to newspapers, from weeklies to major metropolitan dailies. However, the office had little formal censuring power except for materials that left or entered the country.

Fifteen Office of Censorship stations, located in cities where mail was most likely to enter or leave the country, monitored newspapers and magazines shipped to Alaska, Mexico, and other countries, in addition to material being sent to the war zone itself. If the office found objectionable material, it either stopped distribution of the publication or clipped the objectionable paragraph or page and then sent the rest of the publication intact to its destination.[30]

Battle of Midway   Probably one of the most serious breaches of military intelligence occurred in the *Chicago Tribune's* report of the Battle of Midway in June 1942. Stanley Johnston, a *Tribune* correspondent, in an article about the navy repulsing the Japanese at Midway, revealed that the navy had prior word of the Japanese plan to strike. A *Tribune* editor submitted the story to domestic censorship in Washington because the paper was publishing the story under a one-column headline, "NAVY HAD WORD OF JAP PLAN TO STRIKE AT SEA."

What *Tribune* editors did not know was that prior knowledge of the Japanese plan had been obtained by breaking the Japanese naval code. The major question was how Johnston had gotten the information. Johnston claimed that because of his service in the Australian navy and a lifelong study of military and naval subjects, he unraveled for himself the fact that an earlier attack had been a feint. He also claimed that the ships he listed as involved had come from notes mistakenly picked up in the cabin of the ship. Although authorities were never sure of the source of Johnston's list (they believed he had seen the original message transmitted to Admiral Nimitz because of the unusual misspellings in several ships' names), a grand jury in Chicago found the *Tribune* innocent of publishing information that hurt the war effort. The grand jury refused to indict because it was not presented with all available evidence. In order to convict, the government would have had to reveal the classified information it was seeking to protect.[31]

Office of War Information

The Office of War Information (OWI), created in June 1942, handled propaganda and absorbed the Office of Government Reports, the Office of the Coordinator of Information, the Office of Facts and Figures, and several smaller agencies. Elmer Davis, former *New York Times* staffer, directed the operation.

OWI's domestic and foreign operations in May 1945, at the peak of its activity, required the services of 9,600 persons, and its budget was $132,500,000 for its three years of operation.[32] Three experienced editors and publishers directed the domestic operation: Gardner Cowles, Jr., of the *Des Moines Register and Tribune*, the *Minneapolis Star-Journal* and *Tribune*, and *Look* magazine; E. Palmer Hoyt, editor and publisher of the *Portland Oregonian;* and George W. Healy, Jr., publisher of the *New Orleans Time-Picayune*. The government controlled the broadcasting facilities of five companies that had been disseminating shortwave programs from the United States, including CBS and NBC. News and other programs broadcast through these facilities to a variety of enemy and allied countries became known as the Voice of America, an operation still in existence. The Voice of America and related overseas activity comprised 85 percent of the total OWI budget.

The Film Industry Cooperates with the Government

Government opinions of the motion picture industry's activity during the war were mixed. Major producers cooperated to produce war films on what they termed was a nonprofit basis. Nevertheless, during 1941 and 1942, the Army Pictorial Division alone spent more than $1 million in Hollywood. Critics claimed the producers filmed for the government during slack times, or when the studios otherwise would have stood idle, and that by cooperating, the industry managed to remain relatively untouched by the war. Therefore, despite Walt Disney's depiction of Donald Duck as a citizen willing to pay taxes with patriotic enthusiasm and Frank Capra's direction of the "Why We Fight" series designed to train new soldiers, the motion picture industry faced a variety of enemies in Congress.

The Motion Picture Bureau, a division of OWI, attempted to influence Hollywood producers to support the war effort. Among its tasks was to try to motivate producers to incorporate more realistic pictures of African-American life into films.

Figure 14–4   A meeting on military news in the office of Elmer Davis, director of the U.S. Office of War Information. Pictured left to right are Gardner Cowles, Jr., director of Domestic Operations; Nicholas Roosevelt; Milton Eisenhower, associate director; Commander Robert W. Berry, representing U.S. Navy public relations; Colonel F. V. Fitzgerald, U.S. Army Bureau of Public Relations; and Davis. (Office of War Information photo, Division of Prints and Photographs, Library of Congress Collection)

Figure 14–5 The Dust Bowl did not disappear with the end of the 1930s, as this 1942 photograph of a billboard advertising the Dust Bowl Theatre in Pinal County, Arizona, indicates. (Farm Security Administration photo by Russell Lee, Division of Prints and Photographs, Library of Congress)

In response to evidence such as a 1942 survey conducted by the Office of Facts and Figures that indicated that 49 percent of Harlem blacks thought they would be no worse off if Japan won the war, OWI wanted Hollywood to tone down its racist images of African Americans in order to foster a sense of unity in the country.[33]

Although the industry had catered to the Legion of Decency and various other economic groups, when OWI attempted to promote more positive images of African Americans, the industry cried censorship. For example, MGM in 1938 had its script of Robert Sherwood's anti-Fascist play *Idiot's Delight* hand-carried to Italy for approval after drastically altering it to avoid offending Benito Mussolini. Warner Brothers' coal mining saga *Black Fury* was altered to blame labor unrest on union radicals rather than on mine operators—after the National Coal Association protested.

OWI efforts to promote positive African-American images had little effect. A 1945 Columbia University study found that of 100 African-American appearances in wartime films, 75 percent perpetuated stereotypes, 13 percent were neutral, and only 12 percent were positive. OWI hesitated to push very far, claiming the war came first.[34]

Throughout the 1940s, different segments of government attacked the motion picture industry. In 1941, Senator Gerald B. Nye, in a series of committee hearings, charged that motion picture moguls lacked American character. In 1943, a special

Senate committee again questioned whether moviemakers could be counted as loyal citizens. Striking workers and battling unions further provided fodder for the House Un-American Activities Committee to pursue its anticommunism witch-hunt in Hollywood after the war. The industry did not stand solid. Some managers, such as Walt Disney and Louis B. Mayer, cooperated with the government and provided the names of those they termed "known communists," and some workers testified against others as well.[35]

The film industry began its decline in the late 1940s when the Supreme Court forced studios to divest themselves of their theatre chains, thus limiting the monopoly of production and distribution studios that had been built over a thirty-year period. In the industry's peak year of 1946, 90 million Americans, or 75 percent of the population, went to the movies each week. For the next two decades, movie audiences declined dramatically and although studios distributed most major films, independents made some gains in production.

Monitoring the Black Press

Roosevelt's interest in monitoring press attitudes continued from the 1930s through World War II.[36] Aided by J. Edgar Hoover's willingness to investigate journalists, Roosevelt's monitoring policies extended to a variety of groups, including the black press. The black press had been the subject of government interest since World War I, as administration officials during both wars concerned themselves with the possible effects of the attitudes of 13 million African Americans, which comprised 10 percent of the country's population. The black press had grown as an institution during the interwar period, and its increasingly militant stance triggered additional federal concern during World War II. The *Pittsburgh Courier*, the *Baltimore Afro-American*, and the *Chicago Defender* signaled a change in the black press from small sheets of low circulation to mass-circulation, highly influential newspapers in the African-American community. The revival of the Ku Klux Klan in the 1920s, the segregation of black troops, and the general lack of progress toward equal rights for African Americans during the interwar years gave blacks reason to doubt whether another world war was, for them, a war to extend democratic participation.[37]

During World War II, the black press was investigated by seven governmental agencies, including the Department of Justice, the Federal Bureau of Investigation, the Post Office Department, the Office of Facts and Figures, the Office of War Information, the Office of Censorship, and the army. An eighth agency, the War Production Board, may have cut newsprint supplies to some newspapers.[38] In mid-June 1942, John Sengstacke, president of the Negro Newspaper Publishers Association and publisher of the *Chicago Defender*, met with Attorney General Francis Biddle of the Justice Department to discuss increased pressure on the black press to tone down its militancy and to support the war effort without reservation. Sengstacke told Biddle that in exchange for interviews with top governmental officials to obtain information, African-American newspapers would be glad to cooperate with the war effort. For such cooperation, Sengstacke expected that no African-American newspapers would be indicted for sedition.[39] Despite continued investigation by the FBI and by the post office, no black newspapers were indicted during the war. The lack of indictments

Figure 14–6 The *Pittsburgh Courier* was widely read for its "Double V" campaign during the war. (Farm Security Administration photo, Division of Prints and Photographs, Library of Congress Collection)

probably was due to the influence of Biddle and his cooperative agreement with Sengstacke, but it also may have reflected efforts by other black leaders, who worked for increased liberal policies toward African Americans from the federal government.[40] Further, after the bombing of Pearl Harbor in 1941, the black press adopted the "Double V" platform begun by the *Pittsburgh Courier*, which advocated victory at home and victory abroad.

Smith Act Restricts Action

On June 28, 1940, the nation's first peacetime sedition act since 1801, the Smith Act, was passed quietly to prohibit advocacy of the violent overthrow of the government. The act ostensibly would prevent military soldiers from being led astray and made it a crime to "interfere with, impair or influence the loyalty, morale or discipline of the members of the armed forces by encouraging insubordination, disloyalty or mutiny."[41] The second part of the act, modeled after the New York Anarchy and Criminal Syndicalism Act of 1902, prohibited "three kinds of conduct: advocacy of the violent overthrow of the government; organization of a group which advocates the violent overthrow of the government; and membership in a group which advocates the violent overthrow of the government."[42]

▼

March on Washington, 1942

We know that our fate is tied up with the fate of the democratic way of life. And so, out of the depths of our hearts, a cry goes up for the triumph of the United Nations. But we would not be honest with ourselves were we to stop with a call for a victory of arms alone.

—A. Philip Randolph, in an address to the Policy Conference
of the March on Washington Movement, September 1942

Although the act was passed in 1940, it was rarely used before 1949, when public opinion turned violently anticommunist and twelve defendants were indicted for conspiring to organize the Communist party and for advocating the violent overthrow of the government of the United States. The New York case, which became *Dennis v. United States* on appeal, established a pattern for subsequent cases. Judge Harold Medina, who presided at the first communist trial, narrowed the range of punishable speech, stating that the act prohibited only the teaching or advocacy of "action" directed toward overthrowing the government and that it did not mean the accused could not advocate or teach violent overthrow in the abstract.[43] Medina's interpretation later was upheld by the Supreme Court in *Yates v. United States*, 354 U.S. 298 (1957), when it overturned a lower court's decision to convict. Since the Yates case, only one defendant has been convicted. Although it is difficult to predict in what circumstances the Smith Act would be used again, the implications of it remaining on the law books are somewhat frightening. The fact that it exists, wrote Don Pember, is dangerous and could prohibit free expression. "Another national panic, another Red Scare, an alleged conspiracy by Negro militants or the New Left—any of these could create the excuse once again to dust off the Smith Act and begin rounding up 'subversives.'"[44]

Accountability and Freedom

Press critics since the turn of the century had been increasingly concerned about the concentration of ownership, the responsibility shown by publishers and broadcasters, and governmental management of the news. Growing ownership concentration, coupled with sponsorship control of the networks, elicited even greater criticism from various sectors of society during the period between the world wars. Since Theodore Roosevelt's presidency, administrative agencies had flooded news agencies with information, and some publishers, such as Henry Luce, feared that the government, not the press, was controlling the news agenda.[45] After the war, publishers became increasingly concerned about freedom around the world and the lack of access to necessary information.

Hutchins' Commission Seeks Intelligent Account

In December 1942, Luce suggested to Robert M. Hutchins the formation of an independent inquiry into freedom of the press. In 1943, a commission was formed, financed by $200,000 in grants from Time, Inc., and $15,000 from Encyclopaedia Britannica, Inc. The money was disbursed through the University of Chicago and the commission headed by the university's controversial president Robert Hutchins. Although the study was funded at the beginning of the war, its findings were not presented until the war's close.

In its evaluation of the status of freedom of the newspaper press, radio, motion pictures, magazines, and books, the commission elicited testimony from 58 persons connected with the press; recorded interviews with 225 members of industry, government, and private agencies connected with the press; and examined 176 documents prepared by the commission staff. Citing the pressing need for information during a time of world crisis, Hutchins said that the commission concentrated its efforts on determining the "role of the agencies of mass communication in the education of the people in public affairs."[46] The commission did not address the issue of governmental publicity.

In 1947, the commission listed five "ideal demands of society for the communication of news and ideas":

1. A truthful, comprehensive, and intelligent account of the day's events in a context which gives them meaning;

2. A forum for the exchange of comment and criticism;

3. The projection of a representative picture of the constituent groups in the society;

4. The presentation and clarification of the goals and values of the society; and

5. Full access to the day's intelligence.

After evaluating the press in light of its ideal demands, the commission found freedom of the press in the United States to be in danger because of the monopolistic nature of the press. Concentration meant, the commission noted, that fewer people had access to communication channels and that those in charge had not provided a service adequate to society's needs.

Concerned with the potential for either good or evil of new technology yet to be developed, the commission discussed guidelines for the regulation of new technology and international communications systems.[47] The commission chose, however, to assign the press the responsibility of "accountability" rather than recommending increased governmental regulation. The commission suggested that retraction or restatement by the press might better serve victims of libel than suits for damages, and the commission recommended repeal of state syndicalism acts and the Alien Registration Act of 1940, saying they were of "dubious constitutionality." The commission also suggested the government assume responsibility for disseminating its own news, either through private channels or channels of its own.

The commission suggested that the press should accept the responsibility of being a "common carrier" of information and discussion rather than assuming that ownership meant the right to dissemination of a personal viewpoint. It encouraged owners to experiment with new activities, especially in areas in which profits were not necessarily assured. The commission also encouraged vigorous mutual criticism by members of the press and increased competence of news staffs. The commission also chided the radio industry for giving control away to soap sponsors and recommended that it take control of its programs and treat advertisers in the way the "best" newspapers treated them.

Focusing on freedom as "bound up intrinsically in the collective good of life in society," the commission further suggested that the public had a social responsibility to ensure continued freedom of the press, requesting that nonprofit institutions help supply variety and quality to press service. It requested that educational centers be created for advanced research about communications and emphasized the importance of the liberal arts in journalistic training.[48]

Renewing the discussion of the importance of a free and accessible press to a democratic society, the commission finally recommended that an independent agency be established to appraise and report annually on the performance of the press. The commission worried, however, that too much emphasis was being placed on that recommendation. Nevertheless, it seemed the only solution commissioners could agree on, after acknowledging that neither the concept of laissez-faire nor that of governmental control would eliminate the effects of monopoly.[49]

Needless to say, the owners of the agencies of mass communication reacted negatively. Many members of the press were critical because no one from its ranks was included on the commission. Responding to the criticism, the American Society of Newspaper Editors (ASNE) in 1950 appointed ten newspapermen and educators to investigate self-improvement possibilities. The editors' findings reaffirmed the concept of laissez-faire and rejected the commission's recommendations, claiming that improvement of American newspapers depended on "the character of American newspapermen" and their "acceptance of the great responsibilities imposed by freedom of the press." The ASNE study suggested that reporters and editors might be more willing to profit by the "intelligent criticism of the newspaper-reading public" than they would by suggestions made by a commission over which they had no control.[50]

Campaign for International Freedom of the Press

At the same time the Hutchins commission was conducting its study, American news media were waging a campaign to export the First Amendment to the rest of the world.[51] A similar effort was made after World War I, but proposals developed then lay in the archives of the League of Nations, which took no official action on the subject. The 1940s campaign encountered many difficulties from the start. During the war, the press and the government had cooperated on a variety of levels, with the wire services supplying the State Department with news for transmission overseas and with newspapers complying, for the most part, with a voluntary code of censorship. As the war ended, the press became increasingly uncomfortable with its unfamiliar alliance with government. Further, U.S. press motives were suspect in other countries. Other nations often viewed U.S. press demands for freedom of expression as a means of establishing an American domination of news and analysis of that news.

The movement, spearheaded by the American Society of Newspaper Editors, the Associated Press, and the United Press, was based on the hope of newspaper editors that the government would help them to establish international accords that would grant correspondents freedom to travel, to gain access to information, and to transmit information freely to their own countries. Those supporting the movement did not always agree exactly on the goals of the campaign. Kent Cooper, executive director of the Associated Press, argued for an all-inclusive program to export the American press as an institution to all other countries. Speaking to the ASNE, he called for "freedom of the press of the entire world as we know it here." He said the best press in the world existed in the United States and that "it would be wonderful if the force that is available from that success would be directed altruistically toward the extension of the American accomplishments to the rest of the world."[52] Recognizing that other nations might have different opinions about the goals, behavior, and results of American-style press coverage, Hugh Baillie, United Press director, argued for "equal access to news at its source in all countries, equal transmission rates, no peacetime censorship."[53]

ASNE members began talking with the State Department as early as 1943 about end-of-the-war guarantees, and in May 1947, the Subcommission on Freedom of Information and of the Press, organized under the Human Rights Commission, met to establish an agenda for a 1948 Geneva Conference on Freedom of Information. The disputes arising throughout the discussions continued to center on issues that would, in the end, negate the development of an international agreement. Critical areas of discussion included accreditation of correspondents, the privileges of correspondents versus their responsibilities to present the interests of their home countries, permissible levels of censorship, the inequitable distribution of communication facilities and supplies, and permissible sanctions for violations.

Resolution of these issues was complicated by considerations of national self-interest. The United States, for example, consumed more than 65 percent of the international supply of newsprint; however, editors saw no reason to share their wealth. Also, the United States had refused to let some correspondents enter the country on the grounds that they were members of subversive organizations. Furthermore, the Polish delegation at Geneva quoted the Hutchins commission report in their claim that the U.S. press was in the hands of a few and served only special interests in the country.

Disagreement on these issues continued to stall debates and limit effective action until 1950, when the State Department and the American press abandoned the crusade. In the end, these two groups believed that the goal of the provisions as written through compromise at the United Nations was to specify information that could be restricted rather than to increase freedom of access to information. Further, reporting conditions abroad had deteriorated rather than improved, and the murder of CBS correspondent George Polk while working in Greece and the three-year imprisonment of William Oatis of the Associated Press in Czechoslovakia on false charges of espionage discouraged hope for viable international accords.

Television Technology Emerges from the Wings

Variety, in April 1930, advertised that television soon would burst forth in the marketplace. Although tube technology neared acceptable quality in the late 1930s, World

War II interrupted the marketing of sets begun in 1938. Still, several stations broadcast throughout the war, and by 1950 in cities such as Los Angeles, Philadelphia, New York, and Baltimore more people watched television than listened to radio. In 1948, a CBS vice president, Hubbell Robinson, Jr., announced, "Television is about to do to radio what the Sioux did to Custer. There is going to be a massacre."[54]

Technology and Programming

Television technology can be traced in many ways to the same origins as the technology of the motion picture. Experiments in the 1880s with mechanical scanning, and later electronic scanning, had led to development of the iconoscope tube in the 1920s by a Russian émigré, Vladimir Zworykin. From 1935 on, RCA demonstrated television to the trade press, and in 1939 the company presented it publicly at the New York World's Fair. RCA was not alone in the field; CBS and Allen B. DuMont's experimental stations also were telecasting in New York in 1939. By 1940, about twenty-three stations were reported to be broadcasting in the United States. The boom halted temporarily, however, as war and the need for military production dominated the electronics industry. The major figures in the industry joined the war effort. David Sarnoff, who was to become a brigadier general by the end of the war, joined the signal corps; William Paley of CBS worked for the Psychological Warfare Unit; and even Edwin Armstrong, who was experimenting with FM radio, joined the army.

RCA and CBS, which continued to experiment with television, turned their production forces toward domesticity at the end of the war, and by July 1946 the FCC issued twenty-four new licenses. CBS appealed to the FCC to adopt its new mechanical color system, which would provide a superior color system but render prewar black-and-white sets obsolete, while RCA promoted its own compatible electronic color system. In March 1947, the FCC approved RCA's system, registering a major defeat for CBS. Only months after FCC action approved the RCA standards, the FCC chairman resigned to become NBC's vice president and general counsel. In a battle before the war, Sarnoff had persuaded the FCC to establish a national television standard. His postwar efforts were also successful, as RCA's black-and-white and compatible color system dominated the industry and achieved FCC approval. CBS and ABC, created from the Blue Network that RCA had sold in 1943, lagged behind in television development, and in the early 1950s they struggled to catch up.

Television growth was phenomenal. In 1948, there had been 172,000 homes with television receivers. That number grew to 42 million by 1958. The three major networks—ABC, CBS, and NBC—controlled between 50 and 60 percent of all local programming and 95 percent of evening programming.

During the late 1940s, CBS and NBC experimented with newsreel-patterned news broadcasts, operating in conjunction with the movie houses, and they expected radio profits to pay the bills for the as yet unprofitable television operations. However, in 1948 the FCC froze television development one more time in an effort to study the problems of interference. The freeze continued until 1952, near the end of the Korean War. New York and Los Angeles, each with seven stations, had the most complete television operations, while other cities had no more than one station each. Both the inability to guarantee a uniform audience for television and the government freezes caused advertisers to hesitate and continue their radio sponsorship, but some advertisers, like the cosmetic superstar Hazel Bishop, catapulted sales through television advertising. In cities where television succeeded, movie houses closed and night clubs experienced large drops in attendance.[55]

Black Press Reflects Increased Consumer Power

The black press more than doubled its circulation between 1933 and 1940, reaching more than 1,276,000 people by 1940. In 1944, five papers represented a total average weekly circulation of 50,000, representing more than 46 percent of the total circulation. Because pass-around readership was extensive, these circulation figures represented only a fraction of the people reading such papers as the *Chicago Defender*, the *Baltimore Afro-American*, or the *Pittsburgh Courier*.

Growth of Black Dailies

A trend toward consolidation in the black press was apparent from the 1930s onward, just as it was apparent for the press as a whole. In 1956, John Sengstacke converted the famous *Chicago Defender* from a weekly to a daily and developed a newspaper group with nine papers, including the *Pittsburgh Courier*, a paper he acquired in 1966. The second largest African-American newspaper group was the *Afro-American* newspapers. The *Defender* maintained its excellent albeit sensational image through World War II, but the *Pittsburgh Courier* probably gained more notice in the white community because of its twenty weekly editions and its campaign, directed by publisher Robert L. Vann, to remove the radio program "Amos 'n' Andy" from the airwaves. The program's main characters represented two stereotypes—Amos as the classic "Tom," unsophisticated and simple, and Andy as a "coon," domineering and a bit lazy.[56] The "Amos 'n' Andy" show relied on such racial stereotypes and incorporated comedy formats from vaudeville and minstrel shows.

The *Pittsburgh Courier* organized the "Double V" campaign during World War II, pointing out that African Americans needed to work for victory at home on issues of domestic equality as well as for victory abroad. The campaign made it clear to Americans that black newspapers supported the patriotic effort, but they also fought against segregation and discrimination, particularly in the armed forces and war-related industries.

African-American newspapers had benefited from Claude Barnett's Associated Negro Press since 1919; Barnett circulated information for use in black newspapers throughout the nation. In 1940, however, black publishers organized to form the National Negro Newspaper Publishers' Association that competed directly with Bar-

Figure 14–7   John Sengstacke was part owner and general manager of the *Chicago Defender*. (Office of War Information photo, Division of Prints and Photographs, Library of Congress Collection)

nett's service, which finally suspended operations during 1964. The new association gave distinguished service awards to African-American leaders, organized workshops, and provided news services to black newspapers. In 1956, it changed its name to the National Newspaper Publishers' Association, and by 1989 it had 148 member newspapers, to which it offered computerized services and mailing lists.

After the war, African-American newspapers faced new challenges. By the early 1960s, black reporters were in some demand on white newspapers, and the talent drain, although benefiting the image of blacks in the mainstream press, made it more difficult for the black press to succeed. In addition, black newspapers faced competitive factors similar to those faced by mainstream newspapers. Electronic media competed for advertising and viewership.

Johnson and *Ebony*—Magazines for the Middle Class

The major development of the 1950s was the expansion of the African-American magazine industry. In 1942, John H. Johnson, employed by an insurance agency in Chicago, borrowed $500 to start *Negro Digest*. That publication served as the cornerstone for subsequent magazines and a successful corporation. *Negro Digest* summarized articles and comments about blacks found in mainstream publications. It remained popular through 1970, when it was renamed *Black World*, in response to cultural objections to the term *Negro*. Incorporating some themes of the black power movement, the publication began to decline as 1960s-style black nationalism declined, and in 1976 it ceased publication.[57]

Johnson started *Ebony*, patterned after *Life*, in 1945. *Ebony* demonstrated the power of the black person as a consumer and was the first African-American publication to garner enough advertising dollars to shift financial reliance from subscription rates to advertising. *Ebony* chronicled the successes of African Americans in the life of the nation and encouraged interracial understanding and participation in the political process. In 1950, Johnson started *Tan*, and in 1951, *Jet*, a weekly African-American newsmagazine. Other Johnson publications included *True Confessions, Hue, Ebony International, Ebony Jr.,* and *Copper Romance*.

Conclusion

During the years just prior to and during World War II, the U.S. press expanded its overseas operations, placing newspaper, wire service, and broadcast correspondents at many locations throughout the globe. Radio's voice triumphed as it brought news of triumphs and tragedies to the American home. The costs of such coverage were astronomical and continued to escalate throughout the war. The depictions of war varied, seen through the eyes of columnists and cartoonists who commented on the discrepancies between the frontline operation and the propaganda at home, as well as through the eyes of those who photographed not only the action but the results of the war. Issues such as the internment of the Japanese within the borders of the United States provided material for photographic commentary. Although the media reported Nazi repression of the Jews, skepticism stemming from inaccurate World War I atrocity stories and strong anti-Semitic strains within the country moderated editors' coverage of the extermination of 6 million Jews within Germany.

With the advent of war, Congress and the President instituted censorship of correspondents abroad and the media at home. Congress renewed the Espionage Act, and the Office of Censorship monitored news entering and leaving the country and imposed a voluntary censorship code. Broadcasters, wary of the powers of the Federal Communications Act and its regulatory implications, ruled out editorializing. Newspaper editors usually complied with the voluntary code. The Office of War Information established the Voice of America in an overseas propaganda operation and attempted to influence the content of motion pictures. The Justice Department, the Post Office Department, and the FBI continued surveillance of journalists, including those suspected of "leftist" sympathies and the black press. The Smith Act restricted those who advocated violent overthrow of the government, and the legislation remains on the books today.

In 1943, the Commission on Freedom of the Press, concerned about growing governmental news management, the increased concentration of press ownership, and the potential of radio and television technology within a democratic society, reaffirmed a doctrine espousing the importance of a free press in a democratic society. The commission encouraged owners to regard freedom of ownership within the context of the common good and to exercise social responsibility with the right to publish. Editors rejected what they regarded as the commission's interference in private enterprise and established their own study group that reaffirmed the doctrine of laissez-faire.

Toward the end of the war, U.S. editors organized a campaign for international freedom of the press, but questions about whether such a campaign should give license to export U.S. news practices and values or whether it should grant equal access to news at its source in all countries obstructed progress toward international accords.

The increased production of war material and full employment brought the prosperity that had eluded the country during the 1930s, despite the structured New Deal programs designed to end the depression. Americans moved to the suburbs, shunned radical thought, and participated in a decade of consensus politics and cold war ideology.

Endnotes

1. Stanley Cloud and Lynne Olson, *The Murrow Boys: Pioneers on the Front Lines of Broadcast Journalism* (New York: Houghton Mifflin, 1996), p. 60.

2. Robert Desmond, *Tides of War: World News Reporting 1931–1945* (Iowa City: University of Iowa Press, 1984), pp. 77, 83.

3. Cloud and Olson, *The Murrow Boys.*

4. Irving Fang, *Those Radio Commentators!* (Ames: Iowa State University Press, 1977), p. 25.

5. David Holbrook Culbert, *News for Everyman* (Westport, Conn.: Greenwood Press, 1976), p. 72.

6. Hans Kaltenborn, *Fifty Fabulous Years* (New York: G. P. Putnam's Sons, 1950), p. 209.

7. Fang, *Radio Commentators*, p. 34.

8. Kaltenborn, *Fifty Fabulous Years*, p. 301.

9. See Christopher Sterling and John M. Kittross, *Stay Tuned* (Belmont, Calif.: Wadsworth, 1978), pp. 176–77; A. M. Sperber, *Murrow: His Life and Times* (New York: Freundlich Books, 1986); and Eric Sevareid, *Not So Wild a Dream* (New York: Atheneum, 1978, originally published in 1946), p. 83.

10. Cloud and Olson, *The Murrow Boys.*

11. Sevareid, *Not So Wild a Dream*, p. 19.

12. Marlene Sanders and Marcia Rock, *Waiting for Prime Time* (New York: Harper & Row, 1990). The book was first published by the University of Illinois Press in 1988.

13. Fenby, Jonathan. *The International News Services* (New York: Schocken Books, 1986), p. 56.

14. Cited in Margaret Blanchard, "The Associated Press Antitrust Suit: A Philosophical Clash over Ownership of First Amendment Rights," *Business History Review* 61 (Spring, 1987), pp. 43–85.

15. Desmond, *Tides of War*, pp. 5–9.

16. Desmond, *Tides of War*, pp. 17–18, 95–96.

17. Desmond, *Tides of War*, pp. 451, 453.

18. Marion Marzolf, *Up from the Footnote: A History of Women Journalists* (New York: Hastings House, 1977), p. 77.

19. Mary Mander, "Pen and Sword: A Cultural History of the American War Correspondent: 1895–1945," Ph.D. dissertation, University of Illinois at Urbana-Champaign, 1979, pp. 144–45.

20. This account relies heavily on Mary Alice Sentman's entry, "Ernie Pyle," in the *Dictionary of Literary Biography*, vol. 29, pp. 290–300.

21. Bill Mauldin, *Up Front* (New York: Norton, 1944, 1968), p. 78, cited in Mander, "Pen and Sword," p. 147.

22. Lee G. Miller, *The Story of Ernie Pyle* (New York, 1950), p. 427, cited in Ernest C. Hynds, *American Newspapers in the 1980s* (New York: Hastings House, 1980), p. 83.

23. Karin Becker Ohrn, "What You See Is What You Get: Dorothea Lange and Ansel Adams at Manzanar," *Journalism History* 4:1 (Spring, 1977), pp. 14–22, 32.

24. Deborah E. Lipstadt, *Beyond Belief: The American Press and the Coming of the Holocaust, 1933–1945* (New York: Free Press, 1986), p. 57.

25. Arlene Rossen Cardozo, "American Magazine Coverage of the Nazi Death Camp Era," *Journalism Quarterly* 60 (Winter, 1983), pp. 716–18.

26. W. Richard Whitaker, "Outline of Hitler's 'Final Solution' Apparent by 1933," *Journalism Quarterly* 58:2 (Summer, 1981), pp. 192–200, 247.

27. Cited in Whitaker, "Outline of Hitler's 'Final Solution,'" p. 192.

28. Mander, "Pen and Sword," p. 170.

29. Desmond, *Tides of War*, p. 219.

30. Interview with Pat Washburn, Ohio University, January, 1987. Also see Patrick S. Washburn, *A Question of Sedition* (New York: Oxford University Press, 1986), pp. 253–54.

31. A variety of accounts on the Midway incident have been offered, some implying more involvement on the part of the *Tribune* than others. For an explanation of the situation, see Dina Goren, "Communication Intelligence and the Freedom of the Press: The *Chicago Tribune's* Battle of Midway Dispatch and the Breaking of the Japanese Naval Code," *Journal of Contemporary History* 16 (1981), pp. 663–90; and Lloyd Wendt, Chicago Tribune: *The Rise of a Great American Newspaper*, pp. 627–37.

32. Elmer Davis, "Report to the President," ed. by Ronald T. Farrar, *Journalism Monographs* 7 (August, 1968), p. 39.

33. See Clayton R. Koppes and Gregory D. Black, *Hollywood Goes to War: How Politics, Profits & Propaganda Shaped World War II Movies* (New York: The Free Press, 1987).

34. Clayton R. Koppes and Gregory D. Black, "Blacks, Loyalty, and Motion-Picture Propaganda in World War II," *Journal of American History* 73:2 (September, 1986), p. 394.

35. Robert Sklar, *Movie-Made America: A Cultural History of American Movies* (New York: Vintage Books, 1975), pp. 249–51.

36. For an analysis of civil rights progress during the interwar period, see Nancy J. Weiss, *The National Urban League, 1910–1940* (New York: Oxford University Press, 1974).

37. See Washburn, *Question of Sedition*; Lee Finkle, *Forum for Protest* (Cranbury, N.J.: Associated University Presses, 1975); and Harvard Sitkoff, *A New Deal for Blacks* (New York: Oxford University Press, 1978).

38. Washburn, *Question of Sedition*, p. 8.

39. See Washburn, *Question of Sedition*, chap. 4.

40. Richard Gid Powers, *Secrecy and Power: The Life of J. Edgar Hoover* (New York: The Free Press, 1987), p. 277, notes that Biddle blocked almost all of Hoover's recommendations for prosecution under sedition laws. See also Powers, *G-MEN: Hoover's FBI in American Popular Culture* (Carbondale: Southern Illinois University Press, 1983).

41. Don R. Pember, "The Smith Act as a Restraint on the Press," *Journalism Monographs* 10 (May, 1969), p. 5.

42. Section 2385, Title 18, United States Code, cited in Pember, "The Smith Act," pp. 6–7.

43. Pember, "The Smith Act," p. 11.

44. Pember, "The Smith Act," p. 32.

45. Michael Schudson, *Discovering the News: A Social History of Newspapers* (New York: Basic Books, 1978), p. 167. See also Jerilyn McIntyre, "Repositioning a Landmark: The Hutchins Commission and Freedom of the Press," *Critical Studies in Mass Communication* 4 (June, 1987), pp. 136–60.

46. Commission on Freedom of the Press, *A Free and Responsible Press.* (Chicago: University of Chicago Press, 1947), p. vi. See also Margaret Blanchard, "The Hutchins Commission, The Press and the Responsibility Concept," *Journalism Monographs* 49 (May, 1977), pp. 1–59; and D. L. Smith, *Zechariah Chafee, Jr.: Defender of Liberty and Law* (Cambridge, Mass.: Harvard University Press, 1986).

47. McIntyre, "Repositioning a Landmark," p. 141.

48. Quotation is from McIntyre, "Repositioning a Landmark," p. 143.

49. McIntyre, "Repositioning a Landmark," p. 150.

50. John H. Colburn, "What Makes a Good Newspaper?" *Saturday Review* (June 9, 1952), pp. 50, 52, cited in Hynds, *American Newspapers*, p. 29.

51. This discussion relies heavily on the comprehensive account of the movement by Margaret A. Blanchard, *Exporting the First Amendment: The Press-Government Crusade of 1945–52* (New York: Longman, 1986).

52. Kent Cooper, "ASNE and Press Freedom—By Kent Cooper," *ASNE Bulletin* (September 1, 1943), p. 7, cited in Blanchard, *Exporting the First Amendment*, p. 19.

53. Hugh Baillie, "Freedom of Information: Open Channels for News," *Free World* (November, 1944), p. 433, cited in Blanchard, *Exporting the First Amendment*, p. 19.

54. Fred MacDonald, *Don't Touch That Dial: Radio Programming in American Life, 1920–1960* (Chicago: Nelson-Hall, 1979), p. 85.

55. Erik Barnouw, *Tube of Plenty* (New York: Oxford University Press, 1990), p. 114.

56. See Jannette L. Dates and William Barlow, *Split Image: African Americans in the Mass Media* (Washington, D.C.: Howard University Press, 1990), pp. 178–79.

57. See Dates and Barlow, *Split Image*, pp. 370–73.

A Spanish-American boy broadcasts native songs over a parish broadcasting system in Questa, New Mexico, 1943. (U.S. Office of War Information photo, Division of Prints and Photographs, Library of Congress Collection)

PART 4

Corporate Power and Globalization

▼

At the end of World War II, the United States emerged prosperous and confident. Television, put on the back burner during the war, became a triumphant technology promoting a national culture and ethos. Such promotion worked against the preservation of regional culture, and it made national entertainment programming and news a common conversation across geographical barriers.

The nation passed from a short period of euphoria into a long, cold war with the Soviet Union, which had been its ally during World War II. The opposition to communism dominated activity on the foreign front, resulting in a long and unsuccessful struggle in Vietnam, together with protests at home. During the 1960s, Congress passed major civil rights legislation that addressed domestic inequities, but the desire to end racial discrimination was partially achieved only after arduous struggles. In the early anticommunist period, media cooperated with government to try to advance American interests abroad and to convince domestic audiences of the threat.

From 1945 until 2000, technology combined with other business and political factors to ensure that *globalization* was the dominant word. Television was followed quickly by the development of desktop computers that ultimately accessed the Internet, an information system tied together by computers. It was an information system that crossed national boundaries in ways not previously envisioned and that made international freedom of expression more nearly a reality.

Corporate power received more attention than it had since the 1890s, with "merger mania" peaking in the 1980s and 1990s, along with the "going public" of many media companies. Now corporate executives had to worry about stock dividends and public holdings, not only about making reasonable profits for a few owners. Many of these mergers were international, which meant that media companies were bigger and less tied to the national interests of the United States. In addition, the end of the cold war posed a different international landscape to be addressed.

Advertising and public relations developed into full-blown industries as consumer culture became the bedrock for U.S. expansion and industrial growth. Toward the end of the twentieth century, the functions became less distinct, and the two fields began to merge. Global agencies blended the two to achieve goals of promotion and information.

Political communication became a highly sought after professional field when political campaign personnel adapted knowledge of how media work to control delivery of their own messages. President John F. Kennedy (1961–1963) became known as the first President to charm newspeople with his press conferences; President Ronald Reagan (1981–1989) was known as the "Teflon" President who could not be scarred

449

by news messages. Many of his Teflon characteristics were attributed to adept news management.

As the nation crossed into the twenty-first century, it passed into a post–cold war world, in which economic interests, media companies, news content, and entertainment met with and benefited from international interests, audiences, and markets. ▼

CHAPTER 15

Electronic Images in a Cold War

▼

The United States emerged victorious from World War II, a country of prosperity. The land lay unscathed, the war economy created full employment, and soldiers returned home to a welcoming populace. Manufacturing turned domestic as consumers moved to the suburbs, bought appliances and automobiles and the advertising that promoted them. But beneath the surface churned many of the conflicts that had emerged during the depression, along with new ones, such as the proliferation of nuclear weapons. Added to the domestic agenda were new issues, such as housing shortages and inflation.[1] Richard Lingeman of the *New York Times* wrote, "The fifties under Ike represented a sort of national prefrontal lobotomy: tail-finned, we Sunday-drove down the superhighways of life while tensions that later bubbled up in the sixties seethed beneath the placid surface."[2]

Television was a prime cultural force during the 1950s, and questions of television entertainment and the impact of TV on politics forced debates about the role of media and democracy. But like many other issues of the 1950s, some of these lay beneath the surface, only to emerge full-fledged a decade later.

The nation mourned the loss of President Franklin D. Roosevelt. At the end of World War II the Soviet Union secured its position in countries where it had established considerable military influence during the war. The Soviets supported communist takeovers in China and Korea. Journalistic and public support tenuously granted to the Soviet Union during the world war quickly disintegrated, and public opinion leaders spoke of the responsibilities of America in the postwar world, which

▼

FDR Is Dead

The heart of this whole, great city welled over with frank, unashamed grief at dusk last night as the news of President Roosevelt's death spread, by rumor, by radio, and by extra editions of the afternoon newspapers. People told the news to each other in hushed, choked voices. In every corner of the metropolis, people clustered about their radios, hurried into the streets, not wanting to believe it.

When it was true—palpably, hopelessly true—men and women wept open, honest tears at the dread news.

—From the newspaper *PM*, April 13, 1945

some journalists had been demanding since before the war's beginning. Wrote Walter Lippmann in 1939, "What Rome was to the ancient world, what Great Britain has been to the modern world, America is to the world of tomorrow."[3]

In 1947, the United States instituted the Marshall Plan to aid economic recovery in Europe; in 1947, the National Security Act readied a permanent structure for self-defense and aggressive foreign policy by creating the Department of Defense (replacing the Department of War); and the Central Intelligence Agency was created for purposes of spying and carrying out covert actions. In 1953, the U.S. Information Agency became a permanent propaganda unit for dispensing information throughout the world, particularly in Latin America.

Truman's anticommunist rhetoric intensified, and by early 1947 many mass-circulation magazines echoed his pronouncements, supporting the ideology of America as a dominant world power with an altruistic foreign policy. In 1946, *Collier's* labeled the Soviet Union a "gangster government," and the *Saturday Evening Post* characterized postwar tensions as a "worldwide contest between the Soviet Union and the West."[4]

The Soviet Union, expanding into what it considered its own spheres of influence and concerned that the U.S. call for an open-door trade policy was expansionism in disguise, cut off Western access to Berlin in June 1948. Truman airlifted supplies to the western sectors of the city until the Soviet Union was forced to lift its blockade in May 1949. Later in the year, the United States entered its first formal European military alliance since 1778 by creating the North Atlantic Treaty Organization. In Korea, which had been divided by the agreements ending World War II, North Korean soldiers marched across the 38th parallel on June 25, 1950. The United States believed the invasion was Soviet-inspired and took immediate action, although some evidence has suggested that North Korea started the war for nationalistic purposes. The cold war had begun.

The policy of global defense continued unabated as government aid was extended to the French in Indochina, South Korea, and Formosa. James Reston of the *New York Times* reported from Asia in August 1953 that the "range of American activities in this part of the world is unbelievable."[5]

The consensus in the 1950s was that the United States was the most powerful, most free, most wealthy, and most contented nation on earth. A consensus attitude ran through public institutions as well as formed political decisions. High schools used J. Edgar Hoover's anticommunist polemic *Masters of Deceit* to teach American government; historians attempted to explain conflicts as aberrations in society and stressed what had been continuous throughout the nation's political, social, and economic history; and the press ignored the rumbling underneath in favor of the apparent great gains for the nation's population. Broadcasters focused on technological improvement, and although some newsmen strived for greater issue coverage, the commercial dominance of the sponsor limited such scope. It was a press, wrote University of Massachusetts professor James Boylan in the *Columbia Journalism Review,* "mired in a creed of impenetrable smug," of "unquestioning acceptance of authority," and "scorn for matters intellectual." To be a professional, he wrote of his own experience at the Columbia University Graduate School of Journalism, was to get the "technique" right. The fledgling networks joined the patriotic fervor. CBS produced "One Nation Indivisible," a radio program that premiered August 20, 1950. CBS President Frank Stanton announced, "In these broadcasts we feel it is important to discuss the conditions which the American people must face as our country prepares itself for an indefinite period of partial or total mobilization and the sacrifices that they must make in order to strengthen themselves for this ordeal." CBS also produced a television program, "The Facts We Face," that covered aspects of mobilization in the cold war. Stanton said the goal of the series was to "unify the public and to deter U.S. enemies." Many of the scripts were approved by the White House.6

The espoused technique, despite the emphasis on interpretation discussed in many circles in the 1930s, was "objectivity." Although the bylined political columnists and editorial writers practiced as energetically as in the past, many news reporters maintained a conventional attitude, reporting the statements of officials and ignoring the undercurrents, the indications of a discontented African-American population and labor unrest. Publishers and broadcast managers were in collusion, if not consciously, then unconsciously accepting the dominant intellectual frame of the nation's political leaders. Wrote James Boylan, "over the long run even objective journalism disseminates mainly what its managers see as legitimate."7

Alternatives existed, although liberal or critical voices declined after the war, and the media became the object of anticommunist investigations in Congress.

Newspapers faced severe competition from television for the advertising dollar in the 1950s, and the number of cities having multiple newspapers continued to decline. ▼

Media Compete for Audiences and Advertising

Radio in Transition

Radio prospered during World War II, but the popular medium lost listeners in the early 1950s and shifted direction. In heavy competition with television by the mid-1950s, radio turned to music for its content and capitalized on portability.

The 950 stations operating at the beginning of the war years grew to more than 2,000 stations by 1950. Radio station revenue, at $155 million in 1940, reached $310

▼

Radio as Mirror

Radio, if it is to serve and survive, must hold a mirror behind the nation and the world. If the reflection shows radical intolerance, economic inequality, bigotry, unemployment or anything else—let the people see it, or rather hear it. The mirror must have no curves and must be held with a steady hand.

—Edward R. Murrow, September 16, 1945, as reported in *Variety*, September 19, 1945

million by 1945 and $454 million in 1950. Between 1948 and 1958, the number of radios in cars doubled, and by 1963, 75.9 percent of all cars had radios.[8] Radio was firmly established as the major news medium for most Americans. Polls in 1939 indicated that 25 percent of the public relied on the radio for most of its news, and many listeners said they believed radio was more objective than the newspapers. In 1942, other surveys indicated 73 percent of the public received most of its war news from radio; in 1946, 63 percent of the public said radio was its major source of all news.

The magic of live radio rapidly disappeared, as magnetic tape made prerecorded sound palatable. The wire recording available before the war required hand-tying and heat fusion for editing, which rarely produced satisfactory sound. Americans discovered and confiscated prerecorded plastic tape when they entered Germany during the war and found automated radio stations.

Frequency Modulation—A New Radio

Edwin Armstrong, who became a millionaire after inventing circuits for RCA, invented FM in the basement of Philosophy Hall at Columbia University, in response to a comment by RCA president David Sarnoff that he wished someone would invent a black box to take the static out of radio. FM was technically superior to AM, eliminated static, and provided for the high fidelity broadcast of music. When his invention was completed in 1933, Armstrong secured four patents and called Sarnoff to see his invention. After testing the equipment, RCA ignored Armstrong and FM, not wanting to upset the radio structure, and pursued television instead, which Sarnoff saw as competing with FM for the upper ranges of the available frequencies.

After demonstrating the clarity of FM at a November 1935 meeting of the Institute of Radio Engineers, Armstrong went to the FCC in the spring of 1936, seeking spectrum allocation. At the same hearings were David Sarnoff and the RCA attorneys, pleading solely for television frequency allocations. Armstrong managed to obtain an experimental license and began building a 50,000-watt FM station in Alpine, New Jersey. Sarnoff and Armstrong thus began a lifelong battle that eventually ended when Armstrong committed suicide.[9]

In 1940, though, Armstrong achieved a temporary triumph against Sarnoff when the FCC assigned Channel 1, which had been allocated to the television band, to FM. Just as victory seemed imminent for Armstrong, the war began. After World War II, the FCC reversed its earlier position and moved FM to the upper end of the broadcasting spectrum, rendering prewar sets obsolete. In addition, it approved duplicate programming on AM and FM, further reducing the chance of creative FM development. In the years of television development when radio changed to a nearly all-music format, FM finally gained stature because of its superior capability in broadcasting music.

News and Politics

Radio, which had grown to prominence during the 1930s and 1940s with its controversial commentary about the war, its battle coverage, and its top entertainment, searched for new purpose at the end of the war. Performers, news broadcasters, and children's programmers had encouraged bond sales and savings and had been involved in other war-directed efforts. Clearly the time for new programming had arrived. Some industry figures wanted to focus on perfecting existing program genres; others argued that radio should become more controversial and explore issues such as racial and religious intolerance, the threat of the atomic bomb, and antidemocratic tendencies within the country.[10] Radio solved the dilemma to some degree by pursuing both directions. Although it perfected existing programming, it also

Figure 15–1 The rudiments of television viewing were in place as early as 1931, but disputes over color and a wartime freeze halted television's role as an instrument of mass communication until about 1948. (Photo by Underwood and Underwood, Division of Prints and Photographs, Library of Congress Collection)

developed new approaches. In 1945, for example, NBC introduced "Meet the Press," and in 1946 it established a documentary unit.

Radio felt the full impact of the conservative swing of public opinion after the war, and by 1949 sponsors began to withdraw support for liberal commentators. When William Shirer lost his sponsor for his prime-time CBS broadcast that year, he resigned, claiming his liberal views were not compatible with his network employment. Liberal commentators, whose patriotism had been in vogue during the anti-Fascist years, now were draped like weights around the necks of sponsor-dependent and sponsor-dominated networks. Some commentators changed with the times. Walter Winchell, for example, moved from being an outspoken liberal to being so strongly anticommunist that the Soviet ambassador called him a warmonger. In December 1950, when NBC broadcast a public service affairs program sponsored by the American Civil Liberties Union to mark the 159th anniversary of the adoption of the Bill of Rights, hundreds of letters and telegrams protested the airing of "pro-Communist" material.[11]

Change to Music Programming

Nevertheless, liberal versus conservative politics represented only a small portion of radio's real crisis. Despite expansion in the news area, by 1950 radio was beginning an era of "doldrums." More than 100 of the network series had been on the air for at least a decade and the listening audience dwindled, particularly during the evening hours. Furthermore, television had become a real competitor. The networks fought for the best talent in the radio business. William Paley hired some of NBC's best and by December 1949, CBS had sixteen of the top twenty shows in the Nielsen ratings. In contrast, during the first four months of 1949, NBC lost $7 million in advertising revenues.[12] During the early 1950s, despite the fact that radio slashed its advertising rates as much as 25 percent, Kellogg, Pillsbury, and other big advertisers curtailed spending. From 1946 to 1955, the four radio networks' gross revenues declined at the rate of $32 million per year.

Radio continued to fashion new programs, introducing adult fiction and westerns. "Gunsmoke" first was heard on radio in 1952, and "Have Gun, Will Travel" went on the air in 1958. Major dramatic programs such as the "Philco Playhouse" and the NBC "Star Playhouse" nevertheless dropped from the top Nielsen ratings by 1955. Although there were 46.6 million radios in homes, only 768,000 people were listening to evening broadcasts.

So radio simply changed its tune. In a tight economic atmosphere, the networks encouraged local stations to experiment with multiple local sponsorship. Turning away from a single national sponsor increased the level of independence in radio programming as well as the autonomy of the local station. By the 1960s, the networks provided skeletal radio programming: news on the hour, special events coverage, recorded music, and a few features. Commenting on the new developments, Matthew J. Culligan, NBC's vice president in charge of radio, told a group of advertising agency officials in 1958, "Radio didn't die. It wasn't even sick. It just had to be psychoanalyzed." Culligan said the portability of the radio had made it "a companion to the individual" instead of "a focal point of all family entertainment. . . . It has become as personal as a pack of cigarets."[13]

Music had always been a mainstay of radio, with early programming done live from New York ballrooms. Frank Sinatra crooned across the airwaves as well as in intimate night clubs. However, the 1950s witnessed a revolution in music styles as well as in radio music. The rhythm and blues made popular by African-American singers in the 1930s came to radio, often sanitized or "whitened" by the record companies. As blacks moved north, they brought their music to the cities of the North, where it found its way onto local record labels and was termed "race music" by the recording industry.

Alan Freed, a Cleveland, Ohio, disc jockey, was the first to recognize that rhythm and blues held great attraction for a new generation of adolescents, anxious to escape their parents' living rooms, and in June 1951, he started a rhythm and blues program for which he coined the term "rock 'n roll." Armed with plastic-encased radios and transistorized portability, teenagers fled the living rooms to listen to music. Radio stations recognized the commercial possibilities and began to design programs for segmented audiences.

Bill Haley and the Comets sanitized old rhythm and blues lyrics, altering the 1954 lyrics of Joe Turner's "Shake, Rattle and Roll," changing the seductive lines, "Well you wear low dresses, The sun comes shinin' through," to, "You wear those dresses, Your hair done up so nice." The radio version quickly became a hit.

The most popular star of them all, of course, was Elvis ("the Pelvis") Presley, coached by a Memphis producer, Sam Phillips, to have "the Negro sound and the Negro feel." Phillips used an echo-chamber recording technique that made Elvis's voice sound "as if it were ricocheting around inside the listener's skull." Rock 'n roll was here to stay.[14] Radio capitalized on the market.

Payola Scandals and the DJs

Radio, however, faced one more crisis as the decade closed—payola scandals created by disc jockeys who took money, cases of liquor, and other gifts in turn for playing certain records. The scandal ran deeper within the industry than the disc jockeys, however, and two federal communications commissioners and an assistant to the President resigned for accepting gifts that influenced decision making.[15]

Television Moves from New York to Hollywood

Television at first adapted much of its programming from successful radio series. Characterizing what some termed television's "Golden Age" in the early 1950s were live anthologies such as the "Philco Television Playhouse," the "Kraft Television Theatre," and the "U.S. Steel Hour." Each show was individually sponsored by a particular advertiser as the names "Kraft" and "U.S. Steel" indicate. The conservative climate of the early 1950s mitigated against bold or controversial themes, and when Reginald Rose submitted a script entitled "Thunder on Sycamore Street," which depicted neighborhood prejudice against an African-American family, Westinghouse's Studio One theatre on CBS accepted it only on the basis that Rose change the African-American family to "something else" so as not to offend southern audiences. Although Rose agreed to change the family to that of an ex-convict, he built the dramatic plot so that viewers did not know the reason for the neighborhood's ill treatment of the family until the show's end, thus creating a controversial image in viewers' minds.[16]

The anthologies, combined with live spectaculars, provided exceptional fare for the new medium, but between 1956 and 1958 most of the anthologies were canceled. Fashioning new ties to the movie business, the television industry moved from its New York base to the film capital of Hollywood. Detective shows, westerns, situation comedies such as "I Love Lucy," and highly successful quiz shows replaced the older programming.

Quiz Show Popularity Ends in Scandal

The quiz shows, which emulated successful radio quiz shows, offered considerably higher stakes, and by 1957 they constituted thirty-seven hours of the networks' weekly schedule. The "$64,000 Question," which enabled Revlon to sell out of its "Living Lipstick" brand, was quickly emulated by "Twenty-One" and other programs. Public disillusionment ran high, however, when Charles Van Doren, a highly successful "Twenty-One" contestant, admitted in 1959 that he had been given the correct answers by the show's producers. Van Doren's admission led to further investigations, revealing that rigged programs prevailed throughout the quiz show industry.

Figure 15–2   The television quiz hearings of 1959 were lonely indeed, compared to the years of grandiose promotion that preceded them. (*U.S. News and World Report* photo, Division of Prints and Photographs, Library of Congress)

The early days of television bespoke optimism for the possibilities of mass culture. NBC's president Sylvester L. Weaver, Jr., in 1953 described programs that "serve the grand design of television, which is to create an aristocracy of the people, the proletariat of privilege, the Athenian masses—to make the average man the uncommon man."[17] By 1958, however, Edward R. Murrow in a lecture to the Radio and Television News Directors' Association, attacked television content as consisting of "decadence, escapism, and insulation from the realities of the world." He said networks underestimated their viewers and that mass-media content reflected the nation's comfort and complacency.[18] During the early years of the decade, competition among networks, the challenge to defeat the threat of pay television, and the need to program for a new medium promoted the development of superior programming. However, by 1958, nearly 90 percent of all homes had television sets, the growth rates of advertising were leveling off, and the industry decided to contain costs rather than spend lavishly on expensive programming.[19]

Television News

Straight news programming in the early 1950s shifted from radio's analysis to an emphasis on "staged events" in fifteen-minute evening broadcasts. NBC's John Cameron Swayze's "Camel News Caravan" and CBS's "Television News with Douglas Edwards" had to cope with new demands for visuals, resulting in too-often-staged events. The news shows relied on film shipped by plane, either from other parts of the country or from abroad. These delays often meant the news went stale before it was broadcast. In addition, direct sponsorship exacted other tolls: Camel forbade "no smoking" signs from appearing on any of Swayze's shows, and insisted, as part of the advertising contract, that a lighted Camel cigarette remain at Swayze's elbow throughout the news.

Douglas Edwards of CBS led in the ratings until NBC introduced "The Huntley-Brinkley Report" in 1956. David Brinkley, a young southerner, refused to take the news all that seriously, but Chet Huntley carried on the pensive Edward R. Murrow image. Innovative news programs such as Ed Murrow's "See It Now," combined with softer news shows such as NBC's two-hour morning show, "Today," begun in 1952 and starring Dave Garroway, broadened the spectrum of television news.

In 1963, to counteract the growing impact of NBC's Huntley-Brinkley team, CBS introduced a half-hour news show, which incorporated longer reports and more film. CBS rejected as anchorman the superstar commentator Eric Sevareid of World War II fame and Edward R. Murrow tradition for a safer, more objective former wire-service reporter named Walter Cronkite. Cronkite's all-American, trustworthy image balanced the correspondents' reports that unsettled CBS executives and garnered wrath from the White House.[20] NBC quickly expanded its news show to a half hour, and ABC followed suit in 1967.

Cronkite's first news show featured President John F. Kennedy, and eighty-one days later Cronkite relived the terrible events of the assassination of Kennedy as he brought the procession in Washington, as well as the scenes from Dallas, to the American public. Cronkite's broadcast of the Kennedy funeral and events surrounding it signified the growing power of television news. People sat glued to their sets in days of national mourning.

Media and the Advertising Industry

The 1950s represented the second great period of prosperity for the advertising industry. The successes of the 1920s paled by comparison. Although gross advertising expenditures doubled from 1940 to 1950, the relationship to consumer spending remained the same. During the 1950s, however, gross advertising increased by 75 percent, faster than the growth of personal income, the gross national product, or any other economic index. The growth was fueled by the move to the suburbs, which translated into the building of homes, shopping centers, and highways. The advertising expenditures of the automobile industry surpassed those of the heavily promoted packaged goods and cigarettes. In 1957, Chevrolet led in dollars spent on advertising, with a budget of $30.4 million, and Ford followed closely behind, with a budget of $25 million. The only nonautomotive product in the top ten advertisers was Coca-Cola.

Not only were companies spending money on advertising, but advertising agencies profited from the growing belief in the power of advertising. In 1947, J. Walter Thompson (JWT) became the first agency to bill more than $100 million in a single year. Within three years, JWT and its three closest competitors—Batten, Barton, Durstine, and Osborne; Young and Rubicam; and McCann-Erickson—all billed more than $200 million.

As products proliferated and became more like each other, the creative segment of the industry struggled to perfect its advertising appeals. Many of the agencies turned further toward research, creating consumer panels, monitoring consumer tastes, and analyzing the spending habits of America's consumers. The Advertising Research Foundation, started in 1953, started its own research journal. Some advertising personnel, unhappy with a focus on past campaigns, began to investigate ways to predict the success of future campaigns, resulting in a focus on motivational research—or the psychology behind the advertising appeal. The focus on psychology, however, was not widely accepted, and the concepts of motivational research caused great controversy among the old-line agencies.

With the 1957 publication of Vance Packard's nonfiction critique of the advertising industry, titled *The Hidden Persuaders*, the debate on motivation research focused more clearly. Packard told the audience that kept his book on the best-seller list for eighteen weeks that "[l]arge-scale efforts are being made, often with impressive success, to channel our unthinking habits, our purchasing decisions, and our thought processes by the use of insights gleaned from psychiatry and the social sciences." Packard's book initiated a large-scale attack on advertising and its relationship to a consumer-oriented society.

Packard's claims were further substantiated as an independent entrepreneur named James Vicary introduced subliminal advertising, flashing messages urging New Jersey moviegoers to buy popcorn. The messages were flashed so quickly that the audience did not remember seeing them, but nevertheless the purchasing of popcorn increased. Vicary's introduction of subliminal advertising was highly controversial and relatively short-lived; the National Association of Broadcasters banned the messages from the air, thereby eliminating one major market for the technique.

The postwar boom thrust advertising agencies into the status of big business, with predictable results—expansion, international efforts, and mergers.[21]

Advertising and Television

Television programming had first to convince advertisers that it had a target audience for a product. The largely unprofitable early stations (and networks) could not deliver the audiences of the big picture magazines or the local focus of newspaper readers. However, some early buyers of television time were rewarded, and sponsors soon came to the networks. In 1953, Dow Chemical, warehousing a surplus of Saran Wrap, began to advertise on television, only to see its sales go up thirty-fold.

Early advertisers sponsored entire television programs, and it was such advertising that brought profit to television. While in 1951, only 5 of 108 stations made a profit, by 1954 the *Analysts Journal* reported that a network affiliate in a large market could turn a profit of 35 percent.[22] By 1954, CBS was the largest advertising medium in the world, and in three years television's share of billings at the Leo Burnett advertising agency went from 18 percent to more than half.[23]

In the early sponsored shows, advertising agencies teamed with the sponsor to take charge of content, with networks often providing only facilities, air time, and occasional censorship. Critics argued that sponsorship gave the advertiser too much power, and examples such as Procter and Gamble refusing to allow characters to smoke or drink coffee abounded. Some advertisers introduced silly, half-commercial lines into their programs. Many of the larger companies, however, took a longer view, with Alcoa, for example, sponsoring Edward R. Murrow's "See It Now" series for four years of controversy, sticking with him through his broadcast opposing Joseph McCarthy's anticommunist tactics. One of the Alcoa officials said, "We don't think it's proper for a sponsor to influence the news. It's Mr. Murrow's show. We buy what he has to offer. We expect him to attract an audience—and the kind of audience—before which we want to present our commercials." Armstrong, which presented the *Circle Theatre*, noted that it was not "seeking merely to make a quickie impression. What counts is the 'impact' which we feel is more important than exposure."[24]

Through the 1950s, the costs for television production increased, and the cost to produce a single show soon outstripped the budgets of all but the largest advertisers. Additionally, the networks were turning to a "magazine" format, in which they sold time, not shows, to advertisers. By the end of the decade, networks were in full control of programming, and agencies and independents were rarely welcome in the programming business. Networks relied now on ratings to determine the success of programming and the cost of advertising. Stephen Fox argued that although some of the large companies, such as Firestone, were willing to continue to produce the highly prized dramas of the 1950s, the networks canceled such programming for lack of high ratings. Coupled with an emphasis on ratings and increasing costs, the revelations of rigged business-sponsored quiz shows ended the sponsorship approach to television advertising.

Media and Public Relations: The Image of Business

During the twentieth century, advertising and public relations became more intertwined. Public relations campaigns early in the century centered on selling business to the American people, and business was intricately interwound with the expansion of the public relations agency. Business sought to explain itself to the public, to create a favorable image, and to avoid or control government regulation. With the onset of the depression, American business sought to sell capitalism and business to the public, to counteract socialist propaganda, to fight the interests of organized labor, and to portray business leaders as leaders of the nation.

Corporate Public Relations: Image Control

During the 1930s, corporate public relations efforts focused on the efforts of labor to organize. In 1933, Robert L. Lund, president of the National Association of Manufacturers, noted that for the association "the problem of public relations must have an active consideration that the Association has never been able to give it. The public does not understand industry, largely because industry itself has made no real effort to tell its story; to show the people of this country that our high living standards have risen almost altogether from the civilization which industrial activity has set up. On the other hand, selfish groups, including labor, the socialistic-minded and the radical, have constantly and continuously misrepresented industry to the people, with the result that there is a general misinformation of our industrial economy, which is highly destructive in its effect."[25]

The National Association of Manufacturers' campaign differed from the efforts of earlier industrialists. The association commissioned a poll of more than 6,000 employees of large and small manufacturers, showing a sensitivity to employee opinion that had not been manifested before. The public relations program also purchased large amounts of advertising, seeking loyalty from advertising men and women as well as from newspapers. Staffed by former newsmen, the public relations effort used encouragement rather than threats and lectures.

Building on earlier efforts in both the private and public sectors, the association effort targeted a variety of media: radio, motion pictures, film strips, billboards, direct mail, displays for schools, and a speakers' bureau. Public relations efforts included a radio serial, *The American Family Robinson*, which portrayed business leaders as sensitive community statesmen who sought to protect the interests of their employees even at their own expense. The motto of a major newspaper campaign was "Prosperity dwells where harmony reigns," emphasizing class harmony. Richard Tedlow wrote that the organization, often considered the pillar of conservative business practices, "portrayed the businessman as actively working for the best interests of the community as a whole. He was more than a mere automaton with the gumption to pursue exclusively the interests of the stockholders."[26] The National Association of Manufacturers' public relations campaign was investigated in the late 1930s by the LaFollette committee, which labeled it propaganda, pure and simple. Nevertheless, Tedlow claimed, businessmen turned more often from violent action to public relations persuasion techniques. Public relations allowed conversations to exist. By the end of the decade, Tedlow argued, businessmen accorded public relations "recognition as a staff function whose responsibilities included organizing the news that a corporation generated with an eye to maintaining a good reputation for it and keeping the executives up-to-date about trends in public opinion."[27]

With the advent of World War II, business shifted its public relations emphasis to planning and to convincing the public that the success of the war was due to private enterprise rather than centralized governmental planning and the coercion of business. In this effort, the National Association of Manufacturers faced a competitor, the Committee for Economic Development (CED), which had ties to the Department of Commerce and had as its goal to plan for high employment and production after the war. The committee organized a research arm designed to educate businessmen of the necessity for governmental intervention in business to assure prosperity. Both organizations employed public relations techniques, with the CED favoring local publicity and national attention through the business trade journals. In striving to keep a low profile, the CED avoided hiring public relations counselors, although the National Association of Manufacturers often tied its efforts to those of the newly developed public relations firms.

In the immediate postwar world, businesses increased their public relations activities, still placing a good deal of emphasis on management–labor relations although also seeking to tell the public about specific products. In 1947, public relations advertising increased dramatically, as business leaders turned from the uncertain press release to the placement of advertising in which they could be guaranteed accuracy in the exact message that would be delivered. Such advertising campaigns sought to tell the public that productivity had brought about the high standard of postwar living and to refute the charge that companies were earning excessive profits.

Public relations counselors emphasized the need for business to maintain good community relations, and businesses began to encourage personnel to be civic-minded, to serve on the boards of charities, and to ask employees' spouses to minimize news of their social activities, which sometimes led to community charges that business leaders were overpaid. Counselors also emphasized the necessity for research and for obtaining the opinions of employees rather than just delivering messages to them. Counselors advised that good conduct brought good publicity—without coercion. With such advice, businesses sought to be more community-minded and to assure their publics that business was good for America.

Professionalization and Expansion

Edward Bernays had made attempts to organize a professional association for public relations counselors as early as 1927, but these efforts met with little success. During the 1930s and 1940s, however, two dinner clubs formed with the purpose of studying the "publicity profession." The National Association of Publicity Directors was founded in 1937, and a second association, the Wise Men, was founded in 1939. The latter changed its name in 1944 to the National Association of Public Relations Counsel. Despite Bernays' early efforts, he was absent from the membership rolls of these organizations partly because he differed from them ideologically, considering the Wise Men in particular to be too conservative. Businessmen, on the other hand, criticized Bernays for forgetting who his clients were and for publicizing himself, rather than his clients, too much.

Also founded in 1939 was the American Council of Public Relations, which organized as a service group, sponsoring one- and two-week seminars to educate public relations counselors and businessmen on polling, labor relations, and the consumer movement. In 1948, the National Association of Public Relations Counsel merged with the American Council on Public Relations to form the Public Relations Society of America (PRSA), a professional group that is active today. PRSA now publishes professional journals, accredits members, and enforces a code of ethics.

Media, Government, and Politics

During the late 1940s and the early 1950s, the press found itself in an uneasy alliance with government. Cooperation with the executive branch and the State Department during the war years had led editors and broadcasters to question their relationship to federal officials. Although the media promoted the hard-line rhetoric of Truman and other anticommunist political leaders, the media also became targets of its abuse. The convention of objectivity, adhered to in part because publishers had rejected the old partisanship of nineteenth-century and early-twentieth-century press lords as well as because it allowed newspapers to avoid challenging those in power, contributed to the anticommunist hysteria. Often, adherence to objectivity was related to opinions about McCarthy. From 1950 to 1955, the Associated Press Managing Editors Association hotly debated the relative merits of objectivity and interpretation. Those who supported objectivity inevitably supported McCarthy editorially, while those who advocated interpretation opposed the senator and his charges.[28]

The Federal Communications Commission

Created as an independent regulatory agency in 1934, the Federal Communications Commission perpetuated an inequality in the media in relation to the First Amendment, an arrangement originally created by the Federal Radio Act of 1927. Although the FCC had the power to grant and revoke licenses to broadcasters, the print media were free to publish without license. In 1932, a U.S. Court of Appeals upheld the right of the Federal Radio Commission (which preceded the FCC) to revoke the license of a station that made reprehensible attacks on the Catholic church, but a year earlier the U.S. Supreme Court, in *Near v. Minnesota*, held that a "Minnesota rag" scandal sheet could not be shut down even though it was viciously attacking Jews and law-enforcement officials. So, although the government could not censor broadcasts, the threat of license removal acted as a constant caution to station managers.

In addition to allocating licenses, the FCC had been active through the late 1930s in modifying station-network relationships. In May 1941, it issued a report on chain broadcasting in an attempt to limit network control over the affiliates and to increase the diversity of programming. The report also forced the partial dissolution of NBC, specifying that a network could affiliate with only one station in a community.

The Supreme Court upheld the FCC's rules in NBC's challenge to the licensing process in *National Broadcasting Co. v. United States*. The court declared that denial of a station license on the grounds of public interest "is not a denial of free speech," and that the FCC, although charged with technical regulation, had considerably more power than that of a traffic cop.[29] In October 1943, NBC sold the less profitable of its two systems, the Blue Network, which then became ABC.

The FCC continued to express its concern over programming by noting the discrepancies between station license proposals and actual programming. In March 1946, the FCC issued a guide entitled *Public Service Responsibilities of Broadcast Licensees*, more commonly referred to as the broadcasting "Blue Book." Although the FCC stipulated in the Blue Book program standards that were more definite than in the past, those standards never were enforced, thereby creating more controversy than change.

Not only did the courts apply different standards to publishers and broadcasters but also the leaders of the print media often were unsympathetic. In the late 1950s, *Wall Street Journal* editor Bernard Kilgore declared that the First Amendment simply did not apply to broadcasters because the First Amendment, passed in 1791, said nothing about broadcasting.

During the 1950s, the FCC was underfunded and, like most regulatory agencies of the decade, "lost the glamour of the New Deal years, when, so the legend went, the bright young attorneys and academicians rushed to Washington to supervise the American economy."[30] Eisenhower made poor choices in his appointments, and procedural constraints on all regulatory committees limited the possibilities for an activist commission. One chairman dubbed the decade "the whorehouse era," as he noted the 1957 reports of commissioners favoring Republican applicants and accepting gifts and loans from license applicants and lobbyists. In 1957, a House investigation committee revealed that, in at least one case, commissioners had voted in a certain way in return for money to meet personal expenses.

Nevertheless, the activities of the commission in the 1950s lay significant groundwork for subsequent court decisions. In 1959, Congress codified a series of rulings made by the FCC as early as 1949 that became the "Fairness Doctrine." The doctrine required that broadcasters encourage open and robust debate on public issues "by affording reasonable opportunity for the discussion of conflicting views of issues of public importance."

Despite the passing of the Fairness Doctrine, scholars and the public alike questioned the efficacy of the regulatory agency because of its close ties to the industry being regulated. From 1945 to 1971, for example, twenty-one of the thirty-three commissioners (64 percent) who left office went to work for the communications industry.[31]

The House Un-American Activities Committee

Investigation by the House Un-American Activities Committee (HUAC) put fear in the minds and hearts of those who contemplated criticizing the anticommunist stance of the committee. The motion picture industry was the first branch of media to come under the scrutiny of HUAC. Industry leader Jack L. Warner contributed to the hysteria by citing communist propaganda in films that, he said, consisted of "picking on rich men" and "poking fun at our political system." At first, Hollywood assumed a courageous stance and seemed to close ranks to protect those who were attacked, but its courage soon failed. On November 24, 1947, a group of top film executives met in New York and decided to clean house to protect the industry's reputation, blacklisting many industry artists.[32]

Late that same year, the broadcast industry was attacked by the American Business Consultants, a group that consisted of three former FBI agents. Complaints by the group accelerated a few days before the Korean War broke out, when the group published a 215-page booklet, *Red Channels: The Report of Communist Influence in Radio and Television*, with a cover that depicted a red hand closing on a microphone. The report charged 115 individuals in the industry with having communist sympathies. The list, wrote Erik Barnouw, was a "roll of honor," citing many of the people who had made radio an "honored medium." Although the report was seldom discussed publicly, actors soon began to feel its effects, and the industry institutionalized blacklisting, with CBS requiring a loyalty oath and NBC establishing security channels within its legal department.[33] The impact of the charges continued to be felt throughout the 1950s, as networks and sponsors screened actors and writers for any possible leftist ties.

The Press and Joseph McCarthy

One unscrupulous public official who understood how to manipulate the press through its own endorsement of objectivity as a journalistic convention was Joseph R. McCarthy, the Republican junior senator from Wisconsin. Even though McCarthy was to enthusiastically join the hunt for communists in government—in particular, in the U.S. State Department—in March 1950, he had not yet reached the anticommunist bandwagon. Historian Garry Wills suggested that the "McCarthy era"—as it is sometimes called—did not begin in 1950, when McCarthy made his first accusations of communists in government. That era, Wills wrote, started in 1947, under President Harry S. Truman, Attorney General Tom Clark, and FBI Director J. Edgar Hoover. These officials provided HUAC—which helped propel Congressman Richard M. Nixon to prominence—with lists of names and with "the loyalty program for which it could demand ever stricter enforcement, the presumption that a citizen is disloyal until proved loyal, the denial of work to any man or woman who would not undergo such a proving process."[34]

Because he realized that a senator's sensational allegations could make news—and increase his power—Senator McCarthy became an expert in making charges—without supporting evidence—claiming there were hundreds (the figures varied from announcement to announcement) of communists in the State Department. He also identified specific government officials as being communists, making these charges while the Senate or a Senate subcommittee was in session.

Wire services and "objective" newspaper reporters fell easily into Senator McCarthy's trap. He would unleash a sensational charge shortly before a press deadline, minimizing the time available for fact checking by the news media. Refuting the charges required extensive reporter initiative and time, and some media were willing to expend the resources needed to check the facts. However, newspapers that relied on the wire services, which operated on tight deadlines and with limited staff, tended to repeat McCarthy's charges without providing adequate refutation. Nevertheless, a variety of newspapers and magazines, including the *Christian Science Monitor*, the *Washington Post*, the *Milwaukee Journal*, and *Time* challenged McCarthy from the moment on February 9, 1950, that he made his first charges in a speech at Wheeling, West Virginia. The *Post* used in-depth, daily reporting by Murrey Marder not only to report McCarthy's charges but also to examine the charges and to relate McCarthy's comments to earlier charges. Such coverage was supplemented by devastating Herblock cartoons and calm, reasoned editorials by Alan Barth. From the date of the Wheeling speech until McCarthy's death seven years later, the *Milwaukee Journal* published 201 editorials criticizing McCarthy.[35]

Nevertheless, it took four years, charges of communists in the army, and the power of television to finally expose McCarthy in such a way that the American public was no longer willing to believe him. The magic name here—and still a symbol for excellence in television news—was that of Edward R. Murrow of CBS News. The trusted, over-smoked, deep baritone voice that had informed Americans of the bombs being dropped over London, on a program called "See It Now," finally exposed Senator McCarthy.

The winter of 1953–1954 was memorable as the lowest point of the McCarthy era—months during which an Indiana textbook commissioner called Robin Hood a

▼

Murrow Challenges Americans to Think

We will not walk in fear, one of another. We will not be driven by fear into an age of unreason if we dig deep in our history and our doctrine, and remember that we are not descended from fearful men, not from men who feared to write, to speak, to associate, and to defend causes that were for the moment unpopular. This is no time for men who oppose Senator McCarthy's methods to keep silent, or for those who approve. We can deny our heritage and our history, but we cannot escape responsibility for the result. There is no way for a citizen of a republic to abdicate his responsibilities. As a nation we have come into full inheritance at a tender age. We proclaim ourselves—as indeed we are—the defenders of freedom, wherever it continues to exist in the world. But we cannot defend freedom abroad by deserting it at home. The actions of the junior senator from Wisconsin have caused alarm and dismay amongst our allies abroad and given considerable comfort to our enemies. And whose fault is that? Not really his. He didn't create this situation of fear, he merely exploited it—and rather successfully. Cassius was right: "The fault, dear Brutus, is not in our stars but in ourselves."

—Edward R. Murrow, March 9, 1954

Figure 15–3 The television cameras gathered to report the last day of the McCarthy hearings in June 1954. (*U.S. News and World Report* photo, Division of Prints and Photographs, Library of Congress Collection)

communist and recommended purging textbooks of references to Quakers, who did not believe in fighting wars. Further, McCarthy, who had been investigating the army, began to attack individual officers.[36]

On March 9, 1954, Murrow's "See It Now" program devoted all of its thirty minutes to a devastating portrait of Senator McCarthy. As Murrow read the introduction, he offered reply time to the senator. The reply time was offered in that fashion on advice from CBS president William S. Paley. Paley evidently believed the senator was sure to ask for response time, and offering it before the fact would show the network behaving with a fairness that contrasted favorably with McCarthy's bullying treatment of witnesses in the hearings of his Senate Subcommittee on Investigations.[37]

The half-hour show broadcast clips of Senator McCarthy making statements, with a counterpoint of contradictions from the senator himself, or, at times, with corrective statements added by Murrow. For example, in A. M. Sperber's words:

There was McCarthy questioning a witness—"You know the Civil Liberties Union has been listed as a front for . . . the Communist Party?"—with Murrow (intoning an answer) right behind him: "The Attorney General's List (visible in McCarthy's hand) does not and never has listed the A.C.L.U. as subversive. Nor does the F.B.I. or any other federal government agency.[38]

Murrow here stepped far beyond the featureless objectivity upon which McCarthy had fed. Murrow spoke out at a time when few dared to oppose McCarthy publicly. President Dwight D. Eisenhower, despite what evidently was a growing distaste for McCarthy, remained silent or, when out campaigning, gingerly expressed affirmation for McCarthy's anticommunist crusading.

Murrow concluded his broadcast on an intensely personal note. He seemed to look through the camera and talk one-on-one with the members of the audience as he delivered one of the most famous editorial statements in American journalism. He acknowledged that investigation by legislative committees is necessary to gather information needed to create effective laws, but that the line between investigation and persecution is extremely fine. "We must not confuse dissent with disloyalty," Murrow warned, and "must remember always that accusation is not proof."[39]

Murrow's courageous broadcast—with the support of CBS News when it counted most—was the beginning of the end for Senator McCarthy.[40] McCarthy's famous and disastrous confrontation with canny attorney Joseph Welch just months later—in which Welch castigated McCarthy for smearing one of the young lawyers in Welch's firm—symbolized the senator's growing desperation and political impotence. Welch, a slight, gentle Boston lawyer, rose in fury against the alcohol-fueled cruelty of Senator McCarthy with a much-remembered line: "At long last, Sir, have you no sense of decency?"

Eastland Hearings

The press's confrontation with anticommunism did not end with McCarthy's demise. In 1955, the Senate Internal Security Subcommittee, headed by Senator James Eastland, Democrat of Mississippi, held closed hearings to investigate communist influence in American newspapers. The *New York Times* was the focus of the attack. Of the thirty-eight witnesses interviewed, twenty-five were *Times* employees and five others had formerly worked for the *Times*. In January 1956, the *Times* wrote that it had been singled out for investigation because it championed desegregation and protested McCarthyism, issues on which Eastland had opposing views. The *Times* also said it would not knowingly employ a communist on its staff. Actions of the *Times* were remembered differently, however, by its former reporters. Editor Turner Catledge claimed he persuaded the general manager, Julius Ochs Adler, not to fire people for taking the Fifth Amendment.[41] However, James Aronson recalled that the *Times* fired at least three editorial workers.[42]

An Activist News Media

By 1954, then, the elements of an activist news media were in place. The Supreme Court had declared in *Near v. Minnesota* (1931) that it would protect the press from the states' legal meddling, and Murrow had suffered no consequences for his editorial comment on McCarthy. Beyond such legal safeguards, the media had the object

▼

Marvin Kalb (1930–present)

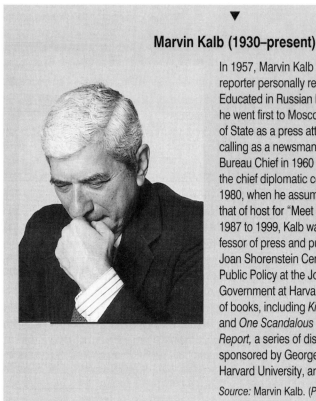

In 1957, Marvin Kalb began his career as the last reporter personally recruited by Edward R. Murrow. Educated in Russian history at Harvard University, he went first to Moscow with the U.S. Department of State as a press attaché but soon found his true calling as a newsman. Kalb became the Moscow Bureau Chief in 1960 for CBS News and served as the chief diplomatic correspondent for CBS until 1980, when he assumed the same post, along with that of host for "Meet the Press," for NBC. From 1987 to 1999, Kalb was the Edward R. Murrow professor of press and public policy and director of the Joan Shorenstein Center on the Press, Politics and Public Policy at the John F. Kennedy School of Government at Harvard. Kalb has written a number of books, including *Kissinger, The Nixon Memo,* and *One Scandalous Story.* He also hosts *The Kalb Report,* a series of discussions about journalism sponsored by George Washington University, Harvard University, and the National Press Club.

Source: Marvin Kalb. (*Photo:* Marvin Kalb)

lesson of the McCarthy era to suggest that simple objectivity was insufficient. Objectivity had to be expanded to reporting the facts fully and fairly; and, if the facts did not speak for themselves, efforts had to be made to put them into meaningful perspective.

Television Goes to the Elections

In 1948, Republicans and Democrats convened their national conventions in Philadelphia because it was in that city of the Founding Fathers that television could reach the greatest audience. Truman deemphasized broadcasting in his campaign, claiming that broadcasters had "sold out to the special interests." He continuously referred to the "kept press" and "paid radio." On the other side, Thomas Dewey refused the advice of the Republican-hired advertising agency of Batten, Barton, Durstine, and Osborne, which urged him to make a number of spot announcements. Instead he relied on lofty speeches. The polls predicted Dewey would win, and on the morning after the election, H. V. Kaltenborn remained convinced, noting that although Truman was ahead, he could not win. Truman's victory was ambiguous at

Figure 15-4   Eisenhower used television to his advantage, both in the 1952 election and in this 1959 press conference. (*U.S. News and World Report* photo, Division of Prints and Photographs, Library of Congress Collection)

best; while he remained in office, he fought an antagonistic Congress throughout his second term.[43]

In 1952, the networks offered sponsored television campaign coverage. As historian Erik Barnouw wrote, Betty Furness opened and closed refrigerator doors hundreds of times for Westinghouse before the issues were settled. General Dwight D. Eisenhower of World War II fame and Richard Nixon of the House Un-American Activities Committee fame challenged Illinois Governor Adlai Stevenson and Senator John Sparkman of Alabama. Eisenhower, on the advice of the same advertising agency that prompted Dewey to use spot announcements, relied on twenty-second "hero-in, hero-out" shots. Saturation coverage during the last two weeks of the campaign cost $1,500,000. Stevenson, refusing to be merchandised "like a breakfast food," relied on speech making, a radio technique not well applied to the visual television era.

Historically, the most studied aspect of the campaign may well have been Richard Nixon's televised "Checkers" speech. The Republican National Committee sponsored a half hour of time for Nixon, accused of irregularity in the use of campaign money, to defend himself. Nixon claimed none of the money ever went for his personal use, and then he added:

One other thing I should probably tell you, because if I don't they'll probably be saying this about me too, we did get something—a gift—after the election. A man down in Texas heard Pat on the radio mention the fact that our two daughters would like to have a dog. And, believe it or not, the day before we left on this campaign trip we got a message from Union Station in Baltimore saying they had a package for us. We went down to get it. You know what it was? It was a little cocker spaniel dog in a crate that he sent all the way from Texas. Black and white and spotted. And our little girl—Tricia, the six-year-old—named it Checkers. And you know the kids love that dog and I just want to say this right now, that regardless of what they say about it, we're going to keep it.[44]

In 1956, recovering from a heart attack, President Eisenhower ran for reelection, relying even more on television than he had in 1952. The networks expanded their coverage of the national conventions, using battery-operated miniature cameras to broadcast live interviews from the convention floor. Other innovations included split screens, devices for flashing vote totals on home screens, and coverage that was coordinated by a TV director instead of the anchor team. However, once the conventions were over, network news about the campaigns consisted only of interview programs and weekly news summaries. The fifteen-minute nightly newscasts provided little daily coverage of political campaigning.[45]

A Few Lonely Voices of Dissent

One of the "lonely voices" on the left was Dwight MacDonald's *Politics*. MacDonald, who spent seven years working for Luce's publications and who flirted briefly with Marxism, began the journal in 1944. *Politics*, which died in 1949, never made a profit, but it kept alive the voice of dissent in the late 1940s.[46] Probably the decade's most consistent critic was I. F. Stone, who published his *Weekly* throughout the Korean War, the McCarthy years, and into the 1960s, when his was one of the first voices to speak against the Vietnam War.

"Izzy" Stone

I. F. Stone, born Isidor Feinstein, challenged the establishment throughout his long career as a journalist. A member of the radical left in the 1930s and a *PM* staffer in the 1940s, Stone cajoled, berated, and challenged government officials and the military-industrial complex.

Stone was born in 1908 and began his first newspaper, *The Progress*, when he was fourteen. His father forced him to stop publishing because the newspaper absorbed Stone so much that he nearly flunked out of school. He attended the University of Pennsylvania but left in 1927 because he claimed school interfered with his reading. He took a job with the *Camden* (New Jersey) *Courier* but quit when he failed to get an assignment to cover the Sacco-Vanzetti anarchist trial. After a short stint with the *Philadelphia Inquirer*, Stone worked from 1938 to 1946 for the *Nation*. He was a staffer on *PM* and then joined the New York *Compass,* which folded in 1952.

In 1946, Stone traveled aboard an illegal ship from Europe to Palestine, writing the account of survivors of the holocaust who ignored Britain's immigration quotas for Palestine to seek a homeland. After spending three months aboard ship and in Palestine, Stone wrote a series for *PM*, which was reprinted in the book *Underground to Palestine*.[47]

In the narrow political atmosphere of the 1950s, Stone was hard-pressed to find a job. Even Frieda Kirchwey, editor of the *Nation*, would not rehire him. His critical work, *The Hidden History of the Korean War*, had garnered attacks from the right, and his criticism of cold war policies of both the West and the East had earned him the label of apologist for the left.

In 1952, Stone began his own news sheet, *I. F. Stone's Weekly*, a critical, liberal publication aimed at a small audience. With $3,500 in severance pay from the *Compass*, $3,000 in loans, and the old *PM*, *STAR*, and *Compass* mailing lists, he gathered 5,300 charter subscribers.

Stone's radical vision of the 1930s faded as the Soviet Union invaded Hungary, and he became fully aware of the lack of regard for human rights within the Soviet system. In May 1956, he traveled through the Soviet Union and returned, noting, "This is not a good society, and it is not led by honest men. No society is good in which men fear to think—much less speak—freely." He called Soviet Russia "a hermetically sealed prison, stifling in its atmosphere of completely rigid and low-level thought control."[48]

Stone's criticism of the Soviet Union alienated many of his readers on the left and, coupled with his defense of a homeland for Palestinians as well as for Jews, lost his *Weekly* about 400 subscribers.[49] Although Stone's fans, ranging from Albert Einstein to Marilyn Monroe, were faithful to his ringing criticism, Vice President Spiro Agnew referred to the *Weekly* as "another strident voice of illiberalism," and David Eisenhower, Nixon's son-in-law, refused to attend his own graduation because I. F. Stone was the commencement speaker.

Stone's unpopularity during the 1950s and early 1960s began to change, however. One of the first to criticize the Vietnam War, he soon became a hero of the American sixties' left. During the 1960s and early 1970s, he received five honorary degrees, including one from the University of Pennsylvania, and a documentary of his life and work was shown at the Cannes Film Festival in 1974 and later on public television.

Stone's wife, Esther, handled the business end of the weekly, which Stone closed down in 1971 because of his own poor health. Though his wife was a Republican at heart, he claimed, she never interfered with his right to be a radical. Although Stone lost his hope for a successful society emerging within a socialist framework, he never lost sight of what he considered to be the necessities of a good society: freedom of speech and protection of other civil liberties.

Stone died in 1989, at the age of eighty-one, of a heart attack. In 1988, he told a Washington reporter, "What I said to my wife a long time ago is that if I lived long enough I'd graduate from a pariah to a character, and then if I lasted long enough, from character to public institution." He had just published a best-selling book on ancient Greece, *The Trial of Socrates*.

Conclusion

Radio, the dominant news medium of the war years, began to give way to television competition and lose both its advertisers and listening audience in the 1950s, despite cutbacks in advertising rates. Reflecting the growing conservatism in the country, the industry withdrew its support for liberal commentators and turned toward a new format of noncontroversial news summaries and music formats. Radio music fostered the growth of rock 'n roll—stolen, then adapted, from African-American blues music. Portability took teenagers out of the home and into their cars—and away from their parents. The new popularity for radio broadened the audience, and the medium remained, throughout the decade, an important news source for most Americans.

Television technology, which had been available since before World War II, found favorable conditions only after two freezes on licenses and the end of the Korean War. Programming in the early 1950s adapted radio's best shows and promised quality fare with anthologies and live performances. Nevertheless, by the end of the decade, industry leaders, assured of large audiences and relieved of the fear of pay television, consolidated costs and turned to less expensive weekly shows. The quiz show scandals of the late 1950s propelled the industry toward a greater interest in public affairs programming. Television was used by both presidential candidates in the elections of 1952 and 1956, and although networks covered the political conventions, fifteen-minute evening newscasts provided little in the way of daily political campaign coverage.

The boom of electronic media coupled with a move to the suburbs and an expansion of automobile ownership fueled advertising growth during the 1950s. The advertising industry began to use social science research in the design of advertising. The growth of consumer products and the advertising that went with them did not escape criticism, and when Vance Packard's *The Hidden Persuaders* hit the newsstands, it was an instant sensation. As television matured, it moved away from sponsorship and toward advertising spots, and advertising agencies specialized in designing the ads.

After World War II, advertising and public relations functions became more intertwined, with some agencies even merging operations. At the forefront of public relations was business—trying to convince the public that the success of the war was due to private enterprise. Public relations activities continued to increase after the war, but businessmen began to recognize that they could control the message through advertising to a much greater degree than they could through news releases.

The media and government participated in an uneasy alliance during the decade. Although the convention of objectivity was employed to join the country's protest against communism, the media also became victims of the anticommunist hysteria. Congressional investigations of the motion picture industry, the broadcast industry, and newspapers led to caution on the part of many editors and managers and slowed progress toward the exposure of Senator Joseph McCarthy.

Endnotes

1. Thomas G. Paterson, *On Every Front: The Making of the Cold War* (New York: W. W. Norton, 1979), p. 119; Andrew Rojecki, *Silencing the Opposition: Antinuclear Movements and the Media in the Cold War* (Urbana: University of Illinois Press, 1999).

2. Cited in Mary Beth Norton, et al., *A People and a Nation*, vol. 2 (Boston: Houghton Mifflin, 1982), p. 862.

3. Walter Lippmann, "The American Destiny," *Life* (5 June 1939), pp. 47, 73, cited in James L. Baughman, *Henry R. Luce and the Rise of the American News Media* (New York: G. K. Hall/Twayne, 1987), p. 132.

4. Ronald Samuel Reinig, "America Looking Outward: American Cold War Attitudes during the Crucial Years, 1945–1947, as Reflected in the American Magazine Medium," Ph.D. dissertation, Syracuse University, 1974, pp. 487 and *passim.*, cited in Baughman, *Luce and the Rise of the American News Media*, p. 150.

5. Norton, et al., *A People and a Nation*, p. 808.

6. James Boylan, "Declarations of Independence," *Columbia Journalism Review* (November/December 1986), p. 30; cited from the Truman Papers [Stanton to Steelman, December 18, 1950, WHCF:OF 575] in Nancy E. Bernhard, *U.S. Television News and Cold War Propaganda, 1947–1960* (Boston: Cambridge University Press, 1999).

7. Boylan, "Declarations of Independence," p. 31.

8. James L. Baughman, *The Republic of Mass Culture: Journalism, Filmmaking, and Broadcasting in America Since 1941* (Baltimore: Johns Hopkins University Press, 1992), p. 66.

9. Erik Barnouw, *Tube of Plenty: The Evolution of American Television* (New York: Oxford University Press, 1975), pp. 77–83.

10. Fred J. MacDonald, *Don't Touch That Dial! Radio Programming in American Life, 1920–1960* (Chicago: Nelson-Hall, 1979), p. 77.

11. MacDonald, *Don't Touch That Dial*, pp. 315, 317, 320.

12. MacDonald, *Don't Touch That Dial*, p. 81.

13. *Variety*, February 12, 1958, p. 49, cited in MacDonald, *Don't Touch That Dial*, p. 88. *Cigaret* was the common journalistic spelling through the 1960s.

14. Todd Gitlin, *The Sixties: Years of Hope, Days of Rage* (New York: Bantam, 1987), pp. 37–44.

15. Barnouw, *Tube of Plenty*, p. 247.

16. Barnouw, *Tube of Plenty*, p. 165.

17. Sylvester Weaver, "Television 1953: The Case for the Networks," *Television Magazine* 10 (January, 1953), p. 17; address by Weaver, 15 June 1953, Broadcast Pioneers Library, Washington, D.C., File 179, p. 16, cited in James L. Baughman, "Television in the 'Golden Age': An Entrepreneurial Experiment," *The Historian*, 47:2 (February, 1985).

18. James L. Baughman, *Television's Guardians: The FCC and the Politics of Programming, 1958–1967* (Knoxville: University of Tennessee Press, 1985), pp. 29, 30. Text of the address is in box 7-B-25 of the Murrow Papers and was reprinted in *The Reporter*, November 13, 1958, pp. 32–36.

19. For an elaboration of this thesis, see Baughman, "Television in the 'Golden Age'."

20. See "Profile of Huntley and Brinkley" in the August 3, 1968, *New Yorker*, pp. 34–60. For CBS, see David Halberstam, *The Powers That Be* (New York: Alfred A. Knopf, 1979), p. 242.

21. Stephen Fox, *The Mirror Makers* (New York: Vintage Books, 1985), pp. 172–210.

22. Baughman, *Republic of Mass Culture*, p. 44–46.

23. Fox, *Mirror Makers*, p. 211.

24. Fox, *Mirror Makers*, p. 213.

25. Cited in Richard S. Tedlow, *Keeping the Corporate Image: Public Relations and Business, 1900–1950* (Greenwich, Conn.: JAI Press, 1979), p. 62.

26. Tedlow, *Keeping the Corporate Image*, p. 68.

27. Tedlow, *Keeping the Corporate Image*, p. 73.

28. Edwin R. Bayley, *Joe McCarthy and the Press* (Madison: University of Wisconsin Press, 1981), pp. 80–85.

29. Baughman, *Television's Guardians*, p. 9.

30. Baughman, *Television's Guardians*, p. 11.

31. Florence Heffron, "The FCC and Broadcast Deregulation," in John J. Havick, ed., *Communications Policy and the Political Process* (Westport, Conn.: Greenwood Press, 1983), p. 43.

32. Barnouw, *Tube of Plenty*, pp. 108–9.

33. Barnouw, *Tube of Plenty*, p. 129.

34. Garry Wills, introduction to Lillian Hellman, *Scoundrel Time* (New York: Little, Brown, 1976), pp. 11–12.

35. Bayley, *McCarthy and the Press*, pp. 135, 148–50.

36. A. M. Sperber, *Murrow: His Life and Times* (New York: Freundlich Books, 1986), p. 426.

37. Sperber, *Murrow*, p. 435.

38. Sperber, *Murrow*, p. 437.

39. Edward R. Murrow, "See It Now" for March 9, 1954, in Edward W. Bliss, Jr., *In Search of Light: The Broadcasts of Edward R. Murrow 1938–1961* (New York: Knopf, 1967), pp. 247–48.

40. Although CBS seemed to support Murrow to some degree in the broadcast, Murrow and Fred Friendly were forced to advertise the program with funds from their own pockets.

41. Turner Catledge, *My Life and the Times* (New York: Harper & Row, 1971), pp. 227–30, cited in Bayley, *McCarthy and the Press*, p. 138.

42. James Aronson, *The Press and the Cold War* (New York: Bobbs-Merrill, 1970), p. 146.

43. Barnouw, *Tube of Plenty*, pp. 111–12.

44. Barnouw, *Tube of Plenty*, pp. 136–38.

45. See Craig Allen, "News Conferences on TV: Ike Age Politics Revisited," *Journalism Quarterly* 70:1 (Spring, 1993), pp. 13–26.

46. Lauren Kessler, "Against the American Grain: The Lonely Voice of *Politics* Magazine, 1944–49," *Journalism History* 9:2 (Summer, 1982), p. 49.

47. Larry Van Dyne, "The Adventures of I. F. Stone," *The Chronicle Review,* supplement to the *Chronicle of Higher Education* (February 5, 1979), pp. 4–6.

48. Robert Cottrell, "I. F. Stone: A Maverick Journalist's Battle with the Superpowers," *Journalism History* 12:2 (Summer, 1985), p. 64.

49. *Washington Post,* July 9, 1979, pp. B1–2.

CHAPTER 16

Affluence and Activism

▼

I t was a time when old values were breaking down; new knowledge exploded all around us; people worried about drugs, hippies, and war. We talked of violence, urban disorder, turmoil. New terms like *polarization, credibility gap,* and *counterculture* crept into the language.[1]

From 1960 through the early 1970s, Americans created and resisted cultural upheaval, dramatic change in value systems, and rebellion and experimentation in journalism as well as in other aspects of American life. John F. Kennedy, in his inaugural address in January 1961 aroused high expectations in the hearts of many intellectuals, young people, and minorities, expectations that remained unfulfilled by the end of the 1960s.[2] Crisis became routine with the Tet offensive of 1968, balance-of-payment and gold crises, the Martin Luther King and Kennedy assassinations, African-American protests, student sit-ins, riots at the 1968 Democratic convention, and the National Guard intervention and subsequent killings at Kent State.[3] The Watergate affair, government corruption at its peak, further dashed the hopes of those who envisioned a new and revitalized nation.

Emerging during the 1960s was a New Left, a radical student mass movement that championed civil rights, challenged authority, and, later in the decade, opposed the Vietnam War. The New Left had few ties to the radical socialist-communist movements of the 1930s, although rather than appealing to the American working class, the movement attracted young, affluent, often alienated adolescents and young adults.[4]

▼

Kennedy Presents a Challenge

In the long history of the world, only a few generations have been granted the role of defending freedom in its hour of maximum danger. I do not shrink from this responsibility—I welcome it. I do not believe that any of us would exchange places with any other people or any other generation. The energy, the faith, the devotion which we bring to this endeavor will light our country and all who serve it—and the glow from that fire can truly light the world.

—John Fitzgerald Kennedy, inaugural address, January 21, 1961

The movement had a profound impact on American institutions, the media being no exception. College students of the early 1960s became reporters, and with them they carried a concept of professionalism that demanded more autonomy in the newsroom and sparked challenges to the authority of the editor. Newsmen and women in television studios across the nation gained respect with the expansion of television news and critical reporting roles in the civil rights movement of the 1960s. James Boylan, reviewing the decade in 1986 for *Columbia Journalism Review,* wrote that the "great surprise, in retrospect, is the speed with which the bedraggled, victimized press of the 1950s came to see itself as an apparently potent, apparently adversary press in the 1960s."

Although the change was apparent in newsrooms and studios, and extremely visible in the alternative press, the effect on the corporate structure and the hierarchy of the media was minimal. Newspaper publishers were concerned with higher costs and competition from television and suburban newspapers; television studios remained dominated by white males climbing the corporate ladder, and media consolidation accelerated.

The emphasis on the reporter and the story, however, coupled with a generational challenge to authority, promoted the development of an adversarial approach—particularly among those who, as foreign correspondents, tackled the job of covering a new kind of war, a war with no frontline, no clear definition of purpose, and a growing opposition at home.

The resistance of daily newspaper hierarchies to expand reporter power and to allow the use of new journalism techniques momentarily energized the magazine industry, and writers adopted magazines as their favorite medium for challenging institutional structures. However, new journalism did not financially enhance the industry; specialization and targeted advertising markets fueled the industry as some of the big circulation leaders died. One of those specialized markets was that of the women's magazines, which flourished during the women's movement.

The changes in the society of which journalism was a part did not enhance the credibility of the media. Journalists had never before been so visible, and at the end of 1968, George Gallup reported that never in his time had media been held in such low esteem. Wrote Ernest Hynds, "As the 1960s closed, it appeared that the press had become the nation's scapegoat for crime, racial troubles, the war in Vietnam and other problems."[5]

Newspapers again declined as the major source of news for Americans, with television rapidly gaining loyal viewers. In 1961, television bypassed newspapers as the most believable news medium. In 1968, it reached a 2-to-1 advantage over newspapers, and by 1974 the margin had widened to a 2+-to-1 advantage.[6] ▼

At Home and Abroad: The Big Stories

Civil Rights

At the end of World War II, black and white soldiers returned home, whites to a world of prosperity and jobs, blacks to a nation still characterized by segregation and unequal opportunity. During the 1950s, protest began in the South, and toward the end of the decade newspapers, television, and the photojournalism magazines such as *Life* recognized civil rights as one of the biggest stories of the postwar world.

Legally, African Americans made gains in the early 1950s, particularly with the 1954 Supreme Court decision in *Brown v. Board of Education of Topeka*, a Kansas case that ruled that separate education was not equal education. Many white communities defied the court order, and in 1957 when a black student attempted to enroll in an all-white Little Rock, Arkansas, high school, Governor Orval E. Faubus called out the National Guard to prevent desegregation of the school. In late 1955, a year-long bus boycott in Montgomery, Alabama, signaled the advent of the type of protest advocated by Martin Luther King, that of nonviolent civil resistance. Volunteers organized by King's Southern Christian Leadership Conference continued to sit in at white lunch counters, libraries, and bus stations, and members of the Congress of Racial Equality and the Student Non-Violent Coordinating Committee encouraged African Americans to resist segregation and to vote.

Southern newspapers and local television stories downplayed the news or refused to cover it at all. Not until network news and national newspapers such as the *New York Times* entered the South to report on the story did it reach the national consciousness. Network news, now thirty minutes long, transmitted the story to homes all over the country, and what had been a regional problem became a national cultural issue.

In the 1960s, civil rights became a story of events, not merely of issues. In 1962, President Kennedy ordered U.S. marshals to protect James Meredith, the first African American to enroll at the University of Mississippi. In August 1963, King addressed a crowd of 250,000 at the Washington Monument, proclaiming, "I have a dream that my four little children will one day live in a nation where they will not be judged by the color of their skin but by the content of their character." In September, white terrorists bombed a Birmingham Baptist church, killing four black girls. Shortly after the assassination of President John F. Kennedy in Dallas, November 22, 1963, President Johnson made civil rights a top priority. Johnson signed the Civil Rights Act of 1964, which outlawed discrimination in public accommodations and in jobs. During the summers of 1964 and 1965, racial violence broke out not only in the South but in northern cities as well. In 1965, Congress passed a voting rights act. On April 4, 1968,

Figure 16-1   By 1964, the networks regularly covered the political party conventions. In 1964, reporters gained experience that would serve them well in the turbulent times to follow. (*U.S. News and World Report* photo, Division of Prints and Photographs, Library of Congress Collection)

Martin Luther King died from an assassin's bullet, and that June, Robert Kennedy lay dead, another assassination victim.

Life magazine was one of the first to focus on the unfolding story of the African-American struggle for civil rights. In 1957 and 1962, *Life* carried extensive coverage on school integration in Arkansas and Mississippi, along with feature stories on racism as a social problem. *Life* assured its readers that the North had done more than the South had for black dignity and regarded the Mississippi incident as "a disgrace to themselves, their state and their nation."[7] However, rarely did *Life* cover contemporary African-American life apart from news events. Critics chastised the media for not having covered civil rights issues as issues and for waiting until civil disobedience commanded their attention.[8] At a University of Mississippi conference in 1987 on journalism and the civil rights movement, veteran reporters recalled that the South's editorial voices had been virtually silent, with occasional exceptions. John Seigenthaler, editor of the *Nashville Tennessean*, noted that "in too many cities cowardice ruled. Retrenchment ruled. It was a profanation of what journalism was supposed to be about."[9]

The civil rights stories were multimedia stories, and despite extensive coverage by magazines and some newspapers, led by the *New York Times*, it was television's story just as surely as World War II had been radio's story. Only the wire services and television carried the daily story to the entire nation, although local southern television stations often refused to carry network feeds. Journalists Robert Donovan and Ray Scherer noted in their book *Unsilent Revolution: Television News and American Public Life*: "Police dogs looked like police dogs in newspaper and magazine photos, but on television the dogs snarled." A reporter for the *Nashville Tennessean* said television "gave that story a color and attraction and emphasis that newspapers couldn't do. Even without any commentary, a shot of a big white man spitting and cursing at black children did more to open up the national intellect than my stories ever could."10

Covering Vietnam

The United States was involved at various levels in Vietnam from the close of World War II. The French had governed much of what became Vietnam, Cambodia, and Laos from the late nineteenth century until World War II. In the 1930s Ho Chi Minh organized the Indochinese Communist party, which was opposed to French rule. During World War II, Japanese troops occupied Indochina but allowed the French to continue their colonial administration of the area. After Japan surrendered in August 1945, Ho Chi Minh established the Viet Minh, a guerilla army, and established the Democratic Republic of Vietnam in Hanoi. The United States subsidized the French and China began to supply weapons to North Vietnam. In 1954, the French were defeated at Dien Bien Phu, and the Geneva Conference declared a demilitarized zone at the 17th parallel.

From 1954 forward, the United States extended direct economic and military aid to South Vietnam. By the end of 1963, President Kennedy had committed $400 million annually in American assistance, and 12,000 military advisers operated in the country.

In July 1964, the U.S.S. *Maddox*, a navy destroyer, was patrolling in the Gulf of Tonkin, seeking reconnaissance about the North Vietnamese. Several smaller ships in the area shelled some offshore islands, and the North Vietnamese retaliated by torpedoing the *Maddox*. The *Maddox* and a companion ship, the U.S.S. *Turner Joy*, believed they were under attack and radioed aircraft carriers for retaliatory air strikes. On August 7, the U.S. Congress passed the Gulf of Tonkin Resolution, which gave President Lyndon Johnson the authority to take any measures to repel attacks and to provide military assistance to Vietnam and other Southeast Asian countries.

Media organizations had pulled most of their correspondents out of Asia after World War II. Until U.S. Marines landed in the spring of 1965, after the Tonkin incident, only five American news organizations maintained staff correspondents in Vietnam. During the early years of the Vietnam conflict, the U.S. press generally supported U.S. military efforts, although Southeast Asian involvement did draw some criticism from the beginning of U.S. involvement.

Figure 16–2   Views of Vietnamese market life and other village scenes conveyed the reality that human beings were being affected by the war. (Photo by Leroy Towns)

For example, in 1961, after a bitter struggle between the U.S.-supported General Phoumi Nosavan and the Pathet Lao, a communist group, President John F. Kennedy said the United States would take action in Southeast Asia if the U.S. S. R. continued to supply the Pathet Lao through Hanoi. At least one reporter doubted the wisdom of the action, asking, "Mr. President, perhaps you could tell us just what our $310 million investment in Laos has bought us?"[11] Kennedy responded by emphasizing the immediate danger of communist control of Laos. Walter Lippmann, whom Kennedy often lunched with, criticized the "bully" position on Laos as a "false and imprudent commitment."[12] Ralph McGill, editor of the *Atlanta Constitution,* noted that in eight years in Southeast Asia the French had failed in their program, and that Southeast Asia could well become a Sino/Soviet battleground. "If Laos falls," McGill wrote, "South Vietnam cannot be defended."[13]

Despite criticism of Kennedy's handling of the Laos crisis, the *New York Times* in the early 1960s described the Vietnam War as "a struggle this country cannot shirk."[14] Overall, the media supported the war and news organizations were slow to staff the conflict. The first TV correspondent, NBC's Garrick Utley, did not arrive until 1964.[15]

Neither Presidents Kennedy nor Johnson was willing to impose full-scale censorship such as that in World War II. Rather, the U.S. Military Assistance Command Vietnam (MACV) established guidelines that newsmen agreed to observe. Under this arrangement, newsmen were never to reveal future plans, operations, air strikes, information on rules of engagement, or amounts of ordinance and fuel available to support combat units. Tactical and troop movements remained secret. Locations and activities of intelligence units and casualties suffered by friendly forces, as well as information on aircraft take offs, were not reported. Efforts to evacuate airmen were off limits while the search was being conducted.[16]

With these guidelines, the Vietnam conflict continued without censorship, which would have required a declaration of war or at least official admission that the conflict was broad enough to require official censorship. By 1963, reporters David Halberstam of the *New York Times,* Neil Sheehan of UPI, and Malcolm Browne of AP had become increasingly critical of governmental policy, although their criticism usually was directed at inefficiencies or ineffectiveness, not at the conflict itself. President Kennedy suggested to *New York Times* publisher Sulzberger that Halberstam was "too close to the story, too involved," hoping to have the reporter removed from Southeast Asia. Sulzberger kept Halberstam in Vietnam for an extended period, just to prove he could not be influenced by such suggestions.[17]

However, government was not the worst critic of the press during those days. Other reporters and editors attacked the Vietnam correspondents. Joseph Alsop accused them of carrying on "egregious" crusades against Ngo Dinh Diem and compared the reporters to Chiang Kai-shek's press critics, whom he blamed for losing China to the Communists. Asserting the still-formidable power of the editor over reporter, Otto Fuerbringer, managing editor at *Time,* commissioned an article that charged the Saigon press corps with pooling "convictions, information, misinformation and grievances" to distort the truth. *Time* correspondents Charles Mohr and Mert Perry promptly resigned in protest. Despite the increased criticism, at the time of the Tonkin Gulf resolution in 1964, opinion polls showed that 85 percent of the public supported the administration; newspaper editorials reflected a similar sentiment.[18]

When Harrison Salisbury, assistant managing editor of the *New York Times,* traveled to Hanoi in late 1966 to cover the war from North Vietnam, the tone of coverage had begun to change. Although President Johnson had been busy convincing the American people that increased recent bombings were aimed strictly at military targets, Salisbury's reports indicated many cities had been hit and civilians killed. Historian Stanley Karnow reported that while Salisbury's stories essentially were accurate, they did convey the wrong impression that the United States "was indiscriminately trying to destroy North Vietnam."[19] What Salisbury wrote, however, was not the only matter of contention. The fact that he employed objective journalistic conventions as he reported from North Vietnam and quoted officials there "as though

Figure 16–3   The faces of Vietnam were portrayed in many U.S. newspapers. (Photo by Leroy Towns)

they belonged to the Sphere of Legitimate Controversy" also raised criticism from American officials and journalists.[20]

In 1967, under the direction of Henry Luce's successor Hedley Donovan, *Time* and *Life* began to alter their perspectives, with an editorial in *Life* claiming the commitment to Southeast Asia was not "absolutely imperative" to America's interests. Two years later, long after Lyndon Johnson claimed Donovan had betrayed him, *Life* ran pictures of the 250 Americans who had died in Vietnam that week.[21]

In January of 1968, television coverage of the Tet offensive by more than 70,000 North Vietnamese troops exploded onto America's television screens. On January 30, the Viet Cong attacked the U.S. embassy and other sites, catching the South Vietnamese army off guard while they celebrated the Vietnamese New Year, Tet. Although the embassy attack was repulsed, the North Vietnamese captured the city of Hue and a number of provincial capitals. That February, a new one-week record of U.S. casualties was set when 543 soldiers were killed. These successes by the North Vietnamese so shocked American elites and American reporters that confidence in the war effort declined. However, the Tet offensive had been accomplished at great expense to North Vietnam, a fact that television ignored and that the print media were slow to report. Peter Braestrup notes that the "disaster" painted by television did not cause the disarray in Washington. "In the absence of presidential leadership and after years of White House ambiguity and claims of 'progress,' LBJ's political crisis was a self-inflicted wound, aggravated but not caused by the Press." On March 31, President Lyndon Johnson said he would scale back the war and not run for reelection. Braestrup argued that polls indicated that the American public had turned against Johnson, not against the Vietnam conflict. By May of that year peace talks began in Paris.[22]

In 1969, shortly after he took office, President Richard Nixon announced that he planned to withdraw U.S. troops and create a process of "Vietnamization," in which the South Vietnamese would defend their own territory. Although troops were withdrawn throughout the summer, in October a national antiwar demonstration attracted huge crowds. The U.S. Air Force bombed Cambodia, even as peace talks continued in Paris.

In May 1970, student protests against President Nixon's announcement of the offensive into Cambodia occurred on many campuses across the nation, including Ohio State, Stanford, Wisconsin, Kansas, and Penn State. Protests at Kent State University in Ohio and Jackson State College, a predominately African-American school in Jackson, Mississippi, however, are the ones etched in blood in the nation's memory.

After several days of demonstrations at Kent State, Ohio Governor James Rhodes—running for the U.S. Senate on a "law and order platform—sent the Ohio National Guard to Kent State. Rhodes declared that the protesters were worse than communists and "brown shirts" (Nazis) and that the student protesters were part of a conspiracy to destroy higher education in America.[23]

Late in the morning of May 4, as a crowd of more than 1,000 students gathered on the Kent State commons, an officer using a bullhorn ordered the students to disperse. When the students stood firm, about 115 guardsmen—armed with loaded M-1 rifles and outfitted with tear gas canisters—took action. When troops pushed the students back with tear gas, some students hurled the canisters back at the troops. As the confrontation seemed to be ending and some students began to walk to their next classes, someone gave the command, "Fire!" About a dozen guardsmen fired into the crowd, squeezing off sixty-seven shots in thirteen seconds, killing four students and wounding nine.[24]

National furor was intense and immediate.[25] While the polarizing shootings at Kent State dominated the news, students at Jackson State found much to protest. Escalation of the war in Vietnam was part of it, as was racism and the historic, slow-to-change exclusion of minorities from higher education. On May 14, 1970, fires

▼

Mert Perry (1929–1970) and Charles Mohr (1929–1989)

Mert Perry and Charles Mohr were correspondents for *Time* magazine during the Vietnam conflict. According to one journalist, Perry was a favorite correspondent of many military officers. Mohr (seen here) was known for being armed with a handgun and standard issue M-16 rifle and was also the first correspondent wounded in the conflict. After an article appeared in *Time* magazine sharply criticizing the Saigon press, both resigned from the magazine. Perry never again achieved the acclaim he did working with Mohr, whereas Mohr received a Bronze Star for bravery after he and two other reporters risked their lives to save a wounded soldier.

Source: M. P. Roth, *Historical Dictionary of War Journalism* (Westport, Conn.: Greenwood Press, 1997). (*Photo:* Time-Pix)

were set on the campus, and police from Jackson and from the Mississippi State Police were called out after gunfire had been reported around the campus area. Police ultimately fired into a jeering crowd of protesters in front of a men's dorm; two students were killed and nine were wounded.[26]

After a four-year halt to bombing, in April 1972 the United States resumed its bombing of Hanoi and Haiphong, and it was not until January 1973 that President Nixon halted the action against North Vietnam. A peace pact was signed in Paris in late January 1973. By March 29, American troops had withdrawn and 590 U.S. war prisoners were released. In January 1975, the North Vietnamese ordered a major offensive directed toward South Vietnam. Saigon, the capital of South Vietnam, fell to the North Vietnamese, and the war ended with the North triumphant.

After the war it became popular for government officials, as well as for some journalists, to blame the news media for losing the war. Because Vietnam was the first war thoroughly covered by television, broadcasters received particularly heavy criticism. In his memoirs, published in 1978, Richard Nixon blamed the news media for reporting "little of the underlying purpose of the fighting." Eventually, he wrote, such "relentless and literal reporting of the war" created a "serious demoralization of the home front, raising the question whether America would ever again be able to fight an enemy abroad with unity and strength of purpose at home."[27] And the *New York Times'* James Reston wrote in 1975:

Maybe the historians will agree that the reporters and the cameras were decisive in the end. They brought the issue of the war to the people, before the Congress or the courts, and forced the withdrawal of American power from Vietnam.[28]

The role of the press in creating public opinion antagonistic to Vietnam has been exaggerated. Historians Stanley Karnow and Daniel Hallin suggested that public opinion and news media reaction *were* intertwined and that media coverage tended to follow, rather than direct, public opinion. Max Frankel of the *Times* was probably accurate when he told Todd Gitlin that when the protest against the war moved "from the left groups, the antiwar groups, into the pulpits, into the Senate, it naturally picked up coverage. And then naturally the tone of the coverage changed. Because we're an Establishment institution, and whenever your natural constituency changes, then naturally you will too.[29] But even after the Tet offensive of 1968, Hallin writes,

> The later years of Vietnam are a remarkable testimony to the restraining power of the routine and ideology of objective journalism. At a time when much of the nation's intelligentsia was in a militant and passionate mood, when members of Congress, employees of the U.S. embassy in Saigon, and business executives could be seen demonstrating in the streets against the nation's foreign policy, most television coverage was dispassionate; "advocacy journalism" made no real inroads into network television.[30]

Nevertheless, President Johnson and others publicly complained that the news media were losing the war in Vietnam. This was particularly true when Walter Cronkite returned from Saigon in February 1968, claiming that the Tet offensive was not a military victory, but rather a definitive statement that "the bloody experience of Vietnam is to end in a stalemate."

Daniel Hallin suggested that media became, in part, a scapegoat for a lack of clarity within the U.S. government and for the lack of consensus in society at large. Stressing that cooperative arrangements worked well, and the press did keep important secrets, Hallin doubted whether more external constraints on the press would have altered the outcome of the war.

Electronic Media and the Global Village

Americans had long been fascinated with the impact of technology on society. In the early 1800s, when Morse invented the telegraph, he told Congress that through electromagnetic telegraphy humankind would be able to create an artificial system to "diffuse, with the speed of thought, a knowledge of all that is occurring throughout the land; making, in fact, one neighborhood of the whole country."[31] In the 1960s, a Canadian literature professor, Marshall McLuhan, declared that the nerve system was no longer "merely a figurative byproduct of telegraphy but an actual expansion of the biological human being."[32] The medium—the mere form of it—was the message, McLuhan claimed:

> This is merely to say that the personal and social consequences of any medium—that is, of any extension of ourselves—result from the new scale that is introduced into our

affairs by each extension of ourselves, or by any new technology. . . . [It] is the medium that shapes and controls the scale and form of human association and action. The content or uses of such media are as diverse as they are ineffectual in shaping the form of human association. Indeed, it is only too typical that the "content" of any medium blinds us to the character of the medium.[33]

Although McLuhan has been attacked for being overly deterministic in terms of technology, his concept of the "global village"—the new scale of the world created by electronic media—has been an enduring concept. In the 1960s, while McLuhan was writing, television and telephone links established between the United States and Europe made possible the technology for live transmission between continents. No longer was isolation possible; the media had united the world—if not in ideology and values, at least in recognition of the interdependence of economies.

Scholars who followed McLuhan recognized the power of television, but they also noted that political and social decisions shaped television; the technology did not shape itself. Neil Postman, in *Amusing Ourselves to Death*, argued that the metaphors of the media explain and organize the world for us, "amusing America to its cultural death."[34] The results of technology, argued Postman, are not always positive.

Satellite Development and the Global Village

Western domination of satellite technology has created considerable controversy about the impact of Western ideology on developing nations. Consistent with his belief that the medium rather than content dictates the message, McLuhan suggested that electronic media in the postindustrial society could become new and "benign" agencies of a collective consciousness. Christopher Brookeman, criticizing McLuhan's corporate connections as well as his naïveté, wrote that McLuhan's ideas appealed to corporations and to the U.S. government alike:

> McLuhan's image of a global village joined by a single universal technology of electric circuitry chimed in with America's world role in reconstructing and maintaining the world economic and political system after the chaos of the Second World War. If McLuhan was right, the new systems of information technology could be the basis for a new world order. In the same way that the new criticism assimilated individual quirkiness, McLuhan's theories aimed to integrate the diversity and individuality of the world's cultures into cybernetic unity.[35]

At the end of his presidency, Dwight Eisenhower encouraged private enterprise to establish and operate satellite relays. His position that satellite development should be commercial rather than governmental was quickly adopted by President Kennedy. Just as the government had rejected control of the telegraph lines many years before, it now rejected ownership of space communications. Congress passed the Communications Satellite Act in August 1962 and, with it, adopted the assumptions that private ownership was necessary for speedy development and efficient operation and that satellites were essentially an adjunct of existing facilities. Although Congress recognized that the State Department and the FCC would need to be involved in the international negotiations needed for satellite communication, it maintained that these would best be handled by the "common carriers." Congress further assumed that capital outlay for a satellite system would be extensive and should be borne by private enterprise.[36]

In February 1963, the Communications Satellite Corporation, COMSAT, became a private U.S. corporation and offered shares to stockholders that summer. The FCC allocated half the shares to individual investors and half to communications carriers. At the end of the trading period, the industry giants, AT&T, IT&T, General Telephone and Electronics Corporation, and RCA Communications held 90 percent of the industry stock and 45.4 percent of the total issue.

The arrangement assured that government would be highly involved in, but not in control of, international satellite transmission. McGeorge Bundy, former chief aide to President Kennedy, testified before Congress in August 1966 that "Comsat was established for the purpose of taking and holding a position of leadership for the United States in the field of international global commercial satellite service."[37] In 1967, James McCormack, chairman and chief executive officer of COMSAT, defined his company "as a unique concept in corporate structure and purpose. It is a privately owned corporation, but it also serves as a representative of the United States Government."[38]

The organization needed customers. The consortium, INTELSAT, organized on August 20, 1964, was designed to fulfill this function. Nineteen countries signed on initially; by 1969, sixty-four countries were affiliated with the consortium. COMSAT held 61 percent of the ownership, which was distributed on the basis of contributions to the capital costs of the system. The United States holds a protected position; no matter how many members eventually join the system, the United States cannot drop below 50.6 percent of ownership.

Questions of Media Monopoly, Regulation, and Technology

One of the truisms about twentieth-century American media history is that technology often surpasses the ability of government to regulate it effectively. The history of radio's introduction to the United States is a case in point. Similarly, the resistance to cable television in the 1960s and 1970s by a broadcast industry–dominated Federal Communications Commission suggested, once again, that technological advances and congressional/FCC planning with the public welfare in mind had little connection with each other.

When the broadcast industry emerged as a commercial enterprise during the 1920s and 1930s, efforts were made to regulate the industry in the "public interest." Despite the rulings regarding equal time and fairness made by the FCC between the 1934 passage of the Federal Communications Act and the 1960s, consumers and legislators have questioned whether the commission operated in the public interest or whether it operated in the interests of the industry alone. Moreover, since 1934, increased attention has been paid to the large corporate structure of broadcasting, the involvement of parent companies in defense contracts as well as communications issues, and the seeming ineffectiveness of the regulatory agency.

When President Dwight D. Eisenhower left office in January 1961, he warned Americans of a growing military-industrial complex and urged the nation to avoid letting "the weight of this combination endanger our liberties or democratic processes." He emphasized the importance of an alert and knowledgeable citizenry to preserve security and liberty.[39]

Although Eisenhower did not specifically address the role of the media in creating an "alert and knowledgeable citizenry," various media critics have questioned the effects on media content and style of media companies' involvement in the military-industrial complex. Sociologist Herbert Schiller argued that a "monopolized informational apparatus" appeared after World War II that is "inseparably connected to the military establishment." In such an arrangement, Schiller contended, "the objectivity and reliability" of communications content comes "increasingly into doubt."[40]

Schiller noted that top executives of the networks often are connected to the power structure in ways that inhibit full and complete coverage of societal issues. For example, Frank Stanton, 1960s president of CBS, served as chairman of the U.S. Advisory Commission on Information, a four-person panel that assesses the role of the USIA and makes recommendations for its future. Until early 1967, Stanton also was chairman of the board of the Rand Corporation, a nonprofit California research organization funded almost entirely by U.S. Air Force contracts. Stanton also chaired the Executive Committee of Radio Free Europe, which in 1967 was uncovered as a conduit for the Central Intelligence Agency.[41]

RCA, the parent company of NBC, ranked twenty-fourth among Defense Department contractors in 1965 and during that year obtained $214 million in military contracts. A year later, as the Vietnam War grew more intense, the value of RCA's military contracts rose to $242.4 million. General Electric, with numerous interests in media companies, earned $824.3 million in 1964 and $1.187 billion in 1965.[42]

The question that emerged in the 1960s was whether network ownership by defense-contracting parent companies and the interlocking responsibilities of network executives altered either the approach or the content of coverage of such issues as civil rights and the Vietnam War. Although legends abound to suggest at least occasional interference with specific stories, more concern has been directed at those stories that did *not* get covered.

Stanton had been a friend of President Johnson since 1938, when Johnson acquired CBS affiliate status for his wife's Austin radio station. During the 1960s, Johnson was regularly infuriated with CBS coverage of Vietnam and relayed his dismay through Stanton to top CBS executives. In August 1965, CBS correspondent Morley Safer filed tape and film of the burning of a Vietnamese village, Cam Ne. CBS executives could not fail to use the film, David Halberstam wrote, because it was "awesome, the full force of television, the ability to dramatize, now fastening on one incident, one day in the war, that was going to be shattering to an entire generation of Americans."[43]

The next morning President Johnson got Stanton out of bed with a telephoned attack: "Frank, this is your President, and yesterday your boys shat on the American flag." Halberstam claimed that CBS made extra efforts during the next two weeks to include positive information on Vietnam in its reports to balance the Safer story and that Stanton would have fired Safer if other executives had not protected him.[44]

Minow and Television as a "Vast Wasteland"

At the beginning of the 1960s, consumer activists challenged the FCC to enforce the Fairness Doctrine and to secure changes in programming. Under the chairmanship of Newton Minow, best known for labeling television programming a "vast waste-land" before the National Association of Broadcasters shortly after his FCC appointment in 1961, the Federal Communications Commission attempted to address complaints about programming, but its efforts met with little success. Despite wide public acclaim for Minow's speech, he faced challenges from conservative commissioners, from Congress, and from the industry. Minow argued specifically for longer news-casts and for improved children's programming. However, whenever Minow commented positively or negatively about programming, congressmen and industry spokesmen accused him of imposing censorship or of decrying public taste. Frank Stanton of CBS responded that broadcasting truly represented a "cultural democracy" and claimed that ratings indicated what viewers preferred. Minow argued for the rights of minorities and for those who did not agree with the ratings, noting that perhaps audiences responded to the stimuli offered, not to alternatives that were not presented.

In 1962, Minow attempted to increase competition and the multiplicity of channels through all-channel legislation that would force the industry to sell sets that received both UHF and VHF channels, thereby ending the preferred position of VHF channels. The industry backed the bill as the least of evils—a way to keep regulation off its backs. Minow continued to argue for increased local, live public affairs programming, as well as for elite cultural offerings, in the face of an industry in which affiliates ran network programming for 95 percent of evening prime-time programming.

Minow, who often stood alone without the support of other commissioners or the public at large, created more controversy than change during the decade. During

What about Television?

Television is more than just another great public resource—like air and water—ruined by private greed and public inattention. It is the greatest communications mechanism ever designed and operated by man. It pumps into the human brain an unending stream of information, opinion, moral values, and aesthetic taste. It cannot be a neutral influence.

—Nicholas Johnson, former federal communications commissioner

his term as chairman, the FCC initiated revocation proceedings against twenty-three stations. Fourteen lost their licenses, but most of those were small radio stations accused of technical violations or of blatantly antisocial programming. When Minow attempted public hearings, those attending often either represented narrow self-interests or defended local stations against federal bureaucrats like himself.[45]

Further, both Kennedy and Johnson attempted to use the Fairness Doctrine to silence the religious right and spokesmen against the Nuclear Test Ban Treaty.[46] Minow resigned in 1963, and Congress halted further attempts by the FCC to turn the National Association of Broadcasters code into official regulation. From 1964 to 1966, the FCC abandoned all attempts to encourage news and public affairs or local programming.

Cable antenna television posed another challenge to network broadcasting and to the FCC. Throughout the 1960s, the FCC heavily restricted the growth of cable antenna television for fear it would destroy the "local" television provided by UHF channels. The industry feared cable would splinter the audience to such a degree that profits would be seriously endangered. The new UHF stations, however, did not provide more diversified programming than the networks; instead the stations kept costs to a minimum by using reruns and network syndications.

Despite broadcasters' continued complaints and efforts to overturn the Fairness Doctrine, the code's constitutionality was upheld by the Supreme Court in 1969. In this case, known as *Red Lion*, radio preacher Billy James Hargis attacked author Fred J. Cook for the views he expressed in the book *Barry Goldwater: Extremist on the Right.* Cook asked for free time to respond over the Red Lion, Pennsylvania, station owned by the Red Lion Broadcasting Company. The broadcaster refused to give Cook time, and Cook complained to the FCC. The FCC, in turn, told the broadcaster to provide Cook with time. Meanwhile, the Radio-Television News Directors Association (RTNDA), along with CBS and NBC, were challenging the complicated and burdensome rules having to do with broadcasters' responsibilities for notifying people who had been personally attacked or people or organizations who had been the subjects of unfavorable editorial comment.

The Supreme Court held that the FCC's creation of the Fairness Doctrine was a constitutional exercise of the regulatory agency's power. It pointed to Congress's 1959 amendment to Section 315 of the Communications Act of 1934, saying that stations were expected to operate in the public interest and to "afford reasonable opportunity for the discussion of conflicting views on issues of public importance." The court held that because of the scarcity of the airwaves, it was "the right of the viewers and listeners, not the right of the broadcasters, which is paramount."[47]

Public Broadcasting as an Alternative

The 1960s reopened the 1930s debate over nonprofit broadcasting. During the 1950s, Frieda Hennock, the first woman member of the FCC, made a heroic and strenuous fight during her term from 1948 to 1951 to convince the commission to set aside television channels for educational use. She made such arguments in the face of dire predictions that the government would use educational programming as conduits for propaganda. Finally, in 1967, after recommendations from the Carnegie Commission—a prestigious study group—President Lyndon B. Johnson advocated and Congress passed legislation creating the Corporation for Public Broadcasting (CPB). This legislation made available several hundred million dollars to support local educational stations and to link together public television stations. In 1969–1970, CPB joined with public broadcast stations to form the Public Broadcast Service (PBS) and National Public Radio (NPR), organizations to distribute television and radio programs to noncommercial educational stations.

At the time the Corporation for Public Broadcasting was created by Congress in 1967, special language was inserted into the Communications Act of 1934 to insulate public broadcast stations from bureaucratic meddling by the FCC. Conservative critics had long wanted to rein in or do away with public broadcasting, that—under the CPB Act of 1967—is charged with providing balanced and objective fare over the public stations. In 1975, a federal court upheld public stations' freedom from FCC content regulation, although public stations still are licensed by the commission. Ironically, this shielding from some FCC oversight has tended to make public broadcasting a political football, with conservative efforts periodically undertaken to get Congress to curtail the federal funding of public stations.[48]

Figure 16–4 WKYS Radio. (*U.S. News and World Report* photo, Division of Prints and Photographs, Library of Congress Collection)

To date, such efforts to hamstring public broadcasting have been defeated in Congress. Furthermore, the Supreme Court has upheld the freedom of public broadcasting stations to editorialize[49] and has given public stations the same editorial freedom enjoyed by commercial broadcasters.[50] One quip has it that commercial television is where people mate and animals talk; public TV is the other way around.

By the late 1980s, two of the most respected television reporters headed an hourlong, noncommercial news broadcast. Robert MacNeil and Jim Lehrer's "MacNeil-Lehrer News Hour" performance lacked the star quality of news anchors Dan Rather (CBS), Tom Brokaw (NBC), or Peter Jennings (ABC), but the "News Hour" helped garner a strong following from those who liked more news. The show's format was shaped around fewer stories, with more "talking heads" and in-depth treatment than were allowed in the major networks' thirty-minute formats. This depth helped PBS to fulfill some of the high hopes for educational TV that had been expressed throughout broadcast history, especially during the 1950s days of TV-channel allocation.

Newspaper Consolidation and Profits

Corporate structure certainly was not unique to broadcasting, and the trend toward conglomerate ownership of diverse media properties continued throughout the decade. Newspapers continued to be consolidated through group or chain ownership. By the beginning of the 1970s, groups or chains accounted for one-half the nation's dailies and two-thirds of its circulation. In the 1950s, the Samuel I. Newhouse group, based in New York, New Jersey, and Pennsylvania, acquired papers in Oregon, Missouri, Alabama, Louisiana, and Ohio. John S. Knight's group in Ohio, Michigan, and Illinois expanded to include newspapers in North Carolina, Georgia, and Pennsylvania. Knight's acquisitions included the prestigious *Philadelphia Inquirer.* The Tribune group, which originally consisted of the *Chicago Tribune* and the *New York Daily News,* took over the top circulation position in the 1960s. The older and influential Hearst Group had begun cutbacks in the 1930s and continued to divest through the 1960s, merging the International News Service with United Press in 1958 to form United Press International and giving up the Sunday supplement, *American Weekly,* in 1963.[51] The Scripps-Howard chain remained stable throughout the period. At the beginning of the 1970s, the Tribune Company, Newhouse, Knight, Scripps-Howard, and Hearst led in circulation, while the Thomson and Gannett groups led in the numbers of dailies.

Although newspapers experienced a steady growth in advertising revenues and circulation during the 1960s, they also faced increasing costs. Circulation had increased from 52 million in the late 1940s to 62 million in the late 1960s. Despite television's inroads into national advertising revenues, ad dollars still had increased from $260 million in the 1940s to over $1 billion in the late 1960s. Total newspaper advertising revenues in 1968 were $5.2 billion, compared to $3.1 billion for television. Although some large metropolitan newspapers suffered, in 1966 medium-sized city newspapers averaged a net profit of 23 percent before taxes.

Another factor affecting cost was a series of strikes that caused extensive shutdowns. The nation's longest strike in late 1967 and early 1968 closed the *Detroit News* and the *Detroit Free Press* for 267 days.[52]

Technology and Resistance

Strikes often occurred over disputes about automation and the role of skilled labor as new technology was introduced to the industry. Three major developments in the 1950s and 1960s revolutionized the printing industry. Teletypesetters, available in the early 1950s, produced punched tape that would activate a Linotype or other type-setting machine. Wire services sent tape with their copy, thereby eliminating the need to typeset wire copy. The improved technology also increased the level of standardization because newspapers could print wire copy without having to hire someone to set it. Computers had been used to produce text as early as 1963, although they were not used widely in newsrooms until the late 1970s. No longer did a reporter have to type a story and have a typesetter retype it into a machine. Further, expanded and improved offset printing that used photographic plates rather than stereotypes provided cheaper printing, especially for smaller papers. Computers affected not only the editorial function but automated mail rooms and accounting systems as well. Facsimile transmission allowed wire services to send pictures and newspapers to auxiliary printing plants.

Figure 16–5 These interior views of a hot-type printing plant were taken in 1957. In the 1960s, many newspapers moved to various forms of cold type. (*U.S. News and World Report* photo, Division of Prints and Photographs, Library of Congress Collection)

Newspaper Preservation Act

The pattern of newspaper consolidation had been evident for many years. Long before Gannett, Knight-Ridder, and other groups had accumulated their many newspaper holdings, some competing publishers hit upon a way to keep two separate newspaper voices alive in a single city. The trends were evident by the 1960s, with big newspaper fish swallowing smaller fish. Inheritance laws made it difficult for many an independent paper to be passed on within a family. Later, certainly by the 1980s, it was apparent that in virtually all communities it was going to be difficult to keep afternoon dailies financially healthy. Advertisers' desires to avoid the duplication of readers resulted in the shutting down of afternoon newspapers, even in cities in which a single owner published the sole morning and afternoon newspapers.[53]

As a result, a group of newspaper owners—with forty-four papers in twenty-two cities—successfully lobbied Congress in 1968 to legalize a limited number of exceptions to the federal antitrust laws. These exceptions allowed joint operating agreements (JOAs) between locally competing newspapers. JOAs permitted two newspapers in one city to merge their printing, circulation, advertising, and business operations while publishing two independent papers with separate identities.

In 1968, the Supreme Court of the United States declared joint operating agreements to be illegal.[54] Congress then passed—and President Richard M. Nixon signed into law—the Newspaper Preservation Act, which in effect overruled the Supreme Court. The adoption of the Newspaper Preservation Act symbolized the end of meaningful efforts on the part of the federal government to regulate newspaper consolidation and legalized the existing agreements.

The act permitted joint operating agreements only if one of the competing newspapers was in financial distress. Passage of the act was triggered by a 1969 decision by the Supreme Court of the United States in what was known as the *Tucson* case. The Supreme Court held that under U.S. antitrust laws, the only legal justification for two companies' combining operations would be proof that one of the companies was failing financially at the time of the combination. Because the Court believed neither one of the Tucson papers was failing, the papers' JOA, or joint operating agreement, violated antitrust laws.

This decision frightened a number of powerful newspaper interests and set off a remarkable scramble in Congress. Within days, legislators from each state with JOA newspapers had submitted bills to create an antitrust exemption for such operations. Despite loud objections from the Antitrust Division of the U.S. Department of Justice, the Failing Newspaper Act—soon to be renamed, more positively, the Newspaper Preservation Act—sailed through Congress with minimal opposition and was signed into law by President Nixon. The theory behind the act was that twentieth-century economics often dictate that no more than one newspaper company can survive in any community, even in a large city, and that allowing JOAs will keep more voices in the marketplace of ideas. Under the JOA concept, the news operations of two newspapers remain separate and "competitive," while the business-printing-circulation departments join together to provide efficiency and reduce costs.

A 1987 study indicated that newspapers produced under JOAs were more similar to competitive newspapers than they were to monopoly newspapers. The study further revealed that in at least four of the twenty-two markets studied, readers had a choice between different op-ed and editorial pages and occasionally between two slightly different news sections.[55]

A large JOA creation raised eyebrows in 1988, however, as Knight-Ridder's *Detroit News* (circulation about 500,000) decided to cohabit with a Gannett-owned newspaper. Creation of this JOA was chancy for a number of reasons. First, it involved the nation's two largest newspaper-ownership groups. Second, under the Newspaper Preservation Act, the attorney general of the United States was required to approve all new JOAs. The attorney general at that time, the nation's chief law enforcement figure, was the controversial Edwin Meese, who resigned from office under a cloud of conflict-of-interest charges.[56] Just before he left office in August 1988, he overruled his own Justice Department lawyers and approved the Detroit JOA linking Gannett and Knight-Ridder in Detroit. That JOA later was upheld by the federal courts.[57] However, it is unlikely that many more JOAs will be created. By the time the Newspaper Preservation Act went into effect in 1970, there were relatively few cities left with independently owned daily newspapers. In 1991, only two dozen cities continued to have joint operating agreements.

Cultural Change in the Newsrooms

During the 1960s and early 1970s, cultural change permeated media institutions just as it permeated other aspects of society. A new generation of publishers assumed control of some of the nation's most prominent newspapers, and reporters challenged the authoritarian structures that held sway in newsrooms. The resulting changes were broad-sweeping, reflected in increasing skepticism of government and experimentation in reporting styles and language.

James Boylan, in an analysis of the changes in the press from 1960 to 1986, attributed some of the changes in journalism to a generational change in the control of major newspapers. In 1960, Otis Chandler took over what Boylan described as "the disreputable old *Los Angeles Times* and began to overhaul it." Arthur Ochs Sulzberger became publisher at the *New York Times* and appointed A. M. Rosenthal as metropolitan editor; Rosenthal subsequently became managing editor. In 1965, Benjamin Bradlee became editor of the *Washington Post.* These individuals shifted to more emphasis on reporting and less on editing.

Changes in the Rank and File

The generational change occurred not only at the top but at the bottom as well. Just as people who were critical of institutional society in the 1960s questioned authority, reporters also rebelled at taking orders from deskmen, whom they considered to be unexciting enforcers of old technical standards. Further, reporters also challenged the authority of those outside the newsroom, public officials in particular. "Being a pro," wrote Boylan, "came to mean more than being a good soldier; it meant allegiance to standards considered superior to those of the organization and its parochial limitations."[58]

The change came early in the decade. In 1962, William Rivers, in a study of Washington correspondents, found that reporters felt considerably less pressure from their home offices to write stories in certain ways and that they experienced greater freedom than had been found in a 1937 study.[59] By 1970, John Johnstone and a group of researchers found that autonomy was highly related to job satisfaction, particularly for younger, participant-oriented journalists. Johnstone also found that older, managerial newsmen tended to be more oriented toward neutral, or objective, journalism than did younger reporters.[60]

Government and the Press

A style of investigative journalism that developed during the civil rights activities of the 1960s and was supported by the Supreme Court in the *New York Times v. Sullivan* case fostered the coverage of Vietnam and culminated in the early 1970s with the publication of the Pentagon Papers, a historical record of the war based on secret governmental documents, and with the coverage of the Watergate affair. As government moved beyond the cooperation mode editors supported throughout World War II and the 1950s and moved into a stage of what editors perceived to be government-imposed, rather than editor-imposed, news management, the press rebelled.[61] Newspaper editors during the 1950s had regarded themselves as members of an American team: They refused an invitation from the Chinese government to send correspondents to China because, as Clifton Daniel wrote, "We did not want to embarrass our government." Editors had withheld information about aerial spying over the Soviet Union before Gary Powers was captured in 1960 in the U-2 incident; in 1961, a *Miami Herald* story about the training of Cuban exile forces in Florida never appeared; and the *New York Times,* the *Miami Herald,* the *New Republic,* and the *Washington Post* all either withheld information completely or altered bits and pieces of the story about the 1961 CIA-sponsored Bay of Pigs invasion of Cuba.

Although editors may have regarded cooperating with the government to suppress information as a civic duty, government excluding the press from the knowledge of power was another issue. Sociologist Michael Schudson traced the outrage of the press at news management to a statement by Arthur Sylvester, spokesman for the Pentagon under Presidents Kennedy and Johnson, who defended news management during the 1962 Cuban missile crisis. Sylvester claimed the government had an inherent right to lie if it meant saving itself when faced with a nuclear disaster.[62] Schudson maintained that Sylvester's statement threatened the role of the press as the "fourth branch of government" by crossing "a thin moral line the press felt an obligation to patrol." The press objected not only to the government lying, but also to its claim that the government had a right to lie:

There was at least this virtue to hypocrisy when the government lied while claiming to be truthful: that if the press discovered the lie, it could embarrass the government. The Sylvester statement placed the government beyond embarrassment.[63]

Further, editors and reporters alike may have objected to Kennedy's handling of the press. Historian and journalist Mark Perry suggested that Kennedy's biographers claimed the President "dazzled" the press, knew how to "handle" them, and enjoyed "bantering" with them. But in actuality Kennedy and his advisers regarded journalists as simpletons to be manipulated.[64]

At any rate, journalists began to take seriously the concept of the profession as a fourth branch of government. The emergence of the press role grew out of cultural changes in the newsrooms in the 1960s but was legitimized by a civil rights court case that assured the right of the press to criticize public officials. In 1971 a second court case underlined the principle that, even in times of protest, prior censorship could not be established.

New York Times v. Sullivan

In 1964, the Supreme Court, hearing a case on appeal by the *New York Times*, extended a decision that Kansas courts had made in 1908 by which public officials carried a heavier burden than did private individuals in libel judgments.[65] The *New York Times v. Sullivan* case assured the news media that random errors in reporting the activities of public officials would not result in large libel judgments. The case was critically important because it allowed the media to report on controversial subjects, such as civil rights demonstrations, on deadline, without fear of heavy recrimination.

The case arose from a *New York Times* advertisement titled "Heed Their Rising Voices," which appeared in March 1960, shortly after whites had used violence at Alabama State College in Montgomery against black demonstrators who were protesting the segregation of public facilities. Sixty-four persons, white and black, signed the advertisement, which appealed for financial support for the Alabama State College students. The ad read, in part:

> In Montgomery, Ala., after students sang "My Country, 'tis of Thee" on the State Capitol steps, their leaders were expelled from school, and truckloads of police armed with shotguns and tear gas ringed the Alabama State College campus. When the entire student body protested to state authorities by refusing to register, their dining hall was padlocked in an attempt to starve them into submission. . . .
>
> Again and again, the Southern violators have answered Dr. [Martin Luther] King's peaceful protests with intimidation and violence. They have bombed his home almost killing his wife and child. They have assaulted his person. They have arrested him seven times—for "speeding," "loitering," and similar "offenses." And now they have charged him with "perjury"—a felony under which they could imprison him for *10 years*.[66]

Police Commissioner L. B. Sullivan, one of three elected commissioners of Montgomery, Alabama, filed suit in a Montgomery court, charging that he was libeled by the ad's general references to the police and that he was accused of padlocking the hall and of intimidating Dr. King and his family. Witnesses testified that much of the material in the ad was in error. For example, students sang "The Star-Spangled Banner," not "My Country, 'tis of Thee." The *Times* advertising acceptability manager testified that he had no reason to believe the ad was false because it was prepared by a reputable agency and signed by persons with good reputations. The Alabama court awarded Sullivan $500,000.

Implications of the lawsuit went beyond the $500,000 penalty for the *New York Times*. Libel suits were being used by southern states to attempt to control news coverage of civil rights demonstrations. For example, the *Times* was facing eleven other libel suits in Alabama courts that totaled more than $5 million. CBS was defending five libel suits in southern states with a total of almost $2 million at stake. These were big dollar amounts in 1964, a time when one could buy an up-scale, luxury-model automobile for about $5,000.

The *Sullivan* case reached the Supreme Court first, and the Court's decision represented a crucial turning point, a reaffirmation of the First Amendment. Even on the surface, the *Sullivan* decision was a great event, because it made difficult the use of defamation lawsuits by public officials as a weapon to punish the press, thus curtailing attempts to sue critics until they shut up or folded up. In writing for the Court's majority, Justice William J. Brennan, Jr., saw that this litigation was not merely a libel suit in which an individual was seeking to protect his reputation. Important as reputation is, there was something far more crucial at stake: the right to be able to discuss and to criticize government and governmental officials.

The lawsuit strategy employed against the *New York Times* was the reprehensible repackaging of an old enemy of freedom, the crime of seditious libel, into a new wrapper—that of civil lawsuits for libel by government officials. Justice Brennan evidently agreed with the late First Amendment scholar Zechariah Chafee: It is not what you *call* the power that is important. Chafee once wrote that it is not the inscription on the sword that matters; it is the existence of the weapon.[67]

The Supreme Court turned aside arguments by lawyers of the plaintiff Sullivan that the *Times* was not entitled to First Amendment protection because the alleged libel appeared in an advertisement. Up to 1964, commercial advertising, the courts had said, was not entitled to First Amendment protection. However, the ruling in *New York Times v. Sullivan* was that editorial advertising—expressing social or political ideas—did have constitutional protection.

The Court's majority in *Sullivan* expressed a willingness to take the risk that freedom of expression entails. Free societies are not always orderly. Justice Brennan's opinion stressed the importance of protecting even erroneous statements in the discussion of public issues:

> Thus we consider this case against the background of a profound national commitment to the principle that debate on public issues should be uninhibited, robust, and wide-open, and that it may well include vehement, caustic, and sometimes unpleasantly sharp attacks on government and public officials. The present advertisement, as an expression of grievance and protest on one of the major public issues of our time, would seem clearly to qualify for the constitutional protection.

The Court then ruled that in order for public officials to recover damages for libel, they must prove that the statements were made with "actual malice"—that is, with "knowledge that it was false or with reckless disregard of whether it was false or not." The decision cleared the way for thorough reporting of civil rights issues and for subsequent investigatory articles on governmental officials, but it did not, as some newsmen and lawyers predicted, abolish the law of libel.

The Pentagon Papers Case

The *New York Times* became embroiled in the federal government's resistance to anti-war protesters on June 13, 1971, when America's foremost newspaper published a front-page story headlined "Vietnam Archive: Pentagon Study Traces Three Decades of Growing U.S. Involvement." That story was published after a Rand Corporation staffer, Daniel Ellsberg, "leaked" photocopies of forty-seven volumes of a security-classified report to *Times* reporter Neil Sheehan. That "Top Secret" study, titled *History of the United States Decision-Making Process on Vietnam Policy,* had been dissected for three months by *Times* staffers before the story about them was published.

The Nixon administration's reaction was swift and severe. Before two days had passed, Attorney General John Mitchell sent a telegram asking the *Times* to voluntarily stop publication of stories based on the top secret report, arguing that "irreparable injury to the defense interests of the United States" would occur if publication continued.[68] The *Times* did not yield to Attorney General Mitchell's request, and the Department of Justice then applied to U.S. District Judge Murray I. Gurfein for an injunction to halt publication. Judge Gurfein, blindsided by this national legal crisis on his very first day of service as a federal judge, issued a temporary injunction on June 15, 1971. Publication, at least by the *Times,* was halted, although a number of other newspapers—including the *Washington Post*—also published excerpts from the secret study.[69]

Put another way, the issue was that most hated and dangerous form of censorship: prior restraint. On June 16, *New York Times* columnist James Reston responded furiously, "For the first time in the history of the Republic, the Attorney General of the United States has tried to suppress documents he hasn't read about a war that hasn't been declared."[70]

The *Times* appealed the district court's order, and the Supreme Court of the United States, which customarily takes months and often years to render a decision, responded quickly after this hot potato of a controversy was passed on to it by the U.S. Court of Appeals for the District of Columbia Circuit. Only two weeks after the *Times* had published its article on June 13, the Supreme Court ruled by a vote of six to three to dissolve the injunctions forbidding the *Times* and the *Washington Post* from publishing. The Court declared

> Any system of prior restraints of expression comes to this Court bearing a heavy presumption against its constitutional validity. *Bantam Books v. Sullivan,* 372 U.S. 58, 83 S.Ct. 631 * * * (1963); see also *Near v. Minnesota ex rel. Olson,* 283 U.S. 697, 51 S.Ct. 525 * * * (1931).[71]

Never assume, however, that the war against prior restraint had been won. A six-member majority of the Supreme Court found in favor of the press in the Pentagon Papers decision. Three Justices voted in favor of prior restraint, even though the "danger" of publishing excerpts from those documents now seems to have been a matter of Vietnam hysteria, not substantive threat. As *Times* columnist Anthony Lewis wrote five years after the Pentagon Papers decision, "the Republic still stands." He added: "Today, hardly anyone can remember a single item of the papers that caused the fuss."[72]

The Pentagon Papers case reinforced journalists' concept of themselves as watchdogs of government, and Harrison Salisbury, referring to Justice Potter Stewart's Pentagon Papers opinion, declared that publishing the Papers meant that the *Times* had "quite literally become that Fourth Estate, that fourth co-equal branch of government."[73]

Watergate and the News Media

In the early 1970s, the *Washington Post* began to investigate a seemingly obscure burglary in the Watergate Hotel in Washington, D.C. That "third-rate" burglary of the national Democratic party headquarters on June 17, 1972, became the beginning of the unraveling of what William Safire called in 1987, an "abuse of the power of government in order to effect an election." Such abuse, wrote Safire, "was an impeachable offense and rightly resulted in the resignation of the President."[74]

Early in February 1972, President Richard Nixon's former law partner, campaign manager, and attorney general John Mitchell resigned from the cabinet to direct the Committee to Re-Elect the President, often referred to by the prophetic acronym CREEP. Former White House aides working with CREEP—G. Gordon Liddy and Howard Hunt—turned out to be macho operatives with a cloak-and-dagger approach to their work. This strategy led to the June 17, 1972, attempted burglary in the Democratic party headquarters in the Watergate complex, where five men were caught not only looking for political information but trying to plant electronic listening devices as well.

Two *Washington Post* reporters, young metropolitan desk staffers Carl Bernstein and Bob Woodward, soon connected one of the burglars, James McCord, to the Central Intelligence Agency.[75] Within days, President Nixon in news conferences denounced electronic eavesdropping as alien to the political process of the United States. As subsequent events showed, Nixon and his aides, H. R. Haldeman and John Ehrlichman, tried to cover up White House connections to the burglars from the outset. Although other newspapers downplayed the story, Woodward and Bernstein's perseverance paid off. They traced a $25,000 check deposited in a Florida bank to the account of one of the Watergate burglars, Bernard L. Barker. The check was written by the Republicans' Midwest finance head, Kenneth H. Dahlberg, and had been given to former secretary of the treasury Maurice Stans, the Republican campaign treasurer in 1972.

With the 1972 election approaching, necessary details of the Watergate story eluded verification no matter how hard the two young reporters—jointly nicknamed

On Watergate

So while Watergate vexes us now as the troubles of the 1860s and 1870s vexed our fore-fathers, there is little reason to despair. Life is trouble, for both men and nations, but this nation retains deep and abiding strength. The present troubles too will pass away, and the American experiment with freedom will endure.

—Robert L. Bartley, *Wall Street Journal*

"Woodstein" by Ben Bradlee—tried to pin it down. While Nixon claimed the White House was cooperating with the FBI and Department of Justice investigators, the *Post* pushed on and on October 10, 1972, broke a major story—that the Watergate burglary was not an isolated incident but was part of a massive Republican campaign of political "dirty tricks," sabotage, and spying.

It was then that Woodward and Bernstein went to press without sufficient verification. Interviewing a likable White House aide, Hugh Sloan, they took his non-committal non-answers to mean that he had told a grand jury that H. R. Haldeman was one of the paymasters who handed out cash in exchange for spying. Sloan denied that he had given the grand jury such information, and the Republican establishment labeled "Woodstein" and the *Washington Post* irresponsible. Some leading Democrats joined the chorus. Sloan later admitted he had not told the grand jury that Haldeman paid for political spying on the Democrats, but only because the jury did not ask him the direct question that would have elicited that specific testimony.

Meanwhile, the burglars obstinately maintained their silence about what they were doing in the Watergate on that June night. The silence continued for more than six months, well past the November 1972 reelection of President Nixon and his vice president, Spiro Agnew. Meanwhile, President Nixon's popularity soared. Shortly after the Paris agreement to initiate a cease-fire in Vietnam was signed on January 27, 1973, a Gallup poll found that 68 percent of the public favored the President.

In March 1973, a major break came in the Watergate story. One of the convicted burglars, James W. McCord, admitted to U.S. district judge John Sirica that he had been pressured to remain silent. McCord was pointing toward the White House when he suggested that persons higher up the political chain were involved.

Disastrous admissions, one after another, then followed. FBI director Patrick Gray resigned late in April, conceding that he had destroyed evidence related to Watergate. White House aides G. Gordon Liddy and Howard Hunt admitted they had broken into a psychiatrist's office to try to obtain the records of former Rand Corporation employee Daniel Ellsberg. Ellsberg was accused, along with J. Anthony Russo, of having stolen and leaked a massive, forty-seven-volume set of classified historical materials dealing with years of U.S. involvement in Vietnam. The materials were classified "Top Secret." Portions of the Pentagon Papers were published by the *New York Times*, the *Washington Post*, and the *St. Louis Post-Dispatch*. Charges against Ellsberg and

Russo were dismissed by a U.S. district judge after word reached him that White House aides Liddy and Hunt had invaded the doctor's office.

Meanwhile, President Nixon announced the resignations of chief aides John Ehrlichman, H. R. Haldeman, and John Dean as well as Attorney General Richard Kleindienst. Nixon told the nation he took responsibility for the actions of his aides, but he denied any knowledge of a cover-up regarding the Watergate incident. Eventually, however, Dean revealed that Nixon was indeed a part of the operation and of the cover-up.

The Nixon Tapes

When Richard Nixon became President, he denounced President Lyndon B. Johnson's procedure of taping many, if not most, of the conversations involving the office of President. As journalist-historian Theodore White observed, "Ego is the disease of great leaders; some leave pyramids, some leave tapes."[76] In fact, Nixon had the Army Signal Corps tear out Johnson's tape machines, and none reappeared until 1971. After Haldeman told Nixon about the insistence of archivists and librarians that tape machines be installed, the President changed his mind and allowed taping to resume. Machines—some with on–off switches and some voice-activated—were installed on White House phones, including those most often used by the President. "Thus the tapes ran," wrote Theodore White, "sporadically stopping and starting, spinning and halting as they wove the web that was ultimately to trap Richard Nixon."[77]

In June 1973, a reluctant witness named Alexander Butterfield appeared before investigators of the U.S. Senate committee investigating Watergate. He grudgingly revealed what he said was "probably the one thing the President wouldn't want revealed"—that the President's conversations had been taped.[78]

Shortly thereafter, Bob Woodward got a tip from his shadowy secret source, the now-legendary "Deep Throat," that there were some suspicious gaps on the tapes. A *Washington Post* story—citing an anonymous source—relayed that assertion to the public. Sure enough, there turned out to be an eighteen-minute gap in one of the tapes, indicating that tampering had occurred.

From then on, the Senate Watergate Committee attracted national attention. Particularly chilling was the series of accusations against President Nixon calmly delivered by John W. Dean, III, former presidential counsel. He accused the President of complicity in Watergate cover-up efforts. The Nixon administration absorbed another damaging blow in the fall of 1973 when Vice President Spiro Agnew resigned from office, charged with tax evasion for accepting illegal payments from contractors while he was Maryland's governor. Nixon replaced Agnew with Representative Gerald R. Ford, the House minority leader.

Other self-inflicted wounds hit the Nixon administration. President Nixon, squirming under the evidence gathering of Special Prosecutor Archibald Cox, a Harvard law professor, demanded that Attorney General Elliot Richardson fire Cox. Richardson and his top assistant, William D. Ruckelshaus, resigned instead of obeying Nixon's order. Solicitor General Robert Bork stepped forward, in what became known as the "Saturday night massacre," and fired Archibald Cox. Bork went on to become a federal appeals judge who in 1987 was nominated for a post on the

Supreme Court by President Reagan. Bork's conservative writings—and memories of his role in Watergate—were among the factors leading to the Senate's refusal to confirm him. Three days after Cox was fired, the House Judiciary Committee—with a majority incensed by the firing of Cox—decided to begin considering impeachment charges against President Nixon. The President, meanwhile, reversed his strategy. Back in July 1973, Nixon had refused to obey a subpoena from the Senate Watergate Committee to hand over the secret tape recordings from the Oval Office. By late October 1973, however, perhaps in response to growing political pressure, Nixon agreed to release the tapes. He later reneged, giving the congressional committee only edited transcripts of the tapes, although the transcripts added up to more than 1,200 pages.

On August 8, 1974, President Richard Nixon at long last announced his resignation on nationwide television, and Gerald Ford assumed the presidency.

The Significance of Watergate

Contrary to popular myth—and to the claims of some journalists—the press, including the *Washington Post*, did not topple President Richard Nixon. As journalist David Schoenbrun wrote, Nixon was doomed neither by his enemies nor by the media. Nixon's ruin was the result of a long record of misdeeds and of violations of the law, as well as his lies and cover-ups. On one level, then, the Watergate debacle can be understood as a breach of faith, as an effort to subvert the electoral and judicial processes of the nation, rather than as a journalistic coup.

Credibility and Ethics

Despite the press's role in Watergate, or perhaps because of it, the public granted less credibility to the press in the early 1970s than it had in previous years. Outside critics charged that journalists "were out of control and out of line with dominant social values; they had come to constitute a separate and subversive class."[79] News organizations responded to the external critique by creating codes of ethics and devices for monitoring the media. The Society of Professional Journalists in 1973 adopted an ethics code, the American Society of Newspaper Editors adopted a revised "statement of principles" in 1975, and the Associated Press Managing Editors acted in a similar vein in 1975.[80] In addition, the National News Council and the use of ombudsmen appeared as attempts to assure fairness in media coverage. Nevertheless, codes and other efforts to assure fairness did not solve the ethics controversy, which came to an embarrassing confrontation in 1981 when Janet Cooke of the *Washington Post* won a Pulitzer Prize for what later was revealed to be a fabricated story about an eight-year-old African-American heroin addict. The *Post* returned the prize when the discovery was made.

Some editors viewed the creation of a National News Council and ethics codes along with the establishment of ombudsmen within larger papers as a long overdue effort by the industry to assume responsibility for its vast power and control over public information. Others, however, rejected the council and other devices as merely efforts to appease government, which would open the door to governmental control.[81] Whatever the motive, the result was that the press seemed as unwilling to criticize itself as it had when the Hutchins commission had released its 1947 report.

National News Council

News councils in the United States have been modeled after the British Press Council, organized in 1964, which required that an individual asking the council to investigate a complaint must also agree not to bring civil action against the newspaper involved in the complaint. In Britain, the council activity corresponded with a drop in libel cases.

The National News Council, begun in the United States by foundation money in 1973, lost its financing in 1984. The National News Council initially had the support of the *Washington Post*, the *Wall Street Journal*, the *Christian Science Monitor*, CBS, the Associated Press, and United Press International. Lined up against the national council was the *New York Times*. Publisher Arthur Ochs Sulzberger announced the *Times'* decision not to participate in the council in a memo to his staff: "We will not be a party to Council investigations. We will not furnish information or explanations to the Council. In our coverage, we will treat the Council as we treat any other organization: we will report their activities when they are newsworthy."[82]

Critics have argued that the failure of this national press council was partly the result of its timidity and early insistence that it limit its cases to "principal national suppliers of news," as well as its reluctance to initiate any investigations on its own.

Ombudsmen

During the 1960s, several U.S. newspapers experimented with the concept of employing an ombudsman. (*Ombudsman* is a Swedish term denoting a government official appointed to receive or investigate complaints.) In the American newsroom, the ombudsman is employed and paid by the employer, not by the government. By 1985, about thirty-five ombudsmen were at work nationwide, responding to criticism from readers and formalizing internal standards and procedures. Many also were writing columns related to their work. Newspapers have experimented with a variety of organizational patterns, sometimes rotating a staff member into the slot and at other times hiring a person from the outside for a limited term. The latter approach has the advantage of reducing staff pressure on the ombudsmen and granting them more independence in their work.

Codes of Ethics

In addition to the adoption of codes of ethics by major journalistic organizations, individual news organizations in the 1970s established codes to limit the involvement of reporters in activities that might embarrass their organizations. CBS, for example, adopted a code of standards for covering demonstrations and other civil disturbances

ASNE Statement of Principles

The First Amendment, protecting freedom of expression from abridgment by any law, guarantees to the people through their press a constitutional right, and thereby places on newspaper people a particular responsibility.

Thus journalism demands of its practitioners not only industry and knowledge but also the pursuit of a standard of integrity proportionate to the journalist's singular obligation.

—Preamble

that encouraged the reporter to relay information factually and without participation.[83] Newspaper codes limited the amount of political involvement management considered appropriate and asked reporters to avoid financial investments that might jeopardize their objectivity.[84]

Language of 1960s Journalism

As young reporters demanded new levels of autonomy in the newsroom and reacted to events of the 1960s, some abandoned the objective, straightforward approach of "Who? What? When? Where? and Why?" The demands of interpretation and the political and cultural context of the decade demanded new techniques, new language, and the incorporation of styles that had distinguished alternative media for many years. The dominant types of new language can be characterized as (1) new nonfiction, (2) alternative/advocacy, and (3) precision.

New Nonfiction

Although the new nonfiction focused on technique, it also raised questions about objective fact. The practitioners of new nonfiction wrote about social trends, celebrities, "little people," and public events. They used fictional techniques to make their articles and books sound like short stories and novels and published their work primarily in magazines. Truman Capote, a fiction writer of some note, catapulted himself into the new nonfiction journalistic world with *In Cold Blood,* an account of a 1959 murder of a western Kansas farm family and the subsequent pursuit, trial, and execution of the murderers five years later. The account stirred considerable controversy and earned Capote $2 million.[85] A good deal of the controversy revolved around the question of accuracy. Capote claimed to have taken no notes during his interviews but said he was able to recall what people said in minute detail. Many reporters, as well as many of the western Kansas people interviewed, questioned his claim. *Commonweal* magazine deplored the "voyeurism" of the book; the *Atlantic Monthly* said that although the publisher of *In Cold Blood* claimed it represented a "serious new literary form," it was, in reality a "high-minded aesthetic excuse for reading about a mean, sordid crime."[86] But others praised the nonfiction work. Tom Greene, writing in *America* (January 22, 1966), praised Capote for capturing in 350 pages "a complete and meaningful human document."

Alternative, advocacy, and underground journalism became names for the issue-oriented discussions alternative media had provided for years.

Alternative and Advocacy Journalism

Alternative journalism might be traced as far back as Ben Franklin's older brother, James Franklin. The elder Franklin in 1721 started the *New England Courant* at least partially as a reaction to the government-dominated views of the postmaster papers of Campbell and Brooker, which were published "by authority." Some of the radical publications of the 1930s and 1940s, including Dorothy Day's *Catholic Worker* and Dwight MacDonald's *Politics* could correctly be labeled alternative publications. Reminiscent of the nineteenth-century reform press, alternative publications during the 1960s provided information not disseminated by mainstream newspapers. Unlike advocacy newspapers, which espoused a cause or a distinct opinion, alternative press stories included a ruthless check for accuracy after intensive investigation. Examples of the best of the alternative papers included the *San Francisco Bay Guardian*, the *Rocky Mountain Journal*, and the *Village Voice*. Alternative editors did not strongly identify with the counterculture movement, but instead they were often middle-aged New Dealers or progressives.

Journalism Reviews as Alternative Media.   Another form of alternative news media that developed during the 1960s was the journalism review. Two leaders still in the field are the *Columbia Journalism Review*, founded in 1961, and the *American* (formerly *Washington*) *Journalism Review*, founded in 1977. Although the Columbia publication had been somewhat managerial in tone, the now defunct *Chicago Journalism Review*, begun shortly after the Democratic convention of August 1968, took a different tack—creating a forum of analytical discussion of the Chicago and national press. The goal was to create an open forum for critical discussion of journalism, which, as the reaction to the Hutchins commission had demonstrated, had been absent from within the profession, although not from without.

Advocacy journalist Hunter S. Thompson, in *Fear and Loathing on the Campaign Trail*, paid scant attention to the journalistic conventions of the regular reporters. In 1972, he wrote, "As far as I was concerned, there was no such thing as 'off the record.' The most consistent and ultimately damaging failure of political journalism in America has its roots in the clubby cocktail personal relationships that inevitably develop between politicians and journalists."[87]

Precision Journalism

Precision journalism incorporated social science techniques in an attempt to empirically measure objective fact. It is at an opposite pole from other types of new journalism. Precision journalists decried the "man-on-the street" interview and the slipshod methods reporters used to gather what they termed *public opinion*. Precision journalists believed in interpretation based on understanding gained through using social science techniques, such as survey research based on random sampling. Philip Meyer, professor in the School of Journalism at the University of North Carolina at Chapel Hill, in 1967 became project director for a project sponsored by the Detroit Urban League and financed by Henry Ford, II, and two foundations. Meyer and his team hired African Americans to interview a random sample of African Americans in the main riot areas of Detroit. After analyzing the results on a computer, Meyer and his team combined the statistical data with photographs and quotes into a highly readable series.[88]

Meyer is still practicing precision journalism, and other individuals and publications have used the approach as well; but although newspapers often have contracted for political poll information, they have failed to use precision techniques in highly creative ways.

Magazines: Death or Specialization

Magazines, unlike newspapers that were aimed at mass audiences, constituted in the 1960s an industry increasingly characterized by a selectivity of audience. Although timely, they did not face the same pressure as the daily newspaper and therefore were more able to treat subjects in depth and to pursue editorial platforms over time. As more permanent vehicles of information than newspapers, they were especially well suited for instructing and educating as well as entertaining. Magazines were national in scope and lacked the local perspective and biases of newspapers, provided low-cost entertainment, and carried considerable advertising.[89]

Although general-circulation leaders like the *Saturday Evening Post, Life,* and *Look* enjoyed great popularity and prosperity during earlier decades of the twentieth century, specialization characterized the vast majority of successful magazines. As early as 1934, the special interest magazine *Model Railroader* capitalized on increased leisure time and successfully appealed to railroad hobbyists. *Skin Diver*, begun in 1951, experienced similar success. The 1960s also witnessed the birth of magazines that were part of the new journalism movement, publications that reflected the political philosophies of the time. Among these were magazines that covered the music industry, such as *Rolling Stone*, and magazines for feminists, such as *Ms.*

Circulation Leaders

Magazine readership increased dramatically across the twentieth century, as a growing population with increased purchasing power attracted advertisers who could target specific buyers. Magazines profited as well from increased educational levels and more leisure time. By 1950, *Life* magazine reached one in five Americans, and by 1961, A. C. Nielsen reports indicated that it reached one-quarter of the adult population. Other big circulation leaders included the *Reader's Digest*, reaching 27 percent of American adults; *Look*, reaching 21 percent; and the *Saturday Evening Post*, reaching 18 percent.

Nevertheless, mammoth circulations did not always indicate health. The push for giant circulations began in 1937, when the *Saturday Evening Post* had garnered 3 million subscribers. From 1942 to 1945, circulations continued to increase, and in the postwar years magazines experienced extensive expansions in circulations. Between 1950 and 1962, *Look* and *McCall's* more than doubled their circulations. Critics argued that magazines were giving up the selectivity of market that had been their strength, and some contended that the "race for circulation was a race to the poorhouse."[90]

Lack of advertisers, not subscribers, sounded the death knell for the big magazines. As costs increased 40 to 50 percent in the 1950s, big publishers were hardest-pressed to respond quickly and effectively. Curtis Publications, with its massive, vertically integrated system of subsidiaries, which did everything from grow trees and produce paper to distribute the *Saturday Evening Post*, found it difficult to maintain large overheads in the face of decreasing advertising revenues. In 1961, Curtis Publishing Company lost $4,194,000; the next year losses jumped to $18,917,000. In 1962, Curtis management attempted to save the *Post*, installing as its editor Clay Blair, Jr., who introduced new journalism and "sophisticated muckraking" to the *Post*. The latter shocked some of the magazine's readers, but more importantly, by the end of 1963 muckraking activity involved the *Post* in $27,060,000 in libel suits.[91] Big publishers were not the only losers. From 1950 to 1960, one out of eight magazines belonging to the Audit Bureau of Circulations died or was merged out of existence.

The one-time circulation leaders such as *Life* and *Look* declined and died in the late 1960s and early 1970s, but their deaths did not represent a decline for the industry as a whole. The large circulations of the *Saturday Evening Post* and other similar magazines resulted in large costs, and television's cost-per-thousand rates prohibited magazines from continuing to increase their advertising revenues enough to keep pace with increasing costs. The mass audience became a television market, and magazines turned increasingly to specialized audiences and advertisers. From 1962 to 1971, 160 magazines were sold or merged, while 753 new magazines appeared on the racks.[92]

The Aged Endure

As the trend toward specialized magazines continued in the 1970s and 1980s, the rescue of three quality monthlies reflected the loyalty of their readership, their importance as cultural artifacts, and their inability to continue to attract advertisers.

Harper's, the quality monthly begun in 1850, continued to earn a prominent place with America's elite readers. In the 1970s, the magazine broke Seymour Hersh's account of the My Lai massacre and devoted a full issue to Norman Mailer, a "new" journalist of the 1960s, and his long essay, "The Prisoner of Sex." In 1962, Harper & Brothers, the original publishers of the magazine, merged with Row, Peterson, & Company to become Harper & Row. The company is now part of the conglomerate HarperCollins. *Harper's* was split from the publishing company when it was purchased by the Minneapolis Star and Tribune Company. In 1980, after suffering major financial losses, the magazine appeared defunct. *Harper's* was rescued in 1980 by the MacArthur Foundation of Chicago and the Atlantic Richfield foundation, which assumed the responsibility for the magazine's operating expenses, including the $4 million debt. MacArthur has continued its support into the twenty-first century.

The *Atlantic Monthly,* another mid-nineteenth-century magazine, was also losing money when it was bought in 1980 by Mortimer Zuckerman, a Boston real estate developer.

The third publication rescued was the *Saturday Review,* which was purchased in 1980 by a successful financial publisher Robert Weingarten. Weingarten altered the *Review* from a general interest magazine to a magazine of the arts.[93]

U.S. News' Mortimer B. Zuckerman moved into the publishing business in the 1980s with purchases of the *Atlantic Magazine* and *U.S. News and World Report.* In the fall of 1984, Zuckerman paid $182.5 million for *U.S. News,* the magazine begun in the 1930s by David Lawrence.

Zuckerman's bid for *U.S. News* guaranteed employees $3,000 for each share of stock they owned. Zuckerman claimed he would not make major changes in *U.S. News:* "It will never be an entertainment-style magazine; it has not been, it is not its tradition. . . . It's not a *People* magazine, and it will never be a *People* magazine. It's a serious magazine—in the best sense of that word."[94]

The *New Yorker,* the envy of the periodical industry from its founding in 1926 until 1967 when the magazine began to lose massive pages of advertising and net profits, shrank from a 1966 level of $3 million to less than $1 million in advertising revenues, although its circulation remained the same. Media critic Ben Bagdikian credited the loss to Jonathan Schell's account of an American assault on the village of Ben Suc in Vietnam. It was that story, Bagdikian claims, that caused nearly 2,500 pages of advertising for products such as Audemars Piguet watches, starting at the price of $10,500, to disappear from *New Yorker* pages.[95]

The late William Shawn, the editor of the *New Yorker* who chose to publish Schell's account, resigned in January 1987. The Newhouse Media Chain bought the magazine in 1985, and Shawn's exit was predicted to cause major changes at the magazine during the next few years. Shawn, the second editor of the *New Yorker,* took over from its founder William Ross in 1952. Replacing Shawn was Robert Gottlieb, former president and editor-in-chief of Alfred A. Knopf, Inc., which is a part of Random House, also owned by Newhouse.

The magazine quickly made some advertising changes, accepting a Calvin Klein "Obsession" advertisement. The ad's risque content would "have been unacceptable under the magazine's once notoriously stolid criteria."[96] Newhouse also launched a $2 million network television advertising campaign promoting the magazine.

Bagdikian described the magazine as "almost the last repository of the style and tone of Henry David Thoreau and Matthew Arnold, its chaste, old-fashioned columns breathing the quietude of Nineteenth Century essays."[97] In 1991, when Tina Brown, former editor of *Vanity Fair,* took over the editorship, the "chaste, old-fashioned columns" underwent redesign. Brown was succeeded in 1998 by David Remnick, in one more attempt to reverse the magazine's financial situation. Remnick began his writing career as an intern at the *Washington Post,* later became a writer at the *New Yorker,* and was an editorial counselor to Brown.[98]

The New Emerge and Last

While the quality monthlies adhered to old values, new magazines invaded the news-stands, shouting unfamiliar headlines and seeking new audiences. Among these were *Rolling Stone*, a counterculture magazine that discussed the politics of drugs and music, and *Ms.*, a new women's magazine that deliberately avoided recipes and kitchen hints. These magazines were irreverent and challenging, and they experienced varied degrees of success. *Rolling Stone* is a money-maker today, but *Ms.* has experienced its share of financial peaks and valleys.

Ms. magazine was begun by Gloria Steinem in 1972, with a spirited voice that championed women in the workplace and discussed many of the issues raised by the women's movement. Early issues of *Ms.* ran articles on date rape, wife battering, pay equity, maternity leave, and sexual harassment. By 1986, however, Susan Milligan of the *Washington Monthly* charged that *Ms.* had lost its focus, differing little from other mainstream women's magazines. She argued that although *Ms.* still occasionally ran articles about poor women and third-world countries, it no longer questioned society's demands on women to be pretty or to be consumers.[99]

By 1989, ownership had changed hands twice. The feminist edge was gone, and during the late 1980s the magazine ran such standard women's fare as how to dress for success and what wine to serve for dinner. Circulation had dwindled to 550,000, a number inflated by giveaways.[100] In October 1989, magazine owner Dale Lang purchased *Ms.*, named Robin Morgan editor, and halted publication of the old-style magazine.

Born again in the summer of 1990, *Ms.* pursued a risky strategy—issuing the magazine bimonthly and advertising-free. Subscribers were asked to pay nearly five dollars per copy. Steinem said that, when the magazine was founded, the initial planners had not considered a no-advertising policy; rather, they had hoped to influence the style of women's portrayal in advertising. As it turned out, *Ms.* had a difficult time procuring advertising and sometimes lost it because of the magazine's strong feminist stance. Nevertheless, Steinem got her revenge. In the first issue after the magazine was reincarnated in the summer of 1990, Steinem attacked the industry for its 1970s positions and identified those advertisers who had refused to support the earlier publication. Philip Morris, she wrote, pulled all its cigarette ads after *Ms.* refused to run ads for Virginia Slims; General Mills and other food companies would not advertise because the magazine did not carry recipes; and Revlon objected to a story of a Soviet woman who did not wear makeup.[101]

In the first issue of the new magazine, Morgan said *Ms.* would avoid reports on fashion, diet, makeup, gardening, and celebrity figures and would include more articles on politics, international news, feminist theory, health, lesbian issues, minority women, and other neglected topics.[102]

The first issue sold out in three days and then sold out a second printing. By late 1991, it had a subscriber base of more than 100,000, newsstand sales of 70,000, and it was operating in the black for one of the few times in its life. By the time the magazine was a year old, it had renewed 75 percent of its subscribers, compared to an average industry renewal rate of about 40 percent. Experts say the critical test comes with the second year of renewals, which normally drops to around 24 percent. *Ms.* needed to beat that average by a considerable margin in order to stay around as an ad-free magazine.[103]

Conclusion

During the early 1960s, it became clear to many television executives—owners, producers, and managers—that television could easily dominate the stories of the decade. Television cameras brought home to a skeptical America the oppression of African Americans in the South just as they brought into America's living rooms the reality of an Asian war. Despite the enormous potential power of television, the medium seemed to pace itself with American public opinion rather than to lead in the formation of that opinion.

In a fifteen-year span, television's coverage of the big stories represented only the simple beginnings of the technological revolution that would follow. Satellite development enabled scholars to speak of a "global village," while simultaneously the international corporate development that accompanied technological progress raised—once more—the old fears of monopoly and government controls. Although the FCC probed programming during the decade, industry pressure saw to it that real change occurred. Critics worried about the effects of interlocking ownership and directorates, noting that many companies that owned media outlets also held huge defense grants. Fearing continued commercial domination of television, Congress acted in 1967 to institutionalize public broadcasting as an alternative to commercial fare.

The trend toward corporate ownership was not unique to broadcasting, and the increased chain-ownership of newspapers intensified fears of what might be the effects of the international consolidation of media interests. Newspaper owners confronted the new technologies that would revolutionize the newsroom by the 1980s, and major strikes shut down some of the nation's major newspapers. Newspapers sought relief from competition in a successful appeal to Congress to pass the Newspaper Preservation Act.

Reporting the dramatic conflicts of the period incurred both governmental interference and legal support. *New York Times v. Sullivan* guaranteed that libel suits would not provide convenient mechanisms for limiting the coverage of public issues. Nevertheless, during the early 1970s, the government attempted unsuccessfully to stop publication of the Pentagon Papers, and government and press alike questioned the validity of early stories that the *Washington Post* printed about the Watergate affair.

The growth of news coverage did not enjoy a parallel growth in public credibility. Journalistic organizations adopted press ethics codes, some newspapers hired ombudsmen, and still other papers participated in an abortive attempt to establish a fully functioning National News Council to hear public complaints.

The cultural controversies that dominated discussion of the Vietnam conflict and the civil rights movement affected the television and newspaper newsroom as well. Reporters, often a part of the generation that comprised the New Left, resisted the authority of the news desk and publisher power, asserting their own autonomy in approaching assignments and writing stories. They often viewed the qualities of professionalism as based on loyalty to an ideal rather than to an organization. Although editors resisted relinquishing power, they too rebelled when government imposed a new style of news management. Willing to cooperate in the 1950s and early 1960s to withhold information from the public that they felt would endanger national security, they mutinied when government tried to withhold information from the editors themselves.

Coverage of the various conflicts of the period and the emergence of reporter power fostered new language and new styles of interpretation, many of which appeared in the few remaining general-circulation or opinion magazines. The magazine industry experienced profound change, as specialization occurred—not only in content but also in the audience targeted by advertisers.

In May 1965, Walter Lippmann, in a speech to the International Press Institute in London, congratulated the press for becoming a profession characterized by intellectual discipline, but he warned against the hazards of the new power and influence gained during the decade of the 1960s, noting that the "crude forms of corruption which belonged to the infancy of journalism tend to give way to the temptations of maturity and power." Lippmann continued by saying, "[T]he most important forms of corruption in the modern journalist's world are the many guises and disguises of social climbing on the pyramids of power."[104]

Endnotes

1. Everette E. Dennis, ed., "The New Journalism: How It Came to Be," in *The Magic Writing Machine* (Eugene: School of Journalism, University of Oregon, 1971), p. 1.

2. For an expansion of this thesis, see Henry Fairlie, *The Kennedy Promise* (Garden City, N. Y.: Doubleday, 1973).

3. Todd Gitlin, *The Whole World Is Watching* (Berkeley: University of California Press, 1980).

4. For an analysis of the "New Left," see Maurice Isserman, *If I Had a Hammer: The Death of the Old Left and the Birth of the New Left* (New York: Basic Books, 1987); and James Miller, *Democracy Is in the Streets: From Port Huron to the Siege of Chicago* (New York: Simon & Schuster, 1987).

5. Ernest C. Hynds, *American Newspapers in the 1980s* (New York: Hastings House, 1980), p. 43.

6. "Changing Public Attitudes toward Television and Other Mass Media," Roper Organization, Inc., 1977, p. 4.

7. "Let Glory Wave Alone over Ole Miss," *Life,* October 12, 1962, p. 6, cited in Mary Alice Sentman, "*Life* in Black and White: Coverage of Black America by *Life* Magazine, 1937–1972," paper presented to Association for Education in Journalism, Michigan State University, August 1981.

8. See Gitlin, *The Whole Word Is Watching,* for a discussion of how issue groups in the 1960s altered their behavior in response to media coverage.

9. Cited in Ray Scherer and Robert J. Donovan, *Unsilent Revolution: Television News and American Public Life* (Cambridge, Mass.: Woodrow Wilson Center for International Scholars and Cambridge University Press, 1992), p. 8.

10. Cited in Scherer and Donovan, *Unsilent Revolution,* p. 6.

11. Transcript of President Kennedy's press conference on Laos, *New York Times,* March 24, 1961, p. 8, cited in Perry, "Damning with Faint Praise: John Kennedy, the Press and the Laos Crisis of 1961," unpublished manuscript, p. 33.

12. "Laos Crisis Mounting, Britain Interceding," by Walter Lippmann, *Boston Daily Globe,* March 23, 1961, p. 1.

13. Ralph McGill, "Inescapable Wrestling Bout," *Atlanta Constitution,* March 24, 1961, p. 1, cited in Perry, "Damning with Faint Praise," p. 24.

14. Stanley Karnouw, *Vietnam, A History: The First Complete Account of Vietnam at War* (New York: Viking Press, 1983), p. 255.

15. Peter Braestrup, "Vietnam, in Retrospect," *Forbes Media Critic* (Fall, 1995), pp. 32–44.

16. William M. Hammond, *Public Affairs: The Military and the Media, 1968–1973* (Washington, D.C.: Center of Military History, United States Army, 1996), p. 4.

17. James Boylan, "Declarations of Independence," *Columbia Journalism Review* (November/December, 1986), p. 33.

18. Karnouw, *Vietnam,* pp. 297, 394.

19. Karnouw, *Vietnam,* p. 490.

20. Daniel C. Hallin, *The Uncensored War* (New York: Oxford University Press, 1986), p. 147.

21. Karnouw, *Vietnam,* p. 489.

22. Braestrup, "Vietnam, in Restrospect," p. 42.

23. "Kent State," May 1–4, 1970 Chronology of Events, http://www.devaughn.com/may4/chronology.htm, 1. July 25, 2001.

24. "Remembering the May 4th Schootings at Kent State," http://www.devaughn.com/may4/chronology.htm, 3; http://www.newsnet5.com/news/stories/ news-990504-102856.html. July 25, 2001.

25. See Gitlin, *The Whole World Is Watching, passim.*

26. "Jackson State May 1970," http://www.devaugn.com/ may4/Jackson%20State/jackson_state_may_1970.htm, 3, July 25, 2001; Tim Spofford, *Lynch Street: The May 1970 Slayings at Jackson State College* (Kent, Oh.: Kent State University Press, 1981).

27. Richard Nixon, *The Memoirs* (New York: Grosset & Dunlap, 1978), p. 350, cited in Daniel C. Hallin, *The Uncensored War: The Media and Vietnam* (New York: Oxford University Press, 1986), p. 3.

28. James Reston, "The End of the Tunnel," *New York Times,* April 30, 1975, p. 41, cited in Hallin, *The Uncensored War,* p. 3.

29. Quoted in Gitlin, *The Whole World Is Watching,* p. 205, cited in Hammond, *Public Affairs,* p. 11.

30. Hallin, *Uncensored War,* p. 163.

31. Cited in J. Herbert Altschull, *From Milton to McLuhan: The Ideas behind American Journalism* (New York: Longman, 1990), p. 339.

32. Altschull, *Milton to McLuhan,* p. 339.

33. Marshall McLuhan, *Understanding Media: The Extensions of Man* (New York: McGraw-Hill, 1964), pp. 7, 9.

34. Altschull, *Milton to McLuhan,* p. 342.

35. Christopher Brookeman, *American Culture and Society Since the 1930s* (New York: Schocken Books, 1984), p. 133.

36. Harvey J. Levin, *University of Pennsylvania Law Review,* 113:3 (January, 1965), cited in Herbert I. Schiller, *Mass Communications and American Empire* (New York: Augustus M. Kelley, Publishers, 1969), pp. 129–130.

37. *Progress Report on Space Communications,* Hearings before the Senate Subcommittee on Communications, 89th Congress, 2nd Session, August 10, 17, 18, and 23, 1966, Serial 89–78, Washington, 1966, cited in Schiller, *American Empire,* p. 131.

38. James McCormack, "Comsat's Role in Communications," *Signal,* May 1967, p. 32.

39. *New York Times,* January 18, 1961, cited in Schiller, *American Empire,* p. 33.

40. Schiller, *American Empire,* p. 53.

41. Schiller, *American Empire,* pp. 54–56.

42. Fred MacDonald, *Television and the Red Menace: The Video Road to Vietnam* (New York: Praeger, 1985), p. 181.

43. David Halberstam, *The Powers That Be* (New York: Alfred A. Knopf, 1979), p. 489.

44. Halberstam, *Powers That Be,* pp. 491–492.

45. For a thorough look at FCC activity during the 1960s, see James L. Baughman, *Television's Guardians: The FCC and the Politics of Programming, 1958–1967* (Knoxville: The University of Tennessee Press, 1985), on which this discussion is based.

46. Edward Fouhy, "Killing Freedom with Fairness," *Washington Journalism Review* (October, 1987), in a review of Lucas Powe, Jr., *American Broadcasting and the First Amendment* (Berkeley: University of California Press, 1987).

47. *Red Lion Broadcasting Co. v. FCC,* 395 U.S. 367 at 385, 80 S. Ct. 1974 (1969).

48. Dwight Teeter and Don Le Duc, *Law of Mass Communications: Freedom and Control of Print and Broadcast Media,* 8th ed. (Mineola, N.Y.: The Foundation Press, 1992), pp. 399–401. For a discussion of constraints on

public television, see B. J. Bullert, *Public Television: Politics and the Battle over Documentary Film* (New Brunswick, Rutgers University Press, 1997).

49. *FCC v. League of Women Voters of California,* 478 U.S. 364, 104 S. Ct. 3106 (1984).

50. *Muir v. Alabama Educational Television Commission,* 688 F. 2d 1033 (5th Cir. 19082).

51. Statistics are from Hynds, *American Newspapers,* p. 88.

52. Hynds, *American Newspapers,* p. 85.

53. Leo Bogart, "The American Media System and Its Commercial Culture," *Journal of Media Studies* (Fall, 1991), p. 23.

54. *United States v. Citizen Publishing Co.,* 394 U.S. 131 (1969).

55. Stephen Lacy, "Content of Joint Operation Newspapers," in *Press Concentration and Monopoly: New Perspectives on Newspaper Ownership and Operations* (Norwood, N.J.: Ablex Publishing Co., 1987), p. 159.

56. Mark Fitzgerald, "Treading Softly," *Editor & Publisher,* July 30, 1988, p. 12; George Garneau, "Detroit JOA Approved," *Editor & Publisher,* August 13, 1988, p. 14.

57. *Michigan Citizens for an Independent Press v. Thornburgh,* 868 F. 2d 1285 (D.D. Cir. 1989).

58. James Boylan, "Declarations of Independence," *Columbia Journalism Review* (November/December, 1986), p. 32.

59. See Leo Rosten, *The Washington Correspondents* (New York: Harcourt, Brace and Company, 1937); and William L. Rivers, "The Correspondents after 25 Years," *Columbia Journalism Review* 1:1 (Spring, 1961), pp. 4–10.

60. John W. C. Johnstone, Edward J. Slawski, and William W. Bowman, *The News People: A Sociological Portrait of American Journalists and Their Work* (Urbana: University of Illinois Press, 1976), pp. 130–132.

61. Michael Schudson, *Discovering the News* (New York: Basic Books, 1978), p. 172–173.

62. *Editor & Publisher,* November 19, 1962, p. 12; "The Right to Lie," *Columbia Journalism Review,* 5 (Winter, 1966–67), pp. 14–16, cited in Schudson, *Discovering the News,* pp. 171–172.

63. Schudson, *Discovering the News,* pp. 172–173.

64. Mark Perry, "Damning with Faint Praise," p. 33.

65. *Coleman v. MacLennan,* 1908.

66. Harold Nelson and Dwight Teeter, *Law of Mass Communications: Freedom and Control of Print and Broadcast Media,* 5th ed. (Mineola, N.Y.: The Foundation Press, 1986), p. 107.

67. Zechariah Chafee, *Free Speech in the United States* (Cambridge, Mass.: Harvard University Press, 1941), p. 467.

68. Don R. Pember, "The Pentagon Papers Decision: More Questions Than Answers," *Journalism Quarterly,* 48:3 (Autumn, 1971), p. 404; *New York Times,* June 15, 1971, p. 1.

69. Pember, "The Pentagon Papers Decision," pp. 404–405.

70. *New York Times,* June 16, 1971, p. 1.

71. *New York Times Co. v. United States,* 403 U.S. 713, 714, 91 S.Ct. 2140, 2141 (1971).

72. Anthony Lewis, "Congress Shall Make No Law," *New York Times,* September 16, 1976, p. 39.

73. Cited in Boylan, "Declarations of Independence," p. 37.

74. William Safire, "Ten Myths about the Reagan Debacle," *New York Times Magazine,* March 22, 1987, p. 22.

75. Carl Bernstein and Bob Woodward, *All the President's Men* (New York: Simon and Schuster, 1974).

76. Theodore H. White, *Breach of Faith—The Fall of Richard Nixon* (New York: Atheneum, 1975), p. 244.

77. White, *Breach of Faith,* p. 245.

78. Woodward and Bernstein, *President's Men,* p. 331.

79. Boylan, "Declarations of Independence," p. 41.

80. Philip Meyer, *Ethical Journalism* (White Plains, N.Y.: Longman, 1987), p. 18.

81. See Meyer's interpretation in *Ethical Journalism,* pp. 168–171; and James Boylan, "Declarations of Independence," p. 42.

82. Meyer, *Ethical Journalism,* p. 170.

83. Clifford G. Christians, Kim B. Rotzoll, and Mark Fackler, *Media Ethics* (New York: Longman, 1987), p. 96.

84. Boylan, "Declarations of Independence," p. 42.

85. Review of *In Cold Blood, Commonweal* (February 11, 1966), p. 561.

86. *Atlantic Monthly,* March, 1966, p. 160.

87. Hunter Thompson, *Fear and Loathing on the Campaign Trail* (San Francisco: Straight Arrow Books, 1973).

88. Dennis Rivers and William L. Rivers, *Other Voices* (San Francisco: Canfield Press, 1974).

89. Theodore Peterson, in *Magazines in the Twentieth Century,* 2nd ed. (Urbana: University of Illinois Press, 1972), argues that magazines, as major carriers of advertising, and therefore of information about new products, were instrumental in increasing the U.S. standard of living. He also claims they played a significant role in creating a sense of national community.

90. Peterson, *Magazines,* pp. 61–63.

91. Peterson, *Magazines,* p. 178–199.

92. Roland Wolseley, *Understanding Magazines* (Ames: Iowa State University Press, 1969), p. 27.

93. Lee Lescaze, "In the Nick of Time: Three General Interest Magazines Rescued . . . For Now," *Washington Journalism Review* (September, 1980), pp. 17–19.

94. Caroline E. Mayer, "Zuckerman: From Boston to Washington, from Property into Publishing," *Washington Post Business* (June 18, 1984), pp. 1, 36.

95. Ben H. Bagdikian, "The Wrong Kind of Readers: The Fall and Rise of the *New Yorker,*" *Progressive,* 47:5 (May, 1983), p. 52.

96. Curt Suplee, "New Editor Chosen at *New Yorker,*" *Washington Post,* January 13, 1987, pp. D1, 10.

97. Bagdikian, "Wrong Kind of Readers," p. 52.

98. "The *New Yorker*'s New Editor Comes to Zellerbach Hall, *Berkeleyan,*" http://www.berkeley.edu/news/berkeleyan/1998/1111/newyorker.html/posted (November 11, 1998), accessed March 11, 2001.

99. Susan Milligan, "Has *Ms.* Undergone a Sex Change?" *Washington Monthly,* 18 (October, 1986), pp. 17–21.

100. See Maria Braden, "*Ms.* Doesn't Miss the Ads," *Quill* (January/February, 1992).

101. Braden, "*Ms.* Doesn't Miss," p. 23.

102. Robin Morgan, "*Ms.* Lives," *Ms.* (July/August, 1990), pp. 1–2.

103. Braden, "*Ms.* Doesn't Miss," p. 24.

104. Boylan, "Declarations of Independence," p. 35.

CHAPTER 17

News as a Corporate Enterprise

▼

During the 1980s, news became a corporate enterprise. The changes, although not comprising a revolution, were major. These business developments occurred during a decade of rapid deregulation under the direction of Republican President Ronald Reagan. The concept of deregulation filtered through the broadcast industry, colored FCC philosophy, and focused more on the competitive nature of the industry and less on concepts of the public interest. Media became a news story of its own.

Many media companies merged and went public. This meant that media company stock sold on the stock exchange. Editors had to answer not only to owners but also to shareholders. Corporate leaders decided that news, to an even greater degree than before, should make money, not simply add prestige to the enterprise or exist to serve the public good. "Softer" journalism crept through local news until it began to influence the prominent evening newscasts.

During the 1980s, new technologies were developed. Cable television expanded and new networks, such as CNN (1980) and Fox Network (1987), developed to compete with the big three: CBS, ABC, and NBC. The underlying structure was created for the Internet, and the personal computer became a popular item in middle-class American homes and businesses. Its development set the stage for heavy reliance on the Internet in the 1990s. By 1980, teenagers sported Sony Walkmans on their way to school and other activities. In the 1980s, the compact disk emerged; coupled with the development of digital audiotape, old technologies for listening to music began to recede.

Coverage of conflict and war changed. The government believed the press had contributed to the loss of the Vietnam War, and during excursions into Grenada, Panama, and the Gulf, journalists were heavily restricted and press pools were created to provide coverage. Despite these restrictions, the public protested very little. The credibility of journalists had dropped to a new low.

Globalization became the buzzword by the end of the 1980s, with increased international ownership reflecting the many mergers that took place in book, magazine, newspaper, and larger media companies. Public relations firms joined advertising firms and became single agencies, blurring the line between the two. Large chain bookstores—coffee shops included—flourished.

These changes resulted in content changes. "Happy talk" local news pleased consumers and made money. The formula, welcomed by media owners, filtered into network news. By the late 1990s, even the venerable CBS anchor Dan Rather was delivering fluffy features on the CBS "Nightly News." "60 Minutes," the first news show to garner top ratings, began in 1979 and retained loyal audiences through the 1990s, as newsmagazines proliferated on network and cable stations. CNN pioneered in twenty-four hour news, with ratings solidly tied to news developments. As political leaders learned the techniques of "happy talk news," they increased their expertise in creating media messages for politics. The political communicator was the new professional.

Figure 17-1 The *Washington Post* gained national prominence after its treatment of the Watergate story. Today the *Post* is the product of a complex, technologically advanced process that combines the talents of more than 3,000 employees. (*Washington Post* photo)

Through it all, consumers were willing to pay for content, and, in 1985, consumer spending on media exceeded advertising expenditures. That meant that consumers bought books and subscribed to cable and to magazines—and paid out money in larger sums than did advertisers.

The investigative journalism that thrived did so to increase ratings, win prizes, and make money. Entertainment was the dominant television force. Writing in 1986, media soothsayer Neil Postman's *Amusing Ourselves to Death* argued that television, with bite-size entertainments sold as units of time, had harmed rational public discourse and damaged democratic processes.[1] ▼

Corporate and Public Ownership

Media Companies on the Stock Exchange

Mass media participated in the accelerating spiral of finance capitalism, mergers, and takeovers of the 1970s and 1980s. In terms of historical perspective, such merging was remarkably rapid, almost sudden. Although group and chain ownership have been structural components of the industry since the eighteenth century, media corporations issuing publicly held stock is a recent phenomenon.

During the 1980s, large media groups, such Capital Cities and ABC, which combined a variety of newspaper and broadcast holdings, merged. Early in 1986, in the biggest non-oil company merger ever, General Electric (GE) acquired RCA for the astounding sum of $6.28 billion. Ironically, the FCC had split these two companies in the 1930s. GE Chairman John F. Welch, Jr., was ecstatic: "This is going to be one dynamite company," he told the *Wall Street Journal.*[2] Included in the RCA corporate partnership was the NBC network. The merger created controversy and outraged consumer advocate Ralph Nader, who pointed out that General Electric was the nation's biggest defense contractor. Nader questioned whether NBC, as part of GE, really could do an adequate job of covering the defense industry.[3]

Accompanying the merger phenomenon was the "going public" of media companies. In newspapers, this trend began in the early 1960s, with Dow Jones, Inc., publisher of the *Wall Street Journal*, issuing publicly traded stock. By the late 1980s, at least fifteen publicly traded corporations owned newspapers. The Times-Mirror Company, headquartered in Los Angeles and formerly a closely held family organization, was listed on the New York Stock Exchange in 1964. Gannett and Media General went public in 1967. In the late 1960s, Ridder Publications and Knight Newspapers—since merged into the mighty Knight-Ridder Corporation—joined the move to go public, as did the New York Times Corporation and Lee Newspapers. In the 1970s, the Washington Post Company (owner of *Newsweek* magazine and, like the others, an owner of big broadcast properties) and Affiliated Publications (owner of the *Boston Globe*) went public. Harte-Hanks Communications went public in the 1970s and then, as hostile takeovers threatened the autonomy of many corporations, bought up enough of its own stock to go private again in the mid-1980s. The 1980s also saw A. H.

Belo Corporation (which owned the *Dallas Morning News* plus broadcast stations) and the Tribune Company (owner of the *Chicago Tribune* and the *New York Daily News*) going public.

"Going public" earns companies certain benefits under the tax code, including the ability to maintain a company after the death of an original owner, at the same time allowing the distribution of shares to heirs and lessening the tax bite the Internal Revenue Service takes out of family-owned businesses when a prime owner dies. Mergers are more easily accomplished, and the liquidity of shares in publicly held corporations facilitates possible stock ownership plans for employees. Proceeds from the sale of stock shares can be used for technological innovations.

However, going public has a negative, as well as a positive, side. Media critics argued that earnings-driven managements worried more about how well shares traded on the stock market and how well regarded they were by financial analysts than about how well the news was covered. Nevertheless, media companies were prized along Wall Street and by hotshot entrepreneurs because they had a high ratio of cash return to investment. Looking back from the end of the 1990s, some critics argued that going public was at least partially responsible for the development of "infotainment," programming that blurred news and entertainment.

Corporate Ownership of Newspapers

Even outside of the megamergers, group or chain ownership of newspapers continued to increase through the 1980s, with purchases of old-line, family-owned newspapers underscoring the trend. In 1970, chains controlled 63 percent of the newspaper circulation in the United States and 50 percent of all dailies; by the end of 1985, chains held 77 percent of the circulation and 71 percent of all dailies. The $315 million 1986 Gannett purchase of the *Louisville Courier-Journal;* the $200 million purchase of the dominant Iowa paper, the *Des Moines Register;* and the Times-Mirror Corporation acquisition of the *Baltimore Sun* papers are examples of the swallowing up of three major independents by newspaper groups.

The Des Moines paper had been owned by the Cowles family since 1903, when Gardner Cowles, an Algona, Iowa, banker had bought the *Register and Leader* for $300,000. Between 1903 and 1986, the combined *Register and Tribune* had won twelve Pulitzer Prizes for excellence. In 1986, the Times-Mirror Company purchased the *Baltimore Sun* and the *Baltimore Evening Sun* from the A. S. Abell Company, paying $600,000. The Baltimore newspapers' prices had shot up because their only competitor, Hearst's *Baltimore News-American*, had folded the day before Abell agreed to sell. Times-Mirror now owned eleven major newspapers, including the *Los Angeles Times;* the *Baltimore Sun;* *Newsday* of Long Island, New York; the *Hartford Courant;* and the *Denver Post*.

It is said that some newspaper owners could learn much by studying the decline of American railroads. Railroaders did little to arrest the decline of rail travel and shipping because they thought they were in the railroad business, not the *transportation business.* Times-Mirror Corporation is an example of a newspaper-based organization that realized it was in the *communication business*; its holdings have not been restricted to newspapers but include broadcasting stations, cable television, and book publishers.

Critics respond differently to the growing incidence of chain ownership. Ben Bagdikian, former dean of the Graduate School of Journalism at the University of California at Berkeley, wrote that "a very large degree of control of the newspaper industry is in the hands of relatively large companies."[4]

Bagdikian's industry snapshots showed that in 1982 a majority of all American media—newspapers, television, radio, books, and movies—were controlled by fifty huge corporations. By 1987, he found that the fifty megacorporations he had studied had merged into only twenty-six major media conglomerates.[5] Brian Brooks of the University of Missouri, however, argued that the newspaper industry remains quite diverse. Of the 1,700 daily newspapers in the country, the biggest chain, Gannett, controlled only ninety in 1986.[6]

Those who argued that U.S. media still represented diverse interests in the late 1980s pointed to the fact that there were 1,610 daily newspapers, with a total circulation of about 60 million each day; 11,500 magazines, many of them highly specialized; 11,000 radio stations; 10,800 cable television systems; and 1,100 television stations.

Figure 17–2 Media companies are big business. Freedom Center, the *Chicago Tribune*'s state-of-the-art production and circulation facility, represents a $186 million investment. (Photo courtesy of the *Chicago Tribune*)

Deregulation and the FCC

The Federal Communications Commission (FCC) was created in 1934 with the full support of the broadcasting industry, indicating that its role would be to "regulate" in the public interest, but not to the detriment of the industry itself. CBS news producer Fred Friendly once called the Federal Communications Commission "the leaning tower of Jell-O." By the mid-1970s, controversy over efforts to create programming change through the FCC led to disillusionment with the agency's effectiveness.[7] The FCC made some concessions to reform groups who had established citizen's rights to challenge broadcast licenses, but these were not major. During the mid-1970s, congressional examinations of FCC policies foreshadowed the deregulatory climate of the 1980s. In 1976, a House of Representatives subcommittee proposed easing of license restrictions and suspension of the Fairness Doctrine.

After 1981, Mark Fowler, who was appointed chairman of the FCC by President Ronald Reagan, led the move to deregulate the broadcast industry. "Free-market forces and competitive forces are better able to serve the public and police companies" than the government, Fowler told a *Washington Post* reporter in 1987. Fowler's efforts helped result in a significant reduction of paperwork and reporting to the FCC (and thus to the public), eliminated the need to keep detailed program logs, and reduced license renewals to a pro forma operation.[8]

On April 1, 1985, the FCC announced that it would expand the number of radio and television stations each person or corporation could own. This policy, which meant that corporations could now own twelve AM radio stations, twelve FM stations, and twelve television stations, instead of only seven of each, accelerated the consolidation of broadcast entities under the umbrella of a single owner. One other limitation set by the FCC was that no one company could have broadcast stations reaching more than 25 percent of the nation's homes. This new policy meant, for example, that Capital Cities Communications, owners of the *Kansas City Star* and the *Fort Worth Star-Telegram,* as well as a number of broadcast stations, could merge with an entity as large as ABC, which owned numerous stations. These companies merged without having to relinquish many of their stations.[9] Deregulation continued unabated and much of this philosophy was incorporated into the Telecommunications Act of 1996, discussed in detail in the final chapter of this book.

Fairness Doctrine Abandoned

The Fairness Doctrine, in force from the 1940s forward, established an expectation that broadcast stations would air opposing sides of controversial issues. Throughout the 1980s, the FCC had asked Congress to repeal the Fairness Doctrine, but Congress refused to act. In 1987, a U.S. Court of Appeals held that the FCC had the authority to repeal it if the doctrine no longer served the public interest.[10] Congress then passed legislation to make the Fairness Doctrine part of federal statute that the agency could not repeal, but the law was vetoed twice by then-President Reagan.[11]

Challenges to remaining vestiges of the Fairness Doctrine continued through the early 1990s, with efforts by some to preserve the Personal Attack Rule, which required a broadcaster to give time to people or groups attacked on the air within the course of public discussion. However, by the year 2000 the courts ordered the FCC to repeal Fairness Doctrine rules that covered personal attacks, as well as those that required stations endorsing political candidates to notify opposing candidates and to offer them equal time. Broadcasters argued that the rules discouraged them from taking editorial positions and airing controversial broadcasts.

The Federal Appeals Court for the District of Columbia, in an opinion written by Judge Judith W. Rogers and joined by Chief Judge Harry T. Edwards, declared that the FCC had failed to respond to the court's requests that the agency justify the rules "in light of the court's earlier findings that the regulations chill at least some speech and impose at least some burdens on activities at the heart of the First Amendment."[12]

New Technology: Networks in Decline

Deregulation and the advance of technology created a new competitive playing field. As the networks strived to enhance profits, the glorious days of large news budgets at the networks were over. In 1987, about 200 employees were fired as part of a $30 million budget reduction. Some long-time reporters who were ousted included highly regarded law correspondent Fred Graham and Capitol Hill correspondent Ike Pappas. In the same sweep, CBS axed the sixteen-year-old children's program, "In the News," and fired its staff. "CBS Morning News" lost twenty-eight job positions. The news division also closed bureaus in Warsaw, Bangkok, and Seattle. Veteran newsmen, such as anchor Dan Rather and Fred W. Friendly, former CBS news president who had been Edward R. Murrow's producer, protested. Friendly argued that news staffs could not be cut to the bare bones and still have sufficient capacity to cover crises and emergencies, as well as routine news. Friendly told the *New York Times*

> [T]he way you judge a news team is how it acts in a crisis. When President Kennedy was shot, the country was on the edge of chaos. CBS held the country together with hundreds of reporters on five continents reporting on the meaning of it.

Friendly noted that CBS news was not losing money; "they're just not making as much as they might make." Asserting that CBS was not in the business of selling cash registers or pork bellies, he maintained, "They're licensed to operate in the public interest, and that's all been forgotten."[13]

CBS news, long the proud leader in network news, by 1987 was trailing NBC and ABC in the ratings game. Dan Rather's "Evening News" lagged behind NBC's Tom Brokaw and ABC's Peter Jennings. CBS also trailed in the prime-time and morning news ratings in 1986, when it became a three-time loser for the first time in at least sixteen years.[14]

Technologies of the 1980s

Cable: Shift of Power

Competition among the three networks was no longer a directly competitive situation. Cable television, which began as Community Antenna Television (CATV) designed to help distribute broadcast signals to communities that had difficulty receiving broadcast signals, challenged the dominance of the broadcast networks. During the early years, cable television was simply a distribution system. An antenna was placed on top of a hill and cables from the antenna fed the homes in a community with a clear signal. However, by the 1970s, cable included programming as well as distribution and challenged the traditional big three networks: ABC, CBS, and NBC. Coupled with satellite delivery of broadcast signals, cable stations and systems became entities in their own right.

CNN

Begun in 1980, Ted Turner's CNN became the first global television channel. By 1990, it was reaching 60 percent of homes in the United States and sending news to Europe and around the world via satellite.[15] A traveler in Moscow in mid-1992, in a room at the Savoy Hotel or the Metropole, could get CNN's Headline News Service in English. Because many Europeans have a working knowledge of English, CNN has remarkable impact worldwide.

FOX

Taking advantage of the FCC's desire to foster competition against the networks, Rupert Murdoch battled the dominant network structure of U.S. television by targeting a young audience with innovative programming. By the mid-1980s, Murdoch established his News Corporation as a major British and Australian media company; owned the *Sun,* Britain's largest-circulation daily, and the prestigious *Times;* and had begun laying the groundwork for a satellite television service called Sky Channel, which beams programs to cable systems throughout Europe.

In 1985, Murdoch expanded into electronic media and became a global power. Murdoch's News Corporation purchased Twentieth-Century Fox Film Corp. and its rich film library. In the same year, Murdoch bought six big-city television stations from Metromedia in New York, Los Angeles, Chicago, Dallas, Houston, and Washington, D.C.[16] The Federal Communications Act prohibits foreigners from owning U.S. television stations, but Murdoch changed his citizenship, and the FCC seemed to ignore the fact that his News Corporation consisted primarily of foreign investors.

Ten years after Murdoch started the network, which he named the Fox Network, the foreign ownership issue resurfaced. After an eighteen-month investigation, the FCC reversed its 1985 decision, declaring that Murdoch's company, despite his citizenship switch, was indeed a foreign company. However, the FCC simultaneously granted Murdoch a waiver from the foreign ownership rule, allowing him to continue business.[17]

The Fox Corporation became highly profitable, and, by 1987, Murdoch's Fox Television Network reached more than 80 percent of American homes.[18] Murdoch wasn't

▼

Bernard Shaw (1940–present)

Bernard Shaw reported on the assassination of Martin Luther King, Jr., reported from Tiana-men Square during student protests there, and moderated two debates. In addition, he reported on countless numbers of national and international events for CNN between 1980, when CNN was formed, and 2000, when he retired from the network. He will be most remem-bered for his live broadcasts from Baghdad with two other CNN reporters as American bombs began to fall in 1991. Shaw, who traveled to Baghdad hoping to interview Saddam Hussein, gave millions of Americans live radio coverage from his hotel room in downtown Baghdad as bombs were falling all over the city.

Source: M. D. Murray, *Encyclopedia of Television News* (Phoenix: Oryx Press, 1999). (*Photo:* Time-Pix)

the only cable success. Although cable audiences were too small to be measured in 1970, by 1987, nearly 80 percent of American households could hook into cable.[19] From 1980 to 1987, prime-time network share had dropped from 90 to 73 percent.

Media Technology Devices

VCRs: Entertainment without Advertising

The growing popularity of cable television was, for the networks, only part of the competitive equation. VCRs (videotape recorders/players) led to a video explosion in the 1980s, which had major implications for broadcast and cable advertising. Using

Figure 17–3   Dan Rather, CBS news anchorman, confers with Howard Stringer. Stringer, executive producer when this photograph was taken in 1983, was later promoted to chief of CBS news. (*U.S. News and World Report* photo, Division of Prints and Photographs, Library of Congress Collection)

VCRs, viewers could record shows to watch later without commercial messages, or buy or rent videotapes, thereby slipping into an advertising-free environment. In 1980, only 1 percent of U.S. households had VCRs; by 1992, more than 75 percent of American households had VCRs.[20]

The VCR spawned a whole new business—the video rental store. Rentals, however, peaked in 1986, when more than 34 million households took home 111.9 million tapes a month, or an average of 3.26 movies per household per month. By 1989, the number of households owning VCRs had increased, but the number of rentals per household slumped to 2.38 a month. By 1990, that number dropped further to 2.07.[21] As rentals slumped, however, sales of movies on video increased. Sales began in 1987 with Paramount's release of *Top Gun* for $26.95—it sold 3.5 million copies. In 1990 *Batman* sold 13 million copies. Another factor affecting video sales and rentals was cable delivery of top-event style movies. These offerings allow the consumer to call the cable company and order a movie on screen for an additional three to four dollars added to their monthly cable bill.

Portability

Music is an art form, but music as content has dominated various media. Once radio made the shift to music, portable radios and other devices for playing music were in demand. In the 1970s, reel-to-reel recorders gave way to portable cassette players, making it possible for people to play tapes on small, portable machines. Once Sony introduced the Walkman in 1979, portability was taken for granted. Records, cassette tapes, and eight-track tapes dominated the market during the 1970s, but in the mid-1980s, they lost ground quickly to the compact disk (CD), with its almost flawless sound reproduction. Sales of CDs soared from $17.2 million in 1983 to $930 million in 1986.

Computers and an Information Society

Although scientists have always been fascinated with developing "counting" machines, the first electronic, working computers were developed during the World War II era. As with most technology, no one person "invented" the computer or the Internet. Computers were not considered devices for the masses, but rather for performing large calculations or aiding military or governmental operations.

The breakthrough can be attributed to a variety of people. John Vincent Atanasoff, an Iowa State University professor, and Clifford E. Berry, an electrical engineering student, were in the process of constructing a computer when the war began. A huge computer, the Colossus, helped the British break German military codes, and Harvard mathematician Howard Aiken developed a computer to calculate artillery ballistics. When U.S. leaders saw the possibilities for defense and space applications of computer technology, they channeled government money to finance computer research and development.

Computers were considered huge memory machines. MIT researcher Vannevar Bush labeled such a machine a "memex," in which an individual could store books, "records, and communications, and which is mechanized so that it may be consulted with exceeding speed and flexibility. It is an enlarged intimate supplement to . . . memory."[22] Bush envisioned the machine as a desktop device with a keyboard; storage would be on microfilm, and dry photography would be used for input.

Doug Engelbart, a young sailor still on duty in 1945, read Bush's article and recognized the problem he described but realized that the computer, not a microfilm machine, was the answer. The computer could manipulate symbols and allow individuals to compare data.[23] Engelbart went on to direct laboratory research at the Stanford Research Institute and was active through the 1970s in developing computer applications. Engelbart's group at Stanford initiated the field of computer-supported cooperative work and invented WYSIWYG word processing, the mouse, multiwindow displays, and electronic meeting rooms.[24]

In 1946, the first electronic, general-purpose computer, Electronic Numerical Integrator and Computer (ENIAC), was developed at the University of Pennsylvania. The construction of the computer reflected the earlier work of Atanasoff and others.[25] ENIAC was eighteen feet tall, eighty feet long, and weighed thirty tons. It used 17,468 vacuum tubes connected by 500 miles of wire to perform 10,000 operations a second. To change its instructions, engineers had to rewire it. The research effort that produced it had been financed by the U.S. government in hopes that a computer would contribute to the war effort, and ENIAC was used to make some of the calculations in the building of the hydrogen bomb in the 1950s.

International Business Machines (IBM) president Thomas Watson, Jr., saw the ENIAC at work and realized that computers could replace mechanical business machines. He rushed to bring out a computer in 1954, only to learn that a competitor would quickly surpass it. Watson rushed development of memory technology that had been planned for later production and had it running in IBM machines within six months, an example of the kind of efforts that made IBM a leader in computer production by the 1960s.[26] By then vacuum tubes had been replaced by small silicon chips.

Engineers recognized at the beginning that computers had many possible applications. Not only could they manipulate numbers and sort information by topic but they also offered a platform for developing graphics programs that could serve as architectural and design tools. Already in the early 1950s, MIT laboratories were experimenting with interactive computing and computer graphics. Ivan Sutherland created "Sketchpad," a graphics program in which the user drew directly on the screen using a light pen. Sketchpad introduced software inventions such as the cursor, the window, and clipping. In 1955, IBM released the computer language FORTRAN, which was designed to aid scientists in solving engineering problems.

Mildred Koss, one of UNIVAC I's initial programmers, commented, "There were no limitations to what you could accomplish. There was lots of vision and new ideas as to where the computer might be used. We looked at the computer as a universal problem-solving machine. It had some rules and an operating system, but it was up to you to program it to do whatever you wanted it to do."[27] But computers could be problematic as well. Grace Hopper, a mathematician who worked in computer research at Harvard and developed the first commercial high-level computer language, gave a name to those problems. While trying to determine what had caused a computer malfunction, Hopper found the culprit—a dead moth on a vacuum tube. From then on, "bug" became a common computer term.[28]

The Microcomputer

With the development of the silicon chip in 1959, the electronics industry began to build microcomputers for individual use. Software, rather than hardware, determined the application. By the early 1960s, this infant industry was garnering annual revenues of more than $1 billion. As computers were used for processing different applications, hardware and software manufacturers began to rapidly develop new products.

In 1974, Intel marketed its first computer chip, the Intel 4004. This chip, which combined memory and logic functions on the microchip to produce a microprocessor, launched the individual computer market. First, workstation terminals that were attached to a large mainframe began to proliferate in the workplace, and then stand-alone desktop computers appeared. However, the personal computer (PC) was designed primarily for ham radio operators and other electronics hobbyists.

In 1975, Paul Allen, a friend of a Harvard student named Bill Gates, was attracted to a newsstand cover of the January 1975 issue of *Popular Electronics*. The cover featured the Altair 8800, the first practical mass-market machine. It was produced by a hobby company called Micro Instrumentation Telemetry Systems (MITS) and sold for $397, about the price of the Intel chip that made its production possible. But there was a catch. To be useful, an Altair required a video display terminal, storage disks, and a printer, which brought the price into the $5,000 range, but for that price the buyer had a computer that did real work, such as word processing, file management, and running BASIC, FORTRAN, COBOL, and PL/I programs. Programmers entered data with switches instead of a keyboard. Hobbyists and entrepreneurs loved the Altair. Personal computing had arrived.[29] Shortly after reading the article, Gates and Allen started the Microsoft Corporation.

In 1977, Steve Wozniak and Steve Jobs, two college dropouts, perfected the Apple II, which sold for about $1,300, contained four kilobytes of memory and came with a jack that converted a television set into a monitor. About the same time, the Tandy/Radio Shack TRS-80s became available; Tandy sported the first truly portable model. In 1981, Osborne introduced a machine with a built-in, 24-line monitor, and in 1981, IBM entered the market with the first IBM PC. "Totables" or "luggables" included the Kaypro, which sold for about $1,800, and Compaq's suitcase-style machine, which was about the size and weight of a portable sewing machine.

By the mid-1980s, the personal computer had been revolutionized with the advent of user-friendly operating systems, such as DOS. DOS-based personal computers became affordable, revolutionizing not only the workplace but also the home. These machines enabled people to use a desktop computer for sophisticated engineering problems and at the same time for other applications, such as word processing, graphics, design, spreadsheets, and database management. Personal computers became even more user friendly in 1984 with the introduction of the Macintosh by Apple. The Macintosh provided an easy-to-use format with a mouse and layers of work files (called the desktop) in a small, light computer.

In 1990, Gates introduced Microsoft's Windows 3.0 (and a 3.1 upgrade), which allowed DOS computers to be as user friendly as the Macintosh while retaining power and speed similar to that of the DOS microcomputer. Windows had sold 60 million copies by 1995, and Microsoft was supplying 80 percent of the operating systems worldwide. The company launched Windows 95 in August 1995, an operating system that better integrated hardware and software and managed complex directories and files. Windows 95 sold 40 million copies in the first year. In 1998, Microsoft introduced Windows 98, further perfecting the system. By 2000, Windows "Me," or the Millennium edition, was introduced, along with Windows 2000, based on Windows NT.

The introduction of user-friendly software, along with the trend toward microcomputers, has made computers a common household item. Some of the earliest users of portable computing technology were reporters, among whom the Tandy Radio Shack model was popular. By the end of the 1980s, reporters and editors were using computers for editing and pagemaking. By the early 1990s the ability to use the Internet and to access the World Wide Web revolutionized the way news was gathered and written.

Information via the Internet

The Internet, widely used by consumers and by news reporters and editors, is available today because the federal government wanted to link computers in such a way that in times of disaster—whether created by humans or nature—defense and communications systems could still operate. In the 1960s, the U.S. Defense Department designed an experimental network called ARPANET.

The crucial breakthrough for ARPANET came from proposals by British physicist Donald Watts Davies and by American Paul Baran of the Rand Corporation. Davies named the concept "packeting." His packet-switching made it possible for computers to divide information into manageable chunks, each with its own address and instructions for reassembly into a coherent message by a receiving computer.[30]

ARPANET began operations in 1969, linking computers at four universities, enabling researchers to share information by establishing computer news groups.[31] The success of ARPANET quickly evolved into many other networking imitators and innovators, linking computers not only to telephone lines but to fiber optic cables or to satellites. This made it possible to trade enormous swatches of information via the system known as Usenet.

As the type and number of network systems increased, it became apparent that using some common system that would allow computers to "talk" to each other would be beneficial to all. In the late 1980s, the National Science Foundation (NSF) created five supercomputer centers. At first, NSF tried to use ARPANET to connect them, but bureaucracy and staffing problems got in the way. NSF, therefore, created its own network, connecting the centers with telephone lines. Then, through a chain system, the network linked universities and other commercial and noncommercial computer groups. In each area of the country a group is linked to its neighbor group or institution, rather than everyone being fed to a central location. This saves primarily in the cost of telephone lines.

The success of the system came close to being its downfall, because users multiplied rapidly and the telephone lines could not sustain the use. In 1987, the old network was replaced with higher-capacity telephone lines. The most important feature of the NSF network has been its commitment to letting everyone use it, thereby opening up enormous sources of data and conversations for people using computers.[32] What is amazing is that connections occur within seconds, despite being linked from one institution to another across hundreds of miles or around the world.

By the 1990s, the various networks combined into the Internet. As Stephen Lubar wrote, "The Internet, as the network of networks came to be called, in 1992 linked more than 17,000 networks in thirty-three countries, all together more than 500,000 computers, and was growing at a rate of 15 percent a month.[33]

The Internet is the carrier of a variety of services, including on-line newspapers, original Internet content, electronic shopping, music that can be downloaded and played through stereo and television equipment, and streaming video that offers real-time news feeds. The Internet distributes almost any content that can be imagined.

Government News Management in Modern War

In war, truth is often the first casualty.[34] One of the fundamental cornerstones of American society is that civilians control the military—the military do not control civilian life. Because the need to protect the country is the foremost task of the military, its belief in a need for secrecy often conflicts with society's need for information. Thus, there are ongoing tensions between the American news media and the U.S. Army, Navy, and Marine Corps. Apparently, as a 1995 report by journalist Frank Aukofer and Vice Admiral William P. Lawrence said of the press and the military, clashes are inevitable.

> The press wants to tell the story, and the military wants to win the war and keep casualties to a minimum. The press wants freedom, and the military wants control. These are fundamental differences that will never change.[35]

As you read in Chapter 16, the freedom to cover the Vietnam conflict gave some military and government leaders pause. Because they believed the media had contributed to the quagmire in Vietnam, they were determined to structure coverage in other ways during conflicts of the 1980s and 1990s. Daniel Hallin argued that because of Vietnam, the British government "imposed tight controls on news coverage of the Falkland crisis of 1982."[36] The British government's success at keeping reporters under control during the Falkland Island incursion, coupled with the myth that Vietnam had been lost by the press, made a profound impression on the Reagan White House.

In 1983, when U.S. military forces invaded Grenada to protect medical students from a purported takeover of the island by communist forces, reporters were kept far from the initial and most important first two days of the military action. Although Larry Flynt, publisher of *Hustler* magazine, sued Secretary of Defense Caspar Weinberger and others, seeking an injunction against being denied access to the scene of the action, the lawsuit was ruled moot. The court argued that the military action had ended and that there was no reasonable likelihood that the Grenada action would happen again.[37]

The smugly excessive secrecy of the Grenada invasion, with its underlying "U.S. reporters are not real Americans" theme, brought fervent protests from the press. These protests resulted in administration and Pentagon acquiescence in the creation of "press pools." As it worked out, a small number of journalists, primarily from the more prominent print and electronic media organizations, were selected by government and media leaders. Journalists who were chosen for such a pool were "on call," expected to be ready to go wherever military action happened. Pool journalists were expected to serve as surrogates for those not selected. In theory, this would enable essential information to reach news outlets as the pool journalists shared their reports with others. Furthermore, because there were fewer reporters for the military to deal with in a pool situation, the military would not have to worry about accommodating large numbers of reporters while trying to win a military action.

Jeffery A. Smith, writing in *War and Press Freedom: The Problem of Prerogative Power,* argued that "no exigency of the nation, not even war, can rewrite the First Amendment and its absolute ban on prior restraint and on subsequent penalties for news coverage and commentary." He cited the Grenada exercise as particularly ludicrous.[38]

Press Pools, the Persian Gulf, and Panama

The first test of the National Press Pool came during the coverage of sea and air battles in the Persian Gulf in 1986–1987, a situation in which the U.S. forces were a looming presence but as observers more than as participants. According to Fred Hoffman, a one-time Associated Press reporter who also had experience as a Pentagon spokesman, reporters acquitted themselves well in the 1986–1987 pool, respecting essential ground rules and maintaining operational security. As Hoffman later said, "Unless the Defense Department's leaders are prepared to extend that trust in hot-war situations, the pool probably will be of little value."[39]

When a hot-war situation came in Panama on December 20, 1989, the sixteen-member National Press Pool, however helpful to military authorities, was an operational disaster for the news media. The pool correspondents were taken to Panama belatedly and had no real chance to cover the important initial actions by 25,000 topflight U.S. troops and some of the most sophisticated U.S. military hardware—from tanks to helicopter gunships to Stealth bombers.[40]

This impressive array of military might resulted in the capture of the Panamanian strongman and former Central Intelligence Agency collaborator General Manuel Antonio Noriega. (Noriega later was tried on drug charges in a U.S. district court in Florida and convicted.) However, what *really* happened in Panama? The U.S. military establishment provided few answers.

A Department of Defense postmortem on invasion coverage criticized Secretary of Defense Dick Cheney (elected Vice President in 2000) for his overactive concern with secrecy and cited numerous other foul-ups that got in the way of pool coverage. Both Cheney and his press aide, Pete Williams (now of NBC news), were assigned blame for the inability of the National Press Pool to allow effective coverage of the Panama invasion.[41]

A year to the day after the U.S. invasion of Panama, U.S. representative Charles Rangel (D–NY) on December 20, 1990, raised questions about the U.S. military withholding videotapes shot from gun cameras on board Apache attack helicopters. He wondered whether those videotapes might help to resolve the discrepant reports about the number of Panamanian civilians killed during the invasion. A year later, the U.S. figures counted 202 dead, but some human rights organizations claimed that more than 2,000 civilians had died.[42]

Press pools or not, civilian reporters in a war zone are largely at the mercy of the military. Correspondents' movements can be controlled, and their dispatches can be censored and/or delayed. Nevertheless, wartime conditions are not the only reasons why war reporting—or any reporting on government—is not as adversarial as

▼

News

The conflict between the men who make and the men who report the news is as old as time. News may be true, but it is not truth, and reporters and officials seldom see it the same way. . . . In the old days, the reporters or couriers of bad news were often put to the gallows; now they are given the Pulitzer Prize, but the conflict goes on.

—James Reston (b. 1909), U.S. journalist. *The Artillery of the Press*, "The Tug of History" (1966)

highly visible TV reporters such as Dan Rather (CBS) or Sam Donaldson (ABC) might claim. Consider Daniel Hallin's assertion in his study of coverage of the Vietnam War:

> Structurally the American news media are both highly autonomous from direct political control and, through the routines of the news-gathering process, deeply intertwined in the actual operation of government.[43]

In time of war, reporters are forced to follow the rules to get access to information. Prior restraint, of course, can be held over all dispatches communicated after battle. Also, military officers can control correspondents' movements, and even have a large say on who talks to reporters and who does not.

The Persian Gulf War and the Media

The U.S. military public relations apparatus not only had the upper hand over the American reporters during the Persian Gulf War of 1991, the military for the most part controlled the pictures in the heads of the public. The first "Bush" President, George H. W. Bush, vowed that the Persian Gulf War would not be "another Vietnam" and—in hindsight—seemed to be talking about two separate matters. First, he announced his determination to commit enough military might to bring the war to a conclusive end. Second, he asserted that, unlike Vietnam, reporters were not going to control the images of the war at home. During the Vietnam conflict, corpses were seen on television and the pictures were plain: War kills people.

With the approved televised coverage of the 100-hour war in the Persian Gulf, camera operators on rooftops sent home, via satellite, nighttime pictures of a light show or fireworks display—an abstract, entertaining picture from hell. Rockets glared and bombs flared and tracers stitched unimaginable light patterns in the skies. With the coverage rules, however, although "smart bombs" were shown being steered down smokestacks, corpses were rarely seen. The bodies of the dead were shown only after television crews and photographers from other nations provided coverage.

A top military correspondent, Malcolm W. Browne of the *New York Times*, saw the limitations placed on news correspondents in the Persian Gulf as a return to what he called "near-total military supervision of their work."[44]

Correspondents were assigned military escorts. Some were helpful and useful but others, because of officiousness or lack of proper training, simply got in the way. Reports filtered back from the Gulf of escorts who would even interrupt interviews, on the grounds that a reporter's questions were improper. For example, a reporter was questioning an enlisted man about his difficulties in worshipping according to his Christian faith in a country that outlawed everything but Muslim rites; the interview was halted by a military escort, a so-called information officer, who said, "Military ground rules forbid questions about things that we don't know about necessarily."[45]

Reporters could understand why in-the-field commanders asked that a battle's location not be given: CNN, for example, which was viewed with great interest in Baghdad, sent satellite-transmitted news from the Kuwait region in an instant to the entire globe. At times, however, the information battlefield commanders asked to be withheld was released almost simultaneously by officials at the Pentagon. As Malcolm Browne observed, the Pentagon was eager to be the first to report the most important news stories.[46] General Norman ("Stormin' Norman") Schwarzkopf, in overall charge of the Persian Gulf operations, became an instant household word and a favorite war hero with the TV briefings he gave, using flip-charts, pointers, and video clips of "smart bombs."

Some journalists complained about Schwartzkopf's passion for "fighting the last [Vietnam] war" and controlling journalists' access to information. *Newsday*'s Patrick J. Sloyan, whose Gulf War coverage won a Pulitzer Prize, rated Schwartzkopf higher on press coverage than he did then-Secretary of Defense (Vice President in 2001) Dick Cheney. Sloyan said Cheney manipulated information fed to the media: "this footage they would spoon feed . . . would dominate perceptions of what was going on."[47]

Despite journalists' problems with access, a total of 186 journalists eventually participated in the press pools in the Gulf War, as compared to only twenty-seven reporters accompanying the troops when the United States and the Allies invaded Normandy in World War II.[48]

The military was in control of its image throughout the Persian Gulf War. The high-tech warfare, the nature of the terrain in the Saudi Arabia–Iraq–Kuwait region, and the restrictions administered by military pools all contributed to polishing the image. Also, with hundreds of reporters brought into the region via the pools, some simply did not have the experience or background to report on the war. The combination of questions at military briefings in Saudi Arabia—some professionally, abrasively pointed from combat-wise journalists and others of the inane, repetitious, slow-pitched variety—infuriated many viewers.[49]

The only way around the pools was for journalists to take off on their own. CBS reporter Bob Simon was captured by Iraqi forces while trying to break free of stultifying pool arrangements and find some real news on his own. Cable News Network broke free of the competition in many ways: Its coverage of the Persian Gulf War was the most comprehensive, and CNN's Peter Arnett scored a remarkable feat by broadcasting reports (obviously censored and sanitized) from Baghdad.

Operation Desert Storm, as the Persian Gulf fighting was called, led to a wave of spread-eagle patriotism, with much of the war coverage by Americans amounting to uncritical support, almost cheerleading. Peter Arnett's reporting from Baghdad was attacked by some flag-waving politicos as the equivalent of treason, and some members of the press joined in. With scattered exceptions such as Arnett and Bob Simon, most of the press submitted tamely to military control of its image. The pictures in American heads during the brief war were directed, by and large, by the military.

Perhaps it might be said that, for the most part, pragmatism ruled the major U.S. news suppliers. If the military was too much in control of access to information in a foreign war zone, there was some sentiment that things could get even worse. In time of war, the military establishment has the whip hand and if challenged in civilian courts is likely to be given the benefit of the doubt.

Evidently for fear of what a conservative Supreme Court might do with the issue of military control of the press in wartime, leading American news organizations chose not to join a lawsuit by Sydney Schanberg, a Pulitzer Prize winner for his coverage of Vietnam. (The motion picture *The Killing Fields* was based on Schanberg's work.) Schanberg, joined by some American publications with a tradition of protest—including *The Progressive* and *Nation* magazines—did not get support from journalistic heavy-hitters such as the *New York Times*, the television network news operations, the *Washington Post*, or the Associated Press. Schanberg, along with famed novelists E. L. Doctorow and William Styron as well as Michael Klare of *Nation* magazine, sued Secretary of Defense Dick Cheney and Assistant Secretary for Public Affairs Pete Williams, seeking an end to what were termed unfair policies. One such policy was a press rule, issued on January 9, 1991, ordering that media reports from combat pools be reviewed by an on-site military public affairs officer before being transmitted. This caused delay and, at times, outright suppression. In addition, even when officers in the field cleared a dispatch, it might be later delayed or stopped outright further up the line.[50]

Astonishingly, the lawsuit failed. Even more astounding, it received only minimal coverage in the establishment news media. Major press either feared losing favored status or reasoned that asking the right question of a conservative Supreme Court could result in a pronouncement encouraging even more restrictive censorship than that of the Persian Gulf crisis. As it stood, the basic law governing military censorship was from the peacetime case of *Near v. Minnesota* (1931), which said that prepublication censorship was constitutionally permissible in wartime.[51]

Management of Special-Interest News

In a society that has grown increasingly complex, public relations and public information specialists carry an enormous responsibility as well as wield immense power in supplying the public with information. These professionals are active in business, science, and the political realm. The connection between public relations and journalism has been an often-debated subject, as journalists argue that public relations specialists have to serve, first, the organization that hires them to create a favorable image and, second—the truth. Public relations professionals argue that journalists too serve more than one master: the organizations that hire them, the public, their sources, and—the truth.

Because government is so large and so complex, there simply are not enough reporters and editors to cover it. Could one or two Associated Press reporters cover all the nonsecret newsworthy reports to be found in the Pentagon on any given day? The answer is no. With 535 members of the House of Representatives and 100 U.S. Senators, could any one person—or news organization—cover the entire Congress? Obviously not.

Without news provided by information officers in the Pentagon or press aides to members of the House or the Senate, Americans would be more poorly informed than they are now. In the average daily newspaper, more than half of the publication's stories are apt to originate from public relations sources. True, the information obtained will be checked out and, with ethical news operations, rewritten, but it should be apparent that public relations is an inseparable part of every American's information stream every day.

Public relations pioneer Edward L. Bernays, looking back over a career of more than three-quarters of a century, saw *public relations* as a term that can be used—and misused—by anyone, from superb practitioner to absolute charlatan. Even so, he defined public relations optimistically, as "an art applied to a science—social science—in which the public interest rather than financial motivation is the primary consideration."[52]

Consider his words—"the public interest." Is there only *one* public interest? Actually, there are many public interests, and public relations specialists and firms, with strategies and techniques carefully arrayed, try to attract or neutralize any number of publics. The interest at Exxon Corporation in "a good environment" will not coincide with that of the salmon fishers of Alaska, the Sierra Club, or the Audubon Society. In public relations, as in law, when an adversary system rewards winning more than justice, the assumption is that the better technician and tactician should win. How that serves "the public interest" is open to conjecture. However, if public relations (PR) is to thrive, it must be further accepted at the corporate chief executive officer (CEO) level. Further, leading PR practitioners urge corporate openness and good citizenship in areas such as environmental awareness and protection.[53]

What Edward L. Bernays called many years ago (in an unintentionally ominous term) "the engineering of consent" is now a collection of huge enterprises. Public relations counseling, according to one forecast, could more than double in the years between 1986 and the first years of the twenty-first century.[54] By the 1990s, PR had been expanding, being given increasing responsibility for product positioning and sales through the orchestration of "integrated marketing campaigns." As ad agencies moved into the twenty-first century, they became increasingly global.

The *Exxon Valdez*—Public Relations Disaster

When a giant oil company's tanker—the *Exxon Valdez*—rammed into a reef and cracked open near Prince William Sound, Alaska, in March 1989, the Exxon Corporation faced a no-win situation. Hundreds of thousands of barrels of oil despoiled more than 1,000 miles of shoreline. Alaska's fishing industry suffered severe damage, and television comedians' wisecracks about Exxon's new recipes for "blackened salmon" did not help.

Things got worse for Exxon when accusations were leveled that Captain Joseph Hazelwood of the *Exxon Valdez* would face criminal charges for being in command of a ship while intoxicated. (A jury later found him guilty.) Meanwhile, Exxon chairman Lawrence G. Rawl and other top Exxon officials decided to stay at the New York corporate headquarters rather than going to Alaska to take personal charge of efforts to clean up the spill. Although New York officials of Exxon would not talk to the press, company statements about the spill and the clean-up work were made from the little town of Valdez, where communications facilities for reporters were inadequate.[55]

At various times, Exxon dug a deeper hole for itself: It squabbled publicly with the government of Alaska and with the U.S. Coast Guard, claiming—falsely, said

Alaska's Governor Steve Cowper—that the oil company had been slowed in its clean-up efforts by official interference. By appearing far less than cooperative on clean-up efforts, Exxon assured itself months of sharply critical headlines, plus lambasting by congressional investigating committees. More than 18,000 customers sent their credit cards back to Exxon. The whole fiasco cost the company billions of dollars: $2 billion in clean-up efforts, plus a fine and an environmental reparation settlement totaling another $1 billion.[56]

Exxon's disaster—and its disastrous handling of the PR problems associated with the Alaskan oil spill—is now a familiar staple of "how not to" case studies. As a leading public relations text points out, the lessons of the *Exxon Valdez* were not lost on British Petroleum when it had a smaller oil spill along the California coast in 1989. The British Petroleum (BP) CEO went to the disaster scene; a well-run clean-up operation was organized quickly, and BP leveled with the press, even providing photos of holes in the hull of the BP tanker *American Trader*. Efforts to assist media communications were substantial, and BP, unlike Exxon, escaped with unscathed and perhaps enhanced credibility.[57]

Politics and Public Relations

Political public relations in North America arguably is older than the United States. After all, the orchestration of protests against British rule that helped lead to the War for Independence can be viewed as one form of political communication. It may also be said that the famous Federalist Papers written by James Madison, Alexander Hamilton, and John Jay to push for adoption of the Constitution of 1787 were likewise excellent examples of political public relations.[58]

Some benchmarks in the practice of modern political PR were provided in the 1950s by the California-based firm of (Clem) Whitaker and (Leone) Baxter. Whitaker and Baxter cut notches as political hired guns with adept sloganeering to short-circuit thought processes. Did the American Medical Association want to oppose a national health insurance plan being considered by Congress? Whitaker and Baxter hung the ominous label of "socialized medicine" on the plan, a tactic dooming it. Did railroads want to defeat a "full crew" referendum vote in California? During the month before the election, 200 radio stations in California ran a musical jingle five to ten times each day, "I've been loafing on the railroad." The railroad's campaign succeeded, and the referendum went down in defeat.[59]

Whitaker and Baxter pioneered in a variety of ways: It was the first firm to specialize in political campaign management. Also, it anticipated modern campaign tactics—first, by looking for a label or "gimmick" (for example, "I've been loafing on the railroad") and second, by having the ability to accomplish everything needed in a PR campaign: generating news releases, preparing press packets, producing radio ads, designing campaign literature and billboards, and organizing "grassroots" supporters and events. What Whitaker and Baxter started in the 1930s and 1940s set a pattern for 1990s campaigns. Televised sound-bites may have replaced catchy musical jingles, but the mass marketing of candidates and issues was here to stay.[60]

Spin Doctors

A 1990s phrase referred to political PR operators as "spin doctors." One major firm that has occasionally corkscrewed itself while trying to put "spin"—a client's special interest—on news is Hill and Knowlton. For example, a fifteen-year-old female Kuwaiti hospital worker known as Nayirah testified before a congressional committee in the fall of 1990 that she had seen Iraqi soldiers throwing babies out of incubators, leaving them to die on the floor. This incubator atrocity story became a prominent part of the debate over whether Congress should declare war on Iraq, which ultimately received a margin of just five votes in the U.S. Senate. It was later revealed that Nayirah was the daughter of Kuwait's ambassador to the United States, and she did not work in a hospital. Months after her testimony and after the warfare in Kuwait, ABC's John Martin was told by Kuwaiti hospital officials that the incubator-dumping incident had not occurred. Later investigations found witnesses to seven Iraqi-caused incubator deaths, although "Nayirah herself admitted to Kroll [an investigator for the Kuwaiti government] that she had seen only one of the fifteen babies mentioned in her written testimony, which was prepared with the aid of Hill and Knowlton."[61]

Hill and Knowlton, paid $11.5 million by the Kuwaiti government–financed Citizens for a Free Kuwait, had been engaged to help the United States decide to go to war. The public relations firm produced a video news release on Nayirah's testimony before Congress, and it was made available to 700 television stations in the United States. Portions of Nayirah's testimony from the video news release were used in a major story on "NBC Nightly News" on October 10, 1990.[62]

Many American reporters accepted as fact the stage-managed news orchestrated by Hill and Knowlton. Reporters eager to get a story and, perhaps, eager to avoid the "unpatriotic news" label assigned to press reports during Vietnam, failed to appropriately question the stories generated by special interest spin doctors. Reporters, editors, and news directors could protect themselves by adopting this attitude: "Fool me once, shame on you; fool me twice, shame on me." Identification by the media of spin doctors who have been known to be, in the British phrase, "economical with the truth" might be one place to start.

Changing News Agenda for Newspapers

In 1950, David Reisman, in a classic work, *The Lonely Crowd*, noted that journalists paid more attention to politics than the audience seemed to demand. Michael Schudson, writing in 1982, observed that the same was still true: "Journalists accord politics a prestige it does not have in the public mind."[63] In 1979, the study *Changing Needs of Changing Readers* by Yankelovich, Skelly, and White for the American Society of Newspaper Editors reinforced the concept that readers wanted information of importance to their own daily lives more than they wanted political news. The study indicated seven hot areas for newspapers to explore: economics, business, financial news, health, personal safety, technology, and international developments. The kind of news readers wanted within these categories, the study emphasized, was news interpreted to explain the impact of events on the local arena. For example, readers wanted to know the effects of decisions made by OPEC (the Organization of Petroleum Exporting Countries) on local oil markets in Texas.[64]

Responding to extensive market research, a highly criticized (but frequently imitated) enterprise was conducted by Gannett Company—the launching of a new national newspaper.

USA Today

"McNewspaper," better known as *USA Today*, was launched in 1982 as a five-day-a-week national newspaper. The brainchild of Allen H. Neuharth, then Gannett's chairman and CEO, *USA Today* helped change American newspapers, both in content and appearance. In preparing to launch this product, Gannett conducted without doubt the most extensive market research in the history of newspapering. The market research indicated that readers wanted short stories, charts, pictures, and graphs, and they wanted information presented in ways that could be absorbed quickly. So extensive was the research that the only addition made after the paper began was a reader-requested crossword puzzle.[65]

USA Today was the first national newspaper, with the exception of Dow Jones' *Wall Street Journal*, to hit the stands since the demise of another Dow Jones publication, the *National Observer*, a serious general interest weekly published between 1961 and 1976. The *Observer*'s audience was so diverse that its "demographics just didn't grab advertisers," reported Lawrence Armour, director of corporate relations for Dow Jones and Company. *USA Today*, on the other hand, is clearly directed. As founder Al Neuharth put it in 1983, the paper is aimed at "several million readers across the U.S.A. who are mobile and curious and have a general interest in what's going on around them, not just finance, not just politics, not just sports."[66] Gannett used its nationwide editorial, production, circulation, promotion, and delivery networks already in place and by January 1983 reported an audited circulation of 531,438. By 1992, *USA Today* had a circulation of over 1.5 million, second only to the *Wall Street Journal*'s 1.8 million.

The editorial product was one of the first to be satellite-beamed to a variety of printing locations. The splashy color and arresting graphics introduced by *USA Today* became standard for many publications, and by the late 1990s, even the *New York Times* and the *Washington Post* began to run color.

In a speech to the Inland Daily Press Association in 1985, Neuharth said readers expect newspapers to "present all the news in the particular arena in which we play. That means the good as well as the bad, the glad as well as the sad. They want reading their newspaper to be as enjoyable an experience as watching television."[67]

Wallace Wright's study of the "good news" qualities of *USA Today* indicated that positioning was the most critical factor, and that 57.4 percent of the good-news stories and only 31.9 percent of the bad-news stories appeared above the fold in that newspaper.[68] Wright said the newspaper's handling of an income-poverty report in 1984 prompted his study. The first six paragraphs of the article in *USA Today* head-

Figure 17–4 Large circulations demand tons of newsprint. These rolls are lifted by overhead cranes with vacuum lifts. (Photo courtesy of the *Chicago Tribune*)

lined "1st Real Income Gain in 4 Years," focusing on a U.S. Census Bureau report that the median income for various U.S. brackets had increased between 1.4 and 3.3 percent over the previous year. In the seventh paragraph, however, the newspaper reported what arguably was the *real* (if bad) news: The national poverty rate reached 15.2 percent of the population, its highest level in eighteen years. The *New York Times* and the *Washington Post* coverage of the same report led with the news regarding the increase in poverty.

Critics have called *USA Today* a fast-food newspaper, with "no serious sense of priorities."[69] The question, asked media critic Ben Bagdikian, is, "[H]ow good is the paper journalistically?" The newspaper represents no gain to the reading public, he declared, claiming that the public "gets a flawed picture of the world each day." He argued that *USA Today* represented "a serious blow to American journalism, since the paper represents the primacy of packagers and market analysts in a realm where the news judgment of reporters and editors has traditionally prevailed."[70] Bagdikian's judgment seems harsh, especially when laid alongside *USA Today*'s editorial page. Developed under John Seigenthaler, respected editor of *The Tennessean* of Nashville, the editorial page and op-ed page take on significant topics, firmly expressing the paper's views and yet also offering contrary opinions, making for a thoughtfully organized presentation of diverse views rather than a collection of scatter-shooting expressions of generally one-sided opinions.

Although critics such as Bagdikian viewed *USA Today* with alarm, others praised its layout, innovative use of color, and clarity of writing and suggested that similar techniques could be profitably applied to newspapers with more serious agendas.

By 1997, *USA Today* had experienced profit during some quarters but it had not become a major money-maker for the Gannett chain. Its ability to attract large numbers of readers, however, had caught the publisher's attention. In another flurry of planning in the early 1990s, Gannett Corporation launched its "News 2000" project, an effort (with overtones of some of *USA Today*'s approaches) to make Gannett's newspapers more attractive and relevant to its readers.

Conclusion

By 1992, the growing number of media companies on the stock exchange and the further consolidation of media companies were facts of life. The networks, dominant since the days of radio, faced hard times and challenges from the cable industry. New technologies challenged old regulations and ideas of scarcity. Yet, in the midst of ever-proliferating channels, critics charged that public discourse had deteriorated and that more channels meant more of the same old content—or less quality and more quantity.

The advent of computers and viewing devices such as VCRs broadened consumers' options. Access to information on the Internet became a reality, at least in the business world, by the end of the 1980s. Such developments set the stage for an on-line revolution during the 1990s.

The Reagan administration during the 1980s chartered a course of deregulation that freed the networks from many of the restrictions and charges to serve the public interest that had surfaced during Newton Minow's chairmanship at the FCC in the 1960s. Gone were regulations about children's and public affairs programming, and the Fairness Doctrine slid into limbo.

Unhappy with the media coverage of Vietnam, the U.S. military organized its news management systems to limit media access to conflicts in Grenada, Panama, and the Persian Gulf. Censorship was imposed in all these conflicts, primarily through limiting access to action and sources. Cable television—CNN, in particular—covered the Gulf War live, and the video footage provided by the Pentagon was so graphically good that networks and cable were unable to resist its use.

Public relations became an increasingly important player in news delivery systems. Faced with challenges such as the oil spill in Alaska, Exxon turned to public relations as a way of handling a highly damaging business operation. Public relations also became a significant player in domestic politics as well as in foreign relations.

In a video and consumer age, newspapers faced a declining readership and began to change the news agenda, hoping to recruit younger readers to their pages. The short stories, emphasis on good news, and graphics displayed by newspapers such as *USA Today* attracted criticism, but they also were adopted by many newspapers striving to stay competitive in the media mix.

Endnotes

1. Neil Postman, *Amusing Ourselves to Death* (New York: Viking Penguin, 1985).

2. "GE's Planned $6.28 Billion Acquisition of RCA Is Expected to Take 9 Months," *Wall Street Journal*, February 13, 1986, p. 1.

3. "GE and RCA: A Sampling of Opinions," *Wall Street Journal*, December 13, 1985, sec. 2, p. 27.

4. Quoted in James L. Rowe, Jr., "Chains Seen Buying More Papers," *Washington Post*, June 1, 1986, p. F2.

5. Ben Bagdikian, "The Twenty-Six Corporations That Own Our Media," *Extra*, June 1987, p. 1.

6. Cited in Rowe, "Chains Buying More Papers."

7. For thorough analysis of the effects of consumer reform, see Willard D. Rowland, Jr., "The Illusion of Fulfillment: The Broadcast Reform Movement," *Journalism Monographs*, no. 79 (December, 1982).

8. *Broadcasting*, December 28, 1987, p. 31; and Caroline E. Mayer and Elizabeth Tucker, "The FCC According to Fowler," *Washington Post*, April 19, 1987, sec. H1, p. 4.

9. David Clark Scott, "ABC Merger Likely to Generate Spinoff Sales," *Christian Science Monitor*, March 20, 1985, p. 19.

10. *Meredith Corp. v. FCC*, 809 F.2d 863 (D.C. Cir. 1987).

11. Dwight L. Teeter and D. R. Le Duc, *Law of Mass Communications*, 7th ed. (Westbury, N.Y.: Foundation Press, 1992), p. 397.

12. Quoted in Stephen Labaton, "Court Rejects F.C.C. Mandate to Broadcast Political Replies," *New York Times on the Web*, October 12, 2000.

13. Tom Shales and Trustman Senger, "At CBS, a Day of Bad News," *Washington Post*, July 2, 1986, p. 6.

14. Alison Leigh Cowan, "Tisch Is Holding a Hot Potato," *New York Times*, March 13, 1987, p. 18.

15. Michael Schrage and David A. Vise, "Murdoch, Turner Launch Era of Global Television," *Washington Post*, August 31, 1986, sec. H1.

16. Stuart Taylor, Jr., "Witch-Hunt or Whitewash?" *The American Lawyer* (April, 1995), p. 60.

17. "Fox and Murdoch Win a Big One," *U.S. News and World Report* (May 15, 1995), pp. 17+.

18. Don R. Le Duc, "Media Ownership: Consolidation and Globalization," in Teeter and Le Duc, *Law of Mass Communications*, chap. 16, p. 701.

19. John W. Wright, ed., *The Universal Almanac* (Kansas City: Andrews and McMeel, 1991), pp. 251–252.

20. Wright, *The Universal Almanac*, p. 253.

21. "Movie Rentals Fade, Forcing an Industry to Change Its Focus," *New York Times*, May 6, 1990, pp. 1, 34.

22. Vannevar Bush, "As We May Think," *Atlantic Monthly* (July, 1945).

23. Larry Press, "Before the Altair: The History of Personal Computing," Communications of the ACM (September, 1993), pp. 27+, via Lexis-Nexis.

24. Press, "Before the Altair." See also D. C. Engelbart and W. K. English, "A Research Center for Augmenting Human Intellect," proceedings of the 1968 Fall Joint Computer Conference (Washington, D.C.: Thompson Book Co.), pp. 395–410.

25. Eugene Marlow, "The Electrovisual Manager: Media and American Corporate Management," *Business Horizons* (March, 1994), pp. 61+, via Lexis-Nexis; see also a Web site describing Atanasoff's contributions at http://www.lib.iastate.edu/arch/jva.html.

26. James Flanigan, "Look to Thomas Watson's Past for IBM's Future," *Los Angeles Times*, January 5, 1994, p. D1, via Lexis-Nexis.

27. Cited in Denise W. Gurer, "Pioneering Women in Computer Science," *Communications of the Association for Computing Machinery* (January, 1995), p. 58.

28. Gurer, "Pioneering Women," p. 50.

29. Michael Swaine, "The Programmer Paradigm," *Dr. Dobbs' Journal of Software Tools*, pp. 109+, via Lexis-Nexis.

30. Katie Hafner and Matthew Lyon, *Where Wizards Stay Up Late: The Origins of the Internet* (New York: Simon and Schuster, 1996).

31. Stephen Lubar, *Infoculture: The Smithsonian Book of Information Age Inventions* (Boston: Houghton Mifflin, 1993), pp. 153–154.

32. For a full discussion of the network, see "What Is the Internet?" in Ed Krol, *The Whole Internet User's Guide and Catalog* (Sebastopol, Calif.: O'Reilly & Associates, 1992).

33. Lubar, *Infoculture*, p. 155.

34. Phillip Knightley, *The First Casualty: From the Crimea to Vietnam: The War Correspondent as Hero, Propagandist, and Myth Maker* (New York: Harcourt Brace Jovanovich, 1975).

35. Frank Aukofer and William P. Lawrence, *America's Team: The Odd Couple: A Report on the Relationship between the Media and the Military* (Nashville: Freedom Forum First Amendment Center, 1995), p. vii.

36. Daniel C. Hallin, *The Uncensored War: The Media and Vietnam* (Berkeley: University of California Press, 1986), p. 4.

37. *Flynt v. Weinberger,* 762 F.2d 134, 11 Med.L. Rptr. 2118 (D.C. Cir.1985).

38. Jeffery A. Smith, *War and Press Freedom: The Problem of Prerogative Power (*New York: Oxford University Press, 1999), p. 4.

39. Quoted in George Garneau, "Panning the Pentagon," *Editor & Publisher,* March 31, 1990, p. 11.

40. Garneau, "Panning the Pentagon," p. 11.

41. Garneau, "Panning the Pentagon," p. 11; and Carter et al., p. 610, citing "DOD Criticizes U.S. Handling of Media Coverage," March 26, 1990, p. 100.

42. Charles B. Rangel, "The Pentagon Pictures," *New York Times* (national ed.), December 20, 1990, p. A19.

43. Hallin, *The Uncensored War,* p. 8.

44. Malcom W. Browne, "Conflicting Censorship Upsets Many," *New York Times,* January 21, 1991, p. A8.

45. Clarence Page, "Gulf between Military, Media Is So Wide That Truth Has Been Put in Choke Hold," *Milwaukee Sentinel,* January 22, 1991, part 1, p. 8.

46. Browne, "Conflicting Censorship."

47. Aukofer and Lawrence, *America's Team,* p. 15.

48. Aukofer and Lawrence, *America's Team,* p. 15.

49. "The Gulf War and the Media," taped excerpts and dialogue of September 13, 1991, conference at the Woodrow Wilson International Center, Washington, D.C., Lawrence W. Lichty, director, Media Studies Project.

50. Other magazines involved in the lawsuit included *Harper's, Mother Jones, In These Times,* and the *Village Voice.*

51. *Near v. Minnesota ex rel. Olson,* 283 U.S. 697, 716 (1931).

52. Edward L. Bernays, Foreword to Dennis L. Wilcox, Philip H. Ault, and Warren K. Agee, *Public Relations: Strategies and Tactics,* 3rd ed. (New York: HarperCollins, 1992), p. xx.

53. See, for example, "What's Ahead in the 1990s," special issue of *Public Relations Journal* (January 1990), *passim.*

54. Robert L. Dilenschneider, "Afterword: The Future of Public Relations," in Wilcox et al., *Public Relations,* p. 659.

55. See Wilcox et al., *Public Relations,* pp. 348–352; and William J. Small, "*Exxon Valdez:* How to Spend Billions

and Still Get a Black Eye," *Public Relations Review* (Spring, 1991), pp. 9–13, 19, 22–23.

56. Small, "*Exxon Valdez,*" p. 10; Samuel Coad Dyer, M. Mark Miller, and Jeff Boone, "Wire Service Coverage of the *Exxon Valdez* Crisis," *Public Relations Review* (Spring, 1991), p. 28; and Wilcox et al., *Public Relations,* p. 351.

57. Wilcox et al., *Public Relations,* p. 348, citing Chris Woodyard, "After Spill, BP Soaked Up Oil and Good Press," *Los Angeles Times,* February 20, 1990, p. BF1.

58. Allan Nevins, "The Constitution Makers and the Public, 1785–1790," address before the Public Relations Society of America, Statler Hilton Hotel, November 13, 1962, Boston, Mass. This was the second PRSA Foundation Lecture.

59. Stanley Kelley, Jr., *Professional Public Relations and Political Power* (Baltimore: Johns Hopkins University Press, 1956), pp. 51, 67–106.

60. Kelley, *Professional Public Relations,* pp. 39–71; and Wilcox et al., pp. 55–56.

61. Arthur E. Rowse, "How to Build Support for War," *Columbia Journalism Review* (September/October, 1992), pp. 28–29; see also Alicia Mundy, "Is the Press Any Match for Powerhouse PR," in *Columbia Journalism Review* (September/October, 1992), pp. 27–34.

62. Rowse, "How to Build Support for War," pp. 28–29.

63. Michael Schudson, "News Conventions in Print and Television," *Daedalus* (Fall, 1982), 111:4, p. 107.

64. Robert G. Marbut, "Economics of the Mass Media in the United States," speech presented to Working Journalist Project, College of Communication, University of Texas-Austin, March 1, 1983.

65. Katherine Seelye, "Al Neuharth's Technicolor Baby," *Columbia Journalism Review* (March/April, 1983), p. 281.

66. Seelye, "Al Neuharth's Technicolor Baby," p. 281.

67. Wallace F. Wright, "*USA Today:* Accentuating the Positive: A Study of the Gannett Flagship Newspaper," paper presented to the Association for Education in Journalism and Mass Communications, 1986, Norman, Okla., p. 4.

68. Wright, "*USA Today,*" p. 10.

69. Ben Bagdikian, "Fast Food News: A Week's Diet," *Columbia Journalism Review* (March/April, 1983), p. 32.

70. Bagdikian, "Fast Food News," p. 33.

CHAPTER 18

New Technologies and Globalization

▼

At the end of the twentieth century, the U.S. media were a dominant force in the world. CNN, the twenty-four-hour news channel, was available in Beijing and Kuala-Lumpur hotels. In addition, U.S. media were imitated in many ways by mature and developing countries. The freedom of expression enjoyed by western media was envied by emerging democracies, many of which were former states of the Soviet Union. However, what was not envied was the highly commercialized content.

New technologies posed a variety of questions regarding governmental regulation and for media content providers, traditional newspapers, schools of journalism, and consumers. Computer-based information was rapidly securing the specialized information market. Tax newsletters, detailed financial news, and other highly technical or narrow subject matter could be delivered quickly to a targeted audience through the Internet and computer technology.

Such technologies also contributed to globalization. The use of the fax machine by students whose protests in Tianamen Square—the place where Mao Tse-tung had declared the New China in 1949—were quelled led to a recognition that technology could transcend international borders and defeat governmental censorship. Despite its efforts to limit the spread of the Internet, China recognized ultimately that it had to support expanded Internet service in order to compete in the world's economies.

Network television functioned more as an entertainment media, with less and less time devoted to news. Cable, with its twenty-four-hour news shows on MSNBC,

Fox, and CNN, ever more aggressively challenged the networks' dominance. Anchors Tom Brokaw (NBC), Dan Rather (CBS), and Peter Jennings (ABC) lost their sparkle as Chris Matthews and Hard Ball, along with shows such as the "O'Reilly Factor," dominated talk and news. During the Clinton campaigns of 1992 and 1996, network television played a critical role televising "town hall" debates, picturing Clinton as a grassroots politician moving popularly among the people. By the time of the 2000 election, cable dominated the political news scene, providing a steady diet of politics as television production.

During the 1990s, several newspapers moved away from their mass media approach to news to target specialized and upscale audiences. Newspapers such as the *Wichita Eagle* reduced its circulation area, no longer claiming to serve the rural audiences surrounding the city.

Consumers were willing to pay for entertainment and news through the purchase of computers, larger televisions, subscriptions to cable services, and Internet access providers. But advertising dominated television, radio, and newspapers. Because of its visual impact, television advertising became synonymous with consumer culture.

The current state of modern media raises questions about the role of media in modern Democratic political processes as well as in cultural evolution. Despite the enormous freedom U.S. journalists enjoy, the corporate nature of the media and journalistic conventions that focus on events rather than issues and political campaigns rather than political processes has caused analysts to doubt whether political coverage fosters good policy making in a Democratic country. Media research indicates that media do have a major impact on individuals' lives but that how individuals use media is related to a variety of demographic and psychological factors. Western media, primarily that emanating from the United States, has a remarkable global influence, and questions about the need for expanded technology and information versus retaining indigenous cultural influences continue to emerge.

U.S. media are diverse in form and content, although mainstream media reflect a high white, male profile. Yet if one looks beyond the prestige media, diverse forms of print and broadcast are available, and ethnic influences are apparent. ▼

Technologies and Regulation

Telecommunications Regulation

The law that governs direct telecommunication underwent its first complete revision in sixty-two years with the 1996 Telecommunications Act. The package of regulations that govern broadcast, cable, and telephone companies ended several years of congressional debate and altered the relationships among the various types of media.

The act removed barriers that prohibited cable and telephone companies from competing against each other and allowed telephone and cable companies to provide entertainment, information, and telephone service. In addition, the Telecommunications Act allows local Bell telephone companies to provide long-distance service if the local companies have competition for telephone service and the FCC decides that it serves the community's interests. Price regulation for cable ended by March 1999.

Ownership regulation changed as well. The number of radio and television stations a company can own nationally is no longer regulated. However, a single company's television stations cannot reach more than 35 percent of all households in the country. Radio stations have no household limit. In radio a company could own multiple stations in a market, but the number varied with market's size. In markets with forty-five commercial stations a company could own up to eight stations but no more than five of a particular type (AM or FM). In the smallest markets, those with fourteen or fewer stations, a company could own five stations but no more than three of a particular type. Three years after the Telecommunication Act, the FCC ruled that one company could own two television stations and six radio stations in a market with twenty or more unaffiliated newspapers, radio stations, and television stations.

Business organizations reacted immediately to the 1996 Telecommunications Act. The removal of ownership limits on radio set off a buying spree among big companies. By the end of 1999, Clear Channel owned 489 radio stations, which was twelve times the legal limit before the 1996 Telecommunication Act. The cable industry took advantage of rate deregulation almost immediately, increasing rates by 15 to 20 percent in some places. Not only did rates go up, but subscribers now have fewer options for complaining about cable companies that have yet to face competition. A little-publicized part of the 1996 act stops the FCC from receiving rate complaints from subscribers. The complaints must now go through the franchising authority.[1]

The 1996 Telecommunications Act did not entirely deregulate the cable industry. In 1992, Congress passed the Cable Consumer Protection and Competition Act, which required cable systems to carry the signals of local television stations. Cable operators argued that the law violated their free speech rights, because they could not open these channels to other cable networks, such as C-SPAN and Comedy Central. If the law did not exist, channels used for smaller local stations would likely be used for cable channels and possibly for pay-per-view programming. In 1997, the Supreme Court upheld the law five to four and required cable systems to continue carrying local station signals.

Regulation and Content

The passage of the Telecommunications Act of 1996 came at a time when control of content had been a serious topic of debate for several years. For example, during the early 1990s some members of Congress were concerned about violence on television and radio and about the content of children's television programming. The Children's Television Act of 1991 forced broadcast stations to program for children and to limit the number of commercial minutes in each hour of children's programming.

Although most of the Telecommunications Act concerns business activities, the most controversial portions cover content regulation. The act prohibits the transmission via computer of pornographic material to minors, requires television manufacturers to include a microchip (called a V-chip) in each set that will allow electronic blocking of programs on the basis of a ratings system, increases fines from $10,000 to $100,000 for television and radio obscenity, and requires cable to scramble programs for subscribers who think the programs are unfit for children.

Because many of the regulations under the act addressed content on the Internet, at issue was whether computer-based information will enjoy the broad protection given print media or even the more narrow rights traditionally ascribed to broadcasting. The regulation against indecent material on the Internet and the V-chip faced court challenges or threats of court challenges immediately after the act went into effect. These law suits involved arguments about the impact of the new regulations on First Amendment rights. In June 1997, the Supreme Court ruled that the Computer Decency Act was unconstitutional. Justice John Paul Stevens wrote the majority opinion for the Supreme Court, noting that the Computer Decency Act cast a "shadow over free speech" and "threatens to torch a large segment of the Internet community." Stevens argued that an attempt to protect children from harmful materials "does not justify an unnecessarily broad suppression of speech addressed to adults."

Most Americans remain concerned about TV violence. A study paid for by the National Cable Television Association found that in 1995, 57 percent of all TV programs contained violence. The researchers concluded that the biggest problem was not the violence itself but how it was treated. In 73 percent of the violent scenes, the perpetrator went unpunished, often the negative consequences of violence were not presented in these programs, and only 4 percent of the programs presented an antiviolent theme.[2]

The industry addressed the concern about violence by adopting a voluntary rating system in 1966. The system identifies six types of content and vary from TV-Y—appropriate for all children—to TV-M—not suitable for children under seventeen.

Napster, MP3, and the Courts

One of the major news stories of 2000–2001 involved the brilliant young Shawn Fanning, a new media tinkerer who devised a program to allow downloading, playing, or CD-ROM recording of popular artists. The program that made this possible was Fanning's "Napster," so named because of his nappy, unruly hair. Downloading "free music" from the Internet had an undeniable appeal to many consumers, but not to many artists who produce that music or their publishers. If a person had a song in the MP3 digital format, it could be shared with others for more digital storing, playing, and recording. Sales of recorded music dropped, and copyright lawsuits flew.[3]

But Bertelsmann, the third largest media conglomerate worldwide, saw great promise in the 38 million file-sharing music lovers who were downloading and sharing and recording music at a furious pace. Bertelsmann's BMG Entertainment agreed to abandon its share of a copyright-infringement lawsuit against Fanning and to offer its music catalog for Fanning's use.[4] In February 2001, to the dismay of lovers of free music without buying CDs, a U.S. Court of Appeals for the Ninth Circuit issued an injunction that halted Napster. Record store owners, predictably, were pleased by the injunction, and reports were broadcast that sales of some companies' CDs were

▼

Shawn Fanning (b. 1981)

Shawn Fanning moved from humble roots to become a computer programmer who changed the music industry. Fanning made his way to Northeastern University, but bored with college life, he spent most of his time on the Internet. Fanning dropped out of college and started Napster. Named after a nickname given to Fanning, Napster is a file-sharing program that allows users to find MP3 music files on other personal computers and download them without charge. Although hailed by computer users and a huge business success, Napster was sued by the music industry over possible copyright infringements.

Source: S. Ante, "Shawn Fanning's Struggle," *Business Week*, May 1, 2000, p. 197. (*Photo:* Time-Pix)

down by as much as 30 percent. Meanwhile, technology moved on, with predictions that services to provide alternatives to Napster would be hard to control.[5]

Media Convergence

Media convergence is defined as the coming together of a variety of distribution systems and using them to convey information. For example, in the 1990s, the *Chicago Tribune* began "converging," or blending, its broadcast and newspaper newsrooms and adding an on-line dimension as well. In the late 1990s, many Washington bureaus—Belo Corporation, Cox, Tribune Company, and others—recognized that consumers could access news produced by their reporters through the Internet, over television or radio, or in newspapers. Combining the news operations within single companies made economic sense.

With deregulation in the 1980s, which culminated in the passage of the Telecommunications Act of 1996, companies became much larger and owned more types of media. By adding convergence to the mix, media companies offered their advertisers and their readers/viewers a powerful combination of television, newspapers, and Internet Web sites. Therefore, when the Chicago-based Tribune Company bought Los Angeles–based *Times Mirror* for the seemingly modest sum of $6.45 billion, plus assuming nearly $2 million in debt, it merely expanded a multimedia pattern it had already created in Chicago. But it also set the stage for even larger conglomerates.

In 2000, the Tribune Company owned eleven daily newspapers, twenty-two television stations, and four radio stations. With this merger, Tribune Company became third nationally in daily newspaper circulation, with 3.6 million subscribers, trailing Gannett with seventy-four newspapers totaling 6.6 million circulation, and Knight-Ridder, with thirty-one papers generating 4.4 million daily circulation. However, the Tribune Company also had positioned itself by making high-technology investments. It now owns a number of on-line publications and is a stockholder in a variety of companies, including America Online.

More Merger Mania

Media conglomerates are a leading and rapidly growing part of business activity in the United States. One week in August 1995, saw Disney's $18.4 billion buyout of ABC-Capital Cities, with Westinghouse bidding $5.4 billion to buy CBS. Disney's $18.4 billion offer to buy ABC-Capital Cities was then the second-highest price ever paid for a U.S. company. The Disney/ABC merger stood to gain a lot, particularly in light of the November 1995 expiration of FCC rules limiting network ownership and syndication of television programs. Now Disney could produce a film for motion picture theatres and cable television and then feed productions to its own TV network.[6]

By acquiring the ABC network, Disney indeed got control of a prime outlet for the production companies it already owned, including Miramax Films, Caravan Films, and Touchstone Pictures. The eleven ABC network-owned television stations were now Disney's, and ABC's network contracts tied Disney into 200 TV network affiliate stations.

If Disney was big in the mid-1990s, Time Warner, Inc., was bigger. In 1996, Time Warner bought Turner Broadcasting System for $7.5 billion, making Time Warner the largest media company—larger than Disney, larger than Germany's Bertelsmann, larger than Rupert Murdoch's News Corp. The merger increased Time Warner's net annual revenue to an estimated $21 billion.[7]

The AOL-Time Warner Merger (2000)

America Online (AOL) was barely fifteen years old in late January 2000, when it purchased Time Warner for $165 billion, which represented the largest media merger in the twentieth century. In a single stroke, an old line media company had access to the Internet, and the thriving on-line company, AOL, had access to Time Warner's cable systems. It was called a merger, but AOL was to be the dominant partner. The *New York Times* described AOL as the "company that brought the Internet to the masses" and noted that the upstart had bought the "largest traditional media company . . . in what would be the biggest merger in history and the best evidence that old and new media are converging."[8]

At the time of the merger, AOL, the nation's largest Internet Service Provider (ISP), had 54 percent of the nation's paying ISP subscribers (22 million), and Time Warner's cable systems accounted for 20 percent of the subscribers nationally (13 million). Cable access provided AOL with the chance to offer faster Internet services.[9]

To understand the impact of this merger, consider a day in the life of a typical American in 2001. Before breakfast, she wants to check the weather and see if she has any e-mail messages, so she logs on to her home computer via her subscription to America Online. While checking e-mail, she plays a CD from a Warner Music Group company, Elektra Entertainment Group. Tiring of that CD, she pops in another, from Rhino Entertainment Group. While heating a bagel, she glances at news summaries from AOL-Time Warner's CNN News Group as a TV provides background chatter. Her husband joins her at the breakfast table; he's leafing through two AOL-Time Warner magazines, *Time* and *Sports Illustrated*. It is not even 7 A.M. and this couple already has read, seen, or heard products from seven of AOL-Time Warner's companies.

This not-unusual couple heads for work. They listen to a few minutes of a Time Warner Audio book on tape before she drops him off at the metro stop as she heads for her job. While riding the metro, he reads a best-selling David Baldacci murder mystery published by Warner Books. At their respective jobs, both may encounter books published by Time Warner Trade Publishing. After work, this movie-loving couple can relax with a TV movie from premium channels owned by AOL-Time Warner, HBO, or Cinemax. Or, if they rent movies or go to the cineplex, they're apt to encounter movies from Warner Bros., Castle Rock Entertainment, or New Line Films, all AOL-Time Warner companies. And if their media-saturated lives include a taste for satire, they might pick up a copy of *MAD* magazine, *also* owned by Warner Bros.[10]

On-Line Accessibility

In July 1999, President William J. Clinton told a California audience, "There is a growing *digital divide* between those who have access to the digital economy and the Internet and those who don't, and that divide exists along the lines of education, income, region and race."

Studies show varying amounts of connectivity. The Department of Commerce in 1999 estimated that 40 percent of all households own computers and more than 25 percent of those have Internet access. An InfoBead survey published in 1999 stated that almost 53 percent of all households owned PCs. Further, a Wirthlin Worldwide study, also conducted in 1999, placed the percentage of U.S. households with Internet access at 33 percent; access outside the home brings the total figure to 66 percent.

Households in an income bracket of $75,000 or more are twenty times as likely to have Internet access as homes at the lowest income levels. African American and Hispanic households are only 40 percent as likely as white households to be on-line.

Research has shown that individuals with higher levels of education generally have more access to mass communication, and they gain ideas and access to new information more quickly than those with less education. If the digital divide increases, certain individuals with access and understanding of how to use technology will gain information even more quickly, thus widening what was referred to in Chapter 1 as the knowledge gap.[11]

However, there is some indication that the digital divide, although it has increased over the past few years, may shift once again. A study by Nielsen indicated use of the Internet by African Americans—at home, school, and work—has increased 50 percent during the single year of 1999.[12] In 1995, Internet use was heavily male. But by late 1997, 43 percent of the people on-line were women. That number jumped to 48 percent by the end of 1998 and was expected to exceed 50 percent by the close of 1999. America Online's membership is 51 percent women.[13] Also, the Department of Commerce report shows that at the high income end of the spectrum, African American households are catching up, going on-line in greater numbers. Some analysts predict the digital divide will shrink drastically, as computers become as ubiquitous as television sets.

Journalism and Convergence

Use of the Internet has brought wrenching changes to the news process. Those who seek to decry Internet news argue that the new medium is full of "wanna-be" journalists. Too often, however, these critics compare Matt Drudge to the *New York Times,* rather than comparing the specialized Internet-delivered content of a respectable news organization. The scholarly journalists Bill Kovach and Tom Rosenstiel talk about the "post O. J. media culture," a reference to massive coverage of the televised criminal trial and 1995 acquittal of sports icon and actor O. J. Simpson. Kovach and Rosenstiel defined that culture as

> [A] newly diversified mass media in which the cultures of entertainment, infotainment, argument, analysis, tabloid, and main-stream press not only work side by side but intermingle and merge. It is a culture in which Matt Drudge sits alongside William Safire on *Meet the Press* and Ted Koppel talks about the nuances of oral sex, in which *Hard Copy* [a "tabloid" TV quasi-news program] and CBS News jostle for camera position outside the federal grand jury to hear from a special prosecutor.[14]

Kovach and Rosenstiel argue convincingly that, with news and entertainment blurring together, argument is being substituted for the verification required in the traditional news process. Round-the-clock news cycles, moreover, encourage less completeness, because far more effort is expended in relaying new facts—some of them minutiae—about the news sensation du jour than really digging into the substance, background, and meaning of a news event.[15]

In addition, the ravenous competition for breaking news too often seemed to value unleashing a story first rather than verifying the facts. While *Newsweek* reporter Michael Isikoff and editors paused before printing a story about then-President William Clinton's affair with Monica Lewinsky, Matt Drudge posted it on *The Drudge Report.* Drudge asserted that *Newsweek* executives killed the story only hours before publication. Once Drudge's scoop hit the Internet, the story and its creation became mainstream news, with Bill Kristol of the *The Weekly Standard* discussing the story (including criticism of *Newsweek*) on ABC-TV's Sunday morning staple, *This Week with Sam Donaldson and Cokie Roberts.*[16]

The Clinton sex scandal resulted in an admission that the President lied under oath. Although the House of Representatives voted articles of impeachment, the Senate failed to convict. The tawdry details of Clinton's personal life, however, both titillated and repelled Americans in a time when traditional media were losing market share to new media and when a growing number of people spent more time at their computers than they did watching television or reading. And in the age of the Internet, as Bill Kovach and Tom Rosenstiel pointed out with pardonable exaggeration, "There Are No Gatekeepers Here."[17]

Consequences of Media Consolidation

Ben H. Bagdikian, who has monitored media consolidation patterns since the early 1980s, wrote in 2000 that continuing media consolidation means that the increasingly diverse population of the United States has its news controlled by a small number of the world's wealthiest corporations. He wrote, "Six firms dominate all American mass media." Each is a subsidiary of a larger parent firm, some of them basically operating in other industries. The six parent firms are General Electric, Viacom (combining CBS and Westinghouse), Disney, Bertelsmann, Time Warner (AOL-Time Warner since late 2000), and Murdoch's News Corp. Bertelsmann is based in Germany and News Corp. in Australia, the other four in the United States.[18]

Bagdikian noted that the total yearly revenue of these six firms adds up to more than the sum of the revenues of the next twenty leading media firms. He asserted the merger creating the megacorporation AOL-Time Warner has the most profound societal implications, because mergers of this size make it clear that news has become primarily an industrial byproduct. Further, as the news component of such giant corporations is pushed to the corporate back burner, the quest for market share and increased profitability encourages if not actually rewards unethical behavior. Bagdikian's concern: news subsidiaries "selecting news that will promote the owning corporation rather than serve the traditional ethical striving of journalism."[19]

Journalism in a Big Media Environment

In 1995, when ABC's "Day One" program accused tobacco manufacturers of "spiking" cigarette tobacco with nicotine extract in order to enhance smoking's addictive potential, Philip Morris sued the network for $10 billion. Philip Morris asserted this claim was untruthful and defamatory, and ABC prepared to defend itself in court, hiring outside lawyers. At the same time, the network's own in-house lawyers were working toward a settlement payment and a public apology to get out of the lawsuit.

The "Day One" broadcast was not slipshod journalism. It was prepared by respected professionals, including producer Walt Bogdanich, whose reporting some years earlier had won a Pulitzer Prize for the *Wall Street Journal*.[20]

Some top libel experts were astonished when ABC settled out of court with an apology and $15 million, in part to pay for the tobacco firm's legal costs in suing ABC. Although the lawsuit seemed clearly defensible by ABC on grounds of truth and

Figure 18–1   The magazine and book industries continue to thrive, as debates over quality and profit persist. (*U.S. News and World Report* collection, Division of Prints and Photographs, Library of Congress)

nonmalicious commentary on a "public figure corporation," the network's settlement showed a profound lack of support and respect for its own producers and reporters. Those journalists understandably refused to sign the settlement agreement.

ABC's lawyer-crafted apology claimed that a "mistake that was not deliberate on the part of ABC" had occurred and that ABC accepted responsibility. The network's apology not only was broadcast at halftime during ABC's "Monday Night Football" but it also appeared in advertisements in several national magazines and newspapers.[21]

Why did ABC duck the opportunity to defend itself and its credibility in a winnable lawsuit? Some have suggested that Disney, having recently purchased ABC, simply wanted to clear the decks of what might be termed a "nuisance."[22] If so, then consolidation of media companies holds little promise for the future of journalism.

The *New York Times* editorialized that the ABC apology was a major victory for the tobacco manufacturers. The newspaper said that the lawsuit should have been the subject of a fight, not capitulation, terming the lawsuit "an ill-disguised effort to chill investigative reporting about smoking."[23]

Did "60 Minutes" Chill Itself?

In November 1995, the successful CBS television magazine program "60 Minutes" was about to break a major antitobacco report. The program was scheduled to broadcast an interview with a former executive of Brown & Williamson Tobacco Co. The executive was willing to go public, charging that the tobacco company purposefully tried to "hook" another generation of young smokers. On November 8, 1995, CBS corporate lawyers decreed that the interview would not be broadcast "until further notice."

The *New York Times* reported that CBS did not fear a libel suit. At stake instead was threatened litigation against the network for interfering with contractual relations with a former employee who had been sworn to secrecy by Brown & Williamson as a condition of employment. That scientist, who initially was a confidential source for CBS, was later revealed to be Dr. Jeffrey Wigand.[24]

Was CBS in real danger from a breach-of-contract lawsuit involving a source's earlier promise? The *New York Times* editorialized pointedly against self-censorship by CBS. The editorial said, "Many legal scholars argue that liability in such cases can be overridden when a public good is served." The *Times* expressed particular dismay that the decision to postpone the interview was made by lawyers and corporate officers, not news executives.[25] There were dissenters from that opinion. P. Cameron DeVore of Seattle, a leading First Amendment attorney, responded to the editorial with the well-supported position that commission of wrongs during news gathering was not protected under the First Amendment.[26]

By the end of September 1995, Wigand was being sued for fraud, breach of contract, and theft by Brown & Williamson; the public records of that suit made his name public. On January 28, 1996, after Wigand had testified under subpoena in a Mississippi lawsuit in which the state sought reimbursement from tobacco companies for medical costs caused by smoking, CBS broadcast the interview.[27]

News is defined as *timely* information—that news is news when it is new. The delaying of the "60 Minutes" broadcast shows that the new corporate landscape in mass media matters a great deal.

Television, Politics, and Democracy

Freedom of expression has been championed over the years because it (1) guards the search for truth, (2) protects and encourages Democratic government, (3) checks government power, and (4) contributes to orderly change and prevents revolution.[28] Alexander Meiklejohn, an early First Amendment theorist, argued that the only expression that should be absolutely protected by the First Amendment is that which relates to the self-governing concept. In the United States, freedom of expression has been granted to a much broader range of issues; nevertheless, one tenet of democracy— and of the Democratic political process—has been that freedom of expression will aid the cause of a governmental responsive to the people.

The invasion of the political process by television has caused a great deal of concern for critics of Democratic processes. Kathleen Hall Jamieson and other scholars of the political process have argued that television has diminished the role of the political party in the nomination of candidates: The televised primary process has popularized candidate selection. "By centering politics on the person of the candidate," she writes, "television accelerated the electorate's focus on character rather than issues."[29] Sociologist Todd Gitlin, however, points out that focus on character is not entirely new. During the 1828 election, supporters of Andrew Jackson charged that the incumbent, John Quincy Adams, had slept with his wife before marrying her, and that while ambassador to Russia, he had procured a young American woman for Czar Alexander I. Adams' supporters charged that Jackson had lived with his wife while she was still legally married to another man.[30]

Another charge leveled at television is that visual emphasis tends to focus on events, not issues, thereby creating horse race coverage of the campaign. Amounts of coverage the press accords to various candidates during the early stages of the primary can affect who is declared a "front-runner," thus giving power to candidates who are widely known and considered potential winners. Yet those very front-runners are the ones most likely to receive the most negative coverage.[31]

Media coverage is achieved not only through decision making by journalists but also through paid media time purchased and designed by the candidates themselves and by their media consultants. Thus, as candidates become familiar with effective media techniques, critics charge that they are able to manipulate the electorate. Through advertising, candidates are able to level charges that can't be counteracted unless the opposition purchases time to refute a specific charge. Thus, many newspapers during the 1992, 1996, and 2000 presidential campaigns began to evaluate political advertising on television as part of their interpretive function. Newspapers printed frames of ads, then commented on their accuracy and implications.

Perhaps the most disturbing part of television's political coverage during the 1990s and 2000 was the brevity of candidate statements. Daniel Hallin documents that from 1968 to 1988, the average sound bite in election news declined from forty-three to nine seconds. Hallin notes that journalists and political experts now dominate more of the election news and commentary than do the candidates. "The rise of mediated TV news," writes Hallin, "is connected with an increasing preoccupation with campaign technique and a kind of 'inside dopester' perspective that puts the image-making at the center of politics and pushes real political debate to the margins."[32]

However, just as Franklin Delano Roosevelt turned to the new popular medium of radio in the 1930s and 1940s to convey his message directly to the people, modern candidates also look to new formats. Bill Clinton in the 1992 campaign ignored conventional wisdom that participating in talk shows was "unpresidential," and used popular TV shows and cable channels such as Oprah Winfrey and MTV to target new audiences. Gone was sedate presidential campaigning, and in its place was a popular appeal to specifically targeted segmented audiences, whatever the tone of the medium—or the message.

The Media and the Election of 2000

The last presidential election of the old millennium was one of the strangest, and most newsworthy, in American history. Although George W. Bush lost the popular vote by nearly a half million votes on November 2, 2000, he won a hotly disputed group of electoral votes in Florida that gave him the numbers he needed in the electoral college.

The final decision on the presidential election didn't come, however, until well into December. And that decision followed an election night in which media miscalls were the topic of the day. By 7:55 P.M. eastern standard time on election night, CBS, NBC, and CNN had all declared Gore the winner in Florida and of the election. Gore's win, however, did not last long. Within two hours, the networks changed Florida from a win for Gore to a "too-close-too-call."[33] Then the election appeared to swing to Bush, leading Gore to phone Bush twice: once to say he was conceding and a second time to retract his concession. The next morning the newspaper headlines were mixed: The *New York Times* declared, "Bush Appears to Defeat Gore, / Hairbreadth Electoral Vote; / Hillary Clinton Goes to Senate." But the *New York Post* declared, "Bush Wins!" Ultimately, the Bush–Gore contest in Florida turned into a dead heat, a photo finish without a camera.

"You're probably disgusted with us right now and you have a right to be," Dan Rather told his viewers. The miscalls by the networks resulted from the fact that all were relying on the same source, Voting News Service (VNS), for their data but still were locked into a traditional desire to "beat the competition." Knowledgeable critics agreed that exit polling data, on which the projections were made, were accurate. But this was a very close election. Pollsters the day before had been unable to solidly predict a winner. One scholar noted, "This gives new meaning to plus or minus 5 percent," meaning that the margin of error—always cited but usually glossed over—came into play during election night.

The scenario was further complicated because VNS was a consortium, organized and funded by the five networks, along with the Associated Press, that were competing against each other. VNS collected data from exit interviews with voters coming out of the polls in predetermined key precincts. The Associated Press, even though it is a subscriber to VNS, wisely held off calling the election early. As National Public Radio's Jean Cochran asked rhetorically, "What if the media had said "too-close-to-call?"[34]

Media critic Steven Brill had a caustic evaluation of VNS. He wrote, "The simple fact is that the news media's election night fiasco happened because the press seems to have violated antitrust laws by organizing a cartel called Voter News Service."[35] The consortium was organized to allow networks to save money by getting rid of their own polling operations. Saving a small amount of money resulted in a loss in diversity of polling approaches and results, to the detriment of the networks' accuracy and credibility.[36] But more than that, the fiasco was caused by the networks' reluctance to wait a few minutes for accuracy.

Writes Louis Liebovich in his study of coverage of presidential elections, "Attempts to hype ratings, restraints on spending for coverage, and lack of a professional environment in the news studio had led to a fiasco. Had the election margin been merely close and not razor thin, few would have noticed, but years of shoddy and amateurish practices at the highest levels in television had caught up with television news."[37]

At the end of the election night miscalls, the Florida vote was so close that it triggered an automatic recounting of votes. At the end of the first recounting, Bush's Florida lead of 1,784 (of more than 5.8 million votes cast) dwindled to 327 votes. Several counties decided—as they could, under Florida law—to recount votes by hand. With incoming absentee ballots, Bush's lead climbed once more, this time to 930.

The process became a political and media zoo, with both campaigns sending armies of attorneys and volunteers to Florida to witness hand recounts in Palm Beach, Volusia, Broward, and Miami-Dade counties. Meanwhile, Secretary of State Katherine Harris declared that she would certify the election on November 17 once the overseas votes were counted. The courts in Florida allowed the recount to continue and blocked Harris from certifying the election. Two days before Thanksgiving, the Florida Supreme Court upheld that decision but also ruled that the recount had to be complete within five days. Miami-Dade stopped its recount, deciding it could not finish in time. The day after Thanksgiving the U.S. Supreme Court said it would hear arguments on December 1 in a suit brought by Bush's lawyers, and a few days later Harris certified a 537-vote victory for Bush. The high court remanded the case to the Florida Supreme Court; the Florida court, by a vote of four to three, ordered a recount of 45,000 so-called "undervotes." These votes were achieved when voters, using punch card systems, failed to punch the card entirely through. The media spent a fair amount of time covering the questions of partially punched votes (i.e., "hanging chads and pregnant chads"). The chief justice of the Florida Supreme Court dissented vociferously.

The Florida Republican legislature was outraged by the Supreme Court's decision, arguing that the state court had overstepped its authority, and prepared to endorse Bush electors despite the ruling of the Court. But the U.S. Supreme Court stepped in, by a vote of five to four, ordering the recount halted and setting a December 11 date to evaluate the Florida court ruling.

On December 12, 2000, the U.S. Supreme Court, in an obviously divided opinion, found the recount unconstitutional. The Court ordered that no standards had been set for how the under votes should be judged. Critics charged both high courts with politicizing the election process. Nevertheless, Albert Gore conceded the following day, thirty-six days after the election.

Election on Cable and On-Line

The election demanded media expertise, and reporters and editors struggled to rise to the demand. When the Supreme Courts of Florida and of the United States released their opinions, reporters scrambled to understand the complex opinions—on camera.

Another factor affected development of election news. Active users of the Internet had more than quintupled from about 4 percent of the country in 1996 to 20 percent in 2000. ABC recorded 23 million Web page visits on election day and CNN recorded 75 million. Both numbers were about twice the hits recorded on any day ever.

Cable news also had a heyday. The talk shows covered the recount nonstop, with legal experts and voting experts testifying on issues such as the quality of the voting machines and the likelihood of the outcome.

The Global Picture

One can look at the global picture of mass media in a variety of ways: (1) by looking at corporate holdings or multinational ownership; (2) by looking at news and entertainment flow—who produces what types of programming to distribute to whom? or (3) by examining the flow of news throughout the world, both in terms of volume and direction and in terms of access.

As pointed out in earlier chapters, the holdings of media corporations grow larger as the numbers of corporations decline. Most of these multinational corporations are western based, and western media dominate news and entertainment production that is distributed to less-wealthy countries. With the collapse of governmental control over Eastern Bloc countries, news production and dissemination in Eastern Europe is undergoing rapid transformation, but many countries now are struggling with how to achieve freedom of media and cope with the commercial demands that accompany such efforts.

The experience during two world wars made it clear that the United States operated under a different set of principles than did the rest of the world. The post–World War II campaign to export freedom of the press failed, as American motives became suspect in other countries, with some nations believing that Americans simply were trying to dominate worldwide news systems. In the mid-1970s that debate was refueled as UNESCO (United Nations Educational, Scientific, and Cultural Organization) took up the cause of communication controversy. By 1984, UNESCO's membership included many third world countries who were disturbed by what they viewed as an imbalance of communication power. For example, in 1984, Latin America imported 42 percent of its media programs; the United States imported only 2 percent. Latin American nations and other media-poor countries expressed grave concern over the fact that most international news flows from the developed West or North to the undeveloped South and East; that the United States and Western Europe receive the largest amount of coverage (although changes in the communist bloc may have altered this momentarily); that western-dominated news neglects progress in developing countries in culture, economics, and politics, and focuses on disasters; that western-dominated news results in a massive consumer culture that erodes national identity in many parts of the world; that American communications policies foster world domination through "media imperialism"; and that communication imbalances promote international instability, global conflict, and national discontent.

Those on the opposing side argue that the United States and other western countries developed a complex communication system early and it became a model for the rest of the world; following that argument media domination occurred naturally. Similar arguments include a claim that the United States has fostered media technology both within the United States and without; that the third world continually invites western media to their countries and to purchase western programming; and that third world countries benefit from improved education and social services because of communications development.[38]

Major questions continue to remain unanswered in understanding and shaping the global mix. Scholars from some newly industrialized countries argue that emphasis on education and economic development fosters the ability to export information and thus to become major players in the communication market. However, one has to ask whether emulating existing models furthers the cultural goals of individual nations. One has to focus on what is measured: Volume of information circulated abroad? Investment in multinational media corporations? If the price for international participation and recognition is playing the competitive game western-style, are we preserving information systems that will provide congruence with other perceived realities within specific cultures? If the goal is to alter international news flow patterns so as to create cross-cultural understanding and respect, do existing models allow such an interchange? In an ideal world, we might picture a pluralistic communications system in which all cultures present and receive messages that are treated with understanding and respect, but we must acknowledge that all cultural systems do not value and respect the same ideals. Western-style feminists, for example, have a great deal of trouble validating societies that, by western standards, subjugate women. Further, information flow at times impedes one culture while liberating another. If you consider the invasion of national media into the southern states in the early 1960s while covering the civil rights movement, you could well argue that national news impeded on distinctive southern value systems, but allowed the culture of a highly repressed minority to emerge. Internationalizing news content, therefore, implies certain value decisions that go beyond money, technology, and power.[39]

Globalization of Media Industries

By 1992, five of America's largest book publishers were foreign owned. Rupert Murdoch's News Corporation, owners of *TV Guide* and the Fox Network, also owned the venerable publishing firm Harper & Row. Bertelsmann, the world's second-largest media conglomerate in 1992, owned Bantam Books, Doubleday, and Dell.[40]

The world recording industry is dominated by five major recording companies: Warner Music Group, Sony Music, BMG, EMI, and Universal Music Group. These produce and manufacture about 85 percent of the cassettes and CDs in the world.[41] Like the periodical industry, the recording industry is global, and although worldwide data are elusive, estimates suggest that five recording companies, owned by American, British, and Japanese corporations, control most of the world's recorded music. The industry's concentration in these countries reflects the concentration of buyers. The United States, Japan, Britain, Germany, and France accounted for 68 percent of recorded music sold during the early 1990s.

The international market is an important factor for U.S. films. For example, Bruce Willis' *Die Hard with a Vengeance* earned $100 million in U.S. revenues and cost $90 million to produce. Willis' salary was $15 million. Did the studios take a loss? Definitely not. Overseas grosses were expected to be between $225 and $275 million.[42] Film has always been an international medium. In 1895, the first public screening of short films occurred in France, the United States, Germany, and Belgium.[43] Today, although American-made films dominate most markets, movies remain essentially international. Three trends demonstrate the global nature of films: strong domestic film industries in many countries, growing exportation of films from many countries, and increasing coproduction of films across national boundaries.

Radio also has been essentially international. This is, in part, because of radio's portability and the ability of radio waves to transcend national borders. With the development of Internet radio in 1995, listeners all over the world could tune in to radio in a variety of countries. By 2000, more than 1,900 U.S. licensed radio stations and hundreds of nonlicensed stations around the world were programming over the Web. Arbitron estimated that in 1999, about 31 million people listened daily to radio over the Web.[44]

Television is probably the medium most susceptible to criticism of cultural imperialism. Not all countries embrace expanding access to television. Many countries in developing areas fear that western programming will corrupt the morals of their people and forever alter indigenous cultures. They see the expansion of television as a form of cultural imperialism, the forcing of one country's culture on another country through media content dominance. In 1995, Iran banned satellite dishes because of concerns about the clash of American programs, such as *Baywatch,* with Muslim beliefs.

Several Asian countries limit the availablity of programs that are produced outside the country. For example, Taiwan requires that 70 percent of its programming be domestically produced; South Korea limits imported television programming to 20 percent of available time.

The Mainstream Newspaper Press

Mainstream newspapers faced three big challenges during the 1990s—declining readership of big-city dailies, shrinking retail advertising, and increased competition not only from electronic media but also from suburban dailies and weeklies.

Although absolute numbers of readers have not declined, household penetration is the key word for the decade—and newspapers are not maintaining circulation per household. As the population grows, newspaper readership does not. Mergers and closures of major department stores during the late 1980s and the early 1990s threatened the big dailies' lifeblood—department store advertising. In the late 1990s, newspapers worried that they were losing classified advertising to the Internet, where ads could be searched for, sorted, and retrieved by various keywords.

Newspaper editors have emulated the graphics of television while still trying to create a product distinct from the short, superficial glances at the news in which television specializes. In 1990, Knight-Ridder initiated a project at the *Boca Raton News* designed to attract Baby Boomers—residents in the twenty-five to forty-three age group. After conducting thirty focus groups, editors redesigned the *News* with shorter stories—no jumps—and careful indexing, grids for movie and classified listings, and a world map that tells readers where news is happening. The *News* also developed seven daily feature areas designed specifically for Baby Boomers, from topics such as "Business" to "Parent and Child." After the change, the *News* increased its circulation by 10 percent during the week and 20 percent on Sunday.

▼

Katharine Graham (1917–2001)

One of the most powerful and successful women in journalism and business, Pulitzer–Prize winning author and former chairperson and chief executive officer of the Post Co., Katharine Graham began her career with the *Washington Post* after her husband's tragic suicide in 1963.

Mrs. Graham's father, Wall Street magnate Eugene Meyer, purchased the *Washington Post* at a bankruptcy sale for a mere $825,000, and developed the Washington Post Co. Katharine worked as a copy girl at the *Post* while still in high school, and again after graduating from college. Her husband, former U.S. Supreme Court law clerk Philip L. Graham, succeeded Katharine's father as publisher of the paper in 1946, and he ran the company until his death. Katharine then took over the Post Co. and soon learned to juggle her roles as mother of four and leader of an emerging journalistic empire. She led the *Post* through the ground-breaking coverage and investigation of the Watergate scandal, during considerable federal crossfire while publishing the Pentagon Papers, and during the months of the 1975 union pressmen strike, missing only one day's publication and establishing her formidable international reputation.

Katharine Graham, the first woman to head a Fortune 500 company, stepped down as chief executive officer of the Post Co. in 1991 and as chairman in 1993. She subsequently wrote her memoirs, winning a Pulitzer Prize for biography in 1998 for *Personal History,* a sensitive and intimate account of her transformation from shy, socialite wife to savvy businesswoman. During her tenure, the Post Co. grew from a modest magazine and newspaper company to a diversified media corporation that included television, newspaper, magazine, cable, and educational services. Mrs. Graham died in July 2001 in Boise, Idaho, after suffering head injuries in a fall. Thousands attended her standing-room-only funeral at Washington National Cathedral, where she was eulogized by former Secretary of State Henry Kissinger, former *Washington Post* executive editor Benjamin C. Bradlee, and her children, among others.

(*Photo:* The Washington Post Co.)

Some critics, such as David Shaw of the *Los Angeles Times,* believe such changes are imitations of television and that what newspapers do best—and should do—are "long, thorough, careful, analytical looks at serious problems." Some newspapers are relinquishing their mass market status and admitting that they are vehicles of news for elites—for those who want more in-depth, analytical information. Newspapers such as the *Philadelphia Inquirer* and the *Washington Post* shun the *USA Today* prototypes but have adopted some of their graphic techniques.

Competition, however, is hitting the dailies from the suburban weeklies and dailies that corner the market of high school sports stories, summer swimming league

Figure 18–2 *Milwaukee Journal* reporters at work in the newsroom. (Photo courtesy of the *Milwaukee Journal*)

scores, and development and transportation news. These, coupled with weekly shoppers carrying some local news but heavily laden with local advertising, are carving a niche out of big daily circulation.

Newspapers also are on-line in greater numbers, but publishers have been unable to determine the profitable formula. If classified advertising continues to shift to the Web, that may provide the profit margin needed to sustain on-line newspapers.

Ethnic Media

Ethnic groups are receiving new attention from mainstream as well as ethnic media, primarily because of increased buying power among some groups. Advertisers study demographics, and buying power buys ethnic images in mainstream media. In addition, the increased ethnic population also encourages the development of African-American media, as well as media targeted to specific language groups, such as Spanish-language television for Hispanics. In California, minorities are becoming dominant and, therefore, are moving toward majority status, a trend predicted for the rest of the nation.

Despite their cultural importance, the minority press has constantly struggled with adequate financing. African-American newspaper publishers still report that their main threat to survival is lack of advertisements.[45] Publishers of minority newspapers believe that a single billing, multiple placement approach to advertising will enable advertisers to improve financial support for minority newspapers. To address the problem, Hispanic newspapers formed the Latino Print Network, which bills an advertiser only once for placement in more than 120 Hispanic newspapers. A similar organization, Amalgamated Publishers, serves about 200 African-American newspapers. In 1999, these two organizations joined the Newspaper National Network, a marketing organization run by the Newspaper Association of America, to make single-billing advertising in 320 minority newspapers available to advertisers.

African-American Media

The black press has always struggled with financing. Advertisers were slow to patronize the pages and screens of black-oriented publications and television programming, and competition for talented reporters with mainstream media in the past twenty years has depleted the talent pool. By 1990, the situation was desperate enough that Benjamin Hooks, then director of the NAACP, announced a campaign to revitalize the black press.

Circulation fell dramatically at many of the big-city African-American dailies during the 1980s. Famous dailies such as the *Afro-American* in Baltimore, Maryland, fared badly; the Baltimore paper declined from 26,400 in circulation in 1980 to 11,614 in 1990.

The general retail decline in the late 1980s that affected the news industry as a whole also had an impact on the black press. Henry LaBrie, who conducts black press surveys for *Editor & Publisher,* argues that many African-American newspapers lost step with a more activist youthful population in the 1960s and never developed a loyal readership of that generation. LaBrie suggests that African-American newspapers need to capture the fervor of the 1930s and 1940s, running more editorials and taking positions with well-argued viewpoints.[46]

After an abortive attempt at an African-American radio network in 1954, two black networks were successfully formed in the 1970s. In 1972, the Mutual Black Network syndicated news and sports under the auspices of the Mutual Broadcasting Network, garnering more than 100 affiliates and 6.2 million listeners. Renamed the Sheridan Broadcasting Network in the late 1970s because of a transfer in ownership, it began to program live events from college campuses, highlighting African-American leaders and journalists. In 1973, a second network, the National Black Network, began to serve black-oriented radio outlets with news and sportscasts, and by 1988 had ninety-four affiliates and expanded programming. Although African-American ownership of radio stations increased during the 1970s, by 1980 the number still remained at less than 1 percent of total stations.[47] By 1986, there were 150 AM stations and 56 FM stations owned by African Americans.

In November 1980, Howard University became the first African-American university to own and operate a public television station—the only black-owned public station in the continental United States. As late as 1981, there was not a single black executive producer or vice president in news at any of the networks. Although images of African-Americans on television have changed over time, public, rather than commercial, television has more successfully altered the use of stereotyped images. By the late 1980s, writes Jannette Dates, "the public broadcasting system at last included a variety of positive images of diverse groups who were treated as respected, valuable members of society, and it had moved closer to such public interests, particularly black interests, than had its commercial counterpart."[48]

Hispanic Media

With the growing Hispanic population in the United States, Hispanics become both new targets for advertisers through mainstream media and also potential readers and listeners of Spanish-language media. The Hispanic edition of Standard Research Data Services lists 103 Hispanic newspapers, 42 major Spanish-language magazines, and 31 English or bilingual Hispanic-oriented magazines. More than three-fourths of Hispanics read newspapers, and more than half read magazines. Thirty-eight percent of those reading newspapers look specifically for Spanish-language papers, and almost a third choose Spanish-language magazines.

Hispanic radio and television stations are attractive commodities. More than 97 percent of all Hispanics in the United States watch television; 81 percent watch Spanish television. Fifty-five percent watch primarily Spanish television.[49]

Conclusion

The media in the United States are among the freest in the world—perhaps the most free. Freedom of expression has been championed over the years because it (1) guards the search for truth, (2) protects and encourages Democratic government, (3) checks governmental power, and (4) contributes to orderly change and prevents revolution. In the United States, freedom of expression has been considered even more broadly—outside, as well as inside—the political process.

The story of media in the 1990s was a story of developing new technologies and experimentation with on-line newspapers, along with new ways of covering campaigns and elections. This led to new concerns about regulation. The Internet revolution forced traditional journalists to deal with "upstarts" who broadcast news on the Internet with little regard—at least at times—for traditional journalistic values.

Media became even larger as megamergers took place during the 1990s. At the beginning of the twenty-first century, AOL and Time Warner merged, creating the biggest media company in the history of the nation. Consequences of conglomeration include a lessening of voices and a tendency on the part of news companies to put profits over values.

Television campaigning brought new criticism in evaluating whether media foster democratic thought. Critics of the media charged journalists with being "bamboozled" by the political communicators. Journalists and political managers often changed places, thus leading the public to wonder about the blurring of political and journalistic lines. Critics also charged that media focus too much on the horse race of an election, not on the issues.

Media research has moved from a theoretical construct of media as all powerful to media with limited effects. Audiences are now perceived to be made up of individuals with varying ethnic, socioeconomic, and educational backgrounds. These variables affect how individuals respond to media. However, critics, alarmed by increasing media violence and life-styles depicted particularly on television, claim that media pervade our lives, structure our experiences, and express varying forms of social power.[50]

In global terms, the media are western. More programming and more telecommunication services originate in northern and western countries. Critics fear that this imbalance of information puts the third world at a disadvantage and sometimes argue for controls that would change the equation. Others, however, contend that the third world benefits from media services and technology transfer.

Ethnic audiences are greater advertising targets than they once were, both through mainstream media and through ethnic publications. African-American and Hispanic publications and broadcast outlets continue to provide an important source of information for those seeking a specialized interpretation of the news. In the case of Hispanics, Spanish-language media are highly sought after.

The mass media of the early twentieth century and the late twentieth century are startlingly different. True, newspapers and magazines spanned the century, but new media riding waves of new technology have changed the lives of Americans, including their work, their leisure, and the knowledge of the world that they can summon with the push of a button or the twist of a dial.

Although the media are much changed, a newspaper critic writing before World War II still can speak to the present. In 1911, after a year of research, the thirty-eight-year-old journalist Will Irwin wrote a "muckraking" series for *Collier's* magazine, titled "The American Newspaper," evaluating the strengths and weaknesses of American daily newspapers. Some of his observations in the fifteen-part series, published from January through July, seem outdated in the 1990s; others ring eerily true.

In the first article of his series, Irwin declared his time to be the "age of the reporter." Of newspapers in 1911, as might be asserted of media today, he said, "No other extrajudicial force, except religion, is half so powerful."[51] Irwin excoriated the debilitating sensationalism of the "yellow press" of Hearst and his followers. His attack on mindless sensationalism might time-travel as criticism of the current round of infotainment—the blurring of news and entertainment.

At the beginning of the twenty-first century, individuals had more access than ever before to news, information, and entertainment. Delivery systems, content providers, journalists—all were more prevalent than in the past. The question for the twenty-first century is whether information in such quantity will foster the continued development of a good society or whether the society will drown in the noise, without being able to perceive the substance in the message.

Endnotes

1. Jim McConville, "TCI Boosts Rates 15%–20%," *Broadcasting & Cable* (March 11, 1996), pp. 12–13.

2. Michael Katz, "Pay Cable Tops Violence Ranking," *Broadcasting & Cable* (February 12, 1996), p. 22.

3. Steven Levy, "The Noisy War over Napster," *Newsweek* (June 5, 2000), pp. 47–54; Jefferson Graham, "Judge Shuts down Napster: Song-sharing Site to Appeal," *USA Today* (July 27, 2000), p. 1A.

4. Jefferson Graham, "Napster Moving toward Monthly Fee," *USA Today* (January 30, 2001), p. 1A; and Frank Gibney, Jr., "Napster Meister: Bertelsmann Boss Thomas Middlehoff Pulls off a Shocking Deal," *Newsweek* (February 5, 2001), p. 58.

5. Mike Flanagan, "Local Fans Split on Napster Ruling," *The Knoxville News-Sentinel,* February 13, 2001, p. A1.

6. Max Robins and Martin Pers, "Goliaths Reel at Disney Deal," *Variety,* August 21, 1995, News Section, p. 1.

7. Anita Sharpe and Eben Shapiro, "Time Warner Offers over $8 Billion in Stock for Turner Enterprise," *Wall Street Journal,* August 30, 1995, p. A1, 6; the sale was completed in 1996 for $7.5 billion.

8. Saul Hansell, "America Online Agrees to Buy Time Warner for $165 Billion; Media Deal Is Richest Merger," *New York Times,* January 11, 2000, p. A1.

9. Hansell, "America Online Agrees," p. A1.

10. These partial listings of AOL-Time Warner holdings were available in February 2001, on http://www.aoltimewarner. com/about/companies/warner_bros.html.

11. P. J. Tichenor, G. A. Donohue, and C. N. Olien, "Mass Media and Differential Growth in Knowledge," *Public Opinion Quarterly* 34 (1970), pp. 159–170.

12. Jeff Gerritt, "Blacks Gaining in Use of Internet," *Detroit Free Press,* March 11, 1999, pp. B1–2.

13. Elizabeth Corcoran, "More Women Are Using Internet," *Lansing State Journal,* February 14, 1999, business sec. p. C1.

14. Bill Kovach and Tom Rosenstiel, *Warp Speed: America in the Age of Mixed Media* (New York: The Century Foundation Press, 1999), p. 4.

15. Kovach and Rosenstiel, *Warp Speed,* pp. 7–8.

16. Kovach and Rosenstiel, *Warp Speed,* pp. 11–12.

17. Kovach and Rosenstiel, *Warp Speed,* title for chap. 6, pp. 51–57.

18. Benjamin Bagdikian, *The Media Monopoly* (Boston: Beacon Press, 2000), 6th ed., p. x.

19. Bagdikian, *The Media Monopoly,* 6th ed., pp. x–xi.

20. Alix Freedman, Elizbeth Jensen, and Amy Stevens, "Why ABC Settled with the Tobacco Industry," *Wall Street Journal,* August 24, 1995, p. B1; Mark Landler, "ABC Settles Suits on Tobacco," *New York Times,* August 22, 1995, p. D1, 6; and Alan Bash and Doug Levy, "ABC, Tobacco Firms Settle Libel Suits," *USA Today,* August 21, 1995, p. 1A.

21. See, for example, the full-page advertisement carrying text of the apology in *People* magazine with a substantial headline in red ink, "Apology Accepted." For an article contending that ABC's nicotine-spiking charges were close to the literal truth, see Timothy Noah, "Congressman Says Data Show Nicotine Was Boosted in Philip Morris Cigarettes," *New York Times,* August 1, 1995, p. B3.

22. Quoted in Bash and Levy, "ABC, Tobacco Firms Settle Libel Suits," p. 1A.

23. "Smoking's Unsettled State," *New York Times* editorial, August 23, 1995, p. A14.

24. Bill Carter, "Tobacco Company Sues Subject of Interview That CBS Canceled," *New York Times,* November 22, 1995, p. A9.

25. "Self-Censorship at CBS," *New York Times* editorial, November 12, 1995, sec. 4, p. 14.

26. P. Cameron DeVore, "In CBS Tobacco Case, Contract Came Before First Amendment," *New York Times,* letter to the editor, December 6, 1995, p. A22.

27. Elizabeth Jensen and Suein L. Hwang, "CBS Airs Some of Wigands' Interview," *Wall Street Journal,* January 29, 1996, p. B10.

28. For elaboration of these points, see Kent R. Middleton and Bill F. Chamberlin, *The Law of Public Communication* (New York: Longman, 1988), pp. 30–45.

29. Kathleen Hall Jamieson and Karlyn Kohrs Campbell, *The Interplay of Influence* (Belmont, Calif.: Wadsworth Publishing Co., 1992), p. 282.

30. "Media Lemmings Run Amok," *Washington Journalism Review* (April, 1992), pp. 28–32.

31. See Richard Davis, *The Press and American Politics* (New York: Longman, 1992).

32. Daniel Hallin, "Sound Bite News: Television Coverage of Elections, 1968–1988," *Journal of Communication* 42:2, (Spring, 1992) pp. 5–41.

33. Seth Mnookin, "It Happened . . .", p. 150.

34. Jean Cochran, "The 2000 Election: What Went Wrong," Freedom Forum Lecture at the University of Tennessee Research Symposium, March 1, 2001.

35. Steven Brill, "Fixing Election Night," *Brill's Content,* February 2001, p. 27.

36. Tom Wolzien, "The Bottom Line," *Brill's Content,* February 2001, p. 97.

37. Louis Liebovich, *The Press and the Modern Presidency: Myths and Mindsets from Kennedy to Election 2000* (Westport, Conn.: Praeger, 2001), p. 242.

38. For opposing arguments, see John Merrill and Everett Dennis, "Global Communication Dominance," in *Media Debates: Issues in Mass Communication* (New York: Longman, 1991), pp. 212–222.

39. Adapted from remarks by Jean Folkerts at the Wichita Symposium: "Beyond Agendas: New Directions in Communication Research," September 1992.

40. Don R. LeDuc, *Law of Mass Communications,* 7th ed. (Westbury, N.Y.: Foundation Press, 1992), p. 695.

41. Geoffrey P. Hull, "The Structure of the Recorded Music Industry," Albert N. Greco, ed., *The Media and the Entertainment Industries* (Boston: Allyn and Bacon, 2000), p. 80.

42. Richard Natale, "Forget Peoria: Will It Play in Paris and Peru?" *Los Angeles Times,* October 7, 1995, p. F1.

43. Patrick Robertson, *The Guinness Book of Movie Facts and Feats* (New York: Abbeville Press, 1993), p. 7.

44. Dave Gussow, "Sites and Sounds," *St. Petersburg Times,* August 21, 1999, business sec., p. 11.

45. Stephen Lacy, James M. Stephens, and Stan Soffin, "The Future of the African-American Press: A Survey of African-American Newspaper Managers," *Newspaper Research Journal* 12:3 (Summer, 1991), pp. 8–19.

46. "Black Papers Are Fighting for Survival," *Wall Street Journal,* October 4, 1990, pp. B1, B6.

47. William Barlow and Janette Dates, *Split Images* (Washington, D.C.: Howard University Press, 1990), pp. 227–228.

48. Barlow and Dates, *Split Images,* p. 338.

49. Sharon Huber, "Hispanic Media, Summer 1992," (St. Louis: D'Arcy Masius Benton & Bowles).

50. Michael Real, *Super Media* (Newbury Park, Calif.: Sage Publications, 1989).

51. Will Irwin, "I.—The Power of the Press," *Collier's,* January 21, 1911.

Index